The Brandeis/Frankfurter Conn

Anchor Books Edition, 1983.
Published by arrangement with
Oxford University Press, Inc.

Library of Congress Cataloging in Publication Data
Murphy, Bruce Allen.
The Brandeis/Frankfurter connection.
Includes index.
1. Brandeis, Louis Dembitz, 1856–1941.
2. Frankfurter, Felix, 1882–1965.
3. Judges—United States.   4. Law—United States—
History and criticism.   I. Title.
KF8744.M87   347.73'2634   82-2104
ISBN 0-385-18374-7   347.3073534   AACR2

Excerpts from the Oral Histories of Henry Wallace, Learned Hand
and Gardner Jackson copyright by the Trustees of Columbia University,
New York, New York, 1976, 1972, 1972
Excerpted by permission of the Columbia Oral History Research Office.

Printed in the United States of America

THE
BRANDEIS/FRANKFURTER
CONNECTION

The Secret Political Activities
of Two Supreme Court Justices

BRUCE ALLEN MURPHY

Anchor Books

ANCHOR PRESS/DOUBLEDAY & COMPANY, INC.
Garden City, New York
1983

For two sources of daily inspiration:
My wife, Carol Lynn Wright,
and the memory of my Grandfather,
Edward Allen Hendrick

Acknowledgments

Since beginning the research on this book I have accrued an astounding number of debts to people for their advice and assistance; it is a pleasure now to express my gratitude to them. Throughout the research I have benefitted from the always patient and wise counsel of my former graduate school advisor at the University of Virginia, Henry J. Abraham. Three other men have been formative influences in my education and in the production of this book: Robert J. Harris of the University of Virginia and Dean Alfange, Jr., and Sheldon Goldman of the University of Massachusetts at Amherst. It has long been my dream to offer these men some tangible evidence of the impact of their labors.

A number of other people have generously provided me with insights which served to guide my research and analysis at different stages of this project: Gary Aichele, Walter Berns, Loren Beth, Alan Betten, Inis L. Claude, Abe Fortas, Al Fortunato, Nechama Gancz, Arthur Goldschmidt, Jr., Gerald Gunther, H. N. Hirsch, J. Woodford Howard, Jr., J. Patrick Jones, Edward Keynes, William Leuchtenburg, David Levy, James Magee, Eileen Mallon, Mary Beth McCabe, Charles McCurdy, Janet Mrazik, Walter Murphy, Roger K. Newman, Elliot A. Rosen, Abram L. Sachar, Glendon Schubert, David A. Shannon, Martin Shapiro, Daniel Stroup, Philippa Strum, John Vile, William Weber, Daniel Winand, and William Wright.

The staffs of the following libraries made my labors easier by cheerfully providing necessary materials and information: the Columbia Oral History Research Office (especially Acting Director Elizabeth B. Mason), the University of Louisville Law School Library (especially Janet B. Hodgson and Tom Owens), the Sterling Library at Yale University (especially Chief Research Archivist Judith A. Schiff), the Library of Congress Manuscripts Division (especially Gary Kohn), the Franklin D. Roosevelt Library (especially Director William R. Emerson), the John F. Kennedy Library, the Harry S Truman Library, The Hoover Institution on War, Revolution and Peace (especially Adorjan I. de Galffy), the University of Colorado Library (especially Cassandra Volpe), the University of Kentucky Library (especially Terry L. Birdwhistell), Alderman Library at the University of Virginia (especially Patti McClung), and the Pennsylvania State University Library. Most importantly, I would like to single out one librarian, Erika Chadbourn, Curator of Manuscripts and Archives at the Harvard Law School Library, for her assistance and friendship. This army of librarians helped to make the book possible.

My sincere thanks to those individuals mentioned throughout the book who kindly allowed me to interview them. I also owe a great debt to the following people (beyond the librarians mentioned above) who permitted me to make quotations from various unpublished materials: Benjamin V. Cohen, Morris L. Cohen, Thomas G. Corcoran, Norris Darrell, Paul A. Freund, Gerald Gunther, Edward F. Prichard, Jr., Elizabeth Brandeis Raushenbush, Rutherford D. Rogers, Grace Tugwell, and Judge Charles E. Wyzanski, Jr.

Grants from a number of sources at various stages of this project made its completion possible. My thanks to: the Eleanor Roosevelt Foundation, the University of Virginia Society of Fellows' Allan T. Gwathmey Foundation, and Forstmann Foundation, the Pennsylvania State University's Faculty Research Initiation Fund, and the Pennsylvania State University's Institute for the Arts and Humanistic Studies. I owe much to Dean Thomas F. Magner, University Vice President R. G. Cunningham, Professor Stanley Weintraub, Ms. Margo Grof and Ms. Beatrice Swift for assistance in the procurement and administration of the last two grants.

In addition, my thanks to a number of friends who provided a wandering researcher with access to their homes (and their refrigerators): Dean and Barbara Alfange, Richard Boudreau, Albert and Stella

Drager (and my good friend Paul Drager), Richard M. Gebhard, and Harold M. and Patricia G. Wright.

The manuscript was improved by a careful reading of all or part of various drafts by the following: Henry J. Abraham, Dean Alfange, Jr., Paul A. Freund, Robert J. Harris, Whittle Johnston, Melvin I. Urofsky, G. Edward White and Patricia G. Wright.

While various drafts of the manuscript were skillfully typed by a number of people, I would like to single out for thanks Earl Davis, Barbara Johnson and Shirley Rader.

My task was made easier by the resources and collegial atmosphere of the Political Science Department at the Pennsylvania State University. I would especially like to thank Department Head John D. Martz for his continual support and interest in every aspect of my work, as well as James Eisenstein, and two former colleagues Bruce A. Williams and Thomas M. Callaghy for their encouragement at crucial junctures.

I have been truly fortunate to receive massive, and uniquely wise, assistance from Oxford University Press, in particular from Laura Brown, Jeffrey Seroy, copyeditors Sally Clark and Elizabeth Fox, and Mary Wander. I am grateful for the opportunity to express my deep gratitude to my editor, Susan Rabiner, for her prodigious efforts on this book. My thanks are extended for her deft editorial judgment and grace under fire, but more so for her having, from the beginning, expressed faith in this project and offered constant encouragement to a first-time author. She has been a beacon of inspiration throughout.

Over the years my parents, Mr. and Mrs. Alfred E. Coe, have provided much support, for which I am very grateful. My parents-in-law, Mr. and Mrs. Harold M. Wright, have defied the stereotype of that status in offering their love, and taking a unique interest in my work.

This book is dedicated to two people, my Grandfather and my wife. My grandfather, Edward Allen Hendrick first instilled in me a love of reading and scholarship. My one regret is that he is not alive to see this work completed. On the other hand, one person probably wonders why she still is here seeing this work through to the end—my wife, Carol Lynn Wright. She has served the usual roles of an author's wife: editor, typist, proofreader, psychiatrist, general whip-cracker, and cheerleader. More than that, though, her sensitivity, wisdom, love, and unflagging optimism have made the completion of this manuscript possible, and also make her an ideal companion.

Only my daughter, Emily Patricia Wright Murphy, remains to be acknowledged. At age seven months she too has provided her own special source of inspiration to the book.

Now perhaps all the people mentioned above will no longer have to dread hearing yet another question about Brandeis and Frankfurter.

State College,   B.A.M.
Pennsylvania
December 14, 1981

Contents

When a priest enters
a monastery, he must leave
—or ought to leave—all
sorts of worldly desires
behind him. And this
Court has no excuse for
being unless it's a
monastery.

Felix Frankfurter,
diary entry dated
January 11, 1943

The Brandeis/Frankfurter Connection

Introduction

On June 26, 1968, President Lyndon B. Johnson nominated Abe Fortas, whom he had appointed to the Supreme Court in 1965, to succeed Earl Warren as Chief Justice. During the subsequent confirmation hearings a storm broke. It was charged that Fortas, while sitting on the Court, had advised the president on the Vietnam War, on ordering federal troops into Detroit during racial rioting there, on dealing with steel industry price increases, and on ending transportation strikes.[1] As the hearings dragged on, the candidate's prospects were further threatened by new reports alleging that he had helped draft an amendment to an appropriations bill providing Secret Service protection for all presidential candidates; had conferred with Johnson about the prospective omnibus crime-control bill; had rewritten portions of LBJ's 1966 State-of-the-Union address; had suggested several executive branch appointments; and had accepted a $15,000 lecture fee to give a law school seminar.[2]

Republican senators, hopeful in an election year of saving the political plum of a Chief Justiceship for a Republican president to award, as well as conservative Democratic senators seeking to embarrass the liberal Warren Court, took the opportunity to argue the issue of the proper separation of the judicial and executive branches. Possibly as important to Fortas's fate, Johnson's own base of support had by this time been very much eroded as a consequence of a general disillusionment with the progress of the Vietnam War.

In an historical sense, Fortas's advisory relationship with his old friend, President Johnson, represented a far less extensive political role than that played by either Louis D. Brandeis or Felix Frankfurter while those two men sat on the Court.[3] How can it be that he was made to pay such a dear price for his extrajudicial activities, while Brandeis and Frankfurter continue to be held in such universally high esteem?

Likely the difference lies in the fact that Fortas's role as advisor to Johnson was presented to the general public as being scandalous, while similar activities by Brandeis and Frankfurter rarely in their own time ever became issues of judicial propriety. Still, why this difference? Was it simply that America's attitude toward what was and was not proper judicial conduct had so radically altered in the years between the terms of Brandeis and Frankfurter and that of Fortas?

Fortas's defense of certain of his actions in testimony before the Senate Judiciary Committee illustrated the basic dilemma of all politically minded people who sit on the Court:

> I don't know how anybody can be a person and not discuss with his friends these days questions about the budget and about the Vietnam war. I'm a person too. I am a Supreme Court Justice, but I talk to people, and people talk to me. I don't see how you can avoid questions like that.[4]

This argument was sufficiently persuasive for the committee, which reported favorably on the nomination by a vote of eleven to six. But the controversy was far from over. During the subsequent filibuster that Fortas's nomination provoked in the Senate, James O. Eastland of Mississippi expressed the concern of many regarding such extrajudicial behavior.

> The judge's role is not known to the public. The nature and scope of his activities are kept secret and are not, therefore, subject to public scrutiny. . . . For instance, a litigant challenging the constitutionality of our involvement in Vietnam might not realize that one of the Justices acted as an adviser to a President on that matter. And when acts hidden from public view are made known, suspicion of wrongdoing may be the natural consequence, damaging public confidence in the Court.[5]

These doubts took their toll as forty-three senators refused to invoke cloture for the debate. As a result, on October 2, 1968, Fortas asked President Johnson to withdraw his nomination. Seven months later, following allegations of financial ties to the family foundation of Louis E. Wolfson, a financier who was subsequently convicted of securities law violations, Justice Fortas, under pressure from the Nixon Administration, resigned from the Court.[6] By July 1969, the Senate had become so interested in the general subject of extrajudicial activities by Court members that it opened hearings on the issue.[7]

Public concern over the ethics and financial integrity of members of the judicial branch continued to be heightened when United States Court of Appeals Judge Clement F. Haynsworth, Jr., nominated to replace Fortas, was charged in his confirmation hearings with having had a conflict of interest in certain cases litigated before his court. This charge was enough to scuttle the nomination of a man many now believe to have been an otherwise competent candidate for the position. But at the time of his nomination, the issue of judicial propriety was receiving so much attention that the Haynsworth nomination was not confirmed by the Senate.[8]

Today, Warren Burger, perhaps the most extrajudicially active Chief Justice since William Howard Taft,[9] has been widely criticized for his off-the-bench activities, even though most of his activities are clearly court related and are rather openly pursued. Seeing himself as a voice for better judicial administration, Burger has been extremely active in pushing for various court reforms and improvements. Yet the intensity and visibility of his role has created some controversy. For instance, when he personally lobbied several congressmen by telephone regarding a bill to revise the bankruptcy law, Burger's action was called by Representative Don Edwards of California "a very serious violation of the constitutional doctrine of the separation of powers."[10] Stung by these comments and subsequent editorial criticism, the Chief Justice defended his actions three weeks later in a public address.

> The separation of powers concept was never remotely intended to preclude cooperation, coordination, communication and joint efforts by the members of each branch with the members of the others. . . .
> To be sure, there is a great and necessary tradition of insulation of judges and justices from political activities generally. *But participation in legislative and executive decisions which affect the judicial system is an absolute obligation of judges, as it is of lawyers.* . . . It is entirely appropriate for judges to comment upon issues which affect the courts.[11] [*Italics mine*]

In fact, as chairman of the Judicial Conference of the United States, which was created by Congress specifically to improve the operation of the federal court system, the Chief Justice had more than adequate grounds to justify his interest in legislative activity that dealt with judicial reform. The fact that he has nonetheless been roundly criticized for these actions, which are substantially no different from those undertaken by nearly every other Chief Justice in history, indicates both the importance of and the confusion surrounding the issue of extrajudicial activity by Supreme Court justices.

By tradition, those who join the judiciary recognize an implicit quid pro quo in the judicial appointment. Given life tenure and relative freedom from partisan political pressure, they are asked, in return, to renounce voluntarily those activities that compromise or appear to compromise the public's belief in the integrity and political independence of the judiciary. They are to behave so as to confirm the portrait of Supreme Court justices as thoughtful, disinterested, and largely apolitical persons of the highest character, sitting at the pinnacle of the American legal system, exercising their powers of judicial review (or refusal to review) based not on personal political philosophy, but on the requirements of justice and constitutional government.

There are a number of solid arguments for requiring this self-policed seclusion of those who join the Court. First, such seclusion sustains the separation-of-powers concept, through which members of one branch of government do not encroach on functions constitutionally delegated to either of the other two. Particularly with the judiciary, maintaining a strict separation precludes the situation in which a member of the Court finds himself ruling on a piece of contested legislation he has earlier helped design or upon which he has previously expressed an opinion. Second, it supports the nonpartisan image of the Court and encourages judicial allegiance to the Constitution rather than to the government then in power. From the other side of the bench, it restrains, by establishing a presumption of impropriety, those who might be tempted to make partisan appeals to individual justices.

Finally, and perhaps most important, public acceptance of Court decisions as expressions of justice requires that justices be apolitical. Much like Caesar's wife, a Supreme Court justice must do more than refrain from personal involvement in political alliances; he or she must be perceived by the public as incapable of having considered such involvement in the first place. For if the Court is to serve the necessary societal function of resolving disputes among its citizenry, and thereby defusing much potential for violence and anarchy, it must avoid activities that risk seriously damaging the expectation that the courts will dispense justice without fear or favor.

On close examination, the whole notion of a judiciary totally secluded from politics appears to be more myth than history. Fully two-thirds of the 102 people who have served on the Court have engaged in some form of extrajudicial political behavior, either informally or in response to official government requests. These activities have taken a variety of forms: advising presidents informally, suggesting legislation to Congress, proposing executive and judicial appointments, participating in informal diplomatic missions, writing articles, delivering speeches, and sitting on official government tribunals.[12]

Students of law and government, who understand that many of those selected for the Court come from intensely partisan political backgrounds and who recognize the "inner-club" nature of policymaking in Washington, should not be terribly surprised by revelations of such extrajudicial activity. Yet, with a few notable exceptions, the literature on the Court barely touches on this subject.[13] While judicial biographies offer the most promise for dealing with this issue, they fail to do so for a variety of reasons. Because of the special insularity of justices a number of these biographies come from the pens of former clerks, devoted followers, or even relatives of the justices, and tend to be overly laudatory and protective.[14] As would be expected, potentially embarrassing information on their subject does not excite these biographers.

There is also considerable evidence that several justices simply combed their private files before their deaths and burned documents that might have damaged their reputations.[15] Further, there has developed a pattern among many of the better, more objective biographers of Court figures to concentrate such studies on the legal—as opposed to the personal or political—philosophy of the justice.[16] Thus, the interaction of the subject justice with society's political tensions is treated only in the context of the exercise of those formal powers granted a justice upon elevation to the Court—of his or her opinions, philosophy, and behavior on the bench. By ignoring the vast informal powers of the justices, biographers, consciously or not, leave undisturbed and maybe even help to perpetuate the myth of judicial seclusion. Consequently, there is a pressing need for more systematic study of the reality of judicial power, including where relevant, the political actions of the justices.

In examining the extrajudicial activities of Louis Brandeis and Felix Frankfurter, my intent here has not been to expose venality in these men or even to chastise them. Perhaps it is time that we question more realistically what we can and cannot expect from all those who sit on our highest Court and what roles these persons should or should not play in formulating public policy. But even if our view of what constitutes the acceptable and unacceptable excursion by a justice into the political world were in no way to be altered by examining the paths chosen by Brandeis and Frankfurter, still the information should be recorded. This book sets out an historical narrative of hitherto unknown, undiscovered, yet rather extensive political activities by two major, highly respected justices of the United States Supreme Court.

For many reasons Justices Louis D. Brandeis and Felix Frankfurter make ideal subjects for such an intensive analysis of extrajudicial behavior. Two of the most renowned justices in American Supreme Court history, both men continue to be universally portrayed as paragons of judicial virtue. According to the vast body of literature on each man, they scrupulously observed judicial proprieties, leaving behind once they had donned their judicial gowns all the political zeal they had honed during their highly visible pre-judicial social reform careers. Brandeis's authorized biographer, Alpheus T. Mason, writing without benefit of access to the very revealing correspondence Brandeis maintained with Felix Frankfurter while Frankfurter was a professor at Harvard, treats only the extrajudicial efforts of the justice during World War I and his involvement in the Zionist cause. Even in these efforts, however, Brandeis is declared to have observed the highest standards of judicial ethics.[17]

Similarly, Frankfurter's biographer acknowledges only a small part of his extensive extrajudicial activities during World War II and explains what she does acknowledge as the actions of a loyal, patriotic citizen during a time of national crisis.[18] Clearly, the prevailing picture of both justices in the literature we have inherited attests to their high sense of ethics and their disinterest in politics, except in extraordinary situations.

This image was carefully nurtured by the justices themselves. Whenever Brandeis was asked to assist in obtaining a government appointment, to accept an honorary degree, to write an article or deliver a speech, he noted on the request "Judicial Propriety Precludes," or simply "precluded."[19] A standard refusal letter was then sent by his law clerk explaining the limitations imposed by Court membership. Likewise, Felix Frankfurter argued on behalf of the nonpartisan, secluded nature of the judicial role with his Supreme Court colleague Frank Murphy.

> When a priest enters a monastery, he must leave—or ought to leave—all sorts of worldly desires behind him. And this Court has no excuse for being unless it's a monastery. And this isn't idle, high flown talk. We are all poor human creatures and it's difficult enough to be wholly intellectually and morally dis-interested when one has no other motive except that of being a judge according to one's full conscience.[20]

Frankfurter's private letters are filled with self-portrayals drawn to convince others of his devotion to this ethical position. There were protests to his friends, and to anyone else who might listen for that matter, that his official position made him a "political eunuch" and a "prisoner of the bench."[21] In fact, there was even one extrajudicial address he gave (something Brandeis always avoided) on the topic of whether a justice ought ever to "think beyond the judicial."[22] Such public relations campaigns, waged by both men, though by each in different ways and to different degrees, were designed to promulgate images of them as paragons of the traditionally nonpolitical justice.

Yet despite these Ophelia-like protests to the contrary, new evidence now reveals that both Justice Brandeis and Justice Frankfurter found it impossible to curb their political zeal after their appointments to the bench. In contradiction to the prevailing understanding of both men in the present body of literature, both remained as involved in politics once on the Court as they had been before appointment. Indeed, the range and extent of their extrajudicial involvement surpassed similar endeavors by all but a handful of Supreme Court justices through the Court's history. While each had a standard refusal position that declared that a justice ought not to make himself available as a political adviser, in the end this proscription seems to have been observed only with those in whose causes the justices had little or no interest.

There are also compelling reasons for treating the political activities of Brandeis and Frankfurter in one study. First, there are the remarkable parallels in their careers. Within a short time after each man had been appointed to the Supreme Court (Brandeis in 1916 and Frankfurter in 1939), this nation was engaged in total war. Such crises tend historically to loosen any standards of propriety governing extrajudicial activities, as every citizen is encouraged to do everything possible to contribute to the defeat of the enemy. Under such similar conditions, it is not surprising that both Brandeis and Frankfurter threw themselves intensely into their extrajudicial activities. The broad political interests and wide-ranging contacts in government each man had would make it virtually impossible for either to remain insulated from the great global struggles being waged to defend democracy and self-determination.

Second, Felix Frankfurter learned the art of being an extrajudicially active member of the Supreme Court at the knee of Justice Brandeis. It now appears that in one of the most unique relationships in the Court's history, Brandeis enlisted Frankfurter, then a professor at Harvard Law School, as his paid political lobbyist and lieutenant. Working together over a period of twenty-five years, they placed a network of disciples in positions of influence, and labored diligently for the enactment of their desired programs. This adroit use of the politically skillful Frankfurter as an intermediary enabled Brandeis to keep his considerable political endeavors hidden from the public. Not surprisingly, after his own appointment to the Court, Frankfurter resorted to some of the same methods to advance governmental goals consonant with his own political philosophy. As a result, history virtually repeated itself, with the student placing his own network of disciples in various agencies and working through this network for the realization of his own goals.

Finally, because of the nature of the personal relationship between Brandeis and Frankfurter, this volume will provide a rare glimpse inside the "marble palace" of the Supreme Court to see how the ethical norms governing the justices are transmitted from one generation to the next. Like their brethren before them, Justices Brandeis and Frankfurter helped to establish the present standards of propriety for individuals on the Court through their own practices and statements. Privately conscious that his behavior could be perceived as unethical by others, Brandeis through his early years on the bench developed specific limits for his own open involvement in extrajudicial conduct. Frankfurter thus observed firsthand the extent of the informal powers of a Supreme Court justice. Consequently, Frankfurter's own decision to adopt selectively and refine these strategies upon coming to the Court himself aptly illustrates his consciousness of such norms. Since both men are portrayed elsewhere as rigidly ethical individuals, we must either revise our picture of them or re-evaluate what have been perceived as the established norms for individuals on the Court.

Until now, no book has detailed the complete story of Brandeis's and Frankfurter's extensive political activities. Both men exercised political influence in relative secrecy, so much so that while both have been the subject of, and mentioned in, innumerable volumes, the full details of their off-the-bench behavior have not yet been revealed. To be sure, some of these activities are partially disclosed in isolated references found in the published letters and writings of Brandeis and Frankfurter.[23] In addition, studies done by other scholars mention, or speculate about, other aspects of the justices' behavior.[24] But this volume is the first attempt to bring together not just these known accounts but also certain unpublished and hitherto unexamined source materials in order to present the entire range of the justices' extrajudicial behavior.

What has become clear is that each of these incidents fits into a larger mosaic, and, that rather than representing isolated actions, each is a part of a vast, carefully planned and orchestrated political crusade undertaken first by Brandeis through Frankfurter and then by Frankfurter on his own to accomplish extrajudicial political goals. Thus, each new piece of material, and the entire picture that is created sheds new light on the prevailing interpretations offered by other scholars regarding these two men, their times, the Supreme Court, and the judicial office itself.

So extensive was the extrajudicial behavior of both Brandeis and Frankfurter that one is left puzzled as to how it could have remained secret for so long. Indeed, the full story of each man's involvement remained hidden not just from the general public, which despite the disclosure of a handful of the justices' actions was never given any reason even to suspect what was actually going on, but also from the closest allies and supporters of these two men. Interviews with the lieutenants of both justices make clear that even they had little knowledge, or even suspicion, of the full extent of their bosses' political roles. Often, during an interview, I would be told of a certain isolated incident, believed by the lieutenant to be atypical of the general pattern of the justice's extrajudicial behavior. It was only when all these "atypical" stories were strung together that the true pattern of behavior was revealed. As a consequence, many of the individuals involved in these events will be discovering for the first time not only the extraordinary behavior of Brandeis and Frankfurter, but also their own individual roles in carrying out the activities described.

Of course, the question must be asked how they could have maintained this secrecy when success for them required the open assistance, or at least acquiescence, of individuals at the highest levels of government—presidents, senators, congressmen, even other judges—as well as, on occasion, writers and editors of magazines, newspapers, and law reviews around the nation. A hint of the knowledge these people possessed regarding Brandeis's and Frankfurter's extrajudicial involvement is reflected today in their personal memoirs, which occasionally mention, often quite casually, their own involvement with, or observation of, the justices' behavior.[25] The key, though, is that each of these many actors was selectively used only in certain roles, or at specific times; none of these people were ever allowed to know the full range and extent of the political activities being orchestrated from the chambers of a Supreme Court justice. In fact, comparisons of the published and unpublished accounts of different allies make clear that each of the justices often refused to divulge even to those enlisted in the cause the full reasons for their own assignments at any particular time. Surely some of these people suspected what was going on in other areas, but no one made it his business to confirm his own suspicions. Also unusual is the fact that when some of the opponents of the two justices occasionally became aware of certain activities, there seems to have been no effort made to mobilize critical opinion by combining what each knew into a fuller picture. Most important in making sure the public remained in the dark as to the full range of their activities were the methods devised by Brandeis and Frankfurter to conceal these activities. Now, after the passage of decades, and years of research, a fuller story can be told.

Unlike Chief Justice Burger, whose political activity concerns mainly the judicial-reform area, and Justice Fortas, whose main extrajudicial involvement was advising a single president, Brandeis and Frankfurter engaged in every conceivable variety of political behavior during a number of different administrations. In many cases their political efforts came to nought; in others they surely helped formulate historic executive programs and design major pieces of legislation. The massive body of unpublished evidence documenting this activity has been made available in the recently opened, unpublished papers and diaries of, among others, Rexford Tugwell, Oscar Cox, Charles C. Burlingham, Raymond Moley, and Henry L. Stimson. Additional evidence, which remained hidden for many years in the private papers of the two justices themselves, their colleagues and intimate friends, and in the papers of four presidents (Woodrow Wilson, Franklin D. Roosevelt, Harry S. Truman, and John F. Kennedy) has only lately become available. Finally, in order to combat the "curse of the telephone," which has made it unnecessary for public figures to commit thoughts to paper in this modern age, the vast resources of the Columbia University Oral History Collection, as well as personal interviews and correspondence with people who knew well and worked closely with the two justices, have been used to help fill in the gaps in the story. From these materials one can construct a portrait of two justices exercising the full range of informal political powers at their disposal to advance the causes most dear to them.

This new biographical data does more than merely satisfy historical curiosity. Even realizing that the effects of many of their extrajudicial actions are now only a memory, the new data is still worth studying because the story is really larger than itself. Such studies provide a necessary perspective for evaluating the charges of improprieties that have appeared in the news over the recent past about other judicial figures. The continuing controversy in such areas as judicial tenure, state judicial-removal commissions, merit-selection plans, allegations of financial conflict of interest by judges, and compulsory disclosure of financial holdings are first cousins to the events and issues outlined in this book. All these proposals are concerned with establishing standards for selecting and retaining judges who are both qualified and above reproach on ethical grounds. Recently intensified interest in the issue has led to the denial of the Chief Justiceship to and then the resignation as associate justice of one man (Fortas), the threatened impeachment of another (William O. Douglas), the refusal to confirm a third (Haynsworth), and the frequent criticism of the present Chief Justice (Burger).*

Such attacks by those crying to save the separation of powers are hardly new, but they are nonetheless compelling. For, unlike the recent removal of an occupant of another high federal office, which seems

---

* The most recent criticism of Burger came as a result of press accounts based on the memoirs of John D. Ehrlichman that the Chief Justice "openly discussed the pros and cons of issues before the Court" with President Richard M. Nixon.[26]

to have had little long-term effect on the prestige of the presidency, similar chastisement of a member of the Supreme Court may permanently lessen public confidence in the Court itself, and hence compromise the ability of the entire judicial branch to have its decisions accepted as law.

It is only natural that new revelations of the activities of Brandeis and Frankfurter will lead necessarily to questions regarding the ethical evaluations to be attached to such behavior. This issue is terribly problematic because there are two dimensions to the judgment. We must first ask whether the actions of Brandeis and Frankfurter were ethical given the standards of propriety that existed at the time during which they served. Such a normative study of past actions requires an examination of the practices by the justices' own colleagues on the bench and by those individuals who served on the Court prior to them. One will also need to analyze carefully the limits Brandeis and Frankfurter themselves set, and claimed to observe. Consequently, if the two justices are to be criticized here for engaging in "unethical" activities, it must be because they transgressed the standards for advisable behavior that were either then in effect or were given voice by the two justices themselves.

There is another normative question, however, that has even greater importance: given this lesson of history, what should be the objective, normative standard for present and future members of the Supreme Court? The search for such a policy recommendation entails an examination of realized benefits measured against the potential risks of actions like those taken by Brandeis and Frankfurter. Given the special advantages available to these two to affect policy extrajudicially—well-conceived programs, access to presidents, willingness to engage in the covert endeavors required, the means to hide the involvement from the public, and a set of allies eager to carry out the plans—how are we to weigh the good that may have been brought about against the potential for future abuse such new precedents allow?

For the other side of the ledger, we should ask what the effect on the Court would have been had either Brandeis or Frankfurter been discovered in his political role in his own time. This latter question assumes added importance when we realize that while the public was never made aware of the full extent of each man's involvement in the political realm, in this current post-Watergate era of investigative journalism, when leaks concerning activities of government figures are beyond the repair of even the most ardent "plumbers," similar activities by present justices would not likely go unreported by the press. As we speculate about what harm might have come to the Court had the extent of each man's activities become known contemporaneously, we are led to the necessity of redefining normative behavior for periods in which such activity would more likely be exposed and could rationally be expected to produce for the Court consequences quite different from those produced during the time in which the behavioral norm was established.

In the end, we must question whether the current concern over judicial ethics represents a significant shift in public expectations regarding the activities of its federal judges since Frankfurter's retirement in 1962. It is hoped that the present study of the informal expressions of power by Brandeis and Frankfurter will provide an improved perspective for considering the capabilities of and normative constraints on any justice seeking to affect public policy through extrajudicial means. With an historically well-based and accurate picture of the role Supreme Court justices can play, and often have played, in determining public policy, we should be able to understand more fully the separation-of-powers concept as it helps shape modern America.

1

Justice Brandeis, Professor Frankfurter: The Problem of Judicial Temperament

A careful reading of the lives of our Supreme Court justices will quickly dispel the myth that the inhabitants of our marbled cloister have, in any fixed pattern, renounced all interest in the ways of the political world. While they may all have donned robes similar to those of monks, many, many have lived lives of less-than-monastic purity when it came to politics.

Nonetheless, by the year 1916—the year in which Louis D. Brandeis was appointed to the Supreme Court—certain limits had established themselves regarding what extrajudicial behavior the American public could reasonably be expected to tolerate from members of its highest bench. Accepted norms dictated that justices might engage in outside literary endeavors and, as long as they were relatively circumspect about it, might make recommendations for appointments to other levels of the judiciary and, to a lesser extent, to positions in the executive branch. Requests that the justices participate in a nonjudicial official government function had to be carefully weighed against the effects such service might have on the Court's image of nonpartisanship. During the War of 1812 the fact of a national emergency had been accepted as a mitigating circumstance in applying standards that might have tended to foreclose all extrajudicial activities by Supreme Court justices. Campaigning for high public office from the high Court, attempted by Associate Justice John McLean from 1832 to 1860, had been eventually greeted with such repugnance that future justices wishing to run (Charles Evans Hughes in 1916) resigned from the Court in order to do so.*

Yet these rather strict standards inherited by Louis D. Brandeis and his brethren on the bench in 1916 are nowhere inscribed in the Constitution. On the contrary, the norms of the time had evolved over the years in response to public acceptance or rejection of specific activities of past Supreme Court justices. The ebb and flow of past public outrage had educated the Court to the fact that if it fell victim to scandal or found itself charged with partisanship, its ability to sustain its decisions as the law of the land would be badly compromised.

The Court Louis D. Brandeis joined was one that generally watched its step, avoiding controversy or political involvement. Following a long period of rather strict self-enforcement of the proscriptions against political activity, the Court had enjoyed, since before the turn of the century, a particularly high degree of public prestige and confidence. As a consequence of this period of rigidly proper behavior, and the pendular effect in these matters, a forgiving public had recently acquiesced for the first time in over forty years to a close advisory relationship between a Supreme Court justice (William Moody) and a president (Theodore Roosevelt). With the door to the outside opened just a crack, then, the opportunity was ripe in 1916 for a politically inclined justice to spread his wings and test the political currents. Remembering Daedalus and Icarus, however, the flight into the political realm would have to be planned very carefully, lest the heat—not from the sun but from the public and press—quickly bring the justice hurtling down to earth.

Nearly all who were exposed to Louis D. Brandeis described him as a reflective moralist, eager to educate others regarding the proper goals for business, government, and even for society in general. Much later, because of his prophetlike visage and demeanor, as well as an air of perfected wisdom he communicated, the members of Roosevelt's New Deal Administration would refer to him as Isaiah. But even from the very beginning of his public life, he was inclined to lecture those who approached him on the ills of the present day, while still maintaining his distance from the controversies. So powerful were his analytical

* For more on the evolution of normative standards governing extrajudicial activity, see the appendix.

skills, and so persuasive his arguments, that a wide variety of people came to him with their problems, either personal or political, and, once the proper solution had been made plain, left wondering why they had been troubled by the problem in the first place.

The roots of these so-distinctive personal qualities can be found in Brandeis's early years. He was born on November 13, 1856 in Louisville, Kentucky, the youngest of the four children of Adolph and Frederika Brandeis.[1] His parents, natives of Prague, had emigrated to the United States after the European revolutions of 1848. Adolph Brandeis became a successful grain and produce merchant in Louisville and was able to raise his family in relative wealth until the post–Civil War depression of 1870 destroyed his business. Louis graduated from the Louisville public schools at age fifteen with a gold medal for excellence. When the family business was dissolved by Adolph in 1872 to conserve capital, the Brandeis family was sent on what turned out to be a three-year trip to Europe. Seeking higher education but lacking the necessary preparation, Louis failed the entrance exam to the *Gymnasium* in Vienna; after a year of travel and self-education he convinced the proctor at the *Annen Realschule* in Dresden to admit him. Studying there from 1873 to 1875, Brandeis later claimed that it was in that period that he learned to think inductively—to derive new ideas from close attention to the facts presented.

Influenced by an extremely brilliant and well-read Zionist uncle, Lewis N. Dembitz, a prominent Louisville attorney in whose honor Brandeis would change his middle name from David to Dembitz, he decided to pursue a career in the law. On September 27, 1875, at age eighteen, lacking formal college training and with his only preparation being the reading of Kent's *Commentaries on American Law,* Brandeis entered the Harvard Law School. Here, two philosophical themes of his later judicial career were formed. First, as one of the earliest products of Professor Christopher Columbus Langdell's new "case method" of studying law, Brandeis continued to develop the inductive analytical abilities formed at the *Annen Realschule.* Second, he fell under the spell of Professor James Bradley Thayer, a teacher of constitutional law and the foremost exponent of the judicial self-restraint theory that would later guide Brandeis's activities on the bench.[2] While Brandeis flourished in the study of law, his successful battles against various obstacles then facing him served to increase his self-confidence. Lacking funds because of the continued difficulties of the family business, Brandeis paid for his education using a loan from his brother Alfred and money earned from various tutoring and proctoring jobs. So diligent and successful was he at these efforts that by the end of his schooling, which included a year of graduate work in 1877–78, Brandeis had paid off the loan, saved between $1,200 and $1,500, and, launching a lifelong practice of wise investment, used part of the money to purchase a railroad bond that he kept long after he had made millions of dollars.[3]

Despite his lack of formal college training and victimized by bad health and failing eyesight so severe that doctors advised him to give up the law entirely, he achieved the highest grade average in the history of Harvard Law School. In so doing, he outperformed classmates who had the advantage of being both older than he—though he was first in his class, the trustees had to pass a special rule to allow him to graduate because he was not yet twenty-one—and from much higher social stations. Likely owing to his obvious brilliance, Brandeis seems to have been accepted by his largely upper-class, college-educated colleagues at Harvard Law School and remained very close to his instructors.

In 1878, Brandeis began his law practice in St. Louis, but yearning for the stimulation of Cambridge and Boston, he accepted, a mere nine months later, an offer to join law school classmate Samuel D. Warren in a Boston law partnership. Warren, a member of a prominent New England family, provided Brandeis with some entrée into Boston's Brahmin society. The firm had a corporate clientele mainly of medium- and small-sized firms. Fearing that Warren would bring in most of the clients and thus put their relationship on an unequal footing, Brandeis developed relationships with the city's rich German immigrant Jews in a highly successful effort to bring in business that would contribute to the firm's growth.[4]

Warren not only introduced him to the important Brahmins in town (among them Oliver Wendell Holmes), but also sponsored his admission to various clubs such as the Dedham Polo Club and Union Boat Club. Though Brandeis sincerely tried to become a part of this upper-class society in these early years, at best he remained on its periphery. As a member of these social clubs, he was accorded such "benefits" as being listed in the Blue Book of Boston in 1886. But while he should have been invited to join other clubs, due to the anti-Semitism of Brahmin society, he was not. He bought a country home in a fashionable Boston suburb, Dedham,[5] and had his wife adopt upper-class dress styles,[6] but as a southern, liberal Jew he was subjected to almost total social isolation, even from his own wealthy clients.

Despite this isolation, Brandeis adopted and advocated those ideals of Boston society that he admired. He was deeply moved by the individualism, ruggedness, love of freedom, and realism of the native New Englanders. Moreover, he was almost puritanical in his adherence to the work ethic and, having experienced the failure of the family business and his years at Harvard on meager funds, excessively frugal. Brandeis was so fond of New Englanders' ways, and so successful in adopting them as his own, that Samuel Warren told him: "In many ways you are a better example of New England virtues than the natives."[7] Indeed, the personal code of Brandeis, as described by G. Edward White, seems almost stereotypical of native New Englanders.

> The Brandeis code justified, among other things, low heat in his law office to save expense, a short working day (to keep one's mind fresh), disdain for drinking, dancing and like pursuits, the zealous molding of the lives of the underprivileged so that paupers might achieve moral growth; and distaste for sloppy and inefficient business practices.[8]

Having been so successful in his life of self-denial and austerity— by age thirty-four he was earning $50,000 a year while the average lawyer was earning less than $5,000 a year, and by fifty-one he was a millionaire[9] Brandeis was eager to impose this life style on others, including his wife, Alice Goldmark, a second cousin from a New York Jewish family, whom he married in 1891, and his two daughters, Susan and Elizabeth, born in 1893 and 1896 respectively.

Another result of Brandeis's personal code opposing bigness, waste, and inefficiency, as well as his zealous pursuit of moral righteousness, was his legendary service in the early twentieth century for public causes. After some reform activity on behalf of honest government in Boston, Brandeis began to delegate more of his routine legal work and to take cases that placed him on the side of Progressivism, safeguarding the interests of the common man in opposition to powerful financial and industrial monopolistic enterprises. As Brandeis became a more and more successful corporate lawyer, he found himself developing greater and greater sympathy for the plight of the common man. This developing compassion led him repeatedly to join battle with the societal power structure in judicial and legislative fights. Each successive battle drove a new wedge between Brandeis and the wealthy

Brahmins he had so desperately attempted to join, and, in turn, pushed him further and further into the camp of the liberal, Progressive reformers.

In fighting these battles, Brandeis's preparation for litigation was such that by the time the case had run its course, he often knew more about the subject than the experts called by each side. In *Muller v. Oregon*,[10] a challenge to maximum-hour legislation for women, he developed what came to be called the "Brandeis Brief," one setting out the sociological as well as legal aspects of an issue. By "impos[ing] some order on the disarray" of facts, Brandeis was guided by his own vision of the "good society."[11] The remainder of his life was devoted to realizing these goals, which would change relatively little throughout his career.

While many saw Brandeis as a philosopher and a "moral teacher" in his efforts for reform, he saw himself only as a "problem solver."[12] Professor Frankfurter later reflected on Brandeis's approach.

> Problems for him were never solved. Civilization is a sequence of new tasks. Hence his insistence on the extreme difficulty of government and its dependence on sustained interest and effort, and on the need for constant alertness to the fact that the introduction of new forces is accompanied by new difficulties.[13]

Brandeis's deep moral convictions gave him a considerable measure of security in suggesting reforms for society. He always recommended solutions to social problems in accordance with his own view of life, very much Jeffersonian in nature. Believing in the "unflagging operation of reason," he encouraged the creation of competitive conditions in order to allow truth to emerge from clashing ideas and interests.[14]

His view of mankind was almost paternalistic. Harvard sociologist David Riesman, after his year of service as Brandeis's law clerk, wrote a four-page letter to Frankfurter entitled "Notes for an essay on Justice Brandeis" that contains a marvelous description of the justice's personal philosophy and jurisprudence. Riesman described Brandeis as having "an extraordinary faith in the possibilities of human development," believing that all men have similar potential and differ only in the advantages created by their life situations.[15] This faith was tempered, according to Frankfurter, by Brandeis's recognition that man has "meagre capacity . . . equipment and comprehension."[16]

Both Frankfurter and Riesman wrote in the same manner regarding the justice's proposed solution for this problem. Lacking fully reliable talent for inquiry and having only limited comprehension, men must restrict the scope of their goals. For similar reasons, no one man ought to be entrusted with too much responsibility in government, business, banking, or even judging. Specifically, he warned against having a single director for more than one corporation and publicly praised the American democracy for its separation-of-powers concept.[17] This last reference is particularly interesting in light of Brandeis's later political behavior while serving on the Court.

Ray Stannard Baker, in unpublished notes of an interview with Justice Brandeis done in preparation for a biography of Woodrow Wilson, amplifies another aspect of Brandeis's personal philosophy. For Brandeis, according to Baker, competition between powers creates a condition allowing man, in his infinite perfectibility, to continue the search for solutions to his problems.[18] Brandeis believed, however, that these searches must be carried on in particular ways. For instance, each person must be prepared to take moral responsibility for his actions;[19] no course of action should be undertaken without careful consideration of its consequences.

Brandeis applied these strictures to himself as well—especially in the area of legal ethics. It was not uncommon for him to win a case for a client and then lecture him on the need to change his ways. Further, he organized and led numerous citizen reform organizations seeking to better the conditions of mankind. For Brandeis, this was just another proper function of a concerned lawyer, and he encouraged others to follow the same road. Finally, he carefully separated these public activities from his private business. Whenever engaged in *pro bono publico* legal work, Brandeis, who was one of the first attorneys to perform such services, would financially compensate his law firm for the time he had spent on the project. On these occasions, to preserve the necessary separation of functions, he simply considered himself to be a client of the law firm.[20]

These public service efforts, which were initiated by his work for "good government" dating from 1891, began in earnest shortly before the turn of the century, when he helped form the Public Franchise League to oppose a proposal that would have led to a transportation monopoly under the Boston Elevated Railway Company. Brandeis succeeded both here and in his subsequent efforts to regulate the rate structure of the newly created Boston Consolidated Gas Company.

During this same time, moved by repeated strikes by unions in various industries, Brandeis became involved in the labor controversies of the time. His investigations led him to become pro-trade union, pushing for more of a voice by labor in company decisions and beginning a lifelong battle against the irregularity of employment, which he blamed for most of labor's problems.

While his early reform efforts had allied Brandeis coincidentally with the Boston financiers and industrialists, his next battle, against fraud and waste in the insurance industry, placed him squarely in opposition to the financial community. For the first time he joined forces with Progressives in the Boston Jewish community to mobilize public opinion. After creating the New England Policy-Holders' Protective Committee and acting as its unpaid counsel, Brandeis beat the insurance companies at their own game by inventing and successfully lobbying for the adoption of savings bank life insurance. Brandeis's final split with the financial community, one that rendered him a target for anti-Semitic attacks, was his brutal battle beginning in 1907 to prevent the merger of the New York, New Haven and Hartford Railroad Company with the Boston and Maine Railroad Company. Brandeis's opposition to such a transportation monopoly was doomed to temporary failure, since virtually all the Brahmin forces united against him. Following this fight, and another equally unsuccessful one against the monopolistic practices of the United Shoe Machinery Company, Brandeis was now firmly in the labor and Progressive camps.[21]

Despite these battles, it was really the Ballinger-Pinchot controversy in 1910 that launched the fifty-four-year-old-Brandeis's national reputation. During the previous year, he had been working with *Collier's Magazine* editor Norman Hapgood and the Western Progressives to fight monopolistic practices by initiating legislation at the national level. In 1910, following charges by Interior Department employee Louis R. Glavis and Gifford Pinchot, chief forester and a conservationist, of irregularities in the opening of public lands in Alaska to mining interests, Brandeis was hired by *Collier's*, which faced possible libel charges for printing the accusations, to represent Glavis in Senate hearings. Though Secretary of the Interior Richard Ballinger was exonerated of charges of wrongdoing by a joint congressional investigating committee on a party-line vote, he later resigned and eventually better conservation practices were adopted.[22]

These repeated clashes with the power structure in the utility, industrial, and financial worlds did more than help mold a Progressive leader; they also helped shape Brandeis as a leader of the American Zionists. Raised without formal religious training, Brandeis tended to follow early in his life the beliefs of his mother, who was more culturally than religiously Jewish, rather than those of his uncle, Lewis Dembitz, the Zionist. For years, Brandeis had a standard routine for dealing with requests from Jewish groups seeking either that he join their association or deliver a speech before them: he would send a standard letter of refusal expressing admiration for their work and, despite his wealth, a relatively small donation. Maintaining this low profile in Boston's Jewish community was necessary to the health of his law practice on the fringes of the Brahmin society.

With each successive reform battle, however, Brandeis was forced to seek a new constituency through which to fight the power structure. More and more he identified with the new wave of East European Jewish immigrants, who were active in various social and liberal reform movements, rather than with the rich German Jews who were his clients. Brandeis came to see in these poorer immigrants the exemplification of the virtues he loved in the American national character and the old New England ways he feared were deteriorating because of monopolistic and dishonest business practices.

It was a series of incidents over a number of years, as chronicled in a recently published study by Allon Cal, that turned the man who had observed no Jewish holidays, and would not speak publicly on a Jewish subject until he was fifty years old, into the leader of the American Zionists.[23] In the first decade of the twentieth century, as Boston became more noticeably anti-Semitic and Brandeis more alienated from the Brahmins, the "People's Attorney," as he was commonly called, became more visible and active in the local Jewish community. His dependence on them for assistance in reform causes, and his recognition of them as a potent political force, became clear in 1905, not only during his quest for savings bank life insurance, but in the effort to defeat the Irish democratic machine of John F. "Honey Fitz" Fitzgerald, grandfather of John Fitzgerald Kennedy, in the Boston mayoral race. One of the most important turning points in Brandeis's conversion to Zionism occurred in 1910 when he was asked to mediate the New York City garment workers' strike. Negotiating with working-class Jews in both labor and management, Brandeis for the first time came to know intimately these first- and second-generation immigrants.

It was an emotional experience as this successful corporate lawyer, who for years had tried to pass in Brahmin society, now sensed his ethnic kinship with the Jewish people. Moreover, in discovering their intellect and sense of morality, he viewed these people—his people— as the new puritans, the true American citizens with all the idealism, industry, innovation, courage, and commitment to hard work that were part of the Yankee spirit.[24] Not only did the experience reawaken Brandeis's personal awareness of his Jewish heritage, it also resulted in Boston's Jewish community beginning to view him as their leader, whether he wanted the role or not.

Still, Brandeis continued to see the Jewish community and the Zionist cause in particular as a political expedient, as a means of furthering his own version of Progressive idealism. At that time he had little knowledge of, or sympathy for Zionism, but his movement toward the cause was inexorable. In 1911 he spoke on Jewish democratic idealism before the Menorah Society of Harvard, an organization formed to promote and study Jewish culture and ideals (a society he joined in May 1913). While still resisting entreaties for other speeches before Jewish groups in 1912, in mid-May of that year he met with Bernard Rosenblatt, honorary secretary of the Federation of American Zionists (composed of East European immigrant Jews as opposed to the rich German Jews in the American Jewish Committee). Their talk on irregularity of employment reinforced Brandeis's understanding of the connection between Zionism and his brand of American Progressivism. During this period Brandeis also wrote a letter to editor Bernard Richards of *The Maccabean*, a journal of the Federation of American Zionists, that some read as a public commitment by him to Zionism. Then, in the summer of that year, the offering of his first gift to the Zionist cause provided tangible evidence of Brandeis's movement toward it.

According to Brandeis's own recollection for Alpheus T. Mason, it was a meeting in August 1912 with Jacob DeHaas that brought him firmly into the Zionist fold.[25] DeHaas, the editor of the Boston-based newspaper, the *Jewish Advocate*, had been a secretary in England to Theodor Herzl, the founder of Zionism. At the close of a meeting on politics, DeHaas spoke with Brandeis about Zionism. Thoroughly intrigued, Brandeis took DeHaas as his secretary and was instructed in the cause during the winter of 1912–13. Still, Zionism for Brandeis was a form of social idealism, and he remained somewhat distant from open, active involvement.

During the latter part of 1912, Brandeis was pushed further toward the cause by anti-Semitic attacks leveled against him. Mobilized by the People's Attorney's efforts against the New Haven Railroad and the United Shoe Machinery Company, some wealthy industrialists established Truth magazine. Issue after issue of Truth portrayed Brandeis as a Jewish radical, a faker, a hypocrite who made money while appearing to back the people's causes, a "sabotageur," and an opponent of upstanding Yankee manufacturers.

Moved by hearing a speech on May 30, 1913 on the nationalist aspects of Zionism from East European Zionist leader Nahum Sokolow and no longer recognizing the Boston that now backed an Immigration Restriction League, Brandeis had nowhere else to turn. But his choice of allegiance was interesting. Rather than join the American Jewish Committee of his German Jewish clients, he chose on April 17, 1913 to join the Zion Association of greater Boston, a subgroup of the Federation of American Zionists available for people who saw themselves as Zionists but did not want to be active participants. Brandeis was truly an American Zionist, seeing the movement not as a nationalist one, but as a social reform effort much like the Progressive movement so dear to his heart. From here it was only a matter of time before he would become the leader of the movement. On August 30, 1914, he was elected chairman of the Provisional Executive Committee for General Zionist Affairs, an ad hoc organization devoted to aiding Jews in the embattled countries of Europe. His acceptance speech at that time aptly captures how he had come to call himself a Zionist.

> I feel my disqualification for this task. Throughout long years which represent my own life, I have been to a great extent separated from Jews. I am very ignorant in things Jewish. But recent experiences, public and professional, have taught me this: I find Jews possessed of those very qualities which we of the twentieth century seek to develop in our struggle for justice and democracy; a deep sense of the brotherhood of man; and a high intelligence, the fruit of three thousand years of civilization.[26]

In 1912, after assessing the other candidates for that year's presidential election, Brandeis threw his support to Woodrow Wilson and urged all his friends to do the same.[27] Very much because of his reformist activities and views, Brandeis was acknowledged by this point as one of the leaders of the informal Progressive party. The initial meeting between Brandeis and Wilson occurred on August 28, 1912, and thereafter the candidate drew from the relationship so many ideas that one scholar has called Brandeis the "architect" of Wilson's New Freedom platform.[28] Brandeis campaigned for Wilson with such vigor that many believed a Democratic victory in November would result in his nomination as attorney general.[29] However, Brandeis's earlier campaigns against big business had antagonized many industrial and Jewish leaders, so much so that these leaders were responsible for Wilson's failure, after his election, to nominate Brandeis for his cabinet. Despite this exclusion from a formal governmental post, Brandeis continued to be one of Wilson's key advisers. His power stemmed from two sources: the near-total compatibility of his views with Wilson's and his willingness to offer such advice while asking nothing in return.

Brandeis used his access to Wilson to translate his vision of the "good society" into concrete policies. By 1912, the two shared the ideal of a society governed by small competitive businesses rather than by the powerful monopolies and trusts that existed at that time. Because the president, also a self-professed reformer, seemed to lack either a cohesive plan to solve the ills of society or confidence in whatever ideas he did have, he was receptive to Brandeis's strategy of minimizing the size of government while still controlling big business.[30] Implementing this plan required that government "establish and then regulate a competitive condition rather than regulat[e] business" directly.[31]

In pursuit of this goal, Brandeis convinced Wilson to adopt two approaches in dealing with big business—create competition in business through a vigorous antitrust policy and then regulate that competition. Breaking up the large monopolies into smaller, more competitive firms would help preserve the values Brandeis cherished. Consequently he became the president's chief adviser on antitrust and financial matters, providing Wilson with general counsel on the subject and even drafting some legislation. Well aware of the abuses committed by the "Money Trust," a somewhat pejorative name given to the nation's largest financial institutions, he advised Wilson in 1913 to back the Federal Reserve System plan proposed by Secretary of State

William Jennings Bryan. Furthermore, in 1914 Brandeis was instrumental in the passage of the Clayton Act, which strengthened the government's antitrust power. Not only did he help draft the final measure, but after lobbying for it with the president, the attorney general, and the Justice Department staff, Brandeis also defended the bill in hearings before the Senate Interstate Commerce Committee. Spurred on by Brandeis's advice, Wilson boldly attacked "the curse of bigness" in industry and finance.[32]

These policies helped implement only a part of the overall Brandeisian program, in that they served to restrict the size of the firms but did nothing about the abuses resulting from unregulated competition. So Brandeis advocated the regulation of competition as well. After all, it was unrestricted competition that had made the monopolies possible in the first place.

> Regulation is essential to the preservation of competition and to its best development just as regulation is necessary to the preservation and development of civil or political liberty . . . Unlicensed liberty leads to despotism. So we have to curb the stronger to protect the weaker.[33]

To accomplish this aim, Brandeis encouraged President Wilson to create the Federal Trade Commission, which would help promote, protect, and regulate competition among the nation's businesses.

So pervasive was Brandeis's influence in the Wilson Administration that he was given a significant voice in several appointments. On his recommendation, William McAdoo was made the secretary of the treasury. In addition, it was common for Attorneys General James C. McReynolds and Thomas W. Gregory to consult Brandeis regarding appointments for the Department of Justice. Clearly, by 1916, Louis D. Brandeis's reputation with the president was that of an indispensable adviser and problem solver.[34] Though still a private citizen, Brandeis was so extensively involved in politics that he was widely viewed as an informal member of the Wilson Administration. For Wilson, the problem of where to put him was a thorny one. As he later revealed to Rabbi Stephen S. Wise, "I need Brandeis everywhere, but I must leave him somewhere."[35]

Wilson's decision to appoint Louis Brandeis to the Supreme Court on January 28, 1916 took the nation by surprise. For many, the nomination of this fifty-nine-year-old champion of social reform, this highly political individual, an acknowledged leader of the American Zionists, seemed inappropriate for the nation's highest Court. Moreover, to the leaders of industry and finance, the Brandeis appointment represented a dire threat. This opposition coalesced to mount one of the longest confirmation battles in Senate history.[36] The most frequently voiced charge was that Brandeis lacked judicial temperament, being both partisan and even radical in many of his views. Furthermore, there were many claims that he had violated legal ethics in his Boston law practice—all of which were unproven. Indeed, what was demonstrated was that Brandeis's unorthodox style of practicing law, in frequently serving as "counsel to the situation" by attempting to strike a fair balance between the litigating parties rather than acting as a hired gun for one particular side, showed that even as a lawyer he maintained the temperament of a judge.[37]

Much of the displeasure with the appointment was summed up by Senator John D. Works, who later voted against confirmation.

> He seems to like to do startling things and work under cover. He has disregarded or defied the proprieties . . . He is of the material that makes good advocates, reformers, and crusaders, but not good or safe judges.[38]

For his part, Brandeis was quickly educated by the confirmation fight regarding the constraints of his new position. Exposed firsthand to the problems a Supreme Court justice might face as a consequence of having associated himself with political issues, he severed all connections with ongoing legislative efforts and continued to work actively only in the Zionist organization.[39] Furthermore, his public stance regarding his own confirmation was one of silence. He told a reporter from the New York Sun: "I have nothing to say about anything, and that goes for all time to all newspapers, including both the Sun and the moon."[40]

While he chose not to answer the charges publicly, Brandeis felt free to supply a group of individuals leading his defense in the hearings—Norman Hapgood, Senator Robert LaFollette, Attorney General Thomas Gregory, Edward F. McClennen (his junior law partner), George W. Anderson (an old friend from earlier reform battles with the Public Franchise League), and Professor Felix Frankfurter—with ammunition for his case. Thus, Brandeis adopted the role of, in his own words, an "interested spectator," remaining apart from the fray but still sending his "campaign managers" long letters providing answers for the charges in the Congressional Record point for point.[41]

For the former People's Attorney, who was far more at home at the vortex of the battle, this role of rear-lines strategist was not an easy one to assume. After six weeks of abuse from his enemies, Brandeis appeared ready to drop the posture entirely.

> It looks to me as if the committee were beginning either to perpetrate an outrage or to make themselves and me ridiculous by these continued hearings. . . . I have accepted the opinion that it would be unwise for me to go down to Washington to appear, but if the proceedings continue on the lines which have been taken, making it appear that we are defending ourselves or excusing our conduct, I think I would rather go down and testify.[42]

Only the cool-headed advice of Edward McClennen and the others calmed the nominee: "Do not let the long continuance of this wear upon you. Do not let anything permit you to harbor the thought for a moment of responding to any suggestion that you testify."[43] In the end this strategy was successful. After four long months, Brandeis was confirmed on June 1 by a vote of forty-seven to twenty-two. This period was additionally fruitful in that it demonstrated to the new justice that he could be a politician in judicial robes simply by continuing to act as the "interested spectator." Soon Brandeis had occasion to further refine this technique.

Even as he prepared to take the oath of office on June 5, 1916, Louis Brandeis was adjusting to the standards of propriety for his new position. Immediately before the ceremony, he asked Chief Justice Edward White whether his substantial investments in long-term municipal and railroad bonds might disqualify him from taking part in certain cases.[44] Much relieved that the Chief Justice anticipated no conflict-of-interest problems so long as the funds were placed in a blind trust, Brandeis left his portfolio undisturbed.[45] However, dealing with his many political associations was a bit more complicated.

Because of the norms against political involvement by Supreme Court justices, Brandeis felt compelled to disengage himself from the many causes and organizations, both public and private, that had occupied his attention for so long. He resigned from the National Economic League, the Economic Club of Boston, the Massachusetts Civil Service Association, the Boston City Club, the Exchange Club of Boston, the Social Law Library, the Massachusetts Bar Association, and the Bar Association of the City of Boston.[46]

The justice hoped, however, to continue his leadership of the American Zionists. In the two years since he had been made chairman of the Provisional Executive Committee for General Zionist Affairs,[47] the movement had become, under his direction, a powerful voice for the interests of Jewish people here and abroad. Unfortunately, as in his other reform ventures, Brandeis had made a number of enemies. These enemies would prove to be particularly troublesome, however, now that he was on the Supreme Court.

In 1915, Brandeis had supported the idea of forming an American Jewish Congress, a democratically elected body that would discuss issues of importance to the Jewish people. This movement was denounced by the wealthier American Jews through their spokesmen in the American Jewish Committee. By mid-1916, Brandeis and his allies seemed to have won the battle and the new congress was about to be formed.

Far from defeated, however, the American Jewish Committee invited Brandeis and his lieutenants to a conference on July 16 at the Hotel Astor. Although Brandeis had been told that the purpose of the meeting was to enable the representatives of the new congress to appeal for unity, the meeting was more like a premeditated ambush. After their remarks, Brandeis and the others offered to leave in order to permit a free discussion of the issues. However, cries from the audience encouraged them to remain, enabling the opponents of the new justice and his allies to hurl insults at them. This personal attack was followed two days later by an editorial denouncing Brandeis in The New York Times, then owned and operated by influential Jews who were associated with the American Jewish Committee. Needless to say, the incident was extremely embarrassing to Brandeis, who had been on the Supreme Court only six weeks. Fearing repercussions for the Court itself, five days after the incident Brandeis officially resigned from the Zionist movement and ended his association with other Jewish relief organizations.[48]

Later that summer, Brandeis was again confronted by the ethical constraints of his new position. The border raids of Pancho Villa into Texas and the retaliatory American incursions into Mexico brought the two nations to the brink of armed conflict. To mediate the dispute,

President Wilson created an arbitration commission. On August 10, he asked Brandeis to serve as one of its members. When the justice immediately accepted "subject to the approval of the Chief Justice," Wilson released the names of the commissioners to the press. Realizing that he was no longer free to act entirely on his own volition, however, Brandeis traveled to Lake Placid in order to consult with Chief Justice White about the request. His discussions with White convinced Brandeis that the nature of the international conflict, combined with the impending presidential elections, made this type of service extremely political and, hence, dangerous to the Court's prestige.[49] In the short note Brandeis sent to Wilson declining the appointment, however, the justice appeared still to be greatly ambivalent about accepting White's advice. He left the door open for future service by declining the appointment "with deep regret," explaining only that "the state of the business of the Supreme Court at the present time" prohibited the acceptance of this additional task.[50]

While in New York, Brandeis had also discussed the appointment with one other person, Professor Felix Frankfurter, a man whose opinion he had come to respect highly. The substance of that discussion is preserved in a letter Frankfurter wrote, more than forty years later, to Professor Paul Freund. Knowing that many of his former students and friends would be engaged in extensive writing about historical events in which he and Brandeis had been involved, Frankfurter, in the later years of his life, took to writing to such people as Philip Kurland, Alexander Bickel, and Paul Freund to make sure that there would be a record of several historical incidents in which he had been a participant and that his views on these events would be "on the record." In the letter to Freund, Frankfurter recounted his reaction to Brandeis's dilemma at that time. He had advised Brandeis, he wrote, against accepting the position. The explanation he gave Freund was only that it would have forced the new justice to begin his new career with a prolonged period of absence.[51]

But as Brandeis began his first term in October 1916, he found himself in a quandary. His temperament was still that of a social activist, but his new position seemingly forbade such involvement. Years later he confessed to Felix Frankfurter that "in the beginning the confinement of work . . . went hard with me" for he was "accustomed to work[ing] when and how he willed" and enjoyed the "freedom in [his] work."[52] Though he had completely avoided all political endeavors since taking the oath of office, Brandeis realized that it would be impossible for him to continue this abstinence. The problem was how to remain influential in politics without violating any standards of judicial propriety.

As he had throughout his career, Brandeis needed to devise a "mechanism" to resolve this seemingly insoluble dilemma. After all, this problem was no more complex than the ones he had faced concerning the artificial gas company monopoly, the abuses in the insurance industry, or the garment workers' strike.[53] Now Brandeis needed only to come up with another creative innovation to deal with the shackles of nonpartisanship that came with his new position. And come up he did.

Brandeis decided that to act freely in the political sphere he would need a lieutenant, one who would be his "eyes and ears" and one who could help implement his programs. To be sure, this method of informal political participation did have distinct disadvantages. He would always have to rely on another to act in his behalf, though Brandeis did have the patience necessary to work in this fashion. The technique also required the right lieutenant, one who commanded Brandeis's complete confidence as to ability and sense of discretion, who was well connected in important circles, and who was both a philosophical ally and a kindred spirit. Fortunately for the justice, there was a friend and ally uniquely qualified for the job in every way, and so the mantle of political reform was passed on—to a thirty-three-year-old professor at the Harvard Law School, Felix Frankfurter. The specific relationship that developed between the two to effect the implementation of Brandeis's programs was unprecedented in Supreme Court history.

Felix Frankfurter was a human dynamo. A man of infinite energy, he walked everywhere with a bounce in his step. Though diminutive in stature, he did everything in a big way. Frankfurter's world was one of vitality and gaiety. He was always singing or whistling to himself—exhibiting his unabashed patriotism, it was often the same tune, "Stars and Stripes Forever." One intimate described Frankfurter as being like champagne, with the same unique ability to make an event livelier by his presence. He would grab people by the arm with a vise-like grip and pepper them with pointed questions that probed their innermost thoughts and beliefs. Yet a simple answer was never quite good enough; it served only as the basis for more questions. When the other party was clever enough and bold enough, a sharp argument on the present topic would ensue. More than just enjoying people generally, Felix Frankfurter had an unparalleled ability to cultivate friendships. He knew everyone and, using his abilities as a broker of individuals, he often sought to bring these people together for various purposes. Relying on his fine wit, and his lively and continual conversation, Frankfurter would capture the undying loyalty of his friends.[54]

For many people, though, Felix Frankfurter also represented an enigma. Often his wife was heard to say, "Whatever you see in Felix, the opposite is true as well." For instance, he was extremely conscious of his Jewish background and appeared at times to many of his intimates to wish that he had been born a WASP. This desire was clearly evident to his law clerks, who noted at their yearly reunion dinners with the justice that it was Elliot Richardson, with his Brahmin family ancestry, who commanded Frankfurter's attention and open admiration. Yet, at the same time, he would clearly show his Jewish background by chuckling whenever one of his favorite Washington restaurants offered their "Ham and Kosher pickle" luncheon special. In another area, while many intimates do reminisce about Frankfurter's love for people, others recall that he also seemed to make snap judgments as to whether a person was interesting and his friendship worth cultivating. Such decisions were made on the basis of the intelligence and sense of humor of the individual, as well as on whether the person could be useful to Frankfurter in any of his endeavors. If a person were found to be unappealing, he would be treated only with distant politeness.[55] Finally, while he constantly professed his aloofness from other people's business and problems, Frankfurter was actually a born meddler. His enormous range of contacts, his incredible intelligence and memory, and his iron courage made Felix Frankfurter a powerful ally and, to some, a formidable enemy.

Born the third son of six children in Vienna, Austria on November 15, 1882, Frankfurter emigrated with his family to the United States at age twelve.[56] His father Leopold sold linens and settled his family initially in New York's Lower East Side. Though he did not know a word of English upon his arrival, young Felix quickly mastered the language and, through voracious reading, became well versed in politics and current affairs. In graduating third highest in his class from City College of New York in 1902, Frankfurter had also gained recognition as a skilled public speaker and debater. Following college he took a civil service job in the New York City Tenement House Department, enrolled, and subsequently withdrew from two New York law schools, and was even considering matriculating at Columbia when a doctor advised him to leave the city for medical reasons. So, in 1903, he enrolled at Harvard Law School where a friend's brother, Samuel Rosensohn, was already attending.

Intimidated by the self-confidence and physical stature of his fellow students, Frankfurter strove diligently in the study of law and soon flourished in the Harvard environment. Despite a rocky start in his first set of midyear exams, he went on to lead his class in each of his three years. Frankfurter's brilliance helped him gain acceptance from his more socially prominent Brahmin colleagues. Not only did he succeed brilliantly in the case method of legal study, Frankfurter profoundly admired and was influenced by the extraordinary collection of teachers there at the time: James Barr Ames, Samuel Williston, John Chipman Gray, and Joseph Beale.

Frankfurter first encountered Brandeis on May 4, 1905, when, as a twenty-two-year-old law student, he heard the People's Attorney deliver an address before the Harvard Ethical Society entitled "The Opportunity in the Law."[57] Brandeis told the next generation of elite lawyers to consider the advantages of working for the people, rather than for rich corporations. Only by struggling against economic irregularities, he said, could their legal training be used to lessen the prospect of class warfare. To Brandeis, working for the people was the highest possible service for an attorney.

Perhaps it was fated that Brandeis and Frankfurter would eventually work together in this mission, for they were cut from similar cloth. Though born twenty-six years apart, they shared the background of being Jewish, raised by Old World parents in financial distress, and educated at the Harvard Law School. Both confronted an anti-Semitic Brahmin society at the school and in neighboring Boston, and both won the grudging respect of these groups by their incisive brilliance in both legal and political affairs. No Harvard students would exceed their performance in school, and few their career accomplishments. Furthermore, their political outlook was nearly identical. Both men were so concerned with what was "right" for the public that they were quickly labeled reformists by their allies and radicals by their enemies.

Both were highly political men yet neither ever ran for public office, choosing instead to serve the interests of society in a role they described as that of "public-private citizen." Like Brandeis before him, Frankfurter believed that his role as an "outside-insider" to the government, with no aspirations for public office, would give him more flexibility to suggest needed reforms and influence the direction of public policy.[58] While both entered private practice immediately after law school, Frankfurter's career then diverged from Brandeis's, in that it did include a short stint in government service. Shortly after joining the prestigious New York law firm of Hornblower, Byrne, Miller and Potter in 1906, Frankfurter took a cut in salary to become the assistant United States attorney for the Southern District of New York under Henry L. Stimson.[59] This was the beginning of a long relationship between the two. Later, reflecting on his service as Stimson's personal assistant, Frankfurter commented, "I don't see how a young fellow coming to the bar could possibly have had a more desirable, more deepening and altogether more precious influence during his formative years than to be junior to Henry L. Stimson."[60] Three years later, Frankfurter briefly joined Stimson in private practice and even managed the latter's unsuccessful campaign for governor of New York in 1910.

In October 1911, when Stimson was named secretary of war by President William Howard Taft, Frankfurter, then twenty-eight years old, traveled to Washington to become the law officer of the Bureau of Insular Affairs. In essence, though, he once again assumed the role of Stimson's special assistant. While the young Jewish immigrant found initial entry into the elitist Washington society to be very difficult, Frankfurter, as always, created his own world of friends. He moved into a lodging house on Nineteenth Street with a group of other young, dedicated, and bright bureaucrats. The house was owned by Robert G. Valentine, then commissioner of Indian affairs, and its other occupants would later make up a roster of prominent individuals: Winfred T. Denison, an assistant attorney general, Lord Eustace Percy, assistant to the British ambassador, and Loring C. Christie, then working in the Department of Justice and a former editor-in-chief of the *Harvard Law Review*.[61] The conversation there was so lively that Oliver Wendell

Holmes soon dubbed it the "House of Truth." Frankfurter later characterized life there: "The parties ran continuously. How or why I can't recapture, but almost everybody who was interesting in Washington sooner or later passed through that house. The magnet of the house was exciting talk, and it was exciting because talk was free and provocative." [62]

It was here that the friendship between Frankfurter and the People's Attorney began. During this time Brandeis frequently came to Washington to testify before various congressional committees, plot strategy with Progressive congressmen, and argue cases before the Supreme Court. After corresponding infrequently, starting in March 1910, regarding their pending cases, Brandeis and Frankfurter formally met in late 1911. They conversed several times in 1911, and exchanged letters in 1912 on important national issues and prospective legislation. [63]

The relationship at this time was one of mutual respect but not intimate friendship. Accordingly, each man's concept of the proper course for governmental policy had not yet coalesced. For instance, on the issue of managing the economy, Frankfurter advocated governmental regulation of monopolistic businesses, while Brandeis suggested that they be broken up into smaller, more efficient companies through vigorous antitrust action. Consistent with these differing views, the two men supported different presidential candidates in the election of 1912. Frankfurter backed the New Nationalism of Theodore Roosevelt while Brandeis's support went to Woodrow Wilson. Brandeis did make an effort, however, to bring Frankfurter over to his side.

> I am glad to know that you feel contented with the state of things politically. I have myself been much disturbed by the repeated divisions of the Progressive forces. If [another candidate] had been nominated substantially all Progressives might have joined in opposition to the Republican and Democratic nominees. With Wilson nominated, after the masterful and masterly handling of the convention by Bryan, it seemed to me that the duty of Progressives was clearly to support Wilson and practically capture the Democratic party. The insistence upon a Roosevelt-Republican party seems to me to postpone the real alignment on national, social and economic lines. [64]

In the end, Frankfurter's opposition to Wilson was not so adamant as to prevent his staying on for a short time in the War Department after the election.

Despite these early philosophical differences, the friendship between Brandeis and Frankfurter quickly deepened. An entry for October 20, 1911, in Frankfurter's diary reveals the breadth of his admiration even then. "Brandeis has depth and an intellectual sweep that are tonical. He has great force, he has Lincoln's fundamental sympathies. I wish he had his patience, his magnanimity, his humor. Brandeis is a very big man, one of the most penetrating minds I know, I should like to see him Attorney General of the United States."[65]

Brandeis came to have a similarly high regard for Frankfurter, as he outlined in this letter to conservationist Philip Wells. "If the War Department seems to be going wrong on water power questions, I hope you will discuss them fully with Frankfurter. He is thoroughly with us on conservation, and is so intelligent that I consider him a power for the right."[66] Moreover, even at this stage of their relationship, Brandeis had grown to appreciate Frankfurter's skill in placing people, as he wrote to one job seeker, "I presume you have written Felix Frankfurter, who has a faculty, rarely equalled, of hearing about 'possible opportunities' for men capable of doing good work."[67]

By 1913 the relationship between the two men had grown to a point that attorney Brandeis assumed an active role in Frankfurter's next career move. Not only did he suggest to Dean Roscoe Pound that the Harvard Law School hire Frankfurter, but Brandeis then went on to suggest some possibilities for funding the position.[68] When the offer to join the faculty was made in November of that year, Frankfurter was so startled that he later commented, "If I had received a letter from an Indian princess asking me to marry her, I wouldn't have been more surprised."[69] For a man who relished the excitement of political controversies, the decision to devote his life to teaching was a difficult one. Consequently, he consulted those friends whose opinions he most respected—Oliver Wendell Holmes, magazine editor Herbert Croly, Theodore Roosevelt, Henry L. Stimson, and, unaware of the earlier efforts he had made on Frankfurter's behalf, Louis D. Brandeis.

Contrary to the advice of all the others, who feared that Frankfurter would be happy only in government service, Brandeis encouraged him to accept the position. When Frankfurter expressed reservations about his qualifications for such an eminent position, Brandeis's answer was simply, "I would let those who have the responsibilities for selecting you decide your qualifications and not have you decide that."[70] With no further argument, Frankfurter at age thirty-one joined the faculty on September 1, 1914, and, for the next twenty-five years, shaped the minds of generations of the nation's most elite law students. Using his penetrating Socratic questioning, he created a "thinking shop" in such courses as Public Utilities, Jurisdiction and Procedure of the Federal Courts, and Administrative Law.[71]

With Frankfurter now teaching in Cambridge and Brandeis practicing law just across the Charles River in Boston, the two men were able to meet more frequently on a face-to-face basis. No longer did they seem to be taking separate roads toward social reform. In the finest Brandeisian tradition, Frankfurter helped establish the Washington-based magazine *The New Republic* and worked with Florence Kelley's National Consumers' League for social legislation. When Brandeis later went to the Supreme Court, it was Frankfurter who was selected to replace him as the unpaid head counsel in several maximum-hours and minimum-wage legislation cases.[72]

During this early period, Brandeis was also able to test Frankfurter's ability as a lieutenant in another area. Just two days before the professor began at Harvard, Brandeis took over the leadership of the American Zionist movement. Then, in March 1915, he created an advisory council—an inner circle of his closest advisers—and appointed Felix Frankfurter as one of its members.[73] Brandeis was pleased with Frankfurter's performance here in all respects. Not surprisingly, as they worked together more closely, the personal philosophy of the Harvard professor gradually came to mirror that of the Boston reformer.

By the time Brandeis went to the Supreme Court in October 1916, he had total confidence in Felix Frankfurter. Their friendship had grown to a point where his letters to the professor were addressed "Dear Felix," making Frankfurter one of the few people in Brandeis's world to be so honored. In a personal letter sent to Frankfurter a few years later, Brandeis characterized the importance of their friendship to him; their relationship was so intimate that Felix Frankfurter had become a "half brother-half son."[74]

Brandeis's confidence in Frankfurter manifested itself in many ways. For the rest of his judicial career, he had Frankfurter send him sight unseen Harvard law students—no others—to be his law clerks. Further, even after his judicial appointment, Brandeis continued to discuss legal issues with Frankfurter, trusting even the secrets of life on the Court to him. Not even Brandeis's intimate friends and Progressive allies like Norman Hapgood, were privy to such information. As

Hapgood complained in a short note to another personal friend, Franklin Delano Roosevelt, "Louis never talks to me about important issues anymore."[75] Other than to his wife, Brandeis was closer to no other person.

With such complete confidence in Frankfurter's ability, views, and discretion, Brandeis had his candidate for a contact to the "outside" political realm. Just one month after the opening of his first term on the Court, he put the relationship on a more businesslike footing. Realizing that Frankfurter, as a professor at the Harvard Law School, would not be able to bear the considerable expenses associated with such a long-term lobbying effort, the justice was very willing to use for such a purpose some of his considerable financial holdings, which were estimated to be worth over 2 million dollars by the time he went to the Court.[76] On November 19, 1916, Brandeis wrote to the professor.

> My dear Felix: You have had considerable expense for travelling, telephoning and similar expenses in public matters undertaken at my request or following up my suggestions *and will doubtless have more in the future no doubt*. These expenses should, of course, be borne by me. [*Italics mine*]
>
> I am sending [a] check for $250 on this account. Let me know when it is exhausted or if it has already been.[77]

Frankfurter returned the check, writing back to Brandeis that he would "treasure [the offer] . . . as one does a deep experience."[78] However, Brandeis was not to be denied and, in his next letter, elaborated more fully what he had in mind regarding their future political relationship, he wrote:

> My dear Felix: Alice and I talked over the matter before I sent the check and considered it again carefully on receipt of your letter. We are clearly of opinion that you ought to take the check.
>
> In essence this is nothing different than your taking travelling and incidental expenses from the Consumers League or the New Republic—which I trust you do. You are giving your very valuable time and that is quite enough. It can make no difference that the subject matter in connection with which the expense is incurred is more definite in one case than in the other.
>
> *I ought to feel free to make suggestions to you, although they involve some incidental expense*. And you should feel free to incur expense in the public interest. So I am returning the check.[79] [*Italics mine*]

This time Frankfurter agreed and the "joint-endeavors-for-the-public-good" fund was established in the Engineers National Bank in Boston.[80]

It was not surprising to find Brandeis prepared to spend his own money to help further the public good, as he had done so throughout his career. He had always considered it a privilege of his wealth to make such contributions to society.

> Some men buy diamonds and rare works of art, others delight in automobiles and yachts. My luxury is to invest my surplus effort, beyond that required for the proper support of my family, to the pleasure of taking up a problem and solving, or helping to solve it, for the people without receiving any compensation. Your yachtsman or automobilist would lose much of his enjoyment if he were obliged to do for pay what he is doing for the love of the thing itself. So I should lose much of my satisfaction if I were paid in connection with public services of this kind.[81]

Over the years, in fact, Brandeis donated nearly 1.5 million dollars to various causes, charities, and organizations.[82] What makes this particular contribution to Felix Frankfurter so unusual is that it was designed to free Brandeis from the shackles of remaining nonpolitical while on the bench and to permit him to engage freely in political affairs simply by sending to Frankfurter a letter filled with "suggestions" for various programs.

Soon these missives flowed in a near deluge to Cambridge. They went far beyond simply proposing policy ideas to suggesting the various means by which these goals might be accomplished. Thus it was that Justice Brandeis and Professor Frankfurter forged in 1916 a potent partnership for the purpose of shaping public policy.

As the expense of the lobbying effort rose, so did the amount of money sent by Brandeis for these purposes. In mid-1917 he placed $1,000 in the special account, and then replenished that amount in each of the next seven years.[83] By this time, Frankfurter quite naturally came to depend on the payments. More than this, the financial aspects of his relationship with Brandeis led Frankfurter to view himself as an employee being compensated for services rendered. Accordingly, when the need arose, he had no qualms about asking the justice for a "raise" in 1925. The expense of psychiatric care for Frankfurter's wife, Marion, who had suffered a nervous breakdown in 1923, led to this extraordinary request.

> After considerable self-debate, I have concluded that it is unfair to withhold from you a personal problem. To carry out the therapy prescribed by Dr. Salmon for Marion will mean the additional expenditure of about $1500 per academic year for this and the following year. There is little doubt that I could fill the gap through odd jobs for some of my New York lawyer friends. But I begrudge the time and thought that would take from intrinsically more important jobs—and so I put the situation to you. Marion knows, of course, of the extent to which you make possible my efforts of a public concern and rejoices over it. But I'm not telling her of this because her sensitiveness might be needlessly burdened where our private interests are involved.[84]

This letter shows clearly both the closeness felt by Frankfurter towards his mentor and benefactor and the change in his own attitude regarding the arrangement between them. Whereas in 1916 he chose to return Brandeis's check, now Frankfurter believed himself to be in a position to ask for six times that amount. Quite understandably, Justice Brandeis did deposit another $1,500 in 1925, telling Frankfurter in a letter written on September 24, "I am glad you wrote me about the personal needs . . . your public service must not be abridged."[85]

Beginning in the following year, perhaps partly in response to Frankfurter's request for his wife, Brandeis raised his contribution to $3,500, which was provided in two separate installments for use by the professor as he deemed appropriate. These payments were made automatically by Brandeis's secretary every year thereafter until Frankfurter himself was appointed to the Supreme Court.[86] By now, the arrangement had grown to a point where Frankfurter fully expected the support and, on the one occasion when it did not arrive as scheduled, he showed no hesitation in inquiring about it. For his part, Brandeis, who was most apologetic for the delay in this instance, gave Frankfurter no reason to reconsider this aspect of their relationship.[87]

It is difficult to judge the actual value of these payments. One indication is to compare them to Frankfurter's yearly salary, which ranged between approximately $6,000 and $10,000 during his tenure at Harvard.[88] However, to fully appreciate the magnitude of these contributions, economic statistics show that the $3,500 Brandeis provided annually to Frankfurter from 1926 to 1938 varied in value in 1981 dollars between $19,150 and $26,150 depending on the year involved.[89]

The political partnership was ideal for both men. For Brandeis, it provided a means by which he could satisfy his own reformist urges while still displaying the "judicial temperament" that critics in the confirmation hearings argued he lacked. More than just being concerned with public appearances, however, Brandeis was genuinely worried about conflicts of interest. Paul Freund, in a personal interview with the author in 1977, recalled that throughout his life Brandeis repeatedly advised bankers to remove themselves from any connection with ongoing businesses.[90] No doubt, this financial relationship with Frankfurter, while open to question by others, satisfied Brandeis's own norms by allowing him to maintain a certain distance from the political issues and actors. His arrangement with Frankfurter not only made it possible for the justice to propose his programs surreptitiously, but, for a man whose life was dedicated to ferreting out all the facts on any particular issue, to get the necessary information on a topic from a reliable source. Thus, Frankfurter provided Brandeis the conduit through which he might both inquire freely in the political realm and influence the course of political decisions.

This arrangement was hardly one-sided, as it benefitted Frankfurter too. To be sure, the Harvard professor cannot be viewed solely as Brandeis's agent, in that he became involved in a wide circle of issues and causes célèbres on his own and in which the justice expressed no strong interest. The investigations in late 1917 into the forced evacuation of striking copper miners in Arizona, known as the Bisbee deportations, and the conviction of labor leader Tom Mooney for a bombing at the Preparedness Day Parade on July 22, 1916, were undertaken by Frankfurter alone as counsel to the president's mediation commission.[91] Yet his love and respect for the justice and for his views made Frankfurter willing to become a lieutenant in other political efforts. Furthermore, the availability of Brandeis's wealth enabled Frankfurter to continue his involvement in such issues without ever being impeded for lack of funds. For a man who was somewhat insulated himself as a professor in a law school in Cambridge, Massachusetts, the deal with Brandeis opened up new vistas for exciting and potentially influential political involvement. Clearly, Frankfurter received as much from this relationship as he gave to it, and he was so successful in carrying out these tasks that by 1928 Brandeis described him in a personal letter to the British philosopher Harold Laski, who was a personal friend of both men, as "the most useful lawyer in the United States."[92]

As extraordinary as this financial relationship between Brandeis and

Frankfurter was, there is no indication from either published or unpublished sources, that any of the justice's colleagues on the bench ever became aware of it. Or, if they did discover what was going on, they cared so little that it was never a cause for either public or private complaint. One indication of the success of this effort to hide the relationship from public view is the silence of Associate Justice William McReynolds. So incredibly anti-Semitic that he avoided speaking to Brandeis for a three-year period, refused to sit next to him in the annual Court picture for 1924 (hence no picture was taken that year), and on one occasion wrote to Chief Justice Taft, "As you know I am not always to be found when there is a Hebrew aboard," McReynolds hardly would have remained quiet had he discovered what was happening.[93] Perhaps it was the fear of people like McReynolds that in part led Brandeis to consider embarking on such a covert relationship in the first place.

Documentary research indicates that Brandeis only mentioned the arrangement to one other person, and then it was to one of his staunchest allies and another Zionist lieutenant—Court of Appeals Judge Julian Mack. Apparently, in early 1922, a suggestion was made by Mack that some of the funds donated to the Zionist cause be diverted to support Frankfurter's activities. Responding that "anything which [Frankfurter] would accept from anyone—should come from me," Brandeis promised to send $1,000, explaining to Mack that "anything I can do for Felix—which is best for him and for the cause he so generously leads—I am glad to do." Yet, the justice also expressed "doubt as to what is best to do," citing his "apprehension" of taking the easier way out by "the removal of financial limitations, [and his] belief in the saving grace of what many call drudgery."[94] Mack could not have known that such "doubt" had actually been resolved five years earlier when Brandeis sent his first check to Frankfurter.

Of course, it would be naive to think that certain congressmen and officials were unaware of, or did not suspect, Brandeis's involvement with Frankfurter on certain legislative proposals. But being old Progressive allies and dedicated admirers of Brandeis, they would have had no motivation to inquire into the exact nature of the relationship, or to reveal whatever they did discover or suspect.

So successful were Brandeis's efforts to hide his varied extrajudicial political efforts that not even his law clerks had any inkling as to what was going on. Unlike other justices on the Court, he had only one assistant and wrote all his opinions and correspondence in longhand. Thus, his political efforts through Frankfurter, and other conduits including Wilson Administration officials Josephus Daniels and William McAdoo, magazine editor Norman Hapgood, and Harlan Fiske Stone (interestingly enough, while Stone was also a member of the Supreme Court), were visible to no one else. When the justice needed on occasion to confer with various officials directly, he nearly always arranged, through intermediaries, for the political figure to approach him for the interview. Personal interviews with three of Brandeis's law clerks, now widely acknowledged as among the elite in their respective fields, law professor Paul Freund, senior Court of Appeals Judge Henry Friendly, and sociologist David Riesman, make clear how it was possible for Brandeis to hide his political efforts even from his closest assistant each year.

Before the completion of the construction of the present Supreme Court building in 1935, space for the justices in the Senate wing of the Capitol building was so limited that many of them worked at home. When Brandeis moved from his apartment at Stoneleigh Court to one on California Street, he converted a two-room apartment directly above his living quarters into a study area and small library for his clerks and himself. With the law clerks working there (and shuttling to the libraries at the Court and the Library of Congress), they were totally unaware of the stream of visitors Brandeis was receiving and counseling on a plethora of topics in the apartment below.[95] While judicial precedent was being forged above, political strategy was being planned below.

Thus did Brandeis make the transition from the People's Attorney to a Supreme Court justice. By employing Frankfurter and developing a style that satisfied the appearance of proper judicial temperament, he set forth, behind the scenes, to attempt to mold American society and government to his liking.

2

Pulling the Invisible Wires:
Brandeis in War and Zionism

The care Brandeis took to hide his political relationship with Frankfurter proved during his early years on the Court to have been unnecessary. Due to a curious amalgamation of factors, few outside restraints were put in the way of his pursuing his political endeavors openly. With a president who had appointed him and members of the executive branch who were his close friends, Brandeis had open lines of communication to all levels of government. In fact, so indispensable had he made himself by his earlier service that his ideas were widely sought on all issues. But these factors alone would not likely have been enough to allay Brandeis's own ethical qualms or more important, the public's general sensitivity to such activities at that time. Rather, it was World War I that overrode any normative proscriptions against extrajudicial activity and helped revive for the first time in nearly fifty years the possibility for open, frequent interaction between a sitting justice and a president on public policy matters.

Despite the ample precedent for open, extrajudicial involvement during such national crises, Brandeis's willingness to ignore the most restrictive restraints on such conduct came with great difficulty. No clearer evidence of this exists than in Brandeis's changed relationship with Woodrow Wilson. Despite their long and intimate friendship, no substantive letters passed between them during Wilson's remaining years in office. Even though Brandeis freely contacted other friends in the administration, he spoke to the president only after observing certain proprieties.

The effort to secure adequate railroad transportation during the war aptly demonstrates Brandeis's continued adherence to a somewhat stricter normative standard for extrajudicial involvement than that which existed for his predecessors during other crises. With supplies becoming bottlenecked in late 1917, and an impending coal famine facing some states, President Wilson determined that the government had to take over the operation of the railroads. However, the right man was needed to run the whole industry, and the president was reluctant to appoint the consensus candidate, William McAdoo, because he was already secretary of the treasury as well as Wilson's son-in-law. So two of McAdoo's supporters, Wilson's personal secretary, Joseph Tumulty, and Interstate Commerce Commissioner Robert Woolley, turned for help to the man who, in their opinion, might have the most influence with the president on this matter—Louis D. Brandeis.[1] When he agreed that McAdoo was the best candidate for the director generalship of the railroad system, Tumulty and Woolley urged Brandeis to make the suggestion directly to Wilson. But Brandeis flatly refused to travel to the White House for such a political purpose; so they spoke to the president and he decided to call on the justice himself.

When Wilson arrived at Brandeis's apartment unannounced, accompanied only by two Secret Service agents, Brandeis was in his upstairs library with books strewn everywhere, struggling to produce a judicial opinion. Alice Brandeis, in a letter to her sister, Susan Goldmark, vividly portrayed the contradiction in the justice's roles this picture presented: "Here surely was the scholar, the student at his work. And yet it is as a practical man of affairs, a statesman, that Louis's advice is so much sought."[2] Wilson explained to Brandeis that, "I could not request for you to come to me, and I have therefore come to ask your advice."[3] After forty-five minutes of conversation, the justice convinced the president to appoint McAdoo, providing only that McAdoo first resign from the Treasury Department.

Brandeis's self-imposed proscription against initiating direct contact with public officials did not, however, extend to members at the lower levels of the administration. Having earlier helped create several agencies and staff many other governmental departments, it was only natural that Brandeis should enjoy ready-made access to a great many officials. From his earlier reform campaigns he had also learned that effectiveness in proposing policies is increased if one advises several persons simultaneously, thus creating a mandate for change. So, the justice cultivated a network of allies and friends in the executive branch for such purposes.

Because of the range of Brandeis's contacts in the administration, his influence, according to one biographer, was "like many invisible wires into many government bureaus."[4] His activities were concentrated, however, in the Treasury, Justice, and War Departments, and in a number of other minor agencies. While he was secretary of the treasury, William McAdoo was a constant correspondent with and visitor to the justice. His dialogues with Brandeis ranged from matters of policy, such as the next Liberty Loan Campaign, to recommendations for future executive branch appointments.[5] Brandeis's working relationship with Felix Frankfurter proved to be very helpful here, as correspondence discovered between the two men confirms. When searching for worthy persons to fill vacant positions, the justice would often forward names to Frankfurter for investigation and approval.[6] With his own vast contacts, and the freedom to ask questions openly, the professor provided a very useful service in the search process.

Thomas Gregory, the attorney general, also provided a willing ear for Brandeis's counsel. Because of their long association, solidified by Gregory's defense of Brandeis in the confirmation battle, the attorney general's requests went beyond the usual discussion of names for appointments and general policies. On occasion, Gregory would ask Brandeis to write memoranda on specific policies then under consideration by the department.[7] Knowing of the attorney general's influential role in recommending judicial appointments to the president, Brandeis also sent Gregory information on potential appointees to the federal bench. Included in one such letter to Gregory was an analysis of District Court Judge Learned Hand's qualifications for elevation to an expected vacancy on the United States Court of Appeals for the Second Circuit.[8]

Further indication of their close relationship was the fact that Brandeis actively promoted Gregory for the Supreme Court vacancy created by the resignation of Charles Evans Hughes in 1916.[9] The justice was so desperate to have another Progressive join him on the Court that he put aside his own fears about open involvement in such matters. Evidence of Brandeis's great interest here, and of his political strategy, was recorded in the personal diary of Colonel Edward M. House. In an entry dated June 19, 1916, House, the president's intimate adviser, described the pressure being placed on him to act in this area.

> I had a telephone message from District Attorney Anderson, who was in Justice Brandeis's office in Boston and was speaking for the Justice as well as for himself. They urged that I use my influence to have Gregory appointed a Justice of the Supreme Court. They had been talking to Gregory and had come to the conclusion that . . . the President would appoint him if I advised him to do so, and Gregory would accept if I thought it best for him to do so.[10]

Other entries in the House diary show that Felix Frankfurter, acting very much on his own, also wrote to the Colonel recommending that either Gregory or former Solicitor General Herbert Lehmann be nominated for the vacancy.[11] But in this same diary, House reported that these entreaties were not entirely persuasive. Because he thought it would be far better to have Gregory remain in a position to recommend the appointment of individuals with the "right" views as federal judges, House declined to approach President Wilson in Gregory's behalf.[12] Instead, the nomination went to federal judge John H. Clarke on July 14, 1916.

Secretary of the Navy Josephus Daniels's relationship with Brandeis was a bit different in that he was often used as a direct emissary from the president. Because of each man's consciousness of the constraints of judicial propriety, Wilson consulted the justice directly only in the most extreme circumstances, such as in May 1917, when an amendment to the pending Espionage Bill threatened to limit his embargo powers.[13] Though now that he had put Brandeis on the Court he had to face getting along without his views on most issues, the president nevertheless felt compelled in emergencies to send intermediaries to glean them. As an intimate acquaintance of both men, Daniels was a likely choice.

> Not once but a number of times discussing humanitarian progressive policies, [Wilson] would say to me: "I wish you would go to see our friend Brandeis, acquaint him with the problem and get his reaction." Brandeis knew he was talking to the President through me, but I learned much in the conversations, which often took a wide range.[14]

Throughout the war, Brandeis also advised Daniels directly on problems within the secretary of the Navy's own domain.

Ample evidence that the justice also developed a vast network of contacts in the lower levels of these departments is also contained in his private letters. From these letters we learn that men such as Assistant Attorney General Charles Warren and Assistant Secretary of the Treasury Leo S. Rowe supplied the justice with departmental gossip.[15] Brandeis also received a steady flow of data and analyses from correspondence and discussions with members of various agencies, such as Federal Trade Commissioner William B. Colm, Tariff Commissioner Edward P. Costigan, and Interstate Commerce Commissioners Clyde B. Aitchison, Charles C. McChord, and George W. Anderson.[16]

The burgeoning bureaucracy that had been created to prosecute the war also gave Brandeis an enhanced opportunity for political involvement. In the summers of 1917 and 1918 he remained in Washington to be more accessible to all these officials. The justice's unpublished private letters are replete with contacts from government officials who were added to his "network of influence" because of this decision. Various other War Department officials, such as Assistant Secretaries William Ingraham and Thomas N. Perkins, administrator William Ripley, and Provost Marshal General John Wigmore freely supplied the justice with useful data and personally consulted him on other issues, such as price controls and the allocation of food resources.[17] In addition, after McAdoo took over the Railroad Administration, his subordinates August Gutheim and Walker Hines were frequent visitors to the Brandeis apartment.[18] Secretary of War Newton Baker took advantage of the availability of such sage advice and consulted Brandeis on the labor situation in the munitions industries. So impressed was Baker with the advice he received that he forwarded it directly to Woodrow Wilson with the recommendation that the president see Brandeis for a "disinterested view of the whole situation."[19] Such general respect for the Brandeis view led Wilson to designate Brandeis and Colonel House to accumulate information for the establishment of a peace treaty at the end of the war.[20]

Of course, there were some officials who were receptive to Brandeis's counsel because they owed their jobs to him. This certainly appears to have been the case with Herbert Hoover—whom Brandeis recommended to the secretaries of war and the treasury to be appointed as food administrator in 1917. Thereafter, Hoover frequently dined with the justice to facilitate discussion of various problems. It was Brandeis who advised him in June 1917 how to secure the enactment of the Lever Food Control bill, an act designed to prevent food shortages and price increases by giving the government absolute authority over the production and distribution of necessary foodstuffs. The justice told Hoover to personally plead the case for passage with one of the most vocal opponents of the act, Senator James Reed. The bill became law on August 10, 1917.[21]

The justice's advice to Hoover, however, was not limited solely to matters of lobbying strategy. Typical of the wide-ranging nature of the intercourse between the two is this response by the justice in November 1918 to a request by Hoover, sent through the food administrator's secretary, Louis Strauss, for his views on "the urgency of the Russian question."

> Thus far we have misunderstood the Russian people and very much underestimated the situation. None of the Commissions which we have sent to Russia has . . . accomplished the least fragment of tangible result, and . . . [they] have been harmful to our prestige among the masses and confusing to individual Russians who may be earnestly trying to discover a way towards stabilization and recovery. Neither military nor diplomatic missions are . . . capable of bringing the proper help, [as] what is needed is an economic mission which would offer its services in an attempt to promote economic recovery and heal the wounds which the transportation and production structures of the Empire have suffered as a result of war and revolution. . . . The present [communist] Government . . . should nevertheless be dealt with in the utmost caution until its intentions are clear and we are convinced of its honesty . . . Any delay in facing the situation will postpone the restoration of normal world conditions and allow the focus of the disorganization to fester and spread.[22]

Though Brandeis's recommendations for a Soviet policy were not followed, his ideas did foreshadow the Marshall Plan concept of reconstructing Europe after World War II through wide-scale economic aid.

Blessed with so many contacts in the government, Brandeis pushed for two main policies. The first was streamlining the governmental machinery for fighting the war. By 1918, it had become apparent that the Wilson Administration was ill-prepared for conducting a major war effort. Blinded by their Progressive instincts, they neglected the large-scale production techniques so necessary to waging modern, mechanized warfare. Despite the use of such methods as competitive bidding for contracts, costs always soared and mobilization efforts lagged. The nature of these problems was plainly evident to the justice, yet he seemed reluctant to offer any solutions without first observing a certain sense of judicial propriety. So, it was left to Felix Frankfurter, who had his own contacts in the administration, to get things rolling. According to an account in House's personal diary, Frankfurter informed the Colonel by letter that if he "requested it . . . Brandeis would write a memorandum pointing out the shortcomings of the War Department." [23] That Brandeis's advice was solicited is evident from the opening words of the letter from Brandeis to House: "You have asked my opinion of the War Department and the War Industry Board and Committees . . ." [24]

Indicating that he "consider[ed] the situation very serious" for both the nation and the Democratic party, Brandeis suggested that "betterment [could] come only through radical changes in systems." [25] The thrust of these suggested alterations was to remove all powers of munitions administration from the War Department and the War Industry Board and vest them "in a single head with full power of delegation." Recognizing the crushing burden of the "Labor Problem" he also recommended that a separate labor administration be created, headed by a single director, to deal with the issues of wages, labor conditions, and strikes. Brandeis also proposed that the War Department, which would be left in sole charge of military policy, be reorganized and coordinated. In addition, the justice called for the creation of a central intelligence office to speed the flow of information and the appointment of a director of shipping to deal with transportation policy. He concluded by suggesting that "effective conduct of the war" required that:

> A small car council independent of all departments and composed of men freed from the detail of administration and of executive responsibility should be created to consider the broad questions of policy in internal and external affairs and submit to the President the results of their deliberations. [26]

On their face, these proposals seem to contradict Brandeis's general desire for small government and suggest his support of a more centralized authority. More likely, however, the justice, ever cognizant of man's limited capabilities, was seeking to reduce the load on Secretary of War Newton Baker. He wanted also to delineate clearly the responsibilities for officials undertaking these different policies and to hold these individuals strictly accountable for their actions. President Wilson and others in the administration found these arguments persuasive. Consequently, they proposed and secured the passage of an executive reorganization bill known as the Overman Act. This measure, which virtually gave the president a *carte blanche* to restructure the various war agencies, was then used successfully to force Brandeis's suggested changes on the War Industries Board.[27]

Quite understandably, Secretary of War Baker attempted to block this reorganization, the effect of which would be to substantially diminish his authority. So, Justice Brandeis tried to sweep him aside as well. After complaining constantly to Colonel House about Baker's inefficiency, the justice then attempted to have him replaced by General Enoch H. Crowder, but here Brandeis's efforts succeeded initially only in raising House's ire. On February 23, 1918, the Colonel recorded in his personal diary: "I cannot understand why a Justice of the Supreme Court should bother about other people's business as Brandeis does."[28] Nevertheless, in the following day's entry, House mentions that he did relay the Brandeis message to President Wilson.

Such concern for any overreaching of judicial authority was not widely shared. When the administration decided in 1918 to adopt Brandeis's suggestion to create a War Labor Policies Board, several people tried to have the justice himself named as its head. One of these was Felix Frankfurter, who even tried to persuade Chief Justice White to allow Brandeis to occupy the new position while simultaneously sitting on the Court. Recalling the earlier Mexican affair, however, the president opposed the appointment fearing it might compel Brandeis to resign from the Court in order to accept the position. Instead, he did the next best thing by tapping Felix Frankfurter to be the chairman.[29]

Now, with Brandeis's own surrogate positioned as a central cog in the war machinery, a surfeit of memoranda, position papers, and general information crossed Brandeis's desk.[30] Other administrators, such as Morris L. Cooke of the Shipping Board, Charles McCarthy of the Food Administration, and Charles Howland of the War Industries Board, also kept the justice amply informed of improvements in these areas.[31] Despite his position on the Court, Brandeis thus continued to act as a member of the Wilson Administration during the war.

One might have expected that extrajudicial activity that was this extensive and wide ranging would have had to take its toll on Brandeis's ability to perform his official duties. In fact it did not. He wrote virtually the same number of opinions during each of the war years as after them,[32] and there was never a suggestion by any of his colleagues or by the Chief Justice that he was not maintaining his share of the Court's workload. However, questions can be raised about his apparent willingness to remain on the bench hearing suits that stemmed from political actions in which he had earlier been involved.

Few would have suggested that Brandeis's intimate connection with the Wilson Administration should have been cause for his disqualifying himself on any case concerning the government's war-related activities. Accordingly, he cannot be faulted for joining a unanimous Court in upholding the Selective Service Act,[33] and the War Time Prohibition Act.[34] Nor can he be criticized for working with Boston Brahmin Oliver Wendell Holmes, a man Brandeis later described to Felix Frankfurter as the Court's "best intellectual machine,"[35] in arguing the need for greater protection of freedom of speech in a series of cases challenging the 1917 Espionage Act and its 1918 amendments.[36]

Brandeis can be questioned, however, for his decision to sit in a number of other war-related cases dealing with matters that had received his attention off the bench. He joined a unanimous ruling in 1919 in upholding an Army Appropriations Act, which gave the president power to seize and operate common carriers.[37] It was this legislation that had spurred President Wilson eighteen months earlier to place the nation's railroads under a director general, and then to talk with Justice Brandeis regarding the appointment of William McAdoo to the post. This, in turn, resulted in the justice's advisory role with McAdoo's subordinates following the appointment. Then, in 1921, Brandeis remained on the bench to hear ten separate challenges to the Lever Food Control bill, despite his having earlier personally advised Food Administrator Herbert Hoover on a strategy for securing initial passage of the measure in the Senate. Here, however, Brandeis agreed with the Court's decision to strike down two parts of the law's fourth section because they were poorly drawn and failed to provide adequate standards justifying the government's actions.[38]

It is intriguing to ask why Brandeis decided to hear these cases despite his earlier involvement, however peripheral, with the legislation being examined. When challenges to the minimum-wage and maximum-hour legislation had come before the Court—an issue that had occupied so much of Brandeis's time and energy when he was still in private practice as counsel to the National Consumers' League—the new justice had withdrawn from considering the cases.[39] But when faced with the suits against the Army Appropriations Act and the Lever Food Control bill, his behavior was quite different, and, as such, very revealing. In each of those cases, Brandeis took part in these decisions as a formal voting member of the Court, but refused to sign the Court's majority opinion and noted that he concurred only in its final result, giving no further accounting of his own reasoning. Perhaps where his private political involvement with aspects of the cases was not known to the public, Brandeis felt no need to disqualify himself, but nonetheless did feel the need to satisfy personal ethical qualms by taking only a very minimal role in the ultimate judicial decision. On the other hand, the fact that his involvement with the minimum-wage and maximum-hour legislation cases was publicly known made it necessary for him to remove himself completely in those instances.

Another possible explanation for Brandeis's decision to remain on the bench in the wartime cases may be evident from his formal ruling in the Lever Act suits, in which portions of the law were overturned. By voting with the Court against the act, after having privately told Herbert Hoover how to get it enacted, Brandeis seemingly demonstrated to those who knew his dual interests and perhaps to himself also the separation that existed between his judicial and political roles. Perhaps privately he saw himself merely as providing political expertise, rather than advocating a particular program, thus leaving him free in his own mind to review, and possibly even oppose, the legislation in his official capacity.[40] Brandeis would repeat this practice of officially hearing cases that had received his attention privately during the 1930s. While this behavior may have satisfied his own personal sense of ethics, it is likely that had the connection between Brandeis's actions on and off the Court been made public, the issue of the "appearance of judicial impropriety" might still have been raised.

Justice Brandeis used all his administration contacts to pursue his second major goal during the war—the establishment of a Jewish homeland in Palestine. Even after the Hotel Astor ambush in 1916 had forced him to resign as official head of the American Zionist movement, Brandeis still continued as its moving force behind the scenes. In fact, in later years, with the formation of the Zionist Organization of America (ZOA), Brandeis would even be listed on the group's letterhead as its "Honorary President."[41] But always the new official leaders of the American Zionists—Judge Julian W. Mack and Rabbi

Stephen S. Wise—remained very much his lieutenants. They would receive detailed instructions in frequent letters from "the Chief" and through conversations with his intermediary, Felix Frankfurter. Still guided by Brandeis, then, the American Zionists acquired substantial political influence in a short period of time.[42]

Because of the way foreign policy was being made at that time, Brandeis had to move directly, and very deliberately, in his effort to secure a Jewish homeland. In this cause, he greatly benefitted from his friendship with Josephus Daniels, who was already sympathetic to the Zionists, and that with Woodrow Wilson, particularly because Wilson, unlike many other presidents of the time, was predisposed to controlling foreign policy from the White House. Yet, the president was highly influenced by two other foreign policy advisers who were less enamored with Brandeis than he—Robert Lansing and Colonel Edward M. House. Lansing, the secretary of state, displayed a distinct anti-Zionist bias, and House a distaste for Brandeis's political meddling. Still, masterminding the lobbying effort through such a political minefield was not an impossible task for Louis Brandeis.

By 1916, the complexity of events in the Middle East had dampened the prospects for establishing a Jewish homeland. The desired land, Palestine, was then part of Turkey, one of the Central Powers in World War I. Moreover, Great Britain and France had already secretly negotiated the Sykes-Picot agreement, which arranged for the division of Palestine between them once the war had ended. For over a year the leader of the World Zionist Organization (WZO), Chaim Weizmann, had been negotiating with no perceptible success with British officials to declare their support for a Jewish homeland in Palestine. The Zionists' only hope came with the election in December 1916 of David Lloyd George as the new British prime minister. He at least was willing to listen to Weizmann. The two men had met several times concerning Zionism beginning in late 1914, and later due to Weizmann's pioneering war-related research as a chemical engineer.[43]

Knowing of Louis Brandeis's enormous influence with the Wilson Administration, Weizmann decided to involve this acknowledged leader of the American Zionists in his effort. This was not the first effort to co-opt Brandeis. Earlier some Zionists had even hoped that the justice might be able to convince President Wilson to bring the United States into war to further the prospects of securing a Jewish homeland in Palestine. Weizmann's plan was a bit more realistic. Not yet aware of the Sykes-Picot agreement, he had already encountered coolness from the French and only vague promises from the British in asking them to commit themselves.[44] Believing that a push from the United States government might tip the scales with British officials, Weizmann cabled Justice Brandeis that "an expression of opinion coming from yourself and perhaps other gentlemen connected with the Government in favor of a Jewish Palestine under a British protectorate would greatly strengthen our hands."[45]

While Brandeis could not speak for the government, he certainly was not constrained from lobbying in private. On May 6, 1917, shortly after the entry of the United States into the war, Brandeis met with President Wilson for forty-five minutes in an effort to clearly define the American government's position on the Palestine question. After hearing Brandeis's arguments, Wilson stated that he "was entirely sympathetic to the aims of the Zionist Movement, and that he believed that the Zionist formula, to establish a publicly assured, legally secured homeland for the Jewish people in Palestine, would meet the situation; that from the point of view of national problems generally, he approved and would support the recognition of the nationality."[46] The president concluded by "expressing himself in agreement with the policy, under England's protectorate, for a Jewish Homeland"[47] and promised that any statement he might make on this matter would be first drafted by Brandeis. However, Wilson said that such a pronouncement would have to wait until he could persuade the French to abandon their interests in the area.

Buoyed by these assurances, Brandeis conferred on the following day with British Foreign Secretary Arthur Balfour, at the invitation of the latter. The justice was pleasantly surprised to discover that there was considerable support within the British government for Zionist goals. Balfour even encouraged Brandeis to secure the support of the United States government for a British declaration on this matter.[48] Knowing the president's willingness to concur only privately at this time, the justice prepared to play a waiting game until he could bring the two governments together.[49]

At this juncture, with the prospects of securing a British declaration looking so promising, events took a very dangerous turn for the Zionists. Part of Wilson's reluctance to act stemmed from his support for the plan of Henry Morgenthau, a former ambassador to Turkey, to negotiate for the withdrawal of that nation from the war. While this

might have shortened the conflict, it would also compromise the plan
to wrest Palestine from the Ottoman Empire.

In the summer of 1917 Morgenthau was about to embark to Turkey
in the hopes of securing this agreement. Using all his contacts and
influence with the Wilson Administration, Brandeis was able to place
Frankfurter on this diplomatic team.[50] Given the potentially fatal results for the Zionists' plans should the mission succeed, one can easily suspect Brandeis's ultimate motives for securing this appointment
for Frankfurter. In fact, the justice further minimized the hazards to
their cause by arranging for Frankfurter and Morgenthau to draft the
news releases for the mission together, for Brandeis and Robert Lansing to then review.[51] Lacking the requisite diplomatic skills, however, Morgenthau failed miserably. Frankfurter quickly convinced
Wilson to recall him before more damage was done.[52]

Simultaneously, the Zionists had secured some movement by this
time by the British government toward their goal. After considerable
negotiation, a declaration favoring Palestine had been drafted, though
it had been greatly watered down by assimilationist forces. These opponents of the declaration were English, anti-Zionist Jews, who were
fearful that a Jewish state might adversely affect their British citizenship and whose most notable spokesman was Sir Edwin S. Montagu,
the secretary of state for India.[53] To the horror of the Zionists, when
this weaker document was sent to Washington for President Wilson's
support, he stated on September 11, 1917, that the time was "not op-
portune" to commit himself to it.[54] Within two weeks, however, the
president would apparently show a willingness to reverse his stance,
an action that has been the subject of considerable speculation by
scholars.[55] The unpublished diaries of Colonel House reveal that it
was Supreme Court Justice Louis D. Brandeis who was able to engineer the change in the United States government's position.

With events at a crossroads, Weizmann had again turned to Brandeis for help. He cabled a copy of the much stronger original draft,
telling the justice that it: "would greatly help if President Wilson and
yourself would support text. Matter most urgent. Please telegraph."[56]
At this point Brandeis became an active participant in lobbying that
took place for the declaration. According to the account discovered in
the House diaries, Brandeis and Rabbi Wise met with House on September 23 in the hopes of securing his support.[57] With House's assistance, Brandeis drafted a private cable to Weizmann, a message that

has been described as "probably one of the most important LDB ever wrote."[58]

> From talks I have had with President and from expressions of opin-
> ion given to closest advisers I feel I can answer you in that he is [in]
> entire sympathy with declaration quoted in yours of nineteenth as
> approved by foreign office and the Prime Minister. I of course hear-
> tily agree.[59]

However, the Colonel also informed his visitors that in his opinion the president should still not make any public statement at all; he suggested that Brandeis and others "bring the French, Italian and Russian governments as near the attitude of Great Britain and the United States as was possible and then leave the matter there." Having said this, House then offered the Zionists some hope by confessing that the president "was willing to go further than I thought advisable" on this issue.[60]

Justice Brandeis wasted no time in playing his trump card of Wilson's sympathy with Zionism. He cabled Weizmann the day after his meeting with Colonel House: "It would be wise for you to get French and Italians to inquire what attitude of President is on declaration referred to in yours of the nineteenth."[61] A copy of this cable, along with other correspondence with the Zionist leader, was forwarded to Colonel House.[62]

Mere reassurances by Justice Brandeis of President Wilson's silent support for the Zionists hardly satisfied Weizmann. There was increasing pressure by anti-Zionists in Britain to stop the British government from making any declaration at all. Moreover, the Americans, still hopeful of a separate peace with Turkey, hesitated to do anything to jeopardize this chance.[63] In a long letter to Brandeis on October 7, 1917, Weizmann explained their plight and the need for "something definite" in favor of a Jewish homeland. He urged the justice to mobilize the opinion of American Jewry, and concluded with a plea.

> I have no doubt that the amended text of the declaration will be again
> submitted to the President and it would be most invaluable if the
> President would accept it without reservation and would recommend
> the granting of the declaration *now*.[64] [*Italics in original*]

Indicating the need for immediate action, Weizmann again cabled Brandeis three days later seeking the president's support for the amended text of the declaration.[65]

The justice, however, was simply not as willing to accept the watered-down wording of the more recent text as Weizmann, who by this time was prepared to support any form of declaration by the British government in behalf of Zionism. So, when Wilson received the "final" version of the text from the British Foreign Office and sent it along to Brandeis, Jacob DeHaas, and Stephen Wise for their suggestions, they redrafted it in a manner that strengthened its wording. On October 16, Colonel House notified the British of Wilson's approval of this revised text, but he reserved the right to make this announcement public at a time of the president's own choosing.[66] With this final assurance, Lord Balfour released on November 2, 1917 the historic British declaration in favor of a Jewish homeland that came to be known as the Balfour Declaration.

> His majesty's Government view with favour the establishment in Palestine of a national home for the Jewish people, and will use their best efforts to facilitate the achievement of this object, it being clearly understood that nothing shall be done which may prejudice the civil and religious rights of existing non-Jewish communities in Palestine or the rights and political status enjoyed by Jews in any other country.[67]

Of course, much remained to be done in translating these words into action, not the least of which was to fend off wholesale attacks on it by the assimilationists in the United States and Europe. The justice was instrumental in these defensive actions as well. However, here he preferred to operate through his numerous lieutenants in the newly formed ZOA: Felix Frankfurter, Judge Julian Mack, Jacob De-Haas, Robert Szold, Stephen S. Wise, and Bernard G. Flexner.[68] Knowing of Brandeis's efforts to maintain a semblance of discretion, President Wilson consulted Rabbi Wise in late August 1918 regarding the preparations for the Paris Peace Conference. Prior to that meeting, Justice Brandeis had supplied Wise with all the information he would need in talking to the president.[69] Persuaded by this conference, Wilson shortly thereafter publicly endorsed the Balfour Declaration for the first time.[70]

The peace negotiations themselves posed new dangers to the viability of Palestine, which, Brandeis and the Zionists believed, depended on the awarding of a mandate over the area solely to Great Britain. Initially, there was talk of a joint British-French directorate of Palestine. Brandeis quashed this discussion with a cable instructing Stephen Wise, who was then in London with the president and Colonel House, to inform them that the justice "favor[ed] and [had] long advocated British trusteeship under the League of Nations; and [the] resolution of [the] American Jewish Congress to this effect expressed the will and judgment of [a] vast majority of Jews in America."[71] Soon, another obstacle became evident to Felix Frankfurter, who was then in Europe as an observer of the Paris Peace Conference for the ZOA— the newly created King-Crane Commission, established by Wilson to investigate the situation in Palestine, might issue a report opposing Zionist interests in that area.[72] This prospect, combined with other dangers, convinced Frankfurter that the matter needed Brandeis's personal attention.

The Harvard professor was laboring under the impression that such help would soon be on the way. In a meeting with Brandeis in early February 1919 to discuss the aims of Frankfurter's upcoming European trip, the justice had vowed, "I shall leave for Palestine [on] the first day [that the] Court closes." Brandeis then went on to explain that he expected Frankfurter "to have been there for some little time before and surmised the situation."[73] By May of that year, though, Brandeis made it clear in telegrams to Frankfurter that he was rethinking his plans.

The collection of Zionist-related documents Frankfurter bequeathed to the Hebrew University in Israel contains letters that illustrate how he was able to influence the reluctant justice. It seems that Brandeis was having second thoughts about the timing of the trip and about the propriety of a Supreme Court justice undertaking such a private diplomatic mission. So, after consulting the British Foreign Office, Frankfurter blitzed the justice with a flurry of cables reasserting the need for such a journey. To further persuade Brandeis, Frankfurter even passed along in one of these letters a message directly from Woodrow Wilson indicating that the president was still in favor of the Balfour Declaration. Not surprisingly, private correspondence discovered in the unpublished papers of Justice Brandeis reveals that this encouraging word from President Wilson was written in response to a direct request from Professor Frankfurter.[74]

In the end, the stakes were simply too high for Brandeis not to become directly and personally involved. On June 14, 1919, the justice set sail. There is no record, either published or unpublished, indicating that any of Brandeis's brethren on the Court questioned the propriety of his journey or found it the least bit unusual. In fact, the routine manner in which the other justices referred to this excursion is suggested by this comment written following Brandeis's trip by Oliver Wendell Holmes in a letter to his long-time correspondent, British philosopher Harold J. Laski: "Brandeis called and seemed to me transfigured by his experiences [in Europe and Palestine]."[75]

It was during this European trip that Brandeis finally met Chaim Weizmann.[76] After conferring with various British officials, Brandeis wrote to his wife: "My coming was very much needed, more than I could have conceived possible, and I feel that I may be of real value all along the line, with the British quite as much as with our own people."[77] Brandeis then traveled to Paris, where he was even more influential. Prior to his arrival, during the months of April and May, the justice's Zionist lieutenants—Frankfurter, Judge Mack, and Louis Marshall—had kept Colonel House informed on developments in the Middle East.[78] Two letters located in the Frankfurter papers indicate that as a Harvard professor Frankfurter had even been able to exchange views with Arab leader Prince Feisal, who expressed the fear that Great Britain and France might replace Turkey as governors of his area.[79] Now Brandeis was able to speak with the various governmental leaders directly.

On June 23, the justice conferred in the French capital with Colonel House and Hugh Gibson, the American minister to Poland. Gibson took the occasion to warn Brandeis about "exaggerated statements of conditions" of Jews in Poland and elsewhere. Unknown to the justice, however, as House privately confessed in a diary entry the following day, the Colonel had coached Ambassador Gibson to deliver his warning to Brandeis for the purpose of deterring the Zionist forces from claiming that Jews had been massacred.[80]

Brandeis also spoke with President Wilson, members of the French cabinet, the Italian ambassador, and Baron Edmond deRothschild.[81] Moreover, Lord Arthur Balfour and Lord Eustace Percy were given the benefit of the justice's counsel in a meeting on June 24, 1919. With each of these officials, Brandeis pleaded that Palestine be made the Jewish homeland and that it be given "economic elbow room" to assure "self-sufficiency for a healthy social life." The justice also pressed for absolute "control of the land and natural resources" by the Jews in Palestine. Balfour agreed with Brandeis on the need for a Jewish homeland and promised to defer any final decision on these matters until Brandeis returned from his upcoming visit to Palestine.[82]

The justice's later moves on this trip were recorded in a group of virtually illegible diary/love letters, many hurriedly written in smudged pencil by the thirty-six-year-old Felix Frankfurter to his fiancée, Marion Denman.[83] Following his short tour of Palestine, the justice returned to Paris for an additional three days of conferences with Colonel House, Lord Balfour, and the American peace commissioners.[84] House had become even more pessimistic regarding the prospects for a British mandate because of a perceived unwillingness on the part of the French, especially Prime Minister Clemenceau, to relinquish their interest in the area.[85] Fortunately for Brandeis, his conversation with British Foreign Secretary Balfour helped turn the tide. Brandeis accused the then-current British administration in Palestine of having a distinctly pro-Arab bias and demanded reform of this position. To the justice's pleasure, Balfour's reaction had indeed been impressive, as described in this report by Jacob DeHaas:

> Mr. Balfour was quite angry at the Palestinian Administration, with the result that on Wednesday all the Administrative officials in Palestine were notified of the Government's attitude in a dispatch. . . . This speedy action, following as it does the appointment of Colonel Minertzhagen to replace Colonel Clayton in Palestine, gives us unbounded satisfaction.[86]

Before sailing back to America, the justice returned to London for a final round of conferences. Speaking with "his characteristic straight-from-the-shoulder method," Brandeis was able to achieve a great deal at these meetings.[87] In fact, he even persuaded President Wilson to ignore the final report of the King-Crane Commission, which called, as Frankfurter had feared it would, for restrictions on Jewish immigration into Palestine and for a united Syria.[88]

In early 1920, the obstacle to the Zionists' aims foreseen by Colonel House, namely the ambitions of France in Palestine, surfaced with renewed discussions on the Sykes-Picot agreement. France wanted to divide the directorate over Palestine, thus threatening the economic viability of the area. Palestine's most powerful American supporter, Justice Brandeis, moved into action again. On February 3, he wrote to Woodrow Wilson—one of the few times they corresponded directly after his appointment to the Court.

> Negotiations in Paris on the Turkish settlement have reached so crit-
> ical a stage in their effects upon the realization of the Balfour Decla-
> ration of a Jewish Homeland in Palestine as to compel me to appeal
> to you. . . . The Balfour Declaration, which you made possible, was
> a public promise. I venture to suggest that it may be given to you at
> this time to move the statesmen of Christian nations to keep this sol-
> emn promise to Israel. Your word to Millerand and Lloyd George at
> this hour may be decisive.[89]

Brandeis then conferred personally with Secretary of State Lansing.
As he related to Judge Mack:

> Saw Lansing this morning. He informs me he sent on Friday under
> President's direction cable to Ambassador [to France, Henry C.] Wal-
> lace transmitting substance my letter and instructing Wallace to see
> French and British authorities and say President agrees with these
> views and urges compliance. This communication directed to be made
> orally because of America's position.[90]

Unwilling to rely solely on efforts to persuade officials in America
during this time, the justice also used his contacts abroad. He cabled
word of his great concern to Lord Balfour and the French peace conference representative, André Pierre Tardieu.[91] Further, the justice
asked Weizmann to pass along his views to British Prime Minister
David Lloyd George.[92] Finally, on April 24, 1920, the Supreme Council of European Powers, then meeting at San Remo, awarded the mandate for Palestine to Great Britain. Certainly, few men had more impact on the creation of the state of Palestine than Louis D. Brandeis, a
sitting justice of the United States Supreme Court.

In undertaking all of these political activities during the Wilson
Administration, Brandeis changed the norms for extrajudicial conduct. His incredibly open and extensive political behavior from 1916
to 1920, made it possible again for members of the Court to establish
intimate advisory relationships with later administrations. Brandeis's
early judicial career, then, is in many ways a paradox. While so concerned about the norms of his position that he hid his relationship
with Frankfurter and greatly limited his direct involvement with
Wilson, his open and extensive actions in other areas seemed to
belie that sense of caution.

Why, one may ask, did this pillar of propriety risk public censure
of himself and the entire Supreme Court by becoming so heavily involved in partisan issues? While the prevailing crisis of war provides

one answer, it is only a partial answer. The main reason may be found in his temperament. He was still, in his soul, both a reformer and a leader. A simple explanation for the justice's willingness to accept the risks of entering the political realm may lie in a brief axiom that Brandeis, according to former presidential adviser and Frankfurter student Benjamin V. Cohen, often offered to people seeking his advice. Whether it was in creating the Federal Trade Commission, designing the war machinery, or securing a Jewish homeland, Brandeis believed: "If you are 51% sure of the solution to a problem, it is far better to act than to leave the choice to others who are less sure of themselves."[93] Because there were few who possessed more self-confidence than Louis D. Brandeis, the thought of having to leave important problems to be solved by others less sure of themselves only because doing otherwise might appear to compromise his judicial position would surely have frustrated him. Consequently, even after the war he felt free to continue his endeavors for the Zionist cause.

While his open involvement on behalf of the establishment of the state of Palestine achieved remarkable success, Brandeis's simultaneous efforts to guide the ZOA by indirect means were beset with problems. Throughout the successful campaign for the awarding of the British Mandate, a widening rift was developing within the Zionist movement itself between the followers of Louis Brandeis and those of Chaim Weizmann. Brandeis, a wholly assimilated, native-born American Jew, saw the Zionist cause as a reform movement, similar to his many earlier Progressive campaigns. Weizmann, on the other hand, a devoted European Jew and a Zionist throughout his entire life, viewed the movement as a religious mission, both immediate and pressing. Although both sought the same ends, so vastly divergent were the approaches of the two men that the feud between them for control of the organization was soon being referred to as "Washington versus Pinsk."[94]

These differences of approach had already become apparent during the earlier successful campaign for the awarding of the British mandate. At that time within the Zionist organization attention was beginning to turn to an examination of the internal operations of the movement itself. Unlike the Weizmann followers, who sought to concentrate on political matters, Brandeis and his lieutenants advocated streamlining the leadership and fund-raising operations of the organization and building up the economy of the Jewish homeland. In refusing even to send a delegation in 1918 to confer with the British-appointed Weizmann Commission, charged with examining conditions in Palestine, Brandeis, writing for the American Zionists, spelled out a set of specific goals very much different from those of Weizmann.

> The utmost vigilance should be exercised to prevent the acquisition by private persons of land, water-rights or other natural resources or any concessions for public utilities. These must all be secured for the whole Jewish people. In other ways, as well as this, the possibility of capitalistic exploitation must be guarded against. A high development of the Anglo-Palestine company will doubtless prove one of the most effective means of protection. And the encouragement of all kinds of cooperative enterprises will be indispensable. Our pursuit must be primarily of agriculture in all its branches. The industries and commerce must be incidental merely—and such as may be required to ensure independence and natural development.[95]

Furthermore, Brandeis organized these ideas into a "five-point social justice code" for the future direction of Palestine, which was adopted at the same Pittsburgh Convention that created the ZOA in June 1918. The so-called Pittsburgh platform governed the later demands of the American Zionists for the development of the Jewish homeland.[96] Weizmann, on the other hand, wanted to raise as much money as possible, even if some was wasted through inefficient management, and to concentrate on the development of Palestine's nationalistic and cultural aspects.

Spurred by his vision for the ZOA, Brandeis quietly guided the movement, through his lieutenants, to a pinnacle of prestige and status.[97] His efforts were so successful that by 1920 the World Zionist Organization was almost completely dependent on American money and members for support.[98] Consequently, at Weizmann's invitation, Brandeis chaired the London Conference in 1920 that discussed the future of Palestine. He was even asked to head the WZO, but declined.[99]

While Brandeis's influence was still rising in the world movement, his conflict with Weizmann would very shortly come to a head in the American movement. Brandeis's resources in this battle were hurt by his unwillingness to become directly involved in the operations of the ZOA. Partially on the advice of his Zionist lieutenants, he chose to remain in the background, believing that the force of his ideas would sustain the movement.[100] Soon, however, supporters of the goals of the World Zionists were able to spread disharmony in the American organization. At the height of the crisis, even the efforts by Judge Julian Mack (then serving on the United States Court of Appeals for the Seventh Circuit) and others to mediate the differences between the two factions failed; the final showdown took place at the American Zionist convention in Cleveland on June 5, 1921.

The specific issue over which the Brandeis faction was deposed from its leadership roles in the ZOA concerned a debate over the operations of the fund-raising organization for the World Zionists, the Keren Hayesod. Chaim Weizmann had come to America to lead the fight for establishing a branch of this agency in America and to secure necessary American funds. The Brandeis group, as in the past, demanded first a strict financial accounting for this money and second that the investment funds not be mixed with other general contributions. When they lost in the formal vote of confidence, all thirty-eight members of the Brandeis-directed Zionist leadership, including the justice as honorary president, resigned.[101]

This heartbreaking defeat hardly dampened Brandeis's enthusiasm for Zionism as an ideal. Throughout the 1920s he maintained an active interest in fund-raising and in developing the "economic-social" aspects of Palestine. The justice occupied himself by seeing key contributors to the movement and by exhorting his lieutenants to work for the development of Palestine.[102] By 1927, following chaotic mismanagement under the leadership of Louis Lipsky, one of Weizmann's followers, some members of the ZOA were seeking Brandeis's return to a position of authority. Despite his continued desire to see better financial management of the organization, Brandeis rejected these pleas, claiming that his position on the Court precluded such involvement. Also in the justice's thinking must surely have been an intention to remain apart in order to be free to oppose the Lipsky regime wherever possible. This he did by lending moral and financial support to opposition forces, while plotting strategy with his own lieutenants during the Court's summer recesses.[103]

Continuing misfortunes for the American Zionists compelled even Chaim Weizmann and his followers in 1929 to seek Brandeis's return to the leadership of the organization. There were now rampant charges of financial mismanagement by the Lipsky administration and the Brandeis-Julian Mack faction was actively pointing out the decline both in membership and in the financial resources of the organization.

At the same time the justice continued to work behind the scenes, as he had throughout the 1920s, exchanging scores of letters with Frankfurter, Mack, Wise, and others regarding the administration of the organization, affairs in Palestine, and the organization's fund-raising efforts. In addition, he was donating his own funds to keep certain parts of the organization afloat.[104] Desperately in need of the funds provided by the Brandeis faction, Weizmann continued reconciliation efforts that culminated in the formation in 1929 of the Jewish Agency, a new fund-raising and development organization for Palestine that included both Zionists and non-Zionists as members. Calls again went out for Brandeis to return to the ZOA. Still, the justice showed little willingness to resume an active role in the official leadership, and, instead, resumed his demand for a complete financial restructuring of the entire Zionist organization.[105]

Though diplomatic efforts to secure Brandeis's renewed leadership of the movement failed, deteriorating conditions in Palestine forced him once again to assume an active role. Arab riots in Palestine spurred new calls in Britain for a limitation on Jewish immigration into the area. Fearing the adoption of such a policy, which would ruin all that he had worked for over the past fifteen years, Brandeis agreed to become more directly involved in the lobbying efforts. When George Young, a British Labour party member who was an expert on the Middle East, visited the United States in September 1929, Brandeis arranged to meet with him. In vigorously opposing Young's suggestion that Britain respond to the Arab riots by eventually relinquishing her mandate in Palestine, the justice "insist[ed] that there should be merely an avoidance of the British blundering [that had been] largely responsible [for such riots]."[106] When British Prime Minister Ramsay MacDonald visited America in October of that same year, Brandeis also presented the Zionist position directly to him. He further asked for British support for the many American projects in Palestine and for assurances that immigration there would not be limited. To the justice's delight, MacDonald pledged that his government would indeed live up to all the obligations it had assumed.[107]

It was the depressing and potentially irreversible trend of declining ZOA membership and funds in late 1929 that finally forced Brandeis to make his first public statement on Zionism in nearly a decade. The occasion was a conference called by Felix Warburg, the wealthy non-Zionist head of the new Jewish Agency, to organize a drive for economic assistance to Palestine. Prior to Brandeis's speech, there had been a good deal of debate by his lieutenants on the advisability of his making a public pronouncement. Even Felix Frankfurter expressed certain qualms of his own regarding such open extrajudicial involvement and was moved to question the fine line of distinction Brandeis had apparently made. In a private, formerly unpublished memorandum for two of Brandeis's lieutenants, Judge Julian Mack and Jacob DeHaas, Frankfurter pointed out that:

> A public appearance on Palestinian matters is bound to involve him in demands for public appearances in non-Palestinian matters. Thus far he had insulated [sic] by his formula "judicial office precludes." Powerful representations have been made to him from time to time for appearance upon professional occasions and I know that it has been felt that he was over fastidious and austere in not giving personal inspiration on important professional occasions. Professional feeling and opinion will not unnaturally take note of the distinction he makes, but more than that, he will subject himself to the drain of increasing and more persistent demands for his presence because of the public appearance now proposed to be made by him.[108]

Nevertheless, Brandeis did decide to speak at the conference, illustrating not only his perception of the need for his active participation in the discussion, but also his disagreement with Frankfurter's lack of distinction between Zionist and non-Zionist-related extrajudicial activities.[109] At the meeting on November 24, 1929, he spoke briefly regarding the efforts in Palestine. In further pledging his support for Zionist endeavors, Brandeis also reaffirmed his optimistic view of the future of Palestine. Thirteen years after the Hotel Astor ambush, the justice had returned to public service in Zionist affairs.[110]

Brandeis continued to confer with visiting foreign dignitaries on Zionist matters. In a memorandum to Frankfurter, Brandeis described his three-hour meeting on June 19, 1930 with British Ambassador Sir Ronald C. Lindsay, who had been sent by Foreign Secretary Arthur Henderson to solicit the justice's views regarding Palestine. According to this memorandum, the discussion ranged over topics such as the seriousness of the situation in the area, the need for further immigration, the duty imposed on Great Britain by its mandate, and plans for the future of Palestine. Overall, Brandeis's message was "that the course of conduct of the local administration conduced to [the] disturbances of 1929 and that the course of conduct since has been inconsistent with the obligations of the mandate."[111] The meeting was helpful in counteracting the impact in Britain of the Shaw report, a policy paper commissioned by the colonial secretary of the Labour government, Lord Passfield, to investigate the causes of Arab riots in Palestine. The report suggested that the British reconsider their promises to the Zionists regarding Palestine.[112]

During this time, the justice also turned his attention to the troubled ZOA. After extensive conciliatory efforts by Brandeis himself, the two factions of the organization resolved most of their differences at the June 1930 national meetings in Cleveland; majority control of the leadership was vested in the Brandeis-Mack faction.[113] However, while the justice refused to assume personally an active and open role in the new administration,[114] he did continue to advise his lieutenants in their search for new members, funds, and goals for the organization.[115] So totally did he command the loyalty of these lieutenants and particularly the loyalty of one special lieutenant, Felix Frankfurter, that his strong guiding influence was never in doubt. Later that year Harold Laski, who had been charged by the British prime minister with finding areas of accommodation between the British government and the Zionists, complained in a letter to Justice Oliver Wendell Holmes: "He [Brandeis] exercises a strange hold over Felix, for the latter who can usually be cool and independent is in these things simply an echo of L.D.B. He gives orders like an omnipotent Sultan and negotiations do not come to a success in that way."[116]

But when events took a potentially fatal turn for the Zionists just a few months later, the justice was forced once again to forego his self-imposed seclusion. Acting on the findings of two separate investigations, the British government issued on October 21, 1930, the Passfield White Paper, which sought to amend the Balfour Declaration in calling for limits on future immigration, industrial development, and Jewish land purchases in Palestine.[117] Justice Brandeis immediately undertook a two-pronged attack. Eight days after the British action, Brandeis met with President Hoover for an hour and vigorously made the case for the Jewish cause.

> [T]he Jews have their backs to the wall . . . they must fight, but . . .
> their fight [is] against the Present government . . . and not against
> the British people; and . . . the American Jews [must] make this clear;
> and . . . insist that the Mandate be lived up to; . . . we consider the
> British people our friends.[118]

Brandeis's sole intention at this time seems to have been to educate the president; when Hoover asked if anything should be done, he responded, "not at present." Then, Brandeis spent the last ten weeks of 1930 showering his friends with ideas for opposing the Passfield White Paper. For instance, an unpublished letter from the justice to Felix Frankfurter now indicates that he even instructed his favorite lieutenant to approach one of his other mentors, Henry L. Stimson, who was then secretary of state.[119] This letter was one of many that Brandeis sent to fellow Zionists to keep them apprised of the situation and to stir them to put to use whatever influence they had.[120] The justice also began to direct some suggestions through a new contact abroad, Oliver Wendell Holmes's English penpal, Harold Laski. The justice hoped that his views would be passed on to various British officials, such as Prime Minister Ramsay MacDonald. These massive efforts were rewarded when the prime minister, on February 13, 1931, released a letter repudiating much of the Passfield White Paper and reaffirming British commitment to the Balfour Declaration.[121]

With the ascension of Robert Szold, a Brandeis lieutenant, to the chairmanship of the new Administrative Committee for the ZOA, the organization was once again being directed by the justice and nearly every move by the organization in the early 1930s was cleared through him.[122] However, an interview with Brandeis's law clerk from 1932 to 1933, Professor Paul Freund, reveals that the alarming rise of Adolf Hitler and anti-Semitism in Germany, combined with the election of a new American government in 1932, convinced the justice of the need to abandon his position backstage and come forward again on Jewish needs. Brandeis made it known in high places that he wanted to confer directly with Secretary of State-designate Cordell Hull on the matter, though there remained in the justice the old concern for appearances. One day in early 1933 Raymond Moley, a member of newly elected President Franklin D. Roosevelt's so-called "Brain Trust," telephoned the Brandeis household to say, "The Justice asked to see Hull and I've been able to set it up." Because Brandeis, according to Freund's recollection, never spoke on the telephone after coming to the Court, the twenty-four year old law clerk had to carry the message to him in the study. Brandeis reacted to Moley's words with general alarm: "No, Secretary of State Hull wants to see me!" When Freund went back and passed this along, Moley said, "Oh . . . yes . . . of course."[123]

During the meeting Brandeis prevailed on Hull to establish a boycott on German goods in order to bring Germany either to its senses or its knees. He even kept Freund on after his official year of clerking to research the American boycott of British goods in colonial days because he saw this as a useful precedent for such a policy. In the end, however, the boycott was never imposed.

The long-term Brandeis involvement in Zionist affairs, stretching from 1921 to 1932, was radically different from his free-wheeling, open work with the Wilson Administration in his initial years on the Court. Most often forced by events and by his own sense of judicial ethics to limit his efforts to working through intermediaries, the justice often witnessed his influence in many sectors being eclipsed by others with more freedom to act. Perhaps, then, he should have been prepared for his lack of success in promoting a number of judicial reforms and Progressive programs during this same period.

3

The Three-Ring Circuit:
Travails of a Frustrated Reformer

During the 1920s, Louis Brandeis's off-the-bench endeavors were certainly not confined to Zionism; he was active in national politics as well. But with Woodrow Wilson's departure from the White House in 1921, and as three consecutive Republican administrations came into office over the next twelve years, Brandeis found his access to the executive branch largely cut off. To continue fostering his ideas, therefore, he had to resort to even more extensive use of intermediaries while simultaneously making himself available for discreet discussions with key political figures.

Ironically, for those of his colleagues on the bench with good contacts within the Republican administrations, such as Chief Justice William Howard Taft and Justice Harlan Fiske Stone, this next decade would prove to be one in which a justice might lobby the executive branch quite openly.[1] Although the end of World War I might have been expected to bring about a return to the more restrictive norms that had governed advisory relationships between a justice and the White House before the war, these norms simply did not re-establish themselves afterwards. Nonetheless, on the now-infrequent occasions when Brandeis sought to influence executive decisions (such as the mandate for the Hoover Commission and appointments to the executive and judicial branches), he chose to go through such conduits as Stone to make his opinions known.[2]

As an exception—although no doubt acting here out of personal affection for Wilson—Brandeis did allow himself during this period to become involved in assisting the retired president in drafting "The Document," a highly partisan platform of Progressive policies designed to guide the Democratic party in 1924. Several drafts of this document, now filed in the justice's unpublished private papers, reveal an intent to battle the Republicans' "promot[ion] [of] the accumulation of wealth as an instrument of power in the hands of individuals and corporations."[3] On few other occasions, however, would Brandeis participate in activities so openly partisan.

Overall, the twelve years of Republican national administrations would be personally frustrating years for the reform activist in Louis Brandeis; few of his extrajudicial endeavors would lead to concrete programs. In another sense, though, these years were highly creative ones. If the executive branch was no longer interested in the ideas of a genius with an eye to the future, there were two other audiences that surely were. The first of these was Congress, where there were still a number of Progressive allies, old friends who had fought alongside Brandeis in earlier times, who would eagerly put forth his current proposals. They included Senators Thomas J. Walsh and Burton K. Wheeler of Montana, George W. Norris of Nebraska, Robert F. Wagner of New York, Robert M. LaFollette of Wisconsin, and Representatives R. Walton Moore of Virginia and Fiorello LaGuardia of New York. The second audience, of course, was made up of those progressively inclined citizens within the general public. Knowing that one day occupancy of the White House would change, Brandeis devoted his efforts to preparing for that day. But what the justice needed at the moment was a way to reach these two currently receptive audiences—a way to present detailed legislative programs, along with supporting information and encouragement, to Progressive politicians and to America's better-educated readers. The person who might best present these ideas would have to be someone who could do so without appearing to be too partisan; someone who also had access to the country's most respected centers of influence and thereby to the press.

It seemed only natural that Felix Frankfurter would once again become the main instrument through which Brandeis would express his political passions, this time to gain intimate access to the legislative arena. Thus, it is not surprising to discover in the files of personal correspondence between Brandeis and Frankfurter that during the twenties letters started to pass between them with much greater regularity—sometimes even on a daily basis. The notes from the justice resembled shopping lists, with numbers running consecutively down the page followed by a paragraph or two containing gossip, words of encouragement, comments on a Supreme Court case, a proposal for reform legislation or perhaps even a strategy for political action. Whenever Frankfurter failed to move on any of these "requests," the next week's mail would bring another plea for action. In turn, the professor's responses kept Brandeis remarkably well informed about what Frankfurter himself had accomplished and about the activities of others.

As a professor at Harvard Law School, Frankfurter was free to present legislative proposals personally to members of Congress. Furthermore, his widespread reputation as a legislative draftsman served to increase his persuasiveness in these efforts, so much so that Brandeis even employed Frankfurter, on occasion, to develop legislation to correct what the justice viewed as erroneous decisions by his colleagues on the bench. In 1931, for example, when the Court would not uphold the power of the Interstate Commerce Commission to assess fees in the reorganization of the Chicago, Milwaukee, St. Paul and Pacific Railroad,[4] Brandeis wrote to Frankfurter, instructing him to draft a legislative remedy, and suggesting how the professor might help get it enacted. Brandeis himself then spoke to Senator Robert LaFollette, Jr., about the issue. This episode is instructive, however, in that none of the three remedial legislative proposals drafted by the Harvard professor were passed.[5] Congress was apparently much too pluralistic for these narrowly focused lobbying efforts to be sufficiently effective. Battles fought there could only be training exercises, useful trial runs until an administration more receptive to these programs would come to power and exert its own political influence in their behalf.

Realizing that these legislative efforts also needed to be supplemented by a campaign to change public opinion, Brandeis simultaneously began to think about ways to present his philosophy and programs in the media. Here again, however, as a member of the Court, he felt constrained in his freedom of action. Once more Felix Frankfurter proved himself to possess extraordinary resources with which to act effectively as the justice's surrogate. His vast personal connections as well as his reputation in legal and general academic circles offered Brandeis a wide range both of publishing outlets and of potential authors.

There was another resource, though, perhaps Frankfurter's greatest single asset, that made it possible for him to investigate and write authoritatively on all topics of interest to the justice—his students at the Harvard Law School. In the 1920s these pupils—the best legal minds of their generation—unwittingly became part of a Brandeis-Frankfurter literary circle. Waves of Frankfurter disciples were utilized as research assistants, and even authors, for producing useful articles. The students who were thus engaged were nearly all members of Frankfurter's senior seminar, "Jurisdiction and Procedure of the Federal Courts." Each had been hand-picked for the class, and more than just possessing special analytical capabilities, every one of them had earned the professor's confidence; they had been chosen more on the basis of Frankfurter's own instinctive reaction to each than on any absolute standard of intelligence. Seeking out students who seemed both interesting and receptive to his inimitable personal charm, he molded them into allies and disciples. The rest of his students were then treated with little more than polite courtesy.

The title for the federal jurisdiction course was really a misnomer. It probably should have been called, as it was by Edward F. Prichard, Jr., one of Frankfurter's favorite students and law clerks, "Felix Frankfurter's View of Current Affairs."[6] No ordinary seminar, its students were assigned to read each week's advance sheets of Supreme Court opinions. Frankfurter would bolt through the door each class day and challenge his charges to explain those decisions. Reflecting the volatile temperament of the teacher, the seminar was just plain noisy all the time. Ideas flew across the room like sparks, inevitably igniting full conflagrations of intellectual argument and excitement. All the questions were challenging in the truest sense of the word. One of Frankfurter's later students, Philip Elman, a man who was destined to serve as law clerk to Frankfurter during the critical period in which he would undergo a fundamental change in his approach to extrajudicial work, remembers an incident that aptly illustrates the lengths to which his mentor would go to imbue the class with his own contempt for imprecision in argument. "Why is this opinion so long?" demanded the professor one day. His eager students responded with a variety of suggestions, ranging over the complexity of the issues presented and the ambiguity of the precedents in the area. "No," Frankfurter explained, "It's because Chief Justice White wrote it—that man is so long-winded he couldn't say anything in less than 50 pages." Often using this "them-and-us" approach, he shaped their young minds and their prejudices and won their undying allegiance.[7]

Frankfurter took as much pleasure from his students as they did from him. He always told colleagues, "To stay young, surround yourself with young people." He might well have said the same thing about "staying bright," for these protégés kept him freshly supplied with new information and lively insights on all issues. Moreover, since Frankfurter had no offspring of his own, his students became his surrogate children. After their graduations, he followed their careers with great interest, offering them assistance in getting jobs and encouragement in performing them well.

These students could not have known, however, about the crucial role their mentor, Felix Frankfurter, was playing in the service of Louis Brandeis. For years, in person and by letter, the justice had been supplying Frankfurter with intimate, detailed information about cases previously decided by the Court, including tidbits on the personalities of his judicial colleagues. In fact, filed in the unpublished papers of Louis Brandeis are two blue notebooks in which Felix Frankfurter kept notes of conversations he had with the justice at Brandeis's summer home in Chatham, Massachusetts from the years 1922 to 1926.[8] These notebooks show that Brandeis kept virtually nothing from his lieutenant, thus making it possible for Frankfurter, using this inside data, to write amazingly perceptive and predictive pieces on the Court and its works. No one was more aware of the gold mine he was tapping than Felix Frankfurter, who described his mining process in a letter to his wife Marion in July 1924:

> Hello, Dearest, from quiet Chatham to quiet Claremont. It's so quiet here . . . And I shall promptly settle down to the "daily stint" on the U.S. Reports—with ample talks with L.D.B. on work of the Court (the inside details there tell everything.) He feels as one continually bottled up and as he puts it "When I talk to you I feel I'm talking to myself"—so out come the innermost judicial secrets . . . LDB and I have the best kind of professional time together, even better than Holmsey would be these days, for L.D.B. nowadays tells me more. You see how much on the make I am professionally.[9]

In further evaluating this process in a letter to Marion mailed five days later Frankfurter added, "I shall have wonderful material for future work in school and, I hope, rich matter for professional literary output." [10]

While the relationship between Brandeis and Frankfurter was one of candor and intimacy, they did observe one limit to their discussions. Following the conventional norm, the two men appear never to have discussed cases pending before the Court. However, even this unwritten rule was stretched to the breaking point by a controversy that gripped the nation and marshalled the fiercest passions of civil libertarians, including Louis Brandeis and Felix Frankfurter.

In one of the most notorious trials of this century, two Italian immigrants, Nicola Sacco and Bartolomeo Vanzetti, a shoemaker and a fish peddler, were convicted and then sentenced to death for the murder of a paymaster and his guard in South Braintree, Massachusetts. [11] The obvious legal irregularities in that trial, which polarized the Boston Brahmins against these "Red Anarchists," so horrified Frankfurter, then forty-four years old, that he was moved to attack the judicial findings in print. His scathing article in the *Atlantic Monthly* and his subsequent book on the same subject published in 1927 revealed the inherent weakness of the state's case. [12] Because of the public outrage aroused by these works, Governor Alvan T. Fuller was forced to appoint an advisory committee, headed by Harvard University President A. Lawrence Lowell, to make recommendations regarding clemency for Sacco and Vanzetti. The subsequent refusal to grant a reprieve merely spurred Frankfurter to increase his efforts to save the convicted men.

In his memoirs Frankfurter recounts that when this case came to the United States Supreme Court, Justice Brandeis announced his self-disqualification because Mrs. Glendower Evans, known as "Auntie B." to his family, had been living in his household while actively involved in the defense effort. [13] In fact, there were reasons for the seventy-year-old justice's recusal other than those Frankfurter cared to reveal. Brandeis's increasingly frequent personal letters to the Harvard professor during this period show the justice's deep interest in both the course of the appeal in the controversial case and the public debate over it. Breaking his own rule never to discuss an issue that might come to his Court, Brandeis wrote a letter to the professor concerning the announced costs of defending the pair in Court: "The Sacco-Vanzetti expense is a terrible indictment of our criminal justice." [14] Then, in two letters written during the early months of 1927, the justice explicitly encouraged Frankfurter's efforts to argue the case for Sacco and Vanzetti in print. [15] Once the article was published, Brandeis's pleasure with the result was self-evident: "Your *Atlantic* article is admirably done. It should produce a profound impression." [16] The Frankfurter papers show conclusively that Brandeis's interest in this case was hardly limited to sending words of encouragement from the sidelines. Any remaining doubt regarding Brandeis's personal involvement in the appeal was removed by this offer to Frankfurter on June 2, 1927.

> I have realized that S[acco]. V[anzetti]., *inter alia*, must have made heavy demands for incidental expense, as well as time, and meant to ask you when we met whether an additional sum might not be appropriate this year. Let me know. [17]

While there is no record of Frankfurter's response, an extra $500 was deposited in the account on August 16. [18]

What makes this involvement so extraordinary is that a mere five days later the unsuspecting lawyers for the convicted murderers visited Justice Brandeis in an attempt to secure a stay of execution pending an appeal to the Supreme Court. Though Frankfurter had by this time receded to the background of the controversy, hoping to avoid prejudicing the appeals process, he continued to influence the actions of the Sacco-Vanzetti Defense Committee from behind the scenes through men like Boston journalist Gardner Jackson and Appeals Court Judge Julian Mack. Having been rebuffed by Justice Holmes in their search for a stay, the group turned their attention to the other liberal Massachusetts justice, now at his summer retreat in Chatham. Indeed, a series of phone calls went out from the headquarters of the Defense Committee and the newly formed Citizens' National Committee for Sacco and Vanzetti imploring Frankfurter to take a more active role in the defense effort and even to present the case to Brandeis himself. [19] Frankfurter demurred; although he could not reveal why, it would have been inappropriate for him to make a formal presentation of the committee's arguments for the case to the justice. Indeed, he told one ally, "I would not be a bit surprised if [Brandeis] disqualified [himself] from sitting and nothing more could clinch it than for me to go down to Chatham. I can't say anything more." [20]

Frankfurter's sense of discretion regarding the justice was such that when asked what the chances were for Sacco and Vanzetti's appeal, he would only say, "It is speculative and I would not express any opinion."[21] Surprisingly, however, he did not feel restrained from advising the group that they "would be wholly justified" in approaching Brandeis about a stay and even went so far as to tell them how to reach him by telephone. Such assistance from Frankfurter was accompanied by a plea "not to talk about this talk between us. Laymen cannot sometimes appreciate."[22] Had these lawyers who were laboring so hard for Sacco and Vanzetti known, as Frankfurter did, that Brandeis was already too personally involved to act in the matter, it is questionable whether they would have appreciated it either.

That we have a record of these conversations between the professor and those others involved in the Sacco-Vanzetti cause comes about through one of those strange tricks history sometimes plays. In what surely must have been one of the earliest uses by law-enforcement authorities of telephonic surveillance, the Massachusetts State Police had wiretapped the headquarters of the Citizens' National Committee, located in the Hotel Bellevue in Boston, Massachusetts, as well as Frankfurter's cottage at Duxbury, Massachusetts. Thanks to those civil libertarians on the Massachusetts State Police force who placed the wiretaps, absent any form of judicial participation, transcripts of these private conversations now exist.

Locked in the personal safe of the Massachusetts public safety commissioner for fifty years, the 310 pages of transcript, marked "confidential" and "to be either DESTROYED or placed in SECRET FILES," provide a vivid demonstration of a man who was cross-pressured between his desire to assist the convicted immigrants and his full awareness of his own limits in dealing with Justice Brandeis.

When the lawyers for Sacco and Vanzetti attempted to approach Justice Brandeis themselves, having been unable to move Frankfurter to speak for them, the justice cited personal connections with the case in refusing even to receive the party. Only the Harvard professor would have known what he really meant. There is, ultimately, little doubt however, that it pained Brandeis to be unable to act in this case. After Sacco and Vanzetti were executed at midnight on August 22, he consoled Frankfurter in a private letter saying; "To the end you have done all that was possible for you and all that was more than would have been possible for any other person I know. But the end of S.V. is only the beginning. 'They know not what they do.' "[23] Six weeks after the execution, the appeal for the case finally reached the Supreme Court and was summarily dismissed.[24]

The recently discovered wiretap transcripts reveal that Felix Frankfurter performed one last service for the justice in this case. In a telephone conversation with Judge Julian Mack, the professor mentioned that Brandeis was "being hammered widely and getting some very abusive letters" because of his announced decision to withdraw from the consideration of the case.

To counteract this criticism, Frankfurter asked that Mack have an editor for The New Republic "put a paragraph in this week's N.R. that L.D.B.'s refusal to act for [the] defense is a striking rebuke to . . . [Trial Judge] Thayer, and point out that it would be a grave wrong for him to have acted." Frankfurter then suggested that this comparison of Brandeis's "purity" with the alleged prejudicial behavior of the trial judge in the case would "please L.D.B. and probably educate a little those that need educating."[25]

It is now apparent that Mack wasted no time in carrying out the instructions to the letter. In the following issue of The New Republic, this item defending Brandeis appeared in the editorial section.

> Bitter criticism of Justice Brandeis for refusing to act in the Sacco-Vanzetti case has been heard from many of the friends of the condemned. It is said that he should have laid aside the scruples arising from the fact that he had intimate personal relations with some of those interested in the defense, that, in a case of this significance, legal niceties were of less importance than anything which might have helped to avert the tragedy of the execution. Nobody can deny that possibly Sacco and Vanzetti had to suffer because Justice Brandeis possessed the same kind of scruple which Judge Thayer should have had, and did not, when he insisted on passing on the question of his own prejudice. But what gave the case its significance? Was it not that the operation of the judicial process in Massachusetts allowed Judge Thayer's lack of scruple—and a similar lack in others— to prevail? Would it not be more to the point for those who are shocked and outraged by the conduct of the case in Massachusetts to insist that no judge, whatever he may consider the importance of a cause, should sit in a case where his own prejudice may be involved, and to cite Justice Brandeis' action as a strengthening of this principle?[26]

The Sacco-Vanzetti incident highlights, oddly, both the limits and the potentially dangerous conflict of interest inherent in the Brandeis-Frankfurter relationship. The bounds to this friendship as viewed by each man are plainly evident here because never once do they seem to have discussed the merits of the case directly. Yet, the problems posed by the monetary aspect cannot be underestimated. To his credit, the justice did in the end avoid any potential violation of judicial ethics by disqualifying himself from the case. On the other hand, it can be said that he had put himself into that compromising position in the first place, thereby helping to deprive convicted men of a right to a fair hearing by the Court's most liberal member. Some may wonder, though, whether the justice would have felt compelled to step down if the only factor had been his secret contacts with Frankfurter regarding the case. His connection with Mrs. Evans, the "Auntie B." of the story, was public knowledge, and could have been the factor that did truly push the justice to his decision.

During the same weeks that the Massachusetts State Police were listening in on Felix Frankfurter's telephone conversations, petitions were filed with the Supreme Court to consider for the first time the constitutionality of police wiretapping. It would be another nine months before the opinion of the five member majority in *Olmstead v. United States*[27] would uphold this practice. But, ironically, the one justice who did not and could not know that he had unwittingly been indirectly involved in just such an investigation, Louis D. Brandeis, took the occasion to write one of the most eloquent dissents of his career. Characterizing wiretapping at various points in his opinion as an "invasion of individual security," an "unjustifiable intrusion by the Government upon the privacy of an individual," and an "unlawful act,"[28] Brandeis closed his discussion with a passage that has been repeatedly quoted over the years.

> Our Government is the potent, the omnipresent teacher. For good or for ill, it teaches the whole people by its example. Crime is contagious. If the Government becomes a lawbreaker, it breeds contempt for law; it invites every man to become a law unto himself; it invites anarchy. To declare that in the administration of the criminal law the end justifies the means—to declare that the Government may commit crimes in order to secure the conviction of a private criminal—would bring terrible retribution. Against that pernicious doctrine this Court should resolutely set its face.[29]

One can only guess what Brandeis's reaction would have been had he discovered the earlier intrusion on the privacy of his own lieutenant,

Felix Frankfurter. But surely his language in condemnation for such practices could not have been much stronger.

The Sacco-Vanzetti controversy, while dramatically pointing up the danger in stretching established limits on judicial propriety, was not, however, at all typical of the collaborative relationship that existed over a number of years between these two men. More typically, the professor served Brandeis in two very different literary capacities. First, by providing him with comments, very nearly always positive, on his judicial opinions, he became one of Brandeis's select critics. The ebullient professor required little prodding to undertake this function: his letters were always filled with glowing praise for the justice's work. Second, Brandeis occasionally used Frankfurter in this period as a research assistant in the production of his judicial opinions. For instance, after asking for the title and location of one of Frankfurter's articles on the commerce clause,* the justice queried Frankfurter for the second time, in a letter dated December 21, 1926: "Thanks for references to your articles. Are you able to give me data as to our overruling ourselves in cases under the Commerce Clause?"[30] This material, once collected, was used by Brandeis in his judicial opinions—in this case, *DiSanto v. Pennsylvania*,[31] which struck down a state law requiring the licensing of steamboat ticket sellers. In his impassioned dissent in that case, Brandeis advocated the need to let the individual states prevent fraud, even if it forced the Court to ignore *stare decisis*† and overrule its earlier interstate commerce decisions. Here he cited Frankfurter's data—two articles, one of which had been written by the professor himself, and a catalog of nearly a dozen earlier instances of Court reversals in this area.[32] That Brandeis, forever concerned with the ethics of his position, would even consider asking an outsider for such assistance, illustrates the intimacy of his relationship with Frankfurter.

---

*Article I, Section 8, Clause 3, of the United States Constitution, reads: "The Congress shall have [the] Power . . . to regulate Commerce with foreign Nations, and among the several States, and with the Indian Tribes." Using this so-called Interstate Commerce power, the authority to regulate commercial transactions among the states, the Supreme Court has expanded Congress's constitutional authority to the extent that it can now regulate virtually any aspect of American life.
†An informal rule of the courts that judges in deciding cases should adhere to the precedents of previously announced decisions. It is thought that by judging in such a fashion the law will be more settled and more predictable.

To encourage the exploration and analysis in legal periodicals of federal jurisprudence, including even his own decisions, Brandeis also became virtually a collaborator in the production of a number of Frankfurter's professional publications. Personal letters from Brandeis to Frankfurter indicate the many ways in which the justice supported such research, even with his own pocketbook. From 1924 to 1939, Brandeis contributed to the support of graduate research fellows working with Frankfurter.[33] The initial recipient was James M. Landis, who went on to become Brandeis's law clerk for the 1925 term, and then to enjoy a fine career as a Harvard Law School professor, a member of the Federal Trade Commission during the New Deal, and later the first chairman of the Securities and Exchange Commission (which was created, in part, due to Brandeis's own extrajudicial lobbying efforts).[34] As an outgrowth of this first fellowship, Frankfurter and Landis became one of the most productive legal research and writing teams of the day. In 1925 they published the first of a series of articles in the *Harvard Law Review* exploring the interrelationship between developing Court procedures and changes in political and economic forces, entitled "The Business of the Supreme Court of the United States—A Study in the Federal Judicial System."[35] Seven other articles were published under the same title over the next two years, benefitted of course by periodic research suggestions offered in letters from Justice Brandeis.[36]

After the eight pieces were published in book form in 1927, whenever Brandeis lobbied a member of Congress concerning judicial reform, which he did frequently, the justice would instruct Frankfurter to send that official a copy of the book and later, drafts of desirable legislative measures.[37] Realizing the potential these "Business" articles held for influencing legislative, public, and even judicial opinion regarding possible Court reforms, Brandeis continued to flood Frankfurter over the years with suggestions and encouragement for future supplements to the series.[38]

In addition, a number of Brandeis's letters to Frankfurter during this period offered suggestions for other articles in legal periodicals and included the necessary evidence drawn from the behind-the-scenes negotiations of the justices on the Supreme Court. For instance, Brandeis's distress over the Court's handling of the writs of *certiorari* * led

---

* Meaning literally "to be informed of," it is a discretionary writ issued by the Supreme Court ordering that the lower court send the records of a case up for review.

to a group of suggestions for what he believed to be necessary articles. The justice became convinced that the expansion of the use of these writs by the Judiciary Act of 1925, which had been drafted and lobbied for by Chief Justice Taft and other members of the Court, had created grave problems.[39] Reviewing the petitions was time consuming, Brandeis argued, and there was a tendency to "improvidently grant" review for many of them. So, the silent partner in the Frankfurter and Landis legal-writing team wheeled into action. On October 29, 1927 Brandeis instructed the professor: "Some day you must have an article in H[arvard] L[aw] R[eview] reviewing the Cert. work since [the] Feb. 13, 1925 act."[40] Then two weeks later the justice informed Frankfurter that he had directed his law clerk to send him "from time to time instances of . . . Certs. granted or denied that deserve study."[41] The result of this deposit of information was a Frankfurter and Landis article in the following year's *Harvard Law Review* entitled "The Supreme Court Under the Judiciary Act of 1925."[42]

Some of these Brandeis ideas, intended for full analysis in an individual article, instead found their way into the continuing "Business of the Supreme Court" series. For example, in four separate letters Brandeis discussed the flooding of the Court's docket with Federal Employers' Liability cases,* which he described as "the most copious and futile of the single wastes of [the] Court's efforts."[43] The justice objected to the willingness of his brethren to use federal jurisdiction in reexamining and reversing such decisions by the states' highest courts.[44] Moved by Brandeis's concern over this matter, in the 1929 edition of his "Business of the Supreme Court," supported by appropriate statistics, Frankfurter and Landis wrote: "Without undue dogmatism, it may be asserted that petitions for certiorari seeking review of the Federal Employers' Liability cases are too readily granted."[45] But none of Frankfurter's readers, indeed quite probably not even his own co-author, was aware of his high source for this statement.

The justice provided Frankfurter's writing operation with more than simply the inspiration and exposition necessary to produce desirable articles. In addition to his yearly support of Frankfurter's political en-

---

* These were cases arising from the 1908 Federal Employers' Liability Act, which made it possible for workers in interstate common carrier industries, such as railroads, to sue their employers for compensation in cases of job-related injuries. Although such suits could be heard by either state or federal courts, they were all ultimately reviewable by the United States Supreme Court.

deavors and his contribution to the graduate research fellow, Brandeis continued to make funds available to support the general research effort. When James Landis ran into monetary problems, it was the justice who bailed him out with a loan.[46] Then in 1929 and 1930, Brandeis paid Frankfurter over $3,500 to hire Wilbur G. Katz to assist in the editing of a case book on federal jurisdiction.[47]

Once Brandeis saw that the number of studies needed on such legal questions far exceeded the time Frankfurter had available for them, the idea of using the Harvard law students presented itself. Issues intriguing to the justice could be explored with a great diversity of approaches, and quite inexpensively. The insights that often accompanied careful scholarship by such talented students could then be used both to develop new pieces of legislation and to influence public opinion. So Brandeis began suggesting to Frankfurter that he delegate the work. For instance, in a letter to Frankfurter dated July 30, 1927, he asked, "Would it not be wise to develop through your seminar a series of articles each dealing solely with a single possible curtailment of jurisdictions of the district courts?"[48] Frankfurter then suggested this and other ideas to members of his seminar as topics for research papers, and continually guided them in their analyses (much of which had already been detailed to him in letters from Brandeis). The justice then continued to supply Frankfurter with useful data and behind-the-scenes information that might aid in the production of the papers.

Eventually, many of these essays were revised into articles, which the professor then helped place in important law journals, including the *Harvard Law Review*. Of course, in each instance, the student-author gratefully acknowledged his debt to Professor Frankfurter for his inspiration both in the selection and analysis of the topic: these students seem to have been completely unaware of the true origin of the ideas. Indeed, judging by the lack of knowledge evident in a personal interview with one of these students half a century later, this author believes that many of Frankfurter's protégés will learn here for the first time about the true chain of inspiration to which they were responding.[49]

Once these articles were in print, the justice would cite the information and analysis, as well as "the mandate of opinion in the Law Reviews," to lobby various politicians and his own colleagues on the Court. It is interesting that these student-authors would later be placed by Brandeis and Frankfurter in a plethora of New Deal agencies, where they could help to implement many of the policies that they had ear-lier been influenced to propose in print.

It should go without saying that the moral and intellectual thrust of these articles almost always supported the positions of Brandeis and Frankfurter. This is not to suggest that these brilliant students were no more than sheep to be led around by the nose. But neither can there by any denying the enormous influence of a professor like Frankfurter on the driven students one would find in any such elite group. With his quick wit and sophisticated intellect he could destroy with a single phrase the pretensions to independence of any young renegade who refused to hop aboard the train while it was still in the station.

Additionally, Frankfurter may very well have been at this time bet-ter informed about the intimate details of the Court's workings than any other American off the high bench itself. Brandeis did not have to reveal the actual deliberations of the brethren in any particular case before the Court for Frankfurter to have gleaned so strong a picture of each of the men on the bench to have appeared to his students almost prescient in his ability to foretell the analytical arguments each of the justices would adopt in their decisions.

Quite naturally, there was not a unanimity of appreciation among Frankfurter's students for this revealed-truth method of being taught. Francis Plimpton, later a lawyer and diplomat (as well as being the father of author/editor George Plimpton), is quoted by Joseph Lash as having put his own impressions of Frankfurter's "Public Utilities" course into verse:

> You learn no law in Public U
> That is its fascination
> But Felix gives a point of view
> And pleasant conversation.[50]

Using the influence of Frankfurter with his students and his con-nection with the *Harvard Law Review*, Brandeis had three types of articles produced. The first group consisted of pieces analyzing the history of activity by the Supreme Court in certain areas. For instance, Brandeis suggested in a June 25, 1926 letter to Frankfurter that an article might be written "on [Supreme Court] cases reversed, in effect, by Congressional action—distinguishing between (a) cases where Congress apparently undertook to correct what it deemed our erroneous construction, from (b) those where its presumed actual intent was not made effective. . . ."[51] Frankfurter's research fellow that year, Malcolm P. Sharp, did later examine this subject in a three-part *Harvard Law Review* article entitled "Movement in Supreme Court Adjudication—A Study of Modified and Overruled Decisions."[52]

The second series of suggestions was designed to illuminate current Court difficulties. Acting on Brandeis's obvious interest in the reform of jurisdiction standards of the federal courts based on diversity of citizenship,* for instance, the professor suggested the idea of writing on this subject to a number of his students.[53] Henry J. Friendly (now a senior judge on the United States Court of Appeals for the Second Circuit) expanded on these notions in an article entitled, "The Historic Basis of Diversity Jurisdiction."[54] In addition, four other Frankfurter students explored this problem in unpublished studies that were then available for Frankfurter himself to use in his own writing on the topic.[55]

In a final series of suggestions, Brandeis's connection with Frankfurter gave him an opportunity to criticize indirectly the actions of his brethren on the Court even after his formal efforts during the deliberation process had failed. For instance, distressed by the Court's frequent use of *per curiam* † opinions to overrule distinguished state courts, and gagged by the tradition prohibiting dissents from such opinions, Brandeis wrote Frankfurter on October 15, 1926 saying that the "H[arvard] L[aw] R[eview] should not miss, or fail to treat [the issue] adequately."[56] The concern was quickly reflected in a *Harvard Law Review* note.[57] Then following his dissent in the wiretap case *Olmstead v. United States*,[58] Brandeis suggested to the professor in a private letter dated June 15, 1928 a line of attack that, he forthrightly stated, could be used by "some reviewer" of that case in the *Harvard Law Review*.[59]

Thus, contrary to the prevailing understanding that Brandeis made no extrajudicial policy statements in the 1920s, either in print or in public speeches, it is clear that while the justice was restrained by his own sense of ethics from personally using such extrajudicial forums,

---

* A suit by a citizen of one state filed against a citizen of another state, thus, according to Article III, Section 2 of the United States Constitution, enabling it to be heard in federal court.

† Meaning literally, "by the Court," it is an unsigned, usually brief, judicial opinion speaking for the entire Court.

he repeatedly engaged an extensive literary network, anchored by Felix Frankfurter, to disseminate his opinions on a wide variety of topics.[60] These indirect literary efforts served to amplify many of the themes that the justice had explored in his formal judicial opinions and in his informal conversations with members of Congress. Thus it was that Brandeis, who was in a favorable position to observe where the law did not seem to serve justice, was able to perceive a needed reform, devise an analysis to support it constitutionally and jurisprudentially, command the introduction of this new analysis into the main currents of legal academic thought, orchestrate its publication in prestigious law reviews, have the abstract ideas then drafted into legislative proposals, and, if all else failed, cite all these independent efforts, as he deliberated with fellow justices on the country's highest bench, as mandate and intellectual authority to use the formal power of the Supreme Court to change the law. Quite naturally, we cannot know for sure what arguments Brandeis did offer his brethren during the deliberative process, but we do know that his formal decisions and dissents, which would logically be expected to rely on those same arguments made in deliberation, did cite the tidal wave of informed opinion his own lieutenant had helped generate.

In attempting to promote Brandeis's Progressive programs with the general public, Frankfurter was, here again, the ideal lieutenant. Frankfurter became the clearing house through which the justice's ideas were passed on to a variety of liberal publications. Seeking to educate the widest possible audience, the two men turned to a variety of authors and editors in such newspapers as the New York World and the Boston Herald, and magazines like Nation, The Survey, and Survey Graphic. Their most extensive efforts, however, were directed toward The New Republic, where Frankfurter served as a trustee and contributing editor, and Brandeis's friend Herbert Croly was the general editor. Other biographers of Frankfurter have documented his role in frequently writing unsigned editorials and articles for The New Republic,[61] but until now no volume has revealed the extent to which the true inspiration for many of these pieces was Justice Louis Brandeis.

This is not surprising, for the justice was extremely careful to conceal his connection with the journal. He never met directly with the editorial board, preferring to pass along his suggestions through letters to Frankfurter and through an occasional chat with Croly at his summer home.[62] Even when the justice sent memoranda regarding what might go into the journal, they were not to be presented in his name. Frankfurter was instructed by Brandeis to propose those ideas that he liked under his own name at future meetings of The New Republic's board of editors.[63] Even by this indirect means the justice did much more than suggest worthwhile topics for exploration. In effect, he became a member of the editorial board in absentia. In a letter to Frankfurter, dated December 1, 1920, Brandeis even tried to instruct the editors regarding the purpose of the journal:

> A. If the N.R. is to justify by its influence and results the sacrifices made for it—it must be—in the period ahead of us more concrete in its undertakings. B. It must be more a journal of fact—than of opinion; which latter is apt to be regarded as mushy. That is—it must make its opinions tell through facts which by their selection and method of presentation argue themselves. And in the end, facts must be presented stripped for action. C. Its task of improving affairs must be accomplished by directing thought, and propelling influence persistently against specific evils. D. It should become the educator of reforming protagonists and . . . should get into close touch, if it does the above suggestions, with Congressmen and other publicity makers who can carry forward the fight.[64]

By his own indirect efforts with The New Republic, Brandeis began to prepare the climate of public opinion for his reform programs in several ways. First, he educated the editorial board on his views so that the whole slant of the journal would favor his philosophy. Just before the beginning of the October 1922 Court term, for instance, he sent Frankfurter his "last will and testament," seven personal letters offering multipage expositions on issues such as prohibition, capitalism, transportation, labor-saving devices, and general economic trends, all designed to influence the entire editorial direction of the journal.[65]

Second, his weekly comments on current events contained in private letters to Frankfurter were often redrafted and printed as unsigned articles in "The Week" section of the journal. Several personal letters from Brandeis to Frankfurter, when compared with subsequent articles published in The New Republic, indicate that the public was exposed unknowingly to the justice's analysis of such a wide range of issues as the 1924 Immigration Act, the McNary-Haugen bill on agriculture surplus, the character and importance of Charles Lindbergh, the silence of Calvin Coolidge on the recurring Teapot Dome scandal, and the high quality of Herbert Hoover's cabinet.[66]

Finally, a number of Brandeis's extrajudicial statements actually appeared nearly verbatim in the journal as unsigned editorials. These pieces, originally sent as personal letters from Brandeis to Frankfurter, found their way into the magazine usually less than a month after they were written. They included expositions on the debilitating nature of coal and railroad strikes, the plight of impoverished farmers, the danger of "big money" in democratic elections, and the inaccuracy of government-reported unemployment figures.[67]

Other ideas offered by the justice for exploration in the liberal journals required much additional research and analysis. On these occasions, he would outline the direction of necessary analysis in some detail and let Frankfurter make the writing arrangements. A search through Brandeis's letters and later editions of *The New Republic* indicate that several times the professor himself took up the cudgel and produced pieces on such subjects as prohibition, the Coolidge Administration's "debauching of the judiciary with inexcusable political appointments," Coolidge's poor handling of the unemployment problem, and the Interstate Commerce Commission's rulings on railroads.[68] Other articles produced in this fashion appeared in the magazine on such diverse topics as the problems of "closed shops" for labor unions and the economic problems of the merchant marine.[69] Periodically, after outlining the topic for an article, Brandeis would even designate his specific choice for the author of the work. This was certainly the case on November 9, 1921, when he asked Frankfurter in a personal letter to persuade author Winthrop D. Lane to write on the problems of the coal industry.[70] The following year Lane did publish a three-part series on this subject in *The Survey* magazine.[71]

Brandeis realized that employing Frankfurter and his many contacts in the legal and literary worlds to prepare public opinion for the acceptance of change by presenting the Progressive ideals in print would only serve as a first step; the achievement of total success, he knew, would require that the legislative machinery be fired up for the campaigns as well. Knowing that the Progressives were only a small minority in Congress, the justice tried in 1925 to band them together for more effective action. During a dinner meeting with Congressman John M. Nelson, he suggested the development of such a coalition and the establishment of a "general staff of thinkers . . . divorced from office and the political task" who could design the programs.[72] When Nelson telephoned the justice seeking the names of people who would serve in this capacity, Brandeis, as he would do frequently during the coming New Deal, turned the actual personnel matters over to his operator in the field, Felix Frankfurter. However, despite a meeting arranged by Brandeis in mid-May between Frankfurter and Nelson, this staff was never formed.[73]

After this organizational effort failed, all the justice could do was propose his legislative ideas to individual allies in Congress. Perhaps the best example of the willingness of the justice during this era to lobby for his programs personally can be found in his promotion of legislation for income tax reform. Brandeis sought to institute a rigidly progressive tax structure that would require the "super rich," a group that included the millionaire justice himself, to pay a much greater share in taxes than the common worker. In addition, Brandeis argued that the tax system could be reformed in a way which promoted competition among businesses by penalizing corporate "bigness."

The justice's lobbying efforts for these ideas were launched on November 19, 1931, when he wrote to Frankfurter: "Senator [Burton K.] Wheeler is interested in [a] progressive tax on bigness. Have you anyone able and willing to draw a bill?"[74] Then Brandeis and Frankfurter met on January 16, 1932, to plan their strategy on the issue. After further analysis of the problem, the justice proposed his solution in a personal letter to Frankfurter written ten days later:

> What would you say to this for a starter in the taxation of corporate bigness: Amend the corporation tax act by adding to the profits tax that all corporations with gross assets of $1,000,000 or more shall have an annual franchise tax of ¼ of such assets held at the end of receiving year, and providing that no such reduction of account should be made for holding of, or in a, subsidiary or other corporation.[75]

Frankfurter immediately designated Max Lowenthal, a Harvard Law School graduate, to draft the bill along with the supporting memoranda. Meanwhile Brandeis had no hesitation in speaking directly to Senators Robert M. LaFollette, Jr., and Thomas J. Walsh on the matter. He also wrote several letters to Frankfurter during the early months of 1932, giving his suggestions for drafting various other tax reforms.[76]

On March 30, 1932, with the revenue act coming up for Senate consideration, Senator Wheeler respected judicial proprieties by writing to Frankfurter, asking him for these Brandeis-inspired proposals.

> Sometime ago, I spoke to you about a bill that a mutual friend of ours talked about, viz:—a tax on the bigness of corporations. You told me you would have something worked out in the matter. In view of the fact that the tax bill will be coming over to the Senate in the near future for consideration, I was wondering if you had worked out the proposition so I could offer it to the tax bill.[77]

Five days later, Frankfurter responded by forwarding a legislative proposal and a supporting memo, which began with a verbatim rendition of Brandeis's suggestion of January 26 to "amend the corporation tax act." The professor also enclosed, without revealing the source, the word-for-word suggestions Brandeis had given him on taxing gifts, estates, and the "super-rich."[78]

On the same day that Frankfurter was writing back to Wheeler, Brandeis was writing Frankfurter telling him that he had already spoken at great length to Senator Hugo L. Black of Alabama about the necessity of taxing great wealth and estates. In that same letter the justice launched his next offensive, proposing to Frankfurter that a levy be placed on corporate trusts to end the use of those trusts for tax evasion. Brandeis instructed the professor to have Max Lowenthal draft such a measure and then to send it to New York Representative Fiorello LaGuardia and the various Progressive senators.[79] Accommodating as always, Frankfurter, once the bill was drafted, immediately sent it to LaGuardia who promised to "take the matter up with the Chairman of the Ways and Means."[80] Then the professor forwarded the entire packet of suggestions on tax legislation to Senator LaFollette.[81] When none of these proposals were immediately adopted by Congress, Brandeis began preparing for future opportunities to present them by suggesting to Frankfurter that "a careful survey of the existing [tax] measures [be] made in the interest of increasing the revenue—and not of protecting the rich."[82] It was now clear to both men that these ideas, together with the justice's proposals for spending the increased revenue on a massive public-works program, which were also forwarded to Senator Robert F. Wagner in 1932,[83] would not receive serious consideration at the national level until public opinion changed and a new administration was elected to the White House.

All was not lost for Brandeis during this early period, though, because one of his programs—unemployment insurance—was adopted at the state level.[84] So important was this proposal to the justice that he had devoted much of his public life to seeking its adoption. According to the personal reminiscences of his daughter, Elizabeth Brandeis Raushenbush, Brandeis first publicly stated the theoretical cornerstone for his policy in 1911 in a speech entitled "The Road to Social Efficiency." He noted that European nations, governed by the nineteenth-century philosophy that unemployment was caused by worker incompetence, had developed relief programs that provided only monetary assistance. In calling for the adoption of a comprehensive unemployment insurance program in the United States, Brandeis was perhaps the first to argue that these precedents should be ignored in favor of a recognition that the cause of the problem lay in the market and not the worker.[85]

The specifics of his plan were outlined in a comprehensive unpublished memorandum that he wrote in June of that year, a copy of which ended up in Frankfurter's private files at the Library of Congress. The proposal called for the employer to deposit a percentage of his wage payroll into an insurance fund that could then be drawn upon by unemployed workers in that firm. At the end of each year, the unused portion of the fund plus the accumulated interest would be apportioned among the owner and workers depending on how that year's work record in the firm compared to "the [national] average number of days employment." Only in the event of full employment in the business for the year would the owner receive the entire fund. By thus tapping the self-interest of the employers, the program sought to provide not only for the immediate needs of the idle workers, but also to minimize the causes of unemployment by encouraging the regularization of work schedules.[86]

While the program made sense in theory, securing its enactment would require a carefully designed legislative strategy and a long-term public education effort. So, during the 1920s the justice dedicated himself to a behind-the-scenes education campaign on the benefits of unemployment insurance. He privately suggested a number of articles to the editors of The Survey and Survey Graphic magazines, which had wide circulations in the business world, on the dangers of "irregular employment." Writing to one of the journals' editors, Robert Bruere, in 1922, Brandeis pleaded, "Refuse to accept as inevitable any evil in business—e.g. irregularity of employment."[87] Throughout this period the justice pressured Bruere's colleague, editor Paul Underwood Kellogg, who was also a close personal friend, on the need to devote a whole issue of his magazine to the problems of "regularity of employment."[88] When Clarence H. Howard, the president of Commonwealth Steel Company in St. Louis, sent Brandeis a booklet in early 1928 outlining his industry's policies, the justice responded in a letter marked "STRICTLY PRIVATE" with a paragraph-long statement arguing that observation of "the right to regularity in employment" was an "obligation" of businesses.[89]

Exactly one year later the Survey Graphic did publish a special issue called "Unemployment and Ways Out," which cautioned people about complacency after the progress of the 1920s. Interestingly, at the request of the editors, Brandeis sent a statement entitled "The Right to Work," which was printed on the initial page of this issue.[90] While the editors gave the impression that this was an old quotation to hide the justice's involvement, in fact it was identical to the one he had privately forwarded to Clarence Howard.

When Brandeis felt the need in the 1930s to advocate specific unemployment insurance legislation, it was only natural, given his Jeffersonian vision of a decentralized governmental system, that his initial efforts were focused on the state level. Fortunately for the justice, his daughter and son-in-law, Elizabeth and Paul Raushenbush, were now two promising economists on the faculty at the University of Wisconsin at Madison.[91] They soon were among the leaders of that state's movement toward unemployment insurance legislation.[92] Consequently, they became virtual lieutenants in the campaign to adopt Brandeis's program and met with him in the summer of 1931 to map out strategy. The justice proposed the same plan he had outlined in 1911 and fully expected that its enactment in Wisconsin would encourage other states to follow quickly. Armed with this overall vision, Elizabeth Raushenbush, at the suggestion of the justice, sent a copy of their idea to Felix Frankfurter, saying:

> It is the only legislative proposal consonant with "the one true faith" (as expounded by LDB). Its basis is that unemployment can be prevented and that the job is to be done by the individual employer—in cooperation with others to some extent if he chooses. We thought you ought to have the bona fide remedy on tap if consulted—there are so many spurious substitutes going around these days.[93]

The Wisconsin bill was drafted initially by Paul Raushenbush and another economist, State Assemblyman Harold M. Groves, who then introduced it to a special session of the Wisconsin assembly in 1931. To the justice's great satisfaction, the original bill was passed by the Wisconsin assembly on January 28, 1932.

During the following summer Brandeis encouraged officials in Massachusetts to adopt their own version of this law. He had begun this campaign in May 1931, when the bill was still being drafted in Wisconsin. At that time, Brandeis urged A. Lincoln Filene, a member of the Governor's Council in Massachusetts who was studying unemployment insurance proposals, to contact Elizabeth Raushenbush for her recommendations. After a series of meetings with other Massachusetts officials in Chatham during the summer of 1932, the justice arranged for these people to confer directly with the Raushenbushes. The administrators were so impressed with Paul Raushenbush's expertise that they asked him to draft their bill as well. Brandeis was truly disappointed when this Massachusetts measure, which was identical to Wisconsin's, was not adopted, and when no other state passed a similar unemployment insurance law during 1933.[94]

In many ways this had been a frustrating era for Louis D. Brandeis. Over a decade had been spent in largely fruitless attempts to secure enactment of desirable Progressive legislation. His proposals were now refined, and his strategies for promoting them were carefully choreographed, but the ethics of his position placed real constraints on the openness and vigor of his activity. Yet, the limited nature of Brandeis's success was due to much more than his self-imposed separation from the political realm. The trend of opinion was simply against him, and while the public could be educated through the media, it was not yet moved to act. Moreover, successive conservative Congresses had proved unwilling even to consider his proposals. Like the proverbial wallflower on Saturday night, Brandeis was all dressed up with no place to go.

What the justice really needed was a new resident in the White House with a sympathetic ear for his Progressive ideals. In October 1929, the New York Stock Exchange crashed and during the months that followed, the nation sank into the Great Depression, the pain of which quickly ended public apathy toward social and economic reform. Mired in the worst economic disaster in its history, the nation called out for a strong leader. But the justice wanted more. For him, the leader had to be flexible enough to accept some of his now finely honed ideas on taxation, public works, and unemployment insurance.

Such an individual, one who might, if enlightened, follow the "Brandeis Way," had been on the political horizon for several years and now moved toward the White House. And so it was that with the election in November 1932 of our thirty-second president, Franklin Delano Roosevelt, a new era seemed to be dawning, not only for the country but for the aging prophet on the high Court. Though in his middle seventies, Louis D. Brandeis might still live to see his blueprint for a better society adopted in his lifetime.

4

A Time of Promise:
The "Prophet" and His "Scribe"
in the Early New Deal

The election of Franklin D. Roosevelt to the White House in November 1932 must have been a particularly heartening event for Louis D. Brandeis. In the twentieth century only one other Democrat—Woodrow Wilson—had held the presidency, and Brandeis must surely have retained a vivid memory of those earlier years and the special relationship he had been able to develop with Wilson. Now a second Democrat was about to take the oath of office, a man who had given both Brandeis and Frankfurter strong reason to believe that he might also be receptive to their counsel. Surely here was the time Brandeis had been waiting for.

Yet, just as certainly, this must also have been a time of great tension for the justice. Throughout the twentieth century he had tried to impose his Progressive values on society. For the past dozen years of Republican rule he had pushed for his programs in most cases with very little success. As 1932 rolled into 1933, Brandeis, who had been appointed to the Court at the age of fifty-nine and was now serving for his seventeenth year, probably knew all too well that this would likely be his last opportunity to bring to fruition his dreams of social reform. Seventy-six years old, with middle-aged children and grandchildren, having suffered the death of his beloved brother Alfred and many other contemporaries, Brandeis must have recognized that whatever reform he hoped to bring about in his lifetime would have to be brought about within the next few years.

But there was another sense in which time was also working against him, and of this he may have been far less cognizant. The Progressive programs he had nurtured had now been with him for quite some time; some of his ideas had been conceived as far back as the early 1900s. While Franklin Roosevelt clearly held out the promise of bringing social and economic reform back into political favor, there was no assurance that the particular reforms FDR would institute would be those that Brandeis had long proposed. All around the nation other Democrats and Progressives were likewise celebrating the fact that a new era was dawning. A man less committed than Brandeis to the absolute correctness of his views might have accepted that no matter how respectfully Roosevelt viewed Progressivism, he was not simply going to pick up exactly where Brandeis and Wilson had left off. But Brandeis, so totally committed to his reform program and so confident of the correctness of his message, may not have been able to step back and observe reality. Rather, he had little patience for those who saw FDR's victory as an opportunity to fulfill their own political dreams, and who, in attempting to do so, might fill the president's head with nonsense.

Fortunately for Brandeis, he and his fifty-year-old lieutenant, Felix Frankfurter, had long been preparing for the possibility that Franklin D. Roosevelt would one day be in the White House. When it finally came to be, Frankfurter could boast that his friendship with Roosevelt was already a long-standing one.[1] Years later, at the request of his friend Grenville Clark, a New York City attorney, then-Justice Frankfurter described the entire history of his relationship with FDR. The notes of this extended conversation, now filed in Frankfurter's personal papers, provide an absorbing account of his friendship with Roosevelt over the years.

According to this account, Frankfurter and Roosevelt, born in the same year and both Harvard alumni,* did not actually get to know each other until late in 1906, when Frankfurter was serving in New York in the U.S. Attorney's Office with Henry L. Stimson and Roosevelt was attending Columbia Law School. Even then, though, the two men saw each other only occasionally, mostly at the New York City

---

*During FDR's last year as an undergraduate at Harvard College, Frankfurter was attending his first year at Harvard Law School.

Harvard Club, and their relationship continued to be that of mere acquaintances. Subsequently, however, from 1917 to 1919, both men served in Washington—Frankfurter as assistant to Secretary of War Newton Baker, and Roosevelt as assistant secretary of the Navy. Their contacts increased when Frankfurter was appointed chairman of the War Labor Policies Board, on which Roosevelt served as the Navy Department's representative. Over the long period of time during which the board met weekly, the relationship was put on a first-name basis, and each grew to respect the other's high degree of competence. Many years later, Frankfurter called FDR "the one man [he] knew well" in the government at that time. According to Frankfurter, each man had come out of the experience with a "great sense of affection [for the other] and regret" when their paths separated at the end of World War I.

Frankfurter's assessment of the intimacy of their relationship during this period lacks a certain credibility, for over the next nine years only once—in 1920 when Roosevelt was stricken with polio—did "F.F.," the prolific correspondent, bother to write him. During Roosevelt's long recuperation and his slow return to political prominence, there was not a letter between them. Their first contact after this long interlude occurred in 1928, with a letter of congratulations on the occasion of FDR's nomination as governor of New York, which was signed quite formally: "Very sincerely yours, Felix Frankfurter." Within three weeks, however, Frankfurter sent two more letters, the last one closing with: "Faithfully yours, F.F."[2] Apparently, the professor's well-renowned powers for creating instant intimate friendships among the powerful had been quickly put in gear.

During this period, Louis Brandeis had encouraged the seeming opportunism of Frankfurter in recultivating FDR's friendship. Realizing the possibility of educating a new, important public official regarding his views, Brandeis wrote his lieutenant shortly before the 1928 gubernatorial election: "If, as I expect, Roosevelt is elected, I should like through you to put in early two requests: (a) Far reaching attack on "the Third Degree," (b) Good counsel in N. Y.'s cases before our Court."[3] Then, following Roosevelt's victory, the justice wrote Frankfurter reminding him of his earlier request.[4] Though he had not seen FDR for a decade, the Harvard professor went to work to promote a relationship between his two friends. On November 21, 1928, he wrote the governor-elect at his Warm Springs, Georgia retreat wondering in it whether a meeting with Brandeis would be possible.[5] Instead, at Roosevelt's invitation, it was Frankfurter who brought Brandeis's message to Albany.

Over the next four years, the friendship between FDR and the professor blossomed. Through letters, telephone calls, and personal visits, Frankfurter advised the governor on such issues as crime control and public utility regulation.[6] During this time he continued to pass along messages from Justice Brandeis. For example, in April 1930,* Frankfurter was instructed to tell Roosevelt that he "should be prepared to pounce upon Hoover at the end of the 60 day . . . [period] when H[erbert] H[oover] said all unemployment trouble would be over."[8]

The 1928 overture to FDR by Frankfurter had, in fact, set in motion one of the most unusual political relationships in American history among a man who would become president, a sitting Supreme Court justice, and a Harvard Law School professor—a triangular symbiotic relationship in which each of the participants offered something useful to the others.

For Roosevelt, who had both the official power of public office and the remarkable gifts that would enable him to secure enactment of his programs, Brandeis and Frankfurter represented valued counsel. Having been exposed to Progressive ideals during his years at Harvard, Roosevelt particularly welcomed this link through Frankfurter to Brandeis's views.

For Brandeis, the visionary prophet later called Isaiah by FDR and other members of the Roosevelt team, a man whose sheer brilliance of

---

* The April 1930 letter in which these instructions are contained is the first of a large cache of over three hundred handwritten, personal missives that the justice sent to Frankfurter during the thirties that somehow managed for decades to remain unpublished; the man who did so much to keep these letters from public view was none other than Frankfurter himself. Alpheus Thomas Mason, in undertaking his authorized biography of Justice Brandeis, was offered access to Brandeis's personal letters but not to those documents relating to his work on the Supreme Court. Despite repeated requests by Mason to see these letters from Brandeis to Frankfurter, Frankfurter refused, on the grounds that, in his opinion, these were part of the justice's "court papers." Upon Frankfurter's death, however, these letters were included in the bequest of Frankfurter's personal files to the Library of Congress. Though they had not been available to Mason, and were not included in the excellent volumes of Brandeis correspondence collected by Melvin Urofsky and David Levy, these letters are, in fact, an important key to understanding the political relationship between the justice and Frankfurter and in describing, in full detail, the true extent of Brandeis's extrajudicial activities during the New Deal.[7]

intellect and intimate knowledge of previous reform efforts enabled him to design workable government programs, the arrangement offered the access to the presidency that he so desperately sought, but one that his position on the Court precluded establishing directly.

For Frankfurter, the man who had the confidence of each of the others and who became the perfect conduit, the arrangement made him the confidant of the two men he most admired, while allowing him to move freely between them. What would not become obvious until much later was the degree to which Frankfurter operated during this period as more than just an intermediary, particularly as his loyalties shifted from the man who had been his first patron—Brandeis—to the man who would be his next—FDR.

Soon after his presidential inauguration, Roosevelt tried to bring Frankfurter into the administration by offering him the position of solicitor general. The professor was told that this was a possible step toward a Supreme Court appointment of his own. Frankfurter declined the post, based on advice he had been given by Brandeis. Instead, he chose the role of "outside-insider" to the New Deal; in his letter of refusal to FDR, he wrote: "I can be of more use to the public . . . by not becoming Solicitor General . . . [but I] should nevertheless like to feel that I am part of the Administration even outside the office."[9] Though FDR responded by calling Frankfurter "an independent pig," he also said, "I guess that's one reason [that] I like you."[10]

In advising Frankfurter that it would be, in his words, "absurd" to accept this governmental position, Brandeis seems to have had mixed motives.[11] The outside role which he chose for Frankfurter was one that the justice knew well from his own days as an adviser to Woodrow Wilson. As Brandeis had earlier learned, because it is rare in politics to find men who offer their counsel but do not seek to feather their own nest by asking for favors or positions in return, such counsel often receives special respect. Yet surely the justice must have also realized that if Frankfurter were to accept the solicitor generalship he would no longer be in a position either to advocate Brandeis's policies or serve as his liaison to the administration.

By refusing the appointment, then, Frankfurter opted for continuing and expanding his long-term role as the central lieutenant for Justice Brandeis. Years later, however, when it would be suggested by historians such as Arthur Schlesinger, Jr., that Frankfurter's views on most matters were not much different from those of Brandeis, Frankfurter would vehemently object. As late as June 1963, after a visit with President John F. Kennedy in which the New Deal was discussed, Frankfurter felt it necessary to write Schlesinger to point out the differences between the two men, arguing that on sociological and economic issues, Brandeis had been the uncompromising "ideologue," while he the "stark empiricist." [12]

That Frankfurter would have so strong a reaction to Schlesinger's thesis is understandable only if one studies carefully the subtlely changing character during the New Deal of Frankfurter's role as Brandeis's extrajudicial lieutenant. In attempting to match up specific requests for action in Brandeis's letters with Frankfurter's eventual recommendations to various political leaders, especially those to FDR, one sees that a number of policies did not survive transmission unaltered by their exposure to the Harvard professor. Particularly as we study the middle thirties it becomes more and more apparent that the solutions Brandeis entrusted to his lieutenant, which continued to be designed as they always had been—to represent the "right" and therefore only approach to the problem—begin to differ considerably from Frankfurter's actual recommendations. At first, it was the professor's pragmatism which accounted for these differences, but later it would be more than a better sense of the possible that would cause a rift between Frankfurter and the man whose ideas he had helped foster for nearly two decades.

Back in late 1932, though, there can be no doubt that Frankfurter was still very much Brandeis's loyal lieutenant and that as such, Frankfurter saw his most important mission the bringing together of Brandeis and FDR. Brandeis was very pleased in October 1932 to receive word from Frankfurter that the confident presidential candidate had requested a meeting after the election to "discuss the problems of the next administration." [13]

Following the twenty minute meeting, which took place at the Mayflower Hotel in Washington, D.C., on November 23, Brandeis sent Frankfurter a handwritten report of his impressions that bubbled with enthusiasm. FDR, he concluded, "seem[ed] well versed [in the] fundamental faith of the situation," and "a new era" was dawning. [14] Brandeis had begun this meeting with a casual offer to Roosevelt that he was "ready to help in any way" he could. As an initial step, two days later he met with former chairman of the Federal Trade Commission, Huston Thompson, who had been charged by the president with gathering proposals for reforming the financial and business communities. Thompson reported to FDR that the justice had explained how to control holding companies (prevalently used by large businesses to evade governmental taxes and regulations), and had suggested that these ideas be forwarded directly to the president.[15]

In late January and early February 1933,* the justice was ready to launch the next step in his crusade. Seeking to get his political affairs in order as quickly as possible, Brandeis sent the battle plan to Frankfurter in four separate handwritten letters. These letters, together with two memoranda Frankfurter wrote for his own files commenting on and analyzing the program, contain the Brandeisian orthodoxy for reforming and reviving the American economy.[16] It was these marching orders that occupied the two men so completely over the next several years.

By now Brandeis had distilled his battle plans into four separate campaigns. First, he proposed massive government expenditures on public-works projects, such as programs for "wholesale afforestation" and the "control of waters."† The plan he envisioned was so comprehensive that it would not only promote economic recovery through government spending, but, if adopted, Brandeis predicted, it would put "two million men to work directly by the United States and the States within six months and another million or so indirectly."[18] While the justice believed that these programs would be partly self-financing, producing revenues by increasing the tax base and providing marketable commodities, a second set of proposals was designed to provide the funds necessary to support the public-works programs completely. Therefore, Brandeis also suggested vast revisions in the federal income tax structure, changes that were designed to make it a much more progressive system. Believing that the burden of taxation should

---

*This was still prior to the inauguration of FDR. At that time the incoming president was not inaugurated until March 4.

†Brandeis's "control of waters" plan, which at times he labelled his "Running Water Control" program, was described in letters to both his daughter, Elizabeth Brandeis Raushenbush, and to Felix Frankfurter (with the intention that his lieutenant pass the idea along to Senator Robert Wagner of New York). The justice proposed that in areas of the country which received between 35 and 50 inches of rain, and had many hills and mountains, that rivers should be dammed to create reservoirs. Thus, he argued, floods would be prevented, irrigation during droughts made possible, navigation improved, soil erosion eased, and new power sources created. All in all, Brandeis's plan was much along the lines of the Tennessee Valley Authority which would subsequently be proposed by the Roosevelt Administration.[17]

be placed on those who could most afford to pay—his "super rich"—Brandeis intended to realize the bulk of the necessary revenue by eliminating this economic class entirely through passage of a "persistent and all-embracing" inheritance tax program. The justice also believed that additional funds could be raised by increasing the taxes for higher income brackets, closing a number of tax loopholes, such as in the gift and estate levies, and passing legislation restricting the "outrageously large" contingency fees charged by tax attorneys filing suits against the government. Brandeis's third campaign was to secure the adoption of a number of reforms in investment and banking practices, such as the holding company idea offered earlier to Huston Thompson. Finally, to insure that the needed revenue would be collected efficiently and that these plans would be implemented correctly, Brandeis wanted the government staffed with "lawyers of ability, training and the right attitude." [19]

Brandeis's plans were laid, but in order to bring them to fruition he had to secure direct access to Roosevelt's inner circle. All his efforts to refine programs, and all Frankfurter's efforts to court FDR would be futile, he and Frankfurter both understood, if the ideas were lost in the crush of supplicants angling for the president's attention on a daily basis. In August 1932, Frankfurter had tried unsuccessfully to place Max Lowenthal, their legislative draftsman prior to the New Deal, at the right hand of the candidate.[20] Then, during the critical time the new administration was being formed, from November 1932 to early 1933, with the president-elect in Albany and the justice's main lobbyist in Cambridge, opportunities for contact had been infrequent at best.[21] In fact, according to the notes of Frankfurter's own recollections of his relationship with FDR, which did not, as a pattern, minimize his own contributions to events, Frankfurter traveled to Albany only twice during the period between Roosevelt's election and his inauguration. Plainly, if Brandeis wanted to be effective he would have to enlist through Frankfurter an ally closer to the president-elect.

This quest for an intermediary was made even more pressing by the fact that the men surrounding FDR at this time were imbued with a concept of the governmental role that was anathema to the justice. Sickened by the power of monopolies and large government, Brandeis and Frankfurter favored measures designed to re-establish competition among industries and businesses, restore trust in the banking and investment communities, and increase the importance of the state governments. But it was Rexford Tugwell, Raymond Moley, and Adolf Berle, three Columbia University professors, who had advised Governor Roosevelt and would come to be known as Roosevelt's "Brain Trust," who were engaged in planning the new administration in a house on 65th Street in New York City. These were the "social planners," the "collectivists," who believed in promoting bigness in the federal government and encouraging monopolistic rather than competitive businesses. They sought to provide central direction for the economy by designing large-scale national programs that instituted cooperation among government, agriculture, and business sectors.[22] It was their philosophy that would guide Roosevelt in the first years of the New Deal despite the monumental struggle for influence waged by Brandeis and Frankfurter.

A generation of writers has described the internecine struggle for influence that took place during the first Hundred Days of the New Deal between these two sets of advisers.[23] Arthur Schlesinger's thesis, which has long been accepted as the most accurate description of what actually occurred, very clearly separates the two camps. Schlesinger notes that "on economic problems, Frankfurter, like Brandeis, distrusted the grandiose schemes of the social planners."[24] The Brain Trusters, he notes, believed just as strongly that the justice's faith in Progressive reform of the economy was "obsolete," "almost as obnoxious as outright conservatism," and a "dead end of liberal reform."[25] Indeed, there is certainly confirming evidence in the published and unpublished accounts of central actors during that period to support the thesis that there was considerable hostility between the two groups. Rexford Tugwell, for example, in his published work shrugs off Brandeis's ideas as "outmoded" and as being promoted by his "satellite" Felix Frankfurter.[26] How at least this one collectivist believed that Brandeis was able nonetheless to gain Roosevelt's ear and hold his respect with these "outmoded" notions was addressed in a highly revealing introduction written by Tugwell for his private, unpublished diary.

Firmly convinced that FDR was looking for a father figure to advise him, Tugwell believed that Brandeis, who, he noted, remained "in the shadows," was the only one in a position to excite the president's "awe and reverence." Once having established himself in this position of authority, Tugwell argued, the justice used a potent "one-two" punch to reinforce his advice—the threat of declaring acts unconstitutional and the enlistment of "hundreds" of lieutenants to sabotage early New Deal policies by staffing its agencies.[27] Further on in this introduction, Tugwell reveals even more of his acrimony toward Brandeis and Frankfurter. He clearly blames these men for his own eventual downfall: "[The Brandeis group] had implacable hostility to me. They were determined to check me everywhere, to discredit and eject me from government [and] they succeeded."[28]

According to Raymond Moley, Tugwell's assessment was right. Contained in his papers is a highly revealing memorandum indicating that Tugwell's distrust of Brandeis and Frankfurter was matched by their distrust of him, and that he, Tugwell, was a particular target of theirs. Moley placed in his files an account of a conversation he had with Thomas Corcoran, a key Brandeis-Frankfurter lieutenant within the administration. When the subject of Tugwell was raised, Moley reports that Corcoran launched into a "fine fury," as evidenced by his "pounding the desk and walking up and down the room," and stated:

> I've never seen anything like him for arrogance. He picked up the draft of a speech the Skipper [FDR] was to make, laid it in front of me, pointed to the word "competition" and said: "That ought to come out." When I paid no attention he turned to the President and said: "You know you don't believe in it." The President ignored him. Can you imagine the nerve of that bastard? Well, we've got the knife in the sheaf and we'll take care of him. Not that he doesn't serve a useful function. He is a sort of catfish to keep the herrings from getting sluggish when the fishermen have taken them back in tanks to port. But the Skipper shouldn't get the idea that he is an edible fish.[29]

Raymond Moley's private papers also contain further evidence of the competition that existed in some cases between members of the two camps, specifically between Frankfurter and Adolf A. Berle, Jr. The opportunity for observing this competition came whenever Frankfurter initially proposed his ideas to the Brain Trust. In early 1933, for instance, the Brain Trusters were considering the endorsement of a complete railroad-reorganization bill.* After forwarding his views on this issue in a letter to Raymond Moley, Frankfurter telephoned their headquarters and spoke with Adolf Berle.[31] According

---

*At the time, this measure was being considered by the Brain Trust as part of a general bankruptcy measure. Frankfurter wanted to keep the railroad-reorganization provisions separate, and to vest the power over the creation of such reorganization plans in the Interstate Commerce Commission, rather than company "insiders," in order to safeguard the public interest.[30]

to Moley, in a matter of minutes the conversation became quite acrimonious, and, after hanging up, Berle kept repeating, "Felix wants to ruin me."[32]

Yet despite these obvious conflicts, and the near universal acceptance of the Schlesinger thesis, two of the alleged combatants—Felix Frankfurter and Raymond Moley—later argued in private correspondence that there had never been any rigid separation between the two sets of advisers. In a private letter to Arthur Schlesinger in 1963, Frankfurter argued:

> I disagree with your view on the Roosevelt Administration in the 30's. . . . I must reject your assumption that there was a real clash of views between Moley-Tugwell and F.F.-Brandeis. This assumes that the respective parties had coherent and systematic views on some of the problems that are involved in Roosevelt's policies.[33]

Frankfurter was not alone in taking exception to the Schlesinger thesis. In 1972, while reflecting on his own work during the New Deal period in a private letter to historian Elliot A. Rosen, Moley claimed that he and Frankfurter "got on very well indeed" because they were both "political men" dedicated to the welfare of Franklin Roosevelt.[34]

Still, scholars writing even recently on this period have continued to portray the relationship between Moley and Frankfurter as one largely of antagonism, failing to discern the actual pattern of collaboration between the two.[35] The reason for the stubborn survival of this impression is that none of these writers have seen unpublished documents that in fact do contradict the Schlesinger thesis and instead show that Moley functioned on numerous occasions during the first Hundred Days as the access to FDR for Brandeis and Frankfurter.

Intrigued by suggestions in Frankfurter's private papers of an apparent warmth between Moley and Frankfurter, I journeyed to California to examine Moley's papers in the hopes of learning something of his view of the relationship. In the recently opened Moley papers I found support for the Frankfurter-Moley refutation of the standard thesis. Letters from Frankfurter and Moley's personal unpublished diary portray a very different picture of the interaction between these two than the one thus far shown.

Frankfurter first met Moley, a man four years his junior, in 1920, when they worked together on a survey of criminal justice in Cleveland.[36] However, their relations suffered when an argument resulted in a long period of noncommunication. When Moley wrote a letter of apology in 1930, the response by Frankfurter was characteristically effusive.

> A letter like yours one is not apt to get twice in a lifetime. The complete clean candor of it, the objectification of the ego is as beautiful as it is rare. I can only say that I covet the capacity for similar self-searching and the avowal of its finding. . . . I hope that I had said enough to indicate the quality of my appreciation. For the rest, the past *is dead* and your letter marks a fresh and mature beginning. [*Italics in original*][37]

Concerned only with the success of the administration after the election in 1932, the two men, despite their philosophical differences, were prepared to join forces on occasion.

The first assistance Moley offered Brandeis and Frankfurter was in setting up a second preinaugural meeting between the justice and the president-elect, which took place in mid-January 1933.[38] As important, however, was that Moley was willing to listen to Frankfurter's entreaties on such matters as the railroad-reorganization issue. Thus encouraged by Moley's initial responses and urged on by Brandeis, Frankfurter decided to take his personal relationship with Moley a step further.

On January 29, 1933, Frankfurter met with Moley for over two hours and discussed Brandeis's numerous tax measures, including the contingency-fee idea.[39] With the groundwork laid, Brandeis, feeling the pressure of time slipping by, abandoned his usual sense of caution and decided that the time had come for him to see Moley personally. The justice signaled his new desire by concluding both an extensive letter and a telegram to Frankfurter detailing his public-works ideas with: "It is this plan that I am eager to talk to Moley about."[40] Just as he had done earlier, when Brandeis wanted to convey a message to Roosevelt, the professor now worked fervidly to arrange a meeting with Moley.

Several letters discovered in Raymond Moley's private papers make it possible to reconstruct Frankfurter's detailed efforts to enlist the Brain Truster's assistance during the month of February 1933. First, he wired Moley at Warm Springs on February 6 that it was "vital [that you] see Brandeis regarding details of a plan most important to [the] early success of [the] administration."[41] Having just discussed these ideas with Frankfurter, the presidential assistant showed no interest in such a meeting. So, Frankfurter wrote again: "[Brandeis] is most anxious to have [a] talk with you about a public works program which seems to him—and I take it also to you—indispensable for achieving recovery."[42] This time, to prod Moley even further, the professor enclosed a copy of that portion of Brandeis's letter that outlined his expenditure proposals, and offered the justice's judgment that Roosevelt's recently announced "control of waters" idea—the Tennessee Valley project—was "fine in quality—but insufficient in quantity for the emergency."[43] To satisfy the "judicial proprieties," Frankfurter closed his plea for the meeting by telling Moley, "of course [these ideas are] not to go beyond yourself and FDR."[44] The next day Moley did phone Frankfurter and promised to speak with Brandeis "at the earliest moment."[45]

When two weeks passed without any further action, Frankfurter launched a new offensive to arrange the meeting. Over the next twelve days he sent Moley four letters on the subject. After an initial reminder, Frankfurter told Moley on February 26: "You ought to see Brandeis because he wants to see you."[46] Moreover, Frankfurter suggested that another direct meeting be arranged between the justice and Roosevelt for the purpose of explaining his programs.* The next day Frankfurter sent a third letter to Moley in which he forwarded an outline of Brandeis's argument that the commissioner of Internal Revenue must effectively use the full range of his powers in order to collect all possible revenue, and asked that it be passed along to FDR.[48]

Since Moley still had not committed himself to a specific date for the conference, Frankfurter's fourth request became even more urgent.

> Meeting with Brandeis . . . seems to me most important on two counts: (1) because of the intrinsic wisdom and far-sighted mastery of Brandeis on financial and economic matters, and (2) because of the heartening effect that it would convey to the people who need most to be encouraged these days that the President is conferring with Brandeis.[49]

* This letter also contained some personal advice for Moley, who was in the process of securing a formal role for himself in the administration. Having discussed this issue twice before, Frankfurter reiterated his advice that Moley have his "status left in unequivocation and . . . as clearly defined as the nature of your duties will demand—that means publicly and candidly declared."[47] Of course, there was a good measure of self-interest on Frankfurter's part here, in that he and Brandeis were seeking an intermediary to Roosevelt.

Moley finally relented and met with the justice two days later. During this conference, Brandeis presented his full plan for economic recovery and claimed that it could be wholly financed through the realization of an additional two billion dollars a year in revenue from tax loopholes that could be closed. Though he did not tell the justice to his face, Moley later wrote that he found the idea of financing such a vast public-works program by "plugging loopholes in the tax law and by waiting for the super rich to die" to be "frivolous to the point of absurdity."[50]

After this meeting, Frankfurter viewed Moley, now serving as assistant secretary of state, as his conduit to the administration. During these crucial first few months of the new administration, Moley provided Brandeis and Frankfurter with their vitally necessary direct access to FDR. It was largely through Moley that they were able to argue their position effectively on a variety of major programs. And argue they did. Indeed, a search of Moley's private papers quite clearly reveals that whenever an administration crisis arose, Moley found on his desk a Frankfurter telegram pleading for him to "call collect" in order to discuss the issue. Of course, the yearly funds provided by Justice Brandeis would help defray the expense of these telegrams and any collect phone calls they engendered. But this only partially explains the phenomenal fact that a count of the documents in Moley's papers and a reading of Moley's personal diary indicates that from January to September 1933 the Harvard professor dispatched over one hundred and fifty letters to Moley discussing various pieces of legislation and possible appointments to the administration.[51]

Apparently, Moley nonetheless managed to keep his distance, for in one letter sent in late March, the professor once again described Brandeis as a "mine of wisdom that is available to the President" that "ought to be tapped before long."[52] Simultaneously, it appears that Moley did not take offense (or at least did not express it) at the barrage of letters Frankfurter sent him; on the contrary, when either man traveled to the other's home city, there would be personal meetings and long discussions. Their personal and professional relationship was such that Moley even offered Frankfurter a position in the State Department. Refusing, Frankfurter took the opportunity to recommend one of Brandeis's old friends, attorney George Rublee, and one of his former law clerks, attorney Dean Acheson, for the position.

As one might expect, he also instructed Moley to confer with the justice himself on the matter.[53]

Later on, after he had been forced out of government, Moley explained to Frankfurter why he had been willing to work so closely with him even though their philosophical outlooks were so different.

> I have always felt that there was a vital point of philosophical disagreement between us. . . . I have been acutely conscious of it and scrupulously fair too, I think, about it, so far as our mutual dealings with F.D.R. and his policies are concerned. When I work for him I *make* myself see that he must draw strength and wisdom from both points of view. [*Italics in original*][54]

By that time, however, Brandeis and Frankfurter were well on their way to placing their own lieutenants at the ear of the president.

Despite the efforts of Brandeis and Frankfurter during the preinaugural months and the first months of the early New Deal to place their own people near the president, and even to proselytize Moley, the president was soon almost completely surrounded by collectivists such as those of the Brain Trust. Consequently, FDR's first Hundred Days were devoted to creating scores of new federal agencies that would attempt to control every facet of the American economy.[55] Large-scale programs such as the Agricultural Adjustment Act and the National Industrial Recovery Act thrust the government into a cooperative partnership with farms and businessmen nationwide in order to promote recovery in those areas. Instead of proposing Brandeis's massive public-works program, FDR and Congress instituted the Civilian Conservation Corps (CCC) and a national relief system known as the Federal Emergency Relief Act (FERA). While the president did support the Tennessee Valley Authority Act (TVA), Brandeis would have preferred a slightly different "control of waters" plan. More preaching would have to be done before the prophet's "fundamental faith," as Brandeis himself called it, would have a convert in the White House.

Having lost the debate over the nature of the early New Deal programs, however, Brandeis and Frankfurter were hardly deterred. Of course, during this time Frankfurter continued his own direct efforts to spread the word throughout the administration. Through letters, phone calls, and personal visits, he sought to educate FDR directly as well as indirectly. But Brandeis had something else in mind. Why not recruit more allies for the crusade? By staffing the many departments and agencies of the executive branch with a sufficient number of "right thinking" individuals in positions of power, he and Frankfurter could create enough contact points in the administration to be able to influence the actual implementation of the new legislation, an exercise possibly more important than having a strong voice in the drafting of it.

Frankfurter's success in placing scores of Harvard Law School graduates throughout the Roosevelt Administration has become legendary.[56] His efforts were so extensive that Rexford Tugwell lamented in his private diary over his impression that "hundreds" of New Deal appointees owed their jobs to the Harvard professor. It was not long before these Frankfurter protégés were commonly being labeled "Felix's Happy Hot Dogs." Typical of the stories about the Frankfurter placement bureau is a statement by George Peek, the head of the Agricultural Adjustment Administration.

> A plague of young lawyers settled on Washington. They all claimed to be friends of somebody or other and mostly of Felix Frankfurter and Jerome Frank. They floated airily into offices, took desks, asked for papers and found no end of things to be busy about. I never found out why they came, what they did or why they left.[57]

Certainly many of the most influential men in the New Deal were appointed on the recommendation of the professor from Harvard. Evidence exists, however, that a number of the suggestions for appointments originated with Louis D. Brandeis. The justice would not only select a candidate but often target exactly where that individual was to be placed in the administration. Of course, these determinations were made on the basis of the individual's qualifications and the likelihood that Frankfurter could engineer the candidate's appointment to such a position.

The justice and his lieutenant were especially successful in placing people in the Departments of Labor, the Interior, and Agriculture. Their task in the Department of Labor was eased by the fact that its secretary, Frances Perkins, was already in their debt. According to the personal recollection of former Brandeis law clerk, Paul Freund, the justice had devoted his entire meeting with President Roosevelt at the Mayflower Hotel in mid-January 1933 to arguing in behalf of Perkins's appointment to the position.[58] While Brandeis had sent other recommendations for cabinet appointments to FDR through two other conduits—Attorney General-designate Thomas Walsh and former Woodrow Wilson cabinet official William McAdoo—it was Perkins, an old Progressive ally in several causes, in whom the justice may have invested the most hope.[59] As he commented in a letter to Felix Frankfurter, Perkins was "the best [that] the U.S. affords."[60]

On March 18, Perkins asked Frankfurter for his suggestions regarding the crucial department solicitor's job. In two letters to the professor, Brandeis suggested for the position either Paul Freund, his then-current law clerk, or Harvard Law School graduate Raymond Stevens. Yet despite his close relationship with Frances Perkins, which was sustained by frequent correspondence on various policy matters, Frankfurter was unable to secure the appointment of either man. However, in April 1933, Frankfurter successfully suggested Charles E. Wyzanski, Jr., a law clerk for both Appeals Court Judges Augustus Hand and Learned Hand, for the post. When problems developed in the Senate proceedings on the appointment because Wyzanski was a registered Republican, Frankfurter was enlisted by Perkins to secure the support of Democratic Senator David Walsh of Massachusetts. Not only did the professor wire Walsh about the matter, but he also reported to Perkins that an "influential friend"* had also spoken to the senator directly.[61] When the confirmation was given by the Senate, Wyzanski, at the tender age of twenty-six, became one of the justice's most useful contacts in the Labor Department.

The Brandeis-Frankfurter placement bureau was even more successful in the Department of the Interior. Because he had great respect for Felix Frankfurter, Secretary of the Interior Harold Ickes not only met with the professor in the initial weeks of the administration to discuss "several matters," but had him arrange an interview with Justice Brandeis on March 12, 1933.[62] After Brandeis suggested in this conference that Nathan Margold be made the department's solicitor, Ickes acted immediately to secure the nomination. Not surprisingly, one of Margold's first acts was to consult both Brandeis and Frankfurter for recommendations on the staffing of his office and procedures for exercising his authority.[63]

Frankfurter's unpublished correspondence files confirm the extent to which this new appointment expanded his and the justice's influence over the policies of the Interior Department. The two men soon

---

* It is quite possible, given their long-standing relationship in various Progressive causes and common roots in Massachusetts, that Justice Brandeis was the "influential friend" who spoke with Senator Walsh.

discovered that having two contacts in the Interior Department created a complementary effect in securing desirable appointments. Frankfurter would begin the process by suggesting a candidate to Secretary Ickes. For instance, on March 23, 1933, Frankfurter recommended that the man Brandeis had defended in the 1910 Ballinger-Pinchot controversy, Louis Glavis, be added to the department solicitor's office. Once persuaded of Glavis's qualifications, Ickes then instructed Solicitor Margold to investigate further the suitability of the candidate, but did not tell him where the idea for the appointment had originated.[64] In this second phase of the process, Margold would almost invariably consult with Brandeis for guidance. In the case of Glavis's appointment, the two men met on March 27 and the justice offered his highest recommendation. With Margold's report back to Ickes confirming Frankfurter's original recommending assessment, Ickes could make the appointment with confidence.

Letters contained in the Frankfurter papers show that there were other opportunities to lobby for Brandeis's candidates for positions in the Interior Department. When additional people were needed to staff Solicitor Margold's office, Felix Frankfurter, acting directly on Brandeis's instructions, suggested the latter's old Progressive allies Harry Slatterly and Gardner Jackson. Neither man was chosen for one of these new openings, but Slatterly was subsequently appointed as personal assistant to Secretary Ickes.[65] Then, with the establishment in 1933 of the Public Works Administration (PWA) to administer emergency relief, Ickes wired Brandeis asking for his suggestions to head the new agency. Within hours the justice proposed the governor of Wisconsin, Philip LaFollette, for the post. In this case, however, Ickes himself was named to the position.[66]

Despite their lack of allies in the highest echelons of the Department of Agriculture, when the related Agricultural Adjustment Administration (AAA) was created Brandeis and Frankfurter achieved considerable success in placing people there. On March 13, 1933, Secretary of Agriculture Henry Wallace brought his assistant secretary, Rexford Tugwell, to a meeting with Brandeis in which they were seeking advice regarding whom to appoint as a solicitor for their department. While Brandeis was the only Supreme Court justice they consulted on the question, neither the officials nor Brandeis regarded this open conference as being either unusual or unethical. The justice suggested several names and then recommended Felix Frankfurter as an additional source of advice. In a letter reporting to Frankfurter on this episode, Brandeis raised the possibility of appointing Dean Acheson to the position, admitting that "it would be a comedown" for him.[67] Here, however, the action Frankfurter took went in another direction. Though he did recommend Dean Acheson as well, the professor had another man in mind for the slot—Jerome Frank—a prominent Wall Street attorney. He wrote to his candidate warning: "If you get any kind of a bid from Washington—however funny it may look on the face of things as being unrelated to your immediate legal experience—certainly don't make a wry face at it until you have had the chance to talk to me about it."[68]

The accounts of Frank, in an oral history, and Rexford Tugwell, in his unpublished diary, enable us to trace the story from that point. Originally, Frank received the solicitorship, but the appointment was blocked by the influential Postmaster General James A. Farley, under the mistaken impression that Frank's father had been an old adversary from Tammany Hall days in New York politics. Once the misunderstanding was discovered and straightened out, Frank was designated general counsel for the prospective AAA and made personal assistant to Tugwell until the agency could be established.

From this point, the oral histories of both Tugwell and Henry Wallace demonstrate how this new appointment quickly expanded Frankfurter's and Brandeis's voice in departmental decisions. In his new capacity, Frank had considerable influence over the drafting of the enabling legislation for the AAA, and then the staffing of it. Acting on Frankfurter's suggestions, he quickly named fellow Harvard Law School graduates Nathan Witt, Lee Pressman, and Alger Hiss to his office.[69] These appointments, together with the fortuitous selection of Gardner Jackson (who had worked with Frankfurter in the Sacco-Vanzetti controversy), as assistant director to the AAA's Consumers' Counsel, created within the agency a Progressive wing through which Brandeis could attempt to influence its policy direction.[70] Given the antagonism of the AAA's first two directors—George Peek and Chester Davis—to Brandeis's ideas, and the justice's inability to place any allies in the National Recovery Administration (NRA), these appointments proved to be especially significant.

Despite a special interest they would naturally have in the policies of the Department of Justice, and numerous efforts to place allies there, Brandeis and Frankfurter had little success in staffing this department. They were simply not as close to Attorney General Homer Cummings as they had been to his predecessor, Progressive Senator Thomas Walsh, who had died shortly after his appointment to the new position. Nevertheless, Brandeis was so eager to have Dean Acheson named solicitor general that for one of the few times he made the recommendation directly to President Roosevelt. But the justice later learned that Attorney General Cummings had an "immediate, violent, and adverse" reaction to the idea, and the post went instead to James Crawford Biggs of North Carolina.[71]

Undaunted by this defeat, Brandeis directed Felix Frankfurter to propose another of his former law clerks, William Sutherland, whom the justice had determined in an earlier interview as being "right" on the question of closing tax loopholes, as an assistant attorney general. Once again, though, despite Frankfurter's efforts to persuade both Cummings and FDR of the merits of this appointment, the choice was passed over.[72] The only real success enjoyed by Brandeis in staffing this department occurred when he asked Frankfurter to help keep Erwin Griswold and Paul Miller in the Solicitor General's office because of their expertise in tax litigation. However, to get what he wanted, Brandeis had to speak directly to the new solicitor general while Frankfurter not only wrote to FDR personally, but, as a letter discovered in the Roosevelt papers at Hyde Park reveals, also forwarded to the president similar views from Justice Harlan Fiske Stone. Brandeis expressed pleasure when the appointments were made, telling Frankfurter that they assured "adequate argument of their tax case at least."[73] When Miller chose instead to leave the government in order to resume private law practice, the justice must surely have been even more disappointed in his overall lack of success in staffing the Justice Department.[74]

Between their joint efforts and Frankfurter's success in placing many of his students on his own, a number of other New Deal vacancies were eventually filled with bureaucrats sympathetic to the Brandeis vision. Justice Brandeis was able to convince Arthur Morgan of the TVA to appoint a Frankfurter protégé, David Lilienthal, as a member of that agency's board. Then, after their lengthy search for the best available position for Dean Acheson, Felix Frankfurter was able to place him as undersecretary of the treasury. Typically, Lilienthal, Acheson, and all the other appointees served as "eyes and ears" for Brandeis and Frankfurter, supplying a constant flow of information on proceedings in their departments.[75]

Utilizing these contacts, the two men were able to monitor the direction of the collectivist efforts as well as to develop a vast store-house of data that eventually proved useful in the battle for accept-ance of the Brandeisian goals. But these new allies could do much more; they could serve as point men in the effort to place more troops in the agencies. The Frankfurter files in the Library of Congress con-tain copies of long lists of possible appointees that were forwarded by the professor to the two department solicitors he had just helped ap-point—Charles E. Wyzanski, Jr., and Nathan Margold.[76] Yet, it was not enough just to have these like-minded individuals in various agen-cies. The justice needed to encourage and educate them. Demonstrat-ing his keen political instincts, Brandeis developed a variety of meth-ods to accomplish this task.

In privately attempting to direct the course of the executive policies in the New Deal, Justice Brandeis on most occasions tried to maintain a certain distance from the principal political actors. To create an appearance of personal detachment, for instance, the justice generally employed intermediaries when approaching President Roosevelt. In-deed, letters stored in Roosevelt's presidential papers show that Bran-deis used a number of persons besides Frankfurter to keep the presi-dent apprised of his position on the issues: Raymond Moley, lawyer Huston Thompson, banker J. Lionberger Davis, speechwriter Samuel I. Rosenman, and even the hostile Brain Truster, Adolf A. Berle, Jr.[77] A constant flow of letters to Frankfurter and these other interlocu-tors made it unnecessary for Brandeis to confer directly with Roose-velt except in rare instances. When such an occasion did arise, Bran-deis would have it arranged for Roosevelt to request the meeting by having an intermediary forward to the White House a message such as: "Justice Brandeis is at home waiting and will gladly come on sum-mons for conference regarding Attorney Generalship and Banking matters."[78]

In working with the lower levels of the executive branch, though, especially in his dealings with those whom he and Frankfurter had initially helped to place, the justice was much more direct with his advice. During these years Brandeis continued his life-long practice of focusing intently on one issue at a time. Upon achieving mastery of a problem area, he was then delighted to instruct other people re-garding his findings and proposed solutions. He did this yearly with his new law clerks, many of whom later received appointments in the Roosevelt Administration, and he continually indoctrinated scores of other young New Dealers by talking with them on the important issues of the day. These administrators never requested such conferences on their own; they were periodically summoned by a phone call from Mrs. Brandeis, saying: "The Justice knows you want an appointment and he will see you at the following time." Of course, such clairvoyance was many times made possible by information that had been passed along by Felix Frankfurter.

Often in these personal conferences the justice would speak in parables drawn from his own earlier reform activities, or in general philosophical terms. In this fashion he could both encourage and educate his visitor without appearing to compromise his judicial position. One time, in a talk with Labor Department Solicitor Charles E. Wyzanski, Jr., the justice convinced him not to resign because of the job's workload by telling him a story about once having advised a close friend, Walter Fisher, who had become secretary of the interior after the Ballinger-Pinchot controversy. Brandeis recounted his having told Fisher that he should "never sign a letter you have not read."[79] Quoting Fisher's response, "You ask the impossible," Brandeis explained to Wyzanski that he now believed his friend to have been correct. Vastly reassured regarding the propriety of delegating more of the workload to his assistants, Wyzanski decided to remain at his post.[80]

On another occasion, when the newly appointed solicitor for the Department of the Interior, Nathan Margold, journeyed to Brandeis's apartment for a conference, he was given this sage advice: "Take [your] time about everything and be sure what [you are] doing before [you do] it."[81] Yet, Brandeis's assistance was hardly limited to providing his allies with general homilies. As Margold made clear in his report to Felix Frankfurter of another meeting with Brandeis, the justice was also willing to serve as a sounding board on specific policy matters.

> I had a long talk with Justice Brandeis yesterday who approved of my method of procedure and who gave me some invaluable suggestions as to how to conduct myself in my new and very trying position.[82]

It should not be assumed that these New Deal administrators were mere puppets on the justice's string who simply carried out his specific instructions on command—though he was always available for specific consultation as needed. Rather, it was more that they were men of a similar mind with Brandeis and, given some general encouragement by him, acted in a manner consonant with his own private wishes.

Other than with Frankfurter, the justice discussed prospective legislation and executive policies directly and in great detail with only a few, carefully chosen, higher level New Deal officials. For these few, Brandeis would use, as he had during the 1920s, the occasion of dinners at his apartment to preach his message. The unique atmosphere surrounding these gatherings contributed to the power of his appeal. James Grafton Rogers, assistant secretary of state in the Hoover Administration, has provided us with a delightful description of this ambience.

Rogers recorded that the justice lived on a crowded street that "smelled of onions." The apartment itself was drab and austere, almost bereft of furniture or "homey touches." Even the legions of books were hidden away in the justice's upstairs study. Dinner was never very much—usually a single boiled chicken and one vegetable platter for a party of six. But *haute cuisine* was not what the guests had come for. Here is Rogers's impression of the nearly mystical experience:

> I came away full of wondering and searching. Brandeis is something between Lincoln and Christ in the strange poetical impression he leaves. Life to him is a great moral web, a complex of good and evil forces, an organ composition. Gentleness, sweetness, yearning, listening, hoping are the sensations you get from him. He distrusts wealth, size, power. He was arguing with me that night for high income taxes as a social measure. . . . He is frail. He had been rereading some Latin books. He quotes Goëthe often. . . . He is not a socialist. He is a moralist. He is scarcely of this world at all. The master of statistics and legal lore is scarcely hinted in his hours at home.[83]

Little wonder that so many guests of lesser mental capacity and greater ambivalence in their political goals often left the occasions, always incidentally at the request of Mrs. Brandeis precisely at the stroke of ten o'clock, fully stimulated and ready to overcome all obstacles in behalf of the justice's Progressive ideals.

Since these sporadic meetings and dinners could have only a limited impact on the implementation and administration of his desired policies, Brandeis developed another ingenious method for indoctrinating his protégés and allies. He held weekly "at home" teas, to which were invited various notable individuals and government officials in

Washington.[84] These social *soirées* were held originally on Monday afternoons, but after a number of years they were scheduled on Sunday, to avoid conflicts with sessions of the Court.

Based on interviews with several Frankfurter protégés and the oral histories of others, each of whom attended these sessions, it is possible to reconstruct something of their nature. Once again, these were hardly the most fashionable occasions from a social standpoint. Noted Washington attorney and former Frankfurter law clerk, Joseph L. Rauh, Jr., remembers that the guests were served by a Supreme Court messenger named Poindexter, who distinguished himself by appearing to be even older and feebler than Brandeis, and who delighted in recollecting about seeing "old man Adams" walking around Washington.[85] Moreover, all that was ever offered was a very weak tea and a single cookie per guest.

The absolute worst time to go to the teas was, apparently, in midsummer, because Brandeis's austerity prevented him from using a fan or even opening the windows to catch whatever breeze there might be. The room was extremely crowded, even more so because everyone brought his spouse. But the spouses of these officials were virtually ignored, often left in a corner of the room to make conversation with one another. The combination of the mass of humanity, the tea, and the heat resulted in a stifling atmosphere. Yet no one ever refused an invitation because, as with all of Brandeis's social affairs, much more than just food was being served.

For the justice these weekly "social occasions" accomplished a twofold purpose: to gather information about ongoing actions in the executive branch and to impart his policy advice. While some people had a standing invitation to the teas, such as presidential assistants Thomas Corcoran and Benjamin Cohen, it was the law clerk's duty to fill out the guest list each week. A typical tea might include fifteen or twenty people—the chairman of one or two federal commissions, some members of the executive departments and agencies, members of the Brookings Institution, one or two ambassadors (most often the representative of Denmark—a country that Brandeis deeply admired), a labor leader, and some heads of corporations. One or two prominent government figures were always invited as well. For example, it was not uncommon to meet here Senators Robert M. LaFollette, Jr., and Harry Truman or Justices Harlan Fiske Stone and Owen Roberts.

While the rest of the guests mingled, Brandeis sat in a corner of the room. Then, led by Mrs. Brandeis, a game of musical chairs was played in which each person was brought over to the justice, either alone or in a very small group, and permitted ten or fifteen minutes with him to confer on matters of mutual interest.

Anyone attending these affairs soon discovered that in order to win the justice's respect, they had to have all the data on their agency fully digested and available in response to Brandeis's inquiries. A story told by former Brandeis law clerk and now Harvard sociologist, David Riesman, confirms this obsession of the justice for the facts. To one tea Riesman invited then-United States Ambassador to the Soviet Union William C. Bullitt. The law clerk had idolized Bullitt from childhood and enjoyed listening to the tales of a man who, after living all over the world, relished explaining about enjoying the "good life" in the different nations. Brandeis, however, was not so easily impressed. Upon being introduced to his visitor, the justice opened the conversation with:"How many tons of cotton are being grown now in Turkestan?" Of course, Bullitt had absolutely no idea and the conversation was quickly abbreviated. When the ambassador left, Riesman remembers, Brandeis was "filled with nothing but contempt for him."[86]

Inevitably, these individual conversations with Brandeis at the teas turned to particular administrative problems that required the justice's assistance. Brandeis often initiated the conversation with the same question, "What are you up to over at your agency?" Then, through a series of cross-examination type inquiries, he would, in the words of Joseph L. Rauh, "squeeze you like an orange" until he "drained you dry of every little bit of information [that] you knew."[87]

Fully informed on all aspects of that agency, Brandeis then used a series of Socratic questions to "stretch the mind" of his guest by leading him in the direction of the desired solution. These questions were always carefully phrased in a superficial attempt to avoid any ethical problems if the issue should ever be heard by the Supreme Court. So the justice would ask "Now if you were given this hypothetical situation and forgetting the legal or Constitutional ramifications, what kinds of actions would you take to remedy it?" Of course, by using a series of these questions dealing with various scenarios, Brandeis was able to make his own views apparent to his visitor without ever discussing the specifics of any particular policy.

Frequently, Brandeis would then launch into a lecture about the need for the listener to probe more deeply into the fundamentals of his field and even suggest undertaking specific long-range studies of problems for the purpose of gathering necessary additional facts. Inevitably, each of these sessions ended with the justice preaching to his guest, regardless of his or her professional capacity or position: "Remember that human beings are fallible and no one can know enough about the nation to single-handedly govern it from Washington—no man can do too much." This combination of intensive inquiry, advice, inspirational homilies, and philosophy could not help but leave the visitor, who was already sympathetic to the "Brandeis Way," quite stimulated regarding his future tasks.

Using all these methods for dispensing advice, Brandeis battled the collectivist trend of the early New Deal on a number of fronts. Of course, his most effective lieutenant in this crusade for securing government action was still Felix Frankfurter. Together they tried to redirect the focus of a number of executive departments and agencies toward their policies of massive, public-works expenditures, financed by a rigorously progressive tax system and augmented by some basic reform legislation to regulate the nation's financial institutions. To accomplish their goal, Brandeis and Frankfurter worked simultaneously on lobbying for the legislative adoption of these new policies while also attempting to convert the administrators of the already created collectivist agencies. It was the appeal of their message, combined with their patience, that led to eventual victory in most areas.

Using Raymond Moley and other contacts throughout the administration, particularly in the Departments of Labor and the Interior, Brandeis initiated his crusade by first lobbying for his massive, public-works program. Initially, President Roosevelt felt it necessary to retrench economically in order to achieve a more balanced budget. This seemingly ruled out any extensive program of public works. When he was later convinced by his advisers of the need for such legislation, Roosevelt relented by proposing only programs of limited, short-term, direct relief for the unemployed. Still influenced by the budget-balancing approach of Budget Director Lewis Douglas, the president continued to resist efforts in behalf of a massive program of government spending to promote recovery of the economy.[88]

On the other hand, Brandeis believed that only such massive government spending, even at the consequence of deficit budgets, was capable of stimulating a recessive economy. The uniqueness of Brandeis's proposals for spending on public-works programs, such as his "wholesale afforestation" and "control of waters" plans, was that he sought both greater employment and the construction of permanent facilities for general social benefit. It was these values that the justice had pressed on the reluctant Raymond Moley in their February 1933 meeting. When this effort had no visible effect, Frankfurter attempted to mobilize public opinion for the Brandeis program by linking the ideas in a magazine article for *Survey Graphic* to noted economic theories and an earlier public-works program proposed by Senator Robert Wagner.[89] Then the two men began using their extensive contacts in the administration to convince the president of the need for more extensive public-works expenditures.

Frankfurter wrote directly to President Roosevelt on March 22, 1933, regarding the need for legislation to promote re-employment and not just relief.

> Of course I rejoice over your message on unemployment relief. The emergency measures of your first few days were indispensable. But putting men to work—gradual but steady re-employment—is the ultimate objective, and your proposals start us on that road.[90]

Since their best contact in the cabinet was Labor Secretary Frances Perkins, who had much to say about any prospective public-works program, both Brandeis and Frankfurter tried to enlist her aid. When, the professor suggested to Perkins in a private letter that she meet with Justice Brandeis on the subject of public works, the secretary indicated that she did intend to use the justice as a source of advice on these matters.[91] Once again, there was no reluctance on the part of either the sitting justice or the labor secretary to confer openly on a public-policy issue.

Seeking a continual direct line of access to President Roosevelt, Frankfurter renewed his efforts to enlist Moley in the crusade. He opened, in late March 1933, with a private letter to Moley, which pressed for another meeting with Brandeis on the subject of public works. When this drew no response, Frankfurter repeated his warning to Moley in early April that the "policy of a large-scale public works program [was] not moving ahead as fast as it should for recovery."[92] But a week later the assistant secretary of state could only find time to promise Brandeis that they would meet on the subject sometime in the future.[93] All was not lost, however, because on that same date Brandeis reported to Frankfurter that he had met directly with the president himself at the White House and had used the occasion to lobby for his extensive public-works program.[94]

To overcome the resistance in the Treasury Department, Brandeis and Frankfurter realized that they needed to place someone in a position of influence in one of the agencies controlling government spending. Despite the fact that only two days earlier they had been put off in their previous request, on April 14, 1933, the two men turned once again to Raymond Moley for help. Frankfurter took to the pen and proposed that Oliver M. W. Sprague, a Harvard economist, be named a governor of the Federal Reserve Board. This recommendation to Moley made it quite clear that it was more than just the candidate's intellectual qualifications that Frankfurter found appealing: "[O. M. W. Sprague has] the technical equipment, real guts, unusual experience, and . . . the right social outlook . . . For instance [he would] be for a vigorous public works program. [Italics mine]"[95] When the appointment was not made, Frankfurter continued to lobby for it in repeated phone calls to the assistant secretary of state.

Events worked out even better than Brandeis and Frankfurter had hoped; Sprague was made financial adviser and executive assistant to Secretary of the Treasury William H. Woodin. Even before the appointment, Frankfurter began to nurture the contact by cabling Sprague: "If call comes be sure to accept it. We have great need of you."[96] Meanwhile, Moley was "heartily" congratulated by the professor for insuring a "real accession" to the administration.[97]

Brandeis immediately enlisted the new ally in the ongoing public-works battle by hosting Sprague at one of his carefully arranged dinner parties. The guest list this time included Labor Secretary Frances Perkins, who was seeking the justice's advice on ways to prevent the enactment of Senator Hugo L. Black's Industrial Control bill, which was intended to prohibit the interstate shipment of goods manufactured by firms using more than a thirty-hour work week. By introducing his two visitors, Brandeis was able to further his personal lobbying efforts with both of them in behalf of his public-works program.[98]

When Roosevelt's monetary and fiscal policies continued to deviate from the justice's, a frustrated Brandeis continued to express to Frankfurter his lack of faith in Roosevelt's program of temporary expenditures for short-term emergency relief.[99] Before leaving to teach at Oxford for the academic year 1933–34 as the George Eastman Visiting Professor, Frankfurter set up another meeting between Brandeis and

Moley on the public-works matter, but the Brandeis side seemed doomed to disappointment. The administration failed to emphasize the long-range permanent construction preferred by the justice. Even Brandeis's administration allies proved to be unsatisfactory. Harold Ickes, after being named to head the new Public Works Administration, and immediately subjected to the customary Felix Frankfurter letter of congratulations containing another plug for the Brandeis orthodoxy, failed to act with the speed that the justice thought necessary to make the program effective.[100] By February 1934, Frankfurter had decided that even Frances Perkins was "too naive" to be as useful as he had originally hoped.[101]

Recognizing the increasing agitation of his mentor over this issue, Frankfurter, even though now lodged in England, set to work to do what he could. His efforts there helped bring about an extraordinary event in the history of the Depression—a lecture on fiscal policy delivered to the president of the United States by a British economist in the pages of The New York Times.

As a first step, the Harvard professor elicited the support of the Cambridge man who would become the guru of a startling new economic philosophy, one that reasoned that in times of business depression, governments did not help matters by struggling to keep their budgets in balance despite falling revenues—the orthodoxy of borrowing to finance public-works projects.[102] That man was John Maynard Keynes, whom Frankfurter had first met at the Paris Peace Conference in 1919, and had later helped to secure a publisher in the United States for his book, The Economic Consequences of the Peace.[103] Now, on December 9, 1933, Frankfurter pleaded with his British friend by letter: "I write because I think that a letter from you with your independent arguments and indications would greatly accelerate the momentum of forces now at work in the right direction."[104]

As it was, Frankfurter was taking no great risk in soliciting Keynes's own "independent arguments," for he had just met with him on Founder's Day at King's College, Oxford. In a letter to Brandeis, Frankfurter reported that he and Keynes had "talked at great length over U.S. affairs," and that the man who would later lend his name to the dominant economic theory of a generation had argued that Roosevelt's economic approach was all wrong and that the United States should invest heavily in permanant public-works projects, such as railroads.

Frankfurter summed up his report to the justice by commenting that Keynes's approach was "substantially yours."[105]

Keynes did not disappoint Frankfurter. His expansive "Open Letter" to President Roosevelt, published in *The New York Times* on December, 31, 1933, recommended a "sound" fiscal policy, one that would include an "increase in national purchasing power resulting from government expenditure," including a public-works program, "financed by loans."[106] In case the president might miss his copy of the *Times* that morning, Frankfurter had forwarded a copy of the letter to the president personally, claiming that Keynes had written it in response to a request by *The New York Times* for his views on the American outlook.[107] In fact, not only had the Harvard professor made the initial request of Keynes, but a letter discovered in Frankfurter's personal papers indicates that the British economist had sent him a "final draft" of the open letter on December 15, 1933, expressing a hope that Frankfurter's critical analysis of the piece would help catch the "Bremen" in it.[108]

Despite all these efforts by Frankfurter, however, it is clear from the president's response that he was not yet convinced that Keynes's ideas could be put to the test. As FDR wrote Frankfurter in England:

> You can tell the professor [Keynes] that in regard to public works we shall spend in the next fiscal year nearly twice the amount we are spending in this fiscal year, but there is a practical limit to what the Government can borrow—especially because the banks are offering passive resistance in most of the large centers.[109]

Knowing that Frankfurter would meet with Roosevelt upon his return from England, Brandeis sent him a complete brief of all the arguments for the public-works programs. He reminded Frankfurter once again that these expenditures involved "permanent investments" and were "an investment in which the returns in direct and indirect income will come later," and expressed the fervent hope that Frankfurter would soon present these matters to the president.[110] Brandeis reasserted in this letter the need to tax the "super rich" and to plug tax loopholes, the two financing proposals Moley had scoffed at as being absurdly paltry sources for the great amount of money that would be needed for the programs Brandeis had been proposing.

Neither this brief nor any of Brandeis's other letters to Frankfurter over the years make clear exactly how strongly committed the justice had become to the radical new economic theories being put forward by Keynes. Several of Brandeis's letters to the Harvard professor during the early 1930s had praised Keynes's work, one even calling it a "powerfully illuminating" answer for a foundering economy.[111] However, the justice's effort in January and February 1933 to outline his program for the New Deal had also betrayed some equivocation when it came to fully endorsing the deficit spending idea. Instead, Brandeis wrote that his program of massive public-works expenditures could be "financed at first by loans then by high estate and income taxes," and that the administration "should treat the early expenditures . . . as advances in anticipation of the large tax [revenues]."[112]

It could well be that the justice sincerely believed that the massive, public-works programs he was advocating would provide the jobs the country needed, would have the long-range benefit of having created permanent capital improvements, and could in fact eventually be financed in large part by his tax schemes without too great a need for new borrowing. Or he could have believed that the programs themselves would serve as necessary pump-priming devices, and that he was prepared to accept any short-term deficits that might result as a small price to pay for the long-range benefits they would provide.

Of course, there is always the possibility that the justice had already fully accepted the then-revolutionary Keynesian theory that in fighting business depressions the government deficit itself was the effective weapon, and that he also understood that attempting to make his case in these terms would leave his plan suicidally vulnerable to devastating attack by the orthodox financial advisors surrounding the president. After all these years, during which we have even had a president as conservative as Richard Nixon claim that "I too am a Keynesian," it is difficult to imagine the full fury of abuse that would have been heaped on any adviser who posited that huge budget deficits themselves could be effective tools in fighting widespread depression. And so it may well have been that the wise Brandeis knew enough about human nature to make his case for a Keynesian solution in terms that would have been intelligible, even if not palatable, to the Brain Trusters, and to talk about the prospect of a budget deficit as a small problem capable of easy solution, rather than as the goal of the program.

But if this last is the most accurate analysis of Brandeis's thinking at the time, he appears to have concealed his full conversion to

Keynesianism even from Frankfurter, for Frankfurter continued in his lobbying for Brandeis's public-works programs to paper over the prospect of the budget deficits that would surely ensue with their adoption.

In late August 1934, Frankfurter met with Roosevelt to discuss the Brandeisian recovery program. In a written report to Brandeis, the professor claimed that he "put it to [FDR] hard" while the president "took careful notes." By his comments in the meeting Roosevelt indicated that the proposal to get people back to work through these programs was slowly winning his approval, though he still had certain reservations. Like Moley before him, he focused on what he perceived to be the central problem of the Brandeis plan—the financing provisions—arguing that he could not "borrow 3 billions a year for 10 years."[113]

In the end, Roosevelt did increase federal spending, but he failed to adopt the precise plan the justice was advocating. While the president pushed the Emergency Relief Appropriation Act through Congress in early 1935, this expenditure of 5 billion dollars, though the largest program in United States history, still was not of the dimensions that Brandeis envisioned; moreover, it emphasized relief for the unemployed, rather than permanent capital investment.[114]

Since realization of their public-works program hinged on the availability of financial resources, Brandeis and Frankfurter pushed simultaneously for their program of taxation. In his letters to Frankfurter, the justice expressed confidence that these massive expenditures could be eventually financed by adopting a rigidly progressive tax. In 1933 and 1934, however, Brandeis and Frankfurter simply did not yet have the necessary contacts in the Treasury Department to lobby successfully for their policies. Nearly the entire department was staffed by "budget balancers," whose ideas were inimical to the justice's plans. Not even the two men they had successfully placed there, Oliver M.W. Sprague and Dean Acheson, could do much because of their open disagreement with the basic financial philosophy of the administration.[115]

Because of this situation, Brandeis and Frankfurter persisted in pressing for the miraculous conversion of Raymond Moley. Frankfurter's initial efforts to sway the Brain Truster, however, were ineffective. Filed in the Library of Congress are copies of two letters in which the Harvard professor tried to influence Moley's thinking on a variety of financial subjects: the importance of the commissioner of Internal Revenue in collecting necessary tax funds, the gold clause in mortgages, and the banking situation in Detroit. When Moley appeared unreceptive to these entreaties, Brandeis decided in mid-August 1933 to seek access to Roosevelt through the president's speechwriter, Samuel I. Rosenman. In a personal conference with the justice on this issue, Rosenman even asked Brandeis what Felix Frankfurter thought of his program, illustrating that more and more members of the administration were becoming aware of the policy-making partnership between the justice and Frankfurter. When Rosenman returned to Brandeis's apartment in September, he reported that the president was so interested in the ideas that he would probably consult with Brandeis about them in the future and then include them in the next message to Congress.[116]

Despite this hopeful sign, Brandeis's concern regarding the nation's financial affairs continued to grow. Seeking to raise prices, administration officials had turned to gold buying—periodic purchases of the metal at steadily increasing prices resulting in a devaluation of the gold-backed dollar—as a solution for the monetary problems.[117] Understandably, both of Brandeis's contacts in the Treasury Department (Acheson and Sprague) voiced immediate objections. In late August, Acheson had seen, and opposed, a Department of Justice memorandum written by Attorney General Homer Cummings which supported the gold-buying policy. After vigorously objecting to the plan, Acheson journeyed to Brandeis's apartment for further instructions. The justice's advice was supportive, but characteristically Delphic: "Dean, if I wanted a legal opinion I would prefer to get it from you than from Homer Cummings."[118]

Eventually Acheson was forced to resign, to be followed shortly by Sprague. Therefore Brandeis and Frankfurter retained only minimal contact in the Treasury Department. In late 1933 they had managed to place Thomas Corcoran, one of their young lieutenants, in an advisory position within the Treasury Department. From that vantage point he had been able to report on activities there. By mid-December, though, Corcoran's position had also become untenable, as he indicated in a letter to Frankfurter.

> I can stay in the Treasury indefinitely: nobody will fire me. But I'm terribly under suspicion as Dean's right hand; and there's transferred to me a lot of the defensive feeling of the Morganthau gang (all fourth

raters) against Dean whom they treated very cheaply and crudely. I have a dozen other offices for my team—It'll take me this week probably to move to R[econstruction] F[inance] C[orporation]. I don't think I'll make a mistake. It's my temporary strategic retreat.[119]

Faced with another disappointing setback in his crusade, Brandeis found that his only recourse for the time being was to complain frequently and bitterly in letters to Frankfurter about the performance of the new acting Secretary of the Treasury Henry Morgenthau, Jr.[120] It would not be until 1935, when FDR would shift the fundamental economic philosophy of the administration, that Brandeis's tax program would be even partially adopted.

The justice and Frankfurter did achieve more immediate successes in advocating some of their financial reform measures.[121] In the hopes of preventing future economic collapses, their most extended efforts were made to improve federal regulation of the stock market and investment practices. But in the long range, the policy successes here would not be nearly as important to Brandeis as the series of legislative drafting relationships that would be forged in this campaign and would serve the justice so well in later battles.

Any discussion of the genesis of such legislation must begin with Thomas G. Corcoran and Benjamin V. Cohen, acclaimed by some as the "greatest legislative drafting team in history."[122] Corcoran, a Harvard Law School graduate and former law clerk to Justice Oliver Wendell Holmes, first came to the government during the Hoover Administration. In response to a request by Eugene Meyer, chairman of the new Reconstruction Finance Corporation, for a "good lawyer," Frankfurter had sent him Corcoran. By remaining as general counsel to the RFC after its reorganization in 1933, Corcoran ("Tommy the Cork" to FDR) had the flexibility to engage in a variety of presidentially directed tasks.[123]

While Brandeis knew Corcoran only slightly before 1933, Ben Cohen, a graduate of Chicago and Harvard, was more familiar to the justice because of his service during World War I as counsel to the United States Shipping Board and later to the American Zionist delegation at Versailles. Cohen was brought to Washington by Frankfurter to become the associate general counsel to the Public Works Administration in 1933. His duties were also vaguely defined and this vagueness permitted him to become involved in legislation concerning a variety of subjects and agencies. Both he and Corcoran were able to do the legwork in drafting the Brandeis proposals while also serving as Frankfurter's eyes and ears in Washington.

These two youthful legislative draftsmen were studies in contrast. Corcoran, a hard-driving, energetic Irish Catholic, was renowned for his outgoing nature. Cohen, a calm, retiring, intellectual Jew who disliked the Washington scene, preferred to remain in the background. Yet, to the amazement of many, and the dismay of the collectivists, the two men forged a legendary partnership for legislative drafting. Working behind the scenes, each used his strength to balance the other in creating and defending their legislative proposals. Cohen was the scholar, who remained in the background and possessed the unique ability of translating abstract ideas into legal language. Corcoran, on the other hand, was the action man who, after developing a wide network of personal contacts, lobbied with amazing vigor on behalf of these proposals.[124]

Unknown to nearly everyone, Corcoran and Cohen in drafting these measures took many of their cues indirectly from Justice Louis D. Brandeis, who advised them through an ingenious circular route of intermediaries. This unique advising technique was described initially by Corcoran himself in an interview for this volume. His recollection was then confirmed by tracing in the various manuscript collections the letters from Brandeis offering advice and those from the other major actors acting upon it during legislative campaigns.

The record in the unpublished Brandeis-Frankfurter letters shows that Corcoran and Cohen would initiate the process by visiting the justice at his apartment, as often as twice a month during some periods, simply to inform him of the situation in the executive branch—discussing both the problems and the proposed solutions.[125] Brandeis confined his comments on these occasions to explicit questions framed with the intention of gathering more information. He made no effort to instruct his visitors regarding possible alternative solutions to the problems.

Following these conferences, the justice would then send his specific legislative proposals to Frankfurter along with suggested areas for future study by his "boys" at Harvard Law School. Frankfurter, in turn, would diligently gather the support material and forward it, together with the Brandeis proposals, to President Roosevelt—sometimes even saying that the justice had "passed" on the idea. The president then completed this circuitous relationship by handing these ideas on to Corcoran and Cohen with instructions to act on them. Already imbued with the teaching of Felix Frankfurter and the philosophy of Louis D. Brandeis, they were prepared to accept the suggestions that they knew well had come initially from the justice. Having participated with Frankfurter in staffing many of the New Deal agencies, Corcoran could then call on a score of his "Harvard Brains," several of whom lived with him in the legendary "little Red house on R Street," to suggest details for the legislation. Finally, both Corcoran and Cohen would edit these proposals, send the legislative blueprint to the president for his action, and shepherd each bill through to enactment by testifying at congressional hearings, providing friendly congressmen with useful arguments, and even drafting speeches for allies.[126]

There is every reason to believe, because of the uniqueness of the Brandeis legislative proposals and the justice's constant contact with these leading actors, that FDR knew precisely where the ideas had originated. Yet, despite its apparent cumbersome nature, Brandeis preferred this type of indirect advising relationship for several reasons. As he had in the 1920s, he still preferred to discuss the specifics of legislation only with Felix Frankfurter. It served to insulate him from public exposure and scandal for having committed what could certainly be characterized by enemies as judicial indiscretion, if not impropriety. Moreover, the justice sought to maintain his distance from Roosevelt and his administration should he later be put in a position of having to rule against him in a Supreme Court opinion. Finally, concerned about the growing anti-Semitic sentiment expressed in complaints that FDR was too heavily influenced by the Jewish community, Brandeis did not feel that public discussion of his relationship with the president would be wise. Overall, this lobbying arrangement served all these needs beautifully. Important parts of the Brandeisian program were eventually enacted as law without the reputation of Louis D. Brandeis ever having been compromised.

This newly established legislative drafting bureau began its work on the Securities Act of 1933, a measure intended to fulfill FDR's campaign promise to prevent future stock market collapses. Unlike the collectivist legislation being considered in this period, the announced aims of this proposed bill, with its emphasis on business regulation, bore the definite imprint of Brandeis's philosophy. While Brandeis left the actual drafting of the new legislation to his young lieutenants, the justice's private letters to Felix Frankfurter confirm that he was extremely active in advising the drafters during the process.[127]

One of Brandeis's earlier conduits to the president, former Federal Trade Commission Chairman Huston Thompson, was charged with drafting a bill to deal with the stock exchange and the sale of securities. By now, though, Brandeis had lost faith in Thompson's intellectual capacity, writing to Frankfurter on one occasion that "as a lawyer he has everything but brains."[128] Totally unaware of this change in the justice's opinion, Thompson remained on reasonably close terms with Brandeis. So, when the first draft of the bill was completed, he brought it to the justice seeking suggestions for any prospective changes. To his surprise, unlike other occasions when Brandeis freely gave his opinion, Thompson recorded in his private diaries that this effort to enlist the justice's support was not successful.[129] During their meeting on March 18, 1933, Brandeis would tell him nothing more than "where to get information" on the subject.[130] Thompson may well have believed that Brandeis refused to comment on the basis of judicial propriety, but more likely, the justice did so in order to enable his own group to take control of the drafting process.

Three weeks later, after the Senate drastically amended the Thompson bill, the Brandeis team was brought in by Raymond Moley to redraft the measure.[131] At Moley's request, Frankfurter sent two men he knew to be supremely qualified for the task, both in terms of their expertise and their usefulness for the justice's purposes. They were Benjamin Cohen, and the key member of the 1920s Brandeis-Frankfurter literary circle, who was now a professor of legislation at Harvard Law School, James Landis. While they worked with Thomas Corcoran in Washington in drafting and lobbying for the measure, Frankfurter supervised from Cambridge. As the work progressed, Raymond Moley's private letters show that Frankfurter kept the Brain Truster apprised by mail and phone of the latest developments.[132] It was left to Moley to inform FDR and Representative Sam Rayburn of Texas, who would be charged with leading the floor fight, of the continuing progress.

For his part, Brandeis became in effect the mediator between the

Thompson and Frankfurter drafting groups.* To this end, he began by suggesting some of his ideas on financial reform legislation directly to the president in a meeting on April 12, 1933.[134] The next day the justice informed Frankfurter: "Huston Thompson was in yesterday much disturbed by delays and possible complications due to the Frankfurter-Landis redrafting of bill. I told him to get in touch with Landis at once and if need be to telephone you."[135] Throughout April and May Brandeis also met individually with the other bill drafters—Cohen, Corcoran, and Landis—to provide them with general encouragement, gather information, and guide their analysis.[136] Very late in the drafting process, the justice again repeated his ideas to Thompson, who, acting on a direct request by Brandeis, duly passed them on to FDR.[137]

Brandeis's pleasure when Thompson's lobbying efforts were slowly superceded by those of the Frankfurter protégés was evident when he reported to the professor that "Tom, Ben and Jim are putting up a significant fight. Tom is proving himself a real general."[138] The justice could not help but be pleased with the direction of the regulations contained in the final legislation. The Federal Trade Commission was given the power to supervise the issuance of new stocks, including the requirement of full disclosure of relevant information about them, and civil as well as criminal penalties were enacted for those company directors who violated these provisions.[139] But more than just securing policy changes, an exchange of letters between Frankfurter and Moley must have given the justice hope that they might indeed have secured a line of access to the upper levels of the administration. After being congratulated on the bill's passage by Brandeis, Frankfurter in turn passed along accolades in a letter to Moley: "Your constant help was indispensable in obtaining a sound securities bill."[140] Moley's response gave them no reason to doubt that

---

* Because of the different perspectives of the two groups, each proposed a very different version of the legislation. Thompson, relying on the federal government, wanted to vest all power to regulate the issuance of new securities in the Federal Trade Commission (even to the extent of being able to disapprove the sale). The Frankfurter group, on the other hand, put their faith in the buyer and sought to minimize the size of the central government. They called only for full public disclosure of all information regarding the proposed new securities. While they did not propose a governmental power to reject the sale of new securities, they did advocate the adoption of a "stop order" which would delay the issuance until full informational disclosure had been achieved.[133]

more might be expected from this relationship. "If you are satisfied with the work that has been done, that is all that can be asked."[141] However, the course of history would soon dictate otherwise.

Before the drafting team could take on their next project, the Securities Exchange Act of 1934, their main White House contact, Raymond Moley, was forced out of government. Interestingly, Moley's diary and unpublished letters show that in mid-June 1933, Frankfurter, perhaps sensing the fickle nature of political fortunes, had tried to convince Moley to place Thomas Corcoran in the White House before the Brain Truster left for the London Economic Conference.* Appearing to act out of the highest motives, Frankfurter explained to Moley that this would be "an excellent adjustment during your absence" in providing FDR with needed advice. Of course, Frankfurter was really seeking to establish a more permanent and reliable contact in the "inner circle." Moley's failure to adopt the idea took on added importance when he was compelled to resign from the administration due to the president's rejection of his policy recommendation from London, and a bitter power struggle with the chairman of the United States delegation to the conference, Secretary of State Cordell Hull.[143] Fortunately for Brandeis, the young legislative draftsmen, Corcoran and Cohen, had by this time secured FDR's confidence and needed no intermediary now to reach him.

As it turned out, the first Securities Act, which emphasized self-regulation by the various companies, seemed inadequate to prevent another collapse of the market in 1933. Since Frankfurter was abroad teaching at Oxford, Justice Brandeis realized that this would be one of those rare occasions when he would have to lobby for his ideas more directly and even step in as supervisor of the legislative drafting operation. In the fall of 1933, Brandeis began to press for more stringent regulations in conferences with Labor Secretary Frances Perkins and Max Lowenthal, who was then a member of Senator Duncan Fletcher's staff.[144] Though another official committee had been formed by the administration to draft the new bill, Corcoran, Cohen, and Landis began once again to work informally on their own Stock Exchange measure.

---

*Formally titled the International Monetary and Economic Conference, this meeting had been arranged by the Hoover Administration in the hopes of realizing economic recovery through international cooperation in monetary policies such as the stabilization of rates of currency exchange.[142]

During this period in late 1933, "Tommy the Cork" and Ben Cohen reported in letters to Professor Frankfurter at Oxford that they were inspired by, in their words, "regular" visits to Justice Brandeis. In one such message Corcoran told Frankfurter: "Long talk with Isaiah sticking. Don't worry."[145] While the bill was being finalized, Frankfurter was reassured by Corcoran as to Brandeis's influence: "Even if you haven't had anything but cables you can always be comfortable that I always take advice—and that I haven't moved and won't move an inch in a general course without going to L.D.B."[146] For his part, Brandeis also reported in letters to Frankfurter that he was guiding the young protégés: "Tom C. has been in several times—doubtless he is keeping you fully informed. The difficulties grow no less."[147] All their efforts were extremely useful, because as Corcoran reported in a private letter to Frankfurter, throughout the drafting process neither formulating committee was ever certain where Roosevelt stood on the issue.[148]

The main question centered on the nature of the regulatory agency itself. The Corcoran-Cohen position advocated continuing the use of the independent Federal Trade Commission (FTC), while the other side wanted to create a new agency composed of members from the Stock Exchange itself. When the advocates for creating the Stock Exchange-staffed regulatory commission gathered forces, Corcoran sent to Frankfurter for reinforcements. Until this time, Frankfurter's involvement from abroad had been confined during the entire process to praising the actions of Corcoran and Cohen in his letters to Brandeis. In these messages, he continually asked the justice to keep in touch with "the boys" because it was a "great comfort" to him. Now Corcoran, in a cable, gave the professor an opportunity to enter the fray.

> Ben's exchange bill well received by press but indications terrific fight in which Skipper's [FDR] position doubtful to remove exchanges from administrative jurisdiction of FTC per bill to new commission dominated by exchange members. Urge all possible help this point particularly soon as possible and the suggestion to Skipper of Ben for F.T.C.[149]

While from today's perspective it seems clear that placing members of the Stock Exchange in charge of this new regulation was like placing the fox in charge of the chicken coop, Corcoran believed at that time that he needed Frankfurter's assistance for another reason. According to a private letter from Frankfurter to Justice Brandeis, Cor-

coran had come to distrust one of the members of the drafting team—
James Landis—whom he perceived as being susceptible to flattery.[150]
Frankfurter, just raring to get involved in the fight, immediately sent
a letter to Corcoran asking that he send him a copy of the bill along
with any supporting statements, and to have the "Skipper" invite his
opinion.[151]

Without even waiting for FDR's request, though, Frankfurter fired
off two personal letters to the president, praising his resolve to reform
the Stock Exchange. The first letter, mailed on February 14, 1934, was
general in scope. However, the follow-up letter, sent a week later, was
carefully crafted so that it praised the overall bill while also presenting Corcoran's warnings regarding the proposed "captive" regulatory
commission. Hoping to insure the proper decision from the noncom-
mital FDR, Frankfurter concluded by disingenuously commenting that
the Wall Streeters' "game must greatly add to your amusement."[152]

After much bargaining in the Congress, the Corcoran-Cohen team,
which had favored having the independent FTC as the regulating body,
had to accept the establishment of a new Securities and Exchange
Commission (to which their colleague, Landis, was appointed). The
new agency, however, while staffed by some exchange regulars, such
as Joseph P. Kennedy, was provided with the necessary independence
from Wall Street to control abuses there. In addition, other reforms
placed limits on credit extended for exchange trading, established rules
for financial reporting by corporations, and more clearly defined the
roles of stockbrokers and company officials.[153] As a result of these
campaigns, at least some of the practices of the investment community would henceforth be governed by the prophet's commandments.

Despite these legislative successes, of even more central interest to
Brandeis in this period were the collectivist agencies that had already
been created. The edicts of these agencies were actively shaping the
course of American society and the American economy, and the longer
this continued, while Brandeis's own ideas remained on the shelf, the
more frustrated the justice would become. There was no guarantee
that his own programs would ever be adopted. For a while, Brandeis
was satisfied with attempting to influence informally the interpretations of the established agencies' powers and privately he continued
to hope that the programs would soon fail. As the sands of time trick-
led inevitably through the hourglass of Brandeis's life, however, the
anxious justice decided that now was the time to throw off his traditional political shackles and try to help this disintegrating process

along. One way to do this was to flash a glimpse of the formidable official powers available to him. From a man so committed to his own sense of right, such an action should not have been surprising. But from a man respected as a pillar of propriety such an act would seem to signal a dramatic abandonment of a life-long posture. If Brandeis had known the consequences of this changed posture, even he might well have acted differently.

Because of the success of the Brandeis-Frankfurter placement bureau in staffing the Agricultural Adjustment Administration, the justice's efforts to influence policies here were quite extensive. The AAA used a system of government taxes, price supports, and subsidies to enforce self-imposed production quotas by the farmers. Combining his expert knowledge of farming, gained through letters from his brother Alfred, a prominent Kentucky farmer, and long hours of study, together with his philosophy of the benefits of small units, Brandeis formulated a powerful argument against what he viewed as the bigness of the AAA.[154]

Brandeis's ideas were offered to a number of listeners in the hopes of creating a "mandate for change." In April 1933, the justice had a chance to argue his philosophy directly with the heads of the Department of Agriculture, Secretary Henry Wallace and Assistant Secretary Rexford Tugwell. In his unpublished diary, Tugwell recorded that in response to Brandeis's now familiar refrain that "bigness is always badness," he had argued instead that bigness "needed only direction and submission to discipline."[155] Tugwell hoped that the justice might give the AAA his stamp of approval; however an oral history by one of Brandeis's allies in the agency, Gardner Jackson, makes clear that LDB had in fact designed a very different agricultural program. Rather than resorting to the national farm-production quotas, Brandeis preferred that the government buy up the land and simply lease it to farmers. For the justice, the ideal agricultural community would be characterized by autonomous, individual farmers working small tracts of land.[156]

Since Wallace and Tugwell were unrepentent, the justice next resorted to issuing grave warnings to the AAA through Gardner Jackson, who throughout his tenure on the agency's Consumers' Counsel consulted Brandeis on a weekly basis concerning developing problems.[157] Before the final passage of the act, Brandeis called in Jackson and prophesied that the projected act would "accentuate the trend . . . of larger and larger holdings in fewer and fewer hands, an increase in tenancy, and absentee ownership," thus leading to an "increase in corporate farming."[158] Acting on the justice's instructions, Jackson conveyed these dire predictions to the agency's counsel, Jerome Frank, Assistant Secretary Tugwell, and several others.

But these messages, as well as Brandeis's frequent talks with Secretary Wallace, produced no observable change in the direction of the AAA. While some might have accepted such defeat, such was not the way of the man they called Isaiah. Even those in the administration who gave the justice this nickname may not have known how close to the mark they had struck. Like Isaiah, who, to insure that his prophecies would be duly noted, remained silent for a full nineteen years, walked around naked for another three years, and even gave his children names that described his predictions, Brandeis was rigidly uncompromising and fully confident of the righteousness of his message. The justice had issued his prophecies, and while most listened, thus far they had refused to change their ways. Such was the difference between having a ready audience and having devoted disciples.

Finally exasperated, in late April 1934, Brandeis decided that the time for patient teaching combined with occasional urgent warnings had passed. Now was the time for nothing short of overt threats. Through Gardner Jackson, the justice sent a message to Rexford Tugwell and Jerome Frank that "he was declaring war" on the New Deal. Though Tugwell was not moved by Brandeis's vision of the AAA, such a threat from a member of the Supreme Court caused great consternation. So he passed the message along directly to President Roosevelt, who promised to see Brandeis as soon as possible to "butter him some." According to Tugwell's account, the administration took this warning so seriously that Jerome Frank "succeeded in postponing the prosecution of an oil code case . . . on the theory that with Brandeis feeling as he does we ought not to take the case up."[159]

A previously unpublished exchange of letters discovered in FDR's personal files at Hyde Park show how far the desperate, aging justice was willing to go in playing political hardball with the president. Knowing that all his indications of displeasure would find their way back to the Oval Office, Brandeis also lectured Jerome Frank and Adolf A. Berle on the issue of "bigness." This time, though, the justice's critical assessment of the AAA and the NRA was followed by an unmistakable warning—which Berle immediately forwarded to Roosevelt—that Brandeis "had gone along with the legislation up to now, but that unless he could see some reversal of the big business trend,

he was disposed to hold the government control legislation unconstitutional from now on." [160] Roosevelt, the consummate politician, was
not one to be bullied by political pressure, even if that pressure came
in the form of a threat from one of the nine men who determined what
the law of the land would be. He wrote Berle:

> As to our friend of the highest court, I expect to have a good long
> talk with him within the next few days. The difficulty is that so many
> people expect me to travel at a rate of one hundred miles an hour
> when the old bus cannot possibly make more than fifty miles an hour,
> even when it is hitting on all eight cylinders. [161]

Whatever action the president did take, if he did take any, there is no
evidence that the promised conference occurred within the next month
or so.

It had to have been a terrible sense of anguish that motivated a man
who had been so cautious in his extrajudicial dealings during the 1920s
to turn around now and issue such overt threats to the administration.
Of course, it can be said in Brandeis's defense that he was, in the end,
very much right about the New Deal's policies serving "bigness," and
that he was as much the prophet here as he ever was. For it is an
ironic fact of American economic history that the period of the New
Deal, so often and so completely associated with the final coming to
political power of the common man in America was a time during
which the corporate giants did well in relative terms, both in business
and in agriculture. But even his being borne out in the end cannot
excuse his failure to observe the most basic stricture for the judiciary,
that against using the power of judicial office to further political goals.

While the president did not rush to mollify Brandeis, others in the
administration became increasingly troubled regarding the future disposition by the Supreme Court of a case dealing with the AAA. Having taken Brandeis's threat seriously, and knowing that some day the
legislation establishing the agency would be reviewed in court, a group
of administrators, led by Gardner Jackson, asked for a conference with
the justice in the summer of 1934. According to Jackson's reminiscences they told the justice that their purpose was to discuss the problems of monopolistic practices in the dairy industry and milk processing firms, but what they really wanted was to get some assurance that
Brandeis would support the AAA when it was tested in his Court.
Despite the fact that the justice made clear to his visitors that he
understood the real reason for their trip, he did speak to them on the
subject for several hours.

In reflecting on the overall legality of the AAA, thus offering the informal advisory constitutional opinion which the Supreme Court had been denying to administrations since the time of George Washington, Brandeis seemed to demonstrate a new flexibility in his position. The justice encouraged the administrators by telling them that now he had come to believe that there were certain industries, such as the steel industry, which by their very nature were so monopolistic that the government had every right to control them. As they left Chatham, Jackson and the others were convinced that Brandeis would view agriculture as just such an industry, and thus vote to uphold the AAA when it came before the Supreme Court.[162]

There can be little doubt, even given the informal, off-the-record nature of the chat, that the justice should not have consented to speak directly with the delegation from the AAA. Both parties expected that this issue certainly would soon be before the Supreme Court. The fact that Brandeis did participate in the discussion indicates once again the pressure he was apparently under to get his political program moving, even if it meant compromising the normal propriety of his judicial position. But Brandeis's behavior when the Court test of the AAA finally did come before him in 1936 may help us to further understand how he viewed the interrelationship of his two roles.

Just as he had during the Wilson Administration in litigation involving agencies on which he had expressed his opinion, Brandeis did sit on the case, *United States v. Butler*.[163] And, illustrating the distinction he was able to maintain between his private political statements and his public legal opinions, Brandeis once again voted contrary to his own informal views. Despite all his admonitions and warnings that he would help dismantle the AAA from the high bench, Brandeis, in dissent, voted to uphold the constitutionality of the act. Once again, though, continuing his earlier pattern, he participated only minimally in the case, by writing no opinion and simply signing Justice Harlan Fiske Stone's dissent.

However, there are many problems here. One, possibly the most serious, is that while this behavior may have satisfied Brandeis's own personal sense of judicial ethics, a group of administrators, led by Gardner Jackson, now could not help but believe that their private lobbying effort in Chatham on a hot summer day had indeed had some effect on the justice's decision in the case. Another is that Brandeis may have recognized that his earlier indiscreet remarks to Adolf A.

Berle had left him at the mercy of his enemies should he have voted to strike down the AAA. While few would venture to ascribe with surety such base motives to Brandeis, there can be no doubt that such off-the-bench opinions by Supreme Court justices, should they become commonplace, would make the personal motives of justices part of the debate surrounding virtually every High Court case.

In delivering his increasingly frequent and vituperative warnings about the direction of the AAA, and the New Deal generally, the justice had stretched to the limit his normal caution regarding extrajudicial behavior. Ironically, though, it was Brandeis's very limited involvement with the other major collectivist agency, the National Recovery Administration, an involvement minimized by his lack of allies there, that resulted precisely in the embarrassing public disclosure he had been trying so hard to avoid.

To pick up the thread of this story we must remember that Brandeis's solution to America's business problems lay in the federal taxing power and not in regulation—certainly not in the fair-trade type regulation the administration seemed to be championing. To him, taxation was the fairest and most easily enforced method of regulation because there were no commissions, hearings, or biased administrators involved. Brandeis advocated taking whatever measures were necessary to eliminate monopolistic practices and to whittle the giants down to size. Then by normal processes in the marketplace, price levels for goods would drop, resulting in the chain reaction of increased demand and increased sales, which would, in turn, rejuvenate the economy. Unpublished documents discovered in three different sets of personal papers reveal that Brandeis preached this message, one that bore great similarity to the ideas he had offered Woodrow Wilson for the New Freedom program, in repeated conversations with young New Dealers, such as Jerome Frank, counsel to the AAA; Harry Shulman, his former law clerk, who was then serving temporarily on the NRA's Consumers' Advisory Board; and Emanuel Goldenweiser, the chief economist of the Federal Reserve Board.[164]

But rather than follow the Brandeisian model, Roosevelt opted for creating the National Recovery Administration. The NRA established a cooperative program between business and government by which the businesses could set up "codes of fair competition" to regulate themselves free from antitrust laws. This program of government-sanctioned monopolies was so antithetic to the justice's notions that his letters to Frankfurter on the subject were filled with vehement complaints.[165] Quite naturally, allies for the justice in the NRA were as rare as hens' teeth. On only rare occasions was Brandeis's opinion solicited by General Hugh Johnson, the head of the NRA;[166] so, the justice and Frankfurter tried to enlist in their crusade Donald Richberg, the counsel for the NRA, who had been appointed on the professor's recommendation.

Brandeis approved only of section 7(A) of the new act, which guaranteed the unions' right to collective bargaining and mandated that the business codes include minimum-wage and maximum-hour standards. Believing that this provision of the law would aid reemployment, and thus economic recovery, Brandeis used Boston department store magnate A. Lincoln Filene to approach Richberg indirectly on "certain phases of the labor situation."[167] When Brandeis reported that these efforts to reach Richberg had failed, an embittered Felix Frankfurter, who had also made similar entreaties, declared in a letter to the justice that their former ally was now "for Business."[168]

Since these contacts with the NRA had not been fruitful, Frankfurter, at the insistence of Brandeis, approached Roosevelt directly on the issue in a two-day conference held in late August 1934. According to the professor's handwritten report to the justice, FDR now appeared to be coming around to their way of thinking on the NRA and openly wished to "keep only [the] (1) minimum wage, (2) maximum hours, (3) collective bargaining and (4) child labor" provisions.[169] Still, to secure his full vision for reshaping America, the justice knew that even more intensive pressure would have to be applied.

At the very time that Brandeis needed to step up his pressure on the administration, however, his care in hiding this extrajudicial conduct was more necessary than ever. None of his colleagues on the bench were involved in any significant political activity at that time, other than occasionally recommending executive and judicial appointments.[170] To be discovered working against the NRA would leave Brandeis open to attack from both the believers in a cloistered Supreme Court and the "social planners" seeking to protect the cornerstone of their program as well as to eliminate their main opponent. Such a victory over Brandeis would lower the Court's prestige and, most assuredly, end any possibility of further work by him in the political realm. Consequently, to his lieutenant Felix Frankfurter fell the responsibility of handling any questions if a member of the public should discover what was going on.

In general, their efforts to maintain secrecy were quite successful. Just as during the 1920s, none of Brandeis's colleagues on the Court appeared to be fully aware of his relationship with Frankfurter; at least none appear ever to have expressed reservations about it. For a while, the only hint of Brandeis's involvement was printed on occasion in the widely syndicated investigative writing of Drew Pearson and Robert Allen.[171] When the storm broke, it came in an ironic twist worthy of an O. Henry short story.

Of all things, the controversy surrounded Brandeis's alleged relationship with NRA head, General Hugh Johnson! In one of the private, unpublished letters discovered in the Frankfurter papers, Brandeis recounted to the professor the full extent of his relationship with General Johnson. The justice explained that his acquaintance with Johnson dated back to World War I, when the latter had been an aid to General Enoch Crowder, a frequent recipient of Brandeis's advice. During 1933 and 1934, Brandeis and Johnson spoke on only five different occasions.[172] Each time they spoke Brandeis's message was exactly the same: "the measure [NRA] is a bad one [because of] the impossibility of enforcement, the dangers to the small industries [and] the inefficiency of the big unit, be it governmental or private." The last encounter was in May 1934, when the NRA head, appearing in a visit with the justice to be a "crushed man," admitted his failure to see the unrealistic nature of the agency's goals and its enforcement provisions. At that time, Brandeis wrote Frankfurter, he felt some compassion for Johnson who "showed manliness in coming to [me, though I] had predicted failure, instead of avoiding [me] as most men would have done, when the predicted failure was apparent." So Brandeis assuaged his visitor by telling him that he, Johnson, had done everything possible to deal with an impossible task, and that the best move now would be to "liquidate" the agency.

After that meeting, Brandeis never again heard from Johnson directly. Instead, the NRA head chose to thank Brandeis by radio. In a speech delivered on September 14, 1934, which criticized textile union leaders and organized labor generally, Johnson added one sentence that seemed almost totally out of context: "During this whole intense experience [of leading the NRA], I have been in constant touch with that old counselor, Judge Louis Brandeis."[173]

The real mystery is why Johnson made such a statement when it was so inaccurate in its implication regarding both the frequency of the contacts and the nature of the advice. Some people thought that Johnson was drunk at the time, but others countered that he always sounded drunk when speaking on the radio. Probably the best explanation is that Johnson, with his agency collapsing all around him, was wallowing in self-pity in describing the trials of the NRA. Faced with outside criticism as well as resistance by his own subordinates, who by slowly adopting the Brandeis philosophy were becoming disloyal, Johnson clutched for support in his hour of need. Since the moral, if not the actual, leader of these critics was Louis Brandeis, a man Johnson apparently considered his friend, he saw no harm in invoking the justice's name to quell the debate. Little did Johnson realize that it was probably the worst thing he could have done in the effort to win Brandeis's and his allies' support, for no statement could have put the justice in more jeopardy.

With a generally quiescent Court in the area of politics, the public outcry over this charge was predictable—immediate, vigorous, and nearly unanimous castigation. Newspaper editorials across the nation criticized Brandeis's involvement. The Baltimore Sun termed the situation "confusion confounded," while the Chicago Tribune called it "a departure from American custom and from judicial ethics which is as truly revolutionary as any project in the program of the New Deal."[174] More important, this paper, along with the New York Herald-Tribune, demanded in unequivocal terms that Brandeis abstain from any Supreme Court case concerning the NRA.[175] The editorial opinion was not completely one-sided, however; the Harvard professor and the justice's other allies had arranged for supportive pieces to appear in The New Republic and the Springfield Republican [Illinois].[176]

Johnson's speech, and the public reaction to it, moved Brandeis to write in a letter to Felix Frankfurter, a copy of which was sent to Judge Julian Mack, that the thought of disqualifying himself from NRA cases was "not agreeable to contemplate." The incident, he calmly explained, "must be regarded as a casualty—like that of being run into by a drunken autoist—or shot by a lunatic."[177] In this fashion, the justice gave his supporters the impression that the incident bothered him only from the standpoint that public opinion might prevent him from exercising his official power in the NRA cases and that he would not be able to battle the "social planners" from the bench. But, just as with Brandeis's public explanation of the reason for his withdrawal from considering the Sacco-Vanzetti case, there was more here than appeared on the surface. Brandeis was never concerned about being compromised in the NRA cases, for in reality he knew that Johnson's statement could not be verified and that his immediate explanation of the incident to Chief Justice Hughes and Associate Justice Van Devanter had eliminated any questions regarding his ethics here. What Brandeis might well have feared was an even greater danger: an in-depth investigation by newspaper reporters and others that would have revealed the incredible extent of his actual extrajudicial involvement elsewhere in the administration. Because of these other political activities, the justice was extremely vulnerable, and unless further exposures could be avoided, his prestige, the Court's reputation, and the possibility of further private efforts on behalf of Progressivism were in dire jeopardy.

The problem then was how best to stem the flood of public criticism as quickly as possible in order to let the issue die down; the Brandeis team conceived and implemented an extended campaign to accomplish this goal. In addition to publishing their own supportive editorials, Frankfurter drafted a statement for Johnson himself to deliver that would "explain" the comment in his speech.* This paragraph, which in the end was never read, is interesting in that it invokes one of the traditionally understood exceptions to the standards of judicial ethics—the duty to discuss general issues, especially in times of national emergency.

> I regret that some newspaper editorials have misconstrued my recent remark that I had consulted Justice Brandeis of the Supreme Court. Of course I never discussed any questions of law or any other controversial matters which could possibly come before Justice Brandeis in his official capacity. He would not permit it and I would never em-

---

* According to a letter written by Frankfurter over a year later (ironically after Johnson had embarrassed him as well with a public attack against the professor's work in the administration), financier and informal presidential adviser, Bernard Baruch, had telephoned him "to say how remorseful Johnson was, and how ready [he was] to make any public statement to correct the outrageously false impression which he had created concerning Mr. Justice Brandeis's observance of judicial propriety." While Frankfurter recollects in this letter that he told Baruch to have Johnson simply let the incident die down, the professor may well have drafted this paragraph in case the explanation strategy was adopted instead.[178]

barrass him by any such action. I talked with Mr. Brandeis on the
general philosophy of present-day trends, having a deep respect for
his profound knowledge. I remember during the War how President
Wilson often talked with Chief Justice White about the prosecution
of the War. It would be a tragic development if, during these times
of great stress where human life is at stake and suffering so great, we
were not able to consult the best minds of this country in this war
against depression.[179]

At the same time, Frankfurter and Judge Julian Mack worked with
President Roosevelt in easing what they believed to be the justice's
acute embarrassment. Initially, Frankfurter wrote FDR that "Hugh
Johnson's outburst about his alleged relations with Brandeis has created a very serious situation, about which I think we had better have
a talk."[180] Roosevelt indicated that he was ready to do whatever would
be advisable and wise to correct the situation. With this opening,
Frankfurter then counselled that a public retraction would not suit
Brandeis because of his "tenderness for [Johnson]."[181] In fact, an examination of Brandeis's letters shows that attributing such tender feelings to Brandeis could not have been further from the truth. In three
unpublished letters mailed to Frankfurter during the week before
Frankfurter's message was mailed to the president, Brandeis proclaimed to his lieutenant his certainty that Johnson's "mind ha[d] gone
astray," and called for his removal from the administration.[182] As
Brandeis warned, "If FD[R] does not shut up the General completely—
or at least remove him—he too will feel the embarrassment."[183]*
Frankfurter apparently was trying to direct the president toward that
alternative without openly expressing the threat.

For FDR, the most immediate concern was how to handle the inevitable questions regarding this incident at an upcoming news conference. In a personal interview, Professor Paul Freund recalled the next
move in the campaign to minimize the negative reaction to this incident. Knowing in advance that Julian Mack would be telephoning in
order to get instructions for the president on this matter, Mrs. Brandeis called in Freund, who had served as the justice's law clerk two
terms earlier, to receive the call. The justice, continuing his practice

---

*Brandeis made his wishes even clearer in a letter to Frankfurter dated September 25,
1934: "Further thought confirms my conviction that neither of the two [FDR or Johnson]
should say a word. . . . On the other hand, if the General's resignation which you say
will be tendered soon and accepted—were tendered and accepted now, it would help
some. The rest must be left to time."

of never speaking on the phone after coming to the Court, awaited the message in his study. Meanwhile, Freund heard Mack say excitedly, "What does Louis want the President to say—some response must soon be made." Brandeis, who was the picture of equanimity even under these trying circumstances, responded just as he had in personal letters to Frankfurter, that neither the president nor Johnson should say anything further because it would do more harm than good.[184] Though Mack repeatedly pressed for permission to say something, Brandeis remained adamant. Unknown to the justice, FDR had already privately revealed in a conference with Harry Hopkins, Harold Ickes, and Charles E. Wyzanski, Jr., that he had decided to fire Johnson because of his intemperate remark. The decision made, Johnson was permitted to resign, and when the action was publicly announced the outcry died down quickly, just as the justice had anticipated.[185]

Despite the public uproar caused by this incident, it had no discernible effect on the extent of Brandeis's extrajudicial behavior. If anything, the justice became even more involved in political affairs. There are two explanations for this continued boldness. First, Brandeis's concern for his policies was so genuine, and his fear of losing this final opportunity to realize their enactment so pronounced, that it overcame any reservations related to notions of "judicial propriety." His almost fatalistic reaction to the Johnson affair indicates that Brandeis simply did not believe that his extrajudicial behavior was unethical in any way. Even faced with the adverse public reaction to this one incident, however, Brandeis may well have had one other reason for deciding not to move toward a posture of extrajudicial restraint and caution. Perhaps he was fully confident that once the uproar subsided, these activities would never again be in jeopardy of discovery. After all, as he wrote Frankfurter, this speech was a freak occurrence involving a "pathological case."[186] No one who was remotely aware of the justice's actual involvement would ever be so indiscreet. Once more, Brandeis's calculation here was correct. The Johnson incident was the only time the justice's involvement in politics became a source of public controversy.

No doubt, part of Brandeis's confidence that he could remain covert in his extrajudicial endeavors was due to his faith in the enormous talents of Felix Frankfurter. This lieutenant was remarkably active in denying the allegations of others regarding Brandeis's political actions. On occasion, he was even able to prevent the publication of such charges to save the justice any "embarrassment." A prime example of this service was revealed through an examination of the correspondence files of Raymond Moley at the Hoover Institution on War, Revolution, and Peace.

In late October 1935, Moley, who was then editing *Today* magazine, notified Frankfurter that an article was about to be printed that discussed some of Brandeis's involvement with the administration. The piece portrayed the clash between FDR's two advisory groups, using the metaphor of a football game, with Frankfurter as one of the "team captains." Before sending Frankfurter an advance copy, Moley himself had already deleted a sentence that mentioned "the aged referee on the sidelines, Louis D. Brandeis [who] was constantly wagging signals to one of the teams."[187]

Frankfurter immediately responded to Moley in a letter in which he still objected to the rather innocuous article for two reasons. First, he disavowed that two such teams even existed. More important, he also objected to the remaining references to Brandeis, who was described as having a "desire for vengeance" against monopolistic practices. Frankfurter argued that this surely could not be true of a man "whose temper of mind and whose feelings are less revengeful, are less concerned with punishment" than were those of most other people.[188]

With the Hugh Johnson incident still so fresh in the public's mind, Frankfurter clearly wanted to keep Brandeis's name out of such articles entirely. Moley argued that this very humorous journalistic approach would serve instead to mitigate any damage from the earlier controversy. Moreover, having not only witnessed these activities but even been part of many of them, Moley, puzzled, amused, or offended by Frankfurter's denial of what both men knew to be true, began his response with "I take it that your personal letter of October 30th is a personal letter, addressed to me as a friend, brother-in-arms, or what you will, and I answer it in that spirit, asking you, 'What the hell?' " Moley went on to defend the piece, writing that if the portrait of Frankfurter and his "boys" was a "misleading picture . . . I have been laboring under a colossal misapprehension for the past three years and in this I am in the company of a goodly number of others." "If the article is false," Moley added, "then I must forget all the things that are the factual foundation for this delusion of mine . . . help me know wherein I have been wrong." After reminiscing about all their earlier mutual political endeavors, Moley, the man to whom Frank-

furter had sent over 150 telegrams and letters in one nine-month period, concluded: "I agree that in spirit [Brandeis] is gentle and kind,"
but "the reference which I deleted as to his quiet advising from the
sidelines . . . was true—he has been a determinative factor in the
guidance of legislative and administrative policy." [189]

To Frankfurter, of course, it did not matter whether the story was
true or not. The important thing was that the public not be encouraged to speculate about such matters. Perhaps the greatest testimonial
to his success in hiding the justice's political activities from view is
the fact that it would be over forty years before the public would discover the full extent of them. For the prophet, Brandeis, the promised
land of true Progressivism was almost visible, and, until forced to
choose between two idols, his scribe, Frankfurter, would make certain
that nothing was permitted to block the path.

5

The Vision is Realized:
Justice Brandeis
and the Later New Deal

Just as Brandeis had prophesied, by early 1935 it was becoming clear that the Roosevelt plan of large-scale, centralized management of the economy was not going to be sufficiently effective to rescue the nation from the Depression. Historian William Leuchtenburg has noted, "From the spring of 1934 to the spring of 1935, the country rode at anchor."[1] The budget deficit and the unemployment rolls grew, and the national income did not. While Roosevelt remained popular as an inspirational leader, many were losing patience with the thrust of the New Deal. Businessmen felt overregulated; workers were unionizing at an incredible rate and violently striking when they did not achieve their demands; and people on relief were rioting for higher payments.

Other charismatic national leaders rose to challenge FDR and propose their own cure-all programs—Louisiana Senator Huey Long's "Share Our Wealth" brand of socialism; radio minister Charles Coughlin's "National Union for Social Justice," designed to replace capitalism; and Dr. Francis Townsend's "Old Age Revolving Pensions." And tens of millions of Americans were listening. Yet people remained loyal enough to Roosevelt personally to elect enough Democrats to occupy over three-fourths of the seats in the House and over two-thirds of those in the Senate in November 1934. Even with this mandate, and while his following clamored for jobs, economic recovery, and financial relief, Roosevelt was able to get only one piece of legislation through Congress in the first months of 1935. Even worse, for the time being Roosevelt seemed either unable or unwilling to chart a new course for his legislative juggernaut.[2] But the president was given new impetus for regrouping his troops on May 27, 1935, when, just as Brandeis had been predicting for so long and to so many people, the day of reckoning came for the early New Deal. Ironically, it was the Supreme Court itself that dealt the telling blow.

Right up to the last moment Brandeis continued to warn the New Dealers about the error of their ways. By mid-March 1935, the justice had become convinced through conversations with Progressive senators that FDR's relationship with them was deteriorating. So he sent word to Frankfurter that these "relations . . . would need much revising."[3] Duly warned, the scribe swung into action. On April 22 Frankfurter forwarded to the president a letter written to him by David K. Niles, the director of the Ford Hall Forum, and a man described by the Harvard professor "as one of the most devoted of [your] followers."[4] In this message, after thoroughly analyzing the political relations between the administration and the liberals and Progressives throughout the nation, Niles called for a "frank talking-things-over" between the president and the leaders of these groups.[5]

Unknown to Roosevelt, the message in this letter and its careful timing had hardly been chance occurrences. Niles was an old Frankfurter ally who was accustomed to doing favors for the professor. During Frankfurter's year of teaching at Oxford, for instance, Niles had made it his business to keep the professor informed about events in Washington and Massachusetts.[6] A few years later, it was Niles who arranged for a mailbox to be placed only one hundred feet from and on the same side of the road as Frankfurter's house on Brattle Street, so that this one-man postal distribution center would not have to cross a busy street to post his mail.[7]

In April 1935, the favor he did for Frankfurter was to write him, apparently at the professor's own request, a letter analyzing the general political situation. Copies of letters to Frankfurter in Niles's private papers reveal how, until he too became part of the administration as FDR's administrative assistant, Niles occasionally acted as a spokesman for Frankfurter's (and hence also Brandeis's) political views. Niles would send his political commentary to Frankfurter, and when the professor was impressed with the letter's message, but not completely satisfied with its style, he would attach his own comments and return it to Niles for redrafting.[8] Once completed, Niles would send the rewritten letter back to the professor, who would then forward it to Roosevelt.[9]

After he had passed along Niles's April 22 letter, which Frankfurter wrote was deserving of the president's "special attention," the professor sent to the White House two additional letters suggesting his own plans for the meeting with liberal leaders.[10] When FDR did meet on May 14 with Frankfurter, Niles, Secretary of the Interior Harold Ickes, Secretary of Agriculture Henry Wallace, and five Progressive senators, the Harvard professor reported that "Justice Brandeis had sent him word that it was 'the eleventh hour' " for the administration.[11]

Indeed it may have been even later, for within two weeks, on May 27, 1935, the clock struck twelve for the National Recovery Administration and the early New Deal when a unanimous Supreme Court in *Schechter Poultry Corporation v. United States* ruled the NRA unconstitutional.[12]* The Schechter brothers, owners of a live-poultry firm in Brooklyn, had been convicted of violating various provisions of the National Industry Recovery Act, including the selling of diseased poultry. Having learned "very, very confidentially" of the Justice Department's intentions to bring this case to the Supreme Court, Felix Frankfurter tried to warn the administration of the danger in pushing it to a final showdown. He instructed Thomas Corcoran to wire the president, who was then on a fishing vacation, not to proceed with the case. This telegram, dated April 4, 1935, and marked "rush-confidential," relayed a warning that Corcoran assumed came straight from the lips of Justice Louis D. Brandeis:

> F.F. suggests most impolitic and dangerous to yield to antagonistic press clamor now *because fundamental situation on Court not changed.* Further suggest you wire Attorney General Homer Cummings not to take hasty action and hold whole situation on N.R.A. appeals in abeyance until you return. [*Italics mine*][13]

The personal papers of Raymond Moley show that Frankfurter also sent a similar message to him. Though Moley was by then editor of *Today* magazine, Frankfurter knew that Moley nonetheless had re-

---

* Brandeis had not been moved by either his occasional contacts with the two NRA heads, General Hugh Johnson and Donald Richberg, or the disclosure controversy with Johnson in September 1934 to disqualify himself from this case either.

tained close contacts within the administration. Roosevelt was ultimately persuaded to delay the case, but his message back to the attorney general did not arrive in time to stop the appeal.[14]

Whether or not Brandeis had, in fact, spoken to Frankfurter about the case, Corcoran's reaction is an interesting indicator of his view regarding the pervasiveness and openness of the justice's extrajudicial activity during this period. Even a most basic knowledge of judicial propriety would dissuade most from believing that a justice, most especially the ethical Louis D. Brandeis, would discuss a case that was about to come before the Court. Yet, in unquestionably believing that this in fact had happened, and in acting on that belief, Corcoran demonstrated that based on his own observations of Brandeis's political behavior, he did not find such action by this justice inconceivable.

When a unanimous Court declared unconstitutional first Roosevelt's dismissal of Federal Trade Commissioner William E. Humphrey, then the Frazier-Lemke Act, a measure that aided farm mortgagors, and finally the NRA,[15] it was clear that another, even stronger message was being sent to Roosevelt that he needed to find new solutions to his problems. But even in his moment of triumph, Louis Brandeis could not help but reveal the anxiety that must have been burning within him. Now seventy-eight, with over two years of the Roosevelt Administration gone, insulated by a doting and extremely persuasive Felix Frankfurter, deeply committed to his causes, and emotionally elevated by the imminent prospect of seeing his programs implemented, Brandeis was eager to make sure that at the last minute they were not compromised.

Immediately after the decisions were handed down, Benjamin Cohen and Thomas Corcoran were summoned to an anteroom in the Court building. Confronting them was Justice Brandeis, arms outstretched to remove his judicial robe, appearing "to Corcoran for a moment like a black-winged angel of destruction."[16] The man they called Isaiah, normally so calm and distant, was later described by Cohen as "visibly excited and deeply agitated" as he "gasped" to them: "You have heard our three decisions. They change everything." Pointing out that the Court was unanimous in its rebuke of the administration, Brandeis twice stated: "The President has been living in a fool's paradise." Moreover, the normally cautious and precise justice began issuing what could only be construed as orders, and repeating them at that:

> You must phone Felix and have him down in the morning to talk to
> the President. You must see that Felix understands the situation and
> explains it to the President. You must explain it to the men Felix
> brought into the Government. They must understand that these three
> decisions change everything. . . . Make sure that Felix is here in the
> morning to advise the President. The matter is of highest importance.
> Everything that you (the administration) have been doing must be
> changed. Everything must be considered most carefully in light of
> these decisions by a unanimous Court.

When Corcoran tried to suggest that some of the Court's comments
might "seriously imperil the holding company legislation," a measure
that both visitors knew well the justice had been actively pressing for,
Brandeis was not willing to be diverted from his main message. Perhaps forgetting for the moment the extent of their knowledge, he answered, "I am not familiar with the various pieces of legislation . . .
but I should not be surprised if everything would have to be redrafted." And what philosophy should guide that redrafting process?
By now the justice's refrain was all too familiar: "All the powers of
the States cannot be centralized in the Federal government."[17]

This was clearly not the same Louis D. Brandeis who was so discreet and restrained in his early years on the Court. Not only was he
delivering threats to members of the administration, he had even
dropped his one unwritten rule never to discuss cases decided by the
Court with anyone but Felix Frankfurter. How highly unusual it is for
a justice to discuss the implications of a decision by the Court cannot
be overstressed here—the judicial opinion is supposed to speak for
itself—but it is even more unusual for a justice to frame that discussion in such a way as to provide general political advice on the new
direction for the administration made necessary by a Court decision.
The statement that "I should not be surprised if everything would
have to be redrafted" seems clearly to have been an advisory statement delivered to members of the administration regarding legislation
not yet enacted.

Clearly, Brandeis seemed no longer even to be as concerned as he
once had been about maintaining his distance from FDR. While it is
true that he left it to Frankfurter to convey the message to the president, Brandeis did venture to speak in this extraordinary manner to
Roosevelt's two top legislative advisers. The justice must have sensed
that for him as well it was the eleventh hour, and may have been too
wedded to his own personal vision of America to let his time expire
without appropriate action.

While the justice intended that FDR take heed from the incident, the prophet's own scribe, Felix Frankfurter, as it turned out, probably should have been warned as well regarding what was in store for him. Always ready to do Brandeis's bidding, for the second time in two weeks Frankfurter boarded a train to Washington on the night of the 27th and the next afternoon was at the White House relaying the justice's message to Roosevelt.[18] The president had been stunned by the Court's unanimous ruling against the NRA, asking aides when he heard the news: "Well, where was Ben Cardozo? . . . And what about old Isaiah?"[19] He had recovered enough by May 29, though, to give a news conference on the implications of the decision. It is interesting that Roosevelt, knowing full well what he was about to tell the newsmen, invited Felix and Marion Frankfurter, who were still in Washington, to attend. Though the professor chose not to go, his wife did. Given the nature of his relationship with Brandeis, it was a wise decision for Frankfurter. FDR spoke to the press corps without notes for an hour and twenty minutes and argued that the Court had "turned back the Constitution . . . to 'the horse-and-buggy days.' "[20] It was not easy for Frankfurter to explain to Brandeis FDR's refusal to come to heel. So difficult was it that he avoided delivering the news to Brandeis face to face, even though he had the opportunity to do so right after Marion had given it to him. It was not until five days later, on June 3, 1935, that he wrote to Brandeis discussing the first issue and papering over the second.

> F.D.[R.] gave me no intimation whatever that he was going to do the press conference talk. I knew nothing of it until Marion told me just as we were coming to lunch with you. I assume F.D.[R.] purposely did not consult me or tell me—why I know not, except perhaps that he had political purposes and so naturally would not consult me.[21]

Why, after nearly nineteen years as Brandeis's political lieutenant couldn't Frankfurter deliver this news to Brandeis face to face? Perhaps he was just as intimidated by the prophet as everyone else, and did not dare to be the bearer of such bad tidings. Or possibly, Frankfurter's great affection for Brandeis made such candor too painful to undertake without some preparation. But there is likely even more here than an uncomfortable moment between two old friends.

This clear precursor of things to come should have suggested to Frankfurter the futility of trying to play indefinitely the role of middle man between these two headstrong historic figures. In the end, the inherent antagonism between the political and governmental views of Brandeis and Roosevelt would lead to repeated and finally grave confrontation between them. When the inevitable rupture did threaten—as it did over the 1937 Judicial Reorganization Act—Frankfurter would be left with a choice to make—to continue his allegiance to his lifetime judicial patron and friend, or to throw his lot in with one of the century's most powerful political figures. Though this first serious clash between Roosevelt and Brandeis should have given Frankfurter this window into the future, likely it did not. Fortunately for him, the difficult decision that would one day have to be made was still far off. Right now, both the prophet and his scribe were focused on the present. Brandeis had all his troops in place and what he saw as the final battle was about to begin.

With the early New Deal programs swept away by the Supreme Court and economic recovery not yet achieved, FDR seemed to have no choice but to come over to Brandeis's "true faith." Unlike the earlier period, Roosevelt was now surrounded by Brandeisians rather than by collectivists. Corcoran and Cohen had, by the spring of 1935, taken positions at the president's right hand.[22] So successful and comprehensive had been Brandeis's and Frankfurter's earlier efforts in staffing the agencies that there was also no further need to operate the Brandeis-Frankfurter placement bureau—allies were already positioned throughout the administration.[23] Frankfurter continued his practice of passing the justice's messages along to the president, sometimes saying only, as he did in one letter, that they came from "one of your most devoted well wishers who is also a most knowing party,"[24] and other times openly naming their source.

An examination of the personal correspondence files of Franklin D. Roosevelt shows that by this time Brandeis had developed one other new conduit through which he would reach the president with regularity and directness. To buck up FDR's resolve to resist the "bigness" message of the collectivists, Brandeis also used Harper's Weekly editor Norman Hapgood, an old ally in Progressive causes and a Brandeis correspondent since the early 1900s. On a regular basis, Brandeis would send supportive messages or new insights on various New Deal policies to Hapgood, who would, in turn, forward the advice, verbatim, to the president. Hapgood made clear where the advice was coming from, attributing it either directly to Brandeis, or, as he did once, to "our well-known friend, the Cape Cod Philosopher."[25] Roosevelt would then respond using the same conduit. In this way, the president and the justice maintained a continual dialogue.[26]

As the congressional session was winding down in late May 1935, word came to Brandeis from Felix Frankfurter that the president had decided "if necessary, to keep [Congress] in extra session for 'must' legislation."[27] Three of those pieces of must legislation were dear to Brandeis's heart: a soak-the-rich tax scheme, government regulation of the holding companies in public utilities, and the establishment of an unemployment insurance program.[28] At long last, after initially creating his program for America, keeping it alive for nearly two decades in Congress, and now, for the second time, having it planted in the inner circles of the New Deal, it seemed likely that the justice would see his years of effort bear fruit in the flood of legislation passed during the so-called "Second Hundred Days."

Over the years, Brandeis had always been willing to supply the president with whatever was necessary for the legislative battle. Despite the lack of enthusiasm by the early New Dealers for his revenue proposals, the justice had continued to send Frankfurter additional legislative ideas, such as a "contingency fee" bill designed to end the practice of tax lawyers receiving as their fees a large percentage of the monetary settlement they might win in a case against the government; an excise tax on what he called "tramp corporations," to discourage them from being chartered for tax purposes in a state different from the location of the majority of their business enterprises; and an intercorporate dividends tax, intended to abolish the practice of establishing holding companies in the public utilities industries.[29] When the justice feared that his tax-reform program, which included a rigorously progressive tax system, the elimination of the "super-rich" strata in society through the imposition of a substantial federal inheritance tax, and the passage of stiff tax levies on large corporations, might be confused with the increasingly popular "Share Our Wealth" program of Huey Long, he had instructed Frankfurter in a letter dated January 10, 1934 to recommend that the president sell the program as a way of "distributing power—consumer power, economic power, political power, and the power of human creative development" rather than as a wealth-distribution scheme.[30]

The inability of the Roosevelt Administration to formulate a comprehensive tax program by late 1934 had given the justice and Felix

Frankfurter another opportunity to press again for the adoption of their revenue measures. Fully aware that the inheritance tax rates were too low to fund public-works programs of the size Brandeis desired, Frankfurter promised the justice in mid-November that he would "plant the seeds" for inheritance and corporate tax reforms.[31] The problem they anticipated in this effort was the same problem that had plagued them through the early New Deal: they had no influential allies on the Treasury Department staff, and its secretary, Henry Morgenthau, Jr., had proven to be a formidable opponent.

By December 1934, though, both of these conditions would change. The Treasury officials, then busily preparing at FDR's request a full-scale reform package for the tax code, seemed to be moving in the direction of the Brandeis philosophy. Under active consideration was a recommendation for increasing taxes to attack corporate and economic bigness as well as to raise revenue.[32] Unknown to them, however, the president had also directed Felix Frankfurter and Thomas Corcoran to work on their own revisions of several features of the income tax code.[33] Then in late December, by which time Frankfurter and Corcoran had made progress in putting Justice Brandeis's tax proposals into legislative form, Frankfurter learned, to his delight, that FDR had now directed Treasury Secretary Morgenthau to consult with him about these new ideas.[34] A transcript of that telephone conversation placed in Morgenthau's personal diary makes clear that while his subordinates were leaning toward the "Brandeis Way," his own personal hostility toward it had not yet abated. Under presidential directive, however, Morgenthau had no choice now but to cooperate with Frankfurter on the development of a tax program designed to raise revenue and promote corporate reform.[35]

By the time of Roosevelt's annual message to Congress on January 4, 1935, the direction of the tax policy was still in flux: so, he called only for "improvement in our taxation forms and methods."[36] When the final version of the Frankfurter-Corcoran tax-reform proposals came to the president's desk later that month, he sent them on to Morgenthau with a memorandum saying that he was "inclined to think that [the secretary] should give serious consideration to the introduction" of these measures.[37] According to Frankfurter's report to Brandeis, shortly thereafter the president declared to Corcoran and Cohen in a conference at the White House that he was now "in favor of [these] excise [taxes] on bigness."[38]

For the next few months, however, Roosevelt's momentum on the issue seemed to stall, and in mid-May, Frankfurter—the consummate political middleman—resorted to his political wile to try to get things moving again. Following the conference between the president and the Progressive senators on May 14, Frankfurter spoke to FDR until late in the night about a variety of issues, including the tax program. With bulldog tenacity and his characteristic eloquence, the Harvard professor followed up this conversation with another plea, mailed in a letter to Roosevelt two days later, this time quoting Justice Brandeis:

> I wish you had seen Brandeis' face light up when I gave him your message about your tax policy and the forthcoming message about it. His eyes became glowing coals of fire, and shone with warm satisfaction. He asked me to tell you how deeply he rejoiced to have had the message from you, and with what eagerness he is looking forward to the enunciation of your policy. When I told him with what tender sadness you said to me that you had hoped the big leaders in finance and business would learn something, he very gravely shook his head and said, "I understand truly his feelings. We have all had that hope from time to time, but apparently they just can't."[39]

These were particularly inspirational words from the justice, almost magically on target—especially so since Brandeis was not actually informed of the nature of the late-night conference until Frankfurter reported on it in a letter written six days after his letter to the president.[40]

Still, one cannot deny the professor's effectiveness. During the early New Deal years he had carefully nurtured his relationship with Roosevelt until, by the summer of 1935, their friendship was one of great intimacy. Thus it was not surprising that, after years of operating at long-range from Cambridge, the fifty-two-year-old Harvard law professor was invited by the president to spend a good part of that summer living in the White House to help plan and execute the crucial, new legislative campaign.[41]

One of Frankfurter's assignments was to help draft FDR's legislative message on tax reform, which was to be delivered to Congress on June 19, 1935. The professor's hand is clearly visible here, as passages of the address sound as though they had come straight from the pen of Justice Louis D. Brandeis. In the speech, President Roosevelt called for increasing the taxes on inheritances and gifts, saying that "great accumulations of wealth cannot be justified" because they foster "un-

desirable concentration of control in a relatively few individuals."[42]
He also advocated increasing the tax rate in the upper-income brackets to prevent "the disturbing effects upon our national life that come from great inheritances of wealth and power." Finally, displaying a definite anti-bigness philosophy, Roosevelt advocated a graduated tax on corporations based on the size of the firm. This measure was designed to protect the small firm, for "without such small enterprises our competitive economic society would cease." Clearly, Roosevelt now supported the use of the federal taxing power to break up great accumulations of capital held by persons and corporations.[43]

While Justice Brandeis was extremely pleased with this tax message,[44] the Congress was not so ready to agree. So, Frankfurter reassured Brandeis in a private letter dated July 10, 1935 that he was spending a great deal of time personally advising Roosevelt regarding the conduct of this legislative battle.[45] Yet despite these efforts, the tax bill was substantially diluted by Congress. While the tax on higher incomes was raised, and a graduated corporate income tax was passed (though not as extensive as the one Roosevelt sought), the inheritance tax idea was completely dropped. Further, the gift tax was increased, but very few of its loopholes were closed to prevent evasion. Nevertheless, when Roosevelt signed the law on August 31, 1935, Brandeis demonstrated his satisfaction by writing Frankfurter: "You have rendered a great service—F.D.[R.] comes out on top."[46]

Brandeis's lengthy crusade for the final piece of his tax-reform package—designed to deal with the holding companies in the utility industry—also came to a successful conclusion in the summer of 1935. For years, the justice and his lieutenant, Frankfurter, had been lecturing people—such as Pennsylvania Governor Gifford Pinchot, NRA official Harry Shulman, Franklin D. Roosevelt, and Raymond Moley—about the "evil" monopolistic practices of the power utilities.[47] Brandeis objected to the practice by these companies of creating pyramids of holding companies in order to maximize profits and increase their control over various operating facilities. Naturally, the justice was concerned with both the bigness of these industries and the virtual monopoly they enjoyed over vital forms of energy.

Brandeis's solution, as indicated in a memorandum written by the chief economist of the Federal Reserve Board, Emanuel Goldenweiser, following one of his conversations with the justice, was really quite direct: "Tax the holding companies out of existence."[48] Only in this manner could the problem be solved without increasing the size of the federal government. With this in mind, he had been instructing the professor and his "boys" how specifically to draft such a device for controlling the practice of corporate tax evasion through the use of holding companies.[49]

Brandeis's prospects for success had started to look quite good in July 1934, when Benjamin V. Cohen was made general counsel to the newly created National Power Policy Committee and given the responsibility for drafting such a bill. Oddly though, Cohen ignored the justice's preferences and argued instead for regulating the operations of the holding companies rather than destroying them completely. However other officials, including several in the Treasury Department, urged instead the total abolition of the holding companies by means of a corporate tax. Even Brandeis tried to make his views known, by sending word in September 1934, through former secretary of the Navy in the Wilson Administration, Josephus Daniels, of his willingness to confer directly with FDR on the pressing issues of "Big Business" and the "evils of monopoly and privilege."[50] However, this time the offer was declined. Indeed, such a meeting turned out to be unnecessary, for Roosevelt announced to a group of his advisers in November that he supported the use of the taxing power to abolish the holding companies completely.

Frankfurter was so encouraged by his latest contacts with the president that he wrote Brandeis on December 20, 1934, "I think that F.D. [R.]'s needs and Tom and Ben's abilities may give us a real opportunity."[51] However, immediate success eluded them because the advisers in the Treasury Department and the National Power Policy Committee, while agreeing that taxation should be the "weapon" to control the holding companies, could not decide whether the overall goal should be mere regulation or total abolition. So, another committee, this one headed by an old Brandeis adversary, Attorney General Homer Cummings, was created in early 1935 to resolve the dispute. This new committee decided to eliminate the tax provisions of the bill entirely and in its place put a much stronger weapon, the "death sentence" provision.[52] Basically this section of the bill required that every holding company be totally abolished after January 1, 1940. Dissatisfied with the departure of this idea from the Brandeis "true faith" of taxation as the weapon, Frankfurter pressed again for that solution in both a letter to President Roosevelt and a personal discussion with him.[53]

When the new proposal was introduced in Congress by Senator

Burton K. Wheeler and Representative Sam Rayburn on February 6, 1935, it was almost immediately in trouble because of the massive lobbying campaign mounted by the utility companies. In addition, Brandeis expressed his personal displeasure with the bill in a talk with John J. Burns, general counsel to the Securities and Exchange Commission (SEC). According to a report Burns forwarded Frankfurter, the justice once again called for using the "tax weapon" as a means of "social reform" and to control "bigness."[54]

With atypical pragmatism, though, Brandeis would decide this time that however better his own approach might be, some attempt had to be made to end abuses of the holding companies. His greatest fear was that neither his idea to tax them to death nor Cummings's plan to sentence them to death would finally be enacted. Even after Roosevelt sent a message to Congress expressing his wholehearted approval of the Wheeler-Rayburn bill, the justice worried in a letter to Frankfurter that the president might "weaken" on it. Fully aware of the intense lobbying pressure that had been applied on this issue throughout the spring, Frankfurter promised Brandeis that he would work continually with FDR.[55]

During the hectic summer legislative session in 1935, Brandeis supplemented Frankfurter's efforts to buck up the president with one of his own, using Norman Hapgood as his intermediary. In a letter to Roosevelt dated June 16, 1935, Hapgood transmitted Brandeis's words of encouragement:

> In a letter received this morning from Mr. Justice Brandeis, on various topics, he says: "If F.D.[R.] carries through the Holding Company bill we shall have achieved considerable toward curbing Bigness—in addition to recent advances."[56]

A grateful Roosevelt responded: "I was glad to hear the comment our mutual friend made on the Holding Company bill."[57]

On the congressional front, Frankfurter and his protégés also did their best to bolster the spirits of Senator Burton K. Wheeler, who was leading the Senate fight for the bill. Corcoran and Cohen remained at Wheeler's side throughout the debate, supplying him with arguments and speeches. Meanwhile, Frankfurter tried to sustain Wheeler's spirits in personal letters to the senator.[58]

When the language of the Senate and the House bills differed, it was Frankfurter who negotiated the compromise measure. The professor drafted a new bill, which greatly modified the death-sentence provisions. This bill, which was eventually passed by Congress, required all holding companies to register with the SEC, forced those holding companies once removed from the operating corporation to justify their existence, and abolished all holding companies more than twice removed from the main firm.[59]

In the end, though the final Public Utilities Holding Company Act was intended to break up monopolies, the justice was not entirely pleased with its wording. So weak were its enforcement mechanisms that companies simply refused to register with the SEC. Brandeis, discouraged but not defeated, continued to send supportive notes to the president through Hapgood urging the vigorous use of this act against "vast concentrations of financial power."[60] Nevertheless, while Brandeis's preferred idea of rigorously taxing these companies was not adopted into law, this legislative battle demonstrated clearly that his antibigness philosophy was taking hold of the administration.

Perhaps the most intensive political effort undertaken by Justice Brandeis during this period was directed toward securing passage of an unemployment insurance law. Ironically, it was in the final stages of this campaign that the justice's political lieutenant, Felix Frankfurter, first began to show signs of less-than-total commitment to the "Brandeis Way." So passionate had been Brandeis's hatred since the early 1900s for "irregular employment," which he had described as the "greatest industrial waste," that he became actively involved in each stage of the formulation and passage of a federal law designed to remedy this condition. To Brandeis's dismay, after his daughter and son-in-law, Elizabeth and Paul Raushenbush, had succeeded in 1932 in securing passage in Wisconsin of the justice's "plant reserves" program, by which each employer contributed to a fund benefitting unemployed workers in their own individual firms, no other state had followed the lead. As Elizabeth Brandeis Raushenbush explained to her father, individual states were not willing to force companies within their borders to pay for a state-mandated program that increased production costs and would place them at a competitive disadvantage with the firms in states that had not yet adopted such a system.[61] It was a bitter irony for Brandeis, the advocate of the Jeffersonian system of decentralized government, that the only hope for his unemployment insurance dreams now lay at the federal level.

The task of lobbying for the enactment of a federal unemployment

insurance law at this time was made more difficult by the public debate over which plan to adopt. Competing with Brandeis's plant-
reserves program was the so-called Ohio plan, being advocated by
Abraham Epstein, the executive secretary of the American Association
for Old Age Security. Instead of creating unemployment funds for individual firms, Epstein's plan mandated that all insurance funds for
an entire industry be pooled at the state level in order to disperse the
monetary risks for each corporation. This program was also a pure
insurance system—with employers, employees, and the government
all contributing to a fund out of which came disbursements for laid-
off workers. The emphasis, then, was on a centralized program dispensing immediate emergency relief to workers, while doing nothing
to discourage erratic employment practices, a main feature of Brandeis's proposal.[62]

In mid-1933, seeing that the state-level lobbying effort was stalled,
Brandeis came up with another of his creative solutions to political
problems. Once again, Elizabeth and Paul Raushenbush served as his
intermediaries. Their recollections for the Columbia Oral History Collection reveal the subtle but effective means used by the justice to
guide his lieutenants in this new endeavor. When the Raushenbushes
visited Brandeis at his Chatham cottage in the summer of 1933, the
conversation inevitably turned to the promotion of the unemployment
insurance idea. Paul Raushenbush observed how impossible it was to
persuade other states to adopt the law, and Brandeis asked simply,
"Have you considered the case of *Florida v. Mellon?*"[63] Some quick
research on the subject made clear that this was indeed the justice's
slightly disguised suggestion for designing a federal unemployment
insurance law that would achieve their goals. For years, Florida had
been attracting millionaires to the state by the absence of a state inheritance tax. To end this practice, a tax-offset provision was included
in the 1926 Federal Estate Tax law, whereby a federal assessment,
which could be avoided only if a similar state inheritance tax program
existed, was placed on all estates. Naturally, every state quickly enacted its own inheritance tax in order to collect the revenue itself.

The analogy between this case and the unemployment insurance
situation was readily apparent to the Raushenbushes. Using the federal taxation power as a lever, Congress could encourage the states to
adopt their own unemployment insurance plans. This could be accomplished by enacting a uniform federal payroll tax for unemploy-

ment insurance against which the employers might credit any payments made to a similar insurance plan adopted by their own state.
Of course, each state would then immediately adopt such a program
in order to utilize the incoming funds themselves. This proposal was
consistent with Brandeis's Jeffersonian philosophy in that it promoted
the direct administration of the insurance plans by individual states,
rather than through a single, large, federal program. In so doing, each
state would be encouraged to experiment in the adoption of its own
particular program.

When pressed by the Raushenbushes for more concrete details of
his suggested measure, Justice Brandeis abandoned his usual practice
of avoiding a discussion of the specifics of a legislative proposal. In
writing them on September 16, 1933 to detail his tax-offset means for
implementing the plant-reserves program, he explained that the federal government could use an excise tax as a "discourager of hesi-
tancy" on the part of states to adopt their own unemployment insurance programs.[64] Meanwhile, through Felix Frankfurter, the justice
received word that the president wanted to discuss the general political situation with him. Deciding to use this opportunity to impress
upon FDR the need to deal with "irregular employment," Brandeis
had Paul Raushenbush draft a bill using the tax-offset/plant-reserves
concept.[65]

The justice was now so excited about the prospects for his program
that he dropped all pretense of abstaining from politics and became
an active lobbyist in its behalf. Private letters and memoranda discovered in the manuscript collections of Felix Frankfurter and Donald
Richberg, as well as the oral history of the Raushenbushes, indicate
that throughout the fall of 1933 Brandeis personally explained his
proposal to a number of individuals, including Raymond Moley, Harry
Shulman, General Hugh Johnson, then head of the NRA, Donald Richberg, then counsel for the NRA, and Columbia University Professor
Walter Gellhorn.

The fact that Brandeis would confer with General Johnson at all, a
man for whom he had very limited respect, indicates the frenzy of his
interest in the proposal. The justice was also able to persuade Isador
Lubin, the United States comissioner of labor statistics, to present the
plan to Secretary of Labor Frances Perkins and the department's solicitor, Charles Wyzanski.[66] Finally, a memorandum in Brandeis's unpublished papers indicates that the justice used two separate inter-

mediaries in an attempt to encourage a "national figure"—either Senator Wagner or Frances Perkins—to read publicly his 1929 quotation from *Survey Graphic* magazine on "The Right to Work." Still cautious about potentially compromising himself on the issue should it ever come before the Court, Brandeis instructed his lieutenants to "make clear . . . that the statement was made many years ago."[67]

Having secured support for the unemployment insurance idea in the upper echelons of the government, Brandeis now sought direct access to those in charge of drafting such a bill. Talking with an old Progressive ally, Massachusetts businessman A. Lincoln Filene, he suggested that a meeting be convened to discuss the subject. The timing and location of this gathering are subjects of some controversy. Historian Arthur M. Schlesinger, Jr., writes that the meeting occurred during that fall of 1933 in the Brandeis apartment.[68] However, one of the participants, Elizabeth Raushenbush, recounts in her oral history that the meeting occurred during early January 1934 in the Georgetown apartment of Filene's daughter, Mrs. Shouse.

While there is also some dispute over who participated in the meeting, it appears that besides Filene and Raushenbush, the other conferees were Charles E. Wyzanski, Jr., Thomas G. Corcoran, Frances Perkins, and Senator Robert Wagner.[69] Filene spoke to the group about a tax-offset/plant-reserves unemployment insurance proposal, which, he said, he had reason to believe would survive a test by the Supreme Court. In the course of presenting Brandeis's plan, Filene was careful never to mention the justice by name; however, everyone in the room seemed to know the identity of the originator. Both Perkins and Wagner were quite excited about the idea—no doubt partly because of their interest in finding a solution that the increasingly obstreperous Supreme Court would accept.[70]

On Perkins's instructions, the bill was drafted by Paul Raushenbush and the assistant solicitor for the Department of Labor, Thomas H. Eliot. Acting on the justice's expressed belief that employers would regularize employment more quickly if the federal payroll tax were greater than the 2 percent in the Wisconsin plan, Raushenbush and Eliot proposed a uniform 5 percent tax on employers' payrolls. The legislation also contained the Brandeis tax-offset provision, by which the employers' federal tax payments would be credited fully for any contribution to a state unemployment insurance plan—thus protecting programs such as the one already adopted in Wisconsin.[71] Introduced in the Senate by Wagner and in the House by David J. Lewis of Maryland on February 5, 1934, the so-called Wagner-Lewis Act was so satisfactory to Brandeis that he referred to it in a letter to Frankfurter as "my federal excise tax . . . to offset irregularity of employment."[72]

While the drafting of the initial bill had gone smoothly, securing its enactment by Congress was another matter. Since Frankfurter was teaching at Oxford during this period,[73] Elizabeth Raushenbush took over the lieutenant's role. Justice Brandeis's personal papers contain a number of letters from his daughter written between January and May 1934, informing and consulting with him regarding moves in the campaign. To build a consensus for the measure, she asked her father to convince his contacts in the League of Women Voters and in the state of Massachusetts of the need for a supportive congressional letter-writing campaign. Then she became concerned about the unwillingness of President Roosevelt to commit himself definitely at this point to the Wagner-Lewis bill. Fearing that Rexford Tugwell might effectively block the plan, Raushenbush suggested to Brandeis that he speak with Tugwell and Harry Hopkins, in order to enlist their support.[74]

As it turned out, her fears were well grounded. Roosevelt was so unpersuaded by the merits of the Wagner-Lewis Act that he wrote Tugwell, in a memorandum drafted in February 1934, that the plan would "require a good deal of overhauling."[75] Despite growing public and congressional support for some type of unemployment insurance plan, and his own public endorsement of the bill in March 1934, FDR decided in May to send only a lukewarm letter of support for the measure to Congressman Robert Doughton, chairman of the Ways and Means Committee.[76] Not surprisingly, given this lack of presidential initiative, the bill was allowed to die in committee. With Felix Frankfurter still abroad, Brandeis was stuck. On his own there was practically nothing he could do about it until the appropriate moment again presented itself.

On June 8, 1934, that moment seemed to arrive. In a message to Congress FDR reaffirmed his interest in unemployment insurance, as part of a more comprehensive program of social security. In a forty-five minute personal conference with FDR that same day, Brandeis tried to convince the president that instead of calling for an overall federal social security program, he should be concerned only with the unemployment insurance aspects. In a pattern typical among FDR's advisers, Brandeis left the meeting believing that he had been much more successful in influencing the president than he actually had been.

Ten days later, Thomas Corcoran reported in a letter to Frankfurter that instead of Brandeis's federal-state, tax-offset/plant-reserves scheme, FDR seemed to be leaning toward an entirely federally administered plan. But, Corcoran added, there still seemed to be some room for compromise.[77] Consequently, Brandeis prepared to mount a final charge to get what he wanted. As he wrote his daughter Elizabeth, "I have left some efficient friends in Washington, who are to work for the true faith during the summer." Of course, he had already taken steps to alert one of those friends, by writing Felix Frankfurter, as did the professor's "boys," Corcoran and Cohen, to return from Europe as soon as possible.[78]

Brandeis knew that he would need his chief political lieutenant in Washington if he were to successfully defend the "true faith" from subversion by the advocates of greater federal involvement in the administration of an unemployment insurance program. Toward the end of June 1934, FDR established the Committee on Economic Security, which was charged with developing in six months a plan that was "national in scope." Since this committee was headed by Frances Perkins, it seemingly provided another avenue for Brandeis to exercise his influence. Not only had she been initially receptive to the Brandeis program as outlined in the Wagner-Lewis bill, but her appreciation of it deepened when Justice Harlan Fiske Stone ignored the norms against issuing informal legal opinions and privately suggested to her that it would be constitutional to use the "federal taxing power" to create an unemployment insurance system. Now spurred by the advance support of two Supreme Court justices, Perkins made a most persuasive argument to those on the committee who were wary of a subsequent Court review of the plan.[79]

But despite her appeal, a majority of the committee's staff was persuaded by other factors to support the development of a centralized, national (rather than state-by-state) administration of the program. Seeking uniformity of benefits and standards throughout the country, some were proposing a subsidy system, by which the federal government would collect the payroll insurance taxes and then return to those states with unemployment compensation laws that met federal standards the funds necessary to support the unemployed workers. From

Brandeis's perspective, though, such a program of direct federal control would entirely thwart state innovation and experimentation in the area.[80]

With the battle lines now drawn, the justice set out to subvert the supporters of the national plan. He instructed Felix Frankfurter to come to Chatham as soon as he returned from Europe in mid-July 1934, in order to discuss the unemployment insurance campaign.[81] Based on this conference with the justice and Elizabeth Raushenbush, as well as other pieces of information in the letters from Corcoran and Cohen, Frankfurter seemed to sense that the momentum had temporarily swung against the Brandeis proposal. So in his next letter to the justice, dated July 18, 1934, the professor suggested delay: "I'm thinking of sending F.D.R. a strong cautionary word . . . against committing himself. We shall have a long, slow, hard job of deflating the grandiose proposals of [other] insurance schemes."[82] For his part, Brandeis also prepared to wage a very careful lobbying campaign.

First, he instructed Frankfurter to contact Raymond Moley once again. Following Brandeis's advice, Frankfurter did confer with Moley and built up the relationship by "catching up with [him on the] past behind the scenes as to events and personalia" in the White House.[83] Then, Frankfurter reported in a letter to the justice dated July 24, 1934 that he had tried to "indoctrinate [Moley] with [the] difficulties and doubts" about the insurance proposals, in order to impress on him "the importance of going slow and avoiding premature commitments" when the administration considered the various plans.

Frankfurter was not only quite proud of his efforts in this conference, but optimistically predicted to the justice: "I think there is a good chance of having Frances Perkins on the right side and of working out [the] program."[84] Both men felt that such additional alliances were necessary because they were wary of working solely through Raymond Moley. As Frankfurter put it in a letter to Brandeis, sent on August 4, 1934, "Yes, Moley is 'mercurial' and subject to evil A[ttorney] G[eneral] influences and very cautious since his repudiation last summer . . . but—it's another case of working with the tools we have."[85]

Unknown to the justice, however, at this critical point in the campaign, Frankfurter's resolve toward Brandeis's tax-offset/plant-reserves program of unemployment insurance seems to have weakened considerably. Frankfurter's devotion to the idea went only so far as its promotion did not adversely affect the political welfare of Franklin Delano Roosevelt. Perhaps Moley had actually convinced Frankfurter that rigid adherence to the Brandeis program would be difficult to put through Congress, or that it would somehow damage Roosevelt's electoral base of support. Possibly Frankfurter came to that conclusion on his own. It is even conceivable that the professor had never really been persuaded by the merits of the program itself.

For whatever reason, at this juncture Frankfurter's usual passion and interest in presenting a Brandeis proposal was missing. Given his closeness to FDR, and his contact with Moley, it was easy for Frankfurter, and not out of character, to advise initial caution in proceeding with the announcement of an unemployment insurance program, only to press hard for the adoption of Brandeis's approach later on. But Frankfurter, while acting as expected in the first instance by advising caution, then defied his own personal nature and his accustomed political style in adopting a scrupulously neutral tone in discussing the various alternative programs. In fact, with everything on the line in this most important of Brandeis's political crusades, there is no evidence that Frankfurter ever seriously pressed the president directly to adopt the plant-reserves aspect of Brandeis's proposal as part of the upcoming Social Security Act. Past history indicates that had he done so, the professor would not have hesitated to boast about his accomplishment in a letter to Justice Brandeis. Apparently torn between the justice's ideological fervor and Roosevelt's political needs, Frankfurter seems to have simply decided to let the president choose his own course.

In his meeting with Moley, Frankfurter had learned that the former Brain Truster was then involved in writing a campaign speech that FDR intended to deliver somewhere in Wisconsin in early August on the subject of social security. After looking over a memorandum that was to serve as a basis for the speech, Frankfurter sent Moley a four-page, handwritten letter on July 25, 1934, which remained hidden in Moley's unpublished papers. This newly discovered missive provides vivid evidence of Frankfurter's intensely divided loyalties on the subject. The professor began by warning Moley: "It is perfectly clear that much and deep investigation and hard thinking . . . will be necessary as a preliminary to formulating a wise and politically sound program of economic-social security."[86] Consequently, Moley was told that

"F.D.R. must avoid the premature formulation of such a program in his . . . Wisconsin speech." Frankfurter argued that as a "campaign speech," the address should be a "call to arms," a "summons to action," and "an inspirational effort" rather than a "blueprint of legislation." Thus it must "restrict itself to a simple diagnosis of economic and social ills and the complementary neglects of society of these ills" until the necessary investigations of the subject have been completed. The professor then amplified on his rationale for delaying a commitment to any program:

> But what the precise methods should be—what schemes of legislation should be evolved appropriate to the various economic needs for security—what are appropriate to a continent like the U.S. as compared with a tight little island like England, what should be the effective relations between the central government and the states, between centralized and decentralized administration, how the wise remedies are to be fitted into our Constitutional scheme—all these questions and more, F.D.R should raise but not even begin to try to answer.
>
> For these *are* very grave questions—not merely of administration but of Constitutionality. [*Italics in original*]

Unlike Frankfurter's usually more vigorous support of Brandeis's "true faith," he exhibits in this letter a tolerance of something other than individual state administration of the program, an idea that was anathema to Brandeis.

> I think F.D.R. should point out emphatically that we need a national program, but a national program does not mean exclusively *national* Congressional legislation. It means nationwide action and national leadership but such leadership may be executed in part by State legislation or by regional legislation in conjunction with Congressional action. [*Italics in original*]

Frankfurter then amplified as to how the program could be administered by regional compacts among several states; in particular he described to Moley the compact by the seven New England and North Atlantic states for dealing with both minimum wages and uniform labor legislation, a viewpoint that would not have pleased Brandeis at all. The professor seemed to be couching his advice in terms that the Roosevelt team could accept. Most interesting, while Frankfurter had always carefully apprised Brandeis regarding each of his steps in his legislative battles, there is no evidence that the justice was ever informed about either this letter to Moley or its contents.

What Frankfurter did allow Brandeis to see was another of his letters, this one hand delivered by Moley to the president, which was designed to convey the same general message—but in very different terms. Here the professor reiterated the warning against making "premature commitments" in favor of a particular "social insurance" program in the upcoming address.[87] Calling on his vast experience as a legislative draftsman, Frankfurter declared that "the extreme intricacy" in formulating wise policies with "effective administration," given "the diversity of conditions in our various regions and even in the various states," made caution even more advisable. Still, the professor revealed even here his uncharacteristic ambivalence regarding which particular program should be adopted:

> The relative advantages and disadvantages of the Wisconsin plan as against the Ohio plan, and still more the relative advantages of a single, national scheme through the States but sponsored by the nation, or fostered by it, calls for long and careful exploration and thereafter a matured process of formation.[88]

This time, however, knowing that Brandeis would be reviewing the letter and had earlier suggested that FDR "ought to say something once about the Wisconsin law if he talks there,"[89] Frankfurter was careful to include a final paragraph that was not part of the first letter to Moley. Frankfurter asked the president: "If you are to speak in Wisconsin on this subject, would it not be well, by way of illustration of a commendable effort, without again committing yourself to the details of legislation, to refer to the characteristic pioneer[ing] legislation of Wisconsin in dealing with unemployment legislation?" From this last paragraph, and what Frankfurter was probably telling him in private talks, Brandeis had no reason to doubt the professor's attachment to the tax-offset/plant-reserves idea. Even still, the justice may not have been entirely happy with the tone of the letter, for, after reviewing it, instead of offering his usual words of praise, he wrote Frankfurter only that it "seem[ed] to be all right."[90] Important to note is that in these letters from Frankfurter, neither the man writing the speech, Raymond Moley, nor the man delivering it, Roosevelt, had been given any positive indication of a commitment by Frankfurter to the Brandeis proposal. Fortunately for the justice, perhaps in response to Frankfurter's primary advice to delay, FDR decided to avoid the social security issue entirely, and in Green Bay, Wisconsin on August 9, 1934, delivered instead a rather stock campaign speech entitled, "A Wider Opportunity for the Average Man."[91]

By this time Brandeis was clearly getting nervous about the outcome of this crusade. In fact, he was distressed to hear from Paul Raushenbush that Edwin Witte, a Wisconsin professor who had worked on the Wisconsin plant-reserves law and was now executive director of Perkins's Committee on Economic Security, was not willing to fight for the inclusion of the plant-reserves proposal in the new federal law; so distressed, in fact, that Brandeis met with him personally to discuss the issue in mid-August.[92] The prophet was now placing a great deal of faith in Felix Frankfurter's long-delayed reunion meeting, following his year at Oxford, with President Roosevelt in Hyde Park. So far as he knew, Brandeis had every reason to expect that his lieutenant would forcefully present to FDR the "true faith" on unemployment insurance. After all, he thought, they had worked side by side throughout the campaign to this point. Moreover, in anticipation of that meeting, Brandeis had even sent Frankfurter some instructions regarding the message he wanted conveyed: "When you see FDR . . . it will be advisable to reinforce what I said to him on employers bearing the whole cost;—which seemed to impress him favorably."[93]

However, when Frankfurter's two day conversation with the president in late August turned to the topic of unemployment insurance, the professor chose to maintain his strict neutrality toward the various plans under consideration. At the very moment when Brandeis's "true faith" could have been most forcefully, and perhaps most effectively, argued with the president, Frankfurter left its basic elements unexplored. Though, the professor proudly claimed in a letter to Brandeis to have "talk[ed] hard what [FDR] must get done through *states*" (*Italics in original*), thus by implication supporting Brandeis's approach to the administration of the plan, the intricacies of the plant-reserves and tax-offset aspects of the proposal were completely ignored. Instead, Frankfurter reported that he had decided to let "Witte's Committee impress F.D.R. with the facts as to the national show."[94] The severe problem with Frankfurter's strategy from Brandeis's perspective was that there was absolutely no guarantee at that point that the committee, now in active deliberations, would recommend anything close to the justice's proposal. The professor had chosen to stay on the middle road between Roosevelt and Brandeis. A fork in that road would come soon.

Fortunately for Brandeis, the president soon seemed to be leaning on his own toward the state-centered approach for administering unemployment insurance. In November 1934, the president delivered before the National Conference on Economic Security an address, written for him by Frances Perkins and her committee, in favor of the federal-state system.[95] By late December, one of the advocates of a central administration for the national program, Rexford Tugwell, realized that the battle was slipping away from him. He presumed in his personal diary that the "Frankfurter and Brandeis influence on FDR has just been too strong."[96]

On January 15, 1935, following bitter debate, the members of the Committee on Economic Security recommended in a report to FDR that the Wagner-Lewis, federal-state system of unemployment insurance be adopted. One of the paramount considerations in this decision was the inevitable constitutional test of the program, particularly of the use of federal taxing power to coerce state action. But in addition to having already received supportive messages from two members of the present Court, the committee also realized that under the federal-state plan, even were the overall national program declared unconstitutional, by the time the issue reached the High Court the individual state plans would be in place to handle the problem. This decision squared with the president's, as by now, Rexford Tugwell protested in his personal diary, FDR "seemed determined [to have] state autonomy" in drafting insurance plans. While Tugwell, writing in his diary, strenuously objected to this idea, he added, "the Brandeis-Frankfurter influence has been sufficient to determine the President's mind on the matter."[97]

The bill Roosevelt eventually decided to include in his 1935 legislative program was a compromise unemployment insurance plan, based on a watered-down version of the Wagner-Lewis proposal. Like that measure, a payroll tax was placed on employers only and there were no federally imposed benefit standards. But the changes from the original idea were quite significant. The payroll tax was limited to 3 rather than 5 percent, and those states choosing to adopt a Brandeisian plant-reserves plan were required to pool one-third of the receipts from each industry.

These alterations were too much for the uncompromising prophet, who was not ready to accept anything less than his "true faith." So troubled had been Brandeis by the 1 percent pooled-funds requirement that he had pleaded with Frankfurter in a handwritten letter dated December 31, 1934 to have "Tom and Ben . . . finish away this compromise and doubtless others which will be troublemakers . . . [and to] strive for the simon-pure article."[98] Despite considerable efforts by supporters of the Wisconsin plan—such as Robert and Philip LaFollette and Paul Raushenbush—the "objectionable features" of the proposal, as Brandeis termed them in a private letter to Frankfurter, were not removed. In the end, the disappointed justice expressed to Frankfurter his belief "that political considerations were the main cause of the unfortunate abandonment [by FDR] of the Wagner-Lewis bill."[99] Unknown to him, though, it was perhaps these same political considerations that had also caused Frankfurter's ambivalence about pushing the Brandeis plan on FDR in the latter stages of the drafting process.

On August 15, 1935, during the ceremony when FDR signed into law the social security measure, including the unemployment insurance provision, there was one person who once again was unable to step forward to receive the souvenir pen he so richly deserved—Supreme Court Justice Louis D. Brandeis. Unique among the lobbyists in this as well as all of the other legislative campaigns, however, Brandeis had one special and very useful tool—fear. There can be little doubt that his position on the Court, one that afforded him a final naysaying vote regarding legislation, undoubtedly added to the persuasiveness of his already formidable intellect and political expertise in his lobbying efforts. As he had openly warned when speaking about other programs earlier in 1935, there was always the possibility that Brandeis might resort to declaring the policy unconstitutional if it was not adopted in accordance with his wishes. While there were no such open threats this time, and Brandeis throughout presented himself only as a private citizen, the administration officials and even the president himself heard the words of the Supreme Court justice.

Despite these private lobbying endeavors, as he had done before, Brandeis remained on the Court when the unemployment insurance provisions of the law were tested in 1937, in the case of *Steward Machine Company v. Davis*.[100] This time, however, in voting with the majority to uphold the measure, Brandeis did not follow his usual practice of minimally participating in the case by concurring separately, but without written explanation, with one of the opinions. The reason for the change, though, was probably not due to a new attitude by Brandeis about such overlaps in his judicial and political roles. Knowing that in a constitutional decision a majority opinion must have five votes to be of full precedential value, Brandeis, as the fifth signer in this case, had no choice but to go along completely with Justice Benjamin Cardozo's opinion, if he wanted the law to be unequivocally upheld.

Throughout Brandeis's whole crusade for unemployment insurance, only Rexford Tugwell privately voiced complaint, or even surprise, about the justice's extensive dual role in this campaign. One can only wonder what would have been the result if Tugwell had followed General Hugh Johnson's lead in educating the general public at that time about the advice offered during the incubation period of the program by an associate justice of the Supreme Court.

After 1937 there was little further danger of public discovery of Brandeis's political activity, for that year marked the severe diminution of his influence, not only with the Roosevelt Administration, but even with his own lieutenants. The relationship the justice had enjoyed with his allies—Frankfurter, Corcoran, and Cohen—had been tempered in recent years by the growing loyalty to FDR of each of these men. Thus far, only once had they been forced to consider choosing between the two men—after the 1935 decisions by the Supreme Court holding so much of the New Deal legislation unconstitutional. However, Roosevelt's Judicial Reorganization Act of 1937, which represented a frontal attack on the Supreme Court as an institution, created the second such setting.

Bolstered by the overwhelming mandate in the 1936 election, Roosevelt proposed on February 5, 1937 a vast reorganization of the federal judiciary. Included in the measure was a Court-packing plan by which one new member would be added to the Supreme Court for each sitting justice over the age of seventy, the total membership not to exceed fifteen. FDR argued that the additional justices were necessary to make the Court more efficient, and to enable it to handle the burgeoning caseload. But the president's true motives were quite plain. By staffing the Court with additional New Deal justices, he could prevent the conservative bench, then commonly called the "Nine Old

Men," from continuing to strike down his programs. Almost immediately, Louis D. Brandeis, at age eighty the oldest member of the high Court, prepared to scuttle the president's program. The precautions he had taken over the years to maintain his distance from the president while still advising him now gave him enough freedom, both politically and psychologically, to wage this battle.[101]

Brandeis conducted his fight in characteristic fashion—through an intermediary. Since his usual allies were unavailable for this campaign, he turned to Democratic Senator Burton K. Wheeler of Montana. His main concern was to expose the plan's true motives by demonstrating the fallacy of the claim that the Court was falling behind in its work. At Brandeis's suggestion, Wheeler called on Chief Justice Hughes and convinced him to write a letter completely rebutting the charges on inefficiency. This document, which carried with it the expressed approval of Justices Brandeis and Van Devanter, was used by Wheeler in Senate hearings, and it proved to be pivotal in the ultimate rejection of the bill.[102]

As the controversy continued to rage, according to the oral history of newspaperman Marquis Childs, Brandeis continued to bolster the spirits of the embattled Senator Wheeler. At one point Childs even passed along Brandeis's news that the plan would soon be unnecessary for the success of the New Deal, because one of the more conservative justices (presumably Willis Van Devanter) was secretly preparing to retire. While Childs was careful never to reveal the source of his information, there could be little doubt in Wheeler's mind that it had originated with Brandeis.[103] In the end, thanks in part to Brandeis's efforts, the reorganization plan was not approved by Congress.

The price paid by Brandeis personally for such open opposition to FDR was extremely high. For one thing, it had an immediate impact on the behavior of the lieutenants they shared. Prior to this time, for instance, Brandeis had enjoyed the unquestioning loyalty of Thomas Corcoran, who had always lobbied for the justice's political programs even if he did not always agree with them. Within a short while after the Court-packing fight, however, Corcoran's opinion of the justice drastically changed. Benjamin Cohen, who was still on close terms with both men, sent a handwritten letter to Frankfurter on October 11, 1937, explaining Corcoran's new attitude. He reported that after being told of Brandeis's interest in seeing him, Corcoran had said:

> I am not going to see him. He did not shoot straight with us last year,
> and it is best not to renew the relationship. The Skipper is very bitter,
> and I think it best that he should not think that we are in touch with
> him.[104]

While Cohen hoped that Frankfurter would speak with Corcoran about
the matter, there is no evidence that the professor did anything to
improve the situation. So, with the exception of one courtesy visit by
Corcoran at the close of the 1937 Court term, he never spoke to Brandeis again.

Perhaps the severest penalty Brandeis paid for his leading role in
opposing FDR's Court-packing plan was that it brought about an end
to his special relationship with Felix Frankfurter. The initial proposal
of the plan left the Harvard professor in a quandary, for it had finally
trapped him between his two friends. The central intermediary between Brandeis and Roosevelt for nearly a decade, he was now forced
to choose between them. The reaction of both of his friends—each of
them within a week of the announcement of the plan seeking to test
the professor's continued loyalty—made that fact eminently clear to
Frankfurter. On February 6, 1937, one day after the Court-packing plan
was initially proposed, a puzzled Brandeis wrote the Harvard professor: "Whom did FD[R] rely on for his Judiciary Messages and bill?
Has he consulted you on any of his matters of late?"[105] Little did the
justice know, in fact there is no evidence to suggest that he ever found
out, Roosevelt also contacted Frankfurter. Though the president had
not consulted with the professor before proposing the program, three
days after Brandeis's query was written, FDR wrote Frankfurter a letter of his own, marked "privatissimo," in which he defended the plan
and asked for assistance in securing its passage.[106]

Only a foolish man would fail to realize that such aid would be
remembered when it came time to make important appointments—
such as to the United States Supreme Court.[107] Yet close friends opposed to the plan, such as New York attorneys Charles C. Burlingham
and Grenville Clark, certain at the time that they could count on
Frankfurter's opposition to the plan, implored him to "speak out loud
and clear against the proposal."[108] Even today, Frankfurter's former
allies speculate and debate over his actual position on the plan.[109]
Unfortunately, we may never know for sure about Frankfurter's own
views, because his crucial 1937 diary was stolen from the Library of
Congress and, despite efforts that included a public plea by columnist

Jack Anderson, it has never been recovered.[110] What is known is that moved either by his greater loyalty to FDR, his intense disapproval of the Supreme Court's callous treatment of one New Deal policy after another, or perhaps even his own sense of self-interest, Frankfurter chose to maintain a public silence on his own position, while privately offering advice and supporting documents to the president's men.[111]

Regardless of his views on the merits of the plan itself, Frankfurter clearly expressed his opinion about Brandeis's public opposition to FDR during this period. Despite their two decades of intimate friendship and near-total agreement on all policy matters, Frankfurter so deeply resented Brandeis's actions in this controversy that it seems to have caused a permanent strain in their friendship.[112] The extent of Frankfurter's anger at the public comment by the Court is revealed in a four-page typed letter he drafted on March 26, 1937 and ultimately chose not to send to the justice.

> I know that some subjects are not to be canvassed. But I should stifle my conscience if I withheld comment on the C.J.'s statement. . . . For one who has watched the Supreme Court for now thirty years as closely as a mother watches a sick child[,] it has been none too easy to keep quiet while this debate has been raging. The C.J.'s statement does not make it easier. . . . I resent the C.J.'s putting you in the front line even with your approval. . . . The core of our difficulty with reference to the Court is the immunity which the Court has enjoyed in being supposedly aloof from politics and, therefore, immune from the conditions under which political controversy is conducted. The Court cannot be allowed to enjoy this immunity and at the same time skillfully take advantage, as does the Chief's statement, of all the opportunities for influencing political action.[113]

Though the attack here was directed against the Chief Justice, it was clearly Brandeis who had disappointed Frankfurter the most. The fact that Frankfurter, who had never openly disagreed with Brandeis, would even consider sending such a strenuously critical letter as this one to the justice indicates the depth of his emotion on this issue.

While their years of intimate friendship made it impossible for the aggrieved professor to fully convey his sense of outrage to the justice directly, he made certain that Brandeis understood his true emotions. Seeking, he wrote in the margin of another letter dated July 15, 1937, "to have as much content of candor in his relationship [with Brandeis] . . . and to let him know as tactfully as [he could], as much as possible of [his thinking]," Frankfurter decided to send a message to the justice that attacked the president's opponents on the Court-reorganization measure. Though the professor recorded that his letter was "perhaps unwise," he wrote Brandeis that Senator Burton Wheeler's "canonization of [Chief Justice Charles Evans] Hughes [was] positively indecent" and that he "deeply resent[ed] his persistent effort to identify [Brandeis] with the Court and to use [him] as a screen for hiding its grave abuses in the past."[114] Since Frankfurter surely knew that these individuals—Chief Justice Hughes and Senator Burton Wheeler—shared Brandeis's views on this matter, the indirect criticism was very thinly veiled. Just to make sure the message was clear, the professor informed mutual friends about the rift that had opened between the two old allies.

Given the events of the prior few years, one might not be surprised that Frankfurter's letter to FDR on this issue read as it did: "That Brandeis should have been persuaded to allow the Chief to use his name is a source of sadness to me that I need hardly dwell on to you."[115] However, by sending a nearly identical statement to Judge Julian Mack on March 24, 1937, and later mentioning the rift to New York attorney Charles C. Burlingham, Frankfurter could be confident that the message would eventually be relayed to the justice.[116]

Frankfurter voiced three areas of objection to this public judicial opposition to the Court-packing plan. Initially, he wrote Burlingham in a letter dated June 9, 1937, that his sense of judicial proprieties was offended by the Chief Justice [and by implication Brandeis] acting "just as political as the President."[117] After two decades of working with such a political justice, however, one has to question the sincerity of this charge. Perhaps it was simply the open discussion of Brandeis's position that bothered Frankfurter. More likely, he was distressed by the fact that it served to oppose and even embarrass his close friend, Franklin D. Roosevelt.

Second, two private letters from Justice Harlan Fiske Stone to Frankfurter, both of which were forwarded to Charles C. Burlingham, provide evidence that Frankfurter objected to the impression left by the Chief Justice that he was speaking for the "entire Court." The professor was fully aware that Justice Harlan Fiske Stone was not consulted regarding the Chief Justice's letter and would never have signed it had he been asked.[118] However, sympathy for Stone's difficulties on the Court hardly explains the intensity of Frankfurter's criticism of Brandeis here.

The third, and perhaps most important objection related to the "gross violation" by the Court of the "settled practice against delivering an advisory opinion on a political issue." These views were made very plain in another private letter, one Frankfurter did mail to Brandeis:

> As to the Chief—I have long written him down as a Jesuit—I deplored his letter and certainly its form. Of course, the President was given unreliable and untrue figures (I know not by whom), but that hardly excuses the Chief Justice for intervening in a political fight by pretending not to, and doing so in the form in which he did. . . . I have just finished with my class the consideration of the problem of advisory opinions and why they are bad and why they should be abjured. What am I to tell them, when they ask me—as they did— about the C.J.'s disregard for solemn Supreme Court doctrine? Not even in a Chief Justice can the end justify the means. I am very sorry to write thus, but I am very, very sad.[119]

Once again, Frankfurter could not bring himself to criticize Brandeis directly, but that did not prevent him from making his true feelings known.

Brandeis chose not to respond to any of these charges by letter, preferring, he wrote Frankfurter, to discuss them in person. While there is no record of their conference on the matter, which was held some time in the month of April, there can be little doubt that the justice knew precisely where the Harvard professor's loyalties now lay.[120]

As a result of this divergence in their views, former Frankfurter law clerk Edward F. Prichard, Jr., remembers, from this point on Brandeis and Frankfurter were much more cautious and reserved with each other.[121] The letters between them after 1937 confirm Prichard's observation by providing vivid evidence of the strained relationship. They wrote much less frequently now, a fact that can, in part, be explained by Brandeis's advancing age. However, these letters also do not have the same sense of intimacy that was present before. The comments of each man were now reduced to occasional gossip and pedantic observations regarding the implementation of their political programs.[122] Moreover, in writing to other friends about the Court-packing incident, Frankfurter made clear by implication that he did not identify with his old mentor's stance in this controversy. This message, penned to Burlingham on June 9, 1937, is typical of Frankfurter's expressions on the subject, if not truly indicative of his feelings.

> I suppose [Harvard Constitutional Law professor] T[homas] R[eed] Powell is right when he says, "It serves you right. You have done more than any one person to build up respect for the Supreme Court." And now I am hoist by my own petard, having built up a myth of infallible respectability behind which all sorts of shennanigan is allowed to go unchallenged. You see I take the law very seriously.[123]

While moving in its sentiment, this self-portrayal by Professor Frankfurter bears little relationship to his own behavior when he later donned the black robes.

After the Court-packing controversy, Brandeis's extrajudicial career came full circle, ending as it had begun. With his influence in the administration virtually ended, and his lieutenant now on another team, Brandeis devoted what energy he had left to one of the issues that had so concerned him throughout his long career in public life— the plight of the Jewish people. During his final two years on the bench, and for the remaining two and one-half years of his life following his retirement, the prophet tried to convince the administration to safeguard the future of the Jewish homeland in Palestine and to relax the immigration quotas for Jews wishing to flee the imminent holocaust.

Throughout the 1930s, a period of declining involvement but not interest in the Zionist cause for the justice, he had warned about the tightening web of Nazism that surrounded Jews in Germany and throughout Europe. Troubled by what he perceived as an anti-Semitic influence in the American government and public, Brandeis repeatedly lectured Felix Frankfurter about these problems and directed him to seek liberalization of the country's immigration policies.[124] While some progress had been made, Brandeis decided by late 1937 to press more forcefully.

Still eager to insure that the British observe their mandate in Palestine, Brandeis met with David Ben Gurion to make clear his emphatic disapproval of any partitioning of the region.[125] Just as important, the British were preventing the oppressed and endangered European Jews from entering Palestine and other British colonies, and in late 1938 Brandeis decided to communicate directly with the president on this matter. Perhaps he believed, and quite rightly so, that this issue was too important to FDR to let their former political squabbles impede their cooperation. After two meetings with the president, the second at FDR's request, the administration did follow up its informal diplomatic efforts with the British ambassador, by issuing a public statement intended to push the British into allowing increased Jewish immigration into Palestine.[126]

The prophet's wide-ranging extrajudicial political crusade was brought to an end by his retirement from the Supreme Court on February 13, 1939. "Isaiah," the oracle, had dreamed such visions for America and now at age eighty-two, in reflecting on his twenty-two years of politics off the bench he had much reason to be satisfied. While the government had not yet absolutely followed his "true faith," it was much closer than it had been in 1916, closer even than it had been in 1933. More people were back to work, and those who were not had governmental support in their time of need; the rich were paying more in taxes; there would be no more Great Depressions brought on by stock market abuses; the holding companies for the utility industry were being pared and regulated; more responsibility was placed in the state governments; and the federal agencies were loaded with Brandeis's allies, protégés, and supporters, who would solidify these gains by their daily decisions.

One perhaps could argue that these accomplishments would not have been lost even if Brandeis had remained in his cloistered existence and allowed his followers to set the legislative agenda by relying solely on his earlier writings. But such an argument—that Brandeis's direct intervention was unnecessary—ignores the realities of American politics. This argument assumes that in the marketplace of government bureaucrats, certain proposals will well up through the agencies on their own merits and come to be adopted by the administration, and pass Congress on their merits. Instead, just as ideas in a pluralistic society need effective presentation by skilled advocates to gather electoral support, so policies in a diffuse governmental structure require action by dedicated lobbyists to secure their adoption. And in this sometimes mad scramble, the prophet well knew, fortune, if not the Lord himself, shines on those who help themselves.

6

The Monk in the Palace Guard I:
Felix Frankfurter
and the Preparation for War

When one considers the intensity of Frankfurter's political passions, and the fact that he had witnessed firsthand the great difficulties and even greater risks that had attended Brandeis's attempts to conduct his wide-ranging political activities from the high Court, one wonders why Frankfurter ever aspired to his own seat on the Supreme Court. But in one of those ironies of human nature, this was precisely where Frankfurter had always longed to be. What other person in America, he must have argued to himself, better understood the Court and its work than he? After all, besides the long-standing special relationship he had had with Brandeis, he had supplied his best students as law clerks for Oliver Wendell Holmes and Benjamin Cardozo, and had been a frequent correspondent of Harlan Fiske Stone, who even asked him to lecture newly appointed Justice Hugo L. Black on what was expected of a member of the high Court.[1] As well, how could the possibility of his own appointment not have been on his mind after Roosevelt had twice mentioned an intention to put him there and he had been told by others that, ironically, only Brandeis's failure to retire may have prevented his appointment earlier?[2]

Still, when Benjamin Cardozo died on July 9, 1938, it seemed that geography and religion might still keep Frankfurter from being Roosevelt's choice. Fortunately for Frankfurter, his friends in high places—

Thomas Corcoran, Benjamin Cohen, Secretary of the Interior Harold Ickes, Secretary of Commerce Harry Hopkins,* and Solicitor General Robert Jackson—were not to be denied.[3] They convinced FDR to appoint Frankfurter to this vacancy, rather than wait for Brandeis to retire. Ironically, exactly two weeks after Frankfurter took his seat on the Supreme Court, Brandeis did retire, to be replaced by William O. Douglas, who was then chairman of the Securities and Exchange Commission.

According to Frankfurter, who frequently was heard castigating others for "trying to re-write and pre-empt history" in their memoirs and diaries,[4] it was his "vivid" recollection that he was shocked at receiving word of his appointment in early January 1939. Caught by a telephone call from the president while dressing for dinner, all he could manage to say was, "I wish my mother were alive." Then, as he recalls the moment, he "probably stuttered and stammered" while making arrangements for an additional call the next day to receive word on congressional reaction to the appointment. In closing Frankfurter records that "this nomination came like a bombshell."[5]

While the "bombshell" reference adds a nice touch, it should be pointed out that the air-raid sirens had been sounding for days. According to one friend's recollection, Benjamin Cohen later commented, "I don't know why Felix was so surprised. Tom [Corcoran] was vigorously lobbying for his appointment and would call him every night to report what had been done. And he did it all on my phone!"[6]

Now that he had his appointment, Frankfurter faced the same hard decision confronting all politically inclined individuals about to enter the judicial "cloister"—whether or not to continue in his pre-judicial interests. Though he had proclaimed to Charles C. Burlingham only two years earlier that he "[took] the law very seriously," it is probably safe to say that the thought of giving up his political activities never even occurred to him.[7] Schooled in the ways of being a politician on the bench, Frankfurter fully understood the illusory nature of any hard-and-fast proscription against extrajudicial work. Moreover, still fired up by that personal drive that had made him such a marvelously effective lobbyist for Brandeis, Frankfurter would have had to beat into

---

*Hopkins was sworn into this post on December 24, 1938, seven days before he and Robert Jackson, who had just been moved from assistant attorney general to solicitor general, discussed the Supreme Court vacancy with the president over lunch. Prior to that time Hopkins had served as Administrator of the Works Progress Administration.

submission his own nature before he could have adopted a totally apolitical posture.

In addition, he knew well the other rewards of politicking off the bench. Here was a means of influencing even those policies that might never come before any court and to do so in a direct fashion and with possibly immediate results. Furthermore, it did not take a crystal ball to foresee in 1939 the terrible road that lay ahead for the United States. For a man like Frankfurter, whose sense of patriotism has been described by Harvard Law Professor Paul Freund as so "unabashed" that it was "almost childlike,"[8] remaining inactive in a time of national crisis would have been unthinkable.

However, Frankfurter began his tenure just as Brandeis had, by publicly associating himself with the popular tradition of judicial seclusion. After the public announcement of his appointment, he told reporters at a press conference: "I am, of course, sensible to the obligation and the honor involved, otherwise, I have nothing to say."[9] Then he shed the outward trappings of his activist, liberal connections, resigning his memberships in such organizations as the NAACP and the ACLU. It was at this point, however, that Frankfurter, the long-time understudy, diverged from the script he had inherited from his mentor and played the role that was now his the only way he knew how—as himself.

Early on in his career as a Supreme Court justice, Frankfurter demonstrated his remarkable political acumen. From the time of his appointment until 1945 Frankfurter used all his political resources to pursue a number of separate extrajudicial campaigns united into one great theme—win the war by aiding the allies, most especially Great Britain. When it became apparent that the network of political power around him was changing dramatically, he proved he could still sustain himself as a potent force. As it became clear that the circle of contacts he had developed in his pre-judicial role as lieutenant for Justice Brandeis would not be adequate to bring his own political plans to fruition, Frankfurter simply went out and recruited new allies from among the more recent waves of newcomers to Washington. Where necessary, he arranged for some of his old allies to be shifted to new governmental positions, placed greater importance on persons who until that time had been on the periphery of his political army, and, relying on his unique ability both to recruit and then shape the attitudes of newcomers, expanded his network by increasing the overall numbers in his force.

There is no question that another factor in Frankfurter's ability to sustain his political prominence and persuasiveness in Washington policymaking circles was his position as a Supreme Court justice. As with Brandeis before him, the force of his ideas, formidable in their own right, seemed to take on added lustre when offered from the pinnacle of the judicial system. But while Brandeis had received special consideration from politicians who were acutely aware of the possibility that he might later be sitting in review of their policies, this apprehension did not exist for those dealing with Frankfurter's political excursions during his early years on the bench. Most of these early activities involved wartime policies, which are seldom litigated in the courts.[10] Moreover, it was commonly understood that even if such issues did reach the Supreme Court, in times of such crisis the patriotic justices almost certainly could be expected to support the government's position.[11]

Nevertheless, Frankfurter's special position as a member of the high Court did increase his influence in one other way. As a justice he was, in a political sense, a free agent. He had no constituency to serve, no bureaucratic turf to defend, no governmental philosophy to implement, and, more important, no apparent personal desires beyond the pure desire to serve the nation. So, while very nearly everyone in Washington could be suspected of jockeying for position and status, special attention would be paid to that "impartial observer, Felix," who had already reached the pinnacle of his career ambitions.

Undoubtedly, though, the most important source of Frankfurter's private political influence in Washington's decisionmaking circles was the fact that he enjoyed the confidence and friendship of the most important public official in the nation—President Franklin D. Roosevelt. By 1939, the relationship between these two men had blossomed into one of great intimacy. After years of having battled side by side with FDR for common political goals, all the while maintaining the ties of friendship through the aid of the postal service, telephone wires, and an occasional overnight visit to Washington or Hyde Park, Frankfurter now was able to walk to the White House, if he so desired, and enjoy cocktails or dinner with the president. Moreover, the invitations to visit overnight at "Frank's" summer retreat in Hyde Park now came with increasing frequency. In fact, according to one inside observer of these events, from 1939 to 1941 Frankfurter remained in almost daily contact with FDR either through personal visits, short, handwritten notes, or phone calls.[12]

Over the years, their relationship had, in fact, developed to a point that Roosevelt, an inveterate prankster, became one of the few people who was able to joke with Frankfurter, even to the extent of occasionally teasing him. For example, there was the time in May 1941 when Frankfurter had received an official United States Army document asking why as a major in the Reserves he had earned no training credits toward a full reappointment. When the adjutant general reassured Frankfurter eight months later that he was doing "very important work" on the Supreme Court and thus would be excused from active service, the justice could not resist forwarding the letter to "My dear C[ommander]-i[n]-C[hief]" and signing his covering letter "Respectfully and martially yours."[13] But FDR was not to be outdone. He told Frankfurter that he "would look awfully well in uniform" and offered to send him to Wake Island where he could "re-capture it single-handed," and then "be buried in Arlington—the ultimate goal of every good soldier."[14] When Frankfurter was later placed on inactive reserve in 1943, the president kidded that an error had been made: "I think [the Army] meant 'Inactive Preserve'. The status is somewhat akin to the process of pickling in alcohol!"[15] With this close relationship Frankfurter would clearly have no trouble in speaking directly to the president on matters of importance.

Despite enjoying this unique access to the president, Frankfurter recognized that to be truly effective in promoting his political ideas he would need to develop other contacts in the highest echelons of the administration. Only in this fashion could the justice remain continually informed as to the policy agenda under consideration, and also be certain that at least if his views were not then being aired, perhaps they might subsequently be solicited. Initially, it appeared that Frankfurter's old allies would provide him with the needed access to the inner White House circle. After all, two of his most devoted political protégés, Thomas Corcoran and Benjamin V. Cohen, were now among the president's closest advisers. Perhaps, the old relationship he had enjoyed with them in drafting legislation during the 1930s could operate with even more efficiency now that he too was in Washington.

No one could deny the success the three had had, with Frankfurter in Cambridge supplying the ideas (many of which had originated with Justice Brandeis), and with Corcoran and Cohen, his two former students, in Washington moving the entire administration in the desired direction. Nor is there any question that during this early period, Frankfurter was the guiding force behind their numerous endeavors; whenever he traveled to Washington, it was as though their commanding general had come to visit. They would gather around him to receive their latest marching orders. For his part, Frankfurter encouraged his "boys" to be forceful, independent, and innovative in pushing the programs. If it became necessary for Corcoran to "break a few eggs" in advocating legislation drafted by Cohen, then that was what was expected. By 1939, however, the situation was different. Frankfurter, then fifty-six years old, was no longer the teacher, and Corcoran and Cohen, then thirty-eight and forty-four years old respectively, had ideas, a following, and reputations of their own. After all, for seven years these two men had drafted and helped to pass some of the most important legislation in this country. They were the ones now owed favors for jobs they had secured for others. Their contacts were now being used to influence the many agencies of the administration. Perhaps Frankfurter should have recognized that dealing with his two former followers would now have to be on an entirely new basis. But he did not.

While other students and former law clerks willingly continued to act as the justice's messenger boys, these two were offended by the prospect. Perhaps Benjamin Cohen said it best when he complained to a friend one day: "Felix is incapable of having adult relationships!" [16] He went on to explain that Frankfurter seemed to relate well to his mentors—men like Brandeis, Stimson, and Holmes—and to his students, but never to his peers. Quite clearly, Cohen, as well as Corcoran, had come to view themselves as having graduated from the second to the third group. Although Frankfurter did indeed have solid relationships with some people who could be considered peers—such as Judge Learned Hand and Dean Acheson—there is no question that the justice was insensitive to the needs of his two oldest protégés. When he steadfastly refused to treat the two men as his equals, a rift gradually developed between them.

The first signs of a break between Frankfurter and Thomas Corcoran came in the first weeks of 1941. Because Corcoran had developed a number of enemies in the earlier legislative battles, there was talk of repositioning him somewhere else in the administration. In the course of this discussion, Frankfurter sent an enigmatic memorandum to FDR in January 1941 offering his view regarding the decision to be taken. After expressing support for Corcoran, the justice went on to describe his former assistant as "lack[ing] mental health just now," and being "in great danger" of doing "vast harm to himself and . . . to the present national effort." What was needed, wrote Frankfurter, was to "find the square hole for Tom's square peg."[17] On the basis of his interviews with the justice, journalist Max Freedman observed that "to Frankfurter's regret," Corcoran had lost FDR's confidence, and though he "mistakenly blamed" the justice for being one of his critics, the presidential assistant had no knowledge "of Frankfurter's repeated praise of the unique gifts brought to the service of the President by the Tommy Corcoran-Ben Cohen team."[18] There are indications, however, that the real motivation for this memorandum was Frankfurter's fear that Benjamin Cohen, whom the justice had described as "indispensable in a variety of ways, because of his extraordinary resourcefulness and imagination and his rare gifts of character," would resign from the government if his long-time ally were forced out.[19]

It is now possible, through the use of unpublished documents gleaned from the official files of the Roosevelt Administration, as well as through interviews with close observers of these events, to reconstruct the events leading to, and the results of, the final falling out between Corcoran and Frankfurter in mid-1941. Searching for a new position in government, Corcoran was then seeking support for his appointment to the one position he most wanted—solicitor general of the United States. It had long been customary for members of the Court to recommend candidates for this job as central litigator for the Department of Justice. Four personal letters from Justices Black, Byrnes, Reed, and Douglas sent directly to the president, and discovered in the files at the Roosevelt Presidential Library, indicate that Corcoran had successfully convinced these four to support his appointment.[20] Needing only one more letter, Corcoran went to visit Frankfurter, certain in the knowledge that here would be his fifth vote. However, according to one interview source who knew both men well, Corcoran did not get the type of reception he had been expecting. In his meeting with the justice, Corcoran explained that four members of the Supreme Court had already signed letters to the president supporting his nomination to the solicitor generalship, and since a majority vote would be more impressive, he asked if Frankfurter would do the same. To Corcoran's amazement, however, Frankfurter, his teacher and the man in whose name he had waged some of the toughest legislative battles seen in Washington for many decades, now not only refused to sign a simple letter of recommendation, but would not even offer an explanation for his action. It is said that from that day forward the two men never spoke again.

When mutual friends later criticized the justice for not supporting Corcoran, who had given the Brandeis-Frankfurter political crusade years of loyal service, he argued that it was only his concern for FDR that had kept him from doing so. "You see," the justice explained to a friend one day, "Roosevelt would have faced a long confirmation fight over this appointment because of Tom's past exploits, and in the face of preparing for war this would be terribly damaging to the President and to the Nation." Of course, it could and should be argued that this political calculation would have been made at the appropriate time by the man with the appointment power—Franklin D. Roosevelt. The possibility presents itself, therefore, that the real reason for Frankfurter's action was neither patriotism nor presidential allegiance, but purely personal antagonism toward Corcoran. By this time, he had become convinced that Corcoran was, in the words of one close observer, "too big for his britches" and needed to be taken down a notch.

The acrimonious rift between Frankfurter and Corcoran became all too evident in May 1942, when Joseph L. Rauh, Jr., the justice's former law clerk, was leaving from Union Station in Washington to join the war effort in the South Pacific. Several of his friends, including Corcoran and Cohen, were gathered on the train platform wishing him well when Frankfurter approached. As soon as their eyes met, Corcoran spun on his heels and left the station without uttering another word or even saying goodbye to Rauh.[21]

A memorandum now filed in the Frankfurter papers at the Library of Congress indicates just how strained the relationship became between the justice and Corcoran by the end of the war. According to this memorandum, written by another one of Frankfurter's law clerks, Edward F. Prichard, Jr., who was then serving as general counsel in the Office of War Mobilization and Reconversion, Corcoran went about telling people that the administration was in "political and moral collapse" because the president had allowed the White House to be "run entirely" by Frankfurter and Harry Hopkins. According to Prichard's account, Corcoran perceived that the justice was interested only "in playing with whatever forces were on top."[22]

Frankfurter's split with Corcoran closed more than just one of the justice's avenues for exerting political influence. Corcoran himself turned out to be no real loss for Frankfurter's purposes because, after failing to secure the solicitor generalship, he left the government entirely, to become a prominent Washington lawyer-lobbyist. However, the incident also adversely affected Frankfurter's relationship with Benjamin Cohen. While these two men remained in contact, Cohen always believed that the justice was entirely wrong in not signing his friend's letter of recommendation. In his opinion, Frankfurter's debt to Corcoran was too great to have done otherwise.[23] Because of what he viewed as Frankfurter's betrayal, Cohen became less available as a political contact in the White House. Consequently in sharp contrast to the earlier Roosevelt years, concerted actions of Frankfurter and Cohen were much less frequent during the war period.

During 1939 and early 1940, though, Frankfurter did have one other possible channel to the White House inner circle—through one of the president's closest advisers, speechwriter Samuel I. Rosenman. On occasion he would send Rosenman long memoranda detailing the need for a speech in a certain area, but even more frequently the justice would forward to Rosenman unsolicited ideas, proposed wording, and even complete drafts for future speeches, many on highly partisan issues. While he also passed some of these same ideas on to Roosevelt directly, the justice found that more could be accomplished by working with the speechwriting team.[24]

Years later, when Rosenman sat down to write an account of his relationship with Frankfurter for his memoirs, a draft copy of the account was forwarded to the justice for corrections and comments, and then placed in Rosenman's private files, which are now held by the Roosevelt Presidential Library. Scribbled on this document, in Frankfurter's unmistakable handwriting, is a plea for the former speechwriter to add to his version that, in each of these events, the justice had "scrupulously observed the restrictions of the Supreme Bench."[25] Contrary to this disclaimer, however, there was an extensive involvement by Frankfurter in every phase of the highly partisan speechdrafting operation, and, unpublished memoranda by Samuel Rosenman, as well as private letters he received from the justice, enable us to reconstruct rather precisely the nature of this role. Knowing Frank-furter's ready availability for personal consultation, the speechwriters would visit his Georgetown home and exchange ideas on the wording of a major presidential address until the wee hours of the morning. Then the justice would review and make necessary revisions in each of the successive drafts. In true Frankfurter style, after the speech had been delivered an effusive message of support from the justice would nearly always be on the president's desk the following morning.[26] There can be little doubt that "F.F." was an essential component of the president's speechwriting operation. But Frankfurter was still dis-satisfied. In the role he had found himself in—that of presidential speechwriting adviser—he was not truly exerting influence on poli-cymaking, but only helping in the packaging and communication of programs to the general public. Thus, while Rosenman gave the jus-tice another line of effective access to the White House, he soon real-ized that it too had its limitations.

Since the old network appeared to offer few prospects for directing the day-to-day administration in the White House, Frankfurter set out to place other friends in positions of influence within the government. Ideally, he wanted to enlist those people with whom he had devel-oped long prior relationships of mutual trust and confidence. Such men would be willing listeners because they were already predis-posed toward Frankfurter's world view; the problem would be in plac-ing them in positions where they would have substantial impact on government policy. With the seeds of international conflict being sown, the justice made the War Department his prime target. His successful effort to restaff the upper hierarchy of this agency with allies illus-trates the special aggressive and personal style of Frankfurter's extra-judicial conduct, in marked contrast to that of his mentor, Louis D. Brandeis.

A marvelous record of Frankfurter's endeavors to help appoint the secretary of war is preserved in a document that Frankfurter himself placed in his personal papers. In the summer of 1947, the justice shared his recollections of the inception of the national military draft with a young Harvard University doctoral candidate, Samuel Spencer, Jr. The notes of this discussion offer Frankfurter's own account of how he and an old Harvard Law School classmate, Grenville Clark, had prepared the administration for the enactment of the Selective Training and Service Act by replacing the upper hierarchy of the War Department with men they knew to be allies in this cause. Though the events this account describes can now be confirmed by private letters written at that time, these unpublished materials were simply not made available during Frankfurter's lifetime to scholars writing about FDR's selection of a new secretary of war in 1940.[27]

According to Frankfurter's recollection, he had long been convinced that Secretary of War Henry Woodring should be replaced. Not only was Woodring overmatched by his official duties, but, in Frankfurter's opinion, his isolationist posture would create obstacles to undertaking the necessary preparations for war. From a conversation with FDR in May 1939, Frankfurter knew that the president shared his view. But Frankfurter also knew that Roosevelt was generally reluctant to remove subordinates directly, and so it did not surprise the justice that no action was taken on this matter for nearly a year.[28]

In late April 1940, Frankfurter was invited to the White House for lunch with the president. From long years of friendship with him, the justice knew that FDR had a particular pattern in dealing with vexatious problems. Though he presented a casual image with his spontaneous wit and flippant style, Roosevelt was always extremely slow and cautious in making final decisions on tough issues. Accordingly, during the two-hour lunch, Roosevelt indicated by repeatedly returning to the same issue that the difficulties in the War Department had reached a crisis point. Seeking Frankfurter's views regarding a replacement for Woodring, the president mentioned three possibilities of his own: former New York Mayor Fiorello LaGuardia, Secretary of the Interior Harold Ickes, and New York Governor Herbert Lehman. The justice raised objections to all three men, finding LaGuardia to be "quixotic and incalculable;" Ickes to be a "chronic complainer;" and Lehman to be "indecisive and inefficient." Finally, the two men parted without reaching a consensus on a candidate. Within a month, however, as German tanks rumbled through France, Frankfurter was suggesting to the president that he request the resignation of his entire cabinet in order to be "free to deal with this new [world] situation."[29]

It was not until May 31, 1940 that Frankfurter settled on his choice to replace the secretary of war.[30] That day he was visited by Grenville Clark, who was then lobbying for a selective service act and was also troubled by the inadequacy of the present leadership in the War Department. After agreeing that a new secretary was needed, the two men considered the prospective appointees. Since he had already discussed the issue with Roosevelt several times, Frankfurter felt confident that he could secure the appointment of whomever they decided would be best suited for the job. Within a few moments they had their man—Henry L. Stimson. As secretary of war in the Taft Administration and secretary of state for Herbert Hoover, he surely had the necessary experience and stature for the job. Here was a man who commanded the respect of other members of the administration as well as of the nation at large. In addition, the president had been toying with the idea of appointing a "coalition cabinet" in preparation for the war, and Stimson's affiliation with the Republican party would be useful here. The idea of placing Stimson in the War Department was even more appealing to Frankfurter for highly personal reasons. He hoped they could resume the working relationship they had enjoyed during the Taft years, when Frankfurter functioned as Stimson's assistant secretary. If not, at the very least, Stimson would be very receptive to the justice's advice, thus giving him a major voice in government policy-making.

The plan had one major flaw—Stimson was seventy-three years old. Not only might he be reluctant to assume such a burden at this time, but Roosevelt himself, having made age in government such a major issue in the "Court-packing" fight of 1937, might resist exposing himself to criticism by making such an appointment. So, Frankfurter and Clark devised a clever strategy of arranging a "dual ticket" for heading the War Department, consisting of both Stimson and a much younger nominee for assistant secretary. The man they settled on for the second post was a former Frankfurter student then serving on the United States Court of Appeals for the Second Circuit, Robert P. Patterson. More than just an extremely capable administrator, Patterson was dedicated to the policy of preparedness for war. In fact, he liked to point out on occasion that he wore a belt he had taken from a German bayoneted by him in World War I.[31] Frankfurter and Clark agreed that his vigor and toughness, combined with Stimson's experience, would provide the ideal combination of qualities necessary to revitalize a War Department plagued by failing leadership.

With his goal now firmly in mind, Felix Frankfurter, the politician, went to work. Since the Court would soon be recessing for the summer, he arranged to pay a farewell visit to FDR before leaving for Cambridge. He also dispatched Clark to investigate the state of each man's health and their willingness to serve in this capacity. The justice already knew that FDR was favorably disposed towards Stimson, having arranged several meetings with him prior to the president's inauguration in 1933 at which the two men reviewed foreign policy issues. Their relationship was nourished by intermittent contacts over the next few years. Then, exactly a month before Frankfurter would propose Stimson for the cabinet post, the justice, apparently coincidentally, organized another informal lunch between Stimson and the president to discuss foreign affairs. At that time, it seems, Roosevelt's high opinion of Stimson was reinforced.[32]

The entire appointment scheme was placed in jeopardy, however, when Grenville Clark ran into some difficulty. He had secured Patterson's agreement to accept the assistant's position. Moreover, since he and Stimson used the same doctor in New York, Clark was able to get private assurances regarding the latter's health. But Stimson himself proved to be a problem. After protesting to Clark that he was simply too old for the job, he agreed to accept the position only if four conditions were met. First, as a Republican, he needed to be released from the traditional loyalty demanded of any cabinet official. Then, Stimson insisted that the War Department adopt a selective service system immediately, a request that pleased Clark enormously. Third, he wanted absolute freedom to advocate publicly that the United States provide aid for the Allies presently fighting in Europe. Finally, Stimson required that he be able to choose his own assistant secretary. This last condition was quickly resolved when Clark explained Frankfurter's plan and mentioned the high regard that the justice had for Patterson. Even though Stimson was positive that the president would never accept these conditions, Clark immediately passed all his information along to Frankfurter.

By the time of their meeting on June 3, 1940, the justice was fully prepared to move to overcome any possible objection FDR might have to the plan. No sooner had their conversation begun when the president gave him a perfect opening by asking, according to Frankfurter's later account, "What am I going to do about the Secretaryship of War— Any ideas since I talked to you last?"

With that, the justice gave an impassioned pitch for his slate of Stimson and Patterson.[33] After pointing out their unique qualifications to fill an increasingly evident need, Frankfurter then carefully explained the four conditions Stimson had placed on his prospective appointment. Finally, Frankfurter preempted any objections to the candidate's age by proposing it as one of the advantages of the appointment. With his great experience, the justice argued, Stimson could quickly analyze important broader issues, while leaving the minor and mundane details to the much more active Patterson.

To Frankfurter's delight, Roosevelt's expression indicated to the justice that he had, in his words, "struck fire" with his suggestion. In fact, the president's only objection during this meeting was that he did not know very much about Patterson. Frankfurter was entirely willing to supervise the administration's legwork here. Grenville Clark later recalled that the justice asked him to draft a memorandum on Patterson's career, and the assignment was duly carried out by Clark's law partner, Elihu Root, Jr.[34]

Meanwhile, in a pattern typical of Frankfurter, he left nothing to chance. When he developed an idea, the justice was simply incapable of allowing fortuitous beginnings to bear their fruit in their own good time. So, the day after his meeting with FDR he wrote the president a long letter reiterating his choice for the position:

> Some things click—they seem just right—and I cannot help but feel that the combination of Stimson and Patterson would take off your shoulders a very great burden and would put the War Department in the charge of men on whom you could rely completely for their understanding and execution of your policies.[35]

On June 5, Frankfurter forwarded to FDR his redrafted version of Clark's detailed memorandum on Patterson's career and fitness for the post. But for the next two weeks there was no movement on the matter. Toward the end of this period a nervous Grenville Clark complained to the justice in a letter that "nothing whatever [was] happening to change the weak administration of the War Department" and asked if something could be done about it.[36]

Unbeknownst to Clark, however, Frankfurter was involved in an aspect of the investigation for the appointment so sensitive that it required his personal attention. In fact, so sensitive was the matter that it was not even mentioned by Frankfurter seven years later in his chat with Samuel Spencer, leaving the student with the impression that he did nothing more in this campaign and merely read about the appointment in the newspaper. But in truth, there was one loose end that remained to be tied up.

While visiting at the home of Thomas Reed Powell, the constitutional law specialist at Harvard, Frankfurter phoned his former student, Charles E. Wyzanski, Jr., who was then in private law practice, and invited him to come over for a chat.[37] It was a bright, sunny day as the two men sat in Powell's garden. There the justice innocently asked for Wyzanski's thoughts regarding the possible appointment of Robert Patterson as assistant secretary of war. Wyzanski had known Patterson for years, having first been introduced to him while serving as a law clerk to both federal Court of Appeals Judges Learned Hand and Augustus Hand, and later working with him on a committee drafting a model code of evidence. But he was quite taken aback at the prospect of this nomination, and told Frankfurter so. For Wyzanski had been visiting the Hands in their judicial chambers one day within the previous year and had observed Patterson in the throes of what appeared to be a complete nervous breakdown. In fact, the situation was so grave that the young lawyer had heard the Hands recommend to Patterson that he resign immediately from the Court of Appeals. Without revealing his motives, Frankfurter then questioned Wyzanski at great length about the specific details of the breakdown and his knowledge of Patterson's condition at the present time.

Wyzanski must have been amazed when, on June 20, 1940, Patterson was appointed assistant to the new secretary of war, Henry L. Stimson. Not until several years later did Wyzanski discover that he had not given Frankfurter disquieting news. It turned out that two men were being actively considered for the post of assistant secretary and that only the justice and Stimson knew that both candidates had previously suffered nervous breakdowns. Frankfurter, charged with investigating the degree of each man's incapacity, apparently gave the nod to Patterson.

Following the appointments, Frankfurter sent the usual congratulatory telegram to the White House praising FDR, this time for his "leadership."[38] Probably, a more accurate version of whose leadership the justice believed had been responsible is contained in a later letter to Grenville Clark. Frankfurter explains: "History is the interplay of . . . anonymous propelling forces and of individuals, so that a few individuals may make the difference in the impact and incidence, the triumph and deflection, of these anonymous forces."[39] Obviously, he believed, and quite rightly so, that he had proved himself one of these formative individuals in playing such a central role in Stimson's appointment.

Frankfurter's efforts to staff the War Department did not end with his successful campaign on behalf of Stimson and Patterson. He needed to place allies in the lower echelons of that agency as well, in order to insure proper implementation of his proposals. The first opportunity came in late 1940 when the Roosevelt Administration was being criticized by the nation's black population for reaffirming its support of racial segregation and for installing only white commanders in all-black military units. These actions, combined with the hostility caused by an assault on a black policeman by FDR's press secretary, Stephen Early, forced the administration, then locked in the 1940 presidential election campaign, to search for immediate means of repairing the damage.

One of Roosevelt's solutions was to suggest that Secretary of War Stimson appoint an assistant to deal with racial issues in the military. When the NAACP became aware of this proposal, its leaders asked Frankfurter to recommend for the post William H. Hastie, dean of the Howard University Law School. The justice required no great prodding to bring this matter before Secretary Stimson. Hastie's performance as a student in Frankfurter's class at Harvard had led the professor to call him "not only the best colored man we have ever had but he is as good as all but three or four outstanding white men that have been here during the last twenty years." [40] As with all his prize students, Frankfurter followed Hastie's career and wherever possible helped him move up. Back in 1930, when the NAACP was organizing a crack legal staff to litigate against segregation throughout society, Frankfurter had recommended to Morris Ernst that a place be found for Hastie "somewhere in your setup." [41] Then, when FDR was considering in 1935 whether to make Hastie the first black appointee to a United States district court judgeship, it was Felix Frankfurter who investigated his former student's qualifications for the post and recommended that the nomination be made. Consequently, by 1941 Frankfurter was only too willing to propose Hastie as an aide to Stimson. While the secretary recorded in his personal diary on October 22, 1940 that he objected to the idea of making the Hastie appointment as a political concession in an election year, he agreed to add him to the staff. [42]

In April 1941, two other Frankfurter allies—both corporate attorneys—were placed in key War Department positions. Realizing that Stimson's spirits had begun to drag because of the pressures of the heavy workload, the secretary of war's personal diary reveals that Frankfurter arranged for Harvey H. Bundy, a former law clerk to Oliver Wendell Holmes and assistant secretary of state under Stimson, to come to Washington as special assistant in the War Department.[43] An even more important addition to the staff for Frankfurter's purposes, however, was one made without his careful preparation. John J. McCloy, one of the justice's former students and a prominent Wall Street attorney, was appointed assistant secretary of war. Having served as Stimson's special assistant on various matters for the previous six months, McCloy needed no letter of introduction. While no documentary evidence was found to support the suspicion, it seems highly likely that Frankfurter also added his recommendation. Though the two men had never been especially close at Harvard, their friendship immediately blossomed in Washington—quite probably because the justice realized that McCloy, whom he now called "Jack," could provide him with an indispensable means for influencing War Department policy.

Because of the diverse responsibilities and personalities of these various individuals, the justice quickly adopted unique methods for working with each of them.[44] A personal interview with John J. McCloy, one of New York City's most prominent attorneys following a distinguished career in diplomacy and banking, has provided some particularly vivid details of life in the War Department at that time, while confirming much of what has been discovered in other unpublished sources.

Stimson required the justice's constant attention. Due to advancing age and the incredible vastness of the departmental problems confronting a secretary of war trying to mobilize the nation before disaster overtook it, Stimson's confidence and energy level periodically waned. A review of the entries during the war years in his personal diary confirms that Frankfurter, at times on as much as a weekly basis, visited Stimson's home either for a chat, an afternoon tea, or dinner. When face-to-face discussion was not possible, the justice utilized the telephone wires between their homes to review the issues of the day. For the secretary, these conversations served a vital function. Knowing of Frankfurter's vast contacts, he would call the justice periodically "just for the purpose of getting the news," and be better informed than if he had devoured The New York Times on a daily basis.[45] Stimson also relied on Frankfurter's counsel and encouragement before making any major decision, much as he had done when they worked together in Taft's War Department. Sensing these needs, the tone of Frankfurter's messages to Stimson greatly resembled the ones he continually sent to FDR: full of praise, reassurance, and flattery.

The justice served another crucial role at this time. The secretary's cold, humorless, rather formal personality and his statesmanlike air simply did not mix well with Roosevelt's relaxed cheerful ways. The uncertain quality of the relationship between the two was accentuated by the fact that Stimson, with his years of experience in two previous administrations, was one of the few officials in Washington fully prepared to speak to FDR as a peer. It was not uncommon for Stimson when he was dissatisfied with an answer to raise a finger to the president and say sternly, "Don't you dissemble with me."

To ease these periodic tensions, Frankfurter became an intermediary between the two men, just as he had been between Brandeis and Roosevelt years earlier. He could feed Stimson's vanity and then later that same day joke about it with FDR over cocktails. When the president became annoyed by Stimson's failure to keep him apprised of policies in the War Department, Frankfurter would save the situation by speaking to the secretary personally. On one such occasion, Stimson recorded in his personal diary entry for January 4, 1941, Frankfurter told him that FDR "was a lonely man . . . [who] was rather proud and didn't like to ask people to come to him," but "he was sure that [Roosevelt] would welcome [Stimson's] approaches if [he] would make them."[46]

Of course, serving in this role, Frankfurter received much in return. Besides the continued loyalty of each man, he was made privy early on in the decisionmaking process to many major actions being considered in the War Department. For example, several entries in Stimson's personal diary during 1940 and 1941 indicate that the justice and the secretary of war spoke frequently about the possibility of moving the Pacific fleet to the Atlantic; at other times the two discussed arranging for a "truce" between the administration and the nation's newspapers.[47] Not only did Frankfurter have a voice in many ultimate decisions through his advice to Stimson, but on those occasions when he was the one to relay Stimson's recommendations to the president, he was able to invest them with even more of his own thinking.

Seeking to expand his influence over War Department policies, the justice approached each of the assistant secretaries regarding day-to-day administrative details. Robert Patterson, in charge of procurement matters, did not receive the lion's share of attention from Frankfurter, but being old friends, the two saw each other enough to make sure there were ample openings for the justice to provide assistance on the occasional troublesome problem. Since John McCloy had been placed in charge of political-military matters, it was he who quickly became the main focus of Frankfurter's attention in the War Department.

McCloy remembers that his political relationship with the justice blossomed when he bought a house around the corner from the one that Frankfurter rented in Georgetown* and the two men began to meet on their evening walks. Quite naturally, discussion on these occasions would turn to departmental matters. Within weeks, the justice and McCloy were phoning each other on a daily basis, as well as visiting each other's homes regularly. Secretary Stimson encouraged this contact because McCloy could then keep abreast of the activities of the New Dealers in Washington. On occasion, he even sent McCloy as an envoy to this group, which Stimson labeled the "caves of Abdullum," to secure their support for a new policy. For his part, Frankfurter enlisted McCloy as one of his main troubleshooters on problems within the administration. Whenever there was a bottleneck in the mobilization drive, the justice would call his good friend, "Jack," asking if there wasn't something he could do. In addition, McCloy provided Frankfurter with a willing ear for his many new proposals. In the early part of the war Frankfurter desperately needed people who could mobilize the entire government, and in McCloy he found just the type of man to help do it.

Even before Frankfurter had fully accomplished his private reorganization of the War Department, he became involved in an extrajudicial endeavor of even greater immediate importance—the re-election of Roosevelt to a third term in 1940. Though he complained in a personal letter to FDR, written on May 3, 1940, that he lived in a "marble prison," far from the wars of partisan politics, in truth Frankfurter could not resist entering the fray.[49] It was not only that he loved FDR and honestly believed that four more years of his regime would be good for the nation, but also that if the current administration were to be voted out of office, all the justice's carefully laid plans for influenc-

---

*Notoriously improvident in his financial affairs, Frankfurter steadfastly refused throughout his life to buy a home of his own. To close friends he explained his hostility toward owning a home by saying that it made one "a hostage to fortune."[48]

ing public policy would be ruined. So, Frankfurter gradually advanced himself till he was virtually an informal campaign manager, playing a central role in every aspect of the campaign, from drafting speeches to plotting election strategy.

The first moves were innocent enough and came at the direct invitation of the president. Debating whether to run for a third term, FDR asked Frankfurter for his opinion and within days received a long memorandum from the justice urging him to run again for the good of the nation. With war imminent, the document argued, Roosevelt's clear vision and continuing leadership were needed to "protect the nation from the convulsions, dangers and upheavals in a period of acute national anxiety, and world strain . . ."[50] The justice also enclosed a memorandum written by Librarian of Congress Archibald MacLeish* at the request of the president, which argued the need for a third term as well as containing suggested wording for the anticipated acceptance speech. FDR used much of this analysis and language in eventually drafting that address.

Since the challenge posed by the Republican candidate, Wendell Willkie, was expected to be a formidable one, Felix Frankfurter psyched himself to meet that threat by stoking up his antipathy to the man he labeled "the wonder boy."† The justice wrote to friends such as Charles C. Burlingham, expressing a "deep curiosity" to know "about the texture of the man's [Willkie's] qualities, his capacities for government, [and] his devotion to the humane ends of a democratic society."[52] Once he had acquired the necessary ammunition, Frankfurter then peppered the president and Samuel Rosenman with ideas for speeches and campaign charges that might be levied against the Republican candidate.[53]

Frankfurter was ready to use all his weapons in order to secure four more years for Roosevelt. With friends, former students, and allies now scattered around Washington in various agencies, the justice had an available force for mounting his own campaign on behalf of the president. The nature of these assignments, which have never appeared in print, were described by former Frankfurter law clerks Joseph L. Rauh,

---

*MacLeish received this appointment in mid-1939 after Frankfurter sent to the president, at the latter's request, a lengthy and effusive letter of recommendation in favor of the selection.[51]
†Ironically, Frankfurter later changed his opinion following Willkie's post-election strong, nonpartisan devotion to the war effort.

Jr., and Edward F. Prichard, Jr., in personal interviews. Frequently during 1940, Frankfurter enlisted them and another former clerk, Philip L. Graham, who later became the publisher of the *Washington Post,* to do what they perversely labeled "Hatch Act Work," so-named because as bureaucrats in various administration posts, they were actually being asked to violate the Hatch Act prohibiting such partisan involvement by government employees. One product of their labors was a pamphlet entitled "Meet the Friends of Willkie," which tried to associate the candidate with arch-conservatism by listing those of his friends who had right-wing views. On several other occasions, Frankfurter's "boys" were called on by the justice and instructed to draft campaign speeches on subjects such as war preparedness for Henry L. Stimson, who preferred not to write partisan statements himself.

Not all these Frankfurter-inspired campaign missions successfully kept the justice's hand in them completely hidden. Joseph Rauh, who went on from his tutelage under Frankfurter to become one of the nation's most prominent civil rights, civil liberties, and labor lawyers, as well as heading the Americans for Democratic Action, recalled a charming story illustrating one such occasion. In October 1940, while working at the Federal Communications Commission, Rauh received a command by telephone from Frankfurter to visit him at the Supreme Court building. The justice told his protégé that Assistant Secretary of War Robert Patterson, a Republican, wanted to make a campaign speech announcing his support for FDR, but hesitated to do so for fear that other Republicans serving in the administration, such as William S. Knudsen, on the advisory commission to the Council of National Defense, might then feel compelled to announce publicly their own support for Willkie. Because this would destroy the appearance of unity in the "coalition cabinet," Frankfurter, who was not averse to trying to have his cake and eat it too, wanted to get Patterson to announce his support for FDR while still forestalling the possibility of Knudsen's doing the same for Willkie.

As was so often the case, the justice had an ally in a perfect position to exert influence. Sidney Hillman, the president of the Amalgamated Clothing Workers of America union and an old friend from the 1930s when both worked in implementing some of the ideas of Louis D. Brandeis, was then serving with Knudsen on the advisory commission. Frankfurter thought that Hillman just might be able to influence Knudsen's behavior. Despite his close relationship with Hillman,

Frankfurter instructed Rauh to visit Hillman and ask if he would be willing to talk to Knudsen about remaining silent. As it turned out, the union official did not think there would be a problem, and told Rauh:

> Look, son, don't you worry about Knudsen. And you tell Felix not to waste your time again. You're a nice young man so don't waste your time. Tell Felix if he wants to know something like that to call me up directly.[54]

Indeed, just as Hillman predicted, Patterson gave the address without any adverse reaction. Frankfurter took Hillman's advice to heart, for rarely again did he make an effort to insulate himself in such a fashion during the war years. Of course, he continued to direct his intermediaries, but while Brandeis had used them to hide his activities from public view, Frankfurter's purpose was simply to extend and broaden his influence.

After his election, FDR thanked Frankfurter for all his assistance during the campaign.[55] Like Louis D. Brandeis's work with Woodrow Wilson on "The Document" in the early 1920s, this partisan effort by Frankfurter was unusual, even for such a highly political member of the Supreme Court. Once again, normal strictures against such activity were seemingly overcome by the individual's loyalty and devotion to a single president, as well as by the pressing exigencies of the period.

Frankfurter's friendship with the president and his vast contacts in the administration finally paid off in his intense campaign to secure American support for Great Britain during the war. The justice's single-minded and at times almost desperate endeavors here are easily explained by his love for that country. He was truly the Anglophile of Anglophiles. The exact beginnings of this devotion to England are difficult to trace. He had always been attracted to its long history of lawful government and its well-ordered way of life, but it was his academic year at Oxford from 1933 to 1934, and the vast number of friendships he established during that time, that may have permanently cemented his special attachment to England.[56] From that time on, he remained in constant contact with friends in British academia, such as Harold Laski and John Maynard Keynes. Whenever any of these scholars ventured to the United States for a lecture series or for some other purpose, they made a mandatory stop in Cambridge for a long discussion with Felix Frankfurter. Over the years, each side kept the other well informed regarding political and social changes in their own countries. The hardships Great Britain was forced to endure after 1939 touched Frankfurter personally. This became even more true when he cared for the three children of Sylvester Gates, a British lawyer and former Frankfurter student, who were dispatched from London to Georgetown to avoid the German bombing.

For their part, members of the British government came to view Felix Frankfurter as one of their central contacts, and perhaps even their best representative, in Washington. Though the justice did not know Winston Churchill personally, he was close to several of the prime minister's colleagues. His friendship with Lord Lothian, the British ambassador in Washington until late 1940, had been forged when they worked together at the Versailles Peace Conference in 1919. When Lothian died and was replaced by Sir Edward Halifax, Frankfurter worked through another of his contacts, Lord Eustace Percy, to see that the new ambassador was properly briefed, supplied with the right staff, and, of course, fully informed of the justice's own special position in Washington.

Another of the justice's allies later in the war was Richard Casey, an Australian serving as minister of state in the Middle East with a seat on the British War Cabinet; indeed, it was on the justice's advice that Casey resigned as Australia's ambassador to the United States to take the new position.[57] All these people, eager to improve relations between Great Britain and the United States, saw their friend Felix Frankfurter as representing one means to accomplish their goal. During a time when a premium was placed in Washington on reliable information regarding the precise needs and survivability of our European allies, Frankfurter was thus properly positioned to be made an informal member of the United States diplomatic corps.

British officials had more than adequate reason, in fact, for viewing the justice as *their* most important contact in Washington. They were well aware not only of his access to an extraordinary array of political figures throughout the administration, but even more important for them, of his intimate friendship with President Roosevelt. Whenever the justice spoke, it was simply assumed in London that the words were coming directly from the president of the United States or, at the very least, had been cleared with the president, and thus represented the will of the American people. Who better, then, to become the central conduit for all the information the British wanted Washington to have and the requests they wanted made? This data was sent in a torrent of mail to Frankfurter in the hopes that he would use it in his daily conversations with other Washington officials. In turn, Frankfurter's mastery of all this information, frequently available to no one else, increased the justice's prestige and influence in Washington even further.

The justice's initial efforts on behalf of Great Britain and the country's other future allies were made more difficult by the prevailing isolationist trend in America. Both before and after the commencement of hostilities in September 1939, the issue in America was quite simply how to stay out of the "European conflict." So, Frankfurter devoted considerable effort in 1939 to pressing the administration to adopt a greater role in the fight against Germany. He sent a number of letters to FDR, reminding him of the worsening conditions in Europe (of which the president was well aware), and imploring that he ask Congress to repeal the 1935 Neutrality Act, an act that mandated that the United States remain strictly uncommitted in such conflicts.

In speaking with the president, Frankfurter argued that while the law professed to preserve our absolute neutrality, it actually favored the aggressor nations by making America a "helpless spectator" while the democracies lay under siege. Henry L. Stimson entered in his personal diary for July 5, 1939 that he too was subjected to a personal exposition by the justice on this matter.[58] In a later memorandum to the president, Frankfurter even went so far as to argue that this act violated international law because war materiel from a neutral nation, America, could actually be supplied to an attacking nation, Germany. In addition, the justice supplied a sentence summarizing his position for possible use in a Roosevelt speech:

> A so-called Neutrality Law which in practical operation favors the forces of aggression must be fundamentally wrong in conception. It runs counter to American traditions and ideals and is in conflict with international law.[59]

No doubt the president appreciated the availability of such legal advice from a member of the Supreme Court. Persuaded by this argument, Roosevelt used it in presenting his case to Congress for repeal of the act. In subsequently lifting the arms-embargo provisions of the law, Congress made it possible for nations to receive war supplies on a "cash-and-carry" basis. This action, it was argued, maintained United States neutrality because, in theory, all nations could purchase goods so long as they were transported in that country's own ships.[60]

By mid-1940, Justice Frankfurter became increasingly concerned about the situation in Great Britain. France had fallen, and Hitler was still in an alliance with the Soviet Union, subjecting the British to the full force of the German war machine. The justice's contacts in Great Britain also informed him of the rapidly depleting financial resources available for purchasing supplies from the United States. Worse still, Frankfurter could see that the ranks of the isolationists at home had grown. In August 1939, Germany and the Soviet Union had entered into what has been called the Ribbentrop-Molotov Pact, and when on September 1, 1939, the two dictatorships started World War II by invading Poland from east and west, much of the American far left, which had once agitated for a stronger stance against Germany, now took a pacifist stance, adding to the German-American Bund and the American Firsters a whole new group of vociferous and articulate voices for peace. When France fell in June of 1940, and Mussolini cast the lot of Italy with Hitler, a grim fatalism set in among many of those Americans formerly in favor of standing up to the dictatorships. Fewer Americans, it seemed, were willing to help Great Britain now that she stood alone and in mortal peril than there had been before the nine-month uninterrupted succession of terrible news had begun for European democracy.

Searching for new ways to aid beleaguered friends and still satisfy these advocates of neutrality, Roosevelt proposed swapping fifty old destroyers for the rights to some of Britain's sea bases. When the Senate refused to approve the deal, Benjamin V. Cohen was instructed to draft a memorandum justifying the legality of a unilateral presidential action. Cohen later recalled, in a personal interview, that Frankfurter convinced him to ask Dean Acheson to help in the writing of the document.* This justification was then put in the form of a letter to *The*

---

*Acheson had been out of government since his resignation from the Department of Treasury seven years earlier because of differences with FDR over the "gold-buying" recovery scheme. The move by Frankfurter to involve him in this destroyer-deal justification turned out to be a fortuitous one for the justice for an entirely different reason. Acheson's fine work here was a step toward his eventual re-entry into the government in 1941 as an assistant secretary of state. Later, when Frankfurter lacked extensive contacts in the Truman Administration, it was Acheson who became his main pipeline to the executive branch.

New York Times that was signed by the venerable eighty-one-year-old Charles C. Burlingham and other attorneys.[61] It seems likely that, given their long friendship, Frankfurter and Burlingham would have discussed this action beforehand. While no written evidence can be found to verify this possibility, the discussion could easily have taken place in person or by phone.*

At this point, Frankfurter did his part for the British by discussing the matter directly with Henry L. Stimson. This conversation, documented in the secretary of war's diary entry for August 15, 1940, aptly illustrates the justice's total lack of restraint at this time in his extrajudicial endeavors. Stimson had asked him not only for his opinion on the Burlingham letter, but also for an analysis of the whole constitutional issue of the "Executive power to [act] in the absence of Congress." Despite long-standing precedent to the contrary, the justice showed no reluctance in offering such an "advisory opinion."† Frankfurter told Stimson that after two or three days of "thinking it over very hard," he had concluded that this trade was valid as a *"quid pro quo"* in which each country received something of value. Furthermore, he noted that since the agreement involved matters crucial to the "national defense," it was well within the inherent power of the executive to take action. Though he had not been asked the additional question of whether the agreement was legal given the contrary dictates of the remaining provisions of the Neutrality Act, Frankfurter showed no hesitation in offering his opinion on that matter as well.

> The statute which lies in the way was a part of the old neutrality laws and was related to the matter of filibustering rather than to the matter of national defense, so that this case is entirely different from the cases [to] which it was intended to apply.[63]

Greatly reassured by this support from a Supreme Court justice, Stimson relayed the message to the president. According to the sec-

---

* Some support for this possibility is provided by the frequent letters from Frankfurter to Burlingham, sent between 1939 and 1945 and now filed in the latter's personal papers at the Harvard Law School, which contained sensitive information on the progress of the war and were each marked with a cautionary "strictly for your eyes."

† An advisory opinion is an opinion on a matter that has not been formally presented to the Court. By giving such advice, the Court or one of its members becomes virtually a legal counsellor to the political branches, thus endangering its objectivity in future tests of such issues. The precedent that advisory opinions are not to be offered goes back to the time of the administration of George Washington, when the Supreme Court refused Secretary of State Thomas Jefferson's request to interpret informally a treaty with France.[62]

retary's account, Roosevelt was "very, very much encouraged" by this opinion and the following day directed the attorney general to begin the appropriate action. In September 1940, acting on his own authority, FDR did send fifty old destroyers to Great Britain in return for rights to certain sea bases around the world. Though this action was never tested in Court, one wonders if the justice would have remained on the bench to hear such a review, especially if the Court could have been anticipated to divide closely.

Soon, though, the British had nothing left to trade, and they desperately needed a direct and immediate commitment by the United States to the war effort. Frankfurter was already working with the president to secure assistance for other countries. For example, he convinced FDR to have food sent to children in Finland,* and, according to a long memorandum discovered in Roosevelt's files, suggested that a military base be established in Ireland to help stabilize the political situation there.[64] However, to achieve the sort of massive assistance program needed for Great Britain, and to overcome the isolationist mentality in America, Frankfurter clearly needed an ally who could provide additional ideas and contacts. Fortunately, exactly the right candidate happened to be available. Curious enough, he was neither British nor American.

Jean Monnet came to the United States in August 1940, after the fall of his native France. Other than Monnet's own memoirs, there is little written about this man who is perhaps best known for his work in bringing about the European Common Market. However, personal interviews with Washington economist Robert Nathan and Harvard Law School Professor Milton Katz, both of whom worked closely with Monnet during the war, have made it possible to offer a more complete portrait of the personality and work of this remarkable man.

Born to an aristocratic family, the fifty-one-year-old Monnet was a superb diplomat who had somehow managed to become attached to the British Purchasing Commission, a liaison agency to the United States government.[65] His position on the commission, which consisted of the heads of the various British diplomatic missions in Washington, gave Monnet a central vantage point from which to plead the case of those fighting the war. Seeking access to various officials in Washington, he very quickly forged a partnership with Felix Frank-

---

*Finland was resisting a Soviet invasion at this time. Until Germany attacked the Soviet Union in June 1941, Finland was considered an ally of the democracies.

furter, who introduced him around the capital. Through the justice, Monnet met decision-makers at the highest levels of government—Harry Hopkins, Ben Cohen, John McCloy, Henry L. Stimson, and even the president—as well as an army of subordinate bureaucrats.

Because he possessed the requisite skills, Monnet, once introduced, became a powerful catalyst for securing government action. Perhaps the French diplomat was best described by Frankfurter himself, who commented in a conversation with his former student, Milton Katz: "Monnet is a man with a ruthless clarity of mind who will not deviate from seeing and describing things as they are and following the facts as he finds them. He never deludes himself." [66] Indeed, Monnet impressed people with his incredible analytical intelligence, his sense of perspective, and his extraordinary gift for separating the important from the irrelevant. Moreover, he was tenacious. It was difficult to disagree with a man who seemed so detached, so objective, and so uncommitted to any single ideological viewpoint. Allying himself with no particular French faction, Monnet was an independent thinker whose influence in Washington increased greatly as it became apparent that he had no ideological ax to grind. His motives were simple and unselfish—to prepare the United States for fighting the war to save Europe from the nightmare of totalitarian suppression. His was the voice of reason itself, speaking to politicians whose constituents were demanding that they avoid this difficult issue, but whose minds and hearts told them they must do otherwise.

Coupled with these qualities of intelligence and temperament was a style of lobbying that always presented his arguments in their best light. As a bureaucrat in various war-related agencies and a Frankfurter ally from his years of service as an economist in the New Deal, Robert Nathan was a frequent target for Monnet's blandishments. In a personal interview he detailed the various skills at Monnet's disposal in his highly successful endeavors. The French diplomat had a gift for working on one campaign at a time and screening out all other influences until the goal was reached. Key administrators would be invited to discuss the issues during a long prebreakfast walk around Rock Creek Park, then referred to by Monnet as "my park." At times these individuals received even more royal continental treatment; they would be invited to his home on Foxhall Road for a magnificent French dinner prepared by his wife Sylvia and their chef. Pressing issues were always discussed before dinner, never during or after, because Monnet maintained that "good food and politics do not mix well."[67] This suited his guests just fine, for they had little energy remaining after consuming the ample repast. The combination of good sense and good will soon placed Monnet in the confidence of the highest administrators in the United States. Within months he was literally drafting memoranda for this government to send abroad and, through his friends elsewhere, composing the answers that were returned.

For the rest of the war, Monnet and Felix Frankfurter were in daily communication, each supporting the other's efforts to communicate the needs of Europe and to formulate plans for meeting them. Though they lacked formal roles within the administration, they were among the most important influences on policymaking during the pre-Pearl Harbor period. Together, they were able to secure aid for the Allies and mobilize the United States for the conflict.

From late 1940 through early 1941 an effort was undertaken to move President Roosevelt even closer to a cooperative effort with the beleaguered British people. In late November 1940, according to the personal diary of Henry L. Stimson, Justice Frankfurter spoke to Secretary of the Navy Frank Knox, regarding the possibility of a summit between FDR and the leaders of other democratic nations. Then Frankfurter tried to persuade FDR to deliver a public message on the need to help Europe, by sending the president a letter introducing Monnet and enclosing one of the Frenchman's memoranda describing the deteriorating situation abroad.[68] However, Roosevelt was having trouble finding exactly the right words to convince a recalcitrant American public of its world responsibilities.

One December night, however, Frankfurter heard Monnet tell a group of friends that the United States "must become a great arsenal, the arsenal of democracy," and instantly recognized that here was the memorable phrase capable of mobilizing popular support for the program the president had in mind. Securing a promise from Monnet that he would never again use the phrase, the justice passed it along to FDR, who incorporated it into a "Fireside Chat" delivered on December 29.[69] It was just the language the president needed to launch his campaign for the Lend-Lease program.

FDR reasoned that the United States might be able to maintain its neutrality and yet further assist the British by merely "lending" or "leasing" them the necessary equipment.[70] Before the plan was finalized, though, other circumstances conspired to jeopardize its success.

Winston Churchill was reluctant to accept the idea, believing that the financial resources of his country were being unfairly depleted by the Americans, who had much to lose should Hitler, Stalin, and Mussolini be allowed to carve up Europe. When Lord Lothian, who held the confidence of both Roosevelt and Churchill died, FDR, who had never met the British prime minister, decided to send his intimate adviser, Harry Hopkins, to London as a special envoy charged with establishing direct communication. Upon hearing about the impending mission Monnet warned Frankfurter about the need for careful preparation. Here was the chance for one of Roosevelt's closest advisers to establish a positive relationship between the two leaders. Yet, it seemed to Monnet that neither side was correctly assessing the true importance of the conference. To help the mission succeed, the justice invited both Hopkins and Monnet to his home for a preparatory briefing.

This was a classic political technique of Frankfurter. Unlike Brandeis, who preferred to confer briefly with individuals in a one-to-one setting, Frankfurter constantly convened long "dinner seminars" at his home. By inviting several people linked by a common interest, he could then direct the course of the conversation and offer a substantial number of his own policy views for consideration. Very quickly everyone in Washington realized that a "social" invitation to the Frankfurter household usually meant that important business would be discussed.

On this occasion Monnet's message to Hopkins was very simple: there was no need to plan for meetings with everyone in London because "Churchill is the British War Cabinet, and no one else matters." Had Monnet been there alone, the recommendation might have had little impact. But as in many of these "dinner-seminars," each man was a close friend of Felix Frankfurter, and looked to him for verification or correction of the views of the other. When Hopkins expressed dismay at Monnet's recommendation that Churchill be courted, Frankfurter scolded him: "Harry—if you're going to London with that chip on your shoulder, like a damned little small town chauvinist, you may as well cancel your passage right now."[71] Duly warned, the man from Sioux City, Iowa, who had never before traveled abroad, readied himself for the conversation with the prime minister of Great Britain.

Before that happened, though, Frankfurter and Monnet had more work to do; the British were no better prepared for Hopkins than he was for them. They, too, needed to be informed regarding the central importance to FDR of this aide with no portfolio, and hence of the crucial nature of this conference to their long-term interests. Consequently, Frankfurter worked with his foreign contacts to smooth Hopkins's mission to London. The justice persuaded Richard Casey, then the Australian ambassador to the United States, to help educate Winston Churchill on the closeness of Hopkins to FDR. According to Casey's memoirs, a draft copy of which was forwarded to Frankfurter in 1960 for comments and corrections, the justice was instrumental in this process.[72] On January 6, 1941, Casey cabled the Australian High Commissioner in London that a "Highly placed and well-disposed person . . . who is a great friend of Hopkins and close to the President," had an urgent message for Churchill before the meeting. After describing Hopkins's personal nature and his reverence for Roosevelt, the minister wrote:

> My informant believes that there is nothing currently more important than that Hopkins' mission should succeed and that Churchill and Roosevelt be brought together through the medi[um] of Hopkins.
>
> My friend therefore urges with great sincerity and conviction that Mr. Churchill go out of his way at early stage to express to Hopkins his great and cordial admiration for the President as a man and as the leader of this American nation and ask that he convey these heartfelt sentiments to the President. There is no surer way of reaching Hopkins' heart and there is no one who can do this more convincingly than Mr. Churchill.
>
> My friend who is a very highly placed person in this country lays great stress on the above. He thinks that in the stress of great affairs Mr. Churchill may take for granted such expressions of regard and that if he does H. may interpret it as indifference.[73]

Two days later the London bureau cabled Casey that Churchill had received the message and would "certainly act on it." Indeed, the prime minister used exactly this strategy in dealing with Hopkins. As a result of the justice's intervention the success of the conference was assured; the month-long series of meetings between Churchill and Hopkins helped greatly to improve the relations between the two nations.[74]

Meanwhile, on the home front, Frankfurter was doing much more to secure aid for the British by openly campaigning for the Lend-Lease program. No detail was too minute to command his attention, and he had all the contacts necessary to shape this bill effectively. In so doing, Frankfurter shattered any thought that he would be willing to observe during what he defined as a time of crisis, the traditional norms proscribing judicial involvement in legislative activities. The official responsibility for the legislation had been placed in the hands of the Treasury Department. Knowing of Frankfurter's consummate interest in the project, Secretary Henry Morgenthau noted in his personal diary entry for January 2, 1941 that he had invited Frankfurter to review their proposals.

While the two men had not been on warm terms during the earlier New Deal, Frankfurter realized that there was something to be gained by carefully cultivating the relationship now. Though Frankfurter knew that nothing was further from the truth, he made a special point of telling Morgenthau how pleased the venerable Louis Brandeis was with his work. Being told that he "seemed to have ideas which fitted in with [Brandeis's] more closely than anybody else connected with the Administration" made Morgenthau even more willing to include Frankfurter in the legislative drafting process.[75] The secretary had only intended, however, that the justice briefly read over the material when he received it.

Little did Morgenthau realize that he could not possibly keep Frankfurter out of the process even if he wanted to do so. The actual drafting of the measure had been assigned to the assistant for the Treasury Department's general counsel, Oscar Cox. As a Harvard Law School graduate, Cox knew Frankfurter, but while the two men liked each other well enough, they were certainly not close friends. Fortunately for the justice, Benjamin Cohen was also included on the drafting team because of his earlier work on the destroyers-for-sea-bases swap with Great Britain. Since he and Frankfurter were still on good terms at this time, this was an opportunity for the justice to have a significant impact on the bill.

From the perspective of Cox and Cohen, it was very important that they have Frankfurter's input. He had developed an encyclopedic knowledge of the proclivities of various members of Congress from his earlier work on New Deal legislation. In addition, even had Frankfurter not taken such a leadership position, the appeal of having a member of the nation's highest judicial body review the bill prior to its passage for any possible difficulties from a legal or constitutional standpoint should not be underestimated. All drafters of legislation harbor a certain dread that language they are creating will one day be criticized by the federal judiciary as being too vague, overbroad, discriminatory, or as having in some other way made the enacted legislation unenforceable. Having an associate justice of the Supreme Court handy with an informal advisory opinion, pointing out and helping to rein in any language that promises to find disfavor with the Court, would surely create a situation in which those drafting the legislation would be willing to go right to the edge in the belief that their proposals would withstand judicial scrutiny.

But of course it was not in Frankfurter's nature to limit himself even to this important role. Having successfully nurtured in the minds of the upper administration the idea of aiding the British, he was now prepared to do whatever was necessary to make sure this assent was translated into effective legislation.* Because of the difficulty of circumventing certain provisions of the Neutrality Act, Cox and Cohen were forced to write over thirty drafts of the enactment, each of which Frankfurter personally reviewed. At meetings with Cox, Cohen, and a variety of other administration officials, each of which lasted several hours, the justice highlighted potential weaknesses in the general focus of the legislation and proposed a number of specific changes in wording. He suggested, for instance, that the title of the bill be altered to read: "Joint Resolution to Promote the Defense of the United States." This and other changes, he believed, would shift the focus of the measure and better tap the patriotic instincts of Congress. In the final stages of the drafting process, the group called in then-special assistant to the secretary of war, John J. McCloy, as a consultant, thus enabling Frankfurter, Cox, and Cohen to provide the War Department some advance notice regarding the prospective bill.

Even after all the bugs seemed to have been removed, Cox and Cohen, before sending the bill to Morgenthau, telephoned Frankfurter one last time to obtain his final seal of approval; as might be expected, the justice had a number of last-minute suggestions to offer, which were duly incorporated into the final measure.[76] Clearly, Frankfurter

---

*This revelation of the justice's intimate involvement in the drafting process for the Lend-Lease bill has never before appeared in print. For years, the evidence has remained hidden in the pages of the personal diary of Oscar Cox, which is now stored at the Roosevelt Presidential Library in Hyde Park. In fact, had it not been for a casual remark by Benjamin Cohen in a personal interview regarding Cox's importance in drafting of the measure, this information might have been overlooked once again.

had played the dominant role in writing the act that, when passed, would provide lifesaving relief to Great Britain in her hour of greatest need.

Next, Frankfurter turned his attention to the problem of securing congressional approval for the bill. His extensive efforts at this stage are detailed in several entries in the personal diary of Secretary of War Stimson. Despite the care taken in drafting the legislation, there was certain to be a battle over its passage in the isolationist Congress. To defuse potential resistance, the justice suggested that the measure be made House Resolution No. 1776. He argued that this would symbolically indicate that the United States was seeking "independence through interdependence." Then Frankfurter and McCloy spoke for many hours forming arguments that the secretary of war could use in defending the measure before Senate hearings. All these ideas were duly passed on to Stimson, who then received a personal visit from the two men while he was preparing his opening address.[77]

John McCloy still vividly recalls a fascinating tale illustrating the intrigue that went into insuring the bill's passage even after it reached the Senate floor. To have help close at hand, Senator James F. Byrnes of South Carolina* had the forty-five-year-old McCloy planted in the Senate chambers dressed as a page. McCloy was chosen for the role not because of his youthful appearance but because he had worked with the drafting team and was seen by Byrnes as the War Department official with the greatest expertise on the subject. Whenever an objection was raised on the floor by one of the opposition, Byrnes would amble over to McCloy for prompting. Once armed with McCloy's information, Byrnes would approach one of his own senators, tap him on the shoulder, whisper in his ear, and then step back and watch the fellow jump to his feet and answer the other side's objection point for point.

Each night McCloy would meet Frankfurter for either a walk around Georgetown or some tea, and the two men would review the day's debate. This gave the justice a chance to offer his own thoughts regarding the ideologies of various senators and to pose arguments for dealing with potential weaknesses in the portion of the measure being considered the following day. Having helped to write each successive draft of the bill, he knew well both its overall problems and just those

---

*In less than a year Byrnes himself would be appointed to the Supreme Court.

sections that would appeal to each politician. This opportunity to influence the Senate debate enabled Frankfurter to insure that the sections of the bill most important to him would be adequately defended and adopted with as few alterations as possible. When the Senate debate dragged on, the justice bolstered the spirits of President Roosevelt by sending him in late February both a short letter and a long memorandum reasserting the necessity for the act. Finally, after a two-month battle, the legislation was passed by Congress on March 11, 1941.[78]

Even after the enactment of the Lend-Lease Act, Frankfurter continued to plead the case for the British. He became, in the words of Ambassador Jay Pierrepont Moffat, the "lawyer for the British" in the debate over how the money should be distributed by the program.[79] Entries in the personal diaries of Stimson and Cox make it possible to trace Frankfurter's final moves in the Lend-Lease campaign.

The justice wanted the funding to be made in a lump-sum payment rather than, as the State Department preferred, through the regular armed-services appropriations procedure. To insure a favorable outcome, the justice enlisted the aid of Secretary of Commerce Jesse Jones in taking the matter directly to Stimson. Eventually the lump-sum approach was adopted. Once the Lend-Lease plan was in full operation, Frankfurter turned his attention to similar discussions regarding aid to China and, after Hitler had abruptly disavowed his nonaggression pact with the Soviet Union by attacking on a five-hundred-mile front, to the Soviet Union as well.[80]

Having provided for the immediate, acute needs of Great Britain, Justice Frankfurter launched into the next of his major wartime political campaigns—mobilizing the American government and industry for the inevitable entry into the war. Seeing that United States involvement in the conflict could not be avoided, both he and Monnet believed that the war would be shortened only if production could be increased beyond the capacity of German industry. For the moment, however, the justice's contacts in government had taken him about as far as they could go in combatting the hardrock isolationism of the American people. Frankfurter needed a new, wider network of contacts to advocate the need for war preparation, and, in a manner reminiscent of his efforts with Brandeis in the 1930s, placed a new set of his "Happy Hot Dogs" in positions where they could do him the most good.

The vanguard of this new group consisted of three of his former students—Philip L. Graham, Edward F. Prichard, Jr., and Joseph L. Rauh, Jr. These men, ranging in age from twenty-six to thirty years old, were among his most brilliant and beloved protégés and assistants. They enjoyed a special relationship with the justice—astonishing people by their brashness and rudeness toward him. They not only spoke frankly with the justice, they argued with him. At the same time, they adored him and willingly served as his point men in Washington, observing the political action for him as well as carrying out his every plan. This was very much a two-way street, though, for Frankfurter reciprocated by promoting their entree into the highest administrative offices. For example, one day Graham and Rauh concocted what, by their own admission, was truly a "crazy" plan to aid the war mobilization. When they insisted that Frankfurter present it to Roosevelt at the next opportunity, he surprised them by agreeing to do so. He later explained with a grin that FDR seemed to be more interested in having his hair cut than in adopting their proposal.

While all three men shared the justice's hatred and fear of Hitler, and agreed that war with Germany was inevitable, with Graham as Frankfurter's law clerk, Rauh in the Federal Communications Commission, and Prichard in the Department of Justice, there was little they could do directly to help bring about America's entry into the war.[81] All that changed when they were brought together in the Office of Emergency Management.

Little has been written on the activities of this vitally important agency, or of Frankfurter's involvement with it. However, personal interviews with two of its former members—Rauh and Prichard—have made it possible to describe these endeavors. The agency was officially established by an executive order on May 25, 1940 to serve, according to its charter, as "extra eyes, hands and brains for the President."[82] Formally, the agency was created so that FDR could delegate broad executive powers to it in times of national emergency.

In the first week of 1941, a subgroup of this agency, the Office of Production Management, was formed to coordinate priorities in industry and government purchases.[83] These offices were quickly staffed with Frankfurter allies—individuals who would all become part of his wider network for influencing the war mobilization. Sidney Hillman, the union official, was made head of the Labor Division. The two economists whom Frankfurter had gotten to know in the 1930s, Isador

Lubin and Robert Nathan, were hired in the Priorities Division and Bureau of Research and Statistics Division respectively. Milton Katz, a former student, was made assistant general counsel to John Lord O'Brian, another Frankfurter friend, in the legal division. James Lawrence Fly, whom the justice had helped place as head of the FCC, was placed in charge of the Defense Communications Board.

But it was when the president realized, after the passage of the Lend-Lease Act in mid-March 1941, that an adequate mobilization effort required the formation of another special troubleshooting group, that Frankfurter was provided with a real opportunity for exerting influence. Presuming that war was not far off, FDR surveyed his administrative bureaucracy and did not like what he saw: there was too much red tape and too little action. Whenever a plea was made for an immediate provision of supplies, the response would always be the same: "Let's first have some competitive bidding." It must have seemed to FDR that for some of these bureaucrats, Hitler could be landing in Baltimore and they would still be waiting for one last bidder to come in with his quote. So, the president decided to place some young human dynamos in a special agency within the OEM, an agency that he hoped would serve as a prod for his sluggish administration. He created a separate operation by which Oscar Cox, general counsel for the new Lend-Lease program, was also made counsel to Wayne Coy, the head of the Office of Emergency Management. Thus, the lawyers in Cox's group were simultaneously members of the two agencies most involved with mobilization efforts. Located in the Lend-Lease offices, Cox surrounded himself with the brightest young lawyers in Washington. Though neither he nor Coy were especially close to Frankfurter, Cox's initial appointments—Philip Graham, Edward Prichard and Joseph Rauh—provided the justice with tremendous inside access to the agency.

Together these individuals cracked whips over the heads of government officials. While others, concerned about the checks and balances in the constitutional system, would wring their hands and apologize that there was nothing they could do to mobilize for war, this dual agency, just as the president wanted, pushed aside those obstacles, performing its task with incredible zeal. For example, there was the day in mid-1941, just after the German invasion of Russia, when a lawyer named Abe Feller got into a discussion with Cox, Rauh, and Graham on the operations of the Lend-Lease program. He mentioned that he had seen a sentence in *Time* magazine detailing the losses in materiel by the Russians during the previous week's fighting with the Germans. Everyone gasped when they realized that the Russians had lost more tanks, planes, and guns in one week than the United States would produce in a single year—even if all the production schedules were met (which, of course, was not happening). Cox attached a copy of the article to a memorandum to Harry Hopkins, telling him that the military had to be instructed to step up their requisitions for supplies.

This sort of dire warning was repeatedly offered by the group. An account of another such incident, related by both Joseph Rauh and Robert Nathan in personal interviews, indicates just how vital these bureaucrats were in ferreting out information for the president. In the summer of 1941, Roosevelt mentioned that "clouds" of U.S. planes were being produced to counteract the German war machine. As lawyers for both the OEM and Lend-Lease, Graham and Rauh had access to the weekly munitions-production progress reports. In surveying that week's statement they noticed that only one four-engine bomber had been delivered to the Army during the previous month. When, over their nightly shot of bourbon, they mentioned the size of this "cloud" to Coy, he too was surprised and signed and sent a memorandum Graham and Rauh had drafted for the president's edification. About ten o'clock the next morning, Coy's secretary called Rauh and Graham saying, "Wayne says, and he doesn't want this diluted, get your ass over here!" When they arrived Coy was waving a responding memo he had just received from Harry Hopkins, saying in effect, "These facts are all wrong and you must never scare the President this way again." Shaken, the two men left to check their statistics with their friend Robert Nathan, who headed the Military Requirement Section in the Statistics Division of the Office of Production Management. While they sat and wondered where they could have gone astray, Nathan shuffled through sheet after sheet of statistics. "No," he finally announced, "I made a mistake." There go our jobs, careers and futures, thought the two lawyers. "There were absolutely no four-engine bombers delivered to the Army last month."[84] Relieved for the personal salvation the information offered but disturbed by what it meant for the country, they returned with the news to Coy, who, in turn, drafted a searing memo for Hopkins. This, then, was a crucial agency for FDR because it foresaw and alleviated industrial bottlenecks, while also providing him with accurate data on the progress of the mobilization effort.[85]

Frankfurter's techniques for dealing with his allies in this agency and others were much more direct and personal than Brandeis's had been in earlier years. In addition to his "dinner-seminars," Frankfurter freely and constantly met with his protégés on an individual basis either at his home or at the Supreme Court building. These talks served as his source of information on the operations of the government. As recalled by Prichard, Rauh, and Nathan in personal interviews, their own command of the facts was improved by membership in what they called the "Goon Squad," a group of fifteen or twenty second-line bureaucrats, who met every Monday evening at Robert Nathan's 18th Street studio apartment. Among the group, besides Nathan, Prichard, Graham, and Rauh, were Lauchlin Currie and Isador Lubin from the White House staff, Leon Henderson from the Office of Price Administration, and at times David Niles, who occasionally came down from Boston. Operating in the strictest secrecy, they kept each other informed of the progress and problems in each of their agencies. It was a very useful group in that it gave each member a much broader view of governmental operations than was possible from behind any one agency desk. At these meetings they hatched their plots to encourage United States entry into the war, and made their plans to speed up military preparation. As would be expected, all this information was passed along to Justice Frankfurter, who commented on it as he thought necessary and used it personally to verify the accuracy of information he was receiving from other sources.

Unlike Brandeis, Frankfurter had no aversion to the telephone and used it regularly to stay on top of his protégés. In fact, he loved using the instrument. A humorous snippet from the transcripts of the wiretap placed on his line by the Massachusetts State Police during the Sacco-Vanzetti controversy in 1927 indicates that even by this early date his love affair with the telephone was already in full bloom and well known among his neighbors. Because Frankfurter's phone at the time was a party line, the conversations of his neighbors were all duly recorded by the police. On one transcript there is this exchange: a caller complains to one of Frankfurter's neighbors, "I finally got through. I've been calling for days but the phone has always been busy." "Oh," replies the neighbor, "that's Felix Frankfurter—he's always tying up the line."[86]

During the 1930s, with his "boys" everywhere, Frankfurter's use of the telephone became even more frequent. Whenever he saw the name of one of his protégés in the newspaper, or a document one had produced, he would call, never identifying himself except by his voice, to give them his opinion of the work. Consequently, these men never did anything in Washington without wondering "what Felix would think about it," and never had to wait long for their grades. Of course, in each of these calls he would pump the individual for information, and nudge him toward the Frankfurter way of thinking.

Once in Washington full-time, the justice developed a weekly ritual of routinely telephoning each of his friends and disciples on Sunday in order to de-brief and counsel them. If one of them did not receive such a call, he would feel left out and wonder what might be wrong. This ready reliance on the phone enabled the justice to operate extra-judicially without leaving a trail of incriminating evidence. Thus, the same man who claimed that he never offered an unsolicited recommendation about an appointment could insure that he would always be asked about filling a particular government vacancy. He could also arrange on the phone for an "unsolicited" invitation to any meeting he wanted to attend. One more Frankfurter ploy involved contacting an individual and asking him or her to write a letter about conditions in a particular branch of government. Then he could forward that "unsolicited" commentary to a higher government official, praising its viewpoint and citing it as evidence of a universal call for reform.

Another fascinating method used by the justice for advising might be described as his own version of the "Brandeis teas." Far less frequent and much less formal than their model, they nonetheless served a similar function. It was in an interview with Edward F. Prichard, Jr.,* that these soirées first came to my attention.

Prichard, Philip Graham, and another former Frankfurter law clerk, Adrian Fisher, then in the State Department, had rented the Hockley House on Foxhall Road in Arlington, Virginia. They lived with a variety of other bright young bachelors: Graham Claytor, a former Brandeis clerk then heading the Southern Railroad, John Ferguson, later ambassador to Morocco, John Oakes, a reporter on the Washington Post, and William Cary, later chairman of the Securities and Exchange Commission. It was an old house on a huge tract of land and with the

---

*"Pritch," as he is affectionately called by his friends, now practices law and politics from his office in Frankfort, Kentucky, and possesses so powerful a memory that he can reel off lists of guests at various functions held forty years ago just as though he attended them the day before. Subsequent interviews with other participants at these affairs confirmed all that I had heard in that initial conversation.

continual conversation, gaiety, and feverish pitch of excitement there, it was reminiscent of Frankfurter's earlier "House of Truth." Periodically, these former Frankfurter clerks would hold parties to which the justice would be invited. Naturally, all the top figures in Washington were also invited and most of them appeared: the Dean Achesons, the Harold Ickes, the Monnets, the Pattersons, the McCloys, the Henry Morgenthaus and others. Just as Brandeis did at his teas, Justice Frankfurter would go off in a corner offering opinions and advice on every conceivable political subject. However, the similarity to the Brandeis soirées ended there. Rather than weak tea and a cookie, a butler served mint juleps and good food. In fact, the monthly food bills were at least $100 apiece for each of the occupants. Unlike the earlier, carefully arranged, conversations at the Brandeis home, the discussion here was always wide ranging with no holds barred on the civilian economy, the draft, the week's events in Congress and foreign affairs. Moreover, people never approached Frankfurter with the same reverence commanded by Brandeis. Instead, there was animated discussion between the justice and his friends, with frequent periods of yelling and screaming so loud that little else could be heard above the din. It was the sort of conversation Frankfurter regularly encouraged. Fully at home in this milieu, he learned and accomplished a great deal in this very sociable atmosphere.[87]

Frankfurter had one other technique in his advising repertoire that made him even more effective than Brandeis. Unlike his mentor, when Frankfurter wanted to influence an individual, he used his unique ability for nourishing friendships to sweep up the entire family in his personal circle. Each time he saw the wife of one of his favorites, the justice would genuinely try to win her affection, not unaware that it could be useful later on. Indeed, on those rare occasions when a Frankfurter suggestion was opposed, that individual would frequently return home to find his wife arguing for the Frankfurter position. When questioned about how she had come to this viewpoint the answer was always, "Oh, Felix called today and we were just talking about the same thing."

Everyone seemed to be aware of the Frankfurter modus operandi. For example, there was the night that the Rauhs were dining with some close friends, including Edward Prichard and Benjamin Cohen, when someone asked Olie Rauh whether she had talked with the justice lately. "No," she said, "I haven't heard from him in quite awhile."

At which point Ben Cohen, who by this time was becoming less enamored of Frankfurter, offered in his characteristically high-pitched
wavering voice, "Well, I guess it's Mrs. McCloy now!"[88] Indeed,
Frankfurter became instant best friends with the wife of the man who
was most important to him at the time, and with the new Lend-Lease
program, as well as the flurry of activities in the War Department, the
newest arrival in Washington, Jack McCloy, seemed to be his latest
target. Though others recognized the justice's intentions, no one else
seemed to mind. It was part of the Frankfurter mystique and charm.
"Isn't that just like Felix!" they would say with affection.

Not surprisingly, these techniques, so well refined, made him one
of the most persuasive lobbyists in Washington. He had all the tools:
the ideas, friendships with the highest officials in the land, contacts
in foreign governments, and an army of dedicated lieutenants who
trusted him and each other. As it turned out, he needed every one of
these weapons to move the nation toward his next goal—preparation
for the war with Germany.

Frankfurter's overall mobilization campaign took the form of four
distinct phases. Each of these programs was linked, and failure to
achieve any one of them would have significantly affected the United
States's ability to wage war. Before the bombing at Pearl Harbor, the
justice worked on two programs designed to increase the country's
readiness in monetary funding and materiel. Working with Treasury
Secretary Henry Morgenthau, he lobbied for a tax program sufficient
to fund the mobilization drive. Then, using his expanded network of
allies, including Jean Monnet, he sought to increase industrial capacity so that an adequate level of war supplies would be produced.

The justice's final two programs were conceived after the entry of
the United States into the conflict. At that time he labored to secure a
reorganized government capable of a sustained, successful management of both production and the fighting. Once that goal was achieved,
the justice endeavored to reduce the possibility that military interests
would become ascendant in the governmental operation. He sought to
keep the military and civilian sectors in balance, if not in harmony,
during the conflict. While Frankfurter was only one of many engaged
in these activities, his efforts were by no means insignificant in realizing their implementation.

Fully aware of the staggering monetary costs that would be run up
during the impending war, the justice, in his initial mobilization ef-

forts in early 1940, urged officials to secure the necessary funding through a revised income tax structure. In a long memorandum to the president, he recommended, just as Brandeis had done, that a more progressive income tax be created by plugging loopholes, raising the capital gains tax, and establishing a levy on the undistributed profits of corporations. This memorandum was passed on to Secretary of the Treasury Morgenthau, who used it extensively in drafting his own tax proposal. An entry in Morgenthau's personal diary dated March 4, 1939 reveals that he was already familiar with these ideas by that early date, having previously discussed them with the justice himself. In fact, during this 1939 meeting with Morgenthau, Frankfurter had even recommended several strategies for increasing Congress's receptivity to the program.[89]

It was not uncommon for Morgenthau to consult members of the Supreme Court before proposing controversial legislation. For example, a memorandum filed in his personal papers indicates that in May 1939, Morgenthau spoke with Justices Frankfurter and Douglas regarding a proposed measure to permit wiretapping by enforcement officers with the authorization of the head of the agency charged with the investigation of a particular statutory violation. Not surprisingly, both civil-libertarian justices argued against the bill. Frankfurter told Morgenthau that "it was better that a hundred guilty men should be at large than that the Government should do an ignoble act." Furthermore, he viewed the proposal as a shortcut for evidence that might easily be obtainable elsewhere. As a former member of the Securities and Exchange Commission, Douglas reasoned that such power was unnecessary for an individual in that position. After a rough count of the votes on the Court, Morgenthau had chosen not to endorse the measure.[90]

Later entries in the personal diaries of both Morgenthau and Vice-President Henry Wallace show that when the tax proposal was under active consideration in 1940 various members of the administration consulted Frankfurter repeatedly over a period of several weeks to get his suggestions on the legislative language. Even after the Treasury plan had been announced, Frankfurter argued with Samuel Rosenman, in a personal letter written on April 16, 1942, which was passed along to FDR, that the plan should have been based even more on the "ability-to-pay" principle. Hence, he called for increasing the corporate excess profits tax 100 percent. Consistent with his progressive tax philosophy, the justice argued that the tax revisions should be made palatable to the "millions of unseen and unheard-from followers of the President."[91]

On June 25, 1940, Roosevelt signed into law the first revenue act of 1940, containing most of, though not all the progressive changes in tax structure sought by Frankfurter. For instance, the excess corporate profits tax enacted by Congress later that year in response to a second presidential message carried a much smaller levy than the 100 percent proposed by the justice.[92]

Frankfurter's next program—to mobilize the industrial sector for war—faced two types of resistance: the isolationist trend in American society and the sluggish nature of the economy, still struggling to rid itself of its depression mentality. His initial effort in this area was simply to convince people of the need to expand industrial capacity. The justice highly favored a plan offered by labor leader Walter Reuther to convert civilian automobile factories into assembly lines for airplanes. However, the problem at this time was much more basic. Still faced with recessionary pressures, businesses had a great deal of idle production capacity and were hesitant to expand production capacity by making additional capital investments. Should the United States enter the war, these industrialists were confident, there would somehow be an automatic increase in industrial output. Frankfurter, though, saw the need to increase production immediately, in preparation for that mobilization. So, he convened "dinner-seminars" at his home and spoke repeatedly with allies such as Isador Lubin on the White House staff and Robert Nathan in the Defense Advisory Commission on the matter throughout the latter half of 1940.

The main focus of these talks, as recalled by Nathan in a personal interview, concerned the crucial steel and aluminum industries. Companies such as Alcoa, the only major aluminum producer at the time, needed to be persuaded to invest immediately in additional machinery. Frankfurter sought to bring in anyone who had any ideas on the subject. At these meetings he was once again the curious professor—asking relevant questions and arming himself with new information. Like Brandeis before him, Frankfurter knew that a command of the facts was absolutely necessary before one could have any effect on decisionmaking. While he could not personally change governmental policies, those who attended these meetings were conscious that the justice was capable of picking up a phone and telling the president something like, "Look, you had better induce the steel industry to expand capacity now or we're in trouble."

On this particular issue, in fact, the justice did serve as a useful channel to the White House until, in early 1941, the battle was won. The steel and aluminum firms finally made a commitment to producing vast amounts of extra tonnage, and additional companies, such as Kaiser and Reynolds Metals, were persuaded by the government to enter the aluminum industry, thus breaking the old monopoly and adding new production capacity. No matter how much was produced, though, wise men realized that even more would be needed if and when the United States did enter the war.[93]

In the spring of 1941 Jean Monnet moved to take advantage of the growing fear in the United States that she might meet the same fate as Western Europe. He, too, was shocked by the underutilization of productive capacity, as well as by the resistance of business and the administration to any change, even in the face of such grave danger. So, he turned to Frankfurter and his network of contacts in initiating wide-ranging discussions on the matter. His message was simple— you must recognize and face up to the incredible magnitude of the all-out production effort that will be necessary to win the war. It was his belief—and it turned out to be a sage one—that only by outproducing the German war machine could the war be shortened. Moreover, he realized that the sleeping industrial giant, the United States, possessed the only economy in the world capable of such an effort before time ran out. While the "cash-and-carry" and Lend-Lease programs were helpful, the United States had to be prepared for its own entry into the conflict.

To accomplish this aim, Monnet conceived and advocated the "Victory Program" for the "Arsenal of Democracy."[94] This program, vital for the success of the allies in World War II, has been inadequately explored in the published literature. Some attention was devoted to it recently with the translation of Monnet's own memoirs into English. Now, interviews with those men, who, as young governmental bureaucrats, worked closely with Monnet—Robert Nathan, Edward F. Prichard, Jr., Joseph L. Rauh, Jr., and Milton Katz—make it possible to reveal more of the story, including the significant role played by Justice Felix Frankfurter.

Monnet's idea was to establish targets for the quantity of armaments needed to be produced in the event that the United States entered the war. This would include American supply requirements plus those for Great Britain, Russia, and the other Allies. By simply predicting the necessary production levels, Monnet hoped to stir the American people and businessmen into sacrificing civilian goods in order to increase industrial capacity even further. Several administrators, including Robert Nathan, were persuaded to create balance sheets of these supply targets. Working with projections of the future size of the Army and the military materiel requirements, they figured out the industrial production requirements for a conflict situation. Out poured thousands of figures displaying the numbers of fighter planes, bombers, transports, tanks, artillery, rifles, and ships of all varieties that would be necessary. These figures were then converted into various measures of limitations: the overall industrial output of the United States in aluminum, steel, and copper, the available financial resources in terms of GNP, and the anticipated unemployment figures.

During this campaign Frankfurter served in various capacities. He remained in continual contact with Monnet—plotting strategy, sharing information, and trading gossip about public officials. Well briefed, the justice could then pass this data along to members of the White House staff and to visitors at his frequent dinner-seminars. Documents peppered with marginal notes in the justice's handwriting indicate that on occasion he would even redraft and then circulate throughout the administration Monnet's memoranda.[95] Moreover, by introducing Monnet to the officials he had previously helped to place in Washington, Frankfurter was able to serve as a conduit between those government employees and the French diplomat. In this way, he was kept fully aware of Monnet's advice to others and was cognizant of every phase of the Victory Program's preparation.

At the same time the justice was serving in an important capacity within the War Department itself, by preparing it for this massive mobilization. Few groups would be more central to the accomplishment of these aims than the labor unions, and in 1940 they were becoming increasingly uneasy about the effect of the impending conflict on their status. Consequently, Frankfurter used his relationship with both Secretary of War Henry L. Stimson and union official Sidney Hillman to promote an air of cooperation between the two groups. A number of notations by Stimson in his personal diary illustrate how the justice accomplished this aim.

Initially, Frankfurter convinced the secretary of war in mid-

November to address personally the American Federation of Labor convention in New Orleans on the position of the War Department toward the labor unions. They needed to be reassured, Frankfurter argued, that times of war would not affect in any way their full rights and privileges and, in fact, would increase the need for the organizational powers of the unions. The justice then adopted his usual role of researcher/speechwriter for Stimson—sending him various government documents, Supreme Court opinions, and clippings from newspapers here and abroad on the importance of labor unions in wartime. Within a day, Frankfurter was actually writing portions of the address himself (drawing on material he had gathered from his "boys" throughout Washington), and Stimson gratefully used nearly every paragraph he received.[96]

While the address was a huge success, it did not end the secretary's difficulties with labor. Knowing of Stimson's austere personality, the justice appointed himself the department's intermediary with the unions for the duration of the war. It was a role Stimson eagerly conceded; he continually consulted Frankfurter whenever any of his department's policies affected the labor unions. In late December 1940, Stimson told Frankfurter about his proposed reorganization of the liaison mechanism between the Naval and War Departments and the Defense Advisory Commission. Knowing that this proposal would affect labor, Frankfurter cleared the idea with Sidney Hillman and helped set up a meeting between the labor official and the two cabinet secretaries. Thanks in part to Frankfurter's mediating efforts, Hillman did agree to the plan, despite his grave doubts about its efficacy.

So effective was the justice in this labor consultant role, that his good offices were even used in 1941 to facilitate negotiations with the unions on certain clauses in War Department contracts. Several entries from Stimson's personal diary provide examples of Frankfurter's service in this capacity. When Henry Ford was accused in mid-January 1941 of shortchanging the unions on a government contract for the production of tanks, Frankfurter had his "boys" investigate the problem and then compared notes with Stimson regarding possible solutions.[97] A month later, an objection was raised by Sidney Hillman to the use of alien workers on government contracts. When Hillman offered as a quid pro quo for accepting these workers the idea that a time limit be put on the lengthy appeals process for the government's Labor Board decisions, Stimson brought Frankfurter in as an adviser.

The justice's solution here was simply to speak with Chief Justice Hughes about the possibility of changing the rules of the Court on such appeals. Toward the end of that year, the secretary of war was troubled by the power of the unions to force unwilling workers to organize, so he held a series of discussions with the justice on the topic. As a result of all these efforts, when it came time to put the Victory Program into operation, the labor unions were ready to provide the necessary support to achieve the desired results. Given the personalities involved, there can be little doubt that Frankfurter's efforts were important in removing any potential obstacles.[98]

The Victory Program was a remarkable success. The military was forced into completely analyzing its production needs on the contingency that the United States might enter the war. Moreover, the administration, industry, and labor were now prepared to implement the plan. By late October 1941, this group had projected the industrial requirements for each of the following years, assuming a variety of economic scenarios. Each time the figures were sent to the White House, administration officials would add to the projections in an effort to push the economy even further. Thanks to the timely efforts of these groups, when Pearl Harbor was bombed on December 7, 1941 the president had available all the figures necessary to put the Victory Program of production into immediate operation. The military knew what type of equipment to order and, as Monnet expected, the industries found a way to meet those demands.

After the entry of the United States into the war, Frankfurter and his newly appointed colleague on the Supreme Court, James Byrnes, realized that these production commitments would be useless without a government structure that was adequate to manage the entire mobilization effort. Not only were they concerned about the lack of preparedness in the administration, they feared the strain this new burden would place on a prematurely aging and increasingly ailing president. So each justice set out to rectify the situation. Byrnes, a long-time supporter of FDR who as a senator from South Carolina had shepherded many of the administration's bills through Congress, now entered the reorganization process at the request of the president. Very soon Attorney General Francis Biddle was conferring with him on all emergency war legislation; in fact, each defense bill was cleared through Byrnes's office as well.[99]

When each of these measures reached the Supreme Court building,

it gave Felix Frankfurter another opportunity to make his own substantial contribution. He appointed himself as one of Byrnes's informal policy advisers and spent even more of his time conferring with
his colleague on these matters. Once again, the locus of power served
as a magnet that riveted Frankfurter's attention on a particular individual. Byrnes had no objections, though, for they had gotten along
well since his appointment to the Court and he could use all the help
available. Together they worked on generating reorganization legislation written in a manner that Congress would immediately pass.

One of the most vital resources Frankfurter brought to this new
partnership was his old network of protégés scattered throughout
Washington. Joseph L. Rauh, Jr., has recounted an incident that aptly
demonstrates how the justice utilized this personal resource to assist
Byrnes. Immediately after the bombing at Pearl Harbor, Rauh received
one of his now routine phone calls from F.F. Without even so much
as a "Hello," the justice hurriedly told his former clerk, "Joe, we need
an Overman Act right away." The protégé tried not to reveal his bewilderment: "An Overman Act, Mr. Justice?" In an insistent tone
Frankfurter said, "That's right, Joe, an Overman Act—you go up to
talk to Jimmy Byrnes and he'll show you how to do this." Rauh's
response was carefully measured: "Fine, Mr. Justice, but just one
question—what the hell is an Overman Act?" Despite the fact that
virtually no one else in Washington would have known either, Frankfurter snapped, "Joe, you simply amaze me—how can a supposedly
educated man not know what an Overman Act is. But then, of course,
you wouldn't know this because nobody reads anything anymore!" [100]

For Rauh, this tone was all too familiar. Years before, there was one
unfortunate day in Professor Frankfurter's class when he had not been
prepared with the reading assignment—the Tom Mooney bombing
case. [101] When he was called on to recite the case he had two equally
bad alternatives: admit his lack of preparation and receive an immediate tongue lashing or double talk for a while in an attempt to bluff
the master. Knowing that sometimes the latter route worked, he chose
it. It was a decision he quickly regretted. He began with "Well, you
have to know what the times were like out there during that period."
Before he could continue, Frankfurter exploded, "You don't know that
I was President Wilson's special assistant, who was charged with investigating that incident, do you? I knew what the times were like out
there, and so did the Administration when I finished my work." It

was one of the few bad lashings Rauh had received at that school, and he never forgot it.

Now in 1941, since he was going to be charged with working on an "Overman Act," Rauh thought it wise to risk the consequences of admitting his ignorance about the original measure. The former law clerk was, of course, subjected to another patronizing lecture from his mentor, who explained that the bill completely reorganized the government during World War I. It was apparent to Rauh that both Frankfurter and Byrnes had been in close contact with the president on this matter, and that it was FDR who had told them of the need for a reorganized bureaucracy in order to function during the conflict.

Rauh immediately journeyed to Byrnes's office to receive his marching orders. The justice, who had been expecting Rauh's visit, outlined a proposal for providing the president with complete reorganization power using the Overman Act as a guide. After having had prolonged discussions with F.F., Byrnes told his caller, he and Frankfurter had both come to the conclusion that only this type of legislation would provide the necessary relief for the overburdened FDR. Then Byrnes picked up the phone and called Hatton Summers, chairman of the House Judiciary Committee, who was selected to manage the floor debate. "Hatton," he said, using a condescending instructional tone, "I'm sending over a young man, someone who has real integrity, to help you on this Overman Act thing." Putting his hand over the phone he asked the puzzled Rauh for his name. Then he continued, "Hatton, his name is Joseph Rauh—he's one of Felix's boys—and he's speaking for the President on this matter. He'll tell you what we have to have. And Hatton," he continued, "This is the way it has to be—there's no time to waste."

Having thus been transformed into FDR's personal emissary to Capitol Hill, Rauh, and several Treasury Department officials drafted what would become the First War Powers Act. The entire process was carefully supervised by Justice Frankfurter. Like the Overman Act before it, the measure provided the president with a blanket emergency authority to reorganize the executive departments for a period extending until six months after the fighting had ceased. In fact, Title I of the First War Powers Act was virtually identical in language to that of the Overman Act, except for some modernization of terminology.[102] Each statute redistributed functions among executive departments, coordinated existing agencies, provided for the expenditure of money for these purposes, gave authority to abolish bureaus, and suspended all conflicting laws.

The danger came when the measure reached the Senate floor and various interest groups vigorously lobbied to add their own provisions to the bill. To combat these forces, Rauh was instructed to sit next to the Majority Leader Alben Barkley, just as John McCloy had done so successfully in the Lend-Lease fight. Whenever a question was raised, the senator would simply whisper to Rauh, "What's the response to that one," and then repeat the young man's words to his colleagues. Consequently, the act was passed on December 18, 1941, eleven days after Pearl Harbor, without substantial alteration. Without a doubt, much of the credit for its passage belonged to two men whose names were never publicly associated with the measure—Felix Frankfurter and James Byrnes, both associate justices of the United States Supreme Court.

One final question plagued Rauh: how had Frankfurter known about this fairly obscure Overman Act? Not until our conversation would Rauh discover that the same thing was true here as with Rauh's embarrassment over the Mooney incident at Harvard. The justice knew about the Overman Act because many years earlier he had had a hand in its formulation. Some twenty-four years earlier, faced with another world war and a similar lack of government preparedness, another Supreme Court justice, Louis Brandeis, proposed the same solution of reorganizing the executive branch. His lobbyist then, Felix Frankfurter, had learned his lesson well.

Even with the success of passing the First War Powers Act, by this time Frankfurter had become acutely aware of the immediate need to reorganize the Office of Production Management (OPM), which was proving to be wholly inadequate for the mobilization task ahead. After discussing the issue thoroughly with James Byrnes, Frankfurter wrote letters and memoranda to both FDR and Harry Hopkins, urging that all responsibility for war mobilization be delegated to one "czar" acting for the administration.[103] In each of these missives, he was careful to say that the issue had been raised with Byrnes and that his colleague was in complete agreement.

Frankfurter had learned well from the failure of the Allies to force themselves to face up to what had to be done to survive. Although France and Great Britain had declared war on Germany in September 1939, over the long winter of the "Sitz War" both allies seemed to rely on the expectation that this war would be fought out as the first had been—as a long, drawn-out, trench war of attrition. As a consequence, neither had been in any frantic rush to prepare to meet the sudden German onslaught that came in May of 1940 and defeated the great French army in six weeks.

Frankfurter was determined that this failure of France and Great Britain to arm themselves aggressively, even after war had been declared, would not be duplicated in the United States. By designating one person to make in the president's name the "day-to-day decisions in the execution of policies," the justice argued in a letter to presidential adviser Harry Hopkins, "the Victory Program adopted [by FDR could be] promptly and effectively carried out."[104] While Hopkins agreed with the proposal, he objected to the heavy-handed pressure being used and responded with a terse: "Dear Felix, I have read your note. I know it is important. Do not be impatient."[105] Within twenty-four hours, Hopkins had on his desk Frankfurter's profuse apology and an expression of total confidence in the ability of the Roosevelt Administration to handle the problem. Nevertheless, these repeated pleas had hit a responsive chord, for Hopkins telephoned Byrnes requesting his views on the need for such a production czar. Perhaps he did not believe that Frankfurter had secured Byrnes's support or, more likely, the president's right-hand man felt that he could work more closely with Byrnes than with Frankfurter. When Byrnes proposed the same solution, he was enlisted to write a memorandum justifying such an appointment. Byrnes's own message was identical to that of his colleague: one person, not a committee like the Office of Production Management, must be given the authority and held responsible for the procurement decisions.[106] Clearly, the two justices were consulting each other regarding the wording of their memos.

Unhappy with the lack of action on the issue and incapable of maintaining his silence, Frankfurter made one last effort in early January 1942 to persuade Hopkins to move. Earlier he had solicited a memorandum from a British lawyer on the problems of industrial production and government control that England had experienced during the early phases of the war. The memorandum began: "What I am terribly afraid of is that the U.S. will not profit sufficiently by our mistakes." The writer then went on to argue that the "all-important" increase in production could only be achieved by "concentration of industry."[107] While acknowledging that turning to monopolistic practices would take "political courage," the writer warned that the United States should not wait two years as England did before taking the necessary action. Frankfurter attached this memorandum to his own cover letter expressing "confidence" in the writer and sent it off to Hopkins.

Even though this letter contained a very important message, and, indeed, predicted how the new agency Hopkins was contemplating would eventually operate, Frankfurter no longer believed that he could persuade the presidential assistant on his own. So, he secured a written message of support from Byrnes as well to insure that the words would be examined carefully and that action would be taken soon.[108] Two letters discovered in the Harry Hopkins papers at the Roosevelt Presidential Library indicate that shortly thereafter the same document found its way to FDR's desk; later in January when the War Production Board was created by executive order to replace the OPM, its new head, Donald Nelson, also received a copy.[109]

This new War Production Board (WPB) was empowered with all the authority the justices had wanted it to have.[110] Not only were all the industrial mobilization powers centralized here, but the office had control over production priorities as well. So, the board dealt with incentives for private plant production, while it also searched for methods to reduce civilian demands in order to meet military requirements. Inevitably, the WPB became involved in determining which civilian services were essential and what limits should be placed on production demands from the industrial sector. The task was a delicate one that required highly skilled, objective administrators who would not be captured by advocates of either the military or civilian sectors. Consequently, Frankfurter made it his special task to watch these officials carefully in order to evaluate their job performance.

The justice was greatly displeased by the initial choice of Donald Nelson to head the WPB. Frankfurter had little personal respect for Nelson, believing from his performance as director of priorities for the OPM that rather than being a strong administrator, he was a puppet of the large industrial interests. Convinced that labor and civilian needs would eventually suffer from Nelson's ineptness, the justice, immediately after Nelson's appointment, encouraged FDR to find a replacement for him, writing: "It took Lincoln three years to discover [General Ulysses S.] Grant, and you may not have hit on your production

Grant first crack out of the box. But the *vital* thing is that you have created the function . . ." [*Italics in original*] [111]

Since Nelson was to be the man in charge, though, Frankfurter did his best at first to try to guide him. Shortly after the appointment, Frankfurter invited several administrators to his home for one of his dinner-seminars and to bring them together for the first time with the French diplomat, Jean Monnet. Among the guests was thirty-five-year-old Milton Katz, a former Frankfurter student who had somehow avoided being characterized as one of his "boys," but who still respected the justice enormously from their repeated contacts over the years. After helping to draft the executive order creating the WPB, Katz was made the agency's solicitor, and soon became the chief policy adviser to Donald Nelson. Naturally, his new position made him a prime prospect for possible use by Frankfurter as a conduit to influence the board's head.

As Katz was soon to discover, the purpose of the dinner invitation was to prepare for Nelson's immediate education in his new job. Over a delicious garden salad, Monnet informed the group that Nelson could never succeed in his post unless, as Katz recalls hearing that day, "he took it on himself to direct but not to administer." The Frenchman was telling Katz quite clearly that the WPB head should not become involved in minute administrative details. Instead, he should stand above the day-to-day issues and ask fundamental questions about basic priorities, objectives, allocation of resources, and the relationship of the production effort to the military effort. Otherwise, Monnet believed, Nelson would quickly become lost in tedious detail.[112]

While he watched Nelson's performance, throughout 1942 Frankfurter used his wide range of contacts in every quarter of the administration to press for a number of other pet projects. No detail of the war machinery was too small for the justice's attention. A memorandum discovered in the Roosevelt papers reveals that in mid-April, when Frankfurter saw an inflationary economy spiraling out of control, he drafted and sent to Samuel Rosenman for the president's attention a complete proposal for a wage-price freeze combined with a rationing plan to prevent the hoarding of goods.[113] The diary and personal papers of Henry A. Wallace indicate that during this same month the justice put the vice-president in contact with chemist and Zionist leader, Chaim Weizmann, who had developed a new technique for processing grain alcohol into rubber, in order that the government might begin to reverse the declining production levels of manufactured rubber in the United States.[114] In late June the justice became concerned that only partially filled supply ships were being sent to Great Britain. A quick Frankfurter phone call to his main troubleshooter in the War Department, "Jack" McCloy, whose brother-in-law, Lewis W. Douglas, happened to be the head of the War Shipping Administration, was followed by an exchange of letters between the justice and Douglas himself, and the problem was quickly rectified.[115]

During this period Frankfurter also became concerned by the sluggish rate of the production of war materiel and began touting the mobilization plan of one of Sidney Hillman's protégés, automotive engineer Alexander Taub.* Taub argued that bottlenecks in the production process could be eliminated by having small businesses around the nation mass produce individual parts of a piece of military machinery and then have the final product assembled at other specially designated assembly plants. In this way, Taub theorized, no single company or plant could create a bottleneck for needed supplies. Since this proposal was in the best Brandeisian tradition, it is not surprising to find Frankfurter putting aside his earlier arguments on behalf of "concentrating industries" in order to present Taub's new plan. Unlike Brandeis, who conceived a program and never wavered until it was adopted, Frankfurter tended to be more flexible, advocating at the moment whatever sound idea seemed most likely to be put into use. In this instance, though, he did not get the reaction from within the administration he would have liked. For when Assistant Secretary of War Robert Patterson first heard about the idea he ridiculed it, saying: "Just how are we going to drag a battleship from San Francisco to Chicago so that all of its parts can be pieced together?" [117]

In October 1942, Congress created the Office of Economic Stabilization, and shortly thereafter, Justice James Byrnes resigned from the Court to become its director. In letters to attorney Charles C. Burlingham and FDR, Frankfurter expressed grief over the loss of his judicial colleague: "For the first time something very good for the coun-

---

* A naturalized American citizen born in England, Taub had made his mark in the administration in 1941, when he argued that by changing the compression ratios of various engines, nearly 70 percent of the existing automotive plants could be converted to defense production. So, he was placed in the conversion section of the government's Division of Contract Distribution in order to implement some of his plans.[116]

try is bad for me . . . [but] I expect great things from Byrnes."[118] However, this sense of loss did not prevent Frankfurter from immediately placing one of his protégés, Edward F. Prichard, Jr., as Byrnes's assistant, thus giving him access to information and decision-making influence in that agency as well.[119]

None of these activities, however, interested Frankfurter more than the work of the War Production Board, which, after all, had been set up to control the crucial production and procurement decisions in the war effort. While Frankfurter kept himself apprised of all the various activities of the board by conferring personally with allies there, his focus was gradually drawn to an impending collision between the military and civilian cliques on the board. Able to sift through first-hand reports of internal power struggles, Frankfurter had, by 1943, become preoccupied with a secret fear that the military might be maneuvering to take complete control of the decision-making process. Bearing the primary responsibility for winning the war, the military felt that it alone had the right, as well as the proper professional qualifications, to determine how the limited supplies of vital raw materials—steel, aluminum, and copper—ought to be allocated among tactical, strategic, and civilian needs. From another side, there were those advancing the view of the industrialists, who believed that they were the only ones qualified to make decisions regarding the most cost-effective distribution of the limited raw materials available. And, of course, there were those who mistrusted any compromise of the American tradition of having generalists exercise ultimate control over all experts, including most especially of having civilians exercise control over the military. As the battle lines were being drawn, and when it seemed that the mood of the country might be leaning toward favoring the position of the Armed Services people, Frankfurter had his next crusade.

This final involvement of Frankfurter with the mobilization effort—reining in the military—proved to be one of his most difficult, for it required that he lobby against positions he had earlier taken. Not only would he be moving against the tide of public opinion, but he would be faced with attempting to prevent the military from exploiting the enormous power of the government's production czar, the enormity of which he had helped legitimize. Worse, the czar, Donald Nelson, turned out to be the wrong man to be entrusted with such power. It quickly became apparent that he tended to bend under pressure, and found it difficult to make decisions, making altogether too inviting a target for those who would co-opt his authority. No doubt, part of his vulnerability could have been laid at the feet of Justice Frankfurter, who had been taking repeated potshots at him in private meetings with important Washington people. Now, to save the War Production Board from the domination by the military, Frankfurter would have to prop up this once-convenient target of his derision.

In the early days of 1943 he arranged a dinner at his home to marshal his troops and try out his tentative plans among friends. His guests, Milton Katz, Jean Monnet, Robert Nathan, and Ben Cohen, quickly agreed that Nelson was not up to the task of holding off the military as things then stood and that a separate administrator was needed to monitor civilian suppliers. The evening ended with a brainstorming session in which the names of various prospective appointees were tossed around. One name that was thrown out drew derisive laughter—Bernard Baruch, elder statesman with a strong pro-military bias, was obviously not their man.[120]

But it was nearly Baruch who had the last laugh, for he became the focus of a plot by the military to replace Nelson and establish military dominance within the War Production Board. Through Katz, the justice learned that two members of the board, Assistant Secretary of War Robert Patterson and Assistant Secretary of the Navy James Forrestal, believing that Nelson's priorities were misplaced, had for months been trying to neutralize the board's powers by making decisions independent of it. In time, Katz added, Nelson had come to rely on Baruch for counsel, thus moving the board even closer to the position of the military.

Eventually, Patterson and Forrestal plotted to have the weakened Nelson replaced by Baruch. Because Baruch was seventy-three years old, it was expected that he would have to rely on his staff for the bulk of the work to be done, which meant that Fred Eberstadt, one of the assistants to the WPB czar would, in effect, be running things. This would certainly please the military, since Eberstadt had been placed on the board by Patterson and Forrestal. When it appeared that James Byrnes had approved the Baruch appointment the military takeover seemed a shoo-in—but only to those who had not figured on the political infighting skills of Justice Frankfurter.[121]

Neither Nelson, in his autobiography, nor Frankfurter, in his published diary,[122] gives a complete account of how Nelson's job was saved, but the recollections of Katz, drawn from a personal interview, now make it possible for the first time to piece together the story. Upon learning of the plan to replace Nelson with Baruch the justice went into action. Not only did he dislike Baruch's policies, he disliked the man personally. "In the world of inflated egos," the justice said, "Baruch has inflated reputation number one."[123] But even if there had not been the element of personal animosity, Frankfurter might still have moved as forcefully, for he truly feared the ascendancy of the military within the WPB that Baruch's appointment as its head would surely have foretold.

Because of his past criticisms of Nelson, however, saving Nelson by ambushing Baruch would not now be an easy matter for the justice. Moreover, Frankfurter was not coming into the fray with his usual army of confederates in place. His only high-level contact at the WPB, Milton Katz, had long ago proved himself not to be a blind follower of the justice but an independent thinker who would follow his own best instincts. Ever flexible, Frankfurter abandoned his usual role of teacher and leader and encouraged Katz to meet with him on several occasions just to "bat the breeze" about current events and problems, with Frankfurter going to great lengths to be subtle in the interpretive gloss he might put on things. Though these meetings were not in the mold of the typical Frankfurter advising sessions, they served a similar purpose. Katz, eager to receive new perspectives on the WPB problem, listened carefully to Frankfurter, and, while he would not accept assignments from the justice, he was, no doubt, influenced by him. These chats also maintained for Frankfurter an open line to happenings at the WPB.

One reason Frankfurter found this independent man so receptive to his overtures was that Katz had his own need of alliances. As a supporter of Nelson he too had found himself under continued verbal assault from the military. Recognizing that there were those in the department who would have loved to force his resignation, Katz saw the utility in keeping at least one person with friends in high places advised as to the job he was truly doing. Felix Frankfurter, whose tentacles were known to reach into very nearly every governmental agency, including the White House itself, seemed to be the ideal person for such a plan. So, Katz used the justice as a sort of disseminator of information, dealing him all the facts about the controversy at the WPB in the hopes that this information would find its way to those in positions to remedy what Katz himself saw as a potentially dangerous situation. The strategy worked well.

Friends in the White House, among them Edward Prichard, advised Frankfurter that an executive order firing Nelson and replacing him with Baruch had been prepared and was sitting on the president's desk waiting for his signature. Though it was late at night, Frankfurter did manage to put those who had given him the information in touch with Katz, and in a subsequent pre-dawn meeting with Nelson, Katz advised his boss to fire Eberstadt. To make a *fait accompli* of it— indeed to keep Nelson himself from changing his mind under subsequent pressure—the firing would be announced at a morning news conference. The reasoning behind it all was that firing Eberstadt would preclude the appointment of Baruch, for as Katz assured Nelson, "Baruch knows he's too old and he'll only take the job if Eberstadt is there to carry the day-to-day burden for him."

Nelson followed his subordinate's instructions precisely, dealing the military a permanent setback in their plan to gain control of the board. Nelson never did learn how Katz came to know about the executive order, but it is unlikely that he would have guessed that his savior had been his old nemesis, Felix Frankfurter. "There is no question," Katz believes today, "that if Justice Frankfurter had not been there, saving Nelson would have been impossible, because no one would have found out about the move in sufficient time." [124]

Discussions between Frankfurter, Monnet, and Katz led to the conclusion that Nelson's rating with FDR had to be buoyed up until the leadership problem in the WPB could be solved other than through yielding to those arguing the position of the military. Frankfurter had an opportunity to advance this view when Samuel Rosenman called that weekend. The justice offered a variety of objections to the continued consideration of Baruch's candidacy—the unlikelihood of his being able to fulfill his duties due to his advanced age, his failure to demonstrate effectiveness in performing certain World War I duties, and most important of all, his association with known critics of FDR. When Rosenman agreed with the thrust of what he was hearing, he prevailed upon the justice to present these arguments directly to the president. Frankfurter declined, saying:

> Of course whenever the President wants to talk to me about anything
> about which I am free to talk, I shall tell him frankly what I think.
> But it is not my business to volunteer views.[125]

However, Frankfurter's newly discovered reticence did not prevent him
from suggesting that Rosenman simply relay the substance of their
talk to the president. Of course, it had been more than a new-found
sense of judicial propriety that had precluded the justice's approaching the president on this matter. There was the unfortunate fact that
his usefulness in making the case against appointing Baruch had been
compromised by his earlier attempts to poison the president's opinion
of the present occupant of the position, Nelson.

Late in May 1943 the president solved the problem his own way,
"layering in" Nelson by creating a new Office of War Mobilization
and placing it under the unassailable leadership of James F. Byrnes.
There was one task remaining, one that the justice reserved for himself. Henry Stimson had to be reassured that it was not *his* authority
that Byrnes's appointment had been intended to undercut, and Frankfurter spent several hours assuring Stimson that the establishment of
the new agency would not substantially affect his own position.[126]

In helping to mobilize the American government, economy, and
public opinion for war, Justice Frankfurter reached the zenith of his
political influence. Despite the fact of his being only one of hundreds
involved in the many decisions that had to be made, his genius for
creating and using friendships gave him a power to move events far
beyond that of most Washingtonians with prestigious portfolios. His
need to, and knack for, finding the center of political gravity allowed
him to enhance the authority of those policymakers whose policies he
favored and to diminish that of those whose policies he found poorly
reasoned.

As the war went on, and eventual victory became inevitable, the
problem facing the government changed from one of organization to
one of administration, from one of devising effective organizational
plans to one of finding the people to carry them out. Even the president found it useful as well as necessary to delegate broad areas of
his authority to others as the conduct of the war became formalized.
And as one would expect, Frankfurter could not maintain the same
level of influence through this stage as he had when the decision-

making was consolidated in the highest echelons of government. Consequently, even though his intense need to be involved never ebbed, he was destined to lose increments of his power to the boulder pushers in the many war agencies. But this was no great loss, for he was already well into a search for new ways to express his political talents.

7

The Double Felix: Brandeis's Legacy, Justice Frankfurter, and the Problem of Judicial Temperament

Louis Brandeis did not witness the end of Frankfurter's war-time campaigns, for at 7:15 in the evening of October 5, 1941 the prophet's own crusade came to a quiet end. At age eighty-four, with his family gathered around him in his California Street apartment, Brandeis succumbed to the effects of a heart attack he had suffered six days earlier. He had spent the thirty-two months since his retirement from the Court in quiet seclusion, keeping in touch with his many friends in and out of government, only rarely venturing out for a car ride, or to lobby for that last crusade of his long, cause-filled life, the welfare of the world's Jewish population. A year after his death his ashes would be buried beneath the porch of the building housing the University of Louisville Law School he had helped establish.[1]

But first, for all he had done for others, it was now time for others to pay tribute to him. The nation's leaders did not hold back in expressing how they viewed the role he had played in reshaping America's government, its institutions, and its society. The prophet's ally in so many old labor battles, Senator Robert F. Wagner, commented that the justice's "achievements are measured not in terms of legal opinions rendered, but of whole institutions shaped to fit the needs of the times." President Roosevelt put aside recent differences to praise "my faithful friend through long years" in saying that "the whole nation will bow in reverence to the memory of one whose life in the law, both as advocate and judge, was guided by the finest attributes of mind and heart and soul."[2]

One of the justice's former law clerks, Dean Acheson, then serving as assistant secretary of state, said of him: "What he has meant to us is not very different from what he has meant to hundreds of young men and women who have grown up under his influence. . . . [T]hroughout these years we have brought him all of our problems and all of our troubles, and he has had time for all of us."[3] From the Zionist Organization of America, which Brandeis had helped create, came this tribute from one of its leaders, Vice-President Solomon Goldman: "To America, he was another Lincoln, to the Jewish people an Isaiah who envisaged with the same glow of passion the world of justice and peace, and in that world a Zion restored."[4]

A public expression of Justice Frankfurter's loss appeared in the December 1941 issue of the journal he and Brandeis had both loved so deeply—the *Harvard Law Review*. In it he portrayed Brandeis as "the one best qualified to judge" and as a man of whom "one is tempted to believe that [the] judicial office was most fitting for his nature." But then Frankfurter began his final paragraph with a statement remarkable for him to have made about his former patron, mentor, and fellow crusader: "A man so immersed in affairs as Louis D. Brandeis must have closed the door on many of his interests when he went on the bench."[5] It was especially remarkable because of its appearance in the very law review that had long been their vehicle for expressing, without identification or attribution, the brilliant insights and analyses of Justice Brandeis in order to exert a powerful political influence within the legal academic community on so many issues of social and political importance.

As it turned out, Felix Frankfurter was more than a faithful lieutenant and defender of Brandeis; he provided him a window through the curtain of death, a means of influencing events not imagined in his own time. Vivid evidence of this can be found on the front page of *The New York Times* of October 6, 1941. Side by side with the announcement of Brandeis's death is a report from Hyde Park that the president was about to decide whether or not to modify the United States's stance of neutrality toward the fighting just going into its third year in Europe. One of the central actors in bringing FDR to the position he then held had been Supreme Court Justice Frankfurter. The prophet may now have been gone, but his former scribe was already doing his own writing on the wall of history.

To appreciate and understand the different approaches of Brandeis and Frankfurter toward extrajudicial politics, one must first reflect on the similarities and differences in their pre-judicial careers and even their personalities. Frankfurter, the man to whom Brandeis had entrusted his fondest dreams and hopes, came to the Supreme Court at approximately the same stage in his life as his mentor had in 1916. Not surprisingly, public perceptions of each man at the time of his own appointment were similar. The exploits of each, frequently reported in the press, had made each among the best known legal figures of his own generation. If Brandeis had been the "People's Attorney" before his appointment, Frankfurter was quite possibly the "People's Professor" before his own. Like his mentor, Frankfurter came to the Court with impeccable credentials as a liberal. He had served with distinction as counsel to the National Association for the Advancement of Colored People, and as an adviser to the American Civil Liberties Union. His reputation as a defender of equal justice under the law and of due-process principles were beyond challenge, having been earned over the course of many long battles fought over these issues—in the Tom Mooney case, the Bisbee deportations, the Sacco-Vanzetti case, among many others.[6] Moreover, he was a legendary scholar, having taught generations of Harvard Law School students and having been published widely in law reviews and in liberal journals such as *The New Republic.*

While there were surely many others of the time with similar credentials, what made Frankfurter appear to be so much a duplicate of Brandeis was the extent to which the two had established reputations as outsiders, battling traditionalists wherever they saw the needs of the common man as not being properly addressed or respected. Like Brandeis, Frankfurter was part neither of the elitism of Harvard, nor of the snobbery of the Boston Brahmins; his ethnic background made both impossible. To the contrary, owing to his well-known endeavors in the Zionist movement, he, like Brandeis before him, was seen primarily as a prominent and respected Jewish-American leader. The public stances he had taken, like those in the Sacco-Vanzetti case, in opposing efforts to impose quota restrictions on the number of Jewish students to be admitted to Harvard, and in defense of a liberal Harvard

Law School professor, Zechariah Chafee, as well as of Amherst College president Alexander Meiklejohn, had placed him squarely in opposition to Harvard University President A. Lawrence Lowell and others in the academic establishment. In 1924, by opposing Attorney General Harlan Fiske Stone's investigation of Progressive Senator Burton K. Wheeler of Montana for alleged improper conduct, he had put himself in conflict with the powerful and conservative American Bar Association.[7] The cumulative effect of the public recollection of all these old battles was to cast him in the public eye, as Brandeis had been cast by 1916, as a defender of the oppressed and as an aggressive advocate of a more just and open society.

Yet despite his many attacks on established authority, Frankfurter was, prior to his judicial nomination, in the same relationship with the government as Brandeis had been prior to his own, serving as a private adviser to an incumbent administration. Frankfurter's connection with the New Deal was as well known as Brandeis's New Freedom link had been, and few in Washington had missed hearing about his "Happy Hot Dogs." If public opinion was not marshalled against Frankfurter's Supreme Court appointment to the degree it had been in 1916 against Brandeis's, it was because Brandeis had paved the way for his protégé by serving with such distinction as the first social reformer, as well as the first Jewish member, ever named to the high bench. The public had reason to expect from Frankfurter the same judicial performance it had had from Brandeis. For that matter, Brandeis himself must have had similar expectations about his former lieutenant. But everyone would be surprised, and perhaps even somewhat disappointed, by Frankfurter's performance. For in reality there were more substantial differences than similarities between Frankfurter and his old patron.

A brilliant philosophizing oracle who dreamt a vast master plan for recreating American society and restructuring its government, Brandeis was a visionary prophet. A millionaire twice over when he came to the Court, he had had the time, as well as the inclination, to conceive his plans. Frankfurter, on the other hand, had long been by necessity a pragmatist and a bit of a hustler, angling for power, friends in high places, financial security, and perhaps even a seat on the Supreme Court. Too busy doing what was expedient, solving today's problems today, he could much less than Brandeis afford to dream grand dreams. His income was limited, in large measure because his public-service work foreclosed the usual opportunities available to prominent law professors to supplement their teaching incomes through outside legal work. Moreover, his modest salary was taxed by the high cost of the psychiatric care required by his wife Marion.

But even had he had the luxury of financial independence, by inclination Frankfurter viewed the world differently than Brandeis ever did. He was at heart a politician. He enjoyed developing important friendships, currying political favor, and constantly pressing for any advantage in the arena of political contest. While he had been Brandeis's lieutenant, formulating brilliant solutions worthy of his advocacy had not been a problem; they came in his mailbox. But when he went on the Court himself, Frankfurter was left to devise his own political philosophy. Not surprisingly, he was, in the end, governed not by any one coherent philosophy but by his own changing biases; his efforts would not serve some ultimate utopian plan, but be applied to the problems of the present, in the form of hard work performed tirelessly and loyally for his two great loves—FDR and the United States of America.

Similarly, while both Frankfurter and Brandeis were passionate in holding their political views, important differences in personal temperament distinguished how each would expound his views. Being, by nature, somewhat of a reserved ascetic, Brandeis had issued his prophecies from a distance and, at least until the final years, had patiently waited for others to secure their adoption. His life style was one of self-denial, his hallmark a personal sense of self-restraint. Frankfurter was entirely the opposite. He was an incessant meddler: aggressive, bold, and relentless in pursuit of each small tactical victory. Perhaps Judge Learned Hand, who knew both men well, put it best: "Well of course [Frankfurter's] got a very passionate nature, and that is rather an initial handicap for a judge . . . [though] not if he has the faculty of adding to it supreme self-restraint. He's learned a good deal of it. But he hasn't it "[8]

Again, some of this difference was perhaps due to differences in the life situation of the two men. As a practicing lawyer, Brandeis had been accustomed to advising important clients from a distance. Whether or not they took his recommendations Brandeis still was paid. It was within this role of detached counsellor that he advised members of the Wilson Administration. Even when his advice was not adopted, Brandeis had the self-confidence and moral certainty to know that he was right; the validity of his ideas did not require confirmation through acceptance by others. Frankfurter, though, was a teacher. His reward came from shaping his students' attitudes about important matters, and through them the attitudes and actions of others. A closeness to his students was necessary to insure the reinforcing feedback. This intimacy may have served another need as well. Because Frankfurter had no children of his own, these students were his link to immortality. Many became his "Happy Hot Dogs" and once having placed them in the Roosevelt Administration, Frankfurter became inextricably intertwined with their efforts, and thence with the progress of their agencies and departments. It would have been very difficult indeed for him to step back upon appointment to the Court and adopt a big-picture view of their efforts in behalf of causes to which he himself had helped foster their commitment.

The best illustration, however, of the effect of these personal-approach differences came in the one area that the public thought it best understood—the relationship of each to the sitting president who appointed him to the Court. Though Brandeis admired Wilson, the president was never more than just another important client seeking advice. On the other hand, Frankfurter loved Roosevelt, basked in his friendship, and sought psychological succor from him whenever possible. One saw Wilson having to travel to Brandeis's apartment or send an emissary to obtain counsel; whereas, not even barring the doors and windows would have kept Frankfurter out of the Roosevelt White House. Consequently, Brandeis became a beacon of light for Wilson, while Frankfurter remained part of Roosevelt's personal retinue.

Not surprisingly, these differences in personal and philosophical traits carried over when each man came to the Court. Brandeis was afforded great awe and reverence. People respected and admired him, paying respectful attention even when they did not agree with the analysis he offered them. In the end, through patience and perseverance, he achieved much of what he wanted for the country. During the 1930s, while Frankfurter was still reflecting Brandeis's ideas and wisdom, he was treated with similar respect. This attitude of respect was reinforced by the perception that he, too, was the distant observer. Because of the physical separation between Frankfurter in Cambridge and his "boys" in Washington, he was still held in awe as their teacher/mentor.

When Frankfurter came to Washington full time, though, he gradually came to be seen by Washingtonians as just one more government figure among many, and by his boys, such as Corcoran and Cohen, many of whom were now in positions of authority, as more of an equal. In Freudian terms, if Brandeis had been their superego, Frankfurter represented their political id. Accordingly, Frankfurter's recommendations commanded no special reverence; he was seen as another political operator, whose proposals went into the political cauldron with all the others. To secure support for his pet projects he would have to offer his support to projects dear to others. In a word, to deal.

In Frankfurter's mind, the most effective lobbyist he could have found for his own pet projects was himself. He surely could not have afforded to subsidize his own political lieutenant, as Brandeis had done. But even had he been able to do so, and even had he been able to find a lieutenant of the quality Brandeis had found, it is unlikely that he would have had the requisite patience to use such a person as Brandeis had used him. Yet more important even than this difference in temperament was another—Frankfurter was, relative to his mentor, more a believer in the power of words, gracefully arranged and forcefully expressed, than of abstract thought. Oddly this particular difference between them may be best illustrated by the way each went about attempting to safeguard the secrecy regarding the extensive political activity in which each was engaged.

While Brandeis did his best throughout his long tenure on the Court to avoid widespread dissemination of information regarding those of his actions he expected could be interpreted by others as improper, Frankfurter relied on strong arguments, indignantly put, to stifle any suggestion that any impropriety had taken place, as if a well-enough reasoned argument could actually change the reality of what had taken place. In this one area Frankfurter showed very little patience and even less of his famous humor, so that especially during his early years of political activism, his young friends and colleagues often had to decide if referring in his presence to what they knew to be true was really worth the angry response such references would occasionally provoke. As one might expect, he was in the end more successful in using this tactic to shield the reputation of the venerable Brandeis from idle gossip than in shielding himself once he became the politically active justice subject to criticism.

But not yet privy to how much less tolerant the future would be of his off-the-bench activities than the past had been of Brandeis's,

Frankfurter was less reluctant once on the Court to approach political figures directly than Justice Brandeis had ever been. As soon as he sensed an opportunity for success, he would fill mail boxes, tie up phone lines, and, at times, even personally occupy the offices of those who might help bring about his ends, offering his own blend of effusive praise and Washington chatter, mixed with a full measure of pleading for action. Rather than direct the battle from afar, he preferred to jump into the political foxholes that had been dug throughout Washington and wage hand-to-hand combat with the most skilled politicians of the day. When his ideas did not receive the same respect that had been accorded those of Brandeis, Frankfurter would compensate by pressing his case even more forcefully and often more openly.

These naturally more aggressive political instincts in Frankfurter were reinforced by the judicial environment of the Roosevelt Court. The Court to which Frankfurter was appointed in 1939 was a Court in transition, his own appointment being the third in a long series of appointments that by 1941 would enable FDR to replace seven of the institution's nine members, making the Supreme Court of the early forties one vastly different from the one on which Brandeis had served for most of his term.

Unlike the "Nine Old Men" of the mid-thirties, the new justices of this Court were all comparatively young and avowed New Deal liberals; more important, they were all highly political persons, both by training and temperament. With the exception of Frankfurter, all were drawn from political backgrounds: Senators Hugo Black and James Byrnes, Solicitor General Stanley Reed, Attorneys General Frank Murphy and Robert Jackson, and chairman of the SEC, William O. Douglas. Moreover, a number of these men—Frankfurter, Douglas, Jackson, and Byrnes—had been chosen partially for the close advisory relationships they had with President Roosevelt.

For these men who would serve during World War II, when the normal proscriptions against political activity would be overridden by the crisis mindset, donning the black robes would only minimally diminish the intensity of their political involvements.[9] Grace Tully, personal secretary to FDR, records that Justices Frankfurter, Douglas, Murphy, and Jackson were "frequent off-the-record White House callers."[10] Still, it was apparently thought prudent to conceal these visits from other White House staffers, as well as from the press and nosey historians, for the names rarely appeared on the various presidential and ushers calendars that listed the daily appointment schedules of FDR.[11] However, a careful reading of letters written during this period between justices and the president confirm that such meetings did occur frequently.

In one public reference to these visits *Time* magazine asserted that Justice Douglas was at least a weekly visitor to 1600 Pennsylvania Avenue. As one of the president's "poker buddies," Douglas's visits were not considered unusual. He advised the president on such diverse issues as the desegregation of the Armed Forces and our relations with Soviet Russia. Occasionally, Douglas was even involved in writing presidential speeches. Together with Justice Black, he also brought pressure upon the secretary of the interior for certain types of government reorganization to help facilitate implementation of the country's war policy.[12]

Stanley Reed, Frank Murphy, and James F. Byrnes were others who repeatedly offered their assistance to the president. While Reed would accept with equanimity a noncommittal response to his advice, Murphy would not. Throughout the war, Murphy showered FDR with advice concerning our relations with the Philippines, all to no avail. Felix Frankfurter at one time expressed annoyance that his "baby brother," Murphy, had the temerity to attempt to use him in approaching the president on this issue.[13] Murphy even expressed a desire to undertake some military assignment, and during the summer of 1942 he trained with the infantry reserves. For him, such nonjudicial work was justifiable because "traditions are being broken everywhere" and he "wanted to be prepared for anything."[14]

Of this group only the help of James Byrnes was truly welcomed by FDR. In fact, Byrnes never really ceased being a government administrator after coming to the Court. In his memoirs, he admits devoting "several hours a day as well as many evenings to conferences and calls about extracurricular affairs."[15] His efforts were essential in the establishment of the War Production Board, and the drafting of the Second War Powers Act. Then during the summer of 1942, he remained in the capital to advise FDR on the inflationary effect of defense procurement on the economy. His advice on the drafting of legislation placing ceilings on wages, prices, and rents was so central that FDR convinced him to leave the Court in October 1942 to become the director of Economic Stabilization—the "Assistant President for Domestic Affairs." Overall, not since the tenures of Chief Justices Salmon P. Chase (1864–73) and Morrison Waite (1874–88) had sitting members of the Supreme Court been so generally active in the political realm.[16]

The views of the new justices on the propriety of extensive political involvement by Court members were not shared by the two holdovers from the earlier era, Owen Roberts and Harlan Fiske Stone. Harvard professor Milton Katz recalls that shortly after the Pearl Harbor bombing, at a dinner party he attended with Justices Owen Roberts, Felix Frankfurter, and James Byrnes, Byrnes mentioned that he was under severe pressure to leave the Supreme Court, to which he had just been appointed, in order to assist in the preparations for fighting the war.[17] Immediately, Roberts responded by insisting that Byrnes must have no doubt in his mind that his primary obligations lay with the Court.*

Chief Justice Harlan F. Stone was even more troubled than Justice Roberts by the extrajudicial actions of his brethren. Although he had earlier worked intensively with Herbert Hoover, Stone, after being particularly embarrassed by one incident in 1939, came to favor greater judicial seclusion. On that occasion, President Roosevelt, after discussing with Stone and Justice Frankfurter a problem in securing congressional appropriations for military housing, had announced both his decision and the fact that the conference had been held. While the criticism that followed did not trouble Frankfurter, Stone withdrew completely from extrajudicial activities refusing several requests from Presidents Roosevelt and Truman to serve on various commissions and tribunals, and from then on chastised those members of the Court who were politically active—including Frankfurter. Stone best explained his change of view in a letter to FDR:

> A judge, and especially the Chief Justice, cannot engage in political debate or make public defense of his acts. When his action is judicial he may always rely upon the support of the defined record upon which his action is based and of the opinion in which he and his associates unite as stating the ground of decision. But when he participates in the action of the executive or legislative departments of government he is without those supports. He exposes himself to at-

---

*Despite these reservations, Roberts did agree to serve, without resigning from the Court, on a commission investigating why the attack at Pearl Harbor had been such a disastrous surprise.

tack and indeed invites it, which because of his peculiar situation inevitably impairs his value as a judge and the appropriate influence of his office.[18]

Despite his holding these strong views, though, Stone did not make an effort, as Chief Justice Edward White had during Brandeis's early years on the Court, to have the brethren observe his own proprietal norms. As a result, throughout the early years of the Roosevelt Court, informal political work off the bench continued with abandon.

This was clearly an atmosphere in which Felix Frankfurter, who had learned his craft as a judicial politician from a master, and in a more difficult time, and who had so strong a need to serve FDR, could move with great freedom. And move he would. Soon it would be clear that the level of his political involvement after his appointment remained at least the same as, and perhaps even increased a bit from that of his days at the Harvard Law School.

Yet even despite the stricter norms of the Court on which Brandeis had sat, Brandeis's style had left him relatively safe from public discovery, while Frankfurter's seemed to invite it. The results were predictable. Frankfurter was identified by some in Washington—including Vice-President Henry Wallace—as a member of FDR's "Palace Guard," the nickname on Capitol Hill for the president's most intimate advisers.* A Washington Post editorial even called for the disbandment of this group.[19] The New York Times, on March 29, 1942, labeled Frankfurter as one of "the men around the President" who was "making as frequent calls upon the President as he did before the war."[20]

Frankfurter's political involvement was criticized particularly harshly by one of his own judicial colleagues—Frank Murphy. Repeatedly, Murphy derisively referred to Frankfurter as "the power behind the throne" and a "sycophant" who was seeking authority with foreign countries. As is often the case, there were personal considerations involved in the making of these charges; Murphy complained to Vice-President Wallace that Frankfurter's influence had denied him an appointment as secretary of war in 1941, and that it was Frank-

---

* The other members of the Palace Guard were reputed to be: presidential assistants Harry Hopkins and David Niles, presidential secretary Steven Early, presidential speechwriter Samuel Rosenman, and the director of the Office of War Information, Robert Sherwood.

furter who had "kicked him upstairs" from the Justice Department to the Supreme Court.*

For Felix Frankfurter, a man sensitive to such criticism, the problem was difficult—how could he follow the Brandeis legacy and still justify to himself and his friends the contradiction between his words and his actions. In this area, he was precluded by his own temperament from following the Brandeis model.

Despite the apparent reluctance of his judicial colleagues to engage in political activities off the bench, Brandeis appears to have had no real compunction about forging ahead when he believed in what he was doing. While always cautious, there is no indication that Brandeis ever felt at all guilty or even uneasy either about his secret lobbying connection with Frankfurter or about any other aspect of his extrajudicial work. Within Brandeis's hundreds of letters to Frankfurter, and the thousands he mailed to others, the subject of the propriety of his political endeavors, or of those undertaken by others in his behalf, is almost never mentioned. There is no discernible attempt by him to deny his own political interests or activities, no breast-beating about normative limits governing the extent of such involvement, no reminder that "laymen cannot sometimes appreciate," and not the slightest hint of criticism of the outside work of any of his brethren. On the one occasion when Brandeis's connections to the administration were revealed, in the Hugh Johnson incident in 1934, he shrugged it off as like "being run into by a drunken autoist,"[22] laid low for a while, and then continued to be just as politically active as before. This is hardly the behavior of a man very much troubled by what he was doing. No Reverend Dimmesdale here.

In contrast Frankfurter seems to have been quietly but deeply troubled by his own activities, to some degree while still Brandeis's lieutenant and then, later, to a much greater degree while on the bench himself. Able neither to separate his political and judicial roles, nor to manage the dual workload as Brandeis had done, Frankfurter sur-

---

* Moreover, Murphy claimed that when, as an associate justice, he later expressed continued interest in the War Department post, FDR suggested that he first be reappointed as attorney general, in order to set up the eventual move. When the offer was mysteriously withdrawn several days later, Murphy became convinced that Frankfurter, in an effort to maintain his influence in the Justice Department, had again been responsible. Whether the claim is entirely valid (an interview with one source who was in a position to observe these actions indicates that parts of it appear to have some validity), it demonstrates the concern others had regarding the power and influence of Frankfurter off the Court.[21]

vived by developing a split personality, a sort of "Double Felix." While the private Felix became in his own time on the bench one of the all-time leaders in political involvement by a Supreme Court justice, the public Felix went to incredible lengths to present just the opposite image. He continually denied his own involvement in activities in which he was deeply involved, set stiff standards for the behavior of others, and, even while violating these standards himself, severely criticized those who failed to observe them.

Such conflict had always been a part of Frankfurter's personality. Unlike Brandeis, who was just as he appeared, Frankfurter, throughout his life, had always had those two sides to his nature. The two elements of the Double Felix—his public protestations and his actual private inclinations—frequently pulled him in opposite directions. Earlier, the public Felix had denied political involvement by Louis Brandeis, while the private Felix assisted those actions. Later, the public Felix disavowed any knowledge of the campaign for his own judicial appointment, while the private Felix waited by the telephone for daily reports from Thomas Corcoran.

Frankfurter's overt displays of hypocrisy were so much a part of his personality that he did not even appear to understand that others could not have helped but see through them. His admonition to friends seemed to be: *Say I do as I say I do, not as you know I do.* To at least some of his friends and protégés, this tendency toward blatant self-exoneration was one of his more appealing traits. "Well, Felix was Felix," commented former Frankfurter law clerk Philip Elman in a personal interview. To which Joseph L. Rauh, Jr., added: "And you just had to love him for being so open about things!"[23] But to his enemies, and others who were troubled by such behavior, this character flaw left him vulnerable to attack for duplicity and a willingness to adapt his principles to his needs.

Frankfurter desperately wanted people to believe that he held great reverence for the ethics of his position. Repeatedly in personal letters to friends, he claimed, as he did once to former New Dealer and political ally Gardner Jackson, that "neither in [this] case nor in any other case have I volunteered recommendations for appointment, but have merely responded to inquiries."[24] When asked for ideas for a speech by the governor of West Virginia on the advisability of Roosevelt's running for a fourth term in 1944, Frankfurter refused by explaining, "I have an austere and even sacerdotal view of the position of a judge on this Court, and that means I have nothing to say on matters that come within a thousand miles of what may fairly be called politics."[25] A strange response indeed from the man who had helped mastermind FDR's 1940 presidential campaign from his seat on the Court.

Another part of Frankfurter's public campaign to establish with others his judicial purity involved criticism of the political actions of his own judicial colleagues. For instance, he once protested to Judge Learned Hand that he was "greatly surprised" by the "free-tongued" nature of Owen Roberts, one of only two members of the Roosevelt Court who turned out to have at least minimally abstained from politics. Nevertheless, Frankfurter pontificated: "Not the least of our problems is the indiscreet speech of him [who] should be the most guarded."[26]

Apparently Felix Frankfurter had evolved some fine distinctions regarding the degrees of impropriety in judicial conduct, for even before his nomination to the Court, he reserved special criticism for those who would run for political office from the high bench. As Frankfurter proclaimed in a private letter written on May 27, 1935 to Geoffrey Parsons, editor of the *New York Herald-Tribune,* "when a man goes on the Supreme Court he permanently takes the veil." Reacting to reports of presidential draft movements for Chief Justice Stone and Justice Roberts, Frankfurter went on to say that "nothing will surely drag the Supreme Court into politics" more than for a member to enter the electoral arena.[27] By throwing one's hat in the ring from the Court, he feared, a justice would call into question the disinterested basis of all his decisions. There would surely be the suspicion that rather than rule solely on the facts and the law, the candidate-justice might be tempted to decide on public-policy grounds.

For precisely this reason, Charles Evans Hughes had resigned from the Court to campaign for the presidency in 1916. But even Hughes's resignation would not, apparently, have satisfied Felix Frankfurter, for in a personal letter to Burlingham, he labeled the incident a "blot on [Hughes's] escutcheon."[28] Whether Hughes had been legitimately drafted or not by the Republican party made no difference to Frankfurter, who explained in a later letter to Professor Alexander M. Bickel, "nobody in our history was truly 'drafted,' excepting George Washington . . . the movement to draft [Hughes] was underway for months and he could have stopped it . . . I think mere receptivity toward a nomination, acquiescence in drinking the hemlock and in having the cup passed, is in itself highly undesirable. It is one of those situations where the interpretation of the act may be as important as the act itself."[29] So, Frankfurter preferred justices to follow the example of Chief Justice Morrison Waite, who in 1876 stopped a similar movement in his behalf at its inception.

Frankfurter's bitterest attacks, though, were reserved for Brandeis's successor on the bench, Justice William O. Douglas, whom he saw as harboring high political ambitions. Frankfurter deeply resented what he viewed as Douglas's "build-up" for the White House. When the behind-the-scenes campaign became public, with the mentioning of Douglas as a possible vice-presidential candidate in 1944, Frankfurter could no longer contain himself. A handwritten marginal note by Frankfurter on a letter discovered in the recently opened Burlingham papers indicates that by July 1944, Frankfurter had been convinced "for months" that Thomas Corcoran's "subterranean skill" was being used in "managing the Douglas candidacy."[30] Since Frankfurter and Corcoran were by this time no longer close, this suspicion merely added to the justice's already considerable disenchantment with Douglas.

The renewed talk in 1946 of drafting a Supreme Court justice for the highest political office, combined with Douglas's apparent interest in the job, troubled Frankfurter greatly. When both Douglas and Chief Justice Fred Vinson were mentioned as possibilities for political office it became too painful. So, Frankfurter penned another letter to Burlingham, expressing his continued frustration:

> Nothing is more important than for every member of the Court to put all other thoughts, than law and Court, out of his consciousness, by consciously foreswearing all other thoughts on the possibility of being amenable to any future ambition. I do not mean Vinson in particular. Unless a man has a dedicated sacerdotal commitment to the Court for life—it plays hell on the Court. [Italics in original][31]

Frankfurter continued to bristle at the way Douglas left the door ajar for several years. One Frankfurter law clerk recalled in a personal interview that Douglas's office was even decorated with a souvenir campaign lunch pail lettered with "Douglas for President—1948."[32]

Frankfurter's intense hostility toward Douglas's ambitions and his claims that Douglas failed to observe standards of judicial ethics were not entirely unjustified. Since the Hughes resignation in 1916—an event that permanently altered the norms in this area—no other member of the Court had sought nomination to high office from the bench.

In fact, during the 1950s two of Douglas's colleagues, when put in similar circumstances, quickly expressed disinterest. Evidence of the first declination is contained in an interesting oral history account by two of Chief Justice Fred Vinson's law clerks, Howard J. Trienens and Newton N. Minow. On a Florida boat cruise Harry Truman privately told Fred Vinson that he would not seek re-election in 1952 and offered to support the Chief Justice's nomination at the Democratic Convention. Without pondering the matter, Vinson declined the offer, saying that as a member of the Court he should not become involved in politics, and that his age and health made such a campaign inadvisable anyway. Before completely closing the door, however, he asked for time to consult his wife. Shortly thereafter, Vinson did absolutely withdraw from any consideration for the position.[33]

When public speculation in 1954 centered on Earl Warren as a possible presidential candidate, his response was just as immediate and even more negative. Not the least bit ambivalent about his intentions, the Chief Justice was, according to a story in the *Boston Globe* on December 16, 1954, "annoyed, displeased, irked, and implacably opposed" to recurring references that he might be drafted by the Republicans if Eisenhower chose not to run again. Warren emphatically stated that he had "donned his judicial robes forever, had put partisan politics behind him forever, [and] it would be prudent to believe him."[34] In letters to his friends, Frankfurter explained that he was pleased by such unconditional denials of presidential ambitions by Warren because they reaffirmed the existing normative standard proscribing such conduct.[35]

The reason for Frankfurter's abhorrence of this particular ambition could have been as much personal as philosophical. The highest office to which he could ever aspire was justice of the Supreme Court, for as a naturalized citizen, he was constitutionally barred from running for the presidency himself. Despite the unquestioned reasonableness of the proscribing norm involved, however, Frankfurter's hostility toward Douglas's behavior seems to have been far more intense than the latter's actions warranted. Douglas never did actively campaign for the presidency. His only sins, if sins they were, were to allow speculation to continue, and to encourage by his silence those individuals who were promoting his candidacy.[36] But while Frankfurter was quick to criticize Douglas's behavior as "disregardful of the duties of the Court,"[37] nothing was said when certain other members of the Court engaged in more active political behavior. For instance, Douglas's ambitions seemed to be the daily focus of Frankfurter's ire, while James Byrnes's continual work in the administration even though still on the Court was supported and praised. This double standard was also evident when Douglas's public comments on United States foreign policy with Mainland China led Frankfurter to protest immediately that:

> Questions may well come before the Court as to the validity of the Mao Government and the status of legitimacy, in view of our policy. Judges shouldn't express views as to matters that may come before the Court.[38]

In contrast, nothing had been said by Frankfurter when Louis D. Brandeis actually became openly involved in international diplomatic negotiations on behalf of the Zionist cause. In addition, Frankfurter's antipathy toward Douglas seems to have clouded his critical judgment, for there is little chance that questions about the legitimacy of the Mao government would ever have come to be heard by the Supreme Court. As Frankfurter surely knew, they would quickly have been dismissed as raising "political questions."* Clearly, it was Douglas the person and not his alleged judicial indiscretions that had so enraged Felix Frankfurter.

This hostility Frankfurter harbored toward Douglas had not always existed. In fact, before joining the Supreme Court within three months of each other, the two men were on extremely cordial terms. The relationship between them had, in fact, been so close that in the early 1930s Douglas consulted Frankfurter on a potential career move. Then a law professor at Yale, Douglas was offered an exorbitant salary to teach at the University of Chicago. Frankfurter, who was not terribly well paid himself, advised against the move, saying that Douglas's wife would find it impossible to get along with the wives of the other professors who were receiving much lower salaries. Their relationship was still sufficiently close in 1939 for Douglas to be a celebrant at a party honoring Frankfurter's Supreme Court nomination.[40]

It is interesting that in his recently published autobiography, *The*

---

* This is a judicial doctrine by which the courts rationalize their avoidance of a review in certain cases by claiming that the power to make decisions in the area has been delegated in the Constitution to one of the political branches. In this case, decisions in the foreign-policymaking realm are almost always seen by the Court as either a prerogative of the president, or, on occasion, of Congress.[39]

Court Years 1939–1975, Justice Douglas plays down the tension between himself and Frankfurter. Indeed, he lists Frankfurter on his "All-American team" of justices, using "basic ability and judicial attitude as yardsticks."[41] Moreover, he claims that "the press was continually rife with untrue stories that Frankfurter and I were always at loggerheads . . . we differed greatly . . . and he was not one to let a difference lie."[42]

Evidence drawn from personal interviews with Frankfurter law clerks and intimates leads one inescapably to the conclusion that Frankfurter would never have been so charitable about Douglas. These individuals were willing to speak now because they felt that the events they were describing were sufficiently remote in time that discussion of them would not violate confidential relationships. It was also approaching the point where if someone did not discuss the events, there might soon be no one alive who could offer historians firsthand information regarding them. While the words varied slightly, each Frankfurter intimate described the justice's attitude toward his colleague in a fashion similar to that of one clerk who said, "Felix sure hated Douglas!"[43]

The reasons and the precise timing of the beginning of the split are variously explained. Two recently published volumes, in examining the philosophical and jurisprudential differences between Frankfurter and Douglas, report that the split between them occurred after they had served together on the Court for a while. In James Simon's illuminating volume, *Independent Journey: The Life of William O. Douglas*, two possible theories are offered. The volume opens with an account of an interview done with Justice Douglas, in which he expressed the belief that the split with Frankfurter began in 1943 with a case deciding the constitutionality of compulsory flag salutes in public schools, *West Virginia Board of Education v. Barnette*.[44] Simon's own research, however, suggests that the genesis of the conflict may have been earlier. In a chapter entitled "The Short Reign of Felix Frankfurter," he traces the divergence to a triumvirate of cases beginning with a First Amendment decision in the 1941 term involving the rights of the press in court trials, *Bridges v. California*,[45] which, for Simon, "marked a constitutional turning point."[46] H. N. Hirsch, in his psychobiography on Frankfurter, offers a different perspective on the origin of the conflict. He traces it to a little known case decided in February 1941 involving the states' power to enjoin labor union picketing:

the *Meadowmoor Dairies* case.[47] Then, Hirsch goes on to agree with Justice Douglas's assessment of the significance of the *Barnette* case in the deterioration of the relationship, saying that this decision "marks a transition for Frankfurter and for the Court [for] the lines of battle [were] sharply drawn."[48]

The personal recollections of Frankfurter law clerks and intimates, however, suggest that Frankfurter himself traced the split to an even earlier case. While Douglas appears not to have perceived it (or would not so admit), in Frankfurter's mind, the relationship with his colleague on the Court ended before it ever had a chance to begin. Moreover, the cause of the split had a highly personal, rather than philosophical, basis. Frankfurter's protégés repeat an identical, and very revealing story, indicating that it was Douglas's behavior in a long-forgotten, obscure tax case, decided a mere eight months after he took his seat on the Court, that irreparably damaged his relationship with Frankfurter. The Frankfurter law clerk that term, Kentucky attorney Edward F. Prichard, Jr., personally observed the origins of the split and by remaining close to Frankfurter was able to follow its development over the years. It is his recollection that after this case, Frankfurter became convinced that Douglas was "play[ing] games with his opinions."[49] Regardless of how much truth there was in Frankfurter's charge, the accounts of his law clerks in later years and the findings of other scholars make clear that this perception hardened to the extent that each Douglas action was placed into this context and interpreted in the light of a presumed insincerity in his Court votes.

The dispute in this early case was so minor that it is easy to understand why Justice Douglas would have overlooked it. The controversy occurred as a consequence of an opinion issued on December 18, 1939 in *Board of Commissioners of the County of Jackson, Kansas v. United States*,[50] a case in which an Indian was attempting to obtain a refund of certain tax payments made to Jackson County, along with interest on the money. Under existing treaties between the federal government and the Indians, lands held in trust for Indians by the United States were not subject to local tax. The issue, then, was simply one of federalism.

Seeking, in Prichard's words, "fairness and equity," Frankfurter and his law clerk worked out a careful opinion that upheld both sides. The Indian could recover his tax payments under federal treaty obligations, but the county would not have to pay interest on the sum it had collected and held. When Frankfurter circulated an early draft of his short, rather turgid decision tracing the history of the Indian treaty and the problems of intergovernmental relations, Justice Douglas offered in a marginal note high praise and gave every indication that he would sign this opinion: "I agree. This is very deftly done—so deftly as to justify the Chief Justice in saying hereafter, 'Felix, my boy.' "[51]

Hugo Black, however, was not so satisfied with the language of Frankfurter's opinion and wrote a separate concurrence. His nine-sentence opinion explained that Congress, by its silence, had specifically intended not to return interest to the Indians in such tax-refund cases as part of a general "policy looking to their eventual absorption into the general body of citizenry."[52] This brief expression of populism was almost indistinguishable from that of the Frankfurter opinion. Nevertheless, on the final day before the Court opinion was to be publicly announced, Douglas walked up to Frankfurter in the robing room and said, "Now really, I think you were right on this [opinion], but I concurred with Hugo."[53]

According to Prichard, Frankfurter "was just furious." His own belief, he told the young law clerk, was that Douglas had switched his vote because he "didn't want Hugo to be alone" in the case. The message Douglas sent over to Frankfurter's chambers attempting to explain his actions, implied as much: "I have decided to go with Hugo on this, not because I have the difficulty he has but for reasons I can tell you sometime. They do not really go to . . . your discussion, which I still think is an excellent one."[54] In fact, pointing up the importance that Frankfurter ascribed to this incident, a full two-and-one-half-years later he placed a note in his scrapbook below Douglas's explanation indicating that he was *still* waiting for a satisfactory explanation: "Douglas *never* thereafter referred to this case, nor to his shift, nor to his reasons for going 'with Hugo.' " [*Italics in original*][55] Following that case, Prichard noted, "Frankfurter never had any more use for Douglas."[56] Thereafter, Frankfurter began to find reason to complain to Justices Murphy and Reed about their colleague's lack of judicial propriety.[57]

In personal interviews, other Frankfurter law clerks have indicated how the personal antagonism manifested itself in later terms. Frankfurter characterized Douglas to his law clerk for the 1941 and 1942 terms, Philip Elman, as being "an absolute cynic," a man who "didn't believe in anything." In fact, the justice was so concerned that Douglas was using the Court as a launching pad for the White House that he lived in constant fear that his colleague was playing politics with every decision, and that his votes were being cast on the basis of whether they might help or hurt his chances for the presidency. Accordingly, Frankfurter would frequently toss a Douglas opinion on Elman's desk and comment, "Well, he's writing for a different constituency this time."[58] Elliot Richardson, who clerked for Frankfurter during the 1948 term, supports this account with a similar one of his own. As a man who professed the need for an objective and independent judiciary, Frankfurter found it difficult to work with Douglas, who, he believed, "betrayed the role of the Court in catering to a liberal constituency."[59] So driven was Frankfurter by the need to defend himself against his "enemies" on the Court, such as Douglas, that, according to a familiar story among the law clerks, he once shouted down one of his assistants who complained that perhaps a full opinion rather than a terse *per curiam* opinion should be written by the justice in a particular case. By writing a full opinion, Frankfurter argued, other members of the Court might be stirred to build a new majority around a different opinion. Frankfurter lectured his bewildered clerk: "Don't you get the idea that this is a *war* we are fighting." [*Italics in original*][60]

Perhaps the split with Douglas was inevitable. Maybe it was just that the personal chemistry between them was never right. Philip Elman speculated that Frankfurter, who tended to place women on a pedestal, might have come to believe that Douglas "lacked character" because of his many marriages. However, several law clerks referred to one other Douglas practice that visibly upset Frankfurter—as one assistant put it, "he was a little bit too sloppy with some of his [opinions]." Frankfurter perceived that his colleague "just didn't come to grips with the tough issues in the case," instead choosing to dash off a personal rather than a judicial opinion on whichever side of the case he favored.[61] Over time, the personal relations between the two deteriorated to the point that by the 1948 term, they literally were not speaking to one another.[62]

While Frankfurter may have had little to say to Douglas, he had plenty to say in later years *about* Douglas to correspondents such as federal Court of Appeals Judge Learned Hand. Frankfurter spilled out enough venom concerning his colleague in personal letters to Hand to easily confirm the worst impressions of their relationship offered by his law clerks. Frankfurter called Douglas, in one personal letter discovered in the Harvard Law School collection, "the most cynical, shamelessly amoral character I've ever known." He went on to add, "With him I have no more relation than the necessities of Court work require. He is too unscrupulous for any avoidable entanglement."[63] Near the end of his Court years Frankfurter was referring to Douglas in private letters as "the cynical, unscrupulous Bill."[64] Finally, in 1959 he complained in another letter that "Douglas's crookery has a depth beyond your plumbing. One has had to live with him for years to appreciate his shamelessness."[65]

While the public Felix was expressing these criticisms of Douglas and engaging in normative philosophizing, the private Felix was making careful preparations to undertake his own informal political endeavors. Frankfurter had learned from watching Brandeis that success in adopting an active role off the bench required rigidly separated political and judicial worlds. Only in this fashion could he act covertly, while still minimizing personal guilt over abandoning publicly enunciated ethical standards. There was also the need to maintain respect from his political allies by appearing to be somewhat detached from his informal lobbying efforts. Interestingly, one segmenting technique that Frankfurter used came straight from the Brandeisian tradition; while he was an activist off the bench, on the bench, he was just the opposite, becoming instead one of the Court's leading exponents of the doctrine of "judicial self-restraint."

Though some have argued that Frankfurter did not completely understand Brandeis's or Holmes's sophisticated self-restraint postures, there can be no doubt that an animus antithetical to judicial activism guided him on the Court.[66] In failing to make decisions in many areas, the new justice disappointed many people who, remembering his earlier years, expected him to pursue an activist civil-libertarian course.[67] No better expression exists of this dichotomy between his inherent judicial and extrajudicial tendencies than in the 1943 case of *West Virginia State Board of Education v. Barnette*. Faced for the second time with the question of whether the children of Jehovah's Witnesses should be forced in public schools to salute the flag,[68] thus violating the tenets of their religion, Frankfurter, the self-avowed civil libertarian, decided in dissent to uphold the regulation. In the opening paragraph of his dissent, Frankfurter tried to defend his decision in terms of preserving the sanctity of constitutional delimitations of judicial prerogative.

> One who belongs to the most vilified and persecuted minority in history is not likely to be insensible to the freedoms guaranteed by our Constitution. Were my purely personal attitude relevant I should wholeheartedly associate myself with the general libertarian views in the Court's opinion, representing as they do the thought and action of a lifetime. But as judges we are neither Jew nor Gentile, neither Catholic nor agnostic. . . . As a member of this Court I am not justified in writing my private notions of policy into the Constitution, no matter how deeply I may cherish them or how mischievous I may deem their disregard. . . . It can never be emphasized too much that one's own opinion about the wisdom or evil of a law should be excluded altogether when one is doing one's duty on the bench. The only opinion of our own even looking in that direction that is material is our opinion whether legislators could in reason have enacted such a law.[69]

As it did for Brandeis, this jurisprudential philosophy offered Frankfurter an easy means of separating, and thus accommodating his two lives. Following his only-one-hat-at-a-time posture Frankfurter allowed himself to resolve only certain types of questions from the bench, while leaving a wide spectrum of issues to be handled privately by working in his capacity as a citizen. Thus could he argue that his informal endeavors were defensible, in that they had no impact on the exercise of his judicial powers. On the surface, at least, his two worlds appeared to be entirely separate.

Beneath the surface, however, Frankfurter discovered that this theoretical separation was difficult to maintain in the real world. He soon discovered that an argument that presented his judicial self-restraint posture as a justification for an active political role relied on false premises. First, not every member of the Supreme Court adheres to the same self-restraint posture. Thus, issues that Frankfurter might prefer to leave to the politicians might still be accepted by his judicial colleagues for review.* Second, the argument presumes that successful political activism by a justice serving in his capacity as a citizen would obviate the need for later judicial review in that area. To the contrary, while the vast majority of the matters in which Frankfurter

---

*Under the rules of the Supreme Court, an appeal will be heard if four of the justices agree that it has substantial merit for review.

became privately involved did not ever come before the Court, appeals of many others did. Finally, the rationale was imperfect in that Frankfurter's self-restraint philosophy was often dropped in cases involving issues of great importance to him. For Frankfurter, then, areas of permissible extrajudicial activity could not be fully separated from those of required judicial activity. The former simply provided the primary and immediate outlet for his zeal and passion on important issues.

While Frankfurter soon realized that the fabrics of his judicial and political worlds would inevitably overlap, he was incapable of following Brandeis's methods for resolving the potential conflicts. Brandeis's personal temperament, the natural distance he kept from others, his well-ordered mind, and his confidence that offering the "true faith" could never be construed by others as being unethical, enabled him to compartmentalize the dual aspects of his work completely on his own. It was enough for him to know that his private advice was absolutely separate from, and would in no way influence, his judicial stances. Furthermore, the fact that Brandeis was able to work so extensively in political endeavors while maintaining his full share of judicial duties becomes even more impressive when one observes that a similarly extensive double workload forced Justice James Byrnes to leave the Court in 1942.

Perhaps seeking to recreate the style and image of Brandeis, and to manage the double workload, Frankfurter, the super pragmatist who lacked his mentor's mental dexterity, devised some artificial means for creating and maintaining the psychological and physical separation between his two worlds. Coincident with the expansion of his extrajudicial interests and duties in 1941, Frankfurter discovered that the solution for compartmentalizing the two sides of his personality lay in a careful use of two distinct sets of lieutenants. To separate fully his public duties from his private interests, the justice used his law clerks only for judicial matters, and an entirely different group of protégés for carrying out his political endeavors. Each group was completely insulated by the justice from his activity in the other realm.

This arrangement, which has never before been described in print, became evident during an interview with Elman, Frankfurter's sole law clerk from 1941 to 1943. The justice's correspondence and diary entries during the period are filled with accounts of political discussions held with visitors from all quarters, during teas and luncheons in his Court chambers. Yet, to my amazement, I discovered that Elman had very little knowledge of either the identities or the missions of these visitors. Interviews with later law clerks confirmed that they were treated similarly. Even today these men remain unaware of the full extent of their boss's extrajudicial behavior.[70] Yet how was it that the justice was able to screen his closest assistants from the constant flood of political visitors coming to see him?

Concealing this activity from his law clerks was made possible by an ingenious arrangement of the justice's chambers. Each justice of the Court is provided with a suite of three offices: a secretarial-reception area, which opens to the hall, a middle office for the law clerk, and the innermost chamber for the justice himself. This last room is larger than the others and comes complete with fireplace, library, and adjoining shower facilities. But Frankfurter switched offices, giving his law clerk the luxurious innermost space and placing himself in the middle office that linked the other two. This made it possible for Frankfurter to receive his visitors without their having to pass through the work area of his law clerk, and for him to have direct access to his secretary should he want to use her services for non-Court-related matters, without the law clerk ever seeing or hearing much.

Frankfurter's efforts to separate fully his law clerk from any of his political activities went to extraordinary lengths. Elman reports that over the years he served as the justice's law clerk he and Frankfurter rarely discussed anything at all of a political nature. The only approved topics of conversation between them were judicial business and personal affairs.

Later on, this would change, but only somewhat. Personal interviews with later Frankfurter law clerks reveal that the older justice would burst into his clerk's office periodically and discuss current world problems in a very general way. One clerk remembers Frankfurter going on at length one day in the late 1940s on the need for negotiating a mutual defense treaty with the Western European nations. Several weeks later the NATO alliance was announced. These "coincidences" occurred so regularly that clerks came to believe that they were being offered, as one put it, "an advance course in what was going to happen in government."[71] From the other side, these chats gave Frankfurter an opportunity to sound out his views on the world's problems and crystallize his solutions. However, during the early years of World War II there seems to have been no such behavior.

For discussion and work in the realm of politics during the early war years, Frankfurter turned to an entirely separate cast of characters. In addition to his wide contacts throughout the government, he operated through the small clique of former protégés—Joseph L. Rauh, Jr., Edward F. Prichard, Jr., and Philip Graham—who were now firmly ensconced in the Washington bureaucracy. When he asked something of them, it was done without question. But because Frankfurter was such a social animal, the requests were not always what the young men expected.

In a personal interview, Prichard tells a marvelous story on himself that illustrates how Frankfurter commanded their unquestioning loyalty. In late 1941, Prichard received a phone call from Frankfurter, who said simply, "Pritch, I'm with Secretary [of the Navy] Frank Knox at my office. Come on over here immediately." On the trip over, the young man's thoughts turned to the prospects of a new government appointment, and he was feeling grateful to the justice for providing him with this opportunity. When he got there, however, Frankfurter implored, "Pritch, do your imitation of John L. Lewis. Frank wants to hear it." [72]

To further insure the compartmentalization of his life, Frankfurter absolutely barred one topic in conversations with this group—issues relating to the Court. To establish this taboo was not easy. After all, in their seminars at Harvard Frankfurter had invited, and even demanded, boisterous criticism and analysis of Supreme Court decisions. When he was appointed to that body, it was too tempting to assume that nothing had really changed with their professor except his uniform. Joseph L. Rauh, Jr., explained in a personal interview how the new rules established themselves. Rauh, Prichard, and Graham, all former law clerks of Frankfurter, made a practice of gathering around the diminutive justice whenever they saw him and treating him as one of the gang, rather than as a Supreme Court justice. Flagrantly ignoring judicial proprieties, they frequently behaved like Peck's Bad Boys and, in Rauh's words "gave him hell for the decisions that were wrong." However, one night in late 1941, the justice inexplicably reacted to their antics by "getting very uppity and telling them all off." "After that," Rauh recalls, "we never had another conversation quite like the ones that we used to." [73] And never again did Frankfurter allow talk with them about Court business.

One other obstacle remained for the politically inclined justice: how could he accommodate all his interests in a twenty-four-hour day? For other colleagues, such as James Byrnes, the answer was simply to ask the Chief Justice for a reduction in the number of opinions assigned to him during the year. An analysis of the number of Frankfurter opinions, either majority, concurring, or dissenting, in the *United States Reports* reveals, however, that, just as Brandeis had done, he maintained a uniformly high output, producing at least as many judicial opinions per year during the war, his period of greatest extra-judicial activity, as he did before and after it. [74] However, to handle the increased workload Frankfurter resorted to a different utilization of his law clerk during this period. A series of personal interviews with Frankfurter law clerks virtually spanning his tenure on the Court reveals quite clearly that a larger share of the judicial duties was delegated to Philip Elman, his law clerk during 1941 to 1943, than to any other assistant. Only in this fashion could the justice devote what amounted to full-time attention during this period to his pressing responsibilities as a member of the Palace Guard.

In sharp contrast to his conduct during the war, from the postwar years on, Frankfurter came to employ two clerks, using them more as drafting assistants than as actual opinion writers. In some cases he would draft an initial opinion, and then ask one of the clerks to rework it. Following that, both would redraft the language and arguments. On other occasions, he would simply vote in the case and then, after stating which way he had decided, ask a clerk to sketch out an opinion on the issue. Sometimes he would offer guidance as to the direction of the opinion, but at other times he wanted the initial draft to be entirely the assistant's work. Of course, the judgment would never appear in the clerk's original form, for Frankfurter would attack it with relish, in effect entirely redrafting it. Each successive redraft was then sent to the Court's printer to obtain a clean copy from which to work. Consequently, it was not uncommon for Frankfurter to sit in the center of the room working with each clerk on a different draft of the same opinion. Once the redrafting process was completed, in fact, it was rare for a clerk to recognize any of his original wording in the final product.

For Elman, who was Frankfurter's only clerk during the hectic early war period, the work experience was entirely different. Because of the external demands on the justice's time, Elman was delegated much more responsibility for producing the judicial opinion. Only once during Elman's tenure did Frankfurter entirely draft an initial opinion in a case—his dissent in the flag-salute case, West Virginia v. Barnette. Even here, however, the process was unusual. Elman was placed at a typewriter while the justice pulled crumpled scraps of paper, envelopes, and napkins containing random sentences from each of his pockets and read them off to Elman. Then the two worked throughout the night trying to organize these thoughts into a cohesive opinion.

In every other case, though, it was Elman's responsibility to produce the original draft of an opinion. When a decision was first assigned to Frankfurter, or when he had decided to write a separate judgment, he might dictate a rough outline, containing an extremely sketchy version of his reasoning. From that, Elman was dispatched to research and write a draft of the opinion, while the justice impatiently checked on his progress. The clerk quickly learned that he was to work on absolutely nothing other than these decisions. Once, when an assigned opinion was not forthcoming, the justice banished Elman to the Supreme Court library in order to free him from "outside distractions." [75] On other occasions, in relatively minor cases, Frankfurter would just tell Elman how he had voted and instruct him to produce an opinion "off the top of his head." With either method, Elman's draft then served as the basis for further work. As soon as Frankfurter received the initial draft, he would call in his personal secretary and immediately dictate another version directly from Elman's work. With his incredible memory for Supreme Court cases, whenever he needed additional support or clarification at a certain point, the justice would leap up and dash to his book shelf for a case citation. Each paragraph was reworked so that the language of the opinion sounded as though Felix Frankfurter had written it from the start. Always, he searched for the bold statement or careful turn of phrase that had become his trademark. These opinions were obviously produced with much less personal attention and much more speed than in his later years. The final decision was his alone and so was the language, but the organization and intermediate stages of the opinion were left entirely to Elman. By using his clerk in this fashion, then, Frankfurter was able to maintain the pace of his judicial duties while also remaining free to

undertake a myriad of other political activities. While Bob Woodward
and Scott Armstrong argue in *The Brethren* that it is not unusual for
present members of the Court to rely heavily on their law clerks for
the actual drafting of opinions, it was not a common practice at that
time.[76]

Frankfurter was extremely conscious of this central role Elman
played for him in maintaining this dual identity. Though Elman was
incligible for military service, he wanted to leave at the end of his
first year as the justice's clerk. Feeling guilty about all his friends who
were involved in the fighting, he intended to find a job that would
more directly aid the war effort. However, Frankfurter convinced Elman to stay on for an additional year (one of only two of his clerks
ever to be so asked), by telling him that *this* was his patriotic duty. At
the end of that year the justice expressed his gratitude by presenting
Elman with a book, *As You Were*, a collection of writings that had
been edited for members of the United States Armed Forces by Alexander Woollcott (one of Frankfurter's friends).[77] The justice had pur-
chased a great many copies of this volume to send to his young friends
around the world. Without further explanation, he inscribed Elman's
copy with the words:

> Dear Phil:
> You will not even think of yourself what Heine said of himself—but
> I can say it, that you, too, are a soldier in the war for liberation.
>
> With every good wish, from your friend,
>
> > Felix Frankfurter [78]

Not until years later, during a personal interview done for this volume, would Elman come to understand that the justice's inscription
actually had a double meaning. In 1943, he presumed the justice "was
simply assuaging my feelings of guilt about being safe at home and
not actively involved in the war effort."[79] But the justice never revealed the even more subtle acknowledgement here, which was more
likely the true message in the inscription. For by his work Elman had
freed Frankfurter from the most time-consuming aspects of creating
judicial opinions, thus making it possible for the justice to undertake
his own war efforts. The young clerk had indeed been a "soldier in
the war for liberation."

8

The Monk in the Palace Guard II: Felix Frankfurter as Diplomat and Post-war Planner

With the Double Felix fully formed, and having achieved many of his political goals by 1942, Frankfurter looked forward to increasing influence in the war effort. However, because most of the decisions made in Washington at that time had to do with military tactics and strategy, it was only natural that Justice Frankfurter would come to have a reduced impact on the main thrust of the government's activities. The strategic position he would have advocated—that American resources should first be directed at saving Europe—was one that virtually everyone in the Roosevelt Administration already held. In addition, the military, accustomed to respecting clearly defined chains of command, would certainly have had little patience with any attempts by a Supreme Court justice to lecture it on how to go about winning the war. Furthermore, many of his boys were now in the military themselves, leaving the justice with fewer operatives in place to bring about his political goals.[1]

Still, he tried. On July 8, 1942 he wrote the president a letter in which he offered his comments on "the invention of an anti-torpedo grid for use on merchant ships."[2] Another letter indicates that he investigated possible appointees to the staff of James Byrnes, then director of the Office of War Mobilization.[3] The one contact through which he was able to exert any significant influence on military policy, however, was located in the Department of War, right at the top. By continuing to act as a sounding board for Secretary Stimson's ideas, the justice was able to have considerable input on at least some of his old friend's decisions. It appears that the secretary was not totally oblivious to Frankfurter's lobbying designs, writing in his diary that "Felix invited himself over once again." But it also appears likely that Stimson still attached a certain weight to the opinions of his old aide, for one discussion between the two—over the possible use of new scientific advances to detect and attack the German submarines that were creating such difficulties for the allies—went on over a period of several months.

But even here, after all, Stimson may have been taking advantage of Frankfurter's political, rather than military, counsel, for Stimson's need appears to have been for a way to overcome an institutional reluctance on the part of the Navy to adopt an offensive attitude toward this relatively new "under-water menace." We do not know just how Stimson did finally prevail, for in those days the Department of the Navy was a full cabinet department, but apparently he was able ultimately to change tactical attitudes toward the manner in which submarines would be fought.[4] When one recalls how hard Frankfurter had fought for the Lend-Lease program, it is clear how agitated he must have been over the inability of the United States to pass the great materials of war to its allies across the Atlantic without substantial loss to U-Boat attack, and how he must have pressed his opinions on all who would listen. But other than in isolated instances such as this one, Frankfurter's influence on military policy was limited.

Yet while there seemed little he could do to direct the course of the great military battles about to be fought, there was still much to be done in maintaining the morale of the American and Allied soldiers and in cementing those international alliances on which he believed the success of the war to be so dependent. The vast network of friends and admirers he had cultivated around the world over the years, together with the smashing success he had had in the Lend-Lease campaign, created the image among many foreigners that here indeed was their best pipeline to America's political leaders and thereby to its resources. Quite naturally, such expectations tend to be self-fulfilling, for the very fact of all these foreign leaders coming to plead their case with the justice created about him an aura of great statesmanship that surely added to his credibility with various administration officials.

Through a myriad of contacts he maintained with the British, the Australians, and the Free French, the center office of Justice Frankfurter's Supreme Court chambers had become by 1942 virtually a one-man annex of the Department of State.[5]

Using these sources of information and influence, the justice pursued a variety of goals. First, he sought to increase the will to win of the Allied armies by securing commitments of foreign governments to political and social reforms, thereby turning the war into a crusade for justice and democracy, and giving the fighting man something of permanent value for which to risk his life. Second, he continued his battle to obtain more aid for America's allies and to increase the harmony between the people of the United States and those of other allied nations. Finally, he went to work on planning what would have to be done to secure an improved world order once the war had ended. To have these ends achieved, the Washington Happy Hot Dog Club would have to start accepting foreign members.

Given all Frankfurter's efforts on behalf of Great Britain, it should not be surprising that the new ambassador to the United States, Lord Edward Halifax, sought out the justice shortly after his arrival in Washington in January 1941. The two men, born a year apart, became fast friends, quickly coming to a first-name basis and spending hours walking in Lafayette Park, across from the White House, discussing world events. A number of personal letters from Halifax and English philosopher Harold Laski written during 1941 make clear that the justice spent the entire year assiduously gathering information from both sides of the Atlantic concerning the state of relations between the United States and Great Britain.[6] By now, British officials viewed Frankfurter as a barometer of American public opinion and so were seriously troubled by his portents of a loss of sympathy on the part of the American people for the plight of their British allies.

As the justice's British friends should have known by now, wherever there was a dramatic Frankfurter delineation of a problem, a Frankfurter solution could not be far behind. The storm clouds, he told his friends, could easily be dissipated by the termination of Great Britain's domination of colonial India. Throughout the war, Frankfurter's personal letters and diary reveal, he kept uniquely abreast of this particular problem by maintaining contact with the Indian ambassador, G. S. Bajpai.[7] After Sir Stafford Cripps, a prominent British Labour Party official, failed in his mission to negotiate a settlement of the dispute, Halifax turned to Frankfurter for advice during a cruise on the presidential yacht Sequoia on June 9, 1942. The British diplomat had become distressed by public comparisons being made between Britain's treatment of India and American relations with the Philippines. Over the next three weeks, the two men exchanged notes on the problem and finally reviewed the entire matter in an hour-long chat at the British embassy on June 28. At Halifax's insistence, the justice set down his views for the British ambassador to present to Prime Minister Churchill in an upcoming discussion on India.[8]

Two days later, Frankfurter wrote a comprehensive memorandum entitled "Notes on India," in which he not only argued the need for Prime Minister Churchill to deliver an immediate speech on the problem, but then, just as he might have done for the president of the United States, went on to offer his own thoughts regarding the contents of such an address. "The rooted feeling of America," Frankfurter began, "is that India is Britain's victim."[9] In his opinion, Americans viewed Britain as having "wronged" the Indians, and thus far little had been done by the British to alter that impression. Furthermore, the situation could become worse if military necessity dictated British suppression of Gandhi and his followers. Since England relied so on American public opinion for future support in the war, the justice explained, bearing the sole burden for these actions in India would foolishly risk British efforts to secure such assistance.

Frankfurter then proposed a dual-pronged remedy. First, Churchill had to act "greatly" and assure India of its eventual independence—just as the United States had done with the Philippines. Second, the United States needed to be brought into a position of guaranteeing this solution. By making India an American, as well as British problem, the burden of sole guilt regarding whatever military actions wartime expedience might demand would be lifted from Great Britain. In concluding, the justice pleaded for action, saying that "the effect upon America of such [a] step and such a declaration will lift Anglo-American relations to a new plane and will be of incalculable benefit for the new international order." This entire argument is interesting in that it shows Frankfurter's pragmatic instincts at work. Though he loved democracy and freedom, he knew enough about human nature to make the future of Anglo-American relations, rather than high-flown philosophical reasoning, the basis of why his plan should be accepted by the British.

Documents discovered in Frankfurter's private papers indicate that during this period the justice was also using his contacts in Great Britain to improve relations between the two countries. Relying on research done by the Library of Congress, Frankfurter had previously drafted a memorandum for his own personal use entitled "Anglo-American Relations." In July 1942, he sent two long letters to Stafford Cripps, in which he incorporated some of the ideas he had earlier developed in that memorandum.[10] Expecting that his letters would be widely circulated in high British circles, Frankfurter conferred with the president, who fully approved of his diplomatic endeavors here, before sending them off.

The first of these missives to Cripps, dated July 9, 1942, indicates how concerned Frankfurter had become over the chasm between the two nations. The justice observed that:

> [There is] a lack of continuing consciousness of comradeship between the two people—comradeship not only in staving off an enemy that threatens everything we hold dear, but comradeship in achieving a common society having essentially the same gracious and civilized ends.[11]

Frankfurter went on to explain his view that the American people did not identify with England as being a democracy like their own. Instead, they pictured it as a divided society ruled by an upper class. This false perception, he argued, diminished the willingness of the Americans to make sacrifices to assist the British. To correct this view, the justice suggested an intensive instructional program designed to show "the inner magnificence of [England's] spirit." In an effort to begin this mutual educational process, he sent copies of this letter-memorandum to both President Roosevelt and Lord Halifax.[12]

But "Ambassador" Frankfurter's mission was far from completed.[13] When little improvement had been realized in the relations between the two countries by the end of the year, Frankfurter became further alarmed by the persistence of blatant Anglophobia in the United States. So, he convened a dinner-seminar on December 18, 1942 to discuss the subject; invited were some of Washington's highest officials: Vice-President Henry Wallace, Secretary of War Henry L. Stimson, Secretary of the Treasury Henry Morgenthau, General George Marshall, James Byrnes, and Harry Hopkins.

A fine documentary record of this gathering is preserved in the personal diaries of Henry L. Stimson and Henry Wallace. Both accounts agree that by the time the meal had ended it was clear to all present why they had been invited. With Lord Halifax also present, Frankfurter launched into an analysis of the Anglophobia in the United States. The justice mentioned a number of statements by administration officials that confirmed the truth of his perception. Pleading for improvement in the relations between "the two great English speaking nations," Frankfurter became, in Stimson's words, "so choked with emotion" that he could not properly express himself. After the discussion had continued into the night, most of those present agreed that only by close contact between the two nations—such as that which had developed between the troops—could relations at the higher levels improve significantly.[14] Subsequently, Frankfurter, more than anyone else in Washington, dedicated himself to this effort.

When no discernible improvement in harmony was realized by the beginning of 1943, the justice increased his pressure on American officials. Seeing his mission in trouble, Frankfurter decided that change could occur only if Prime Minister Churchill were persuaded to take action. Typical of the justice's strategy, he tried to approach Churchill through a variety of intermediaries. By so doing, Frankfurter assured that there would, at worst, be a strong possibility that at least one person would pass the message along. At best, the Prime Minister would be exposed to a barrage of concurring opinions, thus giving an appearance of an overwhelming mandate for change.

Since his work with Halifax had realized little success thus far, the justice initiated his new offensive by discussing the matter with Richard Casey, formerly the Australian ambassador to the United States and now serving in the British War Cabinet. When Casey expressed interest, the justice wrote him a letter on January 8, 1943, urging him to speak directly to Churchill and convince the prime minister to:

> Fire the American imagination by enlightening America with the inner significance of the British spirit the world over as a great democratizing force, and as comrade-in-arms in retaining the democratic society that we have thus far achieved, and in securing the indispensable conditions for its progress.[15]

Then Frankfurter raised the same issues with North Whitehead, an advisor on American affairs in the British Foreign Office. Before his return to his post, even the United States ambassador to Great Britain, J. Gilbert Winant, was subjected to a Frankfurter lecture on the need for Churchill to "creat[e] the right opinion for the right kind of peace."[16] Winant was told that Churchill needed to convince his people that social justice could be the only proper goal for this war.

Upon discovering that Churchill would be giving a speech in mid-May 1943, the justice jumped at the chance to make some suggestions to Lord Halifax regarding what Churchill might say. In a personal letter, the justice unveiled a newly insistent tone:

> Military developments give [the prime minister] an extraordinarily propitious opportunity for promoting the community of feeling between our two peoples that is indispensable to the necessary collaborative action.

By failing to act, the justice pointed out, Churchill would be communicating that he "does not seem to realize that too many Americans are [still] unaware of the commonalities between the two nations."[17] Once again, Frankfurter was disappointed, for Churchill spoke only on matters relating to the actual conduct of the war. Undaunted, the justice for the duration of the war sent extracts of British periodicals to key officials, such as Henry L. Stimson, in order to improve American understanding of British opinion and narrow the gap between the two governments.[18] In time, the two countries did move closer together, and because of his efforts to educate the leaders in both governments on the matter, Frankfurter should be given much of the credit for the special bond that eventually did develop between the two allies. Clearly, the most concerned and effective representative of British interests in this country through that period was this United States Supreme Court justice.

During the war years Frankfurter was involved with officials from the Australian government as well as the British. Entries in Stimson's diary, and letters in the private papers of Charles C. Burlingham, reveal that even before the war, Frankfurter had been advocating to Stimson and others that the naval fleet in the Pacific be transferred to the Atlantic to provide Europe with additional protection.[19] He may now have realized that by working with the Australians, he might find an opportunity to help accomplish this goal.

It is hardly surprising to find that Frankfurter, given his adeptness at cultivating friendships, had quite a crop of contacts to call on even in this area of the world halfway around the globe. Perhaps the best of these was Richard Casey, in 1941 the Australian Minister to the United States, who had proven to be an extremely effective ally in helping save Harry Hopkins's mission to England in order to meet with Churchill. Periodically he conferred with Casey and opened up his vast reservoir of information and contacts to the grateful minister. Moreover, the justice did favors for other Australian officials whenever possible; in March 1941, for instance, he arranged for the visiting Australian prime minister, Sir Robert Menzies, to be honored by the New York City Bar Association.[20] It was inevitable that the Australians would soon come to view this justice-about-Washington as their prime contact to both the Americans and the British delegation in Washington.

After the Japanese launched the war against the United States in December, the Australians turned to their friend for help. Frankfurter's friendships on both sides of the Pacific, as well as of the Atlantic, placed him in an ideal position to affect policy in the particular area that was causing the Australians increased concern. Indeed, Max Freedman, Frankfurter's designated biographer, argues that Frankfurter exerted "helpful intervention in putting Australia's case" to Washington.[21] But a series of letters drawn from Frankfurter's hitherto unpublished correspondence, as well as some newly discovered letters in the Roosevelt Presidential Library, provide evidence that such was not the case. While the Australians were certainly convinced at the time that Frankfurter had their interests at heart, it now seems clear that rather than having a special friend committed to their cause, they may instead have been used by him.

To be able to fully understand the case the Australians expected Frankfurter to make for them, it is necessary first to reflect on how war with Japan came to both the United States and Australia. While there were strong historical and cultural reasons for the United States to be appalled by the threatened overrun of Europe by Hitler in the late thirties, it was the aggressive designs of the Japanese that more directly threatened United States territorial integrity. Those in Washington who saw the need for eventual involvement of the United States in war against the Axis powers were afraid that Japan might, even in the pursuit of its "Greater East Asia Co-Prosperity Sphere," scrupulously avoid the many American possessions and mandates in the Pacific. Indeed, Winston S. Churchill reported that late in 1941 his "deepest fear was that the Japanese would attack [Great Britain] or the Dutch, and that constitutional difficulties would prevent the United States from declaring war."[22] Even after the Japanese obliged Churchill and attacked Pearl Harbor, there was still no sufficiently compelling basis for confidence that the United States Congress would immediately come to the aid of the British in their battle with Germany and Italy. Under the British system, within which the Crown declares war on the advice of its ministers, the British were able to declare war on the Japanese even before the British themselves were attacked anywhere in the Pacific, in fact even before the American Congress was able to declare war on Japan. Churchill's message for America apparently was that if your enemy automatically becomes our enemy, then our enemy should automatically become yours. Still, it is likely that Roosevelt would have been hard pressed to get Congress to reciprocate and declare war on Germany and Italy in response to Japan's attack on Pearl Harbor. It remained for Hitler to solve this difficult constitutional problem for Washington and London; in an act of recklessness that could only have come out of supreme arrogance, Hitler, on December 8, simplified things for the administration, and for the British, by declaring war on the United States.

As the United States directed its attention to the defeat of Hitler in Europe, large areas of the Pacific Ocean fell under the domination of the Japanese. Although garrisons in Bataan and Corregidor in the Philippines fought courageous rear-guard battles, by April 1942 Australia found itself virtually isolated in a Japanese Sea. It was only natural that the Australians should beg that American efforts be directed toward saving Australia from what seemed at the time to be imminent invasion. Should Australia be lost, the argument went, there would be no base from which the Allies might launch offensives to recover the Philippines, the Solomons, the Dutch East Indies, New Guinea, Malaya, Indo-China, and no proper base from which to lend aid to the Republic of China.

Convinced that Churchill was not adequately representing their interests with the American government, the embattled Australian leaders decided to approach the Roosevelt Administration directly. The question was how best to get the ear of the White House in competition with the great partnership and friendship being firmed up between Roosevelt and Churchill.[23] It could not have taken much asking around before the name of Felix Frankfurter came up.

Herbert Evatt, the Australian minister for external affairs had met and become friendly with Frankfurter in 1938 when Evatt, then serving as Chief Justice on the Australian High Court, gave a lecture at Harvard. Frankfurter had arranged for the visiting dignitary to meet President Roosevelt, at which time Evatt surely noted the close relationship between the Harvard Law School professor and the president.[24] Now, in the hour of his country's greatest peril, Evatt was charged with the task of pleading with his friend for help.

In a memorandum dated February 22, 1942, Evatt detailed the conditions in his part of the world in order to provide the justice with information, as he put it, "to do with as he wanted." After analyzing the military situation, Evatt turned to the political front. He explained that despite their admiration for Churchill, the Australians objected to being "informed of decisions and [having] little or no effective voice in their making." They wanted the United States to be aware of the need for reinforcements in the South Pacific. To insure this, "direct contact with the [Roosevelt Administration] in plans for prosecution of the War" was necessary. Evatt asked for the "backing" of Frankfurter and others in establishing this "machinery of allied cooperation." The Australian closed this almost desperate plea with these words: "I hope that the President will take more control of the situation and that you will take a hand."[25]

Despite his high personal regard for Evatt, Frankfurter was put in a very difficult situation by this request. Since this was private communication, outside the normal channels of diplomatic contact, it served to undermine the work of his now close friend, Australian Ambassador Richard Casey. More important, the appeal was directly contrary both to the justice's own preferences for military strategy and the plans that had been explained to him in conversations with Stimson, John J. McCloy and the other War Department officials. The consensus clearly was to save Europe first, which meant that Churchill's requests took precedence, even if the Pacific forces were to be temporarily depleted. So, with the full knowledge of presidential confidant Harry Hopkins and the administration, Frankfurter's decision was simply to decline Evatt's request to argue Australia's case with the White House. However, even in refusing to become that country's main advocate in Washington, he reassured Evatt in his responding letter of February 25, 1942 that there was a "deep feeling of kinship between our two democratic peoples." Further, the Australians were informed that "the most vigilant watchfulness of Pacific affairs" was being exercised.[26] Frankfurter concluded with an extremely glowing recommendation of Casey and implored Evatt to work in the future through his ambassador.

This was Frankfurter's second letter in two days referring to Ambassador Casey's contributions in the United States, but even before the Australian could take any further action, Frankfurter sent the whole file over to Harry Hopkins for his direct approval. Hopkins not only approved of the position Frankfurter had taken, but was quite pleased by it. On March 5, 1942, Hopkins wrote the justice that he "need have no misgivings" about sending the response he had.[27]

For his part, though, Evatt simply changed tactics in approaching the justice: now Casey was used as a messenger between them. The minister forwarded to the Australian legation on March 8, 1942 a cable "for Frankfurter alone," which contained the government's complete proposal for a joint Australia-New Zealand defense operation.[28] Ambassador Casey was also directed to discuss the entire issue of Australian needs with the justice.

Frankfurter, however, was in no mood to be handed such shopping lists. Although he was certainly interested in long-range Australian needs, he objected to the continual pressure for adopting their position immediately. In clearing his new response with Hopkins the next day, the justice complained, "What I most feel like saying [is] 'what the hell—why do you turn to me?' "[29] But once again process was being made the servant of bias, for the justice was chafing under pressure very much similar to that which he had so often exerted on others. Further, had it been the British knocking on doors, his answer might well have been *"what the hell—why not come to me?"* And so it was that the Australians received a personal letter from Frankfurter expressing sympathy for their plight and, as was his custom whenever confronted with a request for extrajudicial action that would not further his own goals, he offered the explanation that judicial propriety prevented his becoming involved.[30]

Events soon dictated that Frankfurter reverse himself and adopt an even more active posture in dealing with the Australians. Anticipating a visit from Evatt to Washington, Frankfurter warned Secretary of War Stimson during a horseback ride that he would be subjected to heavy pressure to open a new military offensive in the Pacific. They spoke at length regarding the future deployment of troops in that theatre and arranged to have lunch two days later. By now, the administration realized that, whether they liked it or not, the justice was their central contact with the Australians, and Stimson decided to brief the justice completely on the Allied plans for a future massive offensive in the European theatre. Since Evatt needed to be "educated," and was close to Frankfurter, the secretary of war reasoned that "Felix [was] a good agent to be well posted on this situation" when the Australians learned of the European plans and reacted to them.[31]

Now that it was convenient for Frankfurter to work with the Australians, he quickly renewed his contacts with officials there, and by mid-May, was reporting to Stimson that Evatt had been "turned around" and now was "very loyal" to the newly planned European drive, but that General Douglas MacArthur had, by his recent statements, given other Australians hope that their requests would be met.[32]

A short while later, Frankfurter was very pleased when FDR arranged a compromise solution: rewarding Evatt's visit to the United States with an agreement to establish a Pacific War Council to include an Australian representative. This at least gave the appearance that, and established a mechanism through which, decisions could be influenced by Australian input. In order to solidify this new relationship with the Australians, Frankfurter then pressed Roosevelt to invite their prime minister, John Curtin, to the United States for a conference. However, after consulting with Secretary of State Cordell Hull, the president decided to delay such an invitation for a while. For the remainder of the war Justice Frankfurter continued to maintain close contact with the Australians through their next diplomatic representative in Washington, Sir Owen Dixon.[33]

During 1943 the justice's diplomatic interests broadened considerably. Since the beginning of the war he had maintained a role in advising FDR on policy with Finland, Yugoslavia, and Russia. Now a constant stream of ambassadors and foreign secretaries, including T.V. Soong of China, President Edward Beneš of Czechoslovakia, Sir Giija Bajpai of India, and Constain Fotitch of Yugoslavia, visited his chambers in search of advice, contacts, and pleasant conversation.[34] While these talks continued to make Frankfurter one of the most informed individuals in Washington's diplomatic circles, his involvement with the affairs of these nations was never very extensive.

During his years on the bench, Frankfurter also was not nearly as active in the problems of world Jewry as one would expect him to have been after his long service as Brandeis's lieutenant in the Zionist movement. To be sure, after Brandeis's retirement Frankfurter remained interested in the subject, gathering information from his numerous contacts whenever he could. One of those sources of information was an old friend and ally, David Niles, now serving as FDR's fourth administrative assistant. With his special expertise on the problems of Palestine and the Middle East, Niles, whom one law clerk remembers as a frequent visitor to the justice's chambers, was able to keep Frankfurter informed regarding White House intentions in this area. Because of Niles's political style—he preferred to rely more on phone conversations than on letters—there is little documentary record detailing the nature of their discussions or of their relationship at this time. However, a letter from Niles to Frankfurter that ended up in the personal papers of Charles C. Burlingham indicates that their relationship proved to be somewhat of an embarrassment to them and the administration on occasion. It seems that certain anti-Semitic groups were aware of the contacts and used them to fuel a character-assassination campaign, portraying both men as having too much of a "communistic" influence on FDR.[35]

Frankfurter had other sources of information as well on the problems of the Jewish people. An entry in Henry L. Morgenthau's personal diary shows that the justice discussed with the secretary of the treasury on June 3, 1941 the question of whether the Palestinians should be enlisted in the British Army. Then, entries in Frankfurter's own diary for 1943 indicate that periodically he would chat in his chambers with men such as Zionist leader Chaim Weizmann, Richard Casey, then-British minister of state for the Middle East, and various officials from the fund-raising Jewish Agency in Palestine, for the purpose of keeping himself informed on what all sides were thinking.[36]

What the Zionist movement needed, though, was not a man gathering information, but a Felix Frankfurter as active a participant in its affairs as he had been earlier in his career. Instead, upon the death of Louis D. Brandeis in 1941, Frankfurter's active interest was seldom translated into active participation in the cause.[37] Given this failure to maintain an active involvement in the movement, the sort of involvement one might expect from the justice in situations in which he had a compelling personal interest, it seems likely that it was more his loyalty to Louis Brandeis than to the cause itself that had spurred his earlier endeavors. During Frankfurter's tenure on the Court, there were only two exceptions to this posture of noninvolvement in Zionist causes—in the first he worked to undermine the Vichy government in Algeria because of its treatment of Jews; in the second, he lobbied for one country's United Nations vote in favor of the partition of Palestine—both matters of such importance that no person even remotely interested in the movement could fail to act.[38]

The question of the treatment of Jews by the Vichy government was brought to a head in late 1942 by the invasion of North Africa by American forces. In 1940, following the defeat of the French army, France had entered into a surrender agreement with the Germans by the terms of which a part of France inland from the Atlantic Ocean and the English Channel was left unoccupied by the Germans. A government, with its capital at Vichy, continued to rule this unoccupied area of metropolitan France as if it were, indeed, an independent nation, carrying on political relations with many nations, including the United States. The surrender arrangement stipulated that this Vichy government would continue to administer the French Empire in North Africa, that the French would remain neutral in the war, and that the Germans would not attempt to use territory under the control of Vichy for military operations against the Allies. While this government enjoyed a nominal independence of German control, it was in the nature of things that its members were soon found currying favor with their conquerors by imitating the anti-Semitism of the Nazi state.

When Dwight D. Eisenhower planned his invasion of Vichy-controlled North Africa, he had little idea what to expect. He would be landing his troops on the shores of a sovereign state, once an ally of the British, but now neutral. He would certainly have preferred a course of action that might assure a friendly reception for his troops, rather than one that would provoke strong resistance from the French. But while there was no question where the sympathies of most of the French North Africans lay when it came to the Americans, the French officials in Algeria and Tunisia had a difficult legal problem of their own. Their home government at Vichy, under the aged Marshal Henri Philippe Pétain and Pierre Laval, directed them to resist the Allied landings. French leaders on the scene were divided. Some favored going directly over to the Allied side, others harbored strong grudges against the British, their former allies, who, many French felt, had abandoned them at Dunkirk to suffer the brunt of German occupation. There was also the unspoken, but unmistakable threat that should the French in North Africa throw in with the Allies, the Germans would quickly retaliate by moving to occupy the remainder of France, causing even greater suffering for the French people at home.

The Allies were in agreement on the importance of having the right man along to plead their case with the French of North Africa, but even here there were problems. The British had made commitments to Charles de Gaulle when he had refused to recognize the surrender of his government in 1940 and had established the Free French movement. But FDR would not go along, having decided that de Gaulle was too provocative a figure among the Vichy French to have any prospect of bringing them over to a stance more accepting of the Allied military operation.[39] Instead Eisenhower was given Henri Giraud, a French general who had made dramatic escapes from German captivity in both wars and around whom Eisenhower had been told all French in the area might rally.

Alas, this was not to be. When Giraud and Eisenhower's emissary, Mark Clark, were flown into Algiers, the local French commanders refused to accept the authority of Giraud. A few days before, the American political representative in Algiers, Robert Murphy, seemed to have the French Military Commander convinced to bring his forces over to the Allied side, but by a strange coincidence Admiral Jean François Darlan, a man notoriously anti-British and a high official of the hated Vichy regime, was brought to Algiers by the hospitalization there of his son. With Darlan present the military commander refused to act on his own.

When Clark saw the reality facing him, he asked Eisenhower by radio for authority to deal with Darlan. The political consequences were immediate. In the end, Admiral Darlan ordered the end of French resistance to the landings in Algeria. French officials in Tunisia were less successful, thus allowing the Germans to come in and establish themselves at important air fields in that area.

While these decisions were being taken on the scene there were many in Washington very agitated about their consequences on the nature of the postwar order that would be established in the region. Further complicating things for Frankfurter was the fate of the many French Jews in Algeria, who had, during rule by the Vichy government, lost certain rights they had long enjoyed in the region. The confused situation in French North Africa generally was also occupying the attention of Frankfurter's powerful ally, Jean Monnet, at this time. The manner of resolution of many of these same questions in North

Africa would also have an important impact in determining the character of the postwar regime in his native France. Hence the team that had worked for United States military aid to Great Britain, and had achieved such success in the American "Victory Program," joined together now for one last campaign.

The combination of Frankfurter's connections in the American government and Monnet's contacts with the many French factions in Algeria had long before given the two men a perfect vantage point from which to observe events and influence policy.[40] On several occasions in fact, Frankfurter had forwarded to Stimson and FDR information he had received, usually from Jean Monnet, on the subject.[41] Thus, it is not surprising that by 1942, Frankfurter had come to be viewed by the Washington community as one of its resident experts on the "French problem." Nor is it surprising that when the question was raised in the administration in late 1942 whether or not General Eisenhower should try to strike a deal with Vichy officials in Algeria, Felix Frankfurter was one of those called in for advice. Secretary of War Stimson invited the justice, Henry Morgenthau, John McCloy, and Archibald MacLeish to his home in mid-November to discuss the problem. Morgenthau became so disgusted by Frankfurter's compromising efforts in the conversation that he later derisively characterized the justice in his personal diary as "Mr. Fixer."[42]

At this point, Monnet, understanding that the Germans would occupy all of metropolitan France should the French not resist the Americans in North Africa, began lobbying with the Americans concerning the need to prepare immediately for the liberation of France. Memoranda and draft speeches covering three basic ideas were sent to Frankfurter, Hopkins, and others. First, Monnet argued that a large French Army had to be equipped and trained in North Africa for use by the French government once that area had been won. Second, he stressed, the French people must be allowed to decide for themselves which government would take power at that time. Finally, neither Admiral Darlan's Vichy group in North Africa nor Charles de Gaulle's National Committee in London should be recognized by the Allies as empowered to do anything other than carry out a limited caretaking role until the liberation of metropolitan France. Pragmatic as always, Monnet positioned himself between the various French factions, hoping to unite them at a later time.[43]

The assassination of Admiral Darlan on Christmas Day, 1942, altered all these careful calculations. Monnet's memoranda to the American officials became even more insistent on the need to preserve the sovereignty of the French people. When the declaration sought by Monnet was not forthcoming from either FDR or Churchill, he sought to influence the thinking of other lesser officials. Monnet and Frankfurter briefed Robert Sherwood and McCloy prior to visits by each man to Algeria on government missions. Furthermore, Monnet kept the justice armed with information in the event that he might be able to influence other key Roosevelt advisers. One such adviser to whom this information was passed on was Samuel Rosenman.

Seeing that General Giraud, who had been established by the Americans as the new Algerian "Civil and Military Commander in Chief," was plotting his own course, Monnet arranged to have himself sent there by Harry Hopkins on behalf of the Munitions Assignment Board. Before leaving, Monnet was persuaded in a two-day conference with Frankfurter not to make any commitments to any French faction and to use his position with the American and British governments as an excuse for doing so. Meanwhile the justice remained informed by debriefing the American diplomats as they returned from the area.[44]

When Monnet arrived in Algeria he discovered a very fluid political situation. Though Giraud was a fine military leader, he vacillated in dealing with civil matters. Being thus open to influence, he had been induced to retain the aides to Admiral Darlan, continuing uninterrupted the anti-Semitic policies of the Vichy regime. Monnet realized that this government's treatment of its Jewish population and political prisoners, as well as its repressive laws, were causing severe criticism in America. A complete "exorcism" of the spirit of the Vichy regime, he came to believe, was a prerequisite to receiving more American assistance.

In addition, Monnet believed, this would be a first step in purging all Frenchmen of the taint of collaboration with the Germans, leading to the eventual uniting of the various factions. To facilitate this change, Monnet convinced Giraud to deliver a progressive speech advocating a move toward democracy. The address, written by Monnet and delivered by Giraud on March 14, 1943, served to bridge the gap between his faction and that of de Gaulle. At the same time, the Algerian government nullified nearly all the Vichy laws.[45]

Despite these accomplishments, Monnet's mission had only been partly successful so far. There was still one Vichy action he had been unable to convince Giraud to reverse—the abrogation of the Cremieux Decree. In 1870, the French had passed a decree granting Jews in North Africa full French citizenship, while denying the same to the Moslems. Arguing publicly that the act was racially discriminatory, Giraud continued the Vichy policy. As he told Monnet, it was his fear of public riots by the Moslems that induced him to keep the abrogation in force. Seeking a positive turn in American public opinion and a stronger commitment to the French, Monnet realized it was "urgent to abolish the laws against the Jews."[46] From a public relations standpoint, Monnet knew that it was courting the contempt of the American public to leave in effect a Vichy action aimed against the very group that was being so brutally persecuted wherever the Nazi gang had left its bootprint. However, Giraud could see the problem from only one side—that of balancing the rights and privileges of Jews and Moslems in the area he was trying to administer. Moreover, the ranking American diplomat in the area, Robert Murphy, was siding with Giraud on this issue.

Monnet knew that restoring the Cremieux Decree would require enlisting the American government in the plan to apply pressure on Giraud. Since the formal diplomatic channels favored a policy different from his own, the situation called for working with someone outside normal official channels. Monnet could see that the job was tailor-made for that one man Department of State, Felix Frankfurter, whose interest would no doubt be heightened by the fact that he was Jewish himelf.

Because of the military situation, the only means by which Monnet could reach the justice was through official communiqués from Robert Murphy to his superiors in Washington. Furthermore, the effort required discretion in that Monnet would be undercutting Giraud, with whom he wished to continue negotiating. Obviously, any messages to Frankfurter would have to be very cleverly disguised.

Indicative of the fact that Monnet had been correct in his assessment of the importance Jews placed on the failure to re-establish the Cremieux Decree, an article appeared in The New York Times on March 19, 1943 which was highly critical of Giraud. The piece contained a statement by Baron Edouard de Rothschild, a leader of the Algerian Jewish community, expressing his "grief and indignation," against the policy that gave "rise to a feeling of anxiety among all those who have been victims of the racial laws and among the miserable human beings tortured by the Nazis."[47] This was precisely the specter that had compelled Monnet to seek a reversal of Giraud's decision.

Asked by the State Department to comment on the statement, Robert Murphy termed it in a cable from Algeria dated March 21, 1943 "a patently false interpretation" and offered a point-by-point refutation of the charges.[48] Murphy argued that this policy was only a minor infringement of Jewish rights and was limited only to Algerian-born Jews. Moreover, a procedure would be established soon whereby these Jews, like the Moslems, could acquire French citizenship if they so desired.

Fully satisfied, Undersecretary of State Sumner Welles used Murphy's data to answer Rothschild's charges in a letter released to the public. It was a very cleverly constructed response, concentrating on the many Vichy laws that had been repealed to the benefit of the Jews, rather than on the one at issue.[49] Monnet was prepared for this move, however. Knowing that only a full restoration of these Jewish privileges would be satisfactory, he brought Frankfurter into the fray with this cryptic request cabled via the State Department:

> I am shocked at the incomprehension shown by certain interpretations in the United States of the measures taken by Giraud wiping out all discrimination against Jews and also by the harmful interpretation of the abrogation of the Cremieux Decree The telegraphic reply sent by Algiers to the Department . . . represents an accurate statement made after consultation with an unbiased and best qualified legal specialist. I hope that you can help in straightening out any possible misunderstanding. If any points remain doubtful to you please cable me through Murphy.[50]

The statement is a masterful deception. Murphy transmitted it in another cable to the secretary of state, written on March 22, 1943, thinking that the "harmful interpretation" in Monnet's view was the one having been made in the Rothschild article, and that Frankfurter, as a leader of the Jewish community, was being asked by Monnet to quiet the Jews down. But because Murphy and Monnet defined their goals differently, each saw the attendant "harms" very differently. The misunderstanding Monnet really wanted the justice to "straighten out" was the one created by the first Murphy cable.[51]

As expected, Frankfurter understood Monnet's request perfectly and began his work to undercut the American diplomat on this side of the Atlantic. Though the normal avenues in the State Department were unavailable, the justice had never been limited by protocol. With Dean Acheson now serving as assistant secretary of state, Frankfurter was able to have this cable forwarded to Monnet:

> Greatly appreciate your message. Have neither knowledge nor concern for deRothschild. For my own understanding should like to be clear about scope and implications of abrogation of Cremieux Decree. Does it deprive of French citizenship anyone who possessed it prior to Vichy Decree? If so, how many and what is the justification for such deprivation.[52]

The question seems to be almost naive, but given the nature of the diplomatic channels available to him, Frankfurter had a very specific purpose. Already aware of the extent of the deprivation, he was clearly trying to begin the process of having the State Department realize and correct its own misinterpretations when faced with additional contradictory evidence.

The response to Frankfurter's inquiry came in two parts: one public and the other by private channel. On April 4, *The New York Times* printed a new letter by Rothschild that renewed charges that Giraud's action was a "vicious discrimination" against the Algerian Jews.[53] Through diplomatic channels Monnet thanked Frankfurter for his letter and called attention to a new cable sent by Murphy to the secretary of state on April 17, 1943, in which the American diplomat admitted that General Giraud, by abrogating the Cremieux Decree, had "deprive[d] Frenchmen [Jews] for the second, third or even fourth generation of their citizenship."[54] Apparently still unaware of what was really happening, Murphy recommended that all this information, even though it was marked secret, be passed along to the justice.[55]

More than a week later it became obvious to Frankfurter that the State Department was not going to press Giraud for change on its own; so he began to use Dean Acheson in a more direct fashion. In a letter to his friend, written on May 3, 1943, the justice first pointed out that Acheson should compare the different cables from Murphy because they were "in rather important details, different."[56] Then, feeling the necessity to make his own views plain, Frankfurter recommended that Murphy be asked to respond to a recent letter by the famed neo-Thomist professor, Jacques Maritain, president of the École Libre des Hautes Études, that had just been published in *The New York Times*. Maritain had charged that the abrogation was "anti-Semitic," "unjust in itself . . . [and] contrary to all the traditions of French law because it penalizes retroactively persons who are in no wise guilty of any offense . . ." He went on to argue that the action "deprive[d] of their citizenship men who are French by birth," a group that numbered over 100,000.[57] Maritain's extremely detailed refutation of the State Department's position also offered a solution for the alleged unequal treatment of Algerian Jews and Moslems: provide the Moslems with French citizenship as well.

An undated memorandum discovered in Frankfurter's papers indicates that the justice had also drafted a comprehensive response to Murphy's argument, one substantially like Maritain's, but, for reasons of his own, chose not to send it.[58] Rather, in closing his letter to Acheson, Frankfurter gave this article a rousing recommendation.

> I attach importance to what Professor Maritain has written. Let me add a redundant thought—that I naturally attach importance to the views expressed by one of the most distinguished of living Frenchmen, a thinker esteemed as much for the seriousness of his intellectual contributions as for the disinterestedness of his spirit.[59]

The justice's message could not be put more strongly—listen to the Catholic philosopher, who was supporting the Jewish position rather than to a diplomat, such as Murphy, who seemingly lacked both expertise and a sense of objectivity. In time, enough pressure was placed on Giraud, and the Cremieux Decree was restored.

This incident and others demonstrate that throughout the war, Felix Frankfurter became one of the most important diplomatic contacts in America—albeit an informal one—for a host of foreign diplomats. By responding to or ignoring the pleas of these foreign representatives, Frankfurter was able to give his own little nudges, this way or that, to foreign policy. While Frankfurter on occasion acted because American officials such as Secretary of War Stimson had asked him to do so, frequently the justice acted in concert with whomever else shared with him a belief in what the government's policy in a particular area ought to be. Thus, the foreign policy goals and priorities of a Supreme Court justice were, in a sense, reflected in the overall thrust of his government's foreign policy.

Toward the end of 1943, the justice turned his attention to the final phase of his wartime extrajudicial work—helping to structure the postwar international order. Frankfurter periodically called his dinner-seminars on the projected needs of the European nations once the fighting ceased. At one such gathering, Jean Monnet was asked to set out for Stimson, McCloy, Acheson, Samuel Rosenman and Lend-Lease Administrator Edward Stettinius "what France needed." [60]

The question of the political directions of various governments after the war concerned Frankfurter a great deal. His uneasiness about Joseph Stalin, for example, led the justice to advise FDR that he needed to involve other members of the Soviet government in the discussions on a prospective peace treaty. Reliance on this one individual, he felt, could prove to be very short-sighted and dangerous. [61] But there was another postwar question to be faced—one of such paramount importance that it occupied even more of the justice's attention at this stage.

From "some distinguished American scientists" whose acquaintance he had made while still in academia, Frankfurter learned about the on-going Manhattan Project, the work on the development of the atomic bomb. The account of Frankfurter's involvement with the Manhattan project is drawn from two memoranda drafted by the justice on April 26 and May 6, 1945, labeled "strictly private" and "top secret" respectively and handed to Secretary of War Henry L. Stimson in order to fill him in on "the details of [the relevant] conversations." [62] Since that time these documents have had an interesting history. To maintain military security for this information, Frankfurter, in May 1945, placed the memoranda in an envelope containing all his documents on the project and turned the envelope over to Major General Leslie R. Groves of the Manhattan Engineer District for safekeeping. Caught up in the intrigue, Frankfurter, when the envelope was returned to him, wrote on the cover letter "The attached envelope . . . was returned to me by Major General Groves in person, in my Supreme Court room, on Wednesday, January 15, 1947, about 11 a.m. I write this upon the General's leaving." Somehow, these documents ended up in the collection of private papers of atomic scientist J. Robert Oppenheimer, which are now stored in the Library of Congress.

The Manhattan Project was such a sensitive secret, former Assistant Secretary of War John J. McCloy recalled in a personal interview, that for a long time not even the other assistant secretary of war, Robert Patterson, who was signing all the requisition forms for its supplies, knew of its mission. McCloy remembers that one day Patterson came into Stimson's office saying, "Since I am in charge of procurement in the Department, don't you think, Colonel, I ought to have a greater knowledge of what is going on there than I now possess."[63] Only then did the secretary, a very discreet man by nature, take the assistant into his confidence.

However, no secret, no matter how closely guarded, was safe from the well-connected and inquisitive Justice Felix Frankfurter and when he learned of the project, he was terrified. To develop such a weapon without fully considering its ramifications for the world balance of power was, in his opinion, extremely dangerous. Something needed to be done to apprise the politicians of this fact.

Unlike his other extrajudicial campaigns, though, Frankfurter was completely powerless to act on his own here and desperately needed an ally. He lacked the technical expertise to understand the weapon, a deficiency that minimized his authority to advocate a particular plan for its control. Moreover, the project's secrecy made it unwise for him to speak about it with anyone other than the president. Since he was not even supposed to be aware of the research, Frankfurter also realized that a discussion with FDR at this point would not be possible. The justice needed an expert in the field who could discuss these issues with him and provide an excuse for revealing his knowledge to FDR.

Fortunately, just such an individual existed—the renowned Danish physicist, Niels Bohr—and, as one might expect, Frankfurter knew him. The two men had met during Frankfurter's year at Oxford, and they conferred again several times in Washington and London in 1939 to discuss "common interests in international cultural relations."[64] Now, in 1943, the justice surmised that Bohr might be just what was needed in his efforts to advise FDR on the issue of the eventual control of the weapon. As it turned out, Bohr himself was seeking a means of approaching the president outside the normal bureaucratic channels to present his own plans for postwar control of the bomb through international scientific cooperation. Felix Frankfurter, with his access to the White House, seemed to Bohr to be a potentially effective conduit. Each man, then, had something very specific to offer the other.

Arranging the wartime meeting with Bohr was so sensitive that it required extraordinary precautions, so much so that for the first and only time after 1941, Frankfurter violated his self-imposed rule for the separate use of his political and judicial assistants. Needing someone in whom he had absolute trust, the justice told his law clerk, Philip

Elman, whose term was nearly finished,* to drive to a particular Washington address, pick up a person there, and bring him back to Frankfurter's Georgetown house.

Elman, now a Washington, D.C. attorney, provides a fascinating account of this unique event. Not having the slightest idea at the time of Bohr's identity or his mission, the former law clerk recalls only picking up a man with a foreign accent and exchanging small talk with him on the return trip. Sometime later, Frankfurter took Elman aside and said in muffled tones, "Phil, I am going to tell you who that man was, but you mustn't tell anyone either about him or that meeting. Does the name Niels Bohr mean anything to you?" As he often did, Elman responded with mock seriousness, "Sure, Mr. Justice, didn't he pitch for the Brooklyn Dodgers?" "Oh, Phil," the Justice chided, "I am truly amazed by your ignorance. How did you attend C.C.N.Y., a great college [having also produced Felix Frankfurter] and not learn anything?" Frankfurter then patiently described the accomplishments of the Nobel Prize winner and closed with this admonition, "Phil, you need only know that Bohr is in this country on a very secret but highly important mission, and yesterday you played a small, but very essential role in accomplishing that mission."[66] This incident displays the incredible caution Frankfurter exercised in this campaign.

Frankfurter recalled his conference with Bohr in his private memorandum of April 26, 1945 for Secretary of War Stimson. The conference began with a discussion of a variety of subjects, ranging from the political affairs of Denmark and England to the probable course of the war. Then, the two men began a conversation about "X"—the Atomic Bomb—and it "became clear to [them] that two such persons, who had been so long and so deeply preoccupied with the menace of Hit-

---

* There is some controversy regarding the date of the initial wartime meeting between Frankfurter and Bohr to discuss the ongoing atomic research. In his memoranda, Frankfurter himself would say only that when Bohr arrived in America after his escape from German-occupied Denmark, they renewed their friendship at a reception given by the Danish ambassador, and arranged to lunch together several days later. Frankfurter's designated biographer, Max Freedman, states that this meeting occurred "late in 1943."[65] On the other hand, Martin Sherwin, in his *A World Destroyed*, says that the conference took place in 1944.

Relying on new evidence derived from a personal interview with Philip Elman, it is now possible to suggest that the meeting occurred closer to the earlier date than the later one, for if Elman was still serving as Frankfurter's law clerk, the meeting could not have taken place after the beginning of the Supreme Court's 1943 term, which opened in October of that year.

lerism and who were so deeply engaged in the common cause, could talk about the implications of 'X' without either making any disclosure to the other."

From that point on they freely discussed with each other the political implications of the project without revealing any secrets or technical information. The justice was in total agreement with Bohr that "X might be one of the greatest boons to mankind or might become the greatest disaster." So, the two men resolved to seek a solution together to the problem of controlling "X" and assuring that it would prove to be a benefit to the world. Bohr expressed the view that the Soviets should be informed about the project immediately, rather than risk their learning about it from other sources. In this way the weapon could be used by the United States "as a means of exploring the possibility of effective international arrangements with Russia."[67] However, the opportunity to use the weapon in such a manner would soon be lost, Bohr believed, because Russia's scientists would discover the secret on their own very shortly, a prediction that history did not bear out.

Fully persuaded of Bohr's position the justice resolved to bring the matter to FDR's attention. In a ninety-minute meeting sometime in February 1944, the president told Frankfurter that he was "worried to death" by the project. Eager for assistance on the subject of control, Roosevelt agreed to meet with Bohr personally. Frankfurter left the meeting believing that he had "plainly impressed" the president and carrying his authorization "to tell Professor Bohr that he might tell our friends in London that [Roosevelt] was anxious to explore ways for achieving proper safeguards in relation to X." There is sufficient reason to believe, though, that FDR was more concerned about how Frankfurter had discovered the project than he was persuaded by the justice's arguments regarding its eventual control.[68]

Bohr's efforts in London to present his ideas to Prime Minister Churchill were completely unsuccessful. The packet of letters and documents Frankfurter later stored in the Manhattan Engineer District reveals the many subsequent efforts the justice made to convince the United States government of the efficacy of Bohr's views. Upon his return to Washington, the scientist gave Frankfurter a full report, which was then quickly passed on to the president. Both the justice and the Danish ambassador then implored Roosevelt to meet with Bohr. When

FDR agreed to the conference, Frankfurter advised the Danish scientist to prepare for the meeting by setting out his proposals in a lengthy memorandum. The justice found this written argument for political and scientific cooperation with the Russians so persuasive that he immediately forwarded it directly to the president.

When Bohr and FDR finally met on August 26, 1944, the full proposal was discussed. Roosevelt appeared to be most encouraging and promised to raise the matter with Churchill at the upcoming Quebec Conference. Nevertheless, before the president left Washington, the justice arranged for Bohr to present his views once more in a "thank you" note and enclosed a supporting letter of his own. Despite these intensive efforts, Churchill induced Roosevelt to continue the policy of withholding the secret from Stalin. In addition, the prime minister suggested to FDR that Bohr might be secretly more sympathetic toward the Russians than he had let on, thus dooming the scientist's later efforts to see the president again.[69]

Frankfurter had not completely given up on his quest for imposing international restrictions on the atomic weapon. Even after FDR's death on April 12, 1945, he searched for methods to approach the new White House occupant, Harry Truman. In early May, believing that Secretary of War Stimson might have influence with Truman, Frankfurter sent him copies of all his memoranda on, and correspondence with Niels Bohr. Included in this packet were the Danish scientist's own plans for creating postwar controls on the use of the bomb.[70] In addition, the justice approached Joseph Davies, U.S. ambassador to Russia from 1937 to 1939, and persuaded him to speak with Stimson and President Truman about the possibility of establishing better relations with Russia. In a long meeting with the president, however, Davies was unable to convince him to adopt a more conciliatory and cooperative posture with the Russians. However, Davies and Harry Hopkins were dispatched during the last week of May 1945 as Truman's special envoys to the Soviet Union to arrange for a possible summit meeting with Stalin. Meanwhile, after "plead[ing] for an interview," the justice conferred with Stimson regarding the proposal of Bohr, whom Stimson referred to as "the great Dane." Furthermore, Frankfurter asked that the secretary confer with the scientist directly. The two men did eventually meet, and Stimson was sufficiently impressed that he advocated in a mid-September memorandum to Truman that the United States undertake a "closer relationship in the matter of the atomic bomb" with Russia.[71] Nonetheless, Bohr's immediate interest in seeing that the U.S. share its atomic secrets with the Russians was never realized.

For Justice Frankfurter, however, this one defeat was a slight mar on a record of many war-related extrajudicial successes. He had helped to prepare the nation for its entry into the war, and had secured assistance, both material and monetary for Great Britain. Then, together with Jean Monnet, he served as a catalyst for the adoption of a mobilization program adequate for the battle that lay ahead. Finally he maneuvered his diplomatic contacts to support the Europe-first priorities that had been adopted by the American military strategists. And these were only his major successes. It is impossible to assess how many mundane, day-to-day decisions were influenced by Frankfurter's constant attention to the major actors—FDR, Stimson, McCloy— and by his genius for helping place allies in key administration posts and then informing, cajoling, directing, and, at times, even commanding them.

Reflecting on Frankfurter's extrajudicial work during the war one has to conclude that he was just as much the politician as anyone else in Washington. He was the consummate operator—using people and in turn being used by others. In undertaking all this extrajudicial political work, Frankfurter was a product of his age, but, in turn, helped to change the normative standards governing the next age. Throughout history, in times of crisis, members of the Supreme Court have been eager and have even been encouraged to adopt a more visible political role. So Frankfurter's work was not much different in kind from the endeavors of other justices, such as Joseph Story in the War of 1812; John A. Campbell and Samuel Nelson in the Civil War; and Louis D. Brandeis in World War I.[72] As in everything else he did, however, Frankfurter pushed his extrajudicial activities to the extreme limits. He became so involved and so concerned, that he made his judicial colleagues—all highly political men in their own right—more comfortable in adopting their own highly active extrajudicial styles.

This general loosening of ethical standards among Court members made Frankfurter uneasy, and perhaps even led him to feel somewhat guilty. He became increasingly aware of the dangers posed by, as Judge Learned Hand described it, the willingness to "lead flaming causes from a cloister."[73] Recalling the occasional problems of Brandeis himself, Frankfurter feared full public discovery of his extensive political involvement during the war. Years after the conflict, Frankfurter worked feverishly to prevent the public from piecing together precisely how politically active he had been. According to Max Freedman, the justice burned literally hundreds of private notes sent to FDR during the war.[74] Moreover, whenever any of the justice's former allies, such as FDR's speechwriter Samuel I. Rosenman, set down their recollections of that era, Frankfurter convinced them to purge all but the most harmless references to his earlier private involvement.[75] Despite these efforts, it was inevitable that there would be reference in print from time to time regarding Frankfurter's political activities. While the justice claimed to observe, as he wrote once in a personal letter to The New Republic editor, Bruce Bliven, "an undeviating rule to be heedless of all the untruths and misrepresentations that . . . appeared in print" about him, Frankfurter actually scoured the newspapers, periodicals, and published books for references to his private political involvement. Each time one came to his attention, the justice made it his business to write an indignant denial.[76] So important was it to Frankfurter that he maintain the image of having been secluded from politics that he continued to express in personal letters to people such as United States Court of Appeals Judge Jerome Frank his allegiance to "a sticky view about the aloofness that one in my position should maintain toward public manifestation, directly or indirectly, on matters of legislative policy."[77]

Despite Frankfurter's vigorous claims of devotion to judicial austerity, his closest friends knew about his activities and some had their reservations about them. Reflecting on the war years, Dean Acheson commented that "the intimate and notorious friendship of one of my closest friends, Justice Frankfurter, with President Franklin D. Roosevelt did harm to the public reputation of both the Court and the Justice."[78] While Acheson's assessment may have been a bit harsh, in that the "harm" was more potential than real, the breadth of Frankfurter's political endeavors may well have contributed to the tightening of the standards of propriety for the entire Court after the war. Even with the change in the political environment after the death of Franklin D. Roosevelt in April 1945, Felix Frankfurter, now sixty-two years old and finishing his seventh term on the Supreme Court, would still have something to say about the question.

9

Staffing the Monastery: Frankfurter's Political Work from 1945 to 1962

While Felix Frankfurter's political activities sharply declined with the death of Franklin Roosevelt and the winding down of World War II, the reduction was, to a degree, more a reflection of changing circumstances than of newly developed attitudes. A thorough analysis of the unpublished papers and documents in various manuscript collections indicates that for the remainder of his years on the Court, whenever the possibility of political action presented itself, Frankfurter was no more able to resist than he had been in the past.

Still, Frankfurter was by no means insensitive to the fact that as an immediate reaction to the end of World War II, some of his brethren were once again taking a less lenient attitude toward outside involvement by Supreme Court justices. While Justice Douglas continued to give advice on foreign policy matters to both President Truman and Secretary of Defense James Forrestal,[1] Chief Justice Stone, attempting to set a new tone for the Court, declined all requests to serve on postwar government tribunals and commissions.[2] Thus, when Associate Justice Robert Jackson announced his decision to accept the role of chief counsel for the Americans at the Nuremberg War Crimes trials, the response he received from his colleagues was not entirely favorable. Strangely, while it was Frankfurter's reaction that Jackson had first worried about, once he reached Germany he found the diminutive justice his staunchest defender back on the Court.

According to a letter written to Frankfurter on January 25, 1946, Jackson ordinarily thought "it [was] unwise for a Justice of the Court to get into . . . outside things."[3] In fact, when he was first offered the assignment, Jackson later confessed, he "had grave doubt . . . [about] whether [he] ought to get into this thing, and [he] did not talk to [Frankfurter] about it for [fear that he] would talk [him] out of doing the job."[4] In the end, though, it appears that Jackson considered the assignment so important, he made the decision that if necessary, he would even consider resigning from the bench to fulfill it.[5]

The support Frankfurter provided Jackson in this decision was indeed badly needed, for Chief Justice Stone was greatly distressed by the whole situation. It seems that Stone opposed the philosophy of the war crimes trials themselves and the image that was being conveyed by the participation of a Supreme Court justice in them.[6] Further, he disliked the idea that Jackson's absence from the Court for a full year increased the burdens on his colleagues and forced several cases, which were deadlocked by a four-to-four vote, to be put over until the following term. Fully aware of the problems caused by his involvement at Nuremberg,* Jackson considered returning to the Court for a brief period in early 1946, but Frankfurter advised against the idea arguing that it was "neither wise nor practicable for him to attempt to participate in the work . . . [of the Court] . . . unless [he] plan[ned] to stay in the United States."[7]

A few weeks later, knowing that Jackson had been stung by criticisms regarding his absence from the Court, Frankfurter wrote him to "dismiss all concern" over these charges because "neither in volume nor in quality [do they] really amount to a hill of beans." He explained that it was common for the Court to reschedule arguments in cases, and so Jackson's absence was "not . . . sacrificing a single interest of importance."[8]

When Jackson seemed unconvinced, Frankfurter's reassurances became even more pronounced, highlighted by the now-familiar ode to his own personal standard of ethics:

---

* Besides the internal problems on the Supreme Court there was a strong body of opinion in American legal circles that because the Nuremberg trials, conducted by an international tribunal, were hearing charges regarding acts that at the time of their commission had not been international crimes, they violated the proscription against ex post facto prosecutions that had, from the time of the drafting of the Constitution, been so important a part of the American sense of justice.

> Whatever I may think about a Justice of the Supreme Court taking on
> other jobs—and I am afraid I am impenitent on that subject—I never
> had any doubt about the profound importance of your enterprise and
> equally no doubt that you would discharge the task according to the
> finest professional standards both intellectually and ethically. That
> you have done so I have said again, and again, and again.[9]

Indeed, a search through the files in the manuscript collections at the
Harvard Law School and Yale University's Sterling Library indicates
that Frankfurter had indeed defended Jackson's involvement, both in
letters to friends—Charles C. Burlingham, Max Lerner, Paul Freund—
and in internal memoranda written for his private files.[10]

This support became even stronger when Stone died in 1945; according to published reports, Justices Black, Murphy, and Douglas
"threatened [President Truman] with resignations" if Jackson were
appointed to the Chief Justiceship.[11] The circumstances surrounding
the appointment of Secretary of the Treasury Fred M. Vinson over
Jackson as Chief Justice led to a very embarrassing situation for Frankfurter, which, in turn, demonstrated the justice's classic technique for
dealing with the problem of public disclosure of his actions. In the
Truman Merry-Go Round, Robert Allen and Robert Shannon reported
in 1950 that Frankfurter had written to Justice Jackson in Nuremberg
informing him of the alleged resignation threat by Justice Black, and
others. An "outraged" Felix Frankfurter personally denied the incident to Justice Black and then wrote Black a letter, dated September
30, 1950, in which he threatened to sue the authors for libel and expressed doubts regarding the value of a First Amendment that pro-
tects such "unqualifiedly unfounded" statements.[12] Frankfurter claimed
that "nothing [could be] further from the truth" than this charge, because "neither *directly* nor *indirectly* did I send *any communication
whatever* to Jackson regarding the vacancy created by Stone's death."
[*Italics mine*][13]

Whether or not Allen and Shannon's allegation that Frankfurter
specifically informed Jackson about Black's resignation threat was true,
a copy of a letter filed in Frankfurter's Supreme Court papers suggests
that his protests of innocence to Justice Black were less than totally
candid. On June 12, 1946, six days after Vinson's appointment as Chief
Justice, Frankfurter had sent the following to Jackson in Nuremberg:

> When Marion and I heard of the appointment of Vinson (whom I very
> much like and for whose work as Chief Justice I have high expecta-
> tions), the following colloquy took place:

> F. "I suppose this is the first time in American History that a man failed of the Chief Justiceship because he showed character when character needed to be shown."
>
> M. "I am glad for Bob's sake that he doesn't have to take on this awful situation."
>
> F. "Yes, and he felt that way himself when he discovered the situation in the Court—that it didn't come his way when Stone was appointed. *But it is not comfortable to have skulduggery succeed.*"
>
> M. "Heavens, no!" [*Italics mine*] [14]

In his grateful (and immediate) response, Jackson indicated that he understood exactly what his colleague was saying. In a personal letter written on June 19, 1946, Jackson objected to the Washington newspapers' detailed coverage of Black's alleged threats to Truman without taking "the slightest interest in finding out whether it was a mere petty and personal opposition or whether there was something serious in my record to warrant such a threat." [15] When the whole matter was exposed by Allen and Shannon four years later, the Double Felix carefully worded his statement to Justice Black denying the role he had been accused of playing. Assuming there had been no other letter on the subject, Frankfurter was technically correct in telling Black that he had written nothing, "regarding the vacancy created by Stone's death," for the letter had been sent *after* the position had been filled, and had not technically informed Jackson of the resignation threats, but had only implied what he and Marion thought of the "skulduggery" that had prevented Jackson's appointment.

Frankfurter's letter to Black was taken at its face value. Not only did Justice Black never suspect what had actually transpired, but he was so moved by his colleague's action that fifteen years later, in writing upon Frankfurter's death a memorial article for the *Harvard Law Review*, he completed the story of this incident. Proving the closeness of their personal relationship, contrary to published reports at the time, Black recalled that he had told Frankfurter that "so far as he was concerned it was as though the statement had never been published." [16] Black's reaction shows clearly that this type of waffling on the part of Frankfurter was successful in protecting his reputation as well as in preserving some modicum of harmony on the Court.

One of Frankfurter's defenses of Jackson—sent to federal Court of Appeals Judge Learned Hand—may have had even broader implications than the issue of Nuremberg itself. Hand had been one of the biggest critics of the trials, noting in a private letter to Frankfurter, dated April 14, 1946, "that [the] Nuremburg business would be a farce if it were not so ominous."[17] Totally in agreement with Chief Justice Stone, Hand argued in another letter that the trials were spurred by the Allies' desire for vengeance and represented "a step towards savagery."[18] However, his anger was even greater toward Jackson's participation in the affair, terming it "unpardonable" and "his Sin Against the Holy Ghost."[19]

Not surprisingly, an examination of the private correspondence of Frankfurter and Hand reveals that the two men debated the issues repeatedly and vigorously but, as the latter phrased it, they remained "chasmally apart."[20] According to Frankfurter's handpicked biographer, Max Freedman, Hand accused his friend of "thinking like a Jew and not like a judge," before ending the discussion permanently to save their friendship.[21]

Freedman also noted that although Frankfurter "never changed his mind about Nuremberg, . . . after this argument with Judge Hand, he became very austere in his attitude to the public duties of a member of the Supreme Court."[22] If this was the beginning of Frankfurter's conversion to judicial asceticism, it was indeed a limited one. It is quite possible that Frankfurter was beginning to question official participation by justices on government commissions and tribunals (something that very minimally touched on his own extrajudicial activities) and there is no doubt that this debate with Hand fueled the constant process of self-examination the justice had long undertaken regarding the ethics of extrajudicial work. But in 1945 Frankfurter still had seventeen more years on the Court and his own political instincts were too strong to consider extrajudicial abstinence at this point in his career.

Still, given the then-current climate of diminishing participation in politics by certain members of the Court, as well as Hand's harsh criticism of Jackson, it was especially embarrassing for Frankfurter when just at this time one of his extrajudicial activities was discovered by the public. Ironically, the incident involved one of his few major efforts for the cause of the Jewish people during his years on the Court.

In late 1947 and early 1948 the United Nations was debating the partition of Palestine to establish the State of Israel. During this discussion, according to Loy Henderson who was then on the Mid-East desk in the State Department, Justices Frankfurter and Murphy telegraphed the president of the Philippines to lobby for a vote in favor of the resolution. When an account of this extraordinary incident was made public in *The Forrestal Diaries*, Frankfurter, as always, indignantly denied any such involvement.[23] Writing the book's editor, Walter Millis, however, he began his disavowal by claiming that he had a perfect right of citizenship to lobby on an issue that was "absolutely unrelated to anything that could be the concern of the Supreme Court."[24] "Certainly," he continued, "one does not cease to be a citizen of the United States, or become unrelated to issues that make for the well being of the world that may never come for adjudication before this Court, by becoming a member of it." Then, in somewhat of a turnaround, he denied any involvement, noting first that upon his ascending to the bench, he had "broke[n] [his] active connection with the Zionist movement" and then that he had observed this separation with "absurd fastidiousness." Finally, he noted, during the U.N. debate, he had "never sent a message by any mode of communication, either direct or indirect, to the *Philippine Delegate of the Assembly or to any other delegate.*" (*Italics mine*) Any charge to the contrary, Frankfurter said, was "an unqualified, unsalvageable, untruth." The justice also claimed that throughout his entire tenure on the Court he never used his judicial position to further the general cause of Zionism, with two exceptions: to send a letter praising a newspaper editorial to Assistant Secretary of State Robert Lovett, and to give Chaim Weizmann a letter of introduction to see General George C. Marshall, who refused to receive the visitor.[25] Frankfurter concluded his letter to Millis by claiming that he had revealed "the totality of all that [he] did, either directly or indirectly, in regard to our Government's dealing with the Palestine problem *in 1947 and 1948—or, for that matter, since.*" (*Italics mine*)

In reality, these assertions were very carefully phrased to hide the truth. First it was the *president* of the Philippines to whom Henderson and *The Forrestal Diaries* claim Frankfurter sent his message, and not the delegate to the United Nations. Next, while the justice was no longer directly a member of the Zionist Organization, he was certainly working at this time on the foreign policy issue that involved their main goal. Finally, there is a disingenuousness in the justice's concluding statement: he had undertaken other efforts on behalf of this cause after ascending to the bench, none of which his statement disclosed—they just happened to occur prior to 1947.

During 1945 and 1946, for example, Frankfurter had used two of his long-time friends to maintain an active lobby for the Zionist cause. Through David Niles, now Truman's presidential assistant and a central figure in the United States government on the Palestine question, the justice was kept fully informed on the American position on this issue.[26] In addition, Frankfurter had a contact, *Boston Herald* editor Frank Buxton, on the Anglo-American Committee of Inquiry on Palestine. Composed of delegates from the United States and Great Britain, this tribunal was charged with making recommendations to their respective governments for dealing with the political, economic, and social conditions in Palestine, the problems of Jewish immigration and settlement in the region, the conditions of the victims of the Nazi and Fascist holocaust, and the problem of continued persecution of European Jews. Since Buxton had corresponded with Frankfurter for decades, it was only natural that he should keep the justice apprised of the proceedings in the committee through frequent extensive letters. In reading through the voluminous file of private letters between Frankfurter and Buxton, one can see that on occasion, Buxton posed questions for the justice that, when answered, were doubtlessly used to guide the group's thinking.

On April 20, 1946, the committee recommended in its final report that 100,000 more Jews be admitted into Palestine, that protection be provided for various Holy Places, that the standard of living of the local Arabs be raised, that large-scale development projects for the area be started immediately, and that the area continue to be governed by mandate, pending a trusteeship agreement that would be reached under United Nations auspices.[27] Even after the committee had issued its report, the chairman of the group, Judge Joseph C. Hutcheson, asked Buxton to secure Frankfurter's reactions to some of their findings and recommendations. The justice, having already de-briefed Buxton in a long conversation, wrote in a letter dated July 25, 1946, that he would be glad to discuss the issue "fully and candidly" with Hutcheson, if he so desired, on his next trip to Washington.[28]

One can certainly understand Frankfurter's interest in this issue. The establishment of Israel, especially after the Holocaust, was a matter of such vital importance to the world Jewish population that Frankfurter, despite his limited commitment to Zionism after Brandeis's death, could hardly have been expected to remain aloof from the struggle. Even though his involvement here was neither extensive nor direct, the justice's explicit denials of what he had done demonstrated that it was certainly more than he wanted to have revealed to the general public.

Following his ascension to the Chief Justiceship, Fred Vinson, an intimate of Truman from their years in the Senate together, reversed the Stone example and personally chose to ignore any standard proscribing political contacts. Years later, it was reported that Vinson and Truman "had telephones by their beds and regularly held long talks at night, in which the President received . . . advice and counsel on many problems."[29] As a member of the White House "inner circle," Vinson even agreed to be sent to Russia as Truman's special envoy to Stalin, but the diplomatic mission had to be canceled when the idea was prematurely disclosed.[30]

Frankfurter would have gladly continued his intensive lobbying efforts in the White House and the executive branch had circumstances not made that impossible. Most of his friends from the Roosevelt Administration were either retired, out of government, or dead. The White House was now staffed by Truman's cronies, with whom the justice had no personal relationships. Not only did this make it unlikely that he would be able to influence the various executive agencies as he had in the past, but it left him with no intermediaries through which to approach the president himself.

A lack of messengers to the White House was not Frankfurter's sole problem, for even if he had been able to reach Harry Truman evidence indicates that his advice would have had little effect. The personalities of the two men simply did not blend very well, for Roosevelt's successor failed to inspire either Frankfurter's respect or admiration. Still, for at least a short period after FDR's death, the justice was somewhat optimistic, stating on April 24, 1945 that "[Truman] is an educable man and it all depends who will do the educating."[31] Frankfurter's efforts to become the political "teacher," however, were apparently not well received by the new president, who referred to the justice in private conversations as the "king maker."[32] As a result, just a year later, the justice rendered in a letter to Learned Hand a much more hostile appraisal of the situation: "God knows what is in store for the country—for I suppose only God knows the considerations which will move Truman."[33]

A search through the official and private correspondence housed in the Truman Presidential Library reveals that for the duration of this administration Frankfurter and Truman exchanged only a few letters on trivial matters, such as discussions of the history of previous secretaries of state and the name of the gun that had, by exploding, killed the first husband of President Tyler's second wife. Perhaps owing in part to these contacts, by the end of Truman's tenure the justice's opinion of him had softened a bit. By 1952, he was writing to Hand:

> As for H.S.T., I've long come to rest in my view of him. His "instincts," his purposes are, I believe, decent and sound, but one cannot—I cannot—think of views as shallow as his in terms of convictions. No, he is not insincere—he is just very shallow.[34]

With Dean Acheson as assistant secretary of state, and later Truman's secretary of state, Frankfurter did have one important contact within the administration. Through him, the justice remained informed on activities and impending decisions in the executive branch. Their daily strolls to work together from their homes in Georgetown have become legendary. While much has already been published about these walks, confidential interviews with a number of Frankfurter's former law clerks now make it possible to add to the legend.

These chats, it seems, grew into such a tradition that even on days of threatening weather the two men would proceed by foot, insuring their protection should the elements turn really foul by having one of Frankfurter's law clerks or a member of the Court staff follow in a car. The discussions on these "walking talks" nearly always began with a review of the foreign news and then proceeded to a myriad of other subjects: the administrative operations of the State Department, books they had read, and ideas for speeches or diplomatic endeavors. There was no set agenda for the discussion, just the ordinary conversation of two of Washington's most visible officials, fueled, of course, by Frankfurter's insatiable curiosity about everything. While we cannot be certain what specific policy advice might have been offered by the justice, there can be little doubt that Frankfurter's opinions and views on the government's actions were vociferously expressed.[35] Still, Acheson was only one friend in a sea of bureaucrats. Due to these minimal contacts in the Truman, and then in the Eisenhower Administrations, following World War II Frankfurter concentrated his extrajudicial efforts in the one arena left open to him—staffing the Federal judiciary. This was the area of interaction with the other branches in which proscriptions against extrajudicial activity, had, historically, been most often ignored.[36]

Even before 1945, the justice had included among his many political activities a number of extensive efforts to secure appointments for various individuals to all levels of the federal court system.[37] Throughout the 1930s he had been supplying memoranda recommending a number of people who were then under consideration for the bench. By the time of his own appointment to the Supreme Court, Frankfurter had become a trusted presidential adviser on judicial selection; it was not uncommon for FDR to request memoranda from him even on prospective appointees to the Supreme Court.[38]

Because of this well-established, informal relationship with the president, Frankfurter was in a central advisory position to recommend a replacement for retiring Chief Justice Charles Evans Hughes in mid-1941.[39] On June 9, Roosevelt urgently requested that Frankfurter join him for lunch in order to discuss the problem of filling the Chief Justiceship. A complete record of this conversation remains in the Frankfurter papers at the Harvard Law Library in the form of a memorandum entitled "H[arlan] F[iske] S[tone] and the C[hief] J[ustice]ship," written from notes Frankfurter made immediately upon leaving FDR. The document shows how willing Frankfurter was to offer suggestions regarding appointments to any governmental position.

According to Frankfurter's account, the president had begun the meeting by asking, "Is there any reason for naming a new C[hief] J[ustice] at once, or wouldn't it do just as well to let it run along, since the Court has adjourned till the fall?"[40] Frankfurter responded by detailing extensively the duties of the Court during the summer months and arguing for the need for a leader during that period. Moreover, he said that Harlan Fiske Stone, as the senior justice, would be the de facto head and it would be unfair to give him the responsibility but not name him to the position later on. Then FDR proceeded to the crux of the conference and asked the justice whether he should appoint Stone or then-Attorney General Robert Jackson as Chief Justice. After a perfunctory protest against being asked this question, Frankfurter launched into a lecture that indicated his acute awareness of the political elements of such appointments:

[On] personal grounds I'd prefer Bob [Jackson]. While I've known Stone longer and our relations are excellent and happy, I feel a closer friendship with Bob. But from the national interest I am bound to say there is no reason for preferring Bob to Stone—quite the contrary. Stone is senior and qualified professionally to be C[hief] J[ustice]. But for me the decisive consideration, considering the fact that Stone is qualified, is that Bob is of your political and personal family, as it were, while Stone is a Republican. Now it doesn't require prophetic powers to be sure that we shall, sooner or later, be in the war—I think sooner. It is most important that when war does come, the country should feel that you are a national, the Nation's President, and not a partisan President. Few things would contribute as much to confidence in you as a national and not a partisan President than for you to name a Republican, who had the profession's confidence, as Chief Justice.[41]

The president, however, was troubled by the ramifications of Stone's elevation. Jackson could be named to replace Stone as associate justice, but, FDR queried, whom could he name to replace Justice Frank Murphy, who was being actively considered for the attorney generalship since he was "very unhappy on the Court." Frankfurter's reply was immediate: "That's easy [General Counsel of the National Labor Relations Board] Charlie Fahy." Since all these recommendations matched those that Chief Justice Hughes had offered to the president, the decision was made easier. On June 12, 1941, Harlan Fiske Stone was made Chief Justice and Robert Jackson appointed to Stone's seat as an associate justice. However, the unhappy Murphy remained on the Court; instead of appointing him as attorney general, FDR selected Solicitor General Francis Biddle for the post.[42] Years later, in referring to this conversation with FDR in a private letter to Philip Kurland, Frankfurter said that he had informed Robert Jackson about his recommendation of Stone and, he claimed, it "only deepened their friendship."[43]

Since the attorney general is generally charged with screening judicial appointments, Frankfurter realized that continuation of his role of counselor in this area required that he quickly establish a good working relationship with Biddle. Soon after the appointment was made, "F.F." sent his usual letter of congratulations, quoting a line of praise frequently used by Oliver Wendell Holmes, "I bet on you."[44] The justice had not yet had time to establish the desired rapport with Biddle when the relationship was put in jeopardy. The new attorney general had heard from Charles C. Burlingham that Frankfurter was trying to have his former student, Charles Fahy, appointed to the now-vacant solicitor generalship. Fearing that a breach of protocol might be perceived, the justice wrote to Biddle:

> If you know anything at all about me you must know that I pay no attention to rumor or gossip, particularly about me. But I do not want my personal indifference to gossip to hurt other people. And so I should like to say to you that Burlingham's reference to my praise of Fahy was a reply to a letter from him urging me to urge Will Chanler for the S[olicitor] G[eneralship]. I wrote to him my high esteem of Chanler, my complete abstention from making any suggestions or recommendations except and unless asked, and an explanation of prophecy that I assumed if you went up Fahy would take your place. But neither then nor at any time have I urged on anybody Charlie Fahy or anybody else.[45]

Of course, the disavowal has an element of truth in that Frankfurter had recommended Fahy not for the solicitor generalship, but for the Supreme Court. There was no need for the justice to worry, though, as the attorney general was entirely willing to enter into an advisory relationship. In a letter sent the following day, Biddle commented invitingly: "I should always welcome such a suggestion from you to the President, and had rather hoped that you had given him your own slant on the vacancy."[46] Indeed, on November 15, 1941, Fahy was appointed as solicitor general.

The arrangement with Biddle soon proved to be extremely useful for the justice. For two years he had been looking for a chance to place his former student, Charles Wyzanski, in the judicial branch. Frankfurter had always taken an active interest in Wyzanski's career, first selecting him as law clerk to Court of Appeals Judge Augustus N. Hand and then working for his appointment as solicitor to the Department of Labor in 1933. In response to a private letter from Learned Hand, for whom Wyzanski had also clerked, suggesting the Boston attorney for a judicial appointment, Frankfurter had written on February 16, 1939: "It has long been my ambition to see him on the Bench, and I shall leave no opportunity unavailed of to express my conviction regarding his pre-eminent judicial qualifications."[47] With the death of Judge Elisha H. Brewster and the retirement of Judge Hugh D. McClellan in 1941, there were two vacancies on the United States District Court for the District of Massachusetts. Using his customary lobbying technique, Frankfurter mobilized allies for a campaign that would create the appearance of a ground swell of opinion in favor of Wyzanski.

One of these allies, among Frankfurter's most prolific correspondents since 1924, was Charles C. Burlingham, who happened to enjoy enormous influence with a number of influential New York City politicians because of his many years of activism in reform movements. So prominent was his role in securing appointments to the federal bench that, according to Professor Andrew Kaufman of the Harvard Law School, he had "the reputation of 'Kingmaker' or the 'Warwick' of the American judicial scene."[48]

In a personal letter written on September 26, 1941, Frankfurter urged his friend to write "FDR in your most seductive style" in favor of the appointment.[49] Then, Frankfurter tried to enlist editor Frank Buxton in the effort, telling him in early September, "I know of no one so well equipped as Charlie [Wyzanski] for the Federal Bench—and I don't care who knows it!"[50] Several months earlier, the editor had indicated a willingness to work in this direction when he wrote Frankfurter that Wyzanski was an "ideal candidate . . . to be pulled out of private practice and put into government service."[51] By now, though, it appears that Buxton had developed some reservations about whether this was the best time to appoint Wyzanski. He suggested that perhaps it would be better to appoint a representative of the "Old Yankees" for this vacancy, rather than a man like Wyzanski, who was Jewish.

Probably no proposal regarding judicial selection could have annoyed Frankfurter more. From his vantage point at the pinnacle of the federal judicial system, he had developed a very specific philosophy to govern such decisions.[52] Indeed, an examination of Frankfurter's personal letters indicates that he was, characteristically, all too willing to outline that philosophy in detail for anyone who cared to hear it. In many letters Frankfurter wrote that it was foolish to appoint persons to the courts because of their party affiliation, prior judicial experience, or to achieve a geographic balance. He was even more disgusted by the effort to fill quotas on the high bench that were established on the basis of "racial or religious considerations." To indicate his horror over this approach, in at least a half-dozen letters to friends in the bar and on the bench around the country—Learned Hand, Frank Buxton, and Charles C. Burlingham—Frankfurter recounted the same story as a parable:

Tempore Taft, his Secretary of War, one Stimson, told me that the President was desirous of putting a Jew on the federal bench in New York and has asked that I make a suggestion to that end. I told Stimson that racial or religious considerations seemed to me not only irrelevant in appointments to the bench but mischievously irrelevant. And that to appoint men for racial or religious reasons was playing with fire. Therefore, I would have no truck with it and I begged to be excused for what I regarded a highly indefensible and dangerous procedure.[53]

Instead, Frankfurter believed that individuals should be chosen for the federal bench solely on the basis of merit. Only the application of this one standard would insure that the candidate possessed the requisite "judicial character." As the justice later defined it:

[A judge needs] open mindedness, with such mind as one has, letting conscience, complete disinterestedness (i.e., indifference to political considerations for oneself, gratitude to the appointing power [and] disregard of "public opinion") [govern his decisions].[54]

In the present case, pure merit selection just happened to favor *his* candidate, Charles Wyzanski. So, after rebuking Buxton for having suggested that religious background be brought into the decision, the justice proposed a way to satisfy even the most persnickety Boston Brahmins. Why not just tell them, he wrote Buxton, that Wyzanski was "the best possible representative of the 'Old Yankees'?"[55] Duly chastened, Buxton did send to Attorney General Biddle a recommendation that, in Frankfurter's later words of praise, "could not have been better."[56]

With the groundwork laid, it was time for the justice to take more direct action. Since the attorney general was now a personal friend and had solicited such suggestions, Frankfurter used an informal lobbying style. At a dinner party, and in Wyzanski's presence, the justice and Learned Hand approached Biddle, who was told that he could "start [his] career with a superlative recommendation" by appointing the thirty-five-year-old lawyer, who, Frankfurter and Hand agreed, was a "natural" for the District Court bench.[57] Biddle agreed to make the recommendation, but "irritated" Frankfurter by asking if Senator David Walsh of Massachusetts had a candidate. Frankfurter, who had so often claimed that partisan factors should not come into the selection process, answered, "Why pay attention to Walsh . . . he's not a friend of the President's."[58] Nevertheless, Biddle did secure Walsh's consent before forwarding Wyzanski's name to the White House; on December 1, 1941 the nomination was made.

Despite all his careful steps to remain a central adviser to FDR's Administration on judicial selection, and his intimate relationship with the president, Frankfurter failed in his attempts to secure the one appointment that probably meant the most to him—to bring federal Court of Appeals Judge Learned Hand to the United States Supreme Court. The two men originally met in 1909 when Frankfurter was assistant United States attorney to Henry L. Stimson and Hand was a newly appointed district court judge.[59] Their correspondence, which began in 1911, became increasingly voluminous and intimate. Addressing each other as "B." and "F.F.," they discussed, among other things, judicial and political philosophy, current events, and personalities on the courts. By the time Frankfurter was appointed to the Supreme Court, Hand was widely acknowledged as one of the most intelligent, respected, and influential judges on any of the nation's federal Courts of Appeal.

Frankfurter's interest in placing Hand on the Supreme Court was only partly due to the latter's outstanding qualifications; the two men shared a very similar judicial philosophy, both adhering to the "self-restraint" position of deference to the legislative will whenever possible. With the developing internecine split on the Court—pitting Frankfurter and Jackson against Douglas, Black, and Murphy—Frankfurter was eager to add an ally, and, even better, a close friend, to the high bench. This impulse became more paramount when James Byrnes, a man who had shown promise as a philosophical comrade-in-arms, left the Court in October 1942 to become FDR's "Assistant President for Domestic Affairs"; Frankfurter dedicated himself to replacing Byrnes with Learned Hand.

The justice was so eager to begin his crusade that he wrote FDR on the subject even before Byrnes officially announced his resignation from the Court. In two separate letters to Roosevelt on September 30, 1942, Frankfurter praised Byrnes, his "most congenial pal," and said that the two men had already discussed the matter of filling the potential vacancy. According to Frankfurter, they had agreed that FDR "again [had] a chance to do something for court and country comparable to what [he] did when [he] made Stone the Chief Justice."[60] Then Frankfurter implied that he, Byrnes, and Stone had the same "notion" regarding a suitable replacement. Over the next few weeks Frankfurter phoned and visited with Roosevelt numerous times to advocate the appointment of Learned Hand. At the same time, Harlan Fiske Stone explained to Attorney General Biddle the need for selecting a man with broad judicial experience and suggested Appeals Court Judges Hand, Wiley Rutledge, and Samuel Bratton as potential nominees.[61]

There seemed to be two major obstacles to Hand's elevation. First, Roosevelt wanted to improve the geographical balance of the Court by appointing a person from west of the Mississippi. With two other New Yorkers already on the Court, Stone and Jackson, the president was reluctant to select another from that state. Second, after the bitter "Court-packing" fight in 1937, FDR was hesitant to appoint the seventy-one-year-old Learned Hand. Again Frankfurter displayed his flexibility on the question of applying or rejecting political arguments in the evaluation of judicial candidates. He wrote to Roosevelt that:

> Especially on the score of politics, L. Hand is the only lad who will create no headaches for you—or, if you will, break no eggs. He is the one choice who will arouse universal acclaim in the press—and the only one who won't make the adherents of other aspirants say, "Why in the hell was X chosen and not my man who is as good as X?" . . . Every other person would divide and opinion [sic] not to speak of other considerations, I never was more sure of anything—as a matter of Politics.[62]

In another missive, sent one month later, Frankfurter told Roosevelt that Hand ranked as an appellate judge with Holmes, Brandeis, and Cardozo. After the announcement of such an appointment, the justice added, "all considerations of age, geography and the like will be seen to have had no relevance." After closing with the comment that Hand would "bring distinction to the Court and new lustre to the President who made it possible," Frankfurter even drafted a version of FDR's nomination announcement for the Senate.[63] *

Despite all these efforts, Roosevelt did not appoint Hand, but instead selected a younger man from Iowa, federal Appeals Court Judge Wiley Rutledge. To soften the blow, FDR wrote a private message to

---

* Max Freedman claims, possibly based on Frankfurter's own recollections, that this December 3, 1942 letter was written in response to a request by the president for the justice's views. However, the evidence does not support such an interpretation. Frankfurter makes clear that he is volunteering the suggestion in his opening line: "If you have decided on Byrnes's successor, do not waste your time reading the rest of this." Moreover, while Freedman argues that FDR's judicial selection was a "last minute change," in fact the decision was not made by FDR until five weeks after this letter was sent.

Frankfurter, confessing that "Sometimes a fellow gets estopped by his own words and his own deeds—and it is no fun for the fellow himself when that happens."[64] The justice conveyed his thanks for the "genrous" note and his appreciation for the "travail through which [FDR] passed," but in a private memorandum he called the failure to select Hand due to the age consideration an "error in judgment."[65]

While these factors of age and geography must surely have influenced Roosevelt, in fact the decision not to appoint the gifted Hand was due more to flaws in the advocate than in the candidate. As Roosevelt told William O. Douglas at a poker party several days before announcing the new appointment to the Court, "this time Felix overplayed his hand . . . Do you know how many people asked me today to name Learned Hand? . . . Twenty, and every one a messenger from Felix Frankfurter." Then, with his expression hardening, FDR added, "And by golly, I won't do it."[66] There is no evidence that Frankfurter ever understood the real reason for the action; in a personal letter mailed to him by Hand the same day that Rutledge's nomination was made the Court of Appeals judge expressed his gratitude for Frankfurter's efforts nonetheless.[67]

There is an ironic twist to this story. Learned Hand, who enjoys almost universal esteem among students of the American legal system, and who may well be the most talented federal judge never appointed to the high Court, went on to outlive the younger Rutledge by nearly twelve full years. If indeed FDR was telling the truth to Douglas about his reaction to Frankfurter's campaign, then the nation was made to pay a dear price for Frankfurter's many prior appointment campaigns, which had had the cumulative effect of diluting the credibility of his exuberance at the very moment he most wanted it taken at full value.

Frankfurter took an active interest in the search to fill a variety of other federal court vacancies, but never to the extent that he had in trying to obtain the Supreme Court nomination for Hand. Over the years, Frankfurter recommended that Court of Appeals Judge Joseph C. Hutcheson be appointed to the Supreme Court and that Professor Calvert Magruder, a former colleague on the Harvard Law School faculty whom Frankfurter had selected as Brandeis's first law clerk, be appointed to the federal Court of Appeals; he was successful in the latter case, but not in the former. On March 17, 1944, Frankfurter solicited the support of James Byrnes in getting Benjamin Cohen appointed to the federal Court of Appeals. Although Byrnes did offer his support, Cohen refused to allow his name to be presented to Roosevelt. In response to a request by Attorney General Biddle, Frankfurter highly recommended the brilliant Professor Charles Houston of the Howard Law School, the man who devised much of the legal strategy of the NAACP Legal Defense Fund and was tutor to Thurgood Marshall, for appointment to the District of Columbia Municipal Court.[68] In addition to these documented cases, it seems likely that there were others in which Frankfurter, with his wide contacts and his propensity for expressing himself on such matters, offered verbal support or condemnation of a variety of other judicial candidacies during the Roosevelt years.

In 1945, however, when Harry Truman became president, Frankfurter's direct efforts to lobby for judicial appointments temporarily came to a halt. There was simply no one in the administration through whom the justice could work. However, Frankfurter had learned from his years as Brandeis's lieutenant that this deficiency alone did not strip him of all possible weapons for influencing decisions; there was always the option of using the indirect approach. So, on May 25, 1950, the justice wrote Charles C. Burlingham, who had earlier asked for Frankfurter's assistance in securing replacements for two vacancies on the United States District Court in New York. The justice stated: "The best chance of having qualified men appointed is not through any wire-pulling here, but to have the Bar Associations raise their voices loud and long. The crowd down here is more sensitive to criticism than you might think, and if you can energize Whitney Seymour to bring the full impact of the Bar to bear you can, I believe, really obtain results."[69] Apparently Burlingham did not respond positively to Frankfurter's expression of political impotence, for the justice wrote again seven days later:

> It's no good telling the Attorney General about the need of appointing good judges, for of course in the abstract he will agree. To be effective, one must be concrete and support men whose names are under consideration. But that requires the kind of relationship with the Attorney General that members of this Court had with Wickersham in the old days or I might have had with Francis Biddle or Bob Jackson in recent days. Neither Jackson nor I have any such relation with the present Attorney General. Apart from the fact that we have

no personal relation with the President, the Attorney General's recommendations are decisive except in rare instances. Such being the
situation you see what little either Jackson or I can do, certainly on
our own initiative.[70]

Though it might have been anticipated that Frankfurter's avenues
for influence on "political" issues would remain cut off with the election of Dwight D. Eisenhower to the White House in 1952, he was
determined to resume a pre-eminent advisory position on judicial selection. This would be difficult: though he identified himself as a political Independent, Frankfurter's close relationship to Roosevelt made
him appear to be an avowed Democrat. Nevertheless, judicial selec-
tions are ideally governed by nonpartisan considerations and Frankfurter believed that he had a chance to re-enter the process if he could
establish a relationship with the agency in charge of such nominations—the Department of Justice. This meant that the justice needed
to find a means of approaching the new attorney general-designate,
Herbert Brownell. Fortunately for Frankfurter, he had available the
perfect conduit to the former corporate lawyer from New York City—
his old friend, Charles C. Burlingham, then ninety-four years old and
being referred to as the "Dean of the New York City bar." [71]

By this time, Frankfurter's relationship with Burlingham had grown
to such intimacy that the justice freely broke one of the cardinal rules
of his position: never discuss outside the Court any issues that might
come to be litigated before it. This breach of propriety occurred in a
debate over the proper relationship between Church and State in the
public schools stemming from the Supreme Court's decision in
McCollum v. Board of Education.[72] At stake here was a released-time
program in Champaign, Illinois, whereby public school children attended religious-instruction classes given in their schools during official school hours. The Supreme Court ruled that this plan violated
the First Amendment "establishment-of-religion" clause, because the
state's public schools were being used to teach Church doctrines.

While the general public furiously debated the merits of the decision, so did Frankfurter and Burlingham in their private correspondence. Burlingham passed along complaints from his friends in the
clergy of the Episcopal Church that Frankfurter was too rigid in his
view regarding the separation of Church and State. They feared, he
wrote in an unpublished letter dated April 13, 1951, that Frankfurter

might oppose Bible reading in schools as well.[73] In an extraordinary response, written on April 18, 1951, the justice offered some advice regarding the future constitutionality of the released-time programs:

> Why don't your clerical friends solve the released time problem in the easy way in which it can be solved, to-wit: let all the children be released from school one hour earlier, to do with that hour as they will. By appropriate arrangements—outside the school building of course—the parents who wish their children to receive their different sectarian instruction will have their children have the benefit of such instruction. The parents who do not want their children to have any sectarian instruction will allow their children to dispose of that extra hour in any way they choose. What's the matter with that?[74]

Perhaps Frankfurter remembered the one time during Brandeis's judicial tenure that he had mentioned an issue then pending in the courts—the *Sacco-Vanzetti* case[75]—and the necessary withdrawal from the litigation that had followed. For after this breach of judicial decorum, Frankfurter indicated that he understood the irregularity of his actions by quickly adding, "Needless to say I cannot give an advisory opinion but I should find it very difficult to think of any ground on which that could be attacked by anybody."[76] When the question of religious teaching in public schools came before the Court again, Frankfurter saw no reason to abstain, and he decided the case precisely along the lines he had indicated in his letter to Burlingham.*

By providing such advance notice regarding his eventual positions on issues presented to the Court, Frankfurter indicated the high level of trust he placed in Burlingham. This confidence, combined with Burlingham's professional status and already expressed willingness to become involved in the judicial selection process, led Frankfurter to believe that here was the man capable of reaching Attorney General-

---

* The next released-time case, *Zorach v. Clauson*,[77] was argued the following year and dealt with a New York City program slightly different from the one Frankfurter had discussed with Burlingham. Those public school children wishing to attend religious instruction during official school hours were released to receive their instruction outside the school grounds, but those students who did not attend the program had to remain in the classroom. Six justices upheld the plan because "neither religious instruction in public school classrooms nor the expenditure of public funds" was involved.[78] Frankfurter, however, dissented because, as he had explained previously to Burlingham, the separation of Church and State required that all public school children be released during the time the religious classes were held. To do otherwise, he argued in his judicial opinion, would be to coerce those students not inclined to leave for religious instruction into doing so simply to remain with their classmates.

designate Brownell. At best, the justice might come to establish a close relationship of his own with the attorney general; at worst, he would still have available an indirect line of communication to him through Burlingham.

Frankfurter's initial move, which occurred within a month after Eisenhower's election, was simply to offer the full range of his experience and expertise to Brownell. In a personal letter to Burlingham marked "Strictly Private," Frankfurter argued there was simply no one as well qualified as he to give advice on the operations of the Department of Justice:

> When Hughes was consulted after his retirement regarding his successor, he told F.D.R.: "You should talk to Justice Frankfurter about the vacancies on the Court for he knows better than anybody else the history of the Court and its present needs." If that was even approximately true regarding the Supreme Court, it is even more true regarding my knowledge of the needs of the Department of Justice. It is the simple truth that I have intimately known the activities of the Department of Justice for a continuous period of 45 years—and of course I have watched it very closely since I came down here in 1939. I need not tell you that there is no better place for watching the Department than from this Bench.[79]

Frankfurter added that he had no qualms about offering such counsel because "[t]he fact that this Court is so vitally concerned with the way in which justice is conducted and the fact that the effective functioning in the Attorney General's office is so deeply involved in the Court's and the Federal Judiciary generally, make me write to you."

The important thing, he explained, was that the attorney general had to act in a manner that respected the "ethics" of Frankfurter's position, as well as with great speed: "Brownell must take the initiative for any help I could be. More than that, the first steps he takes in regard to the Department may very largely bind his future conduct of it. It is no use his talking to me after he has made vital decisions." Quite obviously, these vital decisions involved both the formation of the department's structure and the appointment of key personnel. Since Frankfurter "would not volunteer" to give such advice and information, he proposed that Burlingham have "[New York Governor] Tom [Dewey] suggest to Brownell that he talk with me about the Attorney General's office."[80]

It is somewhat amazing that Frankfurter was willing to help organize and run the Department of Justice—one of the main litigants before his Court. As with his other political actions, though, the justice simply ignored any potential ethical problems here. For him, the department was the "law office of the public" and he, as a citizen, was seeking to insure that it would be run as a "first class law office."

Burlingham did not disappoint the justice. Two days after Frankfurter's letter, Burlingham wrote Governor Dewey, being careful not to reveal that he was acting on the justice's suggestion:

> I know Brownell very slightly but have a great deal of respect for him and know some of his partners well. The Department of Justice is an awful mess. The one man who can advise Brownell wisely and disinterestedly is Felix Frankfurter. He sees the Department almost every day in every way. Why not suggest to Brownell that he have a confidential talk with Felix now?[81]

A week later two different sources informed Frankfurter that his message had been forwarded to Brownell in a manner that hid the justice's initial request. But no meeting was arranged. Instead, Brownell wrote to Burlingham, he would meet with Chief Justice Vinson. Burlingham tried once more to arrange the Frankfurter meeting, arguing in a responding letter that since protocol had now been satisfied, Brownell should speak to Frankfurter, who knew "more about the Department of Justice in a minute than the C.J. could ever know."[82] As it turned out, not until after Brownell had moved to Washington and was personally invited by the justice to his home, however, did the conference take place.*

Though the specific mission had failed, in that the justice did not obtain his early personal contact with Brownell, Burlingham had aptly demonstrated his ability to reach the new attorney general. So Frankfurter decided to continue to use this avenue in his campaign to win Brownell's confidence. Now, though, the justice sought to offer some advice and information on a specific policy issue. After claiming in a letter to Burlingham dated January 5, 1953 that "two former Attorneys General were ignorant of [the] existence" of the Department of Justice's Executive Adjudications Division, Frankfurter delivered a long lecture on its origin and functions. He pointed out that while the division was initially created "as the general legal advisor to the President and the Executive Departments and agencies," the "Special

---

* At that time, Mr. Brownell later recalled, the two men probably discussed policies at the Department of Justice, but he does not remember discussing either judicial or non-judicial appointments.[83]

Counsel to the President" at the White House had supplanted those responsibilities. After condemning this situation, Frankfurter offered his remedy:

> I do not think this subordination of the Department of Justice, as the President's legal advisor, to the legal shop of the White House has been a conspicuous success. I have good reason to believe that the steel seizure* fiasco is attributable to it. The Division with the inappropriate name should be expanded and revitalized, and should exercise the same functions, vis a vis the President, and all the Executive agencies, which the Solicitor General's office exercises in relation to the Supreme Court.[85]

Realizing the true purpose of this letter, Burlingham sent a copy along to Brownell, noting that it "may interest you."[86] This time Frankfurter's strategy met with success as Brownell reacted well to the justice's stroking of his department. Burlingham dutifully reported, in a letter dated January 27, 1953, that Brownell had responded with gratitude for the justice's information regarding the need of the agency to recover lost influence and stated that the matter appeared to require his attention.[87] Now the justice was assured that he could indeed reach the attorney general through the good offices of Charles C. Burlingham.

By this time, Frankfurter's techniques for offering extrajudicial advice were so well honed that he felt certain of achieving his eventual goal—helping to place individuals in the federal judicial system. The situation demanded, however, that he alter his lobbying tactics from those used during the Roosevelt years, when the attorney general was a personal friend. Frankfurter realized that rather than offering advice through informal chats and notes, he would have to use detailed, formal letters of recommendation in addition to choreographed moves by a variety of intermediaries.

Frankfurter began his advisory effort on judicial selection in mid-June 1953. Two vacancies were about to be created on the United States Court of Appeals for the Second Circuit by the retirement of Judges Augustus N. Hand and Thomas W. Swan. Even though he had no particular candidates in mind, Frankfurter was concerned that the ap-

---

* The reference here is to *Youngstown Sheet and Tube Company v. Sawyer*,[84] in which the Supreme Court found unconstitutional President Truman's decision on his own authority to seize and operate the nation's steel mills in April 1952, in order to prevent a strike by the steel workers. Truman had argued that the emergency of wartime gave him the necessary authority to take such action.

pointments not be governed by political considerations, and he wanted to educate the new attorney general regarding the possibilities of appointing truly meritorious persons here. On June 12, 1953 he wrote a letter to Burlingham:

> If I am correctly informed Gus [Hand] and Tom Swan are retiring at the end of their court year. I am writing you in the hope that you will compose one of your deft and wise letters to Brownell with a view to making him conscious of the great opportunity that lies ahead of him to make appointments to the Court of Appeals of a quality to make his Attorney Generalship memorable. Why don't you stir in him the ambition to do what his predecessors in the T.R. and Taft Administration did—appoint men of the caliber of Charlie Hough and Learned Hand. There are undoubtedly men of first-rate quality who are also good Republicans, who would save that court from being degraded with the two Hands and Tom gone.[88]

Here again was the pincer movement in action. Three days earlier, Frankfurter had sent a similar letter to Learned Hand, writing: "There must be men who know Brownell well who ought to tell him to be guided by his own understanding of the needs of your Court—that he should put on the Court men of intellectual distinction as well as of intrinsic authority. . . ."[89]

When no action was forthcoming, Frankfurter again wrote to Burlingham on July 4, 1953, commenting that "the New York appointments in succession to Gus [Hand] and Tom Swan will be a good test of Brownell."[90] This stirred Frankfurter's ally to take action. Three weeks later, after attempting to canvass the retiring judges for their own suggestions regarding replacements, Burlingham reported to Frankfurter that he had written to Brownell "as strongly as [he] could" on the issue.[91] An examination of the unpublished letters filed in the Frankfurter collection at the Library of Congress reveals that later that summer, the justice devoted two more letters to opposing one of the prospective nominees, John A. Danaher of Connecticut, who was then being considered for Swan's seat. While Frankfurter never made clear why he opposed this nomination, it may have stemmed from his perception that political influence, in the person of Senator Robert Taft, was being used to secure it.[92] Subsequently, Danaher was appointed to the United States Court of Appeals for the District of Columbia Circuit instead.

With all his weapons for exerting influence now fully tested, Frankfurter, approaching his seventy-second birthday in late 1954, em-

barked on one of the longest and most complex extrajudicial campaigns of his career—to place Henry Friendly on the United States
Court of Appeals for the Second Circuit. Friendly's record as a law
student was so superb that years later Frankfurter described him as
"one of the two or three towering students during my twenty-five years
at the Harvard Law School."[93] Upon Friendly's graduation, Frankfurter had selected him to be Brandeis's law clerk for a year, where
his work was similarly outstanding. Shortly after he began the clerk-
ship, Brandeis is reported by Frankfurter to have said, "Don't you ever
send me another such man as Friendly . . . If I had another man like
[him], I would not have to do a lick of work myself."[94]

Not surprisingly, given recommendations like these, Friendly went
on to become a prominent Wall Street attorney, serving as general
counsel to such corporations as Pan American Airways. Frankfurter
was so eager to put a man with such excellent intellectual qualifications on the federal Court of Appeals, that he masterminded a fifty-
six-month crusade, involving three separate vacancies, to secure
Friendly's appointment. In tracking the paper trail in unpublished papers left by Frankfurter in the course of this campaign, it becomes
clear that the justice also got involved in waging war against those
politicians who sought to appoint other individuals to the Court for
what he viewed as "irrelevant" political considerations.

The campaign began when Judge John Marshall Harlan was elevated on November 8, 1954 from the Second Circuit to the Supreme
Court, to fill the vacancy left by the death of Robert Jackson.[95] Frankfurter's initial efforts to secure Friendly's appointment to Harlan's old
seat were quite circumspect—reflecting the difficulty of approaching
the Republican administration on such matters. In response to a letter
from Learned Hand proposing Friendly as a possible Appeals Court
appointee, the justice wrote the following on January 4, 1955:

> My interest in your court is, by virtue of my early associations and
> my intimacy with some of you who have been on it for decades,
> almost as deep as yours. Now I have, of course, a close professional
> relation to it. Considering the volume of litigation that is your court's
> concern and, therefore, the relation of the business of your court to
> this Court, it would afford me such satisfaction to further, however
> little, a replacement of [Harlan] by a man who has, as you say the
> "really outstanding quality" that Henry Friendly has. Since coming
> down here, however, I have made it a rule not to initiate any sugges-
> tions for Executive nominations. And so I shall limit myself to send-

ing Senator Ives your letter and placing myself at his disposal, if he cares to make inquiry of me regarding Friendly.[96]

As promised, that same day Frankfurter sent copies of both Hand's letter to him in favor of Friendly and his letter back to Hand, saying he could not "initiate any suggestions for Executive nominations," to Senator Irving M. Ives of New York, along with a cover note stating: "The enclosed letter from Judge Learned Hand and my reply speak for themselves. Let me only reiterate that I am at your disposal."[97]

This subtle approach—sending what appeared to be the incidental private chatter of two eminent judges to the senator—amply demonstrates the keen political awareness Frankfurter had developed over the years in his extrajudicial endeavors. Rather than approaching the Department of Justice, where his relationships were still developing, the justice launched his lobbying effort with Ives, who would clearly be given a voice in the selection by the Republican administration. Though the strategy had many merits, it failed. There is no record of Ives contacting Frankfurter (though it could have been done by phone or in person), and the appointment went to J. Edward Lumbard on July 12, 1955.*

Believing that his first strategy was a failure, the justice determined that with the next vacancy he would approach the attorney general directly and with considerably greater force. When a new position opened up because of the death of Judge Jerome Frank on January 13, 1957, Frankfurter waited less than twenty-four hours before recommending a replacement. In a personal letter to Herbert Brownell, the justice suggested appointing Friendly, whom he described as "an extraordinary creature," possessing "talents and capabilities so far exceed[ing] those even of able men that in talking of him one must indulge in conscious understatement in order to avoid disbelief" by others.

Knowing that political considerations would be influential for this appointment, despite his hostility toward them, Frankfurter also reminded Brownell that his candidate was "a Republican rooted in up-

* As it turns out, none of Frankfurter's strategies would have been successful either for influencing this appointment, or the next one. It seems that unbeknownst to the justice in the first weeks of the Eisenhower Administration, Attorney General Herbert Brownell had persuaded Lumbard and Leonard P. Moore to abandon their lucrative law practices and become United States attorneys for the Southern and Eastern Districts of New York by promising to appoint them to the first two vacancies on the Court of Appeals for the Second Circuit, if at all possible.[98]

state traditions."[99] However, characteristic of the justice's views on these matters, he immediately added in his letter, "The only relevance in mentioning this fact is to reject it as irrelevant." In acknowledging this recommendation, the attorney general's response, written two days later, said only that he knew Friendly well from the days when the two of them were editors-in-chief of the *Yale Law Journal* and the *Harvard Law Review* respectively.[100]

Seeking to build support for this nomination Frankfurter forwarded a copy of his recommendation to Learned Hand asking "What say you to this?" However, Hand had already decided that it would be wise to promote a District Court judge to the Court of Appeals, provided that considerations such as balancing the racial and religious composition of the body were not used for the selection. If that were not possible, he wrote Frankfurter on January 15, 1957, the appointment of Friendly was acceptable to him.[101] This letter seems to have modified the justice's own view regarding the selection, for, contrary to his stated beliefs opposing the use of prior judicial experience as a basis for making court appointments, his second letter on the Frank vacancy, written to the attorney general on January 18, 1957, adopted Hand's position:

> [In my initial letter] I should have added a caveat. Even so surprisingly equipped a member of the bar as Henry Friendly should not be preferred, in my view, if there are available District Judges who have demonstrated the requisite qualifications for the Court of Appeals. On the basis of what I have been observing, limited as it is, there are three such judges in the Southern District of New York: Dimock, Weinfeld and Walsh.
>
> P.S. I do not include Judge Irving Kaufman. He lacks a prime requisite.[102]

The postscript to this recommendation signaled the beginning of a new direction in Frankfurter's judicial-selection campaign, designed to prevent District Court Judge Irving Kaufman's elevation to the Court of Appeals. New evidence gleaned from various collections of unpublished letters makes it possible for the first time in print to reconstruct the justice's efforts here. Through both Learned Hand and John Harlan, Frankfurter learned that Kaufman had become one of the prime contenders for the new Appeals Court vacancy. Now the justice was motivated by more than a mere desire to keep the path open for Friendly's nomination, for he had developed objections to Kaufman personally. This hostility stemmed in part from the justice's intense disagreement with Kaufman's handling of the Rosenberg espionage trial in 1952. With his firm objections to capital punishment, Frankfurter never forgave Kaufman for his manner in sentencing the two convicted atomic secrets spies so harshly. As he wrote in a personal letter to Judge Learned Hand, dated January 25, 1958: "I despise a Judge [Kaufman] who feels God told him to impose a death sentence." Frankfurter reveals the depth of his emotion by continuing his tirade with "I am mean enough to try to stay here long enough so that K[aufman] will be too old to succeed me." [103]

The justice's vehement opposition to Kaufman can best be understood in the context of his earlier hostility toward another District Court judge who had presided in a politically sensitive trial. In 1949, Judge Harold R. Medina heard the *Dennis* case,[104] a prosecution of several American Communist party leaders under the Smith Act, which made it illegal to "knowingly or willfully advocate . . . or teach the duty . . . of overthrowing or destroying any government in the United States by force or violence . . . or to conspire to commit" these acts.[105] Medina's performance in this case and later ones led Frankfurter to label him a "Messianic character" and a "super-egotist," whose "public manifestations go greatly against my grain of what is fitting as a judge." [106] The justice had also begun to see the same qualities in Kaufman, as he stated in an earlier, vitriolic letter to Judge Hand:

> This comes to me from my brother Jackson! BUT let Medina b'ware! or he'll be outshone by a Kaufman with a glitter rare.[107]

Ironically, at that very moment Medina was being considered as a possible replacement on the Court of Appeals for the retiring Learned Hand. Letters in the Frankfurter and Hand collections indicate that in discussing this very possibility, Frankfurter wrote an identical message to both Burlingham and Hand: "If it be true that he is the best available man for a court on which have sat men I have known, then I can only say there is a great diminution in our professional standards." [108] Besides his personal objections to Medina, the justice also abhorred what he perceived as the rationale for such an elevation to the Court of Appeals, which he outlined in a letter to Burlingham on April 25, 1951: "This business of giving judges rewards for presiding in trials that fit in with the passionate prejudices of the day is not very edifying."[109] Nevertheless, Medina did receive the appointment on June 23, 1951, and now, six years later, Frankfurter believed that some politicians were backing Kaufman's elevation for the very same reason.

By mid-February 1957, according to a report in *The New York Times*, a "hot political struggle" was brewing over the Court of Appeals appointment and, while the field of nominees had seemingly narrowed to two men, neither was Felix Frankfurter's candidate. Judge Kaufman, then under attack by various left-wing organizations, was being supported by Senators Estes Kefauver and Styles Bridges, who argued that the promotion would demonstrate presidential and senatorial approval of his handling of the Rosenberg trial. On the other side, United States Attorney Leonard P. Moore had the backing of Thomas E. Dewey and the two Republican senators from New York—Irving Ives and Jacob Javits. They argued simply that the Second Circuit needed another Republican. When a description of this battle appeared in *The New York Times*, Justice Frankfurter responded with his third personal letter to the attorney general, this one written on February 18, 1957, offering the perfect compromise—nominate Henry Friendly:

> On the assumption that the story in this morning's New York *Times* is not fiction, I venture to invoke what I presume to believe is your professional agreement with Grenny Clark that Henry Friendly affords "an extraordinary opportunity to get on the bench, a man who is as certain as can be to be a great judge." After all, the Court of Appeals for the Second Circuit was once composed of Hough and the two Hands. Is it conceivable that a Moore or a Kaufman could contribute any such distinction to that court? (What a claim to a seat on that court that a man presided at a capital trial as he presumably should have presided!) I cudge my brain to think of what public interest it can be that would bar selection of a man whose outstanding qualities are vouched for by Grenville Clark, Learned Hand and John Harlan.[110]

Despite Frankfurter's vigorous campaign in Friendly's behalf, the nomination went to Leonard Moore. This result is hardly surprising given his support from both New York Republican senators as well as the prior arrangement with Brownell. In the following months, though, the justice became aware that Kaufman's powerful political allies would not again be easily denied. They successfully delayed Moore's confirmation by the Senate long enough to force Eisenhower to make a recess appointment.[111]

Twice rebuffed himself, Frankfurter was hardly ready to give up on the possibility of Henry Friendly's placement on the Court of Appeals. The justice's carefully laid plans faced a new potential obstacle on October 23, 1957, when Attorney General Herbert Brownell retired and was replaced by his deputy, William P. Rogers. Rumors about Brownell's resignation had circulated in January of that year, and the possibility of Rogers's subsequent promotion bothered the justice greatly. He wrote to Burlingham:

> I feel about Brownell as you do, but I'm glad he is staying. His most likely successor is more aggressive for the wrong things, to wit: W[illia]m Rogers.[112]

Since as deputy attorney general Rogers was in charge of screening recommendations for judicial appointments, during that year Frankfurter became better acquainted with his views. A personal letter discovered in the Frankfurter files indicates that the two men even corresponded in late February 1957 on the issue of possible reforms to eliminate "unjustifiable delays" in litigation. At that time, the justice advocated the nomination of better rather than more judges, and the narrowing of Court jurisdiction over time-consuming cases such as those involving diversity of citizenship.[113] When Rogers was made attorney general in late 1957, Frankfurter decided to approach him in the same fashion as he had with Brownell when the next opportunity arose.

The possibility of another vacancy on the Second Circuit occurred shortly thereafter with, ironically enough, Judge Medina's announcement on January 28, 1958, that he was thinking of "semi-retirement in a few months." Never one to waste time, Frankfurter wrote a personal letter to the new attorney general that same day recommending Friendly:

> [T]he qualifications of Henry Friendly for the federal bench are, I believe, exceeded by no one at the New York bar and matched, I venture to say, by certainly not more than a handful. I do not know your knowledge of him, but the files of your predecessor bear ample witness that about Henry Friendly you can say with confidence, as one of them put it, that he would turn out to be "a great judge." And the value of his appointment on the actuarial basis of his age will outlast more than one Presidential term.[114]

Later in the same letter, he told the new attorney general that "very few men have been on this court in my lifetime who were fit to be compared with Henry Friendly in legal endowment" and with this appointment "history would acclaim you as it has [your] predecessor Wickersham for putting Learned Hand on the bench." [115]

When Rogers paid a courtesy call on Frankfurter two weeks later, the justice used the occasion to deliver a lecture on his philosophy for making judicial appointments. In the process of this discussion, which he duly reported to Judge Hand, the justice also made plain his view regarding the man whom he knew would be the other main candidate for Medina's seat:

> I was mean enough to let him know that at least one fellow will think of him what he will think of him [sic] for yielding to the pressures on behalf of Irving Kaufman's promotion. [116]

To amplify the point, Frankfurter mentioned to Rogers that Learned Hand agreed with this position. Knowing of Kaufman's powerful support, the justice had clearly decided to increase the level of his attacks on the District Court judge. To Frankfurter's delight, the meeting with Rogers had indicated to him that his channels of communication to the new attorney general were now completely open. Seeking to solidify that new relationship, he began sending encouraging letters to Rogers, such as one discovered in Frankfurter's private papers that praised the new policy of requiring federal attorneys to secure the attorney general's approval before prosecuting defendants who had been previously tried for the same offense by state courts. [117]

Despite Frankfurter's efforts, political circumstances rendered Friendly's appointment difficult. Upon Medina's full retirement on March 1, 1958, Kaufman's congressional backers became even more adamant. They had also gained the support of the extremely powerful senior New York senator, Jacob Javits. Consequently, by March 24, it was widely anticipated that he would be nominated. At this point, Frankfurter's personal opposition to the district judge intensified, because he had now become convinced that Kaufman was lobbying for his own elevation to the Appeals Court. That same day he complained to Burlingham: "Today is a bad day for me to feel too romantic about the judiciary. I refer to the political and other scheming by which Irving Kaufman is having himself put on the Court of Appeals." [118]

In the next few weeks, however, the appointment became entangled in a political battle over the passage of a bill expanding the size of the federal judiciary. What appears to have happened is that after Kaufman had lost out on the last vacancy, one of his supporters, Representative Emanuel Cellar, the chairman of the House Judiciary Committee, secured a promise from Attorney General Brownell that his candidate would get the next Second Circuit appointment. Otherwise, Cellar threatened, he would hold up all legislation dealing with the federal judiciary.

Though William Rogers, upon his appointment as attorney general, agreed initially to honor the pledge, he soon reconsidered. As a compromise, the administration proposed that Kaufman be given one of the newly created seats on the expanded Court of Appeals for the Second Circuit, but *only* after the contested legislation had been passed. This idea did not satisfy Cellar, so he refused to report the bill out of his committee. As a Democrat he was now inclined to hold up the legislation until after the 1960 presidential election, when a victorious Democratic administration might be able to dole out the forty-five new judicial appointments.[119] At this point the issue of Kaufman's promotion was at a complete standoff, with each side accusing the other of using his appointment as a pawn.

Early in 1959, with the Second Circuit's work terribly backlogged due to the unfilled vacancy created by Medina's retirement, many New York Republican leaders and Department of Justice officials began to view Henry Friendly as a compromise candidate for the position. Everything now seemed to hinge on Jacob Javits, who was still supporting Kaufman. So, the ever-vigilant Frankfurter decided to help break the deadlock by trying to move the senator. Since Javits had expressly backed Kaufman, the justice was apparently reluctant to speak with him directly. Instead, he asked District Court Judge Charles Wyzanski, who had attended law school with Javits's law partner, to discuss with the senator the possibility of either giving his support to, or at least withdrawing his political veto* against Henry Friendly. Wyzanski had known Friendly from the days when they took meals at the same eating club at Harvard, so he was happy to phone Javits on this matter.

The results were not promising, for, as Judge Wyzanski remembers the call, the senator responded simply that Friendly "had done nothing for the [Republican] party."[120] Frankfurter was determined not to yield to decisions based on these political considerations. Seeking another avenue of influence, he asked Wyzanski this time to approach

---

* A tradition has been established that no federal judicial appointment will be made if a senator of the administration's party, and from the candidate's home state, objects to the appointment.

Learned Hand and request that he write a recommendation of Friendly to Senator Javits. Not only did Hand agree to send this letter, but he also wrote President Eisenhower.[121] Finally, Javits withdrew his objection and on March 10, 1959, the president sent Friendly's name to the Senate for the seat on the Second Circuit.

Even in victory Frankfurter could not resist taking a parting shot at Kaufman. Writing to Burlingham, the justice gloated:

> I assume you are as delighted as the rest of us with Ike's nomination of Friendly. The essential credit for this nomination belongs to Rogers, the Attorney General. He has shown pertinacious courage in not yielding to the enormous pressure behind Irving Kaufman's greedy ambition. Why Kaufman should have such a drag with so many people of influence is beyond my understanding.[122]

Though Friendly had been nominated, Kaufman's supporters were hardly ready to concede defeat. Just as with Leonard P. Moore's appointment, they were determined to hold up the Senate confirmation for the rest of the congressional session. Senator Thomas Dodd of Connecticut had persuaded fellow Democrat James O. Eastland of Mississippi, the chairman of the Senate Judiciary Committee, to appoint him as head of a special subcommittee dealing only with Friendly's nomination. Though Dodd argued that he was merely protecting his state's interest in the vacancy, he let it be known that his defense of Connecticut's honor would continue until the judicial-expansion bill was passed and the attorney general committed himself to the appointment of Kaufman. Consequently, no hearings at all were scheduled on the Friendly nomination.

While this strategy of delay seemed to be unbeatable, the Kaufman supporters had not counted on the in-fighting skills of Felix Frankfurter. The justice initially tried to dislodge the nomination by asking Professor Alexander Bickel whether Yale Law School might not pass a resolution imploring "their" senator to act.[123] When no statement was forthcoming and the Senate continued to stall throughout the summer months, Judge Learned Hand became part of a new lobbying strategy. On August 10, 1959, he wrote a personal letter to Felix Frankfurter, detailing his anguish over the situation:

> I am increasingly disturbed by the failure of the Senate Judiciary Committee to take any action upon the appointment of Henry J. Friendly. I feel sure that it is seldom indeed when so altogether commendable and outstanding an appointee comes before them—one

qualified in every way for the position—indeed I hazard the guess that he would turn out to be as good as, if not better than, anyone who has been on the Court of Appeals of the Second Circuit. I cannot imagine what is holding up any action, and at least letting us know whether we are to be deprived of him.

After further expressing his bewilderment at the Senate's idleness, Hand wrote Frankfurter the magic words: "If you could find it within the proprieties to lend a hand in urging his confirmation, I am sure that you will be willing to do so, for I know that you share my ardor." [124]

To some it may appear that this letter, no part of which has ever before appeared in print, was a voluntary effort by Judge Hand to bring about some movement on the Friendly nomination. In fact, while the message is carefully crafted, there can be little doubt that the man behind it was none other than Frankfurter himself. Several things indicate that Hand's letter quite probably was solicited by Frankfurter, and written with the intention that it be used in further lobbying efforts. First, contrary to the great intimacy evident in the Hand-Frankfurter correspondence by this time, this particular letter has a formal tone. It reads like a letter of recommendation. Further, the letter carried with it a disclaimer in the form of the following postscript: "By the way, don't be mistaken: Friendly and I, though mentally agreeable acquaintances, are in no sense warm personal friends." If the letter were indeed written solely for Frankfurter, who knew both men quite well and was fully aware of the nature of their personal relationship, why would such a statement have been necessary? Judge Hand and Frankfurter had been discussing the prospects for the appointment of Friendly in their personal letters over the previous four years, so neither the tone nor the content of this message rings true. If these indicators are not enough to show that Hand's actual audience lay elsewhere, the response by Frankfurter to the letter makes the intention even clearer.

With such a "request" for action in hand, the justice went to work immediately. When the effort succeeded, even the justice could hardly contain his enthusiasm in describing the political coup to Hand. In a remarkably candid, and previously unpublished, letter to the retired judge, dated August 19, 1959, Frankfurter reported:

> Your letter [has] done it! Senator Lyndon Johnson just phoned me that he has "seen the gentleman," one Dodd of Connecticut, and "all

will be O.K." A week's notice for a hearing has to be given and that has been done, [and] the hearing will be next Tuesday. L.J. assured me there'll be no difficulty. Armed with your nifty letter, I saw the great man and he started things going at once. I got a good glimpse, incidentally, on how the wheels of government move—or, are made to move. How jejeune almost all books on "political science" are. . . .

P.S. *Please* keep mum about the Friendly matter. These pols like to be their own historians.[125]

The final part of this letter suggests that Frankfurter still believed, just as he had during his work for Brandeis, that the "laymen [might not] appreciate" his actions.

On August 25, 1959, after 168 days of Senate inactivity, the subcommittee opened hearings on Friendly's nomination. Following two weeks of testimony, during which time Senator Javits now offered his "vigorous support" for Friendly, a favorable report was issued to the full Senate, which confirmed the appointment on September 10, 1959. Henry Friendly went on to enjoy an illustrious career on the Court of Appeals for the Second Circuit, where he still serves as a senior judge. Eventually, with the election of John F. Kennedy in 1960, and the passage of the omnibus judiciary bill in 1961, Irving Kaufman was also appointed to fill one of the new seats on the Second Circuit, rising, in 1973, to the Chief Judgeship of this prestigious court.[126]

Frankfurter's extrajudicial efforts—which included two additional, but unsuccessful, attempts to place former law clerks Vincent L. McKusick and Philip Elman on the judiciary in the late 1950s[127]— came to an end on April 5, 1962. Slowed somewhat by a mild heart attack four years earlier, Frankfurter was working at his desk in the Court building when he suffered a mild stroke.[128] According to one account, as Frankfurter recuperated in the hospital after this first of what would be several such attacks, he "was more dead than alive," and when he left the hospital three months later "his eyes were dim, his face awry, his voice weak, [and] his tongue thick."[129] He recovered somewhat, but the man whose energy level burned like that of a super nova had to learn to accept first the flickering, and then the final dimming, of those life forces. He was paralyzed on the left side, and confined to a wheelchair while attended by a full-time nurse (as was his wife Marion, who had been bedridden for nearly a decade with crippling arthritis). At first unable to speak, the voice that returned was slower, softer, and, according to playwright Garson Kanin, even had a trace of the Viennese accent he had worked so hard to lose. His once-awesome memory now came and went on occasion, and he knew that it was time to accept the inevitable and leave his love, the Supreme Court of the United States. And so he did on August 28, 1962.

The body may have failed, but the mind, one so powerful that it had commanded the attention of generations of lawyers, judges, politicians, and scholars, raced on. In the final thirty months of his life, as everyone came to call, he reaped the rewards of his incredible array of friendships. One of his preoccupations, though, was to write to his "boys" around the country, former law clerks, protégés and students—the men who would be writing tomorrow's history—and record his impressions of his life, career, and the course of events. Frankfurter would think of these matters early in the morning and either have them transcribed by his secretary, when she arrived for work, or, if he felt strongly enough about the issue, and was strong enough to do so, slowly and painfully scrawl them himself onto sheets of legal-sized yellow paper. The subject of extrajudicial activities by Supreme Court justices was one of these important subjects.

In the twilight of his life—perhaps reflecting on his forty-five years of activity first as Brandeis's political lieutenant, and then as a political operative from the bench himself—Frankfurter seems to have had a further change of heart regarding the propriety of such behavior. To be sure, he still tried to offer a superficial adherence to a sense of judicial propriety, telling Garson Kanin once, "One of the few pleasant things about retirement is the fact that I can voice my enthusiastic approval of the President [then Lyndon Johnson]."[130] But what would Felix Frankfurter, with all his years of experience in this area, really advise other justices about conducting themselves in office?

In those final days, letters to two of his "boys," eminent law professors both—Alexander Bickel at Yale and Philip Kurland at Chicago—indicate that Frankfurter became very fastidious, perhaps overly fastidious, about political involvement by members of the Court. The seeds of his changing attitude, planted during his work with Brandeis and fertilized by the sharp debate with Hand over Nuremberg, bore fruit when Earl Warren was appointed in late 1963 to head a commission investigating the assassination of President John F. Kennedy. Warren himself recalled that he had not wanted to undertake the task,

but Lyndon Johnson persuaded him by citing the possibility of nu-
clear war if the inquiry were not done properly and headed by a man
of great national stature.[131] Frankfurter was extremely troubled by both
the proceeding and the Chief Justice's participation in it. Writing to
Professors Bickel and Kurland, Frankfurter criticized the secret nature
of the proceedings as well as Warren's public comments, which compromised the possibility of a fair trial for Oswald's own assassin, Jack
Ruby. Then he asked Bickel to draft an article for The New Republic
to explore the entire matter.

Clearly, Frankfurter had now decided that participation by Supreme
Court justices on official government commissions was unwise. According to Max Freedman, he came to believe that involvement in
such a "political investigation" could lessen the "public respect" for
the entire Court.[132] Yet this work differed only slightly from Jackson's
involvement at Nuremberg, which Frankfurter had supported. With
this newly adopted stricter attitude toward extrajudicial conduct by
justices, one can only wonder how Frankfurter would have assessed
the entire history of his own private political behavior.

On this subject, though, there would be no definitive answer. For,
the mighty and prolific Frankfurter pen was finally stilled at 5:05 p.m.
on February 22, 1965, when at age eighty-two he succumbed to the
effects of yet another heart attack suffered the previous day. The judicial politician was gone, and with the dreamer, Brandeis, now only
a distant memory, the Brandeis-Frankfurter connection had come to a
close.

Or had it. For now, throughout the country, were people in the law
schools, in big and little law firms, in government agencies, in the
universities and throughout the federal court system, who proudly labeled themselves as "in the Brandeis-Frankfurter tradition." Some of
these people, his former law clerks and protégés, had trained legions
of students and followers of their own. They would see that the memory was kept alive. And, more than twenty years after the death of
Frankfurter, a few of these individuals would tell an inquiring scholar
how the torch of reform had been lit by the prophet Louis Brandeis
and carried over the years by the scribe of boundless energy, Felix
Frankfurter.

Conclusion

It was never my intention in writing this book to suggest a reevaluation of the many significant contributions of Louis D. Brandeis and Felix Frankfurter to that ever-changing body of analytical reasoning we call constitutional law. Nor was it my intention to tamper with the familiar portraits of the two as men of compassion as well as brilliance, always sensitive to the needs of those less able to protect themselves in the cruel world that existed before so many of their dreams for social justice became reality. While it is the hope of all historians that their work will in some way refine previously held perceptions of their subjects and the major historical events of their times, there can be no question that well after all the material presented in this book has been integrated into our understanding of Brandeis and Frankfurter, both should and will survive as giants of twentieth-century America.

As important, just as this book was not meant to be a comprehensive life study of either Brandeis or Frankfurter, neither was it meant to be a study of the extent to which sitting justices have used their formal powers historically to advance personal political goals. My contention that Brandeis and Frankfurter wielded, *in camera*, enormous political influence through their extensive off-the-bench political activities does not accuse either man of deciding cases before the Supreme Court to suit his own perception of political rectitude. Ironically (but likely not coincidentally), both Brandeis and Frankfurter should properly be classified among those justices who were best able to separate their political views from their judicial decisions. Brandeis was clearly able to make the distinction between what he would like to see come about and what he had a right to help bring about with his from-the-bench vote. Within expected limits of human frailty, he generally respected this distinction. And Frankfurter is perceived by many students of the Court as even more concerned than Brandeis that the Court not expand its powers. We must leave it to psychohistorians to comment on whether or not the extreme judicial restraint of Frankfurter's later years on the bench represented an attempt to assuage a guilt over his past extensive extrajudicial political activity.

Nor did this book ever become a study of the issue of judicial ethics itself. In all the thousands of documents I studied in the preparation of this work, I never came upon even one shred of evidence that even remotely suggests that either Brandeis or Frankfurter ever used his office, or his special position of influence, for his own personal gain. To the contrary, Brandeis committed a large part of his own fortune to the advancement of programs of social reform from which he could not have benefitted. And while Frankfurter did accept money in recompense for his own time and money spent in bringing to fruition many of Brandeis's grand dreams, there can be no doubt that the money played no significant part in his decision to do what he did. He was speaking the plain truth when, in one letter to Brandeis in which he asked for additional funds to help him meet his wife's medical expenses, he reminded his patron that if his time were really his own he might easily be able to earn the additional money he needed doing legal consultation work for any of the many corporations that would gladly have retained him. For all the ethical problems created by the transfer of money from Brandeis to Frankfurter it cannot be said that Frankfurter used the relationship to line his own pockets.

If these two, then, were forces for good on the American political scene, and were good Supreme Court justices, why should we be so concerned that they might have been both at the same time? Is it no more than that revelations about what they did offend a vague patriotic reverence for our own peculiar system of separation of powers? What was the harm of it all? Surely both Wilson and Roosevelt profited immensely from the counsel of Brandeis. The alternative programs to those of the collectivist Brain Trusters, conceived by Brandeis and implemented by the many lieutenants of Brandeis and Frankfurter, may have saved the New Deal after the initial thrust of the First Hundred Days had spent itself on the rough rocks of American antagonism toward collectivism. Frankfurter's contribution to the prewar attempts of FDR to prepare the United States for the dreadful ordeal of World War should not be trivialized.

Such arguments, however, avoid the real issue. That there will always be those who can transcend rules without bringing about the predicted harm is not an argument for dispensing with the rules. For while we establish standards of behavior not to protect us against the sincere but against the insincere, we cannot have one set of rules for the well-intentioned and another for the malevolent.

The two questions we must address are: first, what standards were in place when these two men embarked on their extensive off-the-bench political activities? And second, what standards should prevail now and in the future?

Neither Brandeis nor Frankfurter inherited a tradition of strict observation of an apolitical posture on the part of all Supreme Court justices—fully two thirds of all those who have sat on the Court have engaged in at least some form of off-the-bench political activity. Nor does the Constitution, other than in certain general language establishing the separation of powers concept, specifically proscribe any of the many efforts made by both men to influence the legislative and executive deliberative processes from the chambers of the Supreme Court.

Yet the strongest evidence of the potential danger in having members of the judiciary involved in the very political activities in which Brandeis and Frankfurter involved themselves lies in the attitudes of the two toward their own activities, and in the efforts of both men to conceal them. Both seem to have been convinced, first, that public disclosure of their activities would be sure to bring the Court into disrepute, and, second, that the mission of the Court could not be carried out should their own behavior be used to establish new, more lenient standards allowing more widespread extrajudicial activity by sitting members of the Court. Witness Frankfurter's public protestations of his own almost religious commitment to the concept of the judiciary as a monastery, and to a Supreme Court justice as a political eunuch. And while Brandeis, more confident perhaps than Frankfurter of his own ability to resist corrupting his judicial role by his off-the-bench political involvements, seemed less personally troubled by what he was doing, he too recognized the grave danger to the Court in having his activities become a matter of public debate.

Of course, while the historian may put forward information illustrative of the realities that obtained at various times in any given area of study, it is not for him or her to suggest just which set of standards governing extrajudicial political behavior by sitting justices would best serve the national interest. For example, there is today a new problem that makes strict adherence to standards by all public figures more important than ever before. Though Brandeis appears to have believed that there was nothing inherently wrong in engaging in the activities in which he did engage, there can be little doubt that he was often and seriously troubled by the prospect that revelations about such activity, by exposing the Court to accusations that one of its members had indulged political passions, would undermine the public expectation that the Court could decide the important issues that come before it without concern for political considerations. While it may have been possible once to see the harm not in the activity but in its possible disclosure, and the problem in how best to prevent public scandal, such distinctions are no longer realistic. It is a fact of post-Watergate political life that activities in which past justices participated with impunity can no longer be undertaken without very high risk of disclosure, and this fact alone must change our attitudes toward the enforcement of whatever standards of justice are established.

Whatever these standards, however, they must, in the end, be applied uniformly. Such, after all, is the essence of justice.

APPENDIX

Toward the Monastery:
A Survey of Justices
in Politics from 1789 to 1916

In designing a government of separated powers, the Founders had fought for an independent judiciary.[1] The courts, they argued, could function as another check on the abuses of the legislature[2] and, by strictly enforcing the laws, become the "citadel of . . . public justice and public security."[3] With these as its goals, one would have expected the Founders to have forbidden judges from participating in any extrajudicial political activities. Instead, the prevailing concept of the proper judge's role at that time favored such activity, and it was common practice in the first decade after the ratification of the Constitution for judges to run for political office, to campaign openly for the election of others, and to publicly advise members of the other branches.

While the Framers may have sought an independent judiciary, most of them also believed that judges possessed a "wisdom which should not be limited to adjudication."[4] In fact, several plans had been proposed at the Constitutional Convention that would have formalized the justices' continual involvement in the revision of proposed statutes.[5] These ideas were eventually rejected for fear that judges "might receive an improper bias from having given a previous opinion in their revisionary capacity."[6] However, nothing was ever mentioned at the convention regarding the political roles members of the judiciary might take on voluntarily or be asked to assume informally.

The ambivalent nature of the Framers' commitment to judicial independence is plainly evident in the Constitution itself. Although the Founding Fathers *did* insulate federal judges from political pressure by guaranteeing them lifetime tenure of office and nonreduceable salaries during their "good behavior,"[7] they included only one specific prohibition against the voluntary performance of political duties by judges—that persons were not to sit simultaneously on the bench and in Congress.[8]

Nothing can be found, however, barring judges from holding permanent or temporary positions in the executive branch, or from either formally or informally advising any member of Congress or the president. In fact, the document does not even prohibit judges from openly running for elective office from the bench. *The Federalist Papers,* which both explained and defended the new Constitution, failed even to comment on any of these possibilities in its discussion of the need for judicial independence.[9]

That these potential problems never surfaced (or, at least, that there is no existing record of their ever having surfaced) is likely due to a number of factors. In eighteenth-century England, it was common for judges to advise members of the executive and legislative branches; English norms for judicial conduct actually supported *obligatory* extrajudicial service.[10] The Founders were still being heavily influenced in their thinking by these English norms.

In addition, the lack of institutionalization and the relative unimportance of the early Supreme Court left its members with plenty of time to cultivate their interest in politics. In each of its first three terms, the Court met for no more than ten days and decided no cases. The justices' primary function consisted of circuit riding into the different judicial districts to hear federal Court of Appeals matters. Little wonder that the public, the two other branches of government, and the members themselves saw the institution as being just another political branch, with the justices expected to serve in a variety of additional governmental capacities and to move freely from one public service role to another. The job, in fact, held so little attraction in and of itself that the first Chief Justice, John Jay, resigned from the Court for what he obviously considered a better job—governor of New York.[11]

Last, the public had no real fear of ethically compromising members of the judiciary by having them perform a number of nonjudicial duties. Quite the contrary, their fear was that the nation might unnecessarily lose the valuable talents of the few men capable of performing public service honorably. Because the right to vote was initially limited to white, male landowners, officeholders in all three branches of government tended to comprise a highly homogeneous group, largely the scions of those same well-established families that produced the electorate. These men had all been bred to "behave like gentlemen" in their private dealings and men so raised, it was felt, could be trusted to act similarly once in public office. Their own codes of honor and ethics would set proper limits on their behavior.[12] And indeed, the carriage and demeanor of our earliest political figures—Washington, Jefferson, Hamilton, and Jay—very much reinforced this image of the new nation's public figures as ruling patricians.

So, just as the Framers had anticipated, the public more than accepted the delegation of administrative duties to members of the judiciary. Accustomed to British ways regarding public service by aristocratic generalists, it saw such diverse public service as logical, particularly given the honesty and special fact-finding abilities attributed to those who had been given appointment to the Court.[13]

The actions of President Washington and the early Congresses conformed to these prevailing attitudes. The Supreme Court justices were just another set of advisers, like those at the Departments of State, War, and Treasury, who could be consulted on any political issue. For the first several years of his administration, President Washington freely consulted Chief Justice John Jay on such issues as counterfeiting practices in New York, the scope of the president's appointment powers, and the writing of his State-of-the-Union address.[14] Then, in a series of acts, Congress actually added to the burdens of the Supreme Court by delegating certain official administrative tasks to its justices. For the most part, however, the justices' extrajudicial assignments were restricted to relatively noncontroversial ex officio administrative roles, including supervising the salvaging of French ships stranded off our coast, handling complaints by crews on the seaworthiness of their vessels, examining witnesses in disputed congressional elections, and making the final determination on naturalizing aliens.[15]

In addition, Congress conferred a number of ex officio duties on Chief Justice Jay himself. His talents as a skillful statesman and wise problem solver were cited as the reasons for his appointment as a Sinking Fund commissioner, to work on the problem of reducing the Revolutionary War debt, and then as an inspector of the United States mints.[16] Initially, Chief Justice Jay and his brethren accepted all these additional formal and informal functions, seeing no conflict between this other service and their ability to fulfill their official judicial duties. Soon, however, they realized that the notion of obligatory governmental service was inconsistent with the establishment of an independent judiciary and in three separate actions began to chip away at the transplanted British norms.

In *Hayburn's Case*,[17] the Court evinced its initial concern for the integrity and independence of the judiciary. In 1792, Congress had directed that judges of the federal appeals courts hear the pension claims of veterans disabled in the Revolutionary War.[18] However, these decisions would not be final until reviewed by the secretary of war. Anticipating possible damage to judicial prestige and independence, judges from three appeals courts refused to comply with the act. Instead of serving as members of the bench, they agreed to sit as *ex officio* commissioners.

The Supreme Court upheld the judges' action, finding that the additional review procedures required by the act made the delegated task administrative and not judicial in nature. The language of this opinion was ambivalent, however, in that it proscribed only some administrative actions by the Court as a whole, and said nothing about extrajudicial activity by individual judges.[19] Nevertheless, this was the Court's first tentative step on the road to the seclusion of the judiciary.

John Jay further refined the arguments for judicial insulation in his handling of the congressionally delegated *ex officio* assignments for the Chief Justice. In his charges to various grand juries (a forum used by judges at that time to educate the citizenry regarding the Constitution, the government, and the role of the courts), Jay had long advocated a strict separation of powers between the branches:

> The Constitution of the United States had accordingly instituted these three departments, and much pains have been taken so to form and define them so that they may operate as checks one upon the other, and keep each within its proper limits; it being universally agreed to be of the last importance to a free people, that they who are vested with executive, legislative and judicial powers should rest satisfied with their respective portions of power, and neither encroach on the provinces of each other, nor suffer themselves to intermeddle with the rights reserved by the constitution to the people.[20]

Yet, his own continued work with President Washington would suggest that Jay left to the individual justice's discretion whether or not, and to what extent, political behavior was an "encroachment" on the functions of the other two branches. Jay was himself forced to make such a choice in 1792, when he received an urgent request to attend a Sinking Fund Commission meeting in Philadelphia while he was sitting on the appeals court in New York. By refusing to leave the court, Jay indicated that he regarded his judicial duties as primary. With this small step, Jay removed the obligation of political service from the Chief Justiceship. Thereafter, he and his successors tended to such duties only intermittently.

It was over a request by the executive branch for informal legal advice—an "advisory opinion"—that the issue of obligatory extrajudicial service was finally resolved. When a dispute developed over our treaty obligations to France, Secretary of State Thomas Jefferson sought the advice of the justices, "whose knowledge of the subject would secure us against errors dangerous to the peace of the United States."[21] The administration had every reason to expect an answer, given both the justices' past behavior and the fact that this question involved an interpretation of a treaty, which, under the Constitution, had the force of law.

To Jefferson's surprise, the justices declined to respond, citing the separation-of-powers principle.[22] Acceptance here, they feared, would establish a precedent for a permanent advisory relationship between the judiciary and the president. As the justices put it in their letter to President Washington, such behavior would erode their independence.

> These being in certain respects checks upon each other, and our being judges of a court of last resort, are considerations which afford strong arguments against the propriety of our extrajudicially deciding the questions alluded to, especially as the power given by the Constitution to the President, of calling on the head of departments for opinions, seems to have been *purposely* as well as expressly limited to the *executive* departments. [*Italics in original*][23]

Moreover, they foresaw the future risks to their public prestige should it become known that the Court was deciding cases involving issues the justices had previously discussed in private.

In opting for a standard that proscribed such advisory opinions, the justices spoke only of the delimiting intent of the checks-and-balances provisions of the Constitution, and not of the absolute right of the judiciary to be relieved of conflicting and onerous assignments. Justice Joseph Story, remarking upon the significance of this decision, would later write:

> The functions of the judges of the courts of the United States are strictly and exclusively judicial. They cannot, therefore, be called upon to advise the President in any executive measures; or to give extra-judicial interpretations of law.[24]

Yet, even this interpretation does not address the total problem. Only advice offered by the Court as an institution is banned; informal actions by an individual justice remain undiscussed.[25] In fact, in an earlier letter to President Washington, the justices indicated their acquiescence in assuming such roles, when called upon individually, being "not only disposed, but desirous, to promote the welfare of our country in every way that may consist with our official duties."[26] Each justice, then, was free to interpret his obligations individually. For John Jay, this meant an end to his informal advisory relationship with President Washington, but no prohibition on his running for elective office in New York.

While the early Supreme Court permanently altered the obligatory nature of extrajudicial activity, the justices continued to revel in the tradition permitting unrestricted, voluntary political involvement in other areas. In fact, during this period, they engaged in the widest imaginable range of behavior. Following Jay's example, Justice William Cushing ran for governor of Massachusetts. Then, in the pivotal presidential election of 1800, Chief Justice Oliver Ellsworth was mentioned as a candidate, while Justices Samuel Chase, James Iredell, and Bushrod Washington all openly campaigned for other candidates.[27]

During this period, it was even common for members of the judiciary to serve in two official capacities. Several sitting justices simultaneously held other positions in the government. Chief Justices John Jay and John Marshall each continued to serve as secretary of state for a period of months after his judicial appointment. Moreover, Jay and Oliver Ellsworth were sent as special envoys to negotiate treaties with England and France respectively. Thomas Johnson served as a District of Columbia commissioner during his entire judicial career. Additionally, the practice of "dual judging" was viewed as acceptable behavior. Here a member of the Supreme Court might come to review his own decisions, issued while riding his circuit sitting on the Court of Appeals.[28]

The public's acceptance of this behavior, which would be unthinkable today, reflects the extent of public confidence in the strength of character of these elite patricians. Such open political conduct was considered to be a very distinct part of the judge's role, and it was left to the individual to keep the different tasks separate. The standard of propriety, however, would be further refined with the arrival of Chief Justice John Marshall.

By establishing in 1803 the power of judicial review, in *Marbury v. Madison*,[29] the Supreme Court led by John Marshall made itself the final interpreter of the Constitution. As such, the institution became the ultimate arbiter of conflicts among the governmental branches. This decision necessarily changed the justices' attitudes toward political involvement. The Court could not judge the powers of the political branches unless it was completely independent of them.

With the exception of Marshall's nominal adherence to the ex *officio* tasks assigned to the Chief Justice and Justice Henry Baldwin's participation in the 1830 investigation into Andrew Jackson's campaign against the Seminole Indians, members of this Court refused to participate in any formal nonjudicial governmental functions.[30] Only when Justice Samuel Nelson felt compelled to engage in diplomatic missions during the Civil War would such official extrajudicial work resume.[31]

Consistent with their new proscription against undertaking *formal* duties, the members of the Marshall Court had abstained in the early years from nearly all types of *informal* activity as well. In seeking to further establish their independence and prestige, the justices began to reconsider a more fundamental question—could participation in any form of open political behavior be permitted? By 1810 the Court was meeting for a full six weeks in Washington. Since the justices lived together in the same boarding house during their stay in the capital, each man was fully aware of the political activities of the others. During this period, then, the norms governing political conduct, which established themselves through the justices' peer pressure, were very susceptible to alteration from outside influences. Thus, the War of 1812, and later the reaction of a hostile press in 1819 to the Court's decisions in the areas of federal-state relations and the obligation of contracts, provided the impetus for change.

The Chief Justice had set the standard of political abstinence by exercising only his judicial powers—a practice he generally maintained throughout his tenure. However, the War of 1812 made such a cloistered existence difficult. Several of the justices felt compelled to help wage the war with Great Britain. Joseph Story offered President

Madison general support, as well as the opinion of the "unanimous Court" that the state militias could be nationalized during times of impending invasion.[32] Associate Justice William Johnson lobbied for improvements in the fortification of the port of Charleston.[33] Justice Gabriel Duvall even sought to bring Thomas Jefferson back as secretary of state in order to negotiate during the conflict.[34] In perhaps the most extreme case, Justice Thomas Todd was involved in planning strategy sessions with various war hawks in the Congress, such as Henry Clay. None of these actions were seen as irregular by either the public or other government officials.[35] Thus, the standard was established that, at least in times of crisis, members of the Court could, and even should, undertake any necessary informal extrajudicial tasks that might be useful to the nation.

Owing to the more liberal norms allowed during the war crisis, the next several years were ones of relative freedom for justices interested in political activity. The public was virtually unaware of the activities of Court members, and opinion leaders did little to stir up public concern. Consequently, Justice Joseph Story was able to go to lengths astonishing by modern standards in attempting to reform the judicial process. Efforts by members of the Court to lobby for legislation affecting their powers were nothing new. In the early 1790s, and then again in 1800, for example, various members of the Court had pushed for certain judicial reforms that would have relieved them of the burdens of riding circuit.[36] Story, however, went far beyond simply requesting legislative assistance—he virtually became a legislator on the bench. His stated goal was to increase the power of the federal judiciary, and, hence, the supremacy of the national government. Disappointed by his own Court's refusal in United States v. Hudson and Goodwin [37] to extend the jurisdiction of the federal courts to include all criminal matters, Story sought to establish the authority through legislative means. Initially, he advocated the general idea directly in letters to Attorney General William Pinckney, and indirectly through their mutual friend, Nathaniel Williams. Then, Story even drafted, on his own initiative, some "sketches of improvements in the criminal code" to accomplish the purpose, and forwarded them to Pinckney.[38] Plainly, he saw the distinction between his judicial and political roles as not well defined.

These forays into the legislative realm became even more extensive in 1816. Still seeking to create "judicial courts which shall embrace the whole constitutional powers," Story drafted entire legislative bills, complete with supporting memoranda, which were designed to increase federal jurisdiction at the expense of state courts. These proposals were then forwarded to various Federalist congressmen, such as Charles Jarrett Ingersoll, and anyone else whom the justice could buttonhole.[39] His efforts to extend the jurisdiction of the federal courts took three forms. First, he forwarded to the attorney general an extensive memorandum supporting the passage of a bankruptcy bill, which was then pending before Congress. Then he drafted "A Bill Further to Extend the Judicial System of the United States," along with supporting commentary, which contained his pet provision, that of establishing a national, common-law-crimes jurisdiction. Story also sent this measure to the attorney general, explaining that it was the product of the entire Court. Finally, Story openly defended a pending bill, which would increase judicial salaries.[40] When William Pinckney left the Justice Department to accept an appointment as minister to Russia, these reform efforts were scuttled for the time being. Story then used his opportunity to advocate action in his formal capacity. In *Martin v. Hunter's Lessee*,[41] which established the federal court's power to review appeals from state courts, he stated that it was Congress's affirmative "duty to vest the *whole judicial power*" [*Italics in original*] in the federal courts.[42] More than simply a call for legislative action, this claim, which is taken nearly verbatim from his private communications with various politicians, displays Story's insensitivity to the need for any separation at all between his two roles.

Such open legislative endeavors by Joseph Story continued without abatement for the next two years. In 1816, he began a long-term, working relationship in which then-New Hampshire Congressman Daniel Webster virtually became the justice's legislative surrogate. Story would forward his suggestions for legislation to Webster and make himself available for wide-ranging discussions on necessary statutory revisions and other political issues.[43] In this fashion, they pressed for the extension of federal judicial power and the adoption of the national bankruptcy bill.[44] Neither man was at all self-conscious about this arrangement and, indicative of the loose standards governing extrajudicial activities at the time, there was no public criticism of it. When Webster left the capital in 1817, Story enlisted Senator David Daggett as the voice for his numerous judicial-reform proposals.[45]

Outside pressures, however, brought an end to this era of open, freewheeling political discussion by members of the Court. The main national newspapers, such as the *National Intelligencer* and the *Niles' Weekly Register,* were beginning to report the activities of the Supreme Court on a regular basis. With the increase in the institution's visibility also came a heightened sense of public awareness regarding the outside behavior of its members. This new sensitivity to the judicial role, combined with the reaction to a triumvirate of controversial judicial decisions in 1819, led to a change in the norms governing extrajudicial conduct. As a result of three separate decisions—*Sturges v. Crowninshield,*[46] and *Dartmouth College v. Woodward,*[47] both of which reaffirmed the inviolability of contracts, and *McCulloch v. Maryland,*[48] which, by upholding the charter of the national bank, expanded the implied powers of Congress—the Court became a focal point of public scrutiny and attack. States'-rights advocates throughout the nation criticized the Court for becoming an "engine of the National Government." They characterized the justices as overtly political actors seeking to snuff out the flame of state sovereignty. Accordingly, newspaper editorials appeared with increasing frequency calling for a cutback in the institution's jurisdiction.[49] To protect their power in the face of these attacks and to minimize the risk of additional criticism, either from inflamed enemies or offended supporters, the justices refrained from involvement in any open political activity. Each justice internalized this new norm proscribing open, extrajudicial involvement in a different way—as illustrated by the disparate reactions of John Marshall and Joseph Story.

Chief Justice Marshall was placed in a dilemma by the ferocity of the attacks on the Court following the *McCulloch* decision.[50] The *Richmond Enquirer* (Va.) had printed two series of articles, one signed by "Amphictyon" and the other by "Hampden," probably the handiwork of Virginia judges William Brockenbrough and Spencer Roane, which argued that *McCulloch* removed all limits on congressional authority. Marshall realized that this newspaper was the organ of the Virginia aristocracy, the leaders of the states'-rights movement, and that such articles would also be reprinted and widely distributed. Previously, a member of the Court would openly respond to such criticism by writing articles and delivering speeches. To do so now, however, might fuel the claim that the justices were simply playing politics. On the other hand, offering no defense of the judgment in the face of such a systematic attack might suggest that there was no defense possible of the Court's decision. To resolve this quandary, Marshall resorted to a rather ingenious strategy, which allowed him to explain the Court's reasoning while still observing the newly created norm for extrajudicial conduct.

The Chief Justice decided to debate the Court's critics in the newspapers by writing under a pseudonym. He drafted two responses explaining the long-term benefits of the federal structure: one that appeared in the *Philadelphia Union,* signed "A Friend of the Union," and a more extensive nine-part series that appeared in the *Alexandria Gazette* (Va.) and was signed "A Friend of the Constitution." The severity of the new proscription against such extrajudicial efforts is illustrated by the lengths to which Marshall went to hide his authorship of the essays. Each was sent to Associate Justice Bushrod Washington, who served as intermediary in placing them with a publisher. His instructions were to burn the original handwritten copy once the printer had made his proofs. Furthermore, any correspondence regarding the proofs was to be sent through Marshall's son. These extraordinary measures were so successful, that it was well into the twentieth century before the true identity of the author was discovered.

The more restrictive norms for judicial conduct had an effect even on the extremely active Joseph Story. The change in his behavior, however, was more one of style than of substance. He was still willing to propose his pet legislation to Daniel Webster, who had returned to the House in 1822 as a representative from Massachusetts, but now the justice was a bit more circumspect in his approach. Rather than forwarding unsolicited legislative proposals, Story would either offer to "assist in drawing [them], if necessary," or query "why, will you not ask me to put [a Bankruptcy Act] into shape of a code in articles?"[51] When the congressman did ask for help, Story felt free in 1825 to draft the entire Federal Crimes Act.[52] No doubt, the long-standing personal relationship between the two men, combined with Story's intense interest in these proposals, made him more willing to stretch the newly accepted strictures on extrajudicial activities. In so doing, however, he reinforced the tradition that activity in behalf of judicial reform lies outside any norms proscribing political conduct by members of the Court.

Once the furor over the decisions in 1819 died down, the standard governing extrajudicial conduct was loosened a bit. Because of increased public awareness of the role of the Court, and the need to protect its prestige, it was necessary for the justices, at the very least, to appear to be nonpolitical. Yet, the incomplete institutionalization of the Court and the federal government at that time still afforded justices some leeway for operating in the political realm, provided only that the activity was carried on in a more subdued manner. Again, it was left to each individual justice to draw his own balance.

The justices' reaction to President Monroe's attempt in 1822 to secure an advisory opinion clearly illustrates these different interpretations of the standard. Having vetoed the Cumberland Road bill providing for internal improvements, the president forwarded to each justice a pamphlet giving his reasons. Seeing an obvious effort to secure their informal opinions, Marshall and Story ducked the issue by simply acknowledging receipt of the item. However, Justice William Johnson, sensing the flexibility in the norms governing such conduct, chose to respond directly. Claiming in a letter to be a reporter for his "brother-judges," he defended such federal spending in a rather oblique fashion by telling Monroe that "the Sec'y of State [should] have the opinion of this Court on the bank question printed and dispersed through the Union."[53]

Late in the Marshall Court era, several justices felt free to resume the practice of privately advising government officials. In 1827, Justice William Johnson conferred with President John Quincy Adams, with whom he had a long-standing relationship, on various legal problems concerning the Indians in Georgia.[54] Additionally, Justice Smith Thompson, using his expertise as a former secretary of the Navy, advised the Monroe and Adams Administrations on questions ranging from judicial reform to the regulation of commerce with the British colonies.[55] In each of these cases, though, the justices limited the extent of their involvement, apparently in acceptance of the need to maintain a separation from the political branches.

In response to the rising popularity of the Court after Roger Brooke Taney became Chief Justice in 1835, the standard governing extrajudicial activity changed. Because of the relatively noncontroversial nature of its work over the next twenty years, justices of the Court were able once again to engage freely and openly in politics. For instance, there was a renewed acceptance of the involvement of judicial figures in general elections. Three justices—John McLean, James Moore

Wayne, and Levi Woodbury—actively ran for the presidency, while a number of others openly supported their favorite candidates. Why did this Court resume such behavior after a hiatus of over thirty years?

A study of McLean's justification for his candidacy suggests that the answer lies in his acceptance of a clear distinction between political and partisan activities. While he was somewhat self-conscious about his own presidential ambitions, McLean did not view the pursuit of such ambitions as being a partisan activity. He believed, as did James Monroe, that the president should be above politics and unaffiliated with any individual party. Only this type of nonpartisan posture could harmonize all the factions that divided the nation. McLean's nonpartisan appeal may have been consonant with his role as a Supreme Court justice, but it was not one designed to win political support. He became a sorry figure, placing his hat in the ring in every election from 1832 to 1860 and never even getting a party nomination.[56]

Furthermore, not everyone saw the distinction McLean did between political activity and partisanship, and more were not convinced that a judge should run even a nonpartisan campaign for the presidency. In most of these efforts McLean drew fire from newspapers in all regions, which criticized the political nature of his efforts.[57] Nevertheless, these campaigns established the precedent for ambitious justices to run for the office in the future, which they did with increasing frequency throughout the 1800s. Only when there were changes in the nature of political parties, and the partisan aspect of the presidency clearly established, was such activity by a justice finally precluded.

The apparent relaxation of the extrajudicial norms during this period was certainly evident in the variety of advising roles undertaken by the Taney Court. Now, without hesitation, Joseph Story forwarded to Daniel Webster (and several other congressmen) a number of proposals for judicial reform and even helped draft a treaty that was being negotiated with Great Britain in 1838.[58] In addition, Justices Henry Baldwin and John McLean helped Senator Frelinghuysen of New Jersey draft the 1835 Judiciary Act that realigned the circuits.[59] In fact, Chief Justice Taney became the trend setter for the new norms governing political behavior by his relationship with various White House occupants.

Taney saw no reason to discontinue the long, intimate friendship he had earlier forged with Andrew Jackson as Jackson's attorney general and then secretary of the treasury. So, it was not surprising that he drafted the constitutional arguments supporting a veto of the 1836

Revenue bill, or that he analyzed for Jackson a bill to recharter banks in the District of Columbia that needed the president's signature. Taney's willingness to serve as an informal adviser did not end with a change in presidents. He freely suggested to President Van Buren a number of changes in banking policy that he believed might head off an impending depression.[60]

The curiously transitional nature of the norms governing the acceptance by justices of informal advisory roles during this era is illustrated by the behavior of Justice John Catron. If ever there was a justice in a perfect position to enjoy a long and fruitful advisory relationship with a president it was Catron. Not only was he from the same political party as James K. Polk, but he was also his brother-in-law. Furthermore, Catron had assisted in all of Polk's political campaigns. So, the intimate advisory relationship that existed between them during Polk's tenure as speaker of the House continued when Polk was elected president.

Catron freely peppered his brother-in-law with advice on such matters as organizing the new administration, the problems of Texas and Mexico, the boundary disputes in Oregon, and the revision of tariffs. Yet many of these letters also contained the justice's admonition to "throw this in the fire," indicating that he did perceive some normative constraints on the openness of his behavior. The dangers of violating these standards did not, however, deter Catron from making sure that his political advice was followed by sending it to other governmental officials as well, such as Treasurer of the United States Daniel Graham.[61] Nor, apparently, did Polk see the giving of advice by his brother-in-law as so serious a transgression; quite obviously, he did not always follow the admonition to throw the letters into the fire or we should never have learned of it. The ambivalent nature of Catron's fears regarding the discovery of his extrajudicial activities indicates that the norms governing the justices were indeed in flux.

Were it not for the tragic circumstances surrounding the Dred Scott case,[62] * such advisory relationships might have remained acceptable

---

* Seeking to resolve the growing North-South conflict, the Supreme Court heard the case of a slave who argued that he had become a free man by virtue of traveling into areas designated as "free" by the Missouri Compromise of 1820. The Court, however, ruled that the Compromise was unconstitutional, thus depriving Dred Scott his status as a free man, and ruled further that no blacks, free or slave, were citizens entitled to the protections of the Constitution.

for many years to come. As it was, the justices made two critical mistakes that so damaged the Court's prestige that the lax constraints on political relationships were quickly tightened.

The first error, from a purely practical standpoint, was in choosing to decide the case at all. By the time the *Dred Scott* case came to the Court, the issue of slavery had already been made to suffer through a long history of political controversy and attempted compromise, marred by North-South polarization, extreme factionalism, and even bloodshed. Any attempt by the Court to impose a judicial solution on the century's dominant political issue should surely have been expected to provoke scorn and criticism from both sides. Yet even the Court's decision to hear and decide this case might not have so greatly tarnished the Court's reputation as a body capable of interpreting the law apolitically had not two justices made a second serious error.

Seeking to increase the impact of their judgment, Justices Catron and Grier prematurely leaked the contents of the decision, allowing President-elect James Buchanan to promise in his inaugural address that the slavery question would be "speedily and finally settled by the Supreme Court."[63] To compound the damage done to the Court, Buchanan, in making his startling and, as it turned out, patently absurd statement, made it clear that his information had come from inside sources.

So at a time when the Court's prestige had been jeopardized by having chosen to take a formal action that was sure to be seen as being politically motivated, public attention was also focused on clandestine contacts between its members and one of the country's most prominent political figures.

It can be argued that the justices had been caught engaging in an activity common since the birth of the Court itself. Yet very much as a consequence of these actions, only two justices over the next fifty years would dare venture into such an extensive, intimate relationship with a president.*

The dire effects of the *Dred Scott* decision might well have virtually ended all extrajudicial political activity for many years to come had it not been for the Civil War. Once again, the arrival of a crisis

* The two exceptions were Justice David Davis, who continued to advise Lincoln whom he had previously served as his campaign manager, and Justice William Moody, who continued to advise Theodore Roosevelt after having earlier served as his secretary of the Navy.

tempered any norms that might have established themselves in constraint of such conduct, and the Court, under Chief Justice Salmon P. Chase, soon found itself, in its wartime fervor, expanding its political activities. Like other citizens, the justices were preoccupied with ending the conflict and implementing reconstruction plans; if in the press and chaos of war proper means did not lead quickly to desired ends, well then who could question turning to more expeditious means?

Throughout the course of the war, various members of the Court became involved in pleading the cases of persons who had been adversely affected or unjustly jailed.[64] Further, Justices John Campbell and Samuel Nelson went so far as to try to mend the rift between the North and the South by forwarding several peace proposals to President Abraham Lincoln through various administration officials.[65] Later, Justices Field, Wayne, and Chief Justice Chase were actively involved in shaping the form Reconstruction would take.[66] Unwilling to leave very much to the whims of President Andrew Johnson, Chase labored with Radical Republicans in Congress, such as Senator John Sherman, in drafting two sections of the Fourteenth Amendment.[67] His interest in shaping postwar policies extended even to campaigning publicly in Ohio with Justice Noah Swayne to promote the ratification of the Fifteenth Amendment.[68]

During this period a special dimension was added to the norms governing the participation by members of the Court in political decisions that affected the judiciary. In keeping with well-established custom, several Justices—Chase, Samuel Miller, and Stephen Field— helped draft and then actively promoted the Judiciary Act of 1869, which increased the number of circuit court judgeships.[69] As a new twist, however, this Court also created a precedent allowing sitting justices to promote appointments for future colleagues on the high bench. Before this there had been only a handful of attempts by sitting justices to intervene in the appointment process. Most typically, as in the cases of Gabriel Duvall and John McLean, these attempts had taken the form of efforts by retiring justices to help select their successors.[70] When Chief Justice Taney retired, however, Justice Swayne secured the support of a number of his colleagues and waged a vigorous campaign for his own elevation to the post, thus factionalizing the Court; Justices Miller and Field were engineering their own campaign in favor of the appointment of Salmon P. Chase.[71] Lincoln's selection of Chase, in turn, seems at least in part to have been predicated on the presumption that elevating Chase to the highest seat in the country's judiciary would cure him of his presidential ambitions; alas, Chase, from that seat, actively sought the presidency in the elections of 1868 and 1872.[72]

Although such campaigning for political office outside the judiciary by members of the High Court would soon end, the open efforts of Swayne, Miller, and Field in the highly political appointments process set a precedent that is followed to this day.*

With the end of the Reconstruction era came the inevitable tightening up of those norms governing extrajudicial behavior to approximate those that had existed before the war. While informal advising became nearly nonexistent, the continued acceptability of political campaigning allowed the Court to become the most partisan in history. Three justices, David Davis, Samuel Miller, and Stephen Field, were each candidates in two separate presidential elections.[74] Two others, Chief Justice Morrison Waite and Justice John Harlan, were mentioned for the post but removed themselves from any consideration.[75] Davis, after being elected senator from Illinois in 1876, left the Court to serve in that capacity.[76]

The manner of these "campaigns" by some justices and the refusals by others, however, indicated that even then the normative standard had changed somewhat. The presidency was much more institutionalized by that time and was more clearly identified with intensely partisan interests. Proposing oneself as the "candidate above politics," as John McLean had done earlier, would by then have been considered both naive and terribly ineffective. So those who "ran" for the presidency from the bench ran surreptitiously. They freely encouraged friends to float their names publicly and arranged for editors to picture them as dark-horse candidates. But no one tossed his own hat in the ring or stumped for his own nomination. It was feared that an open campaign might bring the Court as an institution into the political arena and lead an ambitious judge to color his legal decisions according to partisan considerations.

Even if this fear were never realized, it was dangerous enough for

* Indeed, published reports indicate that two of the most influential recommendations for the appointment of Sandra Day O'Connor as the first woman to the Supreme Court came from Justice William Rehnquist and Chief Justice Warren Burger.[73]

the public to think that judicial opinions were being produced to appeal to certain constituencies. Chief Justice Morrison Waite's belief that his predecessor had done exactly that compelled him to refrain from any speculation regarding his potential candidacy. Accepting this standard, however, did not prevent Waite from privately advising Rutherford B. Hayes in his 1876 drive for the post.[77] While openly running for the presidency risked soiling the judicial ermine, a leisurely stroll toward the White House or giving directions to others apparently did not. Nevertheless, after 1884 no other justice was publicly mentioned for the office until well into the twentieth century.

It was the partisanship of the justices on this Court that helped alter the norms governing extrajudicial activity in official governmental capacities. Fully secure in the precedents concerning activity in judicial reform, these justices freely suggested Supreme Court appointments, and, led by Samuel Miller, drafted the 1875 Judiciary Act narrowing the Court's jurisdiction.[78] Furthermore, after Nelson's diplomatic efforts in the Civil War, most saw little danger in resuming service in official government positions. Five justices—Miller, Field, William Strong, Joseph Bradley, and Nathan Clifford—consented to serve on the 1877 electoral commission, which would resolve the outcome of the previous year's disputed presidential election. While the commission was proposed as an impartial one, its composition left Bradley, a nominal Republican, holding the swing vote.

When all twenty disputed electoral votes, and hence the election, went to the Republican candidate, Rutherford B. Hayes, with the justices themselves splitting on all issues in a straight party-line vote, the picture presented to the public was anything but one of nonpartisan decisionmaking.[79] The controversy surrounding the judgment placed the entire Court into the political vortex, thus educating its members regarding the inherent dangers of such official governmental service. So, while all efforts in the past to enlist justices in official tasks had been accepted without question, future requests would now be scrutinized carefully for partisan implications.

These newly instituted restrictions on extrajudicial service made the Court under Chief Justice Melville Fuller, who served from 1888 to 1910, one of the least active in history. Faced with the proscriptions against extensive informal advising, and open campaigning for office, the justices generally avoided any overt partisan involvement. Furthermore, because of the difficulties experienced in 1877, they refused nearly one-half of the requests for service on official governmental tribunals and commissions.[80]

But these restrictions were only part of the reason for the lull in political behavior by members of the Court. This was the period in which the Court fostered the myth of "mechanical jurisprudence," picturing its members as Olympian "finders of the law" rather than as "makers" of it. The projection of this image deflected criticism from their outright policymaking efforts in the area of economic regulation. The conservative decisions were typified by *Lochner v. New York*[81] in 1905, which voided maximum-hour legislation for bakeries, and placed the Court squarely in opposition to prevailing public sentiment favoring such a law.

To further bolster this myth of nonpartisan decisionmaking in their formal capacity, the justices felt compelled to withdraw from the dangers of the political arena. However, they continued to suggest the names of various individuals for appointment to the federal judicial and executive branches, as well as to press for judicial-reform legislation. In fact, such efforts by the justices during this period far exceeded those of their predecessors.[82] Even in these vulnerable times for the Court, such actions, like Fuller's drafting of the 1891 Judiciary Act that abolished circuit riding, were seen as noncontroversial and continued to be undertaken by every member.[83] The only exception to this rule was Justice William Moody, previously a member of Theodore Roosevelt's Administration, who continued after coming to the Court to advise the president as a member of his "Tennis Cabinet." The justice counseled Roosevelt privately on a variety of policy issues and even examined drafts of his public speeches.[84]

The severe restrictions prohibiting extrajudicial activities continued to prevail after Edward White was promoted to Chief Justice in 1910. Generally, the justices limited their political involvement to advocating judicial reform (in helping to draft the 1915 and 1916 acts respecting the Court's jurisdiction), proposing judicial and executive appointments, and occasionally serving on official government tribunals.[85] Moreover, Charles Evans Hughes, who had ignored the norms in 1910 by serving for five months as governor of New York after having been appointed to the Court, now reinforced them by resigning in 1916 to run for the presidency.[86] But by the time Louis D. Brandeis was appointed to the Court in 1916 certain aspects of the external norms governing extrajudicial conduct were ripe for change.

Notes

Introduction

1. Fred Graham, "The Many Sided Justice Fortas," *The New York Times Magazine,* June 4, 1967, pp. 25–27, 86–95.
2. *United States Senate,* Committee on the Judiciary, *Hearings on Nomination of Abe Fortas to be Chief Justice,* 90th Congress, 2nd Session, p. 230 (July 19, 1968), p. 1304 (September 13, 1968), and pp. 1348–49 (September 16, 1968). See also U.S., *Congressional Record,* vol. 114, pp. 26125, 26127 (September 9, 1968), p. 28294 (September 26, 1968); p. 28733 (September 30, 1968).
3. In this book the word political will be used to describe informal, nonjudicial activities undertaken by members of the Court. For those activities, specifically relating to the electoral process, an adjective such as "partisan," will be added.
4. Testimony of Abe Fortas, *Fortas Nomination Hearings,* p. 228 (July 19, 1968).
5. Senate Debate, September 30, 1968, *Congressional Record,* vol. 114, p. 28762.
6. See W. Lambert, "Fortas of the Supreme Court: A Question of Ethics and the Stock Manipulator," *Life Magazine,* May 9, 1969, pp. 32–37. Fortas's explanation of his relationship with the Wolfson Family Foundation can be found in his letter of resignation to Chief Justice Earl Warren, dated May 14, 1969, and reprinted in: *Congressional Quarterly's Guide to the U.S. Supreme Court* (Washington, D.C.: Congressional Quarterly, Inc., 1979), p. 983.

    Two differing interpretations of these events can be found in: Sheldon Goldman and Thomas Jahnige, *The Federal Courts as a Political System* (New York: Harper and Row, 1971), pp. 12–14 and Robert Shogan, *A Question of Judgment: The Fortas Case and the Struggle for the Supreme Court* (Indianapolis: The Bobbs-Merrill Company, 1972). For another account see Bob Woodward and Scott Armstrong, *The Brethren: Inside the Supreme Court* (New York: Simon and Schuster, 1979), pp. 14–20.
7. United States Senate, Committee on the Judiciary, Subcommittee on Separation of

Powers, *Nonjudicial Activities of Supreme Court Justices and Other Federal Judges*, *Hearings*, 91st Congress, 1st Session, 1969.

8. For more on the Fortas and Haynsworth cases, see John Massaro, "Advice and Dissent: Factors in the Senate's Refusal to Confirm Supreme Court Nominees, with Special Emphasis on the Cases of Abe Fortas and Clement L. Haynsworth" (Unpublished Ph.D. dissertation, Southern Illinois University, 1973).

9. See Philip B. Kurland, "The Lord Chancellor of the United States," 7 *Trial* (November/December 1971), pp. 11–28; Arthur Landever, "Chief Justice Burger and Extra-Case Activism," 20 *Journal of Public Law* (1971), pp. 523–41. For more on Burger's activities, see William F. Swindler, "The Chief Justice and Law Reform, 1921–1971," *Supreme Court Review*, 1971, pp. 241–64.

10. Transcript of CBS Evening News with Walter Cronkite, October 6, 1978, p. 11.

11. Manuscript of Warren Burger's remarks in accepting the Fordham-Stein Award, New York City, October 25, 1978.

12. The argument I have made in this chapter, and in the Appendix regarding how standards of propriety governing such behavior have changed relies on information from the following sources. Henry J. Abraham and Bruce Allen Murphy, "The Influence of Sitting and Retired Justices on Presidential Supreme Court Nominations," 3 *Hastings Constitutional Law Quarterly* (1976), pp. 37–63; William Cibes, "Extra-judicial Activities of Justices of the United States Supreme Court, 1790–1960" (Unpublished Ph.D dissertation, Princeton University, 1975); Robert McKay, "The Judiciary and Non-Judicial Activities," 35 *Law and Contemporary Problems* (1970), pp. 9–36; Peter Bell, "Extrajudicial Activities of Supreme Court Justices," 22 *Stanford Law Review* (1970), pp. 587–617; Russell Wheeler, *Extrajudicial Behavior and the Role of the Supreme Court Justice* (Morristown, N.J.: General Learning Press, 1975); Russell Wheeler, "Extrajudicial Behavior of the Early Supreme Court," *Supreme Court Review*, 1973, pp. 123–58, Solomon Slonim, "Extrajudicial Activities and the Principle of Separation of Powers," 49 *Connecticut Bar Journal* (1975), pp. 391–410; and Alan Westin, "Out of Court Commentary by United States Supreme Court Justices, 1790–1962: Of Free Speech and Judicial Lockjaw," 62 *Columbia Law Review* (1962), pp. 633–69.

13. One general work on the Court does discuss some of the political activities of one Chief Justice, William Howard Taft, as well as some of the extrajudicial activities of certain other justices. See Walter F. Murphy, *Elements of Judicial Strategy* (Chicago: University of Chicago Press, 1964). Moreover, several judicial biographies reveal at least some cognizance of their subject's extrajudicial endeavors: see Carl Brent Swisher, *Stephen J. Field, Craftsman of the Law* (Washington, D.C.: The Brookings Institution, 1930); Charles Fairman, *Mr. Justice Miller and the Supreme Court, 1862–1890* (Cambridge, Mass.: Harvard University Press, 1939); Alpheus Thomas Mason, *William Howard Taft: Chief Justice* (New York: Simon and Schuster, 1964); Henry F. Pringle, *The Life and Times of William Howard Taft* (New York: Farrar and Rinehart, Inc., 1939); Alpheus Mason, *Harlan Fiske Stone: Pillar of the Law* (New York: The Viking Press, 1956); and J. Woodford Howard, Jr., *Mr. Justice Murphy: A Political Biography* (Princeton, N.J.: Princeton University Press, 1968). Some of these biographies, though, tend only to hint at the full extent of the involvement of the justice in political activities, perhaps in the interest of the flow of their story.

14. Francis P. Weisenburger, *The Life of John McLean: A Politician on the United States Supreme Court* (Columbus, Ohio: Ohio State University Press, 1937); Clarinda Lamar, *The Life of J. R. Lamar, 1857–1916* (New York: G. P. Putnam's Sons, 1926). For more on the generally weak body of biographical literature on the justices, see

Robert M. Spector, "Judicial Biography and the United States Supreme Court; A Bibliographical Appraisal," II *American Journal of Legal History* (January 1967), pp. 1–24; Wythe Holt, "Now and Then: The Uncertain State of Nineteenth-Century American Legal History," 7 *Indiana Law Review* (1974), pp. 615–83; and G. Edward White, "Some Observations on a Course in Legal History," 23 *Journal of Legal Education* (1971), pp. 440ff.; and J. Woodford Howard, Jr., "Judicial Biography and the Behavioral Persuasion," 65 *The American Political Science Review* (1971), pp. 704–15.

15. Alpheus T. Mason, "Charles Evans Hughes: An Appeal to the Bar of History," 6 *Vanderbilt Law Review* (1952), pp. 1–19; S. Sidney Ulmer, "Bricolage and Assorted Thoughts on Working in the Papers of Supreme Court Justices," 35 *The Journal of Politics* (1975), pp. 286ff.; and Walter F. Murphy, *Elements of Judicial Strategy*, p. viii.

16. For example, Gerald T. Dunne. *Hugo Black and the Judicial Revolution* (New York: Simon and Schuster, 1977); C. Peter Magrath, *Morrison R. Waite: The Triumph of Character* (New York: Macmillan Co., 1963); and James J. Magee, *Mr. Justice Black: Absolutist on the Court* (Charlottesville: University of Virginia Press, 1980).

17. Alpheus T. Mason, *Brandeis, A Free Man's Life* (New York: The Viking Press, 1946), pp. 521–22, 583–85, 628–29, chapters 29, 32, 33, and 37. For more on why Professor Mason was not allowed access to the Brandeis-Frankfurter correspondence in doing his biography, see the introduction to chapter 4.

   For other books attesting to Brandeis's ethics, see Alfred Lief, *Brandeis, The Personal History of an American Ideal* (New York: Stackpole, Sons, 1936); and Irving Dilliard *Mr. Justice Brandeis: Great American* (St. Louis: The Modern View Press, 1941).

18. Liva Baker, *Felix Frankfurter* (New York: Coward-McCann, 1969), pp. 235–38, and *passim*. For a vigorous denial of Frankfurter's political actions and a loyal defense of his sense of ethics see Max Isenbergh, "Felix Frankfurter as a Policymaker," 85 *Yale Law Journal* (1975), pp. 280–98 and Max Isenbergh, "Claims of History? or What the Market Will Bear?," 45 *The Virginia Quarterly Review* (1969), pp. 345–52.

19. See letters of E. C. Burris to Louis D. Brandeis, November 11, 1936, Louis D. Brandeis Papers, Louisville Law School (hereinafter cited as LDB/LLS), Box SC 17. (In this case Brandeis's law clerk that year, Willard H. Hurst, responded, explaining that "judicial proprieties prevent[ed]" the justice from acting. See letter, Hurst to Burris, November 16, 1936, LDB/LLS, Box SC 17.) For an example of the use of "precluded," see letter, FF to LDB, undated, LDB/LLS, Box SC 5. On other occasions Brandeis simply put "declined" on the top of the requesting letter. See, for example, letter, Robert La Follette, Jr., to LDB, January 10, 1929, LDB/LLS, Box SC 8.

   In the first volume of his autobiography, Justice William O. Douglas writes that when faced with such requests, Brandeis wrote "J.P.P." in the corner for "Judicial Propriety Prohibits." (See William O. Douglas, *Go East, Young Man* (New York: Random House, 1974), p. 445. However, a detailed search of the Brandeis papers failed to uncover examples of such behavior.

20. Joseph Lash, ed., *From the Diaries of Felix Frankfurter* (New York: W. W. Norton and Co., 1975), p. 155. Curiously enough, this statement was made on January 11, 1943, during the height of Frankfurter's extrajudicial involvement.

21. See letters, Felix Frankfurter to Henry Wallace, January 27, 1945, Henry Wallace Papers (on microfilm), Franklin D. Roosevelt Library, Hyde Park, New York (hereinafter cited only as FDRL), and Felix Frankfurter to Franklin D. Roosevelt, Septem-

ber 12, 1940, Felix Frankfurter Papers, Library of Congress (hereinafter cited as FF/LC), Box 98.

22. Felix Frankfurter, "Personal Ambition of Judges: Should a Judge Think Beyond the Judicial?" an address before the American Bar Association, as printed in 34 *American Bar Association Journal* (1948), pp. 656–59. This piece was a poorly veiled criticism of the actions of Frankfurter's judicial colleague, William O. Douglas, who was then being touted for the presidency.

23. Clues to some of the justices' many extrajudicial activities can be found sprinkled throughout such volumes as: Lash, ed., *Frankfurter Diaries*; Max Freedman, *Roosevelt and Frankfurter: Their Correspondence, 1928–1945* (Boston: Little Brown and Co., 1967); and Melvin J. Urofsky and David W. Levy, *Letters of Louis D. Brandeis*, 5 vols (Albany, N.Y.: State University of New York, 1971–1978); and Harlan B. Phillips, *Felix Frankfurter Reminisces* (New York: Reynal and Company, 1960).

24. Throughout this book other works will be cited that touch on these matters. A few of the better ones that deal with a time period or major figure and still mention extrajudicial actions are: Arthur M. Schlesinger, Jr., *The Coming of the New Deal* (Boston: Houghton Mifflin Co., 1959), pp. 77, 169, 241–42, 302-3; Arthur M. Schlesinger, Jr., *The Politics of Upheaval* (Boston: Houghton Mifflin Co., 1960), pp. 220–24, 234, 236, 280, and 387–88; William E. Leuchtenburg, *Franklin D. Roosevelt and the New Deal* (New York: Harper and Row, 1965), pp. 147–49, 156, and 233; and Joseph P. Lash, *Roosevelt and Churchill, 1939–1941* (New York: W. W. Norton and Company, 1976), pp. 86, 136, 172, 181, 186, 189–90, 210, 235, 240, 265, 289, and 396.

Two recently published works do much to disclose and analyze some of Brandeis's extrajudicial actions, and both were useful in suggesting the location and dates of some primary and secondary source materials for this study. These works are: H. N. Hirsch, *The Enigma of Felix Frankfurter* (New York: Basic Books, 1981), and Nelson Lloyd Dawson, *Louis D. Brandeis, Felix Frankfurter, and the New Deal* (Hamden, Conn.: Archon Books/The Shoe String Press, Inc., 1980) In the course of examining the actions of Felix Frankfurter, Hirsch discloses some of the considerable political involvement of Justice Brandeis during the New Deal. Dawson's book is devoted exclusively to the study of Brandeis's and Frankfurter's attempts to influence the New Deal. However, because of a difference in focus between my work and Hirsch's (his is an excellent psychological/biographical study of Frankfurter), and due to the great difference in perspective, analytical framework, scope of investigation (in terms of years and figures), and primary document research base between my study and Dawson's, at various points my interpretations and conclusions will diverge from theirs. For the benefit of those who are interested in such historiographical matters, I will point out those differences when they occur.

25. These works will be cited throughout the book. Some examples are: Raymond Moley, *The First New Deal* (New York: Harcourt, Brace and World, 1966), pp. 274–75; Dean Acheson, *Morning and Noon* (Boston: Houghton Mifflin Co., 1975), 161–62, 180–81; Rexford Tugwell, *Democratic Roosevelt: A Biography of FDR* (New York: Doubleday and Company, 1957), pp. 247–48; Samuel I. Rosenman, *Working with Roosevelt* (New York: Harper and Brothers, 1952), pp. 261–62; Francis Biddle, *In Brief Authority* (Garden City, N.Y.: Doubleday and Co., 1962), pp. 192–94.

26. *The New York Times*, December 11, 1981, pp. 1 and A 32, reporting on John D. Ehrlichman, *Witness to Power* (New York: Simon and Schuster, 1982).

Chapter 1

1. This description of Brandeis's early life and career is drawn from the following sources: Alpheus T. Mason, *Brandeis: A Free Man's Life* (New York: The Viking Press, 1956), pp. 11–375; Allon Gal, *Brandeis of Boston* (Cambridge, Mass.: Harvard University Press, 1980), *passim*; Paul Freund, "Louis Dembitz Brandeis," *Dictionary of American Biography*, Supplement III (1941–45), (New York: Charles Scribner's, 1973), pp. 93–100; Philippa Strum, "Brandeis and the Exercise of Judicial Power" (Unpublished paper for the American Political Science Association Convention, Washington, D.C., 1977); G. Edward White, *The American Judicial Tradition: Profiles of Leading American Judges* (New York: Oxford University Press, 1976), pp. 150–77; and Melvin I. Urofsky, *Louis D. Brandeis and the American Tradition* (Boston: Little Brown and Company, 1981), pp. 1–103.
2. Freund, "Louis D. Brandeis," p. 94.
3. Mason, *Brandeis*, p. 48; see also pp. 33, 45.
4. Gal, *Brandeis of Boston*, pp. 11–22.
5. Ibid., pp. 37–41.
6. White, *American Judicial Tradition*, p. 161.
7. Gal, *Brandeis of Boston*, p. 83.
8. White, *American Judicial Tradition*, p. 162.
9. Mason, *Brandeis*, p. 640; Urofsky, *Louis D. Brandeis*, p. 9.
10. 208 U.S. 412 (1908). For more on Brandeis's role in the case, see Gal, *Brandeis of Boston*, pp. 138–42.
11. Paul A. Freund, "Mr. Justice Brandeis," in Allison Dunham and Phillip B. Kurland, eds., *Mr. Justice* (Chicago: University of Chicago Press, 1964), pp. 182, 184. For more on Brandeis's philosophy of the "good society," see White, *American Judicial Tradition*, pp. 160–64; and Melvin I. Urofsky, *A Mind of One Piece: Brandeis and American Reform* (New York: Scribner's and Sons, 1971), *passim*.
12. Freund, "Mr. Justice Brandeis," p. 178, and Felix Frankfurter, "Mr. Justice Brandeis and the Constitution," in Felix Frankfurter, *Mr. Justice Brandeis* (New Haven: Yale University Press, 1932), p. 124.
13. Frankfurter, "Brandeis and the Constitution," p. 124.
14. See Urofsky, *Mind of One Piece*, p. 45; Freund, "Mr. Justice Brandeis," p. 177; and White, *American Judicial Tradition*, pp. 160–63.
15. Memo by David Riesman, "Notes for an Essay of Justice Brandeis," May 22, 1936, FF/LC. Box 127. Riesman was the clerk to Justice Brandeis for the year 1935. See also Osmond K. Fraenkel, ed., *The Curse of Bigness; Miscellaneous Papers of Louis D. Brandeis* (New York: The Viking Press, 1934), p. 45, where the justice is quoted: "I believe that the possibilities of human advancement are unlimited. I believe that the resources of productive enterprises are almost untouched . . ."
16. Felix Frankfurter notebooks on conversations with Justice Brandeis, June 24, 1920, Louis D. Brandeis Manuscripts, Manuscript Division, Harvard Law School (hereinafter cited only as LDB/HLS), Box 114, Folder 8.
17. Riesman memo, May 22, 1936, FF/LC, Box 129.
18. Undated memorandum of interview between Ray Stannard Baker and Louis D. Brandeis, Ray Stannard Baker MSS, Library of Congress (hereinafter cited as LC), Box 21.
19. Fraenkel, *The Curse of Bigness*, p. 37; and White, *American Judicial Tradition*, p. 163. Professor White sees the dual concern for "freedom and self-restraint" as "the core of Brandeis' philosophy." Like Jefferson, Brandeis sought freedom in all walks of life.

20. Ned McClennan, "Louis D. Brandeis as a Lawyer," 33 *Massachusetts Law Quarterly* (1948), pp. 24–25, and *passim*. And David W. Levy, "Lawyer as Judge: Brandeis' View of the Legal Profession," 22 *Oklahoma Law Review* (1969), pp. 391–92, and *passim*. For more on Brandeis's work as a lawyer, see Mason, *Brandeis*, pp. 99–364.

21. For more on Brandeis's early reform battles, see Mason, *Brandeis*, pp. 99–244; and Gal, *Brandeis of Boston*, pp. 22–28; 46–65; and 96–136.

22. For more on the Ballinger-Pinchot controversy, see Mason, *Brandeis*, pp. 254–81.

23. Gal, *Brandeis of Boston*, pp. 137–207 was used as the basis for the following chronicle of Brandeis's conversion to Zionism.

24. Mason, *Brandeis*, pp. 442–43.

25. Ibid., p. 443.

26. Jacob DeHaas, *Louis D. Brandeis, A Biographical Sketch, with Special Reference to His Contributions to Jewish and Zionist History* (New York: Block Publishing Co., 1929), p. 50, as quoted in Mason, *Brandeis*, p. 445. Also quoted in Gal, *Brandeis of Boston*, p. 206.

27. Mason, *Brandeis*, 375–76.

28. Arthur Link, *Wilson: The Road to the White House* (Princeton, N.J.: Princeton University Press, 1947), p. 489.

29. Urofsky, *Mind of One Piece*, pp. 74–75; and Mason, *Brandeis*, pp. 380–85.

30. Urofsky, *Mind of One Piece*, pp. 71–81; and Richard Hofstadter, *The Age of Reform from Bryan to F.D.R.* (New York: Alfred A. Knopf, 1969), p. 247.

31. Urofsky, *Mind of One Piece*, p. 84.

32. For more on Brandeis's activity during this period in his life, see Mason, *Brandeis*, pp. 397–403; and Urofsky, *Louis D. Brandeis*, pp. 76–86.

33. Fraenkel, *Curse of Bigness*, pp. 113–14.

34. Mason, *Brandeis*, pp. 404–8; and Baker-Brandeis Interview Memo, Baker MSS, LC, Box 21.

35. Alfred Lief, *Brandeis: The Personal History of An American Ideal* (New York: Starkpole and Sons, 1936), p. 409.

36. Alden L. Todd, *Justice on Trial: The Case of Louis D. Brandeis* (New York: McGraw Hill, 1964), *passim*; and Mason, *Brandeis*, chapters XXX and XXXI. A brief, engagingly written account of this battle also appears in Urofsky, *Louis D. Brandeis*, chapter VI.

    The author also wishes to thank David W. Levy, my co-author in an article entitled "Preserving the Progressive Spirit in a Conservative Time: The Joint Reform Efforts of Justice Brandeis and Professor Frankfurter, 1916–1933," 78 *Michigan Law Review* (1980), pp. 1252–1304, for suggesting several of the citations that were useful in the following pages. The title of this chapter was also the title for an early draft of that article.

37. John P. Frank finds Brandeis innocent of all charges regarding violations of legal ethics. See, Frank's "The Legal Ethics of Louis D. Brandeis," 17 *Stanford Law Review* (1965), pp. 683–709. See also, Urofsky, *Louis D. Brandeis*, pp. 12, 111–12.

38. U.S. Senate, *Hearings before the Subcommittee of the Committee on the Judiciary . . . on the Nomination of Louis D. Brandeis to be an Associate Justice of the Supreme Court of the United States*, 64th Congress, 1st Session, II, p. 371.

39. Letters, Louis D. Brandeis to Edward Nash Hurley, February 8, 1916, and LDB to Isidor Zai, February 29, 1916, in Melvin Urofsky and David Levy, *Letters of Louis D. Brandeis*, vol. IV (Albany, N.Y.: State University of New York, 1975), pp. 35–36, 98.

40. Quoted by Mason, *Brandeis*, p. 467.
41. See the full body of Brandeis's correspondence from January 28, 1916 to June 5, 1916, in Urofsky and Levy, *Brandeis Letters*, vol. IV pp. 25–295. The term "interested spectator" was Brandeis's own description of his role to his brother Alfred used in a letter of February 12, 1916, in Urofsky and Levy, *Brandeis Letters*, vol. IV, p. 54.
42. LDB to Edward F. McClennen, March 9, 1916, in Urofsky and Levy, *Brandeis Letters*, vol. IV, p. 114.
43. McClennen to LDB, March 10, 1916, in Urofsky and Levy, *Brandeis Letters*, vol. IV, p. 114–15.
44. Mason, *Brandeis*, p. 512; and letter, LDB to Edward White, June 29, 1916, in Urofsky and Levy, *Brandeis Letters*, vol. IV, pp. 241–42.
45. Brandeis explained his entire investment portfolio in a letter to the Chief Justice, LDB to Edward White, July 20, 1916, in Urofsky and Levy, *Brandeis Letters*, vol. IV, p. 249.
46. Letters, LDB to J. W. Beatson, June 16, 1916, LDB to Leon Sanders, June 26, 1916, and LDB to the Massachusetts Civil Service Association, September 25, 1916, in Urofsky and Levy, *Brandeis Letters*, vol. IV, pp. 223, 237, and 260.
47. For more on the American Zionists and Brandeis, see Mason, *Brandeis*, chapter XXIX; Ezekiel Rabinowitz, *Justice Louis D. Brandeis, the Zionist Chapter of His Life* (New York: Philosophical Library, 1968); Melvin Urofsky, *American Zionism from Herzl to the Holocaust* (Garden City, New York: Doubleday, 1975); and Yonathan Shapiro, *Leadership of the American Zionist Organization, 1897–1930* (Urbana, Ill.: University of Illinois Press, 1971).
48. Shapiro, *Zionist Leadership*, pp. 94–96; and *The New York Times*, July 18, 1916, p. 8. Also see letters, LDB to Jacob De Haas, July 21, 1916, LDB to Bernard G. Richards, July 21, 1916, LDB to Felix M. Warburg, July 21, 1916, and LDB to Stephen S. Wise, July 21, 1916, all in Urofsky and Levy, *Brandeis Letters*, vol. IV, pp. 250, 252–53. Also see Urofsky, *American Zionism*, pp. 188–93 and Urofsky *Louis D. Brandeis*, pp. 127–29.
49. Mason, *Brandeis*, p. 512.
50. Letter, LDB to Woodrow Wilson, August 14, 1916, Woodrow Wilson papers, (on microfilm), LC. Also quoted in Mason, *Brandeis*, p. 512.
51. Letters, FF to Paul Freund, January 22, 1957, FF/LC, Box 56.
52. Memorandum, "Conversations Between LDB and FF," p. 1, June 26, [1922], FF/LC, Box 224.
53. For more, see Mason, *Brandeis*, pp. 99–365; Gal, *Brandeis of Boston*, pp. 29–66, 96–137; and Paul A. Freund, "Justice Brandeis: A Law Clerk's Remembrance," LXVIII *American Jewish History* (September 1978), pp. 7–8.
54. Interviews with Philip Elman, July 10, 1979, Washington, D.C., The Honorable Judge Charles E. Wyzanski, Jr., January 13, 1977, Richmond, Virginia, Edward F. Prichard, Jr., June 25, 1979, Frankfort, Kentucky, and Joseph L. Rauh, Jr., July 9, 1979, Washington, D.C. The author wishes to thank Judge Wyzanski for his assistance in the earliest stages of this project.
55. Interviews with the Honorable Judge Carl McGowan, July 19, 1979, Washington, D.C. and Philip Elman, July 10, 1979, Washington, D.C.
56. The following description of Frankfurter's early life and career comes from several sources: Lash, ed., *Frankfurter Diaries*, pp. 3–5; Harlan B. Phillips, ed., *Felix Frankfurter Reminisces* (New York: Reynal and Co., 1960), pp. 3–34; Albert M. Sacks, "Felix Frankfurter," in Leon Friedman and Fred L. Israel, eds., *The Justices of the*

United States Supreme Court, 1781–1969: Their Lives and Major Opinions (New York: Chelsea House Publishers, 1969); and H. N. Hirsch, *The Enigma of Felix Frankfurter* (New York: Basic Books, 1981), pp. 12–40.

57. Liva Baker, *Felix Frankfurter* (New York: Coward-McCann, Inc., 1969), p. 17.
58. For more on this role see Jerold S. Auerbach, *Unequal Justice: Lawyers and Social Change in Modern America* (New York: Oxford University Press, 1976), pp. 191–231.
59. For more on this period in Frankfurter's life, see Phillips, ed., *Frankfurter Reminisces*, pp. 34–50.
60. Phillips, ed., *Frankfurter Reminisces*, p. 48 as quoted in Lash, *Frankfurter Diaries*, p. 6.
61. This picture of the House of Truth can be found in Phillips, ed. *Frankfurter Reminisces*, pp. 105–13.
62. Phillips, ed., *Frankfurter Reminisces*, p. 106.
63. See letter, FF to LDB, March 14, 1910, quoted in Gal, *Brandeis of Boston*, p. 143 (concerning an Illinois maximum-hour law case similar to the Muller case in Oregon; Brandeis sent his case brief to FF). LDB to FF, June 14, 1910 (concerning a response to FF's congratulations of LDB's success in the Illinois maximum-hour case, and notification that LDB was sending FF his brief in the Ballinger-Pinchot controversy), LDB to FF, February 27, 1911 (concerning clippings sent by FF to LDB regarding the latter's work with the Interstate Commerce Commission), LDB to FF, November 15, 1911 (concerning the Sherman Act), and LDB to FF, April 9, 1912 (concerning appointments to the Children's Bureau and the Industrial Commission Board), all in Urofsky and Levy, *Brandeis Letters*, Vol. II, pp. 350–51, 412, 512, and 577–78.
    Allon Gal, in discussing the origins of the Brandeis-Frankfurter relationship, states that the two men first met in the spring of 1912. However, this cannot be the case, as two entries in Frankfurter's diary for 1911 indicate that he held several meetings with Brandeis during the latter part of that year. See Lash, ed., *Frankfurter Diaries*, pp. 103–4, and 119. For Gal's version, consult his *Brandeis of Boston*, pp. 142–44.
64. Letter, LDB to FF, July 12, 1912, in Urofsky and Levy, *Brandeis Letters*, Vol. II, p. 648.
65. Lash, ed., *Frankfurter Diaries*, p. 104.
66. LDB to Philip Wells, July 21, 1913, in Urofsky and Levy, *Brandeis Letters*, Vol. III, p. 146.
67. LDB to Roger Benton Hull, January 31, 1914, in Urofsky and Levy, *Brandeis Letters*, Vol. III, p. 242.
68. See Lash, ed., *Frankfurter Diaries*, pp. 11–12; and letters, LDB to Winfred Thaxter Denison, July 12, 1913, LDB to Roscoe Pound, July 12, 1913, LDB to Roscoe Pound, November 5, 1913, all in Urofsky and Levy, *Brandeis Letters*, Vol. III, pp. 134–36, 209.
69. Phillips, ed., *Frankfurter Reminisces*, p. 78.
70. Ibid., p. 78–79.
71. Roscoe Pound, "Felix Frankfurter at Harvard," in Wallace Mendelson, ed., *Felix Frankfurter: A Tribute* (New York: Benal and Company, 1964), pp. 143.
72. Lash, "A Brahmin of the Law," in Lash, ed., *Frankfurter Diaries*, pp. 16–19; Phillips, ed., *Frankfurter Reminisces*, chapters 9, 10, 11.
73. The other member of the council was Julian W. Mack and other individuals were added (e.g., Jacob De Haas, Stephen Wise, and Bernard Flexner). Letter, LDB to

Julian W. Mack, March 19, 1915, in Urofsky and Levy, *Brandeis Letters*, Vol. III, p. 487.

74. Letter, LDB to FF, September 24, 1925, FF/LC, Box 26. Brandeis had first used this term to describe the professor in a letter he wrote in 1919 to Marion Denman, Frankfurter's fiancee, on learning of Frankfurter's marriage plans. See letter, LDB to Marion Denman, November 3, 1919, FF/LC, Box 26, quoted in H. N. Hirsch, *Enigma of Frankfurter*, p. 85.

75. Letter, Norman Hapgood to Franklin Delano Roosevelt undated, FDRL, Box PPF 2278.

76. For a list of Brandeis's holdings, see Mason, *Brandeis*, p. 691.

77. Letter, LDB to FF, November 19, 1916, FF/LC, Box 26.

78. Letter, FF to LDB, undated, LDB/LLS, Box G 9.

79. Letter, LDB to FF, November 25, 1916, FF/LC, Box 26.

80. This is not the first mention of this "joint-endeavors" fund in print. The matter is also discussed in: Bruce Allen Murphy, "Elements of Extrajudicial Strategy: A Look at the Political Roles of Justices Brandeis and Frankfurter," 69 *Georgetown Law Journal* 101 (1980), at 111–13; Levy and Murphy, "The Joint Reform Efforts of Brandeis and Frankfurter," 78 *Michigan Law Review*, 1252 (1980), at 1261–63; H. N. Hirsch, *Enigma of Frankfurter*, pp. 44, 225; Dawson, *Brandeis, Frankfurter, and the New Deal*, pp. 4–5, and Urofsky and Levy, *Brandeis Letters*, vol. IV, pp. 266–67 and Vol. V, pp. 43, 187–88, 290, 292–93.

   However, this is the first exposition in print of the development and complete extent of both the financial fund and the requests that stemmed from it. This new examination will make clear that this money was given by Brandeis not merely out of generosity, but as part of an entire package that over the years included literally hundreds of requests for political action by Frankfurter.

81. Fraenkel, ed., *The Curse of Bigness*, p. 266.

82. For a complete list of Brandeis's extraordinary contributions to charity see Mason, *Brandeis*, p. 692.

   Over the years Brandeis attempted to imbue his daughters Elizabeth and Susan with his own sense of obligation to charitable and public causes. For instance, in June 1931, he transferred $10,000 bonds to each of his daughters, explaining to Elizabeth: "As you know, mother and I have, for many years, given a large part of our income to public causes in which we took an active part; thus rendering our own work more effective. We think you and Susan may wish to do the like." Letter, LDB to Elizabeth Brandeis Raushenbush, June 3, 1931, in Urofsky and Levy, *Brandeis Letters*, vol. V., p. 478.

83. The early development of the financial relationship is detailed in: letters, LDB to FF, May 3, 1917, January 3, 1923, January 16, 1923, and March 17, 1925, and LDB to Julian Mack, January 12, 1922, FF/LC, Boxes 26, 27.

84. Letter, FF to LDB, undated, FF/LC, Box 29, as quoted in H. N. Hirsch, *Enigma of Frankfurter*, p. 225. Because of these circumstances, FF also asked for Brandeis's assistance in another letter: FF to LDB, September 29, 1924, FF/LC, Box 29. The nature of Marion's psychiatric problems, and speculations regarding their causes can be found in: Lash, ed., *Frankfurter Diaries*, p. 31; Hirsch, *Enigma of Frankfurter*, pp. 47–51, 58–62, 64, and 81–5. Relying on the letters between Felix and Marion, Hirsch makes a persuasive case that while his wife had certain psychological weaknesses, it was Frankfurter who, by his dominating personality, caused her problems.

85. Letter, LDB to FF, September 24, 1925, FF/LC, Box 27.

86. See letters, LDB to FF, October 2, 1926, June 5, 1927, August 15, 1927, April 11, 1929, September 26, 1929, and July 30, 1934, FF/LC, Boxes 27, 28.

87. When the payment was missed, Brandeis responded this way: "Yours of 31st just received. I am deeply chagrined at my oversight in not having Miss Malloch make the deposit of $2,000 on January 1st/27. I am writing her by this mail and asking her to advise you immediately on making the deposit . . . If, by any chance, the deposit is not regularly made, please inquire of Miss Malloch or let me know." Letter, LDB to FF, June 2, 1927, FF/LC, Box 27.

88. Interview with Harvard Law School Dean Albert M. Sacks, August 3, 1979, Cambridge, Massachusetts.

89. These figures were computed as of September, 1981, using consumer price indices listed in: *Statistical Abstract of the United States* (Washington, D.C.: Government Printing Office, 1957), p. 328; *Statistical Abstract of the United States* (Washington, D.C.: Government Printing Office, 1980), pp. 478, 487; *The Wall Street Journal*, February 26, 1979, p. 1; *The New York Times*, December 24, 1980, p. 1, col. 1; *The New York Times*, March 25, 1981, p. 1, col. 1., and *Washington Post*, September 25, 1981, p. 8. A range of values for the money has to be given because of fluctuations in the value of the dollar from year to year.

90. Interview with Paul A. Freund, October 26, 1977, Cambridge, Mass.

91. L. Baker, *Felix Frankfurter*, pp. 62–75.

92. LDB to Harold Laski, November 29, 1927, LDB/LLS, M18. The author wishes to thank Professor William Leuchtenburg for calling this letter to his attention.

93. Henry J. Abraham, *Justices and Presidents: A Political History of Appointments to the Supreme Court* (New York: Oxford University Press, 1974), pp. 166–67.

94. Letter, LDB to Julian W. Mack, January 12, 1922, FF/LC, Box 27. Twelve years later, Brandeis sent another letter to Mack confessing that he had been sending Frankfurter $3,500 "for years," see letter, LDB to Mack, March 11, 1934, as quoted in Dawson, *Brandeis, Frankfurter and the New Deal*, p. 4.

95. Interviews with Brandeis's former law clerks: Paul A. Freund, October 26, 1977, Cambridge, Massachusetts, the Honorable Judge Henry Friendly, April 14, 1978, (by phone); and David Riesman, July 26, 1979, Cambridge, Massachusetts. Some of the material discussed by Professor Freund in our interview was later published by him in "Justice Brandeis: A Law Clerk's Remembrance," LXVIII *American Jewish History* 1 (September 1978), pp. 7–18.

Chapter 2

1. Alpheus Mason, *Brandeis: A Free Man's Life* (New York: Viking Press, 1946), pp. 521–22; and letter, Alice Brandeis to Susan Gilbert, April 20, 1918, LDB/LLS, Box M 4-2. Also see Alfred Lief, *Brandeis: The Personal History of an American Ideal* (New York Stockpole Sons, 1936), pp. 407–8; and Ray Stannard Baker, *Woodrow Wilson: Life and Letters*, vol. VII (New York: Doubleday, Page and Company, 1939), p. 401.

2. Letter, Alice Brandeis to Susan Goldmark, April 20, 1918, LDB/LLS, Box M 4-2. The letter was written several months after the visit by President Wilson on December 9, 1917. Quoted also in Mason, *Brandeis*, p. 522.

3. Quoted in Baker, *Wilson Letters*, p. 401.

4. Lief, *Brandeis*, p. 407.

5. Letters, William McAdoo to LDB, January 31, 1918, LDB/LLS, Box WW 3; and William McAdoo to LDB, February 5, 1917, March 19, 1917, LDB/LLS, Box SC 3.

6. For example, one case involved possible appointments for Raymond Ingersoll and Hugh McLean. See letters, William McAdoo to LDB, January 30, 1917, February 12, 1917, LDB/LLS, Box SC 3, and FF to LDB, January 3, 1917, and February 5, 1917, FF/LC, Box 26.

7. Letters, Thomas Gregory to LDB, January 27, 1919, April 20, 1918, and April 18, 1917, LDB/LLS, Boxes, SC 4-2 and SC 3.

8. Letter, LDB to Thomas Gregory, March 15, 1917, LDB/LLS, Box SC 3.

9. Mason also says that Brandeis suggested John Clarke's name for this appointment. See Mason, *Brandeis*, p. 513.

10. Diaries of Colonel Edward M. House, June 19, 1916, Edward M. House MSS, Box 45, p. 215, Sterling Library, Yale University. There is no evidence that Gregory was told of *Brandeis's* support for the nomination, but because of their close friendship, it is quite likely that he knew.

This technique of advising politicians through intermediaries would become a trademark of the Brandeis extrajudicial approach.

11. There is no evidence that Frankfurter was acting on Brandeis's instructions. He wrote Colonel House that both men were excellent lawyers, "but also statesmen," with "open and vigorous mind[s]." See House Diaries, June 14, 1916, Edward M. House MSS, Box 45, Sterling Library, Yale University. For more on this incident see letter, FF to House, June 19, 1916, "Supreme Court file," Number 3522, House MSS, Sterling Library, Yale University.

This "free-agent" role was not typical of Frankfurter when dealing with the Department of Justice. Generally, he acted as an intermediary between Brandeis and the attorney general, For example, he passed on Brandeis's recommendation for the appointments of Phil Miller and Edward Costigan as assistant attorneys general. See letters, FF to LDB, "Thursday 1917 [undated], and February 1, 1917, LDB/LLS, Box SC 3.

12. Gregory's name was also suggested for the Supreme Court vacancy by Justice John H. Clarke, House Diaries, January 11, 1917, House MSS, Box 45, p. 17, Sterling Library, Yale University.

13. Baker, *Wilson Letters*, vol VII, p. 53.

14. Josephus Daniels, *The Wilson Era: Years of Peace, 1910–1917* (Chapel Hill, N.C.: University of North Carolina Press, 1946), p. 548.

15. Letters, Warren to LDB, March 18, 1918, LDB/LLS, Box WW 3, and Rowe to LDB, July 28, 1917, LDB/LLS, Box WW 1.

16. Letters, Colm to LDB, May 10, 1918 and April 4, 1917, LDB/LLS, Boxes SC 4-2, SC 3; Costigan to LDB, December 21, 1918, LDB/LLS, Box WW 3; McChord to LDB, July 17, 1918, LDB/LLS, Box WW 2-2; Aitchison to LDB, January 8, 1919, LDB/LLS, Box WW8; and Anderson to LDB, October 30, 1918, LDB/LLS, Boxes WW 2-2, WW 3.

17. Letters, Perkins to LDB, November 8, 1918, November 9, 1918, LDB/LLS, Box WW 4; Ripley to LDB, August 9, 1918, November 14, 1918, November 26, 1918, LDB/LLS, Box WW 4; Ingraham to LDB, April 6, 1917, April 11, 1917, and April 12, 1917, LDB/LLS, Box SC 3; Wigmore to LDB, November 11, 1918, LDB/LLS, Box WW 5. See also Mason, *Brandeis*, pp. 520–21, 526–27.

18. Letters, Gutheim to LDB, July 26, 1918, LDB/LLS, Box WW 3; Hines to LDB, May 1, 1918, LDB/LLS, Box SC 4–2.

19. Mason, *Brandeis*, pp. 522–3.

20. This occurred in October 1917. See Lief, *Brandeis*, pp. 406–7; and Ezekiel Rabinowitz, *Justice Louis D. Brandeis, the Zionist Chapter of His Life* (New York: The Philosophical Library, 1968), p. 72.

21. Mason, *Brandeis*, pp. 519–20. For more on the congressional battle over the Lever Act see Alfred H. Kelly and Winfred A. Harbison, *The American Constitution; Its Origins and Development* (New York: W. W. Norton & Company, 1963) pp. 660–61.

22. Memorandum of meeting between Lewis Strauss and Brandeis, November 18, 1918, FF/LC, Box 26. Strauss had visited the justice to ask for an appointment for his boss. To save Hoover some time, Brandeis gave this advice to Strauss. In the course of this discussion, the justice said that he also distrusted the "Kerensky group" because they were too "Czarist" and autocratic. Also quoted in Mason, *Brandeis*, pp. 527–28.

23. Edward M. House Diaries, January 9, 1918, House MSS, Vol. 13, Box 45, Sterling Library, Yale University.

   Frankfurter stayed on in the War Department after Theodore Roosevelt left office and, as a consequence, had built up a number of contacts. Then in April 1917 he was asked by Secretary of War Newton Baker to work in Washington, D.C. on various war-related problems. Later that year he worked on Woodrow Wilson's Mediation Commission. In 1918 he was asked by the Secretary of War Baker to write a report on the conditions in the department. This report was very critical of the operations of the secretary and his whole department and greatly offended Baker. Frankfurter called for a complete reorganization of the department, including "the creation of a singleheaded manager to direct the industrial energies of the war." See letter, Frankfurter to Newton Baker, January 8, 1918, House MSS, Box 45, Sterling Library, Yale University.

24. Letter, LDB to Edward M. House, January 9, 1918, FF/LC, Box 26. This letter is also quoted in Mason, *Brandeis*, pp. 523–24.

25. It is interesting to note here the concern of the justice for the fate of the Democratic party as well as for the nation.

26. Letter, LDB to Edward M. House, January 9, 1918, FF/LC, Box 26.

27. For more on the operations of the War Department during this time and the changes that were made see Robert C. Cuff, *The War Industries Board* (Baltimore: John Hopkins University Press, 1973), pp. 135–47, and Daniel R. Beaver, "Newton D. Baker and the Genesis of the War Industries Board, 1917–18," *The Journal of American History*, 1965, pp. 43–58.

28. Edward M. House Diaries, February 23, 1918, House MSS, vol. 13, Box 45, and letter, LDB to House, March 3, 1918, House MSS, Box 18, Sterling Library, Yale University. Before anything could be done, Baker named Secretary Crowell to the position. Thus, there was nothing more for House to do on this matter.

29. Frankfurter's efforts to have Brandeis named to the War Labor Policies board probably occurred without the justice's knowledge. See letter, FF to Newton Baker, April 30, 1918, (on microfilm), Frankfurter MSS, Harvard Law School (hereinafter cited only as FF/HLS). Also, see Mason, *Brandeis*, pp. 524–25.

30. Undated memorandum, FF to LDB, 1918, LDB/LLS, Box WW 4, (concerning wage rates in the lumber industry). See also letters, FF to LDB, September 28, 1918, August 5, 1918, LDB/LLS, Box WW 4 and Walton Hamilton to LDB, October 28, 1918, LDB/LLS, Box WW 4.

31. Letter, Cooke to LDB, April 13, 1918, July 13, 1918, LDB/LLS, Boxes WW 4, WW 3; McCarthy to LDB, June 17, 1918, October 7, 1918, LDB/LLS, Box WW 3.

32. A count of Brandeis's opinions (majority, concurring, and dissenting) during his early years on the Court reveals the following: 1916 Court term—23 opinions; 1917 Court term—28 opinions; 1918 Court term—opinions; 1919 Court term—25 opinions; 1920 Court term—26 opinions; 1921 Court term—26 opinions; 1922 Court term—31 opinions; and 1923 Court term—28 opinions.

33. *The Selective Draft Law Cases* (*Arver v. United States*), 245 U.S. 366 (1918).

For more on the Court's decisions in cases involving the war powers used in World War I, see Kelly and Harbison, *The American Constitution*, chapter 25. The cases that are discussed in the following section are drawn largely from the citations on pp. 662–64 of that book.

34. The Court upheld this act in two separate cases: *Hamilton v. Kentucky Distilleries Co.*, 251 U.S. 146 (1919), and *Rupert v. Caffey*, 251 U.S. 264 (1920).

The story of how the Court came to have a unanimous decision in the *Hamilton* case is most interesting. According to Brandeis's account for Felix Frankfurter years later, the initial conference vote in the case was five to four with Brandeis in the majority and Oliver Wendell Holmes in dissent. Chief Justice White realized that Brandeis was the associate justice most likely to write an opinion that might sway Holmes so he assigned the majority opinion to him, hoping to bring Holmes over to the majority opinion. Not only was Brandeis successful in swaying Holmes's vote, but he secured the votes of his three other reluctant colleagues as well. See Memorandum, "Conversations Between LDB and FF," (p. 23), FF/LC, Box 224.

35. Memorandum, "Conversations Between LDB and FF," (p. 1), FF/LC, Box 224. In another section of this document, though, Frankfurter records Brandeis's complaint about what he viewed as his colleague's penchant for deciding cases on the basis of philosophical rather than "real world" factual bases: "Holmes has no realization of what moves men—he is as innocent as a girl of sixteen is supposed to have been . . . he doesn't understand or appreciate facts." (p. 3).

36. In these cases Holmes and Brandeis articulated and developed the "clear-and-present-danger" standard. According to this standard, "the United States constitutionally may punish speech that produces or is intended to produce a clear and imminent danger that it will bring about forthwith certain substantive evils that the United States constitutionally may seek to prevent." *Abrams v. United States*, 250 U.S. 616 (1919), at p. 627.

In the early cases, Holmes and Brandeis used this standard to uphold what amounted to government censorship, on the grounds that during times of war one must grant wide leeway to the government. (See *Schenck v. United States*, 249 U.S. 47 (1919), *Debs v. United States* 249 U.S. 211 (1919), and *Frohwerk v. United States*, 249 U.S. 204 (1919). Years later, Brandeis confessed to Frankfurter that he was "never quite happy" with his acquiescence to these decisions. He attributed his action to the fact that he "had not then thought the issues of freedom of speech out— [he had] thought at the subject, not through it." (Memorandum, "Conversations Between LDB and FF," p. 23, FF/LC, Box 224).

Beginning in *Abrams v. United States*, however, Holmes and Brandeis began to use the clear-and-present-danger test to uphold the interest of free speech in the face of such government regulation. As Brandeis put it in dissent in *Schaefer v. United States* (251 U.S. 466 (1920)): "Correctly applied, [this test] will preserve the right of free speech both from suppression by tyrannous, well-meaning majorities and from abuse by irresponsible, fanatical minorities." (at p. 482). It would be another three decades before the Supreme Court adopted the Holmes-Brandeis standard, and, even then, the test, as utilized, would have been unrecognizable to its original authors and probably repudiated by them. (See *Dennis v. United States*, 341 U.S. 494 (1951)). As in his work off the Court, throughout the 1920s Brandeis was doomed to speak from a minority position on this matter. (See also *Pierce v. United States*, 252 U.S. 232 (1919)).

37. *Northern Pacific Ry. Co. v. North Dakota ex. rel. Langer*, 250 U.S. 135 (1919). See also Kelly and Harbison, *The American Constitution*, p. 663–69.

38. The two cases that overruled portions of section four of the Lever Food Control Act

were: *United States v. L. Cohen Grocery Co.*, 255 U.S. 81 (1921), and *Weeds Inc. v. United States*, 255 U.S. 109 (1921).

39. See *Bunting v. Oregon*, 243 U.S. 426 (1917); *Stettler v. O'Hara*, and *Simpson v. O'Hara*, 243 U.S. 629 (1917), and *Adkins v. Children's Hospital*, 261 U.S. 525 (1923). Brandeis's decision to disqualify himself from hearing the first three cases is not surprising since he had helped to write the brief for the *Bunting* case, had argued the *Stettler* case before the Oregon and United States Supreme Courts, and had already argued the *Simpson* case before the Oregon Supreme Court. Felix Frankfurter argued the cases for the National Consumers' League, seeking to have the Supreme Court uphold the law in each instance.

40. No challenge to the Overman Act, which gave the president vast powers to reorganize the government, ever came before the Supreme Court. It would have been interesting to see whether Justice Brandeis would have disqualified himself from that case, since it was his suggestion that seemingly led the Wilson Administration to seek the adoption of this legislation.

41. See letter, Louis Lipsky to LDB, February 11, 1919, LDB/LLS, Box ZP 26. For Brandeis's rise in the organization, see Gal, *Brandeis of Boston*, pp. 202–7; Urofsky, *Mind of One Piece*, 95–108.

42. The following account greatly benefitted from Melvin I. Urofsky, *American Zionism from Herzl to the Holocaust* (Garden City, New York: Doubleday, 1975), and Robert Silverberg, *If I Forget Thee, O Jerusalem* (New York: Pyramid Books, 1970).

43. Chaim Weizmann, *Trial and Error, The Autobiography of Chaim Weizmann* (New York: Harper and Bros., 1949), pp. 149–50, 238–39.

44. Silverberg, *O Jerusalem*, pp. 85–89. The British were privately rethinking their position.

45. Letter, Chaim Weizmann to LDB, April 8, 1917, quoted in Silverberg, *O Jerusalem*, p. 76.

46. Memorandum by Jacob DeHaas, May 9, 1917, quoted in Rabinowitz, *Brandeis*, p. 63. Also quoted in Melvin Urofsky and David Levy, *Letters of Louis D. Brandeis*, vol. IV (Albany, N.Y.: State University of New York, 1975), p. 286.

47. Ibid.

48. Letter, Brandeis to DeHaas, May 8, 1917, in Urofsky and Levy, *Brandeis Letters*, vol. IV, pp. 288–89; Urofsky, *American Zionism*, pp. 207–8.

49. Letter, Brandeis to DeHaas, May 10, 1917, in Urofsky and Levy, *Brandeis Letters*, vol. IV, p. 290. The justice held another meeting with Balfour on May 9.

50. William Yale, "Ambassador Henry Morgenthau's Special Mission of 1917," I *World Politics*, pp. 308–20. On page 310, Yale says: "Interestingly enough it was Justice Brandeis, one of the leading American Zionists, who suggested that Mr. Frankfurter should accompany Mr. Morgenthau on his special mission."

51. Letter, LDB to Jacob DeHaas, June 7, 1917, in Urofsky and Levy, *Brandeis Letters*, vol. IV, p. 296.

52. Urofsky, *American Zionism*, p. 209.

53. Ibid., pp. 204, 210–11.

54. Urofsky and Levy, *Brandeis Letters*, vol. IV, p. 310.

55. For the various theories concerning these events see Leonard Stein, *The Balfour Declaration* (London: Vallentine and Mitchell, 1961), chapter 34; Isaiah Friedman, *The Question of Palestine; British-Jewish-Arab Relations* (New York: Schocken Books, 1973), *passim*; Selig Adler, "The Palestine Question in the Wilson Era," X *Journal of Jewish Social Studies* 4 (1948), pp. 304–44; Herbert Parzen, "Brandeis and the Balfour Declaration," V *Herzl Yearbook* (1963), pp. 309–50; Mason, *Brandeis*, p. 453, Urofsky, *American Zionism*, p. 211–12; Urofsky and Levy, *Brandeis Letters*, vol. IV, pp. 310–11.

My interpretation agrees with that of Richard Lebow, who, unlike the scholars cited above, also had the opportunity to consult the House diaries on these matters. See Richard N. Lebow, "Woodrow Wilson and the Balfour Declaration," 40 *Journal of Modern History* (1968), pp. 501–23.

Wilson was caught between the advice of Brandeis and that of Colonel House, who urged caution in all these matters. See Urofsky, *American Zionism*, pp. 210–11; see also Silverberg, *O Jerusalem*, p. 91.

56. Letter, Chaim Weizmann to Brandeis, September 19, 1917, Urofsky and Levy, *Brandeis Letters*, vol. II, p. 310. Weizmann also cabled DeHaas urging him to press Brandeis for more action on these matters and for taking no chances in negotiations.

57. House Diaries, September 22, 1917, House MSS, vol. II, Box 45, pp. 286–87, Sterling Library, Yale University.

58. Urofsky and Levy, *Brandeis Letters,* vol. IV, p. 311.

59. Letter, LDB to Weizmann, September 24, 1917, House MSS, Box 18, Sterling Library, Yale University.

60. House Diaries, September 23, 1917, House MSS, vol. 11, Box 45, p. 290, Sterling Library, Yale University. Brandeis also advised the colonel in this meeting on such matters as appointments to the Interstate Commerce Commission and on "our future relations with South American" and "several other matters."

On foreign policy the views of the justice were that "Germany will try to penetrate South America with the civilization, and that we should meet it at every point and try to offset it. He thought if Germany was successful, sometime in the future, another conflict would occur and perhaps on this Continent."

61. Letter, Brandeis to Weizmann, September 24, 1917, House MSS, Box 18, Sterling Library, Yale University.

62. Letter, LDB to House, September 24, 1917, House MSS, Box 18, Sterling Library, Yale University.

63. Silverberg, *O Jerusalem*, pp. 92–93.

64. Letter, Weizmann to Brandeis, October 7, 1917, quoted in Rabinowitz, *Brandeis,* pp. 68–71.

65. Letter, Weizmann to Brandeis, October 10, 1917, quoted in Rabinowitz, *Brandeis*, p. 71.

66. Urofsky, *American Zionism*, p. 212; Silverberg, *O Jerusalem*, p. 94; and Rabinowitz, *Brandeis*, pp. 72–73. For example, Brandeis wanted the term "Jewish people" substituted for "Jewish Race." Wilson did not publicly support the document until ten months later.

67. Text quoted in Urofsky, *American Zionism*, pp. 212–13.

68. See Urofsky and Levy, *Brandeis Letters*, vol. IV, pp. 301ff. There is a good account of the actions of Judge Julian Mack in Harry Barnard, *The Forging of an American Jew: The Life and Times of Judge Julian W. Mack* (New York: Herzl Press, 1974).

The ZOA was created from the various Jewish organizations at the Pittsburgh Convention on June 25, 1918. For the details see Urofsky, *American Zionism*, pp. 255–56.

69. Letter, Jacob DeHaas to Brandeis, August 26, 1918, quoted in Rabinowitz, *Brandeis*, p. 43.

70. Urofsky and Levy, *Brandeis Letters*, vol. IV, pp. 354–55.

71. Letter, Brandeis to Stephen S. Wise, December 29, 1918, quoted in Mason, *Brandeis*, p. 455.

72. Urofsky and Levy, *Brandeis Letters*, vol. IV, p. 397; Phillips, ed., *Frankfurter Reminisces*, chapter 16 was useful in this section.

73. Letter, FF to Marion Denman, February 9, 1919, FF/LC, Box 6.

74. Letters, Frankfurter to Brandeis, May 19, 1919, May 21, 1919, May 22, 1919, and May 30, 1919, FF/HLS (on microfilm). See also letters, Frankfurter to Wilson, May 14, 1919, and Wilson to Frankfurter, May 16, 1919, LDB/LLS, Box ZP 26. Also of interest are letters, Brandeis to Frankfurter, June 5, 1919 and June 9, 1919, quoted in Urofsky and Levy, *Brandeis Letters*, vol. IV, pp. 396–97.

75. Letter, Oliver Wendell Holmes to Harold J. Laski, October 5, 1919, quoted in Mark DeWolfe Howe, ed., *Holmes-Laski Letters: The Correspondence of Mr. Justice Holmes and Harold J. Laski, 1916–1935* (Cambridge, Mass: Harvard University Press, 1953), p. 212. Howe confirms, in a footnote on the same page, that these "experiences" were the ones enjoyed by Brandeis on his European trip.

76. Mason, *Brandeis*, p. 456.

77. Brandeis to Alice Brandeis, June 22, 1919, in Urofsky and Levy, *Brandeis Letters*, vol. IV, p. 404. Also quoted in Mason, *Brandeis*, p. 456.

78. House Diaries, entries for March 26, April 15, and April 29, 1919, vol. 15, pp. 161–80; also letters, Frankfurter to House, April 14, and 30, 1919, House MSS, Box 45, Sterling Library, Yale University.

79. Letter, Frankfurter to Feisal, March 3, 1919, and Feisal to Frankfurter, March 3, 1919, FF/LC, Box 27.

80. House Diaries, June 23, 1919, June 24, 1919, House MSS, vol. 15, p. 250, Sterling Library, Yale University.

81. Mason, *Brandeis*, p. 456.

82. Memorandum of Brandeis meeting, June 24, 1919, quoted in Rabinowitz, *Brandeis*, pp. 112–15.

83. Letters, Frankfurter to Marion Denman, June 24, 1919; June 25, 1919, August 14, 1919, August 16, 1919, August 22, 1919, August 29, 1919, and a number of undated letters written in this period, FF/LC, Box 8.

84. Letter, Brandeis to Alice Brandeis, August 8, 1919, in Urofsky and Levy, *Brandeis Letters*, vol. IV, p. 421.

85. House Diaries, August 7, 1919, House MSS, vol. 15, Box 46, p. 19, Sterling Library, Yale University. Also letter, Frankfurter to Marion Denman, August 7, 1919, FF/LC, Box 9.

86. Rabinowitz, *Brandeis*, p. 92.

87. Ibid., p. 92, see also letter, Brandeis to Alice Brandeis, August 8, 1919, in Urofsky and Levy, *Brandeis Letters*, vol. IV, p. 421.

88. Rabinowitz, *Brandeis*, pp. 99. Urofsky, *American Zionism*, pp. 236–37.

89. Letters, Brandeis to Wilson, February 3, 1929, in Urofsky and Levy, *Brandeis Letters*, vol. IV, p. 446–47.

90. Letter, Brandeis to Julian Mack, February 9, 1920, in Urofsky and Levy, *Brandeis Letters*, vol. IV, p. 447.

91. Rabinowitz, *Brandeis*, pp. 116–17. There were letters from Brandeis to Balfour on February 1, 1920 and to Tradieu on February 2, 1920.

92. Mason, *Brandeis*, p. 458. The letter to Weizmann was dated February 16, 1920.

93. Brandeis repeated this rule to virtually everyone with whom he spoke. Interview with Benjamin V. Cohen, Washington, D.C., September 29, 1977. See also Paul and Elizabeth Raushenbush Reminiscences, Columbia Oral History Collection (hereinafter cited only as COHC), p. 115, Butler Library, Columbia University.

94. Urofsky, *Mind of One Piece*, p. 106.

95. Letter, LDB to Weizmann, January 13, 1918, FF/HLS (on microfilm). Colonel House also advised against any encouragement by the Americans for this conference because we were not yet at war with Turkey and President Wilson did not want a joint American-British protectorate over the area.

96. Mason, *Brandeis*, pp. 454–55.
97. See letters, LDB to DeHaas, February 6, 1917, LDB to DeHaas, July 5, 1916, LDB to DeHaas, November 22, 1917, LDB to Mack, Wise, Louis Lipsky and DeHaas, October 25, 1919, and LDB to Clarence I. DeSola, June 23, 1916, in Urofsky and Levy, *Brandeis Letters*, vol. IV, pp. 272, 244–47, 322–23, 435, 227–28. See also Urofsky, *Mind of One Piece*, p. 103.
98. See, e.g., Brandeis to Frankfurter, October 13, 1919 and December 4, 1919, in Urofsky and Levy, *Brandeis Letters*, vol. IV, pp. 431, 439–40.
99. Mason, *Brandeis*, pp. 458–60.
100. It appears that Brandeis also avoided the leadership role on the advice of his lieutenants in the organization. See letter, LDB to FF, May 22, 1921, FF/LC, Box 27.
101. For a short account of this incident, see Urofsky and Levy, *Brandeis Letters*, vol. IV, p. 563; see also Urofsky, *American Zionism*, pp. 285–98.
102. Letters, FF to Jacob DeHaas, July 26, 1921, FF/LC, Box 26; and LDB to FF, February 3, 1922, LDB to Solomon Rosenbloom, June 25, 1922, LDB to Julian Mack, October 20, 1923, and October 30, 1923, LDB to Nathan Strauss, April 25, 1922, and LDB to FF, October 24, 1923, LDB to Julian Mack, January 4, 1924, and LDB to Jacob DeHaas, February 14, 1924, in Urofsky and Levy, *Brandeis Letters*, vol. V, pp. 43–44, 51, 54–55, 102–4, 417–18, and 420–22.
103. Letters, LDB to FF, January 1, 1927, February 15, 1927, and February 26, 1927, LDB to Jacob DeHaas, June 5, 1927, LDB to Jacob Gilbert, April 18, 1928, and LDB to Julian Mack, May 21, 1928, and July 5, 1928, all in Urofsky and Levy, *Brandeis Letters*, vol. V, pp. 291–92, 336, 343, 347–48, 427–28, and 472–73. See also Urofsky, *American Zionism*, pp. 314–16.
104. Letters, LDB to FF, September 20, 1929, and LDB to Mack, September 20, 1929, September 29, 1929, and October 1, 1929, also October 20, 1929, and January 29, 1930 on Brandeis's concern with the discriminatory operations of the government there and the operation of the Hadassah (the women's Zionist fund-raising operation), all in Urofsky and Levy, *Brandeis Letters*, vol. V, pp. 385–89, 397–98, 407–9.

 On Brandeis's financial contributions, see letters, LDB to Mack, February 7, 1930, February 13, 1930 and March 9, 1930, March 16, 1930, LDB to Israel Brodie, February 6, 1930. These letters show that the justice was paying $400 a month to finance DeHaas's salary in the organization (LDB to Szold, January 18, 1931), and was also financing the publication of *Davar English Supplement*, on the Zionist labor groups (LDB to Nathan Kaplan, June 15, 1930), all in Urofsky and Levy, *Brandeis Letters*, vol. V, pp. 417–19, 420–22, 427–28, and 472–73.
105. At this point in his life Brandeis also decided that even his private efforts for Zionism had to be controlled. Due to advancing age and the Court duties imposed on him, LDB told FF that he could meet with Zionists only in the summer recess months. When the Court was in session the justice wished to "confine his activities to thinking and exercising judgement," with the results communicated privately to these leaders by the Brandeis lieutenants. See letter, LDB to FF, September 23, 1929, in Urofsky and Levy, *Brandeis Letters*, vol. V, pp. 389–91.

 For more on the long negotiations during the 1920s leading to the formation of the Jewish Agency, see Urofsky, *American Zionism*, chapters 8 and 9.
106. Letter, LDB to FF, September 6, 1929, in Urofsky and Levy, *Brandeis Letters*, Vol. V, pp. 383–85.
107. Letter, LDB to Julian Mack, October 9, 1929, in Urofsky and Levy, *Brandeis Letters*, vol. V, pp. 400–2.
108. "Memorandum for Judge Mack and Mr. DeHaas," written by Felix Frankfurter,

October 3, 1929, FF/LC, Box 83. See also, Urofsky, *American Zionism,* p. 362–63.

109. Later letters by the justice show that he was very reluctant to come out publicly and speak at that meeting. See letters, LDB to FF, October 5, 1929 and November 29, 1929, in Urofsky and Levy, *Brandeis Letters,* vol. V, pp. 398–99.

110. *The New York Times,* Nov. 25, 1929, p. 3; also Urofsky, *American Zionism,* pp. 362–64.

111. Memorandum by Brandeis on his meeting with Lindsay, undated, FF/LC, Box 28. See also letter, Lindsay to LDB, June 10, 1930, FF/LC, Box 28.

112. Urofsky, *American Zionism,* p. 381.

113. Urofsky, *American Zionism,* pp. 366–89, 380–81.

114. Letters, LDB to Mack, June 11, 1930, June 19, 1930, and June 27, 1930, all in Urofsky and Levy, *Brandeis Letters,* vol. II, pp. 426–29.

115. Letters, LDB to Julian Mack, July 4, 1930, July 6, 1930, July 12, 1930, July 16, 1930, July 20, 1930, August 6, 1930, LDB to Szold, August 3, 1930, August 18, 1930, August 19, 1930, and August 20, 1930, LDB to DeHaas, August 31, 1930, all in Urofsky and Levy, *Brandeis Letters,* vol. V, pp. 430–40, 443–52. See also letters, LDB to Mack, August 4, 1930, and LDB to FF, September 12, 1930, September 19, 1930, October 9, 1930, FF/LC, Box 28.

116. Letter, Laski to Holmes, December 27, 1930, in Howe, *Holmes-Laski, Letters,* pp. 1301–02, as quoted in Lash, ed., *Frankfurter Diaries,* pp. 41–42.

117. Urofsky, *American Zionism,* pp. 381–83. The report was issued on October 21, 1930.

118. Letter, LDB to FF (on meeting with Hoover), October 29, 1930, FF/LC Box 28.

119. Letters, LDB to FF, November 13, 1930, and also LDB to FF, November 15, 1930, and December 17, 1930, FF/LC, Box 28.

120. See letters, quoted in Urofsky and Levy, *Brandeis Letters,* vol. V, pp. 459–71.

121. Urofsky, *American Zionism,* pp. 383–84. MacDonald gave Brandeis the perfect entree when he asked Laski for a visit to offer advice on the situation. It is impossible to know exactly what influence the justice had on these events.

122. See letters, from LDB to Szold, November 15, 1930, December 6, 1930, December 19, 1930, January 10, 1931, January 18, 1931, March 3, 1931, May 29, 1931, and June 10, 1931, all in Urofsky and Levy, *Brandeis Letters,* vol. V, pp. 461–62, 468–69, 469–71, 472–73, 474, and 478–79; also see generally, pp. 461–92.

123. Interview with Paul A. Freund, October 26, 1977, Cambridge, Massachusetts. Freund subsequently recorded this story, and resserts that Brandeis never spoke on the phone following his judicial appointment, in: "Justice Brandeis: A Law Clerk's Remembrance," *American Jewish History,* 1978, p. 16.

Chapter 3

1. On Taft's activities see Alpheus T. Mason, *William Howard Taft: Chief Justice* (New York: Simon and Schuster, 1964), pp. 158–60, 278, and 297–98; Walter F. Murphy, "In His Own Image: Mr. Chief Justice Taft and Supreme Court Appointments," *Supreme Court Review,* 1961, pp. 167–77; and Walter F. Murphy, "Chief Justice Taft and the Lower Court Bureaucracy," 24 *Journal of Politics* (1962), pp. 453–59.

   On Stone's activities see Alpheus T. Mason, *Harlan Fiske Stone: Pillar of the Law* (New York: Viking Press, 1956), pp. 266, 270–71, 285, 474 fn., and 707 fn.

2. Letters, LDB to FF, March 17, 1929, March 17, 1930, April 15, 1930, February 3, 1932, February 13, 1932, February 16, 1932, and February 25, 1932, FF/LC, Boxes 27, 28; also see letters, LDB to FF, March 6, 1929, March 13, 1929,

March 17, 1929, April 3, 1929, June 15, 1929, September 6, 1929, and December 2, 1929, in Melvin Urofsky and David Levy, ed., *Letters of Louis D. Brandeis*,
vol. V, Albany, N.Y.: State University of New York, 1975), pp. 371–415. For information on Brandeis's role in the appointment of Justice Benjamin Cardozo, see Ira
Ho Carmen, "The President, Politics, and the Power of Appointment: Hoover's
Nomination of Mr. Justice Cardozo," 55 *Virginia Law Review* (1969), pp. 620–51.

3. Several drafts of "The Document" are in LDB/LLS, Box M 17-3. See also letter to
Woodrow Wilson, June 25, 1921, in Urofsky and Levy, *Brandeis Letters*, Vol. IV, p.
568; Alpheus Mason, *Brandeis; A Free Man's Life* (New York: Viking, 1946), pp.
534–35; and Melvin Urofsky, *A Mind of One Piece; Brandeis and American Reform*
(New York: Charles Scribner's Sons, 1971), p. 127.

4. *United States v. Chicago, Milwaukee, St. Paul and Pacific Railroad*, 282 U.S. 311,
(1930). This case was decided on January 5, 1931.

5. See letters, LDB to FF, January 26, 1931, and February 2, 1931, FF/LC, Box 28; and
Senator Robert La Follette, Jr., to FF, February 10, 1931, and February 19, 1931,
FF/LC, Box 80.

   For a more-extended example of how Brandeis used Frankfurter to get congressional legislation passed, in this case seeking to alter the diversity-of-citizenship
jurisdiction, and to overturn the Supreme Court's decision, in *Black and White
Taxi Co. v. Brown and Yellow Taxi Co.*, 276 U.S. 518 (1928), see David W. Levy
and Bruce Allen Murphy, "Preserving the Progressive Spirit in a Conservative Time:
The Joint Reform Efforts of Justice Brandeis and Professor Felix Frankfurter, 1916–
1933," 78 *Michigan Law Review* (1980), pp. 1252–1304.

6. Interview with Edward F. Prichard, Jr., June 25, 1979, Frankfort, Kentucky.

7. Interview with Philip Elman, July 10, 1979, Washington, D.C.

8. The notebooks are in LDB/HLS, Box 114, Folder 8. A transcription of portions of
these conversations is filed in FF/LC, Box 224.

9. Letter, FF, to Marion Denman Frankfurter, July 7, 1924, FF/LC, Box 12, as quoted
in H.N. Hirsch, *The Enigma of Felix Frankfurter* (New York: Basic Books, 1981), p.
86.

10. Letter, FF to Marion Denman Frankfurter, July 2, 1924, FF/LC, Box 12, as quoted in
H. N. Hirsch, *Enigma of Frankfurter*, p. 86.

11. Some good books on the Sacco-Vanzetti case are: Herbert B. Ehrmann, *The Case
That Will Not Die* (Boston: Little, Brown and Co., 1969); M.S. Musmanno, *After
Twelve Years: The Sacco-Vanzetti Case* (New York: Alfred A. Knopf, 1939); and F.
Russell, *Tragedy in Dedham—The Story of the Sacco-Vanzetti Case* (New York:
McGraw-Hill, 1962).

12. See Felix Frankfurter, "The Case of Sacco and Vanzetti," *Atlantic Monthly*, Vol.
139 (March 1927), pp. 409–32; Felix Frankfurter, *The Case of Sacco and Vanzetti:
A Critical Analysis for Lawyers and Laymen* (Boston: Little, Brown and Co., 1927);
and Harlan Phillips, ed., *Felix Frankfurter Reminisces* (New York: Reynal and Co.,
1960), chapter 20.

13. Phillips, ed., *Frankfurter Reminisces*, p. 210. There is a discrepancy in the spelling
of Mrs. Evans's nickname. Quoting Frankfurter, Phillips uses "Auntie Bee," but I
rely on the spelling that Brandeis uses in his personal letters. See letters, LDB to
FF, July 22, 1927, Urofsky and Levy, *Brandeis Letters*, vol. V, p. 297.

   Apparently, Brandeis's wife and daughter Susan joined Mrs. Evans's efforts to
defend Sacco and Vanzetti. See *The New York Times*, August 22, 1927, p. 1, col.
8, cited in Urofsky and Levy, *Brandeis Letters*, Vol. V, p. 299.

14. Letter, LDB to FF, November 8, 1925, FF/LC, Box 27. My explanation of the meanng
of this letter relies on Urofsky and Levy, *Brandeis Letters*, Vol. V, p. 194.

15. "We are glad to hear that the S.V. article is so far advanced." Letter, LDB to FF, January 1, 1927, FF/LC, Box 27, and "there are rumors of an S.V. article in the forthcoming March *Atlantic* to which we are looking forward," letter, LDB to FF, February 26, 1927, FF/LC, Box 27.

16. Letter, LDB to FF, March 4, 1927, FF/LC, Box 27. Brandeis also asked Frankfurter for a copy of his Sacco-Vanzetti book on March 9, 1927; see letter, LDB to FF, March 9, 1927, FF/LC, Box 27. For more letters in which LDB discusses Frankfurter's involvement with the case, see letters to Frankfurter dated: March 29, 1927, April 6, 1927, April 26, 1927, April 27, 1927, April 29, 1927, May 2, 1927, May 6, 1927, May 21, 1927, and May 25, 1927, FF/LC, Box 27.

17. Letter, LDB to FF, June 2, 1927, FF/LC, Box 27. This letter is of interest not only because it contains the overt offer of financial assistance but because Brandeis seems here to be communicating to Frankfurter that he is aware of the likelihood that as a consequence of Sacco-Vanzetti, Frankfurter has likely dipped into some of the money Brandeis had sent him that year for the joint-endeavors fund. The justice was thus offering to restore some of those funds in order to underwrite the many other political activities that would be undertaken at his request that year. Consequently, even without this new offer of monetary assistance, one might argue that Brandeis already realized that his long-term financial relationship with Frankfurter might in and of itself compromise his ability to hear the appeal on this case when it reached the Supreme Court.

18. Letter, LDB to FF, August 16, 1927, FF/LC, Box 27.

19. For more on the formation and actions of the two separate Sacco-Vanzetti defense committees, see Russell, *Tragedy in Dedham*, pp. 427–28.

20. Transcripts of state police wiretaps on Felix Frankfurter, dated August 21, 1927, p. 3, Secretary of State's office, Government Center, Boston, Massachusetts.

21. Ibid., August 9, 1927, p. 1.

22. Ibid., August 9, 1927, p. 6 and August 20, 1027, p. 17.

23. Letter, LDB to FF, August 24, 1927, FF/LC, Box 27.

24. The appeal was dismissed by the Supreme Court on October 3, 1927. *Sacco and Vanzetti v. Commonwealth of Massachusetts*, 275 U.S. 574 (1927).

25. Note 20, above, September 6, 1927, p. 5.

26. *The New Republic*, September 14, 1927, p. 83.

27. 277 U.S. 438 (1928).

28. Ibid., at pp. 474, 478, and 483.

29. Ibid., at p. 485.

30. Letter, LDB to FF, December 21, 1926, FF/LC, Box 27. Brandeis had asked for this information in an earlier letter, see LDB to FF, December 16, 1926, FF/LC, Box 27.

31. 273 U.S. 34 (1927).

32. Ibid., at pp. 42–43. Here Brandeis cited the article by Frankfurter and James Landis, "The Compact Clause of the Constitution—A Study in Interstate Adjustments," 34 *Yale Law Journal* (1925), pp. 685ff. Of course, this research assistance was fine training for the man who would become a Supreme Court justice in 1939.

33. See James M. Landis, "Mr. Justice Brandeis and Harvard Law School," 55 *Harvard Law Review* (1941), p. 189, and letter, LDB to FF, March 17, 1925, FF/LC, Box 27.
   Verifying Landis's statement about Brandeis's contributions to this fellowship are a series of yearly letters to LDB from FF reporting on the accomplishments of the research fellow, which begin by saying that this is "a report on the workings of the Research Fellowship which you helped to make possible." See letter, FF to LDB, September 30, 1925, September 28, 1926, February 3, 1928, and November 12, 1928, LDB/LLS, Box SC 8.

34. For more on Landis, see Donald Ritchie, *James M. Landis: Dean of the Regulators* (Cambridge, Mass.: Harvard University Press, 1980).
35. 38 *Harvard Law Review* (1925), pp. 1005–59.
36. Frankfurter and Landis, "Business of the Supreme Court of the United States—A Study in the Federal Judicial System," 39 *Harvard Law Review* (1925–26), pp. 35–81, 325–67, 587–627, and 1046–71; and 40 *Harvard Law Review* (1926–27), pp. 431–68, 834–73, and 1105–29.

    Some of the suggestions made by Brandeis for study in this initial series can be found in letters, LDB to FF, April 20, 1924, May 2, 1926, August 15, 1926, and August 23, 1926, FF/LC, Box 27.
37. The book citation is Felix Frankfurter and James M. Landis, *The Business of the Supreme Court, A Study in the Federal Judicial System* (New York: Macmillan Co., 1927).

    After lobbying with Senator George W. Norris on the Supreme Court's diversity-of-citizenship jurisdiction in May 1927, Brandeis had Frankfurter send the senator copies of the *Harvard Law Review* "Business" articles, since the book was not yet in print. See letter, LDB to FF, May 17, 1927, FF/LC, Box 27. The following year, after lobbying with Senators John J. Blaine and Robert LaFollette, Jr., as well as with Representative R. Walton Moore concerning the same issue, Brandeis asked Frankfurter to send each man a copy of the book. See letters, LDB to FF, February 11, 1928, and March 4, 1928, FF/LC, Box 27. For more on Brandeis's lobbying efforts for judicial reform see Levy and Murphy, "Preserving the Progressive Spirit in a Conservative Time," 78 *Michigan Law Review* 1252 (1980), pp. 1273–78.
38. These articles, co-authored by Frankfurter over the years, highlighted the decisions and various problems encountered by the Supreme Court in an individual term. See Frankfurter and James M. Landis, "Business of the Supreme Court at October Term, 1928," 43 *Harvard Law Review* (1929), and "Business of the Supreme Court at October Term, 1930," 45 *Harvard Law Review* (1931), pp. 271–306; Frankfurter and Henry M. Hart, Jr., "Business of the Supreme Court at October Term, 1933," 48 *Harvard Law Review* (1934), pp. 238–75; and Frankfurter and Adrian S. Fisher, "Business of the Supreme Court at October Terms, 1935 and 1936," 51 *Harvard Law Review* (1938), pp. 577–609. Interestingly, a modified version of this series, which reviews the Supreme Court's actions on a yearly basis, still continues to appear in the *Harvard Law Review*.

    Examples of the letters Brandeis sent to Frankfurter enclosing ideas, evidence, and even partial outlines for some of these "Business" articles are: letters, LDB to FF, April 20, 1927, June 5, 1927, July 29, 1927, March 16, 1928, October 18, 1928, December 5, 1929, and December 21, 1929, FF/LC, Box 27.

    The initial series on the Supreme Court was so successful that Brandeis even tried unsuccessfully to convince Frankfurter to begin a similar study of the lower federal courts. See letters, LDB to FF, July 7, 1928, and October 10, 1928, FF/LC, Box 27.
39. For more on lobbying by members of the Court for the Judiciary Act of 1925 see Walter F. Murphy, *Elements of Judicial Strategy* (Chicago: University of Chicago Press, 1964), pp. 138–45; and Mason, *William Howard Taft*, pp. 109–16.
40. Letter, LDB to FF, October 29, 1927, FF/LC, Box 27.
41. Letter, LDB to FF, November 13, 1927, FF/LC, Box 27. Brandeis's law clerk that year was Henry J. Friendly, now senior judge for the United States Court of Appeals for the Second Circuit.

    Brandeis knew that Frankfurter would be able to understand this new information because five months earlier he had sent the professor a long letter detailing

topics to be explored from the Court's new procedures under the Judiciary Act of
1925. See letter, LDB to FF, June 5, 1927, FF/LC, Box 27.

42. 42 *Harvard Law Review* (1928), pp. 1–29.

43. Letters, LDB, to FF, May 2, 1926, March 16, 1928, October 18, 1928, and December
5, 1929, FF/LC, Box 27.

For more on the Federal Employers' Liability Acts of 1906 and 1908 see: *The
Constitution of the United States of America: Analysis and Interpretation* (Wash-
ington, D.C.: Government Printing Office, 1973), pp. 162, 766; and C. Herman
Pritchett, *The American Constitution* (New York: McGraw-Hill, 1968), p. 152.

44. Here the Court was operating under its power according to the *United States Statutes*, vol. 39, chapter 448 (1916).

45. Frankfurter and James M. Landis, "Business of the Supreme Court at October Term,
1928," 43 *Harvard Law Review* (1929), pp. 33–62, 52–53.

46. Letters, LDB to FF, August 8, 1926, January 18, 1928, FF/LC, Box 27.

47. Letters, LDB to FF, March 6, 1929, April 11, 1930, September 26, 1929, and February 14, 1930, FF/LC, Box 27.

48. Letter, LDB to FF, July 30, 1927, FF/LC, Box 27. As will be shown below, this
suggestion was certainly followed by Frankfurter and his seminar students in the
diversity-of-citizenship-jurisdiction area.

More Brandeis seminar suggestions appear in: letters, LDB to FF, June 16, 1922,
December 25, 1926, May 31, 1927, June 20, 1927, July 29, 1927, July 30, 1927,
March 16, 1928, July 11, 1928, July 14, 1928, December 5, 1929, and December 21,
1929, FF/LC, Box 27.

49. Interview with the Honorable Judge Henry J. Friendly, April 14, 1978 (by phone).
On occasion, Frankfurter would send Brandeis lists of the topics that had been
chosen by his students for their seminar papers. See letter, FF to LDB, February 7,
1917, LDB/LLS, Box SC 3.

50. Liva Baker, *Felix Frankfurter* (New York: Coward-McCann, Inc., 1969), p. 13, from
Francis Plimpton's "Reunion Runes," as quoted in Joseph Lash, ed., *From the Diaries of Felix Frankfurter* (New York: W. W. Norton and Co., 1975), p. 15.

51. Letter, LDB to FF, June 25, 1926, FF/LC, Box 27.

52. 46 *Harvard Law Review* (1932–33), pp. 361–403, 593–637, and 795–811.

Another example of articles produced by Frankfurter's seminar students on actions by the Courts comes from late 1926. Employers were continually securing
injunctions to stop labor strikes by simply claiming in federal courts sitting in
equity that a stoppage of work would result in "irreparable damage" to their industry. So Brandeis asked Frankfurter to have his students detail, in an article, how
by "appropriate changes in state criminal administration . . . the whole illegiti-
mate brood of such resorts to equity . . . could be stamped out." See letter, LDB to
FF, November 30, 1926, FF/LC, Box 27. Two separate articles were eventually published by Frankfurter's students in the *Harvard Law Review*, acknowledging, of
course, the professor's assistance, which touched on aspects of this issue. However,
little action was taken at the state level. See John E. Lockwood, Carlyle E. Maw,
and Samuel Rosenberry, "The Use of Federal Injunction in Constitutional Litigation," 43 *Harvard Law Review* (1929–30), pp. 426–63, and Erwin N. Griswold and
William Mitchell, "The Narrative Record in Federal Equity Appeals," 42 *Harvard
Law Review* (1928–29), pp. 483–515.

53. For an indication of Brandeis's intense interest in the subject, as well as many of
the thoughts and pieces of evidence drawn from the Court's actions in this area
that he offered Frankfurter for use in research and writing, see letters, LDB to FF,
April 2, 1925, January 28, 1926, February 1, 1926, May 11, 1927, July 30, 1927,

March 28, 1928, and July 11, 1928, in Levy and Murphy, "Preserving the Progressive Spirit in a Conservative Time," 78 *Michigan Law Review* (1980), pp. 1275–78.
54. 41 *Harvard Law Review* (1927–28), pp. 483–510.
55. A. H. Feller and N. Jacobs wrote a paper entitled "Proposed Limitations on the Diversity Jurisdiction of the Federal Courts," which Frankfurter acknowledged as useful for his own understanding of the issue in his article, "Distribution of Judicial Power Between United States and State Courts," 13 *Cornell Law Quarterly* (1928), pp. 499–530, at 523. (Brandeis was so pleased with this article on the diversity-of-citizenship jurisdiction that the normally reserved justice literally bubbled with enthusiasm for it: "Your Cornell article is admirable—informing, suggestive, wise." Letter, LDB to FF, July 7, 1928, FF/LC, Box 27).

Also, two of Frankfurter's graduate research fellows, Harry Shulman and Lowell Turrentine, undertook studies on the *Swift v. Tyson* case (the cornerstone of this issue), and the general topic of diversity of citizenship respectively. See letter, FF to LDB, November 12, 1928, LDB/LLS, Box SC 8. Years later, Professor Shulman, who would also serve as a Brandeis law clerk, did publish an article incorporating material on this problem area. See Shulman and Edward C. Jaegerman, "Some Jurisdictional Limitations on Federal Courts," 45 *Yale Law Journal* (1936), pp. 393–421.

All these materials were available for Frankfurter's later writing on the topic in his many "Business of the Supreme Court" articles, as well as his other writing on the topic directly. See Frankfurter, "A Note on Diversity Jurisdiction—In Reply to Professor Yntema," 79 *University of Pennsylvania Law Review* (1931), pp. 1097–1100.
56. Letter, LDB to FF, October 15, 1926, FF/LC, Box 27. This case was *State Industrial Board of New York v. Terry and Tench Co., Inc. and United States Fidelity and Guaranty Co.*, 273 U.S. 639 (1926).
57. See 40 *Harvard Law Review* (1926–27), pp. 485–91. The justice's concern over misuse of the power to reverse state courts by *per curiam* opinion was repeated on other occasions. See letters, LDB to FF, March 7, 1920 and December 6, 1927, FF/LC, Box 27.
58. 277 U.S. 438 (1928).
59. Letter, LDB to FF, June 15, 1928, FF/LC, Box 27. There is no evidence that the *Harvard Law Review* acted on this suggestion.
60. See Alan Westin, "Out of Court Commentary by United States Supreme Court Justices, 1790–1962," 62 *Columbia Law Review* (1962), pp. 633–53.
61. Lash, ed., *Frankfurter Diaries*, pp. 16–40; L. Baker, *Frankfurter, passim;* and H. N. Hirsch, *Enigma of Frankfurter*, pp. 45, 71, 73, and 77.
62. This triangular relationship is made clear in: letters, LDB to FF, December 1, 1918, December 10, 1920, March 2, 1921, and in Urofsky and Levy, *Brandeis Letters*, Vol. IV, pp. 367, 517, and 538. See also letter LDB to FF, September 29, 1922, FF/LC, Box 27.
63. Letter, LDB to FF, October 2, 1922, FF/LC, Box 27.
64. Letter, LDB to FF, December 1, 1920, FF/LC, Box 27.
65. Letters, LDB to FF, September 4, 1922, September 6, 1922, September 19, 1922, September 24, 1922, September 25, 1922, September 30, 1922, October 2, 1922, FF/LC, Box 27.
66. Letters, LDB to FF, June 3, 1924, December 5, 1926, May 25, 1927, March 4, 1928, March 1, 1929, FF/LC, Box 27. Less than a month after these letters were written (for most of them it was only a matter of two weeks), their messages appeared in *The New Republic* in varying forms. See *The New Republic*, vol. 39 (June 11, 1924),

p. 61–62, vol. 39 (June 18, 1924), p. 84, vol. 49 (December 15, 1926), p. 95, vol. 51 (June 22, 1927), p. 107, vol. 54 (March 4, 1928), pp. 112–13; vol. 58 (March 13, 1929), p. 81.

67. Letters, LDB to FF, September 4, 1922, January 24, 1926, June 25, 1926, and March 29, 1928, FF/LC, Box 27. The printed articles appear in *The New Republic*, vol. 32 (October 4, 1922), pp. 136–37; vol. 45, vol. 54 (April 4, 1928), p. 201.

A wonderful example of this technique by Brandeis of having his ideas routed through Frankfurter and printed as editorials in *The New Republic* involved the Judiciary Act of 1925. Seeking to influence public opinion in favor of the court reorganization measure, on February 6, 1925, Brandeis sent the following analysis, intended for *The New Republic*, to Frankfurter:

> Our jurisdiction bill will doubtless become a law within a few days. When it does, this story, with a moral, may well be written:
>
> U.S.S.C.—venerated throughout the land. Despite the growth of population, wealth and governmental functions, and developments particularly of federal activities the duties of the Court have, by successive acts passed from time to time throughout a generation been kept within such narrow limits that nine men, each with one helper, can do the work as well as can be done by men of their calibre, i.e., the official coat has been cut according to the human cloth. Congress, Executive Departments, Commissions and lower federal courts.—All subject to criticism or execration. Regardless of human limitations, increasing work has been piled upon them at nearly every session. The high incumbents, in many cases, perform in name only. They are administrators, without time to know what they are doing or to think how to do it. They are human machines. (Letter, LDB to FF, February 6, 1925, FF/LC, Box 27).

This "insider's view" of the work of the Supreme Court appeared nearly verbatim as portions of the second of a two-paragraph unsigned editorial on the Judiciary Act in *The New Republic* for February 25, 1925 vol. 40, pp. 3–4.

68. Letters, LDB to FF, September 25, 1922, February 29, 1928, March 29, 1928, and July 21, 1929, FF/LC, Box 27. The articles written by Felix Frankfurter as follow-ups were: "Enforcement of Prohibition," *The New Republic*, vol. 33 (1923), p. 150, "National Policy for Enforcement of Prohibition," Annals, vol. 109 (1923), 19. 193ff., "Federal Courts," *The New Republic*, vol. 58 (1929), pp. 273ff., "Rationalization in Industry and the Labor Problem," 13 *Academy of Political Science Proceedings* (1928), pp. 171ff; and "Public Services and the Public," 20 *Yale Law Review* (1930), pp. 1–39.

69. Letters, LDB to FF, November 26, 1920, and September 20, 1921, FF/LC, Box 27. See *The New Republic*, vol. 24 (December 8, 1920), p. 28, (December 15, 1920), p. 59, and (December 22, 1920), p. 92. The second letter was a full outline for an article on this subject and was written by E. J. Clapp, "The American Transportation System," *The New Republic*, vol. 30 (March 15, 1922), pp. 72–75.

70. Letter, LDB to FF, November 9, 1921, FF/LC, Box 27.

71. See "Miners in Distress," 47 *The Survey* (February 18, 1922), pp. 786–87; "Breaking the Miners," 47 *The Survey* (March 4, 1922), pp. 887ff; and "Black Avalanche," 47 *Survey Graphic* (March 25, 1922), pp. 1002–6.

72. Nelson was a Progressive Republican from Wisconsin (and a follower of LaFollette) who served in the House from 1906 to 1919 and then from 1921 to 1933. See letter, LDB to FF, January 1, 1925, Urofsky and Levy, *Brandeis Letters*, vol. V, pp. 155–56.

73. Letters, LDB, to FF, February 21, 1925 and June 2, 1925, in Urofsky and Levy, *Brandeis Letters*, vol. V, pp. 165–66, 174–75.
74. Letter, LDB to FF, November 19, 1931, FF/LC, Box 28.
75. Letter LDB to FF, January 26, 1932, FF/LC, Box 28. Brandeis anticipates the January 16 meeting in a letter to FF on January 2, 1932, FF/LC, Box 28.
76. Letters, LDB to FF, February 25, 1932, March 11, 1932, March 24, 1932, March 30, 1932, and FF to LDB, March 22, 1932, April 3, 1932, FF/LC, Box 28.
77. Letter, Senator Wheeler to FF, March 30, 1932, FF/LC, Box 110.
78. Letters, FF to Wheeler, April 4, 1932, FF/LC, Box 110. Also see letter, LDB to FF, January 26, 1932, FF/LC, Box 28.
79. Letter, LDB to FF, April 4, 1932, FF/LC, Box 28.
80. Letters, FF to LaGuardia, April 13, 1932, and LaGuardia to FF, April 14, 1932, FF/LC, Box 80.
81. Letter, FF to LaFollette, Jr., May 3, 1932 and LaFollette, Jr., to FF, June 17, 1932, FF/LC, Box 80.
82. Letter, LDB to FF, June 12, 1932, FF/LC, Box 28.
83. Brandeis had given much thought to the potential uses for the additional revenue created by his tax proposals. Accordingly, he developed and promoted a large-scale, public-works program designed to bolster the economy and aid specific sectors of the population. The campaign was set in motion when Senator Robert F. Wagner of New York, who had drafted a legislative proposal mandating that the government undertake those "public works . . . which it is already committed to construct" and finance it through "a long term bond issue," wrote Felix Frankfurter for advice. This measure, Wagner explained, was intended to increase employment, stimulate industry, and increase demand for industrial goods. The senator then made clear the purpose of his letter:

> My purpose in writing to you is to secure the reaction of an expert who by his training is especially equipped to pass judgement upon this proposal. May I, therefore, ask you to write me freely and candidly? (Letter, Senator Wagner to FF, April 20, 1932, FF/LC, Box 109.)

There is good reason to believe that Wagner, knowing that Frankfurter worked with Brandeis, fully expected that the justice would be consulted as well. Indeed, the professor wasted no time in securing the opinion of the other "expert" opinion and Justice Brandeis responded with his suggestions on the bill nine days later:

> [Wagner is] entirely right. [However,] instead of spending more on highways (which we have enough of and which hurt railways). [Spend on] (a) extensive afforestation (b) controlling rivers—so as to prevent floods and store water for irrigation and power and improving navigation (c) parks and sanctuaries (d) expenditures for adequate penal institutions. (Letter, LDB to FF, April 29, 1932, FF/LC, Box 28.)

Without providing any indication as to where the ideas originated, Frankfurter forwarded a verbatim account of Brandeis's suggestions to the senator. Wagner thanked the professor for his judgment, but, writing that plans had already been made for spending the money intended for this purpose, the senator refused to adopt the wording proposed by Brandeis. However, like the tax proposals, this public works program would be revived in the Roosevelt Administration. Letters, FF to Senator Wagner, April 30, 1932, and Wagner to FF, May 3, 1932, FF/LC, Box 109.

84. The discussion here and elsewhere on the unemployment-insurance-law views and efforts of Justice Brandeis benefitted greatly from the reminiscences of his daughter, Elizabeth Raushenbush, and her husband, Paul Raushenbush, in the Columbia Oral History Collection. In the 1930s they worked as lieutenants for the justice in his campaign for unemployment insurance legislation (see chapter 5).

This information also appears in Raushenbush and Raushenbush, *Our "U.C." Story, 1930–1967*, (Madison, Wisconsin: private publication, 1979).

85. See Louis Brandeis, *Business—A Profession* (Boston: Small, Maynard and Co., 1914), pp. 57–58, 70ff.

86. A complete description of this plan can be found in "Memorandum of Mr. Brandeis on Irregular Employment," June, 1911, FF/LC, Box 226.

87. Letter, LDB to Bruere, February 25, 1922, in Urofsky and Levy, *Brandeis Letters*, vol. V, p. 45. During the period from 1922 to 1932 the same editorial board was responsible for publishing both *The Survey* and *Survey Graphic* magazines. *Survey Graphic* was published at the beginning of each month, and *The Survey* was published in the middle of each month.

88. Letter, LDB to Kellogg, June 9, 1924 and March 11, 1928, in Urofsky and Levy, *Brandeis Letters*, vol. V, pp. 133, 329.

89. Letter, LDB to Clarence H. Howard, April 1, 1928, LDB/LLS, Box G 2.

90. Part of that statement is: "For every employee who is 'steady in his work,' there shall be steady work. The right to regularity in employment is co-equal with the right to regularity in the payment of rent, in the payment of interest on bonds, in the delivery to customers of the high quality of product contracted for. No business is successfully conducted which does not perform fully the obligations incident to each of these rights. Each of these obligations is a fixed charge . . ." entitled "The Right to Work as Formulated Long Since by Louis D. Brandeis," *Survey Graphic*, April 1, 1929, p. 1. Also, Raushenbush's Reminiscences, COHC, pp. 129–31.

91. Brandeis asked for Frankfurter's assistance in placing the Raushenbushes in a teaching position. However, there is no record in the private letters whether either man was responsible for the appointments at the University of Wisconsin. See letters, LDB to FF, January 10, 1927 and January 21, 1927, FF/LC.

92. For more on their views, see the influential explanatory article written by Elizabeth Brandeis Raushenbush; "Wisconsin Tackles Job Security," *The Survey*, vol. 67 (December 15, 1931), pp. 295–96.

93. Letter, Elizabeth Raushenbush to FF, September 21, 1931, FF/LC, Box 92. See also, Raushenbush Reminiscences, COHC, p. 135.

94. Letter, LDB to Elizabeth Raushenbush, May, 1931, in Urofsky and Levy, *Brandeis Letters*, vol. V, p. 475: "A. Lincoln Filene who is on the Governor's Council to study unemployment insurance was in with his secretary, Edwin S. Smith to get my advice. I told them that they should apply to you for the best possible 1) noncontributory, 2) state fund, 3) individual (proposals). You will probably get a letter of inquiry." See also, Raushenbush Reminiscences, COHC, pp. 137–39.

Later that year Brandeis received from Edwin Smith a letter describing plans to push the unemployment insurance program in New York. The justice sent that letter, dated November 23, 1931, along to Elizabeth Brandeis Raushenbush with a note of his own, dated December 2, 1931, which read: Dearest E.: E. A. Filene was in—Asked me (after he had talked to Senate Comtee) what I thought on Unemployment Insurance—I told him to learn the true gospel by writing for your and Paul's bill and memo. Father" Letter, Edwin Smith to LDB (containing note to ERB), November 23, 1931, LDB/LLS, Box G 4.

Chapter 4

1. The following account of Frankfurter's and Roosevelt's relationship relies on a memorandum transcribing a discussion among Frankfurter, Grenville Clark, and Harvard University doctoral candidate Samuel Spencer, Jr. See "Sam Spencer's Notes on FF Conversation," summer 1947, FF/LC, Box 44. For more information on this relationship see Harlan B. Phillips, ed., *Felix Frankfurter Reminisces* (New York: Reynal and Co., 1960), pp. 235–37.

2. See letters, FF to FDR, October 9, 1928, November 8, 1928 and November 21, 1928, in Max Freedman, ed., *Roosevelt and Frankfurter: Their Correspondence, 1928–1945* (Boston: Little, Brown and Co., 1967), pp. 38–39.

3. Letter, LDB to FF, November 4, 1928, FF/LC, Box 27.

4. Letter, LDB to FF, November 14, 1928, FF/LC, Box 27.

5. Letter, FF to FDR, November 21, 1928, in Freedman, *Roosevelt and Frankfurter*, p. 39.

6. Letters, FDR to FF, July 5, 1929, August 5, 1929, January 24, 1930, October 16, 1930, and January 10, 1931, and FF to FDR, July 13, 1929, July 29, 1929, January 17, 1930, June 13, 1931 and October 27, 1931, in Freedman, *Roosevelt and Frankfurter*, pp. 41–59.

7. These letters from Brandeis to Frankfurter can be found in FF/LC, Boxes 27, 28, and 29; for the correspondence between Professor Mason and Frankfurter on these letters see Box 83.

8. Letter, LDB to FF, April 16, 1930, FF/LC, Box 27.

9. Letter, FF to FDR, March 14, 1933, FDRL, Box PPF 140.

10. Memorandum, "Sam Spencer's Notes on FF Conversation," summer 1947, FF/LC, Box 44. Also see letter, FDR to FF, April 5, 1933, in Freedman, *Roosevelt and Frankfurter*, pp. 123–24.

11. "Memorandum by Frankfurter of a visit with Roosevelt on March 8, 1933, the President asked Frankfurter to become Solicitor General," in Freedman, *Roosevelt and Frankfurter*, p. 114.

12. Arthur Schlesinger's three-volume series on the New Deal, *The Age of Roosevelt*, vol. I: *The Crisis of the Old Order 1919–1933*; vol. II: *The Coming of the New Deal*; vol. III: *The Politics of Upheaval* (Boston: Houghton Mifflin Co., 1957–1960), is widely acknowledged, and deservedly so, as among the best volumes on this period of U.S. history. Frankfurter's statement (letter to Arthur Schlesinger, June 18, 1963, FF/LC, Box 101), while obviously somewhat self-serving, can be verified through letters that became available after Schlesinger's work was published.

13. Letter, FF to LDB, October 20, 1932, FF/LC, Box 28; see also letters, FF to LDB, November 17, 1932 and November 19, 1932, FF/LC, Box 28. Another account of this request from FDR can be found in Phillips, ed., *Frankfurter Reminisces*, pp. 238–40. Here, however, Frankfurter's memory is only partially correct. He refers to a request for a meeting "Two days or three days before inauguration." In fact, this was the second meeting between Brandeis and FDR, and it had been arranged by Raymond Moley. In "Sam Spencer's Notes on FF Conversation," Summer 1947, FF/LC, Box 44, Frankfurter did correctly recall that there were two meetings.

14. Letter, LDB to FF, November 24, 1932, FF/LC, Box 28.

15. Letter, Huston Thompson to FDR, November 25, 1932, FDRL, Box PPF 1333.

16. The following account of the Brandeis "platform" relies on a series of letters in which the justice described and analyzed all aspects of his plans: letters, LDB to FF, January 21, 1933, January 31, 1933, February 5, 1933, and February 9, 1933, FF/LC, Box 28. See also two memoranda by Frankfurter giving his interpretations

and analyses of facets of the program: "Memo on Public Works Program" and "Memorandum Regarding Financing of the Public Works Program," undated, FF/LC, Box 226.

17. Letters, LDB to FF, April 29, 1932, FF/LC, Box 28; and LDB to Elizabeth Brandeis Raushenbush, November 19, 1933, in Melvin Urofsky and David Levy, eds., *Letters of Louis D. Brandeis*, volume V (Albany, New York: State University of New York Press, 1978), pp. 527–28.

18. Letter, LDB to FF, January 31, 1933, FF/LC, Box 28.

19. Letter, LDB to FF, January 21, 1933, FF/LC, Box 28.

20. Letter, FF to LDB, August 7, 1932, LDB/LLS, Box G–9.

21. According to Frankfurter's own account, which never minimizes the assessment of his own contributions to events, he went to Albany only twice during the period between Roosevelt's election to the presidency and his inauguration. See memorandum, "Sam Spencer's Notes on FF conversation," Summer 1947, FF/LC, Box 44.

22. There is a mountain of literature on the New Deal and the views of the various sets of FDR's advisors. See John Braeman, "The New Deal and the Broker State; A Review of the Recent Scholarly Literature," 46 *Business History Review*, winter 1976, pp. 409–29. Since my own book concentrates on the political work of Brandeis and Frankfurter while on the Court, I have kept to a minimum a review of these findings in the text. However, I will mention helpful general material in the footnotes. I found the following articles and books very useful as general sources on the period explored in this and the next chapter: Schlesinger, Jr., *The Age of Roosevelt;* William Leuchtenburg, *Franklin D. Roosevelt and the New Deal* (New York: Harper and Row, 1963); and Rexford Tugwell, *The Brains Trust* (New York: Doubleday and Company, 1968); Frank Freidal, *Franklin D. Roosevelt: the Triumph* (Boston: Little Brown and Co., 1956); Raymond Moley, *After Seven Years* (New York: Harper and Bros., 1939); Bernard Sternsher, *Rexford Tugwell and the New Deal* (New Brunswick: Rutgers Univ. Press, 1964).

23. This battle is described as leading to FDR's decision to follow the advice of one set of his advisors—the "collectivists" —for a period of time, leading to what has been called the First New Deal. Then, after these programs failed to achieve their stated goals, the president turned to the other set of advisors—the "atomists"—leading to the Second New Deal. This concept of two New Deals was first conceived by Basil Rauch, but it was popularized by Arthur Schlesinger, Jr. in his work on that period. See Rauch, *The History of the New Deal* (New York: Creative Age Press, 1944), and Schlesinger, Jr. *The Coming of the New Deal, passim.* Two fine bibliographies outline the followers of this conceptual framework: Otis L. Graham, "Historians and the New Deals: 1944–1960," 54 *The Social Studies*, 1963, pp. 133–40, and William Wilson, "The Two New Deals: A Valid Historical Concept," 28 *The Historian*, June 1966, pp. 268–88.

One scholar argues that there were not two New Deals that Roosevelt simply moved between advisors as the need arose. See Elliot A. Rosen, "Roosevelt and the Brains Trust: An Historical Overview," 87 *Political Science Quarterly*, December 1972, pp. 531–37 and *Hoover, Roosevelt and The Brains Trust: From Depression to the New Deal* (New York: Columbia University Press, 1977).

My book will not treat the merits of the issue of two New Deals directly. Rather it is my purpose to show, using unpublished source materials that were not available to these other scholars, that the two sets of presidential advisors were not totally separate and hostile toward one another. In fact, I will argue that Felix Frankfurter (at the urging of Justice Brandeis) and Raymond Moley—were quite close on occasion.

24. Schlesinger, Jr., *The Crisis of the Old Order*, 419.
25. Ibid.
26. This language is taken from Tugwell's *Roosevelt's Revolution: The First Year—A Personal Perspective* (New York: Macmillan Co., 1977), pp. 284–86 and is typical of the descriptions offered by this author in his other volumes on the New Deal. For an excellent summary of Tugwell's philosophical and political clash with Justice Brandeis and Felix Frankfurter, see Sternsher, *Rexford Tugwell and the New Deal*, chapter 10.
27. Rexford Tugwell, "Introduction" to his New Deal Diary, pp. 13–15, Rexford Tugwell papers, FDRL, Box 13. The evidence indicates that this introduction was not written contemporaneously with the events but nearly twenty years later. Tugwell is not unusual in his tendency to add material to his files in order to present his retrospective view of these events to researchers. This was also a favorite technique of Felix Frankfurter, who would occasionally add "memoranda for the file" to "explain" some incidents. Similar charges are made by Tugwell in his *Democratic Roosevelt, A Biography of FDR* (New York: Doubleday and Co., 1957), pp. 247–48.
28. Tugwell Diary, "Introduction," p. 29. This clash was also obvious to the other presidential advisors: see Raymond Moley, *27 Masters of Politics* (New York: Funk and Wagnall's, 1949), p. 114.
29. Undated memorandum, Raymond Moley papers, Hoover Institution on War, Revolution and Peace (hereinafter cited only as Hoover Institution), Stanford, California Box 1.
30. For more, see telegram, FF to Fiorello LaGuardia, January 12, 1933, in Freedman, *Roosevelt and Frankfurter*, p. 104.
31. Letter, FF to Moley, January 11, 1933, Moley papers, Hoover Institution, Box 68.
32. Raymond Moley Diary, January 11, 1933, Moley papers, Hoover Institution, Box 1. Undaunted, Frankfurter kept forwarding his views to Moley. See letter, FF to Moley, January 12, 1933, Hoover Institution, Box 68; and Moley Diary, February 12, 1933, Moley papers, Hoover Institution, Box 1.
33. Letter, FF to Arthur Schlesinger, Jr., June 18, 1963, FF/LC, Box 101. Frankfurter believed that Schlesinger had been misled by Thomas Corcoran, who had split from the justice in 1941.
34. Letter, Raymond Moley to Elliot A. Rosen, May 7, 1972. My thanks to Professor Rosen for supplying me with a copy of this letter. In this letter, Moley argues that the portraits of his relationship with Frankfurter crafted by the historians of the period—he cites specifically, Arthur M. Schlesinger, Jr., William Leuchtenburg, and James MacGregor Burns—reflect the fact that none of these men consulted his personal papers or interviewed him. Of course, Moley may well have denied these men permission to carry out such tasks.
35. For scholars portraying only the differences between the two groups of advisors, see Joseph Lash, ed., *From the Diaries of Felix Frankfurter* (New York: W. W. Norton and Co, 1975), p. 44; and H. N. Hirsch, *The Enigma of Felix Frankfurter* (New York: Basic Books, 1981), pp. 104, 111, 113. Nelson Dawson, *Brandeis, Frankfurter and the New Deal* (Hamden, Conn.: Archon/Shoestring Press, 1981), pp. 33–39, offers both views of the relationship. At one point he mentions Moley's criticism of Brandeis's program, later he argues that Moley and Frankfurter "cooperated closely for some time," but then he returns to a discussion of Moley's distant relationship with Brandeis and Frankfurter. (Dawson writes without having seen the Moley papers.) Only historian Elliot Rosen describes the close relationship between Moley and Frankfurter, see his "Roosevelt and the Brains Trust," pp. 532–33. Even this

discussion is truncated, however, perhaps due to the unavailability of the Moley papers at that time.

36. Moley was the director of the survey and hired Frankfurter to supervise the actual research. See Lash, ed., *Frankfurter Diaries*, p. 134, and Urofsky and Levy, *Brandeis Letters*, volume IV, p. 552.

37. Letter, FF to Moley, December 1, 1930, Moley papers, Hoover Institution, Box 17.

38. Letter, FF to Moley, January 19, 1933, Moley papers, Hoover Institution, Box 68.

39. Moley Diary, January 29, 1933, Moley Papers, Hoover Institution, Box 1.

40. Letter, LDB to FF, January 31, 1933, FF/LC, Box 28. The justice also sent Frankfurter a telegram with the same suggestion, dated January 31, 1933, FF/LC, Box 28.

41. Letter, FF to Moley, February 6, 1933, Moley papers, Hoover Institution, Box 68.

42. Letter, FF, to Moley, February 9, 1933, Moley papers, Hoover Institution, Box 68.

43. This letter from LDB to FF, February 5, 1933, (can also be found in FF/LC, Box 28), was enclosed in a letter from FF to Moley, February 9, 1933, Moley papers, Hoover Institution, Box 68. FDR announced the new TVA plans on February 2, 1933.

44. Letter, FF to Moley, February 9, 1933, Moley papers, Hoover Institution, Box 68.

45. Lash, ed., *Frankfurter Diaries*, pp. 134–35 (entry dated February 10, 1933).

46. Letter, FF to Moley, February 26, 1933, Moley papers, Hoover Institution, Box 68. The first letter was dated February 23, 1933, FF/LC, Box 84.

47. Letter, FF to Moley, February 26, 1933, Moley papers, Hoover Institution, Box 68. The Frankfurter diary entry, cited note 45 above, reveals that the two men also discussed this precise issue on the telephone.

48. Letter, FF to Moley, February 27, 1933, Moley papers, Hoover Institution, Box 68.

49. Letter, FF to Moley, March 6, 1933, Moley papers, Hoover Institution, Box 68.

50. The meeting was held on March 8, 1933. Moley, *The First New Deal* (New York: Harcourt, Brace and World, 1966), p. 275.

51. This figure reflects the total of those documents I actually counted from FF to Moley in the Moley papers, Hoover Institution, Box 68 and those I read about in the Moley Diary in Box 1. Some samples of this advice offered are: FF to Moley, February 27, 1933 (recommending Nicholas Kelley for undersecretary of the treasury), January 24, 1933 (in Box 1) (on meeting with Eugene Meyer regarding gold policy) and March 20, 1933 and March 23, 1932 (discussing U.S. relations with Soviet Russia).

52. Letter, FF to Moley, March 21, 1933, Moley papers, Hoover Institution, Box 68.

53. Letter, FF to Moley, March 24, 1933, Moley papers, Hoover Institution, Box 68.

54. Letter, Moley to FF, October 31, 1935, Moley papers, Hoover Institution, Box 17.

55. A succinct summary of the policies enacted during this period can be found in: Leuchtenburg, *Roosevelt and the New Deal*, pp. 41–63.

56. Tugwell claimed that the number of appointees owing their jobs to Frankfurter were in the "hundreds." See Tugwell diary, "Introduction," pp. 15–22, Tugwell papers, FDRL, Box 13. For an excellent background description of Frankfurter's "placement bureau," see Jerold S. Auerbach, *Unequal Justice: Lawyers and Social Change in Modern America* (New York: Oxford University Press, 1976), chapter VII.

57. George Peek, "In and Out: The Experiences of the First AAA Administrator," *Saturday Evening Post*, May 16, 1936, vol. 208, p. 7. Also quoted in Schlesinger, Jr., *Coming of the New Deal*, p. 16.

58. Interview with Paul A. Freund, October 26, 1977, Cambridge, Massachusetts. Professor Freund's recollection of this meeting is particularly vivid because he drove with the justice after the incident and spoke to him about the contents of the discussion. Brandeis had long been associated with Ms. Perkins in various Progressive actions over the years. For more on Perkins's life and work, see George Martin,

Madam Secretary: A Biography of Frances Perkins (Boston: Houghton Mifflin Co., 1976).

59. Letter, LDB to FF, January 13, 1933, FF/LC, Box 28. Brandeis asked for Frankfurter's suggestions on appointments here as well (he especially wanted recommendations of people from the western United States).

60. Letter, LDB to FF, February 23, 1933, FF/LC, Box 28.

61. For information on the appointment, see letters, Frances Perkins to FF, March 18, 1933, and FF to Perkins, March 11, 1933 and March 16, 1933, FF/LC, Box 150; LDB to FF, March 22, 1933 and March 25, 1933, FF/LC, Box 28.
    For more on the confirmation battle here see letters, FF to Perkins, April 3, 1933, April 11, 1933, Perkins to FF, April 6, 1933, FF/LC, Box 150; FF to Perkins, April 3, 1933, April 6, 1933, May 9, 1933, and May 11, 1933, Frances Perkins papers, Manuscripts Division, Columbia University, Box 15; FF to Senator Thomas Walsh, April 11, 1933, FF to Senator Robert Wagner, May 8, 1933, and Wagner to FF, May 9, 1933, FF/LC, Box 150.

62. Harold Ickes, *The Secret Diaries of Harold Ickes* (New York: Simon and Schuster, 1953), vol. I, p. 5 (entry for March 10, 1933). The meeting also concerned the legal set-up of the Department of the Interior. Also, letter, Ickes to FF, March 8, 1933, FF/LC, Box 149.

63. Margold had been one of Frankfurter's students at Harvard Law School, and after a one-year stint as an instructor there, followed by service in a number of agencies, he accepted the position in 1930 as special counsel to the NAACP. See letters, Ickes to FF, March 14, 1933, FF to Ickes, March 16, 1933, and Margold to FF, March 27, 1933, FF/LC, Box 149; LDB to FF, March 13, 1933, FF/LC, Box 28; also see Ickes, *Diary*, vol. I p. 6 (entry for March 12, 1933).

64. Letters, FF to Ickes, March 23, 1933, Ickes to FF, March 25, 1933, and Margold to FF, March 27, 1933, FF/LC, Box 149. It is in a letter from Brandeis to Frankfurter dated March 28, 1933 (referring to a letter sent by Frankfurter the previous day on the same issue) that the justice makes clear how the two men were working in conjunction, not only to secure Glavis's appointment through Margold, but, by implication, how they were also working for other appointments in the Department of the Interior. See letter, LDB to FF, March 28, 1933 (referring to Frankfurter's letter dated March 27, 1933), FF/LC, Box 28. Dawson, in his account of the Glavis appointment, misses the crucial role of Justice Brandeis in the affair. See Dawson, *Brandeis, Frankfurter and the New Deal*, p. 49.

65. Letter, FF to Margold, March 30, 1933, FF/LC, Box 149. Gardner Jackson, as will be seen, was appointed elsewhere in the Roosevelt Administration. Jackson, a Boston newsman, was well known to Justice Brandeis and Felix Frankfurter from his work in defense of Sacco and Vanzetti.

66. See letters, Ickes to LDB (telegram), June 13, 1933, LDB/LLS, Box G–6; LDB to Ickes, June 14, 1933, in Urofsky and Levy, *Brandeis Letters*, volume V, pp. 518; and LDB to FF, June 15, 1933, FF/LC, Box 28.

67. Wallace, who got along with Brandeis, had made the appointment for the two men. See letter, LDB to FF, March 13, 1933, FF/LC, Box 125. The other men suggested by the justice for this position were Nathan Margold, Paul Miller, and Erwin Griswold. Dean Acheson later was named an undersecretary for the Treasury Department.

68. Letter, FF to Frank, March 15, 1933, Jerome Frank papers, Sterling Library, Yale University, Box 12.
    Frankfurter nominated Frank for the job in a letter, FF to Tugwell, March 15, 1933, FF/LC, Box 125. Also suggested for the post was William O. Douglas. Frank-

furter was, of course, no stranger to Tugwell and even sent a letter of congratulations to Tugwell on his appointment. See FF to Tugwell, March 11, 1933, FF/LC, Box 125.

67. Of course, Frankfurter offered his assistance in securing Frank's confirmation and revealed that he "had asked Tom Corcoran to talk to you [Frank] about personnel." See FF to Frank, April 24, 1933, Frank papers, Sterling Library, Yale University, Box 12. For more on the appointment process for this staff see Reminiscences of Rexford Tugwell, COHC, pp. 43–45, and Reminiscences of Henry Wallace, COHC, pp. 375, 533–34. Also see Reminiscences of Jerome Frank, COHC, pp. 13–15, 64–65; and Tugwell Diary, "The Hundred Days," April 21, 1933, Tugwell papers, FDRL.

70. See letters, LDB to FF, March 28, 1933, FF/LC, Box 28; FF to Margold (in which the recommendation is passed along), March 30, 1933, FF/LC, Box 149; and Reminiscences of Gardner Jackson, COHC, pp. 412–13.

George Peek makes clear in his writing his bitterness towards Frankfurter and the other "radicals" and "communists" who had infiltrated his department. Peek, "In and Out," *passim*.

71. Dean Acheson, *Morning and Noon* (Boston: Houghton Mifflin Co., 1965), p. 161–62.

On Brandeis's and Frankfurter's efforts here, see letters, LDB to FF, February 5, 1933, March 13, 1933, April 12, 1933, and April 26, 1933, FF/LC, Box 28. Brandeis also asked Dean Acheson to visit him and suggested that he secure William O. Douglas's assistance in seeking the assistant attorney generalship.

72. Letters, FF to Cummings, June 7, 1933, FF/LC, Box 149; LDB to FF, May 28, 1933, FF/LC, Box 28; FF to FDR, July 10, 1933, and Cummings to FDR, July 19, 1933, in Freedman, *Roosevelt and Frankfurter*, pp. 139, 144.

See also letters, Sutherland to FF, July 7, 1933, July 16, 1933, July 19, 1933, LDB/LLS, Box G–6. Sutherland ended up working with another Frankfurter-Brandeis ally, David Lilienthal, in the TVA.

73. Letter, LDB to FF, August 14, 1933, FF/LC, Box 28. See also letter, FF to FDR, July 10, 1933, in Freedman, *Roosevelt and Frankfurter*, p. 139; and letter, Justice Harlan Fiske Stone to FF, May 17, 1933, FDRL, Box PPF 140 (this letter was also sent along to the president).

74. Letter, Paul Miller to LDB, August 4, 1933, LDB/LLS, Box G–6. Acting on his own initiative, Frankfurter also used his friendship with Assistant Attorney General Harold Stephens to make "confidential suggestions" regarding the placement of other middle-level officials in the Department of Justice. See letter, Harold Stephens to FF, September 16, 1933, FF/LC, Box 149. (In this case discussing a job offer to "Mr. Huberman" in the antitrust division).

75. On Acheson's appointment, see letters, FF to Moley, March 24, 1933, March 29, 1933 and April 1, 1933, Moley Papers, Hoover Institution, Box 68. Also see letter, FF to Moley, April 2, 1933, FF/LC, Box 84. In the first of these letters proposing Acheson, Frankfurter urged Moley to consult Justice Brandeis on the matter as well.

Thomas K. McGraw, *Morgan vs Lilienthal* (Chicago: Loyola University Press, 1970), p. 19. There are a number of letters from Lilienthal in the files of both Brandeis and Frankfurter. These missives both provide information on the TVA and request answers to various questions. See, for example, letter, Lilienthal to LDB, August 26, 1933, LDB/LLS, Box G–6.

76. To Wyzanski, Frankfurter sent lists of names for appointments as Labor Department mediators. See letters, FF to Wyzanski, July 15, 1933 and July 18, 1933, FF/LC, Box 113. For the Margold assistance, see letters, FF to Margold, March 30, 1933, May 11, 1933, and Margold to FF, March 27, 1933, April 3, 1933, and May 9, 1933,

FF/LC, Box 149. Of course, many other appointments were suggested through the good offices of Frankfurter's Washington lieutenant, Thomas Corcoran.

77. See letters, Huston Thompson to FDR, November 25, 1932, FDRL, Box PPF 1333; J. Lionberger Davis to Marvin McIntyre (presidential appointments secretary), July 7, 1934, August 9, 1934, September 18, 1934, FDRL, Box PPF 86. Davis had a long meeting with Brandeis on the subject of government banking policy and successfully secured an appointment with Roosevelt to pass along this information. Also see letters, LDB to FF, September 10, 1933, FF/LC, Box 28 and Adolf Berle to FDR, April 30, 1934, FDRL, Box PPF 1306.

78. Letter, Claggett to McIntyre, March 3, 1933, FDRL, Box PPF 140. Walsh had died, thus creating the vacancy.

79. In his research on Brandeis, Alpheus T. Mason discovered the original correspondence between Fisher and Brandeis. Mason reports that the full advice to Fisher was: "approve no documents the contents of which you do not understand; sign no letters which you have not read." Alpheus T. Mason, *Brandeis: A Free Man's Life* (New York: The Viking Press, 1956), p. 282.

80. Interview with the Honorable Judge Charles E. Wyzanski, Jr., January 13, 1977, Richmond, Virginia. The author wishes to express his gratitude to Judge Wyzanski for his invaluable assistance in the earliest stages of this research.

81. Letter, Margold to FF, April 3, 1933, FF/LC, Box 149.

82. Letter, Nathan Margold to FF, March 27, 1933, FF/LC, Box 149.

83. Letter, James Grafton Rogers (assistant secretary of state under Herbert Hoover) to Robert Stearns, undated, James Grafton Rogers papers, Hoover Institution, Folder 19025–10V.

84. The details for this account of the Brandeis teas (except where noted) were drawn from the following sources: interviews with Paul A. Freund, October 26, 1977, Cambridge, Massachusetts, Edward F. Prichard, Jr., June 25, 1979, Frankfort, Kentucky; Thomas G. Corcoran, September 29, 1977, Washington,, D.C.; Judge Charles E. Wyzanski, Jr., January 13, 1977, Richmond, Virginia; and Judge Henry Friendly, April 14, 1978, by telephone; Reminiscences of James Landis, COHC, p. 67; Reminiscences of Marquis Childs, COHC, pp. 66–67; Reminiscences of Frances Perkins, COHC, Book 7, pp. 94–95; and a personal letter to the author from Elizabeth Brandeis Raushenbush, August 23, 1977.

   Other useful published accounts of the Brandeis "teas" appear in Melvin I. Urofsky, *A Mind of One Piece: Brandeis and American Reform* (New York: Charles Scribner's Sons, 1971), pp. 131–32; Paul A. Freund, "Justice Brandeis: A Law Clerk's Remembrance," *American Jewish History*, 1978, pp. 14–16; and Merle Miller, *Plain Speaking: An Oral Biography of Harry S. Truman* (New York: G. P. Putnam's Sons, 1973), p. 379.

85. Interview with Joseph L. Rauh, Jr., July 9, 1979, Washington, D.C.

86. Interview with David Riesman, July 26, 1979, Cambridge, Massachusetts.

87. Interview with Joseph L. Rauh, Jr., July 9, 1979, Washington D.C.

88. FDR was not a strict budget balancer, but he wanted to limit spending as much as possible. So, he liked having men such as Lewis Douglas in the administration. See Leuchtenburg, *Roosevelt and the New Deal*, pp. 45–46, 52–53, and 84–86.

89. Felix Frankfurter, "What We Confront in American Life," *Survey Graphic*, March, 1933, p. 136.

90. Letter, FF to FDR, March 22, 1933, in Freedman, *Roosevelt and Frankfurter*, pp. 121–22.

91. Letters, FF to Perkins, April 4, 1933, and Perkins to FF, April 5, 1933, Perkins papers, Butler Library, Columbia University, Box 15. Perkins was particularly re-

ceptive to Frankfurter's advice, as he had been supplying information to her regarding labor standards (at Perkins's request) over the previous month. See letters, FF to Perkins, March 26, 1933 and March 29, 1933, Perkins papers, Butler Library, Columbia University, Box 15. Later on, Frankfurter once again pressed Perkins to adopt the Brandeis public-works program. See letter, FF to Perkins, May 2, 1933, FF/LC, Box 150.

92. Letter FF to Moley, April 5, 1933, FF/LC, Box 84. See also letter, FF to Moley, March 28, 1933, FF/LC, Box 84.

To demonstrate that some "old Treasury influences hostile to a constructive program [were] still operating," the professor also enclosed an earlier exchange of correspondence with former Undersecretary of the Treasury Arthur Ballantine, who greatly opposed a similar public-works plan put forth by Senator Robert Wagner. Letter, FF to Moley, April 5, 1933, Moley papers, Hoover Institution, Box 68. Also see letters, FF to Robert Wagner, April 30, 1932, Arthur Ballantine to FF, May 13, 1932, and FF to Ballantine, May 16, 1932 and June 11, 1932, Moley papers, Hoover Institution, Box 68.

93. Letter, LDB to FF, April 12, 1933, FF/LC, Box 28. There is no evidence that this other meeting between Moley and the justice ever took place.

94. Letter, LDB to FF, April 12, 1933, FF/LC, Box 28.

95. Letter, FF to Moley, April 14, 1933, Moley papers, Hoover Institution, Box 68. There is no indication that Brandeis initially recommended Sprague, though perhaps it was done in person or by phone. However, Sprague's philosophy on financial issues was exactly the same as the justice's. Also, as events would soon show, Brandeis was fully aware of what Frankfurter was doing here.

96. Letter, FF to Sprague, May 10, 1933, FF/LC, Box 84.

97. Letter, FF to Moley, May 21, 1933, Moley papers, Hoover Institution, Box 68.

98. Letters, LDB to FF, May 14, 1933, and May 23, 1933, FF/LC, Box 28. There can be little doubt that Brandeis, who used dinners at his apartment for advising purposes, designed this guest list deliberately for such a discussion.

99. Letters, LDB to FF, September 28, 1933, and November 24, 1933, FF/LC, Box 115; also letter, Benjamin Cohen to FF, October 9, 1933, FF/LC, Box 115. Frankfurter spoke to Moley personally on this matter as well.

100. Letter, FF to Ickes, July 10, 1933, FF/LC Box 149.

101. Letter, FF to LDB, February 8, 1934, LDB/LLS, Box G9.

102. Frankfurter had already been working with his contacts in England seeking to influence FDR's judgment on the issue of public works programs. On November 23, 1933, he had sent the president a letter from an Oxford don, Roy Harrod, praising this use of government resources. See letter, FF to FDR, November 23, 1933, in Freedman, Roosevelt and Frankfurter, pp. 167–73.

103. Roy Harrod, The Life of John Maynard Keynes (New York: Harcourt, Brace and World, 1951), p. 290.

104. Letter, FF to Keynes, December 9, 1933, FF/LC, Box 117. In also quoting this letter, Dawson, Brandeis, Frankfurter, and the New Deal, p. 32 argues that Brandeis and Frankfurter were unequivocally "Keynesians." He posits that as Keynesians they "believed that massive public works spending financed by rigorous, progressive taxation could end the depression." Keynes, however, was not interested in increasing taxes to pay for increased public works programs, but was instead advocating massive deficit spending for such programs in order to promote economic recovery. It will be argued below that the extent of Brandeis's adherence to the Keynesian philosophy is a matter of some conjecture.

105. Letter, FF to LDB, December 9, 1933, LDB/LLS, Box G9.

106. A copy of the letter can be found in Freedman, *Roosevelt and Frankfurter*, pp. 178–83.
107. Letter, FF to FDR, December 16, 1933, in Freedman, *Roosevelt and Frankfurter*, p. 177. Frankfurter also sent a preview copy to Brandeis on December 18, 1933, LDB/LLS, Box G9.
108. Letter, Keynes to FF, December 15, 1933, FF/LC, Box 117.
109. Letter, FDR to FF, December 22, 1933, in Freedman, *Roosevelt and Frankfurter*, pp. 183–84. Frankfurter wrote to Brandeis that he hoped the advice would have a good effect on the president, FF to LDB, January 7, 1934, LDB/LLS, Box G9.
110. Letter, LDB to FF, August 3, 1934, FF/LC, Box 28. This meeting was delayed until the last days of August. See note 113 below.
111. See letters, LDB to FF, June 11, 1931, September 28, 1931, January 23, 1932, and December 18, 1932, FF/LC, Box 28.
112. Letters, LDB to FF, January 31, 1933, and February 5, 1933, FF/LC, Box 28. Moreover, these letters make clear that Brandeis expected part of the expense to be offset by new revenues brought in by the sale of commodities produced as a direct result of the public-works programs (i.e., timber, electricity, etc.). This author did not find any evidence that Brandeis recognized or accepted the possibility of long-term, massive deficit budgets.
113. See letter, FF to LDB, August 31, 1934, LDB/LLS, Box G9, which completely describes this meeting between Frankfurter and Roosevelt.
     This entire issue was particularly vexing for Brandeis, as he showed in a letter to Frankfurter, which proposed this overall massive-borrowing campaign. See letter, LDB to FF, August 3, 1934, FF/LC, Box 28.
114. For more, see Leuchtenburg, *Roosevelt and the New Deal*, pp. 124–25. Also see Schlesinger, Jr., *The Politics of Upheaval*, pp. 263–70.
115. Brandeis did not like the FDR program of balancing the budget, preferring instead an emphasis on "a postal savings plan and heavier estate taxes." See LDB to FF, May 14, 1933, FF/LC, Box 28.
     In addition to the people they had placed successfully in the Treasury Department, they had also tried to place Donald Richberg, but he ended up at the National Recovery Administration. Raymond Moley Diaries, March 12, 1933, and March 15, 1933, Moley papers, Hoover Institution, Box 1.
116. Letters, FF to Moley, February 27, 1933, and March 6, 1933, FF/LC Box 84; LDB to FF, August 14, 1933, and September 10, 1933, FF/LC, Box 28; and FF to LDB, August 16, 1933, LDB/LLS, Box G9.
117. For more, see Schlesinger, Jr., *Coming of the New Deal*, pp. 238–47.
118. Acheson, *Morning and Noon*, p. 181.
119. Corcoran was originally the assistant to Acheson in that department. See Corcoran to FF, December 11, 1933, FF/LC, Box 116.
120. For example, see letter, LDB to FF, November 24, 1933, FF/LC, Box 115.
121. For years, Brandeis had been inveighing against the excessive salaries paid corporate heads. In early 1933, Professor Frankfurter suggested to Progressive Senator James Couzens, a Republican from Michigan, that he "initiate the inquiry into excessive salaries" because "the country is most ripe for such legislation." The senator responded that members of his political party had no influence in the Congress then, and suggested that Frankfurter raise this issue with friendly Democrats. Heeding this advice, Frankfurter, on the very next day, began his correspondence with Democratic Senator Edward Costigan of Colorado on both this issue and desirable bank reforms. Letters, FF to Sen. Couzens, February 23, 1933, Couzens to FF, March 4, 1933, FF to Couzens, March 14, 1933, and FF to Couzens,

March 28, 1933, FF/LC, Box 50. Earlier the senator had agreed with Frankfurter that there was a need for such an investigation. Letters, Couzens to FF, March 30, 1933, FF/LC, Box 50; FF to Senator Costigan, March 31, 1933, April 11, 1933, and April 18, 1933, Costigan to FF, April 8, 1933, and April 15, 1933, FF/LC, Box 49.

When little action was taken, Brandeis himself tried to set up a meeting with Senator Costigan. However, other moves taken by the justice with the White House inner circle soon made the conference unnecessary. A private discussion on August 11, 1933, with Samuel Rosenman regarding the need for "smaller executive corporation salaries" achieved substantial results. In October the president's speech writer informed Brandeis that Roosevelt had directed the Federal Trade Commission to investigate the excessive salaries being paid to corporate officials. Letter, FF to LDB, October 20, 1933, LDB/LLS, Box G9. See also letters, September 16, 1933, August 14, 1933, and September 10, 1933, FF/LC, Box 28.

During this same period, Brandeis spoke to anyone who would listen about the need for extensive bank reform. The justice sought to establish an extensive program of "postal savings," to use federal tax powers to break up the nation's largest banks, to end the practice of interlocking directorates between banks and businesses (which required a single corporate head to "serve two masters"), and to have others undertake a study of why banks had failed around the nation. Despite extremely open lobbying with various executive branch administrators—such as NRA official, Harry Shulman, and Federal Reserve Board official, Emanuel Goldenweiser—and even an attempt to send these ideas to the president through a banker, J. Lionberger Davis, none of Brandeis's suggestions were adopted into law in the early New Deal. Letters, LDB to FF, April 3, 1933, FF/LC, Box 28; and FF to LDB, February 2, 1934, LDB/LLS, Box G9. "Memorandum on talk with LDB," Harry Shulman, December 8, 1933, FF/LC, Box 28; Memorandum, "Visit with Brandeis," Emanuel Goldenweiser, February 23, 1934, Emanuel Goldenweiser papers, LC, Box 7; and letter, J. Lionberger Davis to Marvin McIntyre, August 9, 1934, and September 18, 1934, FDRL, Box PPF 186. Davis said he spent three-and-a-half hours talking to Justice Brandeis on FDR's legislative program and the justice "begged him" to speak to the president on these ideas. He got the appointment on October 24, 1934.

During the later New Deal, Brandeis once again pursued the issue. With the banking bill of 1935 under consideration, the justice once again lectured Emanuel Goldenweiser about the need for reform. In regard to the conflict-of-interest problems created by interlocking directorates banks and businesses, Brandeis told his visitor that "the limitations of human wisdom   [were] a reason why administrative machinery should not make demands upon human nature that are greater than human nature could meet." Then the justice renewed his call for an "autopsy" of the banks that had failed in the early 1930s. The available statistics on banks were useless, he claimed, because the rising deposit figures only signified an increase in the amount of credit extended. Improved information on these institutions would serve to prevent future depressions. While Brandeis was pleased with the direction of the prospective banking reforms, they simply were not extensive enough for his tastes. (Memorandum, "Visit with Justice Brandeis," by Emanuel Goldenweiser, May 19, 1935, Emanuel Goldenweiser papers, LC, Box 17). The subsequently adopted banking reform bill, written by Marriner Eccles and revised by Senator Carter Glass, significantly tightened up the Federal Reserve System. There is no evidence of involvement by Justice Brandeis in this legislation other than this meeting with Goldenweiser.

122. Alva Johnson, "White House Tommy," *Saturday Evening Post*, July 31, 1937, pp. 5, 65–67.

123. Gerald Nash, "Herbert Hoover and the Origins of the Reconstruction Finance Corporation," 46 *Mississippi Valley Historical Review*, December 1959, p. 458. For a time, in late 1933 to 1934, Corcoran served in the Treasury Department as an assistant to Dean Acheson.

124. Sometimes Corcoran did his job with such exuberance that congressmen complained that he was ramming the Roosevelt policies down their throats. Corcoran was said to generally precede his message by noting: "I have just come from the White House," and go on to make threats to take away pork barrel legislation if the right votes on policy were not forthcoming. For more on this extraordinarily effective team see Johnson, "White House Tommy," "Twins: New Deal's Legislative Architects: Corcoran and Cohen," *Newsweek*, July 13, 1935, pp. 24–25; "Necks In: Irishman and Jew Keep Quiet Behind Today's Rooseveltian Brain Trust," *Literary Digest*, May 22, 1937, pp. 7–8; Max Stern, "The Little Red House," *Today*, May 19, 1934, p. 5ff. Also see Reminiscences of David Morse, COHC, pp. 105, 112, and Reminiscences of James Landis, COHC, pp. 158–63.

125. The extensiveness of these visits appears to have been at least this great, if not more so, during Frankfurter's trip to Oxford from 1933 to 1934. A precise count of the total number of visits is made difficult by references to multiple visits in some letters and uncertainty as to whether all the visits are recorded in the letters. See letters, Corcoran and Cohen to Frankfurter, and Brandeis to Frankfurter, FF/LC, Boxes 28, 115, and 116 (many of which are cited and quoted below).

126. Interview with Thomas G. Corcoran, September 29, 1977, Washington, D.C. Letters offering and transmitting advice from all the major actors in the various legislative campaigns that concerned Justice Brandeis confirmed Corcoran's descriptions of these events.

127. Letters, LDB to FF, March 18, 1933, and May 24, 1933, FF/LC, Boxes 28, 115; also interview with Benjamin V. Cohen, September 26, 1977, Washington, D.C.

128. Letter, LDB to FF, April 13, 1933, FF/LC, Box 28.

President Roosevelt gave the overall responsibility for drafting the bill to Secretary of Commerce Dan Roper, who then passed it on to Thompson and former Pujo Committee investigator Samuel Untermeyer for the specifics. For more on the drafting process for this legislation see Reminiscences of James Landis, COHC, pp. 158–63; Michael Parrish, *Securities Regulation and the New Deal* (New Haven: Yale University, 1970), pp. 1–72; and James Landis, "The Legislative History of the Securities Act of 1933," 28 *George Washington Law Review*, October, 1959, pp. 29–49.

129. For an example of a time that the justice was willing to speak with Thompson at length about issues—in this case on holding company regulation—see note 15 above.

130. Huston Thompson Diaries, March 18, 1933, Huston Thompson papers, LC, Box 1. See also letter, Thompson to LDB, March 17, 1933, LDB/LLS, Box G–12.

131. Raymond Moley Diaries, April 7, 1933, Moley Papers, Hoover Institution, Box 1.

132. Letters, FF to Moley, April 12, 1933 and April 15, 1933, Moley Papers, Hoover Institution, Box 68.

133. For more on the clash between the two groups in the drafting of this statute, see Schlesinger, Jr., *Coming of the New Deal*, pp. 434–42.

134. Letter, LDB to FF, April 12, 1933, FF/LC, Box 28. At that time the justice also discussed postal savings plans and " [w]resting the power from the Bankers," as

well as the need for greater safety measures for the savings accounts. The president seemed "much interested in the Postal savings idea and as   [Brandeis] was walking out of the door he called after him to that effect."

135. Letter, LDB to FF, April 13, 1933, FF/LC, Box 28.

136. Letters, LDB to FF, April 26, 1933, and May 24, 1933, FF/LC, Boxes 28 and 115.

137. Huston Thompson Diaries, May 7, 1933, Thompson papers, LC, Box 1. In this meeting, Brandeis once again pressed his postal savings idea, telling Thompson to relay to the president the need for lifting the "limitation on deposits in Postal Savings."

138. Letter, LDB to FF, May 24, 1933, FF/LC, Box 115.

139. Leuchtenburg, *Roosevelt and the New Deal*, p. 59.

140. Letter, FF to Moley, May 24, 1933, Moley papers, Hoover Institution, Box 68. Later, Justice Brandeis gave the reasons for his satisfaction with the proposal. He was pleased that the new law had not curtailed financial investments, as others had warned it would. See letter, LDB to FF, August 3, 1933, FF/LC, Box 28.

141. Letter, Moley to FF, May 25, 1933, Moley papers, Hoover Institution, Box 68.

142. For more on the London Economic Conference and Moley's role in it see Schlesinger, Jr., *Coming of the New Deal*, pp. 213–32.

143. Before taking any action toward resignation Moley conferred with Frankfurter, who by now had become one of his main advisors. See Raymond Moley Diaries, July 13, 1933, and July 29, 1933, Moley Papers, Hoover Institution, Box 1, and letters, FF to Moley, June 16, 1933, and September 26, 1933, Moley Papers, Hoover Institution, Box 68. For more on the causes of the Moley resignation, see Schlesinger, Jr., *Coming of the New Deal*, pp. 217–32. Moley had recommended that the president support a declaration from the conference regarding stabilization of international monetary rates.

144. Letters, LDB to FF, September 20, 1933, FF/LC, Box 28; and Max Lowenthal to FF, October 26, 1933, FF/LC, Box 117. Fletcher, the chairman of the Senate Banking and Currency Committee, co-sponsored this new law with Sam Rayburn.

   For more on the formulation of the law, see Parrish, *Securities Regulation*, pp. 112–44.

145. Letter, Corcoran to FF, November 16, 1933, FF/LC, Box 116. Corcoran's claim about "regular" visits can be found in letter, Corcoran to FF, October 13, 1933, FF/LC, Box 116. This assertion is easily documented by reports of meetings in other letters: Corcoran to FF, September 8, 1933, FF/LC, Box 182; and Benjamin V. Cohen to FF, November 8, 1933, FF/LC, Box 115. Also, see notes 146–49 below.

146. Letter, Corcoran to FF, December 30, 1933, FF/LC, Box 116. Also quoted in Dawson, *Brandeis, Frankfurter and the New Deal*, page 96.

147. Letter, LDB to FF, December 17, 1933, FF/LC, Box 20. See also letter, LDB to FF, December 7, 1933, FF/LC, Box 115.

148. Letter, Corcoran to FF, December 11, 1933, FF/LC, Box 116. Corcoran's concern over this lack of knowledge about the president's intentions are detailed in this letter.

149. Cable, Corcoran to FF, February 11, 1934, FF/LC, Box 116. Other letters from Frankfurter on this issue are: FF to LDB, November 17, 1932, and December 28, 1933, LDB/LLS, Box G9.

150. Letter, FF to LDB, February 19, 1934, LDB/LLS, Box G9.

151. Letter, FF to Corcoran, February 13, 1934, FF/LC, Box 116.

152. Letter, FF to FDR, February 22, 1934, FF/LC, Box 34; and FF to FDR, February 14, 1934, in Freedman, *Roosevelt and Frankfurter*, pp. 192–94.

153. For more on the final measure see Schlesinger, Jr., *Coming of the New Deal,* pp. 466–67.
154. See letters, LDB to FF, July 17, 1933, and August 30, 1933, FF/LC, Box 28. On Brandeis's interest in farming, see letters, LDB to Alfred Brandeis, September 26, 1920, January 16, 1921, March 1, 1921, and June 17, 1921, in Urofsky and Levy, *Brandeis Letters,* vol. IV, pp. 487–88, 527, 535–36, and 566–67.
155. Rexford Tugwell Diaries, "The Hundred Days" section, April 15, 1933, Tugwell papers, FDRL, Box 15.
156. LDB's overall plan can be found in: Reminiscences of Gardner Jackson, COHC, pp. 417–21, and letter, LDB to FF, August 30, 1933, FF/LC, Box 28. For general background information in this area, see Donald H. Grubbs, *Cry from the Cotton: The Southern Tenant Farmer's Union and the New Deal* (Chapel Hill, N.C.: University of Northern Carolina Press, 1971).
157. In these sessions with Jackson, the justice gathered information and gave advice on all sorts of issues. For example, he advised Jackson to leak a damaging memorandum to the press regarding a new AAA price regulation in order to protect the public's interest. The justice's clear intent was that much of this information would be passed on by Jackson to his superiors in the AAA. See Reminiscences of Gardner Jackson, COHC, pp. 429–31, 483–85, and 493–94.
158. Reminiscences of Gardner Jackson, COHC, pp. 417–18.
159. Rexford Tugwell Diaries, "The Hundred Days," April 26, 1934, p. 75, Rexford Tugwell papers, FDRL, Box 16; letter, LDB to Henry Wallace, December 5, 1934, Henry Wallace papers (on microfilm), FDRL, Reel 19; also letter, LDB to FF, January 19, 1934, FF/LC, Box 28. Tugwell does not cite the oil-code case that was postponed. The Supreme Court did not decide the major case in this area until the following year (*Panama Refining Co. v. Ryan,* 293 US 388 (1935)).
160. Letter, Berle to FDR, April 23, 1934, FDRL, Box PPF 1306.
161. Letter, FDR to Berle, April 30, 1934, FDRL, Box PPF 1306. The indications are that the president did not meet with Brandeis until that June, see letters, LDB to FF, February 7, 1935, FF/LC, Box 28.; and LDB to E. Raushenbush, June 8, 1934, in Urofsky and Levy, *Brandeis Letters,* vol. V, pp. 539–40.
162. The account of this meeting, can be found in the Reminiscences of Gardner Jackson, COHC, pp. 490–94, 584–87. The others who went to Chatham were Thurman Arnold, Wesley Sturges, and Lee Pressman. These men were sent by Jerome Frank as part of an overall process of review for the goals and methods of the AAA.

From Brandeis's standpoint, the AAA took a giant step backwards in early 1935 with the "purge" of his "allies," Jerome Frank, Gardner Jackson, and more than fifteen other "radicals." Reminiscences of Gardner Jackson, COHC, pp. 593–617. Henry Wallace told the president that this mass firing was an administrative necessity. However, he told Jackson that it was because of his lobbying with members of the Supreme Court regarding the AAA (which of course was true to an extent). The secretary simply believed that these "radicals" were subverting his programs. Brandeis's reaction to this mass firing was to become even more disappointed with the direction of that agency: "The removal of Jerome Frank should not have involved the others. It is disappointing. I should be sadder about it even than I am, if I were not convinced that this whole AAA production curtailment policy will not prove disastrous." Letter, LDB to FF, February 24, 1935, FF/LC Box 28. Others viewed Jerome Frank as a protégé of Frankfurter. However, the letters in his private papers show that the two men differed radically on matters of policy. See FF to Frank, January 18, 1935, January 18, 1936, and January 21, 1936, Jerome Frank Papers, Sterling Library, Yale University, Box 12.

The justice made one last ditch effort to educate these administrators in a June meeting with Agriculture Undersecretary Milo Perkins. Brandeis pontificated with familiar zeal against "bigness" in government. Specifically, in discussing the "sanctity of littleness," the justice warned about "jobs calling for superhuman abilities," which make "tyrants of men." When it was suggested that the AAA might be such a decentralized approach, Brandeis disagreed, saying that this "program was imposed from above, and did not arise locally out of understanding from below." Brandeis pleaded with his visitor for a return to "economic democracy" in the farming industry by adopting local schemes of production. Memorandum, Milo Perkins, "A Meeting with Justice Brandeis," June 5, 1935, Rexford Tugwell papers, FDRL, Box 17. The justice was searching for a method to achieve some "economic democracy" in the agency. He also urged Perkins to go back to his native Texas and revitalize the government in that state.

163. 297 US 1 (1936). Brandeis and Benjamin Cardozo joined Harlan Fiske Stone's dissent in the case. They voted to uphold the act on the basis of its tax provisions.

164. Jerome Frank memorandum, "Notes on Conversation with Brandeis," Jerome Frank papers, undated, Sterling Library, Yale University, Box 19. Judging by the account of this meeting, Brandeis's message to Frank was typical of the philosophical and political advice he was offering all the other executive branch officials who visited with him. Frank quotes Brandeis as saying:

> [I am] of the opinion that our economic difficulties are due in considerable measure to the existence of the huge corporation. [I] believe that such corporations cannot adequately be controlled by Government. [I] therefore think that by means of excise taxes huge corporations should be broken up.
>
> Let it be assumed that the diagnosis, i.e., that unregulated big business has caused our major economic difficulties, [is correct]. At the moment it would appear that the country is not prepared to try the proposed remedy. The present temper is apparently in accord with the view that unregulated big business is undesirable. But the dominant attitude seems to be that the remedy is to be found in governmental regulation of big business.
>
> Even if it be assumed that regulation cannot succeed and assumes further that the attempt to regulate over a long period will be undesirable and is avoidable, nevertheless serious consideration should be given to this fact.

Shulman and Goldenweiser have left similar accounts of meetings with the justice. See "Memorandum on talk with LDB," written by Harry Shulman, December 8, 1933, FF/LC, Box 28; and "Visit with Brandeis," written by Emanuel Goldenweiser, February 23, 1934, Emanuel Goldenweiser papers, LC, Box 7.

165. Letters, LDB to FF, August 2, 1934, August 3, 1934, August 5, 1934, and FF/LC, Box 28.

166. For example, see letter, LDB to FF, August 14, 1933, FF/LC, Box 28 (discussing personal visit by General Johnson). See also, letter, LDB to FF, September 22, 1934, FF/LC, Box 28.

167. Letters, Filene to Richberg, September 4, 1933, and Richberg to Filene, September 5, 1933, Donald Richberg Papers, LC Box 1. See also letters, FF to Grace Abbott, May 30, 1933, FF to Senator Robert Wagner, May 30, 1930, memorandum, "The National Industrial Recovery Bill and Wage Standards," undated, FF/LC, Box

159. Also, see letters, FF to Richberg, June 6, 1933, and July 7, 1933, Richberg papers, LC, Box 1.

168. Letters, LDB to FF, November 16, 1933, FF/LC, Box 28; and FF to LDB, November 28, 1934, LDB/LLS, Box G9. The two men also feared the influence of Richberg on FDR.

169. Letter, LDB to FF, August 31, 1934, LDB/LLS, Box G9. See also letters, LDB to FF, August 3, 1934, and September 29, 1934, FF/LC, Box 28.

170. There were some notable exceptions to the Court's general abstinence from political activity. One example was the effort by several of the justices, some working against others, to secure an appointment for their candidate in 1932 to replace Oliver Wendell Holmes on the Supreme Court. For more, see Ira Ho Carmen, "The President, Politics and the Power of Appointments: Hoover's Nomination of Mr. Justice Cardozo," 55 *Virginia Law Review*, 1969, pp. 620–51. Another notable exception came in 1937, when several members of the Court (including Brandeis) lobbied to defeat the Court-packing reorganization plan of FDR. For more, see chapter 5.

171. Drew Pearson and Robert S. Allen, *The Nine Old Men* (Garden City, N.Y.: Doubleday, Doran and Co., 1937), pp. 165–67, 257–58.

172. This was Brandeis's own account of the relationship, sent to Frankfurter after the controversy broke, with the idea that someone should be aware of his side of the story. Of course, this letter could easily have been interpreted by Frankfurter as an effort to arm the lieutenant should he decide to continue his active defense of the justice. And so he did. See letter, LDB to FF, September 22, 1934, FF/LC, Box 28 for the quotations that follow, until otherwise noted.

173. *Chicago Tribune*, labelled "September 19 or 20, 1934," copy found in FF/LC, Box 28.

174. Ibid., see also, *Baltimore Sun*, September 16, 1934, copy found in FF/LC, Box 28.

175. Ibid.; and *New York Herald-Tribune*, September 26, 1934, copy found in FF/LC, Box 28.

176. See letter, LDB to FF, September 22, 1934, FF/LC, Box 28.

177. Letter, LDB to FF, September 25, 1934, FF/LC, Box 28. Frankfurter's files (Box 28) show that an exact copy of the letter was sent on to Mack, but it is not made clear by whom.

178. Letter, FF to Alfred E. Cohn, October 30, 1935, in Freedman, *Roosevelt and Frankfurter*, p. 290.

179. Undated memorandum, FF/LC, Box 28.

180. Letter, FF to FDR, September 20, 1934, in Freedman, *Roosevelt and Frankfurter*, p. 233.

181. Letter, FF to FDR, September 27, 1934, (on microfilm), FDRL.

182. Quotation from letter, LDB to FF, September 22, 1934, FF/LC, Box 28. The two letters in which Brandeis calls for Johnson's ousting are: LDB to FF, September 19, 1934, and September 25, 1934, FF/LC, Box 28.
    A careful reading of Frankfurter's September 27 letter to Roosevelt (cited note 181 above) shows just how distorted a picture the president was receiving regarding Brandeis's true feelings about Johnson and the events that had transpired. After writing to FDR about Brandeis's "tenderness" for Johnson, Frankfurter quotes Roosevelt that part of Brandeis's September 25 letter to Frankfurter that states that disqualification from the NRA cases in the future was "not agreeable to contemplate" and that the "incident must be regarded as a casualty." (see text for note 177 above). Then the professor concluded his September 27 letter to the president by reminding him of an earlier assessment of Brandeis by FDR: "Brandeis has and

is a great soul." In truth, however, charity was not in Brandeis's heart on this occasion. For Frankfurter did not inform the president about the remainder of the September 25 letter, in which Brandeis called in unequivocal terms (and for the second time) for Johnson's immediate resignation (see unnumbered footnote appended to footnote 183 below).

183. Letter, LDB to FF, September 19, 1934, and September 25, 1934, FF/LC, Box 28.

184. Interview with Paul A. Freund, October 26, 1977, Cambridge, Massachusetts.

185. Interview with Judge Charles E. Wyzanski, Jr., January 13, 1977, Richmond, Virginia. According to Arthur Schlesinger, Johnson formally tendered his resignation on September 24, 1934 and announced FDR's acceptance of it to members of the NRA in a meeting on October 1. See Schlesinger, Jr., *The Coming of the New Deal*, pp. 155–57.

When Brandeis was told about the resignation by Frankfurter, his reaction was predictable. He wrote the professor on September 29, 1934: "I am glad the resignation was so promptly accepted." Letter, LDB to FF, September 29, 1934, FF/LC, Box 28.

186. Letter, LDB to FF, September 19, 1934, FF/LC, Box 28.

187. Letter, Raymond Moley to FF, October 26, 1935, Moley Papers, Hoover Institution, Box 17.

188. Letter, FF to Moley, October 30, 1935, Moley Papers, Hoover Institution, Box 17.

189. Letter, Moley to FF, October 31, 1935, Moley Papers, Hoover Institution, Box 17.

Chapter 5

1. William E. Leuchtenburg, *Franklin D. Roosevelt and the New Deal* (New York: Harper and Row, 1963), p. 94.

2. The description in this paragraph is drawn from Leuchtenburg, *Roosevelt and the New Deal*, pp. 91–142, 146.

3. Letter, LDB to FF, March 12, 1935, FF/LC, Box 28. See also Arthur M. Schlesinger, Jr., *The Age of Roosevelt. Vol. III: The Politics of Upheaval* (Boston: Houghton Mifflin Co., 1960), p. 326.

4. Letter, FF to Miss LeHand, April 22, 1935, Max Freedman, ed., *Roosevelt and Frankfurter: Their Correspondence 1928–1945* (Boston: Little Brown and Co., 1967), p. 260.

5. This letter to FDR was very carefully drafted to make it seem that the problem was that the liberals were too impatient and needed the meeting for some "straightening out," see Niles to FF, April 22, 1935 (sent on to FDR by FF), in Freedman, *Roosevelt and Frankfurter*, pp. 261–62. Niles was later assistant to Harry Hopkins in the WPA, and to both FDR and Truman.

6. See Felix Frankfurter file, e.g., letter, Niles to FF, March 8, 1934, David Niles papers, in possession of Dr. Abram L. Sachar, chancellor, Brandeis University, Waltham, Massachusetts (hereinafter cited as Niles papers). My thanks to Dr. Sachar for his kindness in allowing me to view these files.

7. Letter, J. A. Latimer (special assistant to Postmaster General) to FF, October 28, 1937, Niles papers.

8. For an example of this process see letter, Niles to FF, July 22, 1935 (returned to Niles with Frankfurter's penciled revisions on the original letter), Niles papers.

9. For an example of Frankfurter's action with a different message, see letter, FF to FDR, April 22, 1935, Freedman, *Roosevelt and Frankfurter*, p. 260.

10. Letters, Niles to FF (sent along to FDR), April 22, 1935, in Freedman, *Roosevelt*

and Frankfurter, pp. 261–62, and FF to FDR, April 30, 1935 and May 3, 1935, FF/LC, Box 98.

In his account of this incident, which relies solely on the files of Brandeis, Frankfurter, and Roosevelt, Nelson Dawson *Louis D. Brandeis, Felix Frankfurter and the New Deal,* (Hamden, Conn.: Archon Books/The Shoestring Press, Inc., 1981) pp. 115–16) only speculates that such "Byzantine manuevering" by Frankfurter in the use of a letter from Niles "may have" been possible. Based on my examination of the Niles papers, though, I believe that the likelihood of this strategy being used by Frankfurter is much stronger than has been previously described.

Strengthening the view that this whole episode was part of a larger strategy is the fact that Frankfurter, a meticulous file clerk of his personal letters, had placed in his Roosevelt folder a copy of his earlier letter to Brandeis, dated April 3, 1935, which praised Niles highly. See letter, FF to LDB, April 3, 1935, FF/LC, Box 98.

11. The Senators attending the meeting were George Norris, Edward Costigan, Hiram Johnson, Robert LaFollette, Jr., and Burton Wheeler. See Harold Ickes, *The Secret Diary of Harold L. Ickes,* vol. I (New York: Simon and Schuster, 1953), pp. 363–64 (May 15, 1935 entry).

12. 295 US 495 (1935). This was actually the second court test which the Justice Department had prepared for the NRA. The first case, involving violations of the Lumber Industry Codes by mill owner W. E. Belcher, was dropped when the government discovered various weaknesses in the facts of the suit. Faced with adverse press reaction to this decision, the administration quickly prepared its new case, which proved to be an even worse measure of the value of the NRA. For more, see Schlesinger, Jr. *The Politics of Upheaval,* pp. 276–77.

13. Telegram, Thomas G. Corcoran to FDR, April 4, 1935, FDRL, PPF 140 (*Italics mine*). Quoted also in Schlesinger, Jr., *The Politics of Upheaval,* p. 278; and Dawson, *Brandeis, Frankfurter and the New Deal,* p. 69.

Interview with Thomas G. Corcoran, September 29, 1977, Washington D.C.

14. According to the account of Arthur Schlesinger, which was the basis for this sentence, Thomas Corcoran believed that the message from the president was "deliberately held up." See Schlesinger, Jr. *The Politics of Upheaval,* p. 278.

For the message sent to Moley on the matter see letter, FF to Moley, dated only "1935," Moley Papers, Hoover Institution, Box 17.

15. Besides *Schechter,* the other decisions by the Court were *Humphrey's Executor v. U.S.,* 295 US 602 (1935) and *Louisville Joint Stock Land Bank v. Radford,* 295 US 602 (1935).

16. Schlesinger, Jr., *The Politics of Upheaval,* p. 280.

17. Memorandum, Benjamin V. Cohen to FF, untitled, May 28, 1935, FF/LC, Box 28. Parts of this memorandum are also quoted in Dawson, *Brandeis, Frankfurter and the New Deal,* p. 129–30; and another version of this incident, drawn from interview sources, is quoted in Schlesinger, Jr., *The Politics of Upheaval,* p. 280.

18. See telegram, FF to Grace Tully, May 27, 1935. Also, the nature of their discussion can be inferred from two letters, dated May 29, 1935 and May 30, 1935, written by FF to FDR following his trip and dealing with the subjects of "the Supreme Court vs. The President" and "a program for *immediate* action in dealing with the consequences of the Schechter decision." All these letters are quoted in Freedman, *Roosevelt and Frankfurter,* pp. 272–75.

19. Leuchtenburg, *Roosevelt and the New Deal,* p. 145.

20. This quotation and account is drawn from Schlesinger, *The Politics of Upheaval,* pp. 285–86. See also Leuchtenburg, *Roosevelt and the New Deal,* p. 145–46. Leuchtenburg argues, contrary to others, that FDR had not hoped for the Court to

strike down the NRA in order to allow him a free hand in choosing a new programmatic direction.

21. Letter, FF to LDB, June 3, 1935, LDB/LLS, Box G9. Also quoted in H. N. Hirsch, *The Enigma of Felix Frankfurter* (New York: Basic Books, 1981), p. 120; and Dawson, *Brandeis, Frankfurter, and the New Deal*, p. 133.

22. See Leuchtenburg, *Roosevelt and the New Deal*, p. 149; Schlesinger, *The Politics of Upheaval*, pp. 225–30; and Dawson, *Brandeis, Frankfurter and the New Deal*, pp. 96–97.

23. A search of all relevant files in the various collections revealed only one instance of Brandeis and Frankfurter combining to secure an appointment during the later New Deal period. In response to a request by the president, directed through Felix Frankfurter, Justice Brandeis recommended John Fahey for a position at the Department of Commerce. See letter, FF to FDR, September 14, 1935 (with Brandeis telegram attached), FDRL, PSF 150.

24. Letter, FF to FDR, November 15, 1935, FDRL, PPF 140. In this letter Frankfurter was passing along a message he had received from Brandeis (dated November 14, 1935, FF/LC, Box 28) concerning the election preparations. Obsessed with the need for studying the banks which had been bankrupted in the depression, Brandeis urged Frankfurter to suggest it to the president as a possible "campaign weapon."

Interestingly, in two other letters (dated December 15, 1935, and February 9, 1936, FF/LC, Box 28), Brandeis recommended to Frankfurter that the president and Thomas Corcoran begin gathering figures on the rapid increase in business profits as a demonstration of the positive achievements of his administration and on the recent business efforts of his opponent, Al Smith. While none of these suggestions appears to have been adopted by FDR, the willingness of Brandeis to involve himself even slightly in the upcoming highly partisan presidential campaign is surprising. Perhaps it is an indication that Brandeis was by this time so concerned with the adoption of his programs that he was less willing to observe the traditional standards of propriety for that era.

25. Letter, Norman Hapgood to FDR, January 25, 1937, FDRL, PPF 2278. Hapgood's code name for Brandeis is drawn from the location of the justice's cottage in Chatham, Massachusetts, which is on Cape Cod.

26. See also letters, Hapgood to FDR, July 5, 1935, July 13, 1935, July 15, 1935, July 17, 1935, July 30, 1935, August 3, 1935, August 7, 1935, August 11, 1935, August 26, 1935, November 30, 1935, February 20, 1936, May 25, 1936, July 31, 1936, January 7, 1937, and January 25, 1937, also see letters, FDR to Hapgood, June 22, 1935, February 24, 1936, and January 7, 1936, FDRL, PPF 2278, 2235.

27. Letter, FF to LDB, May 24, 1935, LDB/LLS, Box G9.

28. Two other pieces of FDR's "must" package of legislation were a banking regulation bill and a labor measure which eventually was passed as the National Labor Relations Act. See Leuchtenburg, *Roosevelt and the New Deal*, pp. 150–51.

29. For more on Brandeis's ideas as to how federal taxation could be used as a weapon for reforming society, see memorandum, "Visit with Justice Brandeis," written by Emanuel Goldenweiser (of the Federal Reserve Board), February 23, 1934, Emanuel Goldenweiser papers, LC, Box 7. See also letters, LDB to FF, January 21, 1933, March 18, 1933, September 10, 1933, and October 29, 1934, FF/LC, Box 28.

Justice Brandeis was so anxious to see the "contingency fee" bill enacted that he abandoned his usual practice and became actively involved in both the drafting of specific legislation and the lobbying campaign for its acceptance. After his initial suggestions of the need for such legislation in letters to Frankfurter (August 11, 1928, January 21, 1933, and March 18, 1933, FF/LC, Box 28), Brandeis wrote his lieutenant that the fee bill should "apply to all suits in the Court of Claims" (April 13, 1933, FF/LC, Box 28). Once drafted, the original bill was sent to Brandeis for his comments. The justice, however, did not believe that his allies had gone far enough. So, in a second letter to Frankfurter, dated April 30, 1933 (FF/LC, Box 28), Brandeis provided specific criticisms of each portion of this draft bill. He argued that the fees charged by lawyers in government claims cases should "in no way be dependent on the result of the agent or attorney's efforts." The bill was then revised in accordance with Brandeis's instructions, and Frankfurter brought it to the president's attention in a personal conference. In later sending a copy of the measure and a supporting memorandum to the White House, the professor made no secret of the actual inspiration for this proposal:

> L.B.D. thinks—this is of course solely for your own ears—that large losses to the revenue are directly traceable to evils connected with contingent fees in tax and other suits against the Government and that this Bill will plug up at least some of the holes that should be plugged up.
>
> This is, of course, the most opportune time to secure this legislation. (Letter, FF to FDR, May 29, 1933, Freedman, *Roosevelt and Frankfurter,* p. 135.)

When nothing was done on the bill during the initial months of the Roosevelt Administration, Brandeis wrote to his lieutenant at Harvard on July 14, 1933: "I hope the contingent fee matter will not sleep." (FF/LC, Box 28). But even Frankfurter could see that the time was not right for this idea, so he waited eight months before making a final plea to FDR in January, 1934:

> I hope you will secure at this session of Congress legislation to put a crimp into one of the most corrupting influences of our profession, namely, the big fees for nursing claims against the Government. This is all the more essential legislation because the hope of large fees for tax refunds is one of the great leverages for raids on the Treasury. You will remember that . . . last spring . . . I drafted at your suggestion, [a bill] putting a limit upon the fees that may be charged in cases of claims against the Government. Between ourselves, L.D.B. passed on that bill before I submitted it to you. (Letter, FF to FDR, January 29, 1934, FF/LC, Box 97.)

On February 2, 1934, Frankfurter proudly reported to LDB that he had pressed the idea on the president once again (LDB/LLS, Box G9). Then on January 30, 1936, Frankfurter sent another letter to Roosevelt urging once again the passage of the "contingency fee" law. This was followed by another encouraging letter from the Harvard professor mailed over two weeks later. See letters FF to FDR, January 30, 1936 and February 19, 1936, quoted in Freedman, *Roosevelt and Frankfurter,* pp. 314–18.

Despite all of these efforts, the idea never seems to have been seriously considered by the administration. Although it was finally included as one part of the president's tax message on March 4, 1936, it was never passed. See Sidney Ratner, *American Taxation, Its History as a Social Force in Democracy* (New York: W. W. Norton, Co., 1942), pp. 472–74; and letter FF to FDR, March 4, 1936, quoted in Freedman, *Roosevelt and Frankfurter,* p. 333.

30. Letter, LDB to FF, January 10, 1934, FF/LC, Box 28.
31. Letter, FF to LDB, November 17, 1934, LDB/LLS, Box G9. In another letter Brandeis

had reviewed in great detail the figures for tax returns in America in order to arm Frankfurter with necessary information. Letter, LDB to FF, September 29, 1934, FF/LC, Box 28.

32. This tax proposal was designed by Herman Oliphant, a neo-Brandeisian in the Treasury Department, and Morgenthau, who himself mistrusted large concentrations of power. The proposal had most of the provisions which Brandeis sought: inheritance and gift taxes, an intercorporate dividend tax, a graduated tax on income, and an undistributed profits tax for corporations. See Schlesinger, Jr., The Politics of Upheaval, p. 326.

   For a full description of the background of all these tax philosophies, see Ratner, American Taxation, passim.

33. At the president's request they drew up three bills on "contingency fees," "tramp corporations," and an excise tax by "insiders" between corporate officers. These were all originally Brandeis ideas which had been proposed to Frankfurter and Corcoran. See "Memorandum to the Secretary of the Treasury," sent by FDR on January 16, 1935, FDRL, PPF 140.

34. In his letter to Brandeis reporting the conversation, Frankfurter could not contain his glee: "Poor H.M. Jr. evidently inferred from F.D.'s talk that the President cares for what I say—for this is practically the first time H.M. Jr. and I ever talked." Letter, FF to LDB, December 20, 1934, LDB/LLS, Box G9.

35. Henry Morgenthau Presidential Diary, December 19, 1934, vol. 2, pp. 332–35, Henry L. Morgenthau papers, FDRL.

36. Roosevelt's address, delivered on January 4, 1935, can be found in Samuel Rosenman, ed., Public Papers and Addresses of Franklin D. Roosevelt, vol. IV (New York: Random House, 1938), p. 15.

37. "Memorandum to the Secretary of the Treasury," from FDR, January 16, 1935, with enclosed letter, Corcoran to FDR, dated January 14, 1935 (with bills and supporting memorandum for Congress), FDRL, PPF 140; also letter, FF to LDB, January 18, 1935, LDB/LLS, Box G9, in which FF called tho bills "well drawn "

38. Letter, FF to LDB, January 22, 1935, LDB/LLS, Box G9. Interestingly, he reported also that Robert Jackson, then in the Treasury Department, was supporting the bill.

39. Letter FF to FDR, May 16, 1935, in Freedman, Roosevelt and Frankfurter, p. 271. Also partially quoted in Dawson, Brandeis, Frankfurter and the New Deal, pp. 116–17.

40. This report was actually the second letter written by Frankfurter to Brandeis after his return from the visit to Washington; in addition, it appears to be in response to a direct request from the justice for information. The letter from Frankfurter, dated May 22, 1935, makes it clear that the two men spoke during the visit, but apparently only before the conference between FDR and the liberal/Progressive leaders. Frankfurter also reported that Herman Oliphant, the general counsel for the Treasury Department, was consulting Corcoran and Cohen for their ideas on tax policy. See letters, FF to LDB, May 22, 1935 and May 21, 1935, LDB/LLS, Box G9; and LDB to FF, May 19, 1935, FF/LC, Box 28.

41. Hirsch, Enigma of Frankfurter, pp. 116–18.

42. For more on the drafting process see Morgenthau Diary, June 16, 1935, and June 19, 1935, vol. 7, Morgenthau papers, FDRL; also Schlesinger, Jr., The Politics of Upheaval, p. 327; and Raymond Moley, The First New Deal (New York: Harcourt, Brace and World, 1966), p. 531. In a letter to Brandeis, Frankfurter said that FDR was determined on tax policy and the Treasury Department was helpful. See FF to LDB, June 14, 1935, LDB/LLS, Box G9. See also letter, FF to LDB, May 21, 1935, LDB/LLS, Box G9.

43. The quotations from the tax revision message, which was delivered on June 19, 1935, and in Rosenman, *Public Papers of FDR*, vol. III, pp. 271–75.

    One of the problems which FDR claimed would be solved by his program was the use of "tramp corporations" to increase profits. Also, large industries would be prevented from splitting up to evade taxes. Though this program used an indirect approach, it was clearly heading in the direction Brandeis and Frankfurter had long advocated.

44. Letter, LDB to FF, June 20, 1935, FF/LC, Box 28.

45. Letter, FF to LDB, July 10, 1935, LDB/LLS, Box G9. Frankfurter also noted that one of his efforts had achieved success: The Progressives were now happy with FDR following their meeting.

    See also letters, FF to LDB, July 21, 1935, LDB/LLS, Box G9; and LDB to FF, July 19, 1935, FF/LC, Box 28; as well as Ickes, *Secret Diary*, vol. I, pp. 412–15 (August 10, 1935 entry).

46. Letter, LDB to FF, August 30, 1935, FF/LC, Box 28. Also quoted in Dawson, *Brandeis, Frankfurter and the New Deal*, p. 119. For more on the final tax bill and its ramifications, see Ratner, *American Taxation*, pp. 469–72.

47. See letters, LDB to Gifford Pinchot, November 23 (?), 1931, quoted in Philip Funigiello, *Toward a National Power Policy: The New Deal and the Electric Utility Industry, 1933–1941*, (Pittsburgh: University of Pittsburgh Press, 1973), p. 21. This book was also extremely useful as background material for this section of the chapter. See also letters, Pinchot to LDB, November 18, 1931, Gifford Pinchot papers, LC, Box 1622; FF to LDB, August 7, 1932, LDB/LLS, Box G9; FF to Moley, February 28, 1933, FF/LC, Box 84. Both of the FF letters report on meetings he held with FDR in order to put forward LDB's views on utility regulation. See also memorandum, Harry Shulman, "A Visit with Justice Brandeis," December 8, 1933, FF/LC, Box 28.

    The Shulman memorandum makes clear a view which Brandeis had been expressing in his letters to Frankfurter over the years: the problem of holding companies could not be solved by the much-discussed Federal Incorporation Law. The justice was fearful that Congress would be content only to pass such a licensing law regulating the operation of the interstate power industries, which, he believed, would only serve to increase the size of the governmental structure without solving the basic problem.

    Also useful as background information for this section were Ellis W. Hawley, *The New Deal and the Problem of Monopoly*, (Princeton: Princeton University Press, 1966) and Schlesinger, Jr., *The Politics of Upheaval*, pp. 303–5. By this time, the practice of holding companies in the utility industry was so pervasive that by 1932 thirteen holding companies controlled fully 75 percent of the electric utility industry.

48. Memorandum, "Visit with Justice Brandeis," Emanuel Goldenweiser, February 23, 1934, Emanuel Goldenweiser papers, LC, Box 7. The justice said that the only exception to the tax should be the holding company stock held in foreign countries. The justice preferred to find a way to exercise this control through the states if possible. See memorandum, by Harry Shulman, December 8, 1933, FF/LC, Box 28.

49. Letter, LDB to FF, June 15, 1933, FF/LC, Box 28. The Brandeis idea was to tax all their profits by counting the dividends in the various subsidiaries of a corporation.

50. Letter, Daniels to FDR, September 26, 1934, FDRL, OF 237. The details on the formulation of this piece of legislation can be found in Funigiello, *Toward a National Power Policy*, pp. 32ff.; Hawley, *Problem of Monopoly*, pp. 330ff.; and Schlesinger, Jr., *Politics of Upheaval*, pp. 300–309.

51. Letter, LDB to FF, December 20, 1934, LDB/LLS, Box G9.
52. In a letter dated January 22, 1935, Frankfurter reported to Brandeis that the "boys," Corcoran and Cohen, had discovered in a personal conference with the president that Roosevelt was "really hot on holding co[mpanie]s and for drastic action." See letter, FF to LDB, January 22, 1935, LDB/LLS, Box G9.

    It was during this process that Frankfurter was tickled when Secretary of the Treasury Morgenthau was moved to call "practically for the first time." See transcript of the phone conversation in Morgenthau Diary, December 19, 1934, Morgenthau papers, FDRL.

    The Corcoran and Cohen report, delivered on January 22, 1935, called for a tax to induce streamlining by the corporations as well as the registration of these companies. For details see Michael E. Parrish, *Securities Regulation and the New Deal*, (New Haven: Yale University Press, 1970), pp. 157ff.
53. Letter, FF to LDB, January 24, 1935, in Freedman, *Roosevelt and Frankfurter*, pp. 251–53; and Henry L. Stimson Diaries, February 10, 1935, Sterling Library, Yale University. Stimson reports that during this meeting Frankfurter criticized the drastic nature of the "death sentence" provision, an action which led to the professor being "rapped" by the president.
54. Letter, Burns to FF, March 1, 1935, FF/LC, Box 28. Burns totally agreed with the suggestion.
55. Letter, LDB to FF, March 25, 1935, FF/LC, Box 28. See also letter, FF to LDB, March 15, 1935, LDB/LLS, Box G9. The presidential message can be found in Rosenman, *Public Papers of FDR*, IV, pp. 98–102.

    See also letters, FF to LDB, May 21, 1935, April 13, 1935, May 2, 1935, and June 14, 1935, LDB/LLS, Box G9. Frankfurter praised the president for his "obstinate courage" in pressing for the bill.
56. Letter, Hapgood to FDR, June 16, 1935, FDRL, PPF 2278.
57. Letter, FDR to Hapgood, June 22, 1935, FDRL, PPF 2278.
58. Letter, FF to Wheeler, May 3, 1935, FF/LC, Box 111. See also Reminiscences of Samuel Rosenman, COHC, p. 124. Corcoran and Cohen were also brought in to help on FDR's speeches and messages in this area.
59. For more on this, see Leuchtenburg, *Roosevelt and the New Deal*, p. 159.
60. In one letter Brandeis, through Hapgood, urged FDR to use this act vigorously to break up "vast concentrations of financial power." Letter, Hapgood to FDR, February 13, 1936, FDRL, PPF 2278. In a later letter the justice expressed approval to Felix Frankfurter for a Roosevelt speech which called for taxing existing holding companies. Letter, LDB to FF, January 17, 1938, FF/LC, Box 29.

    For more on the final bill see Funigiello, *Toward a National Power Policy*, pp. 94–97; and Hawley, *Problem of Monopoly*, pp. 335–37.
61. Letter, Elizabeth Raushenbush to LDB, dated only "Thurs." 1933, LDB/LLS, Box SC 12–2.

    See also, letters, LDB to Elizabeth Raushenbush, September 19, 1932, in Melvin Urofsky and David Levy, eds., *Letters of Louis D. Brandeis*, vol. V (Albany, N.Y.: State University of New York, 1975), pp. 510–11; and Reminiscences of Paul and Elizabeth Raushenbush, COHC, p. 137.
62. For general background on the entire unemployment insurance law see Daniel Nelson, *Unemployment Insurance: The American Experience, 1915–35* (Madison, Wis.: University of Wisconsin Press, 1969), chapter 9. See also Arthur M. Schlesinger, *The Coming of the New Deal* (Boston: Houghton Mifflin Co., 1958), pp. 301–3; Elizabeth Brandeis, "Security for Americans," *The New Republic*, December 5, 1934, p. 95; and Abraham Epstein, "Enemies of Unemployment Insurance," *The New*

Republic, September 16, 1933, pp. 94–96. For information on the approaches of Senator Robert Wagner to this problem, see J. Joseph Huthmacher, *Senator Robert F. Wagner and the Rise of Urban Liberalism* (New York: Atheneum, 1968), pp. 174–75.

Another proposal for unemployment insurance came from Senator Robert Wagner of New York, who called in 1933 for a federal-state approach in which tax incentives would be offered to encourage the establishment of private insurance funds for unemployed workers by their individual employers. One other group would eventually call for exclusively federal action to solve the problem.

63. Paul Raushenbush, "Starting Unemployment Compensation in Wisconsin," 4 *Unemployment Insurance Review* (April–May, 1967), p. 22. See also Reminiscences of Paul and Elizabeth Raushenbush, COHC, pp. 140–41; and letter, Thomas H. Eliot to author, May 26, 1978.

64. Letter, LDB to E. Raushenbush, September 16, 1933, in Urofsky and Levy, *Brandeis Letters*, vol. V, p. 520; and Reminiscences of Paul and Elizabeth Raushenbush, COHC, p. 141.

65. Ibid. Elizabeth Raushenbush responded that her husband would be "simply delighted" to draft a bill and then went on to criticize the other programs then being proposed. Letters, E. Raushenbush to LDB, September 20, 1933 and September 24, 1933, LDB/LLS, Box G7–1.

66. See letters, LDB to FF, September 20, 1933, FF/LC, Box 28; memorandum of talk with LDB by Harry Shulman, December 8, 1933, FF/LC, Box 28; letters, LDB to E. Raushenbush, September 30, 1933 and November 17, 1933, in Urofsky and Levy, *Brandeis Letters*, vol. V, pp. 523, 526–27; LDB to Donald Richberg, December 10, 1933, Richberg papers, LC, Box 1. Lubin said that he would take this idea straight to the secretary of labor, Frances Perkins, and the department's solicitor, Charles E. Wyzanski, Jr. The justice also spoke on this matter with Walter Gellhorn of Columbia University. Reminiscences of Paul and Elizabeth Raushenbush, COHC, p. 143. The fact that Brandeis would take this matter to General Johnson, a man for whom he had very limited respect, demonstrates the depth of his interest in this proposal.

67. Memorandum, Mr. Stoddard to A. Lincoln Filene, December 27, 1933, entitled "Justice Brandeis' statement on Unemployment," LDB/LLS, Box G–7.

68. Schlesinger, Jr., *Coming of the New Deal*, pp. 302–3. Dawson, *Brandeis, Frankfurter and the New Deal*, p. 106, is also in error on this question, placing the meeting "during the Christmas vacation of 1933," at Filene's home in Washington. No other source, published or unpublished, agrees with this contention as to location.

69. My account relies on the recollections of two of the participants: the Reminiscences of Elizabeth Raushenbush, COHC, pp. 142–48; and portions of an account in an interview with Judge Charles E. Wyzanski, Jr., January 13, 1977, Richmond, Virginia. Even here, however, there is disagreement. Judge Wyzanski contends in the interview, and in an article ("Brandeis," *Atlantic Monthly*, November, 1956, p. 69), that the meeting was held in Justice Brandeis's apartment. However Ms. Raushenbush specifically denies this contention. She recalls that the meeting was arranged by Filene in his daughter's Georgetown apartment. For more on this account see P. Raushenbush, "Starting Unemployment Compensation," p. 22.

Another source of disagreement revolves around the list of participants. For instance, Arthur Schlesinger Jr. (*Coming of the New Deal*, p. 302) places Thomas H. Eliot, assistant solicitor for the Department of Labor (who eventually ends up drafting portions of the bill under discussion), at the meeting. However, in a personal letter to the author dated May 26, 1978, Mr. Eliot denies that contention.

70. For more, see the Reminiscences of Paul and Elizabeth Raushenbush, COHC, pp. 142–48.

71. See Reminiscences of Paul and Elizabeth Raushenbush, COHC, pp. 149–55; and P. Raushenbush, "Starting Unemployment Compensation," p. 23.

Nelson, in *Unemployment Insurance*, p. 199, argues that the Brandeis program was neutral toward the different state insurance plans because it enabled all the various programs to flourish under his federal-state structured system.

72. Letter, LDB to FF, January 25, 1934, FF/LC, Box 115.

73. Of course, Frankfurter maintained a close watch on these events and responded to Brandeis's news of January 25 with an expression of his "delight . . . over the introduction of your excise tax on payrolls to effect regularity." Letter, FF to LDB, February 8, 1934, LDB/LLS, Box G9.

74. Letters, E. Raushenbush to LDB, January 8, 1934, February 5, 1934, February 10, 1934, February 12, 1934, February 15, 1934, May 26, 1935, LDB/LLS, Boxes G7–1, G11–3.

75. Memorandum, FDR to Rexford Tugwell, February 28, 1934, FDRL, PSF 73. See also Nelson, *Unemployment Insurance*, pp. 199–200.

76. Nelson, *Unemployment Insurance*, pp. 202–4 has full details on this delay. FDR was hesitant on this issue because the business community was upset about it.

See also letter, LDB to E. Raushenbush, April 22, 1934, in Urofsky and Levy, *Brandeis Letters*, vol. V, p. 537; Rosenman, *Public Papers of F.D.R.*, Vol. III, p. 162; and Leon Keyserling, "The Wagner Act," 29 *George Washington Law Review*, pp. 209–11. Keyserling, then administrative assistant to Wagner, argues that even the senator was not fond of this plan because it set up separate state plans rather than the overall national insurance plan he preferred.

77. Letters, Thomas Corcoran to FF, June 18, 1934, FF/LC, Box 149; and LDB to E. Raushenbush, June 8, 1934, in Urofsky and Levy, *Brandeis Letters*, vol. V, pp. 539–40.

The meeting was arranged by Corcoran and Raymond Moley. FDR was even more disposed to listen to Brandeis, having just recently received the justice's stern warning regarding the ill-advised direction of the administration's legislative program.

78. Letters, LDB to E. Raushenbush, June 8, 1934, in Urofsky and Levy, *Brandeis Letters*, vol. V, pp. 539–40; Corcoran to FF, April 22, 1934 and May 11, 1934, FF/LC, Box 116. Although Corcoran wrote the letters, it was made clear to Frankfurter that these were the sentiments of both himself and Cohen.

For Brandeis's similar messages to Frankfurter, see letters, LDB to FF, March 18, 1934 and May 24, 1934, FF/LC, Boxes 28, 115.

79. Letter, Corcoran to FF, June 18, 1934, FF/LC, Box 115; Frances Perkins, *The Roosevelt I Knew* (New York: Viking Press, 1946), pp. 286–87. See also Nelson, *Unemployment Insurance*, pp. 206–8. Nelson notes that the argument for the need to find a *constitutional* insurance program was even used in later discussions with state officials to secure their support for the Wagner-Lewis Act.

Also on the committee were Morgenthau, Cummings, Harry Hopkins, Edwin Witte (a Wisconsin professor serving as the executive director), and Arthur Altmeyer (as the chairman of the technical committee). For the full story of this committee see Edwin Witte, *The Development of the Social Security Act* (Madison, Wis.: University of Wisconsin Press, 1963).

80. This new plan also called for an increase in the benefits to unemployed workers. For more, see Nelson, *Unemployment Insurance*, p. 208; and Schlesinger, Jr., *Coming of the New Deal*, p. 305.

81. See letters, LDB to FF, June 7, 1934 and July 7, 1934, FF/LC Box 28.
82. Letter, FF to LDB, July 18, 1934, LDB/LLS, Box G9. Frankfurter's strategy seems to have been drawn from the letter by Thomas Corcoran, which gave him a picture of what was going on in Washington. Letter, Corcoran to FF, June 18, 1934, FF/LC, Box 115. Here, Corcoran also advised to "delay" on the unemployment insurance matter. In a follow-up letter, Brandeis approved of this strategy. Letter, LDB to FF, July 20, 1934, FF/LC, Box 28.

The conference between the justice and Frankfurter, which was held at Brandeis's summer cottage in Chatham, seems to have taken place shortly after July 7, 1934. See letter, LDB to FF, July 7, 1934, FF/LC, Box 28.

83. Frankfurter was particularly anxious to impress Moley because he had been informed in Corcoran's letter of June 18, 1934 (FF/LC, Box 115) that Moley was still well-connected with the White House and through the month of May had been writing speeches for the president.
84. All these quotations are from letter, FF to LDB, July 24, 1934, LDB/LLS, Box G9. In this same meeting, Frankfurter, seeking to gain better inside access to the decision-making process on this matter, tried to convince Moley to have Benjamin V. Cohen named as directing secretary of the Commitee on Economic Security which was drafting the law.

Moley's willingness to work with Frankfurter on this matter can be inferred from his diary entry for June 24, 1936 (Moley papers, Hoover Institution, Box 1).

85. Letter, FF to LDB, August 4, 1934, LDB/LLS, Box, G9. Years later, Brandeis was still calling Moley "mercurial." Letter, LDB to FF, August 1, 1938, FF/LC, Box 29.
86. The following quotations are all from one letter-memorandum: FF to Moley, July 25, 1934, Moley papers, Hoover Institution, Box 17.
87. Unless otherwise, noted, the following quotations are from letter, FF to FDR, July 29, 1934, FF/LC, Box 244. Contained herein is the undated Frankfurter memorandum on the subject of the speech discussing unemployment insurance.
88. This particular phrasing is very close to that which Frankfurter offered in his letter to Moley.

Relying on this same quotation and others from this memorandum by Frankfurter to Roosevelt, Dawson (*Brandeis, Frankfurter and the New Deal*, p. 109) fundamentally misinterprets Frankfurter's position on unemployment insurance. He argues that "Frankfurter's neutral facade was thin; he was clearly urging the Wisconsin plan on Roosevelt." In fact, the tenor of this entire memorandum, the companion letter to Raymond Moley, and the particular configuration of Brandeis's comments in his own letters and Frankfurter's phrasing of this memorandum to FDR (all of which Dawson missed) makes clear that the professor was in no way "clearly urging" Brandeis's solution on the president.

89. Letter, LDB to FF, July 20, 1934, FF/LC, Box 28.
90. Letter, LDB to FF, July 26, 1934, FF/LC, Box 28. In noting that he was enclosing Frankfurter's proposed letter with his own, Brandeis also offered this one criticism: "I assume he [FDR] will understand what premature commitment means—before his committee reports." Accordingly, Frankfurter adjusted his own letter to FDR to make this matter clear, writing, "I venture strongly to urge against premature commitment i.e. before your social investigator [sic] reports to you on the details of the program for social insurance." Letter, FF to FDR, July 29, 1934, FF/LC, Box 244.
91. Rosenman, *Public Papers of FDR*, vol. III, pp. 370–75.
92. Letters, LDB to FF, August 8, 1934, FF/LC, Box 28; and FF to LDB, August 8, 1934, August 24, 1934, LDB/LLS, Box G9. FF told the justice that there was indeed a

special need to influence Witte, and after the visit he reported that Witte was "well invigorated" by the talk with LDB.

93. Letter, LDB to FF, July 26, 1934, FF/LC, Box 28. At that time they were expecting the meeting to occur in early August. However, it was repeatedly postponed until the very end of the month. See letter, FF to LDB, August 24, 1934, LDB/LLS, Box G9.

94. Letter, FF to LDB, August 31, 1934, LDB/LLS, Box G–9.
    Frankfurter met with FDR again in October on this issue, but no record of their conversation remains. Letter, FF to LDB, September 17, 1934, LDB/LLS, Box G–9; see also letter, LDB to FF, October 28, 1934, FF/LC, Box 28.

95. Nelson, *Unemployment Insurance*, pp. 208–11; Witte, *The Social Security Act*, p. 118; and Rosenman, *Public Papers of F.D.R.*, vol. III, pp. 452–53. Undoubtedly, the plan was approved because of its political benefits as well as its constitutional basis. However, we cannot be certain that FDR was fully in favor of the policy because of the fact that the speech was drafted and approved by Perkins and her committee. See Perkins, *The Roosevelt I Knew*, p. 292.

96. Rexford Tugwell Diary, "The New Deal Diary," December 31, 1934, Tugwell papers, FDRL, Box 16. The report was issued during Christmas week after severe pressure by Perkins (*The Roosevelt I Knew*, pp. 292–93). Tugwell claims that Harry Hopkins joined him in this fight for a national plan. However, the evidence from other sources shows that Hopkins was quite clearly in favor of the federal-state approach. Partly because of this pressure, though, the final program emphasized "works programs" rather than "unemployment pensions."

97. Rexford Tugwell Diary, "The New Deal Diary," January 16, 1935, Tugwell papers, FDRL, Box 17.

98. Letter, LDB to FF, December 31, 1934, FF/LC, Box 28. See also letter, FF to LDB, January 4, 1935, LDB/LLS, Box G–9, in which FF says that "FDR was furious against the subsidy plan."

99. Letter, LDB to FF, February 7, 1935, FF/LC, Box 28. Despite Brandeis's great anxiety at that time regarding this legislation, there is no evidence that Frankfurter tried to get the president to change his mind and adopt the Wagner-Lewis tax offset idea for the 1935 Social Security Act.
    However, the LaFollettes wired FDR to protect the Wisconsin insurance plan. Also, Paul Raushenbush did some investigating in Washington to see what could be done on this matter (he was in town to draft a model insurance law for other states). See letter, FF to LDB, January 18, 1935, LDB/LLS Box G9; and LDB to FF, January 23, 1935, FF/LC, Box 28.
    Privately the justice hoped that Senator LaFollette would be able to amend this bill in the Senate to restore the "purity" to the act. Letter, FF to LDB, January 22, 1935, LDB/LLS, Box G9.
    Two months later the justice had become so disillusioned by the failure to return to the "pure" program that he wrote Frankfurter of his wish that the measure "go over to 1936" because "anything passed this year will be unalterably bad." Letter, LDB to FF, March 25, 1935, FF/LC, Box 28.

100. 301 U.S. 548 (1937).

101. The best work on the battle over this program, William Leuchtenburg's "The Origins of Franklin D. Roosevelt's 'Court-Packing' Plan," 1966 *The Supreme Court Review*, pp. 347–400, was used as a background reference for this section.

102. Alpheus T. Mason, *Brandeis: A Free Man's Life* (New York: Viking Press, 1946), pp. 624–27.

103. Reminiscences of Marquis Childs, COHC, pp. 65–70, Childs's recollection is in-

correct in one respect. He believed that Sutherland had retired when, in fact, it was Willis Van Devanter.

104. Letter, Benjamin V. Cohen to FF, October 11, 1937, FF/LC, Box 115. Interestingly, Cohen also reported that one of the reasons for Corcoran's ill feeling toward Brandeis was his belief that it was Brandeis's personal friendship with Frankfurter that had kept the professor from announcing his support of the "Court-packing" program.

105. Letter, LDB to FF, February 6, 1937, FF/LC, Box 38.

106. Letter, FDR to FF, February 9, 1937, quoted in Freedman, *Roosevelt and Frankfurter*, p. 381.

    Although FDR did not consult Frankfurter on the issue, he did give him a warning in advance that something unusual would occur and asked for his temporary silence. In a letter dated January 15, 1937, FDR wrote: "Very confidentially, I may give you an awful shock in about two weeks. Even if you do not agree, suspend final judgment and I will tell you the story." Frankfurter's response, dated January 18, 1937, displayed his suspense: "Are you trying to find out how well I can sit on top of a Vesuvius by giving me notice that 'an awful shock' is in store for me 'in about two weeks'? Well, I shall try to hold my patience and fortify my capacity to withstand 'an awful shock,' but you certainly tease my curiosity when you threaten me with something with which I may not agree. That, certainly, would be a great surprise." After the plan was announced, Frankfurter sent the following, dated Sunday (February 7, 1937): "And now you have blown me off the top of Vesuvius where you sat me some weeks ago." Then Frankfurter went on to hint that he might be willing to support the program when he said: "Dramatically and artistically you did 'shock' me. . . . But I have, as you know, deep faith in your instinct to make the wise choice—the choice that will carry intact the motley aggregation that constitutes the progressive army toward the goal of present-day needs, and that will, at the same time, maintain all that is good in the traditional democratic process." It was this last letter to which FDR was responding when he asked for Frankfurter's assistance. See Freedman, *Roosevelt and Frankfurter*, pp. 378–81. Also partially quoted in Dawson, *Brandeis, Frankfurter and the New Deal*, pp. 139–40; Hirsch, *Enigma of Frankfurter*, p. 121; and Joseph Lash, ed., *From the Diaries of Felix Frankfurter* (New York: W. W. Norton and Co., 1975), p. 61.

107. If there was any doubt in Frankfurter's mind about the stakes here for his own career, they must have been removed when, according to Max Freedman, FDR phoned him after the plan had been announced asking not only for his assistance, but for a public silence and neutrality toward the plan. According to Freedman, Roosevelt told Frankfurter that he "intended one day to put him on the Supreme Court, and he did not want him entangled in this particular controversy." Freedman, *Roosevelt and Frankfurter*, p. 372; also quoted in Hirsch, *Enigma of Frankfurter*, pp. 120–21.

108. Letter, C. C. Burlingham to FF, February 7, 1937, Charles C. Burlingham papers, Harvard, Box 5. Grenville Clark to FF, March 18, 1937, FF/LC, Box 42. See also Freedman, *Roosevelt and Frankfurter*, pp. 391–97.

109. None of the individuals interviewed for this volume knew first-hand about Frankfurter's position or were in a position to offer unimpeachable evidence regarding it. However, each has their own private opinion and their own story to tell about those days. For example, Joseph L. Rauh, Jr., remembers Harold Laski being very upset with Frankfurter for not publicly putting himself on the firing line in opposition to the program. Interview, July 9, 1979, Washington, D.C.

    James Landis argues that Frankfurter opposed the plan in his reminiscences for the Columbia Oral History Collection (pp. 301–2). One other scholar, Alpheus Mason, has argued that Frankfurter supported the plan (*Brandeis*, p. 625). While we may never know for sure about the nature of Frankfurter's position, it is clear that he was torn among three loves: for Brandeis, for Roosevelt, and for the Supreme Court as an institution.

110. The diary for this year and several others, along with a large batch of letters and documents, were discovered missing from the Frankfurter collection in late 1972. Jack Anderson's public plea for return of the documents appeared on September 14, 1973, (*Washington Post*, p. D21). About a month later the columnist received photocopies of some of the documents in the mail (many others had been copied by scholars around the nation and they too were returned), but even today some of this material is still missing.

111. Freedman, *Roosevelt and Frankfurter*, p. 372, relying on his interviews with Frankfurter, says that the professor had been privately "a central and constant adviser of the President, and, a few days before joining the Supreme Court himself, had actually helped to edit the official version of the court-packing controversy for the Public Papers of President Roosevelt." See also Hirsch, *Enigma of Frankfurter*, pp. 120–21; and Lash, *Frankfurter Diaries*, p. 61–62.

112. My position will differ here from others who have written on this subject. Quoting from some of the same letters which I will use, H.N. Hirsch (*Enigma of Frankfurter*, pp. 123–24), who sees more of a break between Brandeis and Frankfurter, and thus is closer to my position than any of the others, argues that the two men "came close to a break," but in the end Frankfurter's "friendship with Brandeis was too precious." Dawson (*Brandeis, Frankfurter and the New Deal*, pp. 144–47) also quotes from some of the same letters I will use and concludes that "this was undoubtedly the closest they ever came to an outright split," but then adopts the position of Max Freedman that "once tempers had cooled, they agreed not to discuss the Supreme Court crisis for a time to avoid placing such a strain on their friendship again" (*Roosevelt and Frankfurter*, p. 396). Lash (*Frankfurter Diaries*, p. 61) says only that the professor "quarrel[ed] with the revered Brandeis" over the issue.

Relying on personal interviews, a letter dated July 15, 1937, from Frankfurter to Brandeis, which the others do not use, and an analysis of the remainder of their personal correspondence, I see more of a break between the two men than has been previously depicted.

113. Letter, FF to LDB, March 26, 1937, (not sent), FF/LC, Box 28. That FF would direct such an attack against an action which was supported by LDB shows the depth of his emotion on the issue. This was one of the few times when he openly disagreed with his mentor.

114. Letter, FF to LDB, July 15, 1937, FF/LC, Box 28. As will be shown, this letter was written three months after he had discussed the issue with Brandeis personally. So, the justice's stance was obviously still a source of considerable annoyance to Frankfurter.

115. Letter, FF to FDR, March 30, 1937, in Freedman, *Roosevelt and Frankfurter*, p. 392.

116. Letter, FF to Mack, March 24, 1937, FF/LC, Box 81. Here FF said, "I greatly deplore that L.D.B. should have lent himself to the Chief's statement."

With Burlingham, Frankfurter discussed his objections to the justices' actions in the "Court-packing" fight and then proudly added: "I talked pretty plainly to LDB about this." Letter, FF to CCB, June 9, 1937, Charles C. Burlingham papers, Harvard Law Library, Box 4, Folder 15.

117. Letter, FF to Charles C. Burlingham, June 9, 1937, Charles C. Burlingham papers, Harvard Law Library, Box 4, Folder 15.
118. Letters, Stone to FF, April 8, 1937 and December 21, 1939, Charles C. Burlingham papers, Harvard Law Library, Box 5.
    Frankfurter remained fully informed on this matter because of his close contact to Justice Stone. For years the professor had been an informal political lobbyist for Stone as well and thus tended to take his side in this controversy. As a result, for years Frankfurter continued to be bitter toward Hughes. He only changed his mind after coming to the Supreme Court and seeing Hughes operate in that setting. See Alpheus Mason, *Harlan Fiske Stone: Pillar of the Law* (New York: Viking Press, 1956).
119. Letter, FF to LDB, undated and sent, FF/LC, Box 28.
120. Letters, LDB to FF, April 5, 1937 and April 25, 1937, FF/LC Box 28, cited in Dawson, *Brandeis, Frankfurter and the New Deal*, p. 147.
121. Interview with Edward F. Prichard, Jr., June 25, 1979, Frankfort, Kentucky. As a law student with Frankfurter, and then his law clerk in the 1939 term, Prichard was in a position to observe the change in the relationship between the two men. His assessment is entirely verified by an examination of the letters which passed between them following the Court-packing controversy.
122. Compared to the letters which were travelling between the two men on a weekly, and at times even daily basis, the number of letters between them during this later period represents only a mere handful.
123. Letter, FF to Charles C. Burlingham, June 9, 1937, Charles C. Burlingham papers, Harvard Law Library, Box 4, Folder 15.
124. Throughout the 1930s the justice had mobilized Felix Frankfurter for action on this issue. In April, 1933, the justice sent two private letters to the professor describing the conditions for European Jews and imploring him to take the matter up with the president. Instead, evidence in the Frankfurter files and the Raymond Moley papers indicates that over a four-month period, Frankfurter wrote Moley half a dozen times requesting help in liberalizing U.S. policy toward Jewish refugees. In each of these letters he felt it necessary to reassure the Brain Truster that "there isn't the slightest danger of mass immigration" of German Jews to America. Frankfurter then met personally with Moley and Herbert Feis attempting to "open the doors" for these refugees. Furthermore, Justice Brandeis met directly with Secretary of State Hull, who did not seem to appreciate the gravity of the problem.
    None of these efforts, however, were as effective as Frankfurter's work with Secretary of Labor Frances Perkins. After contacting her, in two letters written on April 27, 1933, and April 29, 1933, copies of which were forwarded to Raymond Moley and are now filed in the latter's personal papers at the Hoover Institution on War, Revolution and Peace, the department informally instructed the U.S. consuls to interpret the relevant immigration laws and quotas liberally. Seeing that even this action was insufficient, the Harvard professor continued to press for more official changes. See letters, LDB to FF, April 12, 1934 and April 13, 1934, FF/LC, Box 28; FF to Raymond Moley, April 24, 1933 and May 29, 1933, FF/LC, Box 84; FF to Raymond Moley, April 24, 1933, May 10, 1933, June 7, 1933, and June 13, 1933, Frances Perkins to FF, April 25, 1933, and FF to Frances Perkins, April 27, 1933 and April 29, 1933, all in Raymond Moley papers, Hoover Institution, Box 68; and Reminiscences of James Warburg, COHC, p. 638, (diary entry for May 3, 1933).
    Frankfurter's year of teaching (1933–1934) at Oxford gave Brandeis an opportunity to influence British policy regarding immigration to Palestine. Their private

correspondence during the period indicates that while the two men continually discussed possible avenues of assistance for the Jewish people, their actual accomplishments during this period were minimal. According to a private letter written on December 16, 1933 from Raymond Moley, then editor of *Today* magazine, to Frankfurter, Brandeis was able to delay the publication of an article by Moley on this issue pending a decision by the attorney general. In 1934, after additional pressure by the justice on Secretary Perkins and President Roosevelt, the immigration regulations prohibiting people likely to become "public charges" from entering the country—an excuse for artificially restricting entry quotas—was liberalized. While this was a beginning, much more needed to be done for the refugees. See letters, LDB to FF, December 30, 1933, FF/LC, Box 115; LDB to FF, August 27, 1933, FF/LC, Box 28; FF to LDB, November 7, 1933, LDB/LLS, Box G–9; Raymond Moley to FF, December 16, 1933, FF/LC, Box 117; and interview with Charles E. Wyzanski, Jr., January 13, 1977, Richmond, Virginia. An excellent background source on this immigration issue as it concerned the refugees before and during the war is Henry L. Feingold, *The Politics of Rescue: The Roosevelt Administration and the Holocaust, 1938–1945* (New Brunswick, N.J.: Rutgers University Press, 1970)

Letters stored in the Frankfurter papers at the Library of Congress show that during the mid-1930s Justice Brandeis resorted to reminding Frankfurter of the deteriorating political situation of the European Jews. At the same time he continued to advise and fund the operations of the Zionist organization (since his lieutenants were now firmly in control of the organization). Letters, LDB to FF, July 19, 1936 and August 20, 1936, FF/LC, Box 28; LDB to Stephan Wise, January 22, 1935, June 2, 1936, September 5, 1936, LDB to Felix Warburg, July 11, 1935, LDB to Robert Szold, July 12, 1937, January 2, 1938, January 16, 1938, all in Urofsky and Levy, *Brandeis Letters*, vol. V, pp. 571–72, 576–77, 590–91, 593–94.

125. LDB to Stephan Wise, September 23, 1937 and October 3, 1937, LDB to Julian Mack, October 4, 1937, and LDB to FF, December 12, 1937, FF/LC, Box 28; FF Memorandum on Zionism interests, untitled and dated "September, 1937," FF/LC, Box 28.

126. Letters, LDB to FF, October 16, 1938, LDB to Robert Szold, November 24, 1938, in Urofsky and Levy, *Brandeis Letters*, vol. V, pp. 603, 605–6. Benjamin Cohen to FF, November 21, 1938, FF/LC, Box 45; and LDB to FF, November 23, 1938, FF/LC, Box 29. See also Feingold, *The Politics of Rescue*, p. 13.

Even after the justice retired on February 13, 1939, he continued to personally lobby the president on this issue. In a lengthy private letter, dated April 17, 1939, Brandeis asked FDR to intercede with the British once again—this time in order to delay their imminent issuance of even more restrictive immigration regulations. Although the president had succeeded in such a mission twice before and an official memorandum dated May 10, 1939 shows that he instructed Undersecretary of State Sumner Welles to act on the matter, this time the effort was futile. On May 17, 1939, the British, succumbing to Arab pressure, issued a new White Paper restricting immigration. Thereafter, the files show that Brandeis continued to advise and consult with Roosevelt in person and by mail, seeking to influence United States policy toward Jewish immigration. See letters, Gardner Jackson to FF, December 8, 1938, Gardner Jackson papers, FDRL, Box 5; LDB to FDR, December 21, 1938, April 17, 1939, and December 4, 1939, and FDR to LDB, December 27, 1938, May 11, 1939, December 16, 1939, and May 5, 1941, FDRL, PPF 2335; FDR's memo for General Watson on meeting with LDB, October 19, 1939, FDRL, PPF 2335; LDB to FDR, April 26, 1941, in Urofsky and Levy, *Brandeis Letters*, vol. V, p. 651;

memorandum for Undersecretary of State Sumner Welles from FDR, May 10, 1939, FDRL, OF 700; and phone message from LDB, May 18, 1939, FDRL, PPF 2335. In May, Brandeis sent Dr. Solomon Goldman to see FDR, but the appointment was given instead to Secretary of State Cordell Hull.

Chapter 6

1. Stone was upset when Black issued a long dissent to a per curiam opinion. At that time, reports Stone's biographer, Alpheus T. Mason, such a practice of dissenting to short, unsigned opinions was virtually unprecedented. See letter, Stone to FF, February 8, 1938; and memorandum, FF to Black, undated, quoted in Alpheus T. Mason, Harlan Fiske Stone; Pillar of the Law, (New York: The Viking Press, 1956), pp. 468–70. See also H. N. Hirsch, The Enigma of Felix Frankfurter (New York: Basic Books, Inc., 1981), pp. 140–41.
2. FDR had mentioned the possibility to Frankfurter when he wanted to place the professor in the administration as solicitor general and when he asked for assistance during the "Court-packing" fight. The theory that Brandeis's retirement was preventing the appointment of Frankfurter to the Court came from Thomas Corcoran, as reported in a letter from Benjamin Cohen to Frankfurter. See "Memorandum by Frankfurter of a Visit with Roosevelt on March 8, 1933," in Max Freedman, ed., Roosevelt and Frankfurter: Their Correspondence, 1928–1945 (Boston: Little, Brown and Co., 1967), p. 112, see also p. 372; and letter, Benjamin V. Cohen to FF, October 11, 1937, FF/LC, Box 115.
3. For more on the efforts by these men to bring about the Frankfurter appointment, see Liva Baker, Felix Frankfurter (New York: Coward-McCann, Inc., 1969), pp. 201–7; Joseph Lash, ed., From the Diaries of Felix Frankfurter (New York: W. W. Norton and Co., 1976), pp. 63–65; and Hirsch, Enigma of Frankfurter, pp. 124–26.
4. Confidential interviews, July 9 and July 10, 1979, Washington, D.C. Frankfurter not only dictated his reminiscences to Harlan B. Phillips (Felix Frankfurter Reminisces (New York: Reynal and Co., 1960)) and Max Freedman (Roosevelt and Frankfurter), but also had a highly personal diary, which has now been published under the editorship of Joseph Lash (Frankfurter Diaries). Moreover, throughout Frankfurter's unpublished papers are explanatory memoranda, some quite obviously written years after the events took place, which "explain" the incidents being documented.
5. Phillips, Frankfurter Reminisces, pp. 283–84.
6. Confidential interview, July 9, 1979, Washington D.C.
7. See letter, FF to Burlingham, July 9, 1937, Burlingham papers, Harvard Law Library, Box 4, Folder 15.
8. Felix Frankfurter: Talks in Tribute, February 26, 1965 (occasional Pamphlet Number Eight, Harvard Law School, Cambridge, Mass.), quoted in Sanford Levinson, "The Democratic Faith of Felix Frankfurter," 25 Stanford Law Review (1973), p. 430. See this article for more on Frankfurter's patriotic instinct and its effect on his general philosophy.
9. Baker, Frankfurter, p. 207.
10. In fact, none of the programs that Frankfurter worked on during the war years were ever brought before the Supreme Court for review. So he was never put in the situation, which repeatedly confronted Brandeis, of having to decide whether to judicially review his private political endeavors. While we cannot know for certain whether Frankfurter would have disqualified himself from such litigation, perhaps one can speculate about his decision from his behavior in United States v. United

Mine Workers. In this case, despite having earlier helped to draft the Norris-La-Guardia Anti-Injunction Act, Frankfurter remained on the bench when that legislation was tested in the Supreme Court. Apparently, like Brandeis before him, Frankfurter considered his private political and subsequent official judicial work to be completely separate.

11. No more vivid evidence exists of this attitude than the Court's decisions in: *Ex parte Quirin,* 317 U.S. 1 (1942) and *Korematsu v. United States,* 323 U.S. 214 (1944).

   In the first case, the highly activist, civil libertarian Roosevelt Court upheld the death sentences issued by a military court to eight German saboteurs who had landed on American shores during the war. Interestingly, the full opinion in the case was not issued by the Court until after the executions had been carried out. For more, see Mason, *Harlan Fiske Stone,* pp. 653–66. In the *Korematsu* case the Court upheld the internment of one hundred thousand persons of Japanese ancestry who were then living on the West Coast of the United States.

12. Interview with Thomas G. Corcoran, September 29, 1977, Washington, D.C. The statement by this source is confirmed by the fact that during the spring and summer of 1939 Frankfurter had sent nearly three hundred short notes to FDR on the progress of the war. Apparently, though, these notes were partially destroyed by Frankfurter, and the rest were not kept by the president. See Freedman, *Roosevelt and Frankfurter,* pp. 496–97.

13. Letters, FF to FDR, May 16, 1941, and United States Army to FF, May 9, 1941, in Freedman, *Roosevelt and Frankfurter,* pp. 597–99.

14. Letters, FDR to FF, January 16, 1942, and FF to FDR, January 13, 1942 and January 20, 1942, in Freedman, *Roosevelt and Frankfurter,* pp. 642–43.

15. Letters, FDR to FF, September 28, 1943, and FF to FDR, September 15, 1943 and September 28, 1943, in Freedman, *Roosevelt and Frankfurter,* p. 702.

16. Confidential interview, July 9, 1979, Washington, D.C.

17. Letter, FF to FDR, January 8, 1941, in Freedman, *Roosevelt and Frankfurter,* pp. 577–78.

18. Freedman, *Roosevelt and Frankfurter,* p. 578.

19. Letter, FF to FDR, January 8, 1941, in Freedman, *Roosevelt and Frankfurter,* pp. 577–78.

20. Letters, Hugo Black to FDR, September 10, 1941, James Byrnes to FDR, August 26, 1941, and Stanley Reed and William O. Douglas to FDR, June 23, 1941, FDRL, Official File, Box 1560.

   Another short account of the Frankfurter-Corcoran split, written solely on the basis of interview sources, can be found in Joseph C. Goulden, *The Super Lawyers: The Small and Powerful World of the Great Washington Law Firms* (New York: Weybright and Talley, 1971), p. 155.

21. Confidential interview, July 9, 1979, Washington, D.C...

22. Memorandum, Edward F. Prichard to FF, January 6, 1945, FF/LC, Benjamin V. Cohen file, Box 45.

23. Confidential interview, July 9, 1979, Washington, D.C.

24. Letter, FF to FDR, November 10, 1942, FDRL, President's Secretary's File, Box 151.

25. Rosenman had sent the justice a draft of his memoirs to be entitled *Working with Roosevelt* (New York: Harper and Brothers, 1952), and FF added these comments. See Samuel Rosenman papers, FDRL, Box 1. Rosenman did use these changes in his published account (pp. 207–8).

26. This paragraph is based on a variety of sources: memorandum, untitled, September 20, 1940, speech file, Samuel Rosenman papers, FDRL, Box 1; letters, FF to Rosenman, April 13, 1942, FDRL, PPF 1820; FF to Rosenman, December 29, 1940, Samuel

Rosenman papers, FDRL, Box 1. At this time the justice was helping draft Roosevelt's third inaugural address. FF to Rosenman, October 7, 1940, and FF to FDR, August 12, 1940, in Freedman, *Roosevelt and Frankfurter*, pp. 540–46; draft pages of Rosenman memoirs, Samuel Rosenman papers, FDRL, Box 1; and Henry L. Stimson Diaries, October 23, 1940, Henry L. Stimson Papers, Sterling Library, Yale University.

27. Unless otherwise indicated, the basics of this account of FF's campaign for Stimson/Patterson is drawn from Notes by Samuel Spencer of a conversation with FF and Grenville Clark, summer, 1947, FF/LC, Box 44; also Samuel Spencer, "A History of the Selective Training and Service Act of 1940" (Unpublished Ph.D. dissertation, Harvard University, 1949), pp. 104–125.

It seems that Spencer's handwritten notes were given to Grenville Clark, who then lost them in a box in his office attic for a period of ten years. While Spencer used his own copy to finish his dissertation in 1949, Frankfurter repeatedly pressed Clark to retrieve the notes and place them with his private papers. This was finally done in 1957. See letters, Clark to FF, May 1, 1957, FF/LC, Box 44; and FF to Clark, May 16, 1957, FF/HLS, Box 184. Consequently, these notes were not available to Henry L. Stimson when he was writing his autobiography with McGeorge Bundy (*On Active Service in Peace and War* (New York: Harper and Brothers, 1947). Seeking perhaps to foster a certain myth about this appointment, the former secretary of war writes only that he was "surprised" and "astonished" to receive the presidential call and fails even to mention Frankfurter's role in the affair (p. 323). This may explain why Frankfurter wrote Clark on January 8, 1952 complaining about "the whole incredible distortion and falsification of much pertaining to FDR's administration, including my [F.F.'s] relations with him." Clark quotes this letter in his missive to FF, May 1, 1957, FF/HLS, Box 184. As late as mid-1957, Clark was commenting to Frankfurter that no one had "written a reasonably accurate account as to the appointment of Stimson and Patterson." Clark to FF, May 1, 1957, FF/HLS, Box 184. Apparently, Frankfurter also withheld the notes from Elting E. Morison when he was writing his biography of Stimson, *Turmoil and Tradition: A Study of the Life and Times of Henry L. Stimson* (New York: Houghton Mifflin Co., 1960), chapter 26. Morison does cite on pp. 480–82 conversations with both FF and Clark concerning these events.

Writing after Frankfurter's papers were opened to the public, Richard Danzig does cite the Spencer dissertation in his fine article on Frankfurter's jurisprudence, "How Questions Begot Answers in Felix Frankfurter's First Flag Salute Opinion," 1977 *The Supreme Court Review* pp. 257–74. However, this account of the Frankfurter effort, for obvious reasons, is extremely abridged (pp. 269–70).

28. According to Frankfurter's account, apparently FDR had asked on one occasion for Harry Woodring's resignation from that position.

29. Letter, FF to FDR, May 26, 1940, in Freedman, *Roosevelt and Frankfurter*, p. 523.

30. On p. 521 of *Roosevelt and Frankfurter*, Max Freedman argues that FF's campaign for Stimson began on May 3, 1940. At this time he brought Stimson and FDR together at a luncheon for a discussion on foreign affairs. However, there is no evidence in the papers of FF, FDR, or Stimson to support this idea. The fact that the luncheon was a coincidence and that the campaign did not formally begin until nearly a month later is indicated in Spencer's notes of conversations with FF (summer, 1947, FF/LC, Box 44), and confirmed in a letter from Grenville Clark to McGeorge Bundy, July 18, 1947, FF/LC, Box 44.

31. Interview with Judge Charles E. Wyzanski, Jr., January 13, 1977, Richmond, Virginia.

32. See Henry L. Stimson Diary, May 3, 1940, Henry L. Stimson papers, Sterling Library, Yale University; and Henry L. Stimson and McGeorge Bundy, *On Active Service in Peace and War* (New York: Harper and Brothers, 1947), pp. 292–93.

33. One of the reasons for the appeal of this proposal to FDR was the fact that Stimson was a Republican. At that time, the president was contemplating forming a "Coalition Cabinet" for the prosecution of the war.

34. As reported in letter, Grenville Clark to McGeorge Bundy, July 18, 1947, FF/LC, Box 44.

35. Letter, FF to FDR, June 4, 1940, FF/LC, Box 98. This letter also contains some of the justice's impressions of Robert Patterson.

36. Letter, Clark to FF, June 14, 1940, quoted in Spencer, "A History of the Selective Training and Service Act," p. 168; see also letter, FF to FDR, June 5, 1940, FF/LC, Box 98.

37. This story is based on interviews with Edward F. Prichard, Jr., June 25, 1979, Frankfort, Kentucky; and Judge Charles E. Wyzanski, Jr., January 13, 1977, Richmond, Virginia. Neither of these sources is certain of the identity of the other candidate being considered for the post of assistant secretary of war.

38. Letter, FF to FDR, June 20, 1940, FF/LC, Box 98. One week before this appointment was made Frankfurter did send the president a letter discussing the qualifications of Patterson for the position. See letter, FF to FDR, June 13, 1940, FF/LC, Box 98.

39. Letter, FF to Grenville Clark, May 16, 1957, FF/HLS, Box 184.

40. Letter, FF to Morris L. Ernst, June 5, 1930, quoted in August Meier and Elliott Rudwick, "Attorneys Black and White: A Case Study of Race Relations in the NAACP," 62 *Journal of American History* (March, 1976), p. 933; see also Richard M. Dalfiume, *Desegregation of the U.S. Armed Forces: Fighting on Two Fronts, 1939–1953* (Columbia, Mo.: University of Missouri Press, 1969), pp. 34–36; Walter White, *A Man Called White: The Autobiography of Walter White* (New York: Viking Press, 1949), pp. 187–88; and Jonathan J. Rusch, "William H. Hastie and the Vindication of Civil Rights" (unpublished Master's thesis, University of Virginia, 1974), *passim*. My thanks to Mr. Rusch for pointing out many of the sources used in this section on Hastie.

41. Letter, FF to Ernst, June 5, 1930, quoted in Meier and Rudwick, "Attorneys Black and White," p. 933.

42. Henry L. Stimson Diary, October 22, 1940, Henry L. Stimson papers, Sterling Library, Yale University.

43. Henry L. Stimson Diary, April 3, 1941 and April 6, 1941, Henry L. Stimson papers, Sterling Library, Yale University; and Reminiscences of Harvey Bundy, COHC, pp. 149–50.

44. Unless otherwise noted, the following portrait of FF's work with the War Department and with Stimson is based on interviews with John J. McCloy, August 10, 1979, New York, N.Y.; and with Joseph L. Rauh, Jr., July 9, 1979, Washington, D.C.

45. This description is given by Stimson in his Diary, March 28, 1941, Henry L. Stimson papers, Sterling Library, Yale University. A review of those diaries written during the war years reveals the scores of occasions that the two men met to discuss policies of all varieties.

46. Henry L. Stimson Diary, January 4, 1941, Henry L. Stimson papers, Sterling Library, Yale University. Also quoted in Joseph Lash, *Roosevelt and Churchill: 1939–1941* (New York: W. W. Norton and Co., Inc., 1976), p. 186.
    The analysis of the relationship among the three men comes not only from my

interview sources but is also confirmed by a close reading of their personal correspondence and the diaries of FF and Stimson.

47. Henry L. Stimson Diary, July 23, 1940, May 7, 1941, May 25, 1941, and May 26, 1941, Henry L. Stimson papers, Sterling Library, Yale University.

48. Interview with Edward F. Prichard, Jr., June 25, 1979, Frankfort, Kentucky.

49. Letter, FF to FDR, May 3, 1940, FF/LC, Box 98.

50. Undated memorandum, FF to FDR (probably written in June or July, 1940), in Freedman, *Roosevelt and Frankfurter*, pp. 531–35. See also Lash, *Roosevelt and Churchill*, p. 172.

51. Letter, FF to FDR, May 11, 1939, in Freedman, *Roosevelt and Frankfurter*, pp. 492–94.

52. Letter, FF to Burlingham, July 24, 1940 and September 29, 1940, Charles C. Burlingham papers, Harvard Law School, Box 5, Folder 2.

53. Letters, FF, to FDR, July 23, 1940, September 4, 1940, September 12, 1940, September 21, 1940, and FF to Missy Le Hand, August 12, 1940, in Freedman, *Roosevelt and Frankfurter*, pp. 539–41, 551–52.

54. This quotation and the account of the "Hatch Act Work" is based on interviews with Joseph L. Rauh, Jr., July 9, 1979, Washington, D.C.; and with Edward F. Prichard, Jr., June 25, 1979, Frankfort, Kentucky.

55. Letter, FDR to FF, November 8, 1940, in Freedman, *Roosevelt and Frankfurter*, p. 551.

56. For more on the disparity between Frankfurter's religion and his desire for social status, see Lash, *Frankfurter Diaries*, pp. 1–98; and Hirsch, *Enigma of Frankfurter*, *passim*.

57. FF had met Lord Lothian when he was working with Woodrow Wilson at Versailles and Lothian was secretary to Prime Minister Lloyd George. On the briefing of Halifax, see letter, FF to Percy, December 23, 1940, FF/LC, Box 89.

    FF became friends with Casey when the latter served as Australian Minister to the United States. See Raymond Moley, *The First New Deal*, (New York: Harcourt, Brace and World, 1966), p. 383; and Richard Casey, *Personal Experience 1939–1946* (New York: David McKay Company, Inc., 1962), pp. 51–53.

58. Letters, FF to FDR, February 2, 1939, June 3, 1939, June 13, 1939, September 3, 1939, and September 13, 1939, in Freedman, *Roosevelt and Frankfurter*, pp. 486–500. See also Henry L. Stimson Diaries, July 5, 1939, Henry L. Stimson papers, Sterling Library, Yale University.

59. Memorandum by FF to FDR, September 28, 1939, in Freedman, *Roosevelt and Frankfurter*, pp. 499–500. Also quoted in Walter J. Cibes, "Extra-Judicial Activities of the United States Supreme Court, 1790–1960," (unpublished Ph.D. dissertation, Princeton University, 1975), p. 1151.

60. Roosevelt, in his speech on September 21, 1939, called for repealing the arms embargo portion of the Neutrality Act of 1935. See Samuel Rosenman, *Public Papers and Addresses of Franklin D. Roosevelt*, vol. 8 (New York: Random House, 1938), pp. 512–25, especially p. 516.

    By taking this action, Congress favored the British in reality because the German ships would not be able to safely cross the Atlantic in order to secure the American supplies. See Lash, *Roosevelt and Churchill*, chapter 12, for more details.

61. This account is based on an interview with Benjamin V. Cohen, September 26, 1977, Washington, D.C.; Lash, *Roosevelt and Churchill*, pp. 210–20; and Emmet John Hughes, *The Living Presidency* (New York: Houghton Mifflin Co., 1972), p. 324.

62. For more on the development of this normative standard, see the book's appendix.

63. This and the previous quotations are drawn from the Henry L. Stimson Diary, August 15, 1940, Henry L. Stimson papers, Sterling Library, Yale University. Also quoted in Lash, *Roosevelt and Churchill*, p. 210.

64. In 1941, the president finally compromised and put a base on Iceland for the protection of both areas and the entire North Atlantic. For more, see letter, FF to FDR, December 30, 1940, FDRL, President's Secretary's File, Box 140. On December 31, according to marginal notes, FDR sent this letter along to Sumner Welles, an assistant secretary of state. FF repeated the message in a memorandum dated June 15, 1941, in Freedman, *Roosevelt and Frankfurter*, pp. 608–9.

    On the Finland matter, see letter, FF to FDR, November 29, 1940 (includes Lothian's memorandum), in Freedman, *Roosevelt and Frankfurter*, pp. 561–64; and FDR phone message for FF, December 2, 1940, FDRL, President's Secretary's File, Box 150.

65. This agency later became the British Supply Council. For more on Jean Monnet's actions during the war, see his *Memoirs* (London: William Collins Sons and Co., 1978), chapter 7.

66. Interview with Milton Katz, August 3, 1979, Cambridge, Massachusetts.

67. Interview with Robert Nathan, July 11, 1979, Washington, D.C. This interview, along with the one cited in footnote 66 above, was helpful for the entire description of Monnet's personality and goals.

68. See Henry L. Stimson Diary, November 25, 1940, Henry L. Stimson papers, Sterling Library, Yale University. Also see letter, FF to FDR, December 19, 1940 (includes Monnet's memorandum on the "New Order" in Europe), Freedman, *Roosevelt and Frankfurter*, pp. 566–68.

69. Monnet, *Memoirs*, p. 161; Samuel I. Rosenman, *Working with Roosevelt* (New York: Harper and Brothers, 1952), pp. 261–62; and Lash, *Roosevelt and Churchill*, pp. 262–80.

70. According to Benjamin V. Cohen's recollection, it was the president himself who first conceived the "lend-lease" idea, and the proposal was subsequently developed by his aides. Interview with Benjamin V. Cohen, September 26, 1977, Washington, D.C.

71. Robert Sherwood, *Roosevelt and Hopkins: An Intimate History* (New York: Harper and Brothers, 1948), p. 232. For reasons known only to Sherwood, he does not identify Frankfurter as the third party at this meeting. Lash, in *Roosevelt and Churchill* (p. 274), also makes this quotation and correctly speculates that it "may have been Justice Frankfurter" who was at the meeting. Subsequently, Monnet, in his *Memoirs*, pp. 164–66, positively identifies Frankfurter as the "friend" who lectures Hopkins.

72. Draft of Casey memoirs sent to FF for correction, October 25, 1960, FF/LC, Box 244.

73. Letter, Casey to Australian High Commissioner, January 6, 1941, FF/HLS, Box 195. This letter is reproduced in slightly different form in Casey, *Personal Experience*, pp. 51–53. It is this latter published version which is quoted by Lash, *Roosevelt and Churchill*, p. 274.

74. Lash, *Roosevelt and Churchill*, pp. 274–86.

75. Henry L. Morgenthau Diary, January 2, 1941, Morgenthau papers, FDRL, vol. 344, p. 91.

76. The final bill was drafted on January 10, 1941.

    The account of this drafting process is drawn from a variety of sources: interview with Benjamin V. Cohen, September 26, 1977, Washington, D.C.; and Oscar Cox Diary, entries for January 2 to January 5, 1941, Oscar Cox papers, FDRL, Box 145.

77. Henry L. Stimson Diary, January 26, 1941, Henry L. Stimson papers, Sterling Library, Yale University.
78. The account of the legislative campaign for Lend-Lease is drawn from an interview with John J. McCloy, August 10, 1979, Washington, D.C. The supportive letters from Frankfurter to Roosevelt, dated February 25, 1941 and February 27, 1941, are in Freedman, *Roosevelt and Frankfurter*, pp. 582–86.
79. Jay Pierrepont Moffat, *The Moffat Papers* (Cambridge, Mass.: Harvard University Press, 1952), p. 354. Also quoted in Lash, *Roosevelt and Churchill*, p. 289.
80. Henry L. Stimson Diary, February 16, 1941, Henry L. Stimson papers, Sterling Library, Yale University; and Oscar Cox Diary, August 2, 1941, August 3, 1941, and August 19, 1941, Cox papers, FDRL, Box 145.
81. This account is based on interviews with Edward F. Prichard, Jr., June 25, 1979, Frankfort, Kentucky; and Joseph L. Rauh, Jr., July 9, 1979, Washington, D.C. For more background on this group, see David Halberstam, *The Powers That Be* (New York: Alfred A. Knopf, 1979), pp. 163–75.
82. This duty is described in *O.E.M.; Functions and Administration* (Washington, D.C.: Government Printing Office, April, 1941), p. 3. For a brief explanation of the functions of this agency, see Alfred H. Kelly and Winfred A. Harbison, *The American Constitution: Its Origins and Development* 3rd edn. (New York: W. W. Norton and Company, Inc., 1963), p. 830.

The authority for this agency was initially granted in an executive order, number 8248, dated September 8, 1939.
83. Created by executive order, number 8629, January 7, 1941.
84. Virtually nothing has been written on the activities of this vitally important agency or of Frankfurter's wartime protégés. This story, and the entire account of the work of these two groups, is drawn from interviews with Joseph L. Rauh, Jr., July 9, 1979, Washington, D.C.; Edward F. Prichard, Jr., June 25, 1979, Frankfort, Kentucky; and Robert Nathan, July 11, 1979, Washington, D.C.

A similar version of the "bombers" story based on his interviews appears in Halberstam, *The Powers That Be*, p. 174.
85. Two other examples of the sort of tasks assigned to this group are provided by the interview with Joseph L. Rauh, Jr., July 9, 1979, Washington, D.C. When Roosevelt wanted to ensure that the Russians would get needed supplies for the war, the legal team from the OEM was placed in charge of supervising the effort. Later, when there was a threatened march by Blacks on the Capital to protest segregation in the Armed Services, this agency was charged with drafting the conciliatory memorandum which defused the controversy.
86. Wiretap Transcripts, August 3, 1927, Secretary of State's Office, Government Center, Boston, Massachusetts.
87. The account of these soirees was drawn from an interview with Edward F. Prichard, Jr., June 25, 1979, Frankfort, Kentucky. The story is confirmed by interviews with two visitors to these parties: John J. McCloy, August 10, 1979, New York, N.Y., and Judge Carl McGowan (who lived at one time in Hockley House), July 10, 1979, Washington, D.C.
88. Confidential interview, July 9, 1979, Washington, D.C.
89. Henry L. Morgenthau Diary, March 14, 1939, Henry L. Morgenthau papers, FDRL, Volume 169; see also memorandum, FF to FDR, October 8, 1939 in Freedman, *Roosevelt and Frankfurter*, pp. 500–503.
90. Memorandum from Morgenthau to Edward Foley, Jr., March 9, 1939, Henry L. Morgenthau papers, FDRL, Box 20.
91. Letter FF to Samuel Rosenman, April 16, 1942, FDRL, President's Personal File,

Box 140. Also see Henry L. Morgenthau Diary, March 14, 1939, Henry L. Morgenthau papers, FDRL, Volume 169; see also Henry Wallace Diary, December 20, 1943, in Reminiscences of Henry Wallace, COHC, p. 2933.

92. For more on these tax programs, see Sidney Ratner, American Taxation (New York: W. W. Norton Co., 1942), pp. 493–96.

A month before the signing of the Revenue Act, Frankfurter's attention was focused on another mobilization problem—that of securing the necessary manpower in the eventuality of a war. Grenville Clark, a member of the Military Training Camps Association, sought the adoption of a Selective Service Act, which had been drafted by the group. In late May, Clark convinced Frankfurter to secure a hearing for the group with FDR. When the chances for such a meeting fell through, Clark, realizing the inadequacy of the War Department Administration, planned with the justice to secure the appointment of Henry L. Stimson as secretary of war. Two years later, the issue was raised again in the form of a National War Service Act, which required some form of national service during the crisis. Not only did Justice Frankfurter take an active interest in the passage of the law, but when the Manpower Commission was created to coordinate such a mobilization effort, he continually advised Henry L. Stimson regarding its operations and personnel. See Henry L. Stimson Diary, November 5, 1942, December 21, 1942 and May 29, 1943, Henry L. Stimson papers, Sterling Library, Yale University; Reminiscences of James Curtis, COHC, p. 335; Reminiscences of Frances Perkins, COHC, book 8, p. 137; and Spencer, "A History of the Selective Training and Service Act," pp. 102–25.

93. Interviews with Robert Nathan, July 11, 1979, Washington, D.C.; and Joseph L. Rauh, Jr., July 9, 1979, Washington, D.C. One such lecture by FF to FDR on the war needs occurred when he sent the Monnet memorandum in December, 1940, on the need for the United States to become the "Arsenal of Democracy." See memorandum, FF to FDR, December 19, 1940, in Freedman, Roosevelt and Frankfurter, pp. 566–68.

94. This account of the "Victory Program," another vital exercise which has been inadequately explored in the literature, is based on Monnet, Memoirs, pp. 150–77; and interviews with Robert Nathan, July 11, 1979, Washington, D.C.; Edward F. Prichard, Jr., June 25, 1979, Frankfort, Kentucky; Joseph L. Rauh, Jr., July 9, 1979, Washington, D.C., and Milton Katz, August 3, 1979, Cambridge, Mass.

95. There are several such untitled and undated Monnet memoranda with Frankfurter corrections in the margins which can be found in FF/LC, Monnet file, Box 85.

96. See Henry L. Stimson Diary, November 11, 1940, November 12, 1940, and November 13, 1940, Henry L. Stimson papers, Sterling Library, Yale University.

97. Henry L. Stimson Diary, January 2, 1941, see also Stimson Diary, December 18, 1940 and January 4, 1941, Henry L. Stimson papers, Sterling Library, Yale University.

98. Henry L. Stimson Diary, February 5, 1941 and November 6, 1941, Henry L. Stimson papers, Sterling Library, Yale University.

99. For more, see James Byrnes, All in One Lifetime (New York: Harper and Brothers, 1958), pp. 147–57.

100. The account of this entire incident involving the "First War Powers Act" is based on an interview with Joseph L. Rauh, Jr., July 9, 1979, Washington, D.C.

101. For more on Frankfurter's involvement in this case, see chapter 1.

102. Cf. the wording used in "The First War Powers Act," Public Law Number 354, 55 Stat., 77th Congress, Chapter 593, with the "Overman Act," Public Law Number 152, S. 3771, 65th Congress, Chapters 77, 78, pp. 556–57.

103. Letters, FF to Hopkins, December 17, 1941, and FF to FDR, December 17, 1941, in Freedman, *Roosevelt and Frankfurter,* pp. 627–31.

104. Memorandum from FF to FDR, December 17, 1941, FF/LC, Box 98.

105. Letter, Hopkins to FF, December 18, 1941, in Freedman, *Roosevelt and Frankfurter,* pp. 643–44.

106. See letter, FF to Hopkins, December 19, 1941, in Freedman, *Roosevelt and Frankfurter,* p. 632; and Byrnes, *All in One Lifetime,* pp. 149–52.

107. The writer of this memorandum was never identified. See letter, FF to Hopkins (memorandum enclosed), January 9, 1942, Harry Hopkins papers, FDRL, Box 143.
    The letter went on to point out that the other two possible methods for meeting military industrial requirements—limiting the supply of raw materials to nonessential industries and limiting sales of nonessential goods to the public—were harmful because they reduced the production capacity of the entire nation.

108. Letter, James Byrnes to Harry Hopkins, January 9, 1942, Harry Hopkins papers, FDRL, Box 153.

109. Letters, Harry Hopkins to James Forrestal, January 14, 1942, and FDR to Hopkins (with a copy sent to Robert Patterson), January 20, 1942, Harry Hopkins papers, FDRL, Box 153.
    The W.P.B. was created by executive order, number 9040, on January 24, 1942.

110. For more on the W.P.B., see Donald M. Nelson, *Arsenal of Democracy: The Story of American War Production* (New York: Harcourt, Brace and Company, 1946), pp. 194–417.

111. Letter, FF to FDR, January 17, 1942, FF/LC, Box 98.

112. The account of this entire incident involving Frankfurter's defense of Nelson relies heavily on an interview with Milton Katz, August 3, 1979, Cambridge, Mass.

113. Letter, FF to Rosenman, April 16, 1942, FDRL, President's Personal File, Box 140.

114. Letter, FF to Henry Wallace, April 23, 1942, Henry Wallace papers, FDRL; Henry Wallace Diary, April 24, 1942 and April 26, 1942, COHC, pp. 1510, 1515. There is no evidence that Weizmann used this opportunity to press Zionist claims. FF pushed Weizmann on FDR for this purpose nearly one month later. See FF to FDR, June 6, 1942, in Freedman, *Roosevelt and Frankfurter,* p. 661. At that time the State Department was not receptive to these requests, according to FDR.

115. Interview with John J. McCloy, August 10, 1979, New York, N.Y.; and letters, Douglas to FF, June 20, 1942, and FF to Douglas, June 22, 1942, FF/LC, Box 52.

116. Taub's ideas are detailed in *Fortune,* December, 1941, pp. 116–18; *Business Week,* December 6, 1941, p. 22; *Newsweek,* February 20, 1950, p. 50; and *Scientific American,* February, 1950, pp. 16–19.

117. Interview with Joseph L. Rauh, Jr., July 9, 1979, Washington, D.C.

118. Letter, FF to Charles C. Burlingham, October 9, 1942, Burlingham papers, Harvard Law School, Box 5, Folder 4. A nearly identical letter was sent by FF to FDR, December 30, 1942, FF/LC, Box 98.

119. Reminiscences of Gardner Jackson, COHC, p. 538; and interview with Edward F. Prichard, Jr., June 25, 1979, Frankfort, Kentucky.

120. Lash, *Frankfurter Diaries,* pp. 143–44 (entry for January 4, 1943).

121. Lash, *Frankfurter Diaries,* pp. 166–67, 185–86 (entries for January 23, 1943, February 8, 1943, and February 9, 1943).
    A new biography has been published on Bernard Baruch, unfortunately too late in the production process for use in this volume. Jordan A. Schwarz, *The Speculator: Bernard Baruch in Washington, 1917–1965* (Chapel Hill, N.C.: University of North Carolina Press, 1981).

122. Nelson (*Arsenal of Democracy,* pp. 388–89) writes only that at the last minute

one of his "most trusted assistants" warned him about the plot in a breakfast meeting which had been arranged by a post-midnight telephone call. Frankfurter neglects the incident entirely. See Lash, *Frankfurter Diaries*, pp. 190–93 (entries for February 17–21, 1943).

123. Interview with Edward F. Prichard, Jr., June 25, 1979, Frankfort, Kentucky.

124. This quotation and the basis for the entire account of this incident are drawn from an interview with Milton Katz, August 3, 1979, Cambridge, Mass.

125. Lash, *Frankfurter Diaries*, pp. 191–92 (entry for February 20, 1943); see also pp. 190–91 (entry for February 17, 1943).

126. Henry L. Stimson Diary, May 29, 1943, Henry L. Stimson papers, Sterling Library, Yale University; and Lash, *Frankfurter Diaries*, pp. 246–48 (entries for May 28, 1943 and May 30, 1943).

Chapter 7

1. Alpheus T. Mason, *Brandeis: A Free Man's Life* (New York: The Viking Press, 1956), pp. 635–38; *The New York Times*, October 6, 1941, p. 1, col. 4.; *Washington Post*, October 6, 1941, p. 1, col. 2.
   My thanks to Professor James Magee of the University of Delaware for initially suggesting the title for this chaper.

2. *Washington Post*, October 7, 1941, p. 4, col. 4.

3. Quoted in Mason, *Brandeis*, p. 637

4. *Washington Post*, October 7, 1941, p. 4, col. 4.

5. Felix Frankfurter, "Mr. Justice Brandeis," 55 *Harvard Law Review*, (1941), p. 183.

6. For more on Frankfurter's involvement in these issues see chapters 1 and 3.

7. For more, see H. N. Hirsch, *The Enigma of Felix Frankfurter* (New York: Basic Books, Inc., 1981), pp. 65–81.

8. Reminiscences of Learned Hand, COHC, p. 101. Also quoted in Joseph Lash, ed., *From the Diaries of Felix Frankfurter* (New York: W. W. Norton and Company, Inc., 1975), p. 77.

9. For more on the effect of a national wartime emergency on the normal standards of propriety governing extrajudicial conduct, see the book's appendix.

10. Grace Tully, *F.D.R., My Boss* (New York: Charles Scribner's Sons, 1949), p. 140.

11. The various Daily Presidential Calendars are at the Franklin Roosevelt Library in Hyde Park, New York.

12. See *Time Magazine*, March 10, 1941, p. 15; William O. Douglas, *Go East, Young Man* (New York: Random House, 1974), pp. 332–33, 345, 349, and 453; and Harold L. Ickes, *The Secret Diary of Harold L. Ickes*, vol. III (New York: Simon and Schuster, 1953), pp. 148–49, 191, 199, 204, and 208.

13. Letter, FF to FDR, February 12, 1941, in Max Freedman, ed., *Roosevelt and Frankfurter: Their Correspondence 1928–1945* (Boston: Little Brown and Co., 1967), p. 581. On the activities of Stanley Reed, see Walter J. Cibes, Jr., "Extra-Judicial Activities of the United States Supreme Court, 1790–1960" (Unpublished Ph.D. dissertation, Princeton University, 1975), p. 1266. On the activities of Murphy, see J. Woodford Howard, *Mr. Justice Murphy, A Political Biography* (Princeton, N.J.: Princeton University Press, 1968), pp. 273–74, 326–27.

14. Howard, *Mr. Justice Murphy*, p. 273.

15. James F. Byrnes, *All in One Lifetime* (New York: Harper and Brothers, 1958), p. 148. Also quoted in part in Cibes, "Extra-Judicial Activities," p. 1173. Much more will be said about Byrnes's political activities off the bench later in this chapter.

16. For more on the extrajudicial activities of the Supreme Court during these periods, see the book's appendix.
17. Interview with Milton Katz, August 3, 1979, Cambridge, Mass.
18. Alpheus T. Mason, "Extrajudicial Work for Judges: The Views of Chief Justice Stone," 67 *Harvard Law Review* (1953), pp. 203–4, and *passim*. Stone refused to serve on the War Ballot Commission, the Hague Arbitration, the National Traffic Safety Commission, and the Atomic Energy Commission.
19. Henry Wallace Diary, August 19, 1943 and December 20, 1943 entries, COHC pp. 2637, 2933; *Washington Post*, August 19, 1943, p. A17.
20. *The New York Times*, March 29, 1942, sect. 7, pp. 8–9.
21. Henry Wallace Diary, May 31, 1943, December 8, 1943 and November 15, 1944 entries, COHC, pp. 2486–88, 2490, 2889, and 3541. Also, interview with Thomas G. Corcoran, September 29, 1977, Washington, D.C.
22. Letter, Brandeis to Julian Mack, September 25, 1934, FF/LC, Box 28.
23. To a man, this response was given by Frankfurter's law clerks in commenting on his various activities. These words, however, come from interviews with Philip Elman, July 10–11, 1979, Washington, D.C.; and with Joseph L. Rauh, Jr., July 9, 1979, Washington, D.C.
24. Letter, FF to Gardner Jackson, October 19, 1940, FF/LC, Box 69; see also letter, FF to Louis Lande, June 12, 1943, FF/LC, Box 74.
25. Lash, ed., *Frankfurter Diaries*, p. 228 (April 21, 1943 entry).
26. Letter, FF to Learned Hand, April 8, 1944, Learned Hand papers, Harvard Law School, Box 105.
27. Letter, FF to Geoffrey Parsons, May 27, 1935, FF/LC, Box 88.
28. Letter, FF to Charles C. Burlingham, September 7, 1950, Charles C. Burlingham papers, Harvard Law School, Box 5. See also letter, FF to Alexander Bickel, January 17, 1956, FF/LC, Box 24.
29. Letter, FF to Alexander Bickel, January 23, 1956, FF/LC, Box 24.
30. Letter, Harry Hopkins to Frankfurter, July 10, 1944, Charles C. Burlingham papers, Harvard Law School, Box 5, Folder 5. See also letter, Learned Hand to FF, September 7, 1942, FF/LC, Box 64; and Mason, "Extrajudicial Work for Judges," pp. 215–16.

   In a recently published biography of William O. Douglas, James Simon indicates that Corcoran's involvement in such a presidential campaign for the justice may have been as extensive as Frankfurter feared. Just as interestingly, Douglas, in an interview done by Simon, indicated his belief that Frankfurter was pushing Justice Robert Jackson for the presidency. See James F. Simon, *Independent Journey: The Life of William O. Douglas* (New York: Harper and Row, Publishers, 1980), pp. 257–75 and 9.
31. Letter, FF to Charles C. Burlingham, June 24, 1946, Charles C. Burlingham papers, Harvard Law School, Box 5, Folder 7.
32. Confidential interview with Mr. Justice Frankfurter's law clerk, July 10, 1979, Washington, D.C.

   One indication that Frankfurter continued to believe that Douglas was *actively* seeking the nominations is in Lash, *Frankfurter Diaries*, pp. 339–40 (January 16, 1948 entry).
33. Interview with Vinson's former law clerks, Howard J. Trienens and Newton N. Minow, February 27, 1975, Fred Vinson Oral History Project, University of Kentucky Library, Louisville, Kentucky. Thanks to project director Terry L. Birdwhistell for his assistance on these materials.
34. *Boston Globe*, December 16, 1954, p. 14. Copy in FF/HLS, Box 172.

35. Letter, FF to Alexander Bickel, January 17, 1956, FF/LC, Box 24.
36. In his interview with James F. Simon, Justice Douglas denied that he ever held such presidential ambitions. Instead, he claimed to have spoken about the matter with his predecessor on the bench, Louis D. Brandeis, who argued "that a member of the Court could not have political ambitions because it would hurt the Court" (p. 9). Following this advice, Douglas claimed, he had no such political ambitions.

    In chapter 20 of this biography, Simon offers his own conclusions regarding Douglas's involvement in politics. He argues that by 1946 Douglas was "slightly bored" by the Court's work, and found that it was "confining and did not fully satisfy his intellectual appetite or temperament" (p. 267). Though others, led by Thomas Corcoran, pushed first for Douglas's appointment to the Cabinet and then for his nomination to run for the highest office, Simon portrays Douglas as an interested observer, but not an overly active campaigner for the nomination. For more, see Simon, *Independent Journey*, pp. 257–75.
37. Letter, FF to Charles C. Burlingham, September 9, 1951, Charles C. Burlingham papers, Harvard Law School, Box 5, Folder 1.
38. Ibid.
39. For more on the nature of political questions, see Henry J. Abraham, *The Judicial Process: An Introductory Analysis of the Courts of the United States, England and France*, 4th edn. (New York: Oxford University Press, 1980), pp. 384–89; and C. Herman Pritchett, 2nd edn. *The American Constitution*, (New York: McGraw Hill, Inc., 1968), pp. 176–77.
40. Interview with Judge Charles E. Wyzanski, Jr., January 13, 1977, Richmond, Virginia. See also, Lash, *Frankfurter Diaries*, p. 64.
41. William O. Douglas, *The Court Years, 1939–1975; The Autobiography of William O. Douglas* (New York: Random House, 1980), p. 42.
42. Ibid., p. 22.
43. Confidential interview, July 9, 1979, Washington, D.C.
44. 319 U.S. 624 (1943); Simon, *Independent Journey*, p. 11–12.
45. 314 U.S. 252 (1941).
46. Simon, *Independent Journey*, p. 211. Simon argues (pp. 211–15) that the other two cases which marked the split among the justices were a Sixth Amendment right to appointed counsel case, *Betts v. Brady*, 316 U.S. 455 (1942); and a First Amendment free exercise of religion case, *Jones v. Opelika*, 316 U.S. 584 (1942). Later in the book Simon lends support to Douglas's own assessment of the importance of the *Barnette* case in the development of the split with Frankfurter. According to this account, Frankfurter became embittered when he was convinced that Douglas and Hugo Black, reacting to public pressure, had switched their votes on the issue and opposed him "for political reasons" (p. 262).
47. *Milk Wagon Drivers Union of Chicago v. Meadowmoor Dairies*, 312 U.S. 287 (1941).
48. Hirsch, *Enigma of Frankfurter*, p. 176, and pp. 152–75.
49. Interview with Edward F. Prichard, Jr., June 25, 1979, Frankfort, Kentucky. Virtually the same story was recounted in additional interviews with Judge Charles E. Wyzanski, Jr., January 13, 1977, Richmond, Virginia; and Joseph L. Rauh, Jr., July 9, 1979, Washington, D.C.
50. 308 U.S. 338 (1939).

    H. N. Hirsch does assign some importance to this case in indicating a split developing between Frankfurter and Douglas. In his words, this was one of two cases decided during the 1939 term which indicated "some faint signs of discord between Frankfurter and Black and Douglas." My sources indicate, however, that from Frankfurter's perspective this case was not just the beginning of the end of his relationship with Douglas; instead it marked the end of their judicial relationship entirely. See Hirsch, *Enigma of Frankfurter*, pp. 145–47.

51. Douglas wrote this on FF's slip opinion in the case. See FF Supreme Court scrapbook, 1939, FF/HLS, quoted in Hirsch, *Enigma of Frankfurter*, p. 146.
52. 308 U.S. 338 (1939), at 353.
53. Interview with Edward F. Prichard, Jr., June 25, 1979, Frankfort, Kentucky.
54. Douglas wrote this on FF's later draft of the slip opinion, FF Supreme Court scrapbook, 1939, FF/HLS, quoted in Hirsch, *Enigma of Frankfurter*, p. 146.
55. Ibid.
56. Interview with Edward F. Prichard, Jr., June 25, 1979, Frankfort, Kentucky.
57. For some of these complaints, see Lash, *Frankfurter Diaries*, pp. 154–56, 339–40 (January 11, 1943 and January 16, 1948 entries).
58. Interview with Philip Elman, July 10, 1979, Washington, D.C.
59. Interview with Elliot Richardson, April 29, 1981, State College, Pennsylvania.
60. Ibid.
61. The quotation is from a confidential interview, July 11, 1979, Washington, D.C. However, each of my interview sources who had served as a law clerk to Frankfurter said virtually the same thing.
62. Interview with Elliot Richardson, April 29, 1981, State College, Pennsylvania.
63. Letter, FF to Learned Hand, November 5, 1954, Learned Hand papers, Harvard Law School, Box 105.
64. Letter, FF to Learned Hand, October 12, 1957, Learned Hand papers, Harvard Law School, Box 105.
65. Letter FF to Learned Hand, April 27, 1959, Learned Hand papers, Harvard Law School, Box 105.
66. For more, see H. N. Hirsch, *Enigma of Frankfurter*, pp. 127–37.
67. Some have argued that Frankfurter was indeed true to his activist, civil libertarian views on the bench. See William T. Coleman, "Mr. Justice Felix Frankfurter: Civil Libertarian as Lawyer and as Justice," 1978 *Law Forum*, (1978), pp. 279–99; and Joseph L. Rauh, Jr., "Felix Frankfurter: Civil Libertarian," II *Harvard Civil Rights-Civil Liberties Law Review* (1976), pp. 496–520.
68. In the first public school flag salute case, decided in 1940, (*Minersville School District v. Gobitis*, 310 U.S. 586 (1940)), the Court, with Frankfurter writing the majority opinion, had upheld the compulsory exercise. Press and public opinion regarding this decision was swift and highly negative. See Alpheus T. Mason, *Harlan Fiske Stone: Pillar of the Law* (New York: The Viking Press, 1956), pp. 525–34.
69. 319 U.S. 624 (1943), at 647.
70. Interview with Philip Elman, July 10 and 11, 1979, Washington, D.C. Cf. Lash, *Frankfurter Diaries*, pp. 141–262.
71. Confidential interview, July 11, 1979, Washington D.C.
    In the remainder of this chapter, the account of other law clerks' experiences with Mr. Justice Frankfurter is drawn from a number of confidential interviews with these men, held in Washington, D.C., July 9 and 10, 1979, and in Cambridge, Mass. on July 26, July 27, August 3, and August 4, 1979.
    Interestingly, FF's use of his judicial chambers is reminiscent of LDB's earlier creation of an upstairs "study" for his law clerks, which also prevented them from observing the constant flow of visitors to his home.
72. Interview with Edward F. Prichard, Jr., June 25, 1979, Frankfort, Kentucky.
    For more on FF's relationships with Philip Graham, see David Halberstam, *The Powers That Be* (New York: Alfred A. Knopf, 1979), pp. 166–78.
73. Interview with Joseph L. Rauh, Jr., July 9, 1979, Washington, D.C.

74. Byrnes, *All in One Lifetime,* pp. 148–49. A count of Frankfurter's opinion output (including majority, concurring, and dissenting opinions) reveals that it actually increased during the war years: 1938 terms—15; 1939 term—24; 1940 term—18; 1941 term—30; 1942 term—28; 1943 term—31; 1944 term—32; and 1945 term—40.
75. Interview with Philip Elman, July 10, 1979, Washington, D.C.

  A confidential interview with a later law clerk indicates that Frankfurter found this technique to be so effective that on occasion he used it with his other assistants as well. Confidential interview, July 26, 1979, Cambridge, Mass.
76. Bob Woodward and Scott Armstrong, *The Brethren: Inside the Supreme Court* (New York: Simon and Schuster, 1979), *passim.*
77. Alexander Woollcott, ed., *As You Were: A Portable Library of American Prose and Poetry Assembled for Members of the Armed Forces and the Merchant Marine* (New York: The Viking Press, 1943).
78. The note from Frankfurter to Elman is dated April 8, 1943.
79. Letter to author from Philip Elman, July 30, 1979.

Chapter 8

1. Frankfurter did try unsuccessfully to keep Joseph Rauh from going to the battle front by placing him with Harry Hopkins. See letters, FF to Hopkins, March 10, 1941 and March 11, 1942, Harry Hopkins papers, FDRL, Box 153.
2. Letter, FF to FDR, July 8, 1942, FDRL, President's Personal File, Box 140. On the letter FDR referred the matter to a Captain McRea and said, "Please see this man and give him a chance to present his plan to the proper officers."
3. Letter, FF to Byrnes, February 19, 1944, FF/LC, Box 41, regarding "President Sproul's qualifications."
4. Joseph Lash, ed., *From the Diaries of Felix Frankfurter* (New York: W. W. Norton and Co., 1975), pp. 168–71, 200, 205–6, 231–32, and 259–60 (entries for January 25, 1943, March 1, 1943, March 6, 1943, May 2, 1943, and June 17, 1943); and Henry L. Stimson papers, Sterling Library, Yale University.
5. According to Jean Monnet, who was in a unique position to observe both sides of the diplomatic exchanges, Frankfurter and Harry Hopkins were the most influential advisors to FDR on the issue of relations with France. Jean Monnet, *Memoirs* (translated by Richard Mayne) (St. James Place, London: William Collins Sons and Co., Ltd., 1978), p. 182.
6. Letters, FF to Halifax, October 14, 1941, November 14, 1941, December 16, 1941, and Halifax to FF, December 29, 1941, FF/LC, Box 62; and Laski to FF, February 7, 1941 and July 8, 1941, FF/LC, Box 75.
7. Letters, Bajpai to FF, July 7, 1942, August 8, 1942, November 17, 1942, November 21, 1944, March 14, 1945, and March 16, 1945, and FF to Bajpai, December 7, 1943 and March 8, 1944, FF/LC, Box 23; and Lash, *Frankfurter Diaries,* pp. 145–95 (entries for January 5, 1943 and February 22, 1943).
8. Letter, Halifax to FF, June 30, 1942, FF/LC, Box 62; see also letters, Halifax to FF, June 13, 1942, July 1, 1942; and FF to Halifax, June 16, 1942, FF/LC, Box 62.
9. Until otherwise noted, the following quotations and summary regarding Frankfurter's position on this issue are taken from a document entitled "Notes on India," June 30, 1942, FF/LC, Box 62.
10. Letters, Cripps to FF, April 24, 1942, FF/LC, Box 47; FF to Cripps, July 9, 1942 and July 24, 1942, FF/LC, Boxes 62, 126; and memorandum, "Anglo-American Relations," May 26, 1942, FF/LC, Box 126.

11. This quotation and, until otherwise noted, the following summary and quotations are drawn from a letter, FF to Cripps, July 9, 1942, FF/LC, Box 62; see also Max Freedman, ed., *Roosevelt and Frankfurter: Their Correspondence, 1928–1945* (Boston: Little, Brown and Co., 1967), p. 66.

12. Letters, FF to FDR, July 9, 1942, in Freedman, *Roosevelt and Frankfurter*, pp. 664–66; and FF to Halifax, December 19, 1942, FF/LC, Box 62.

13. Frankfurter did his best to maintain his friendship with the British ambassador, writing him on June 30, 1942, "You will let me say how finely you represent the idea of the United Nations in your function as your country's ambassador." Letter, FF to Halifax, June 30, 1942, FF/LC, Box 62.

14. The account of this dinner is drawn from two sources: Henry L. Stimson Diary, December 18, 1942, Henry L. Stimson papers, Sterling Library, Yale University; and Henry Wallace Diary, December 19, 1942, COHC, pp. 2083–87; Henry Wallace Diary, December 19, 1942, COHC, p. 2093.

15. Letter, FF to Casey, January 8, 1943, FF/LC, Box 126. See also Lash, *Frankfurter Diaries*, pp. 146–47 (entry for January 6, 1943). There is every reason to believe that Casey passed this information on to Prime Minister Churchill.

16. Lash, *Frankfurter Diaries*, pp. 198–99 (entry for February 26, 1943). Winant was on his way back to London. It is impossible to verify this incident through Winant's papers because they have been selectively purged. It seems likely, however, that Frankfurter would have actively maintained this contact with Winant.

On FF's work with North Whitehead, see also Lash, *Frankfurter Diaries*, p. 156 (entry for January 11, 1943).

When Sir Anthony Eden visited this country later that year, Frankfurter supplied him with the necessary evidence and arguments for his meetings with the House and Senate Committees on Foreign Relations. See Lash, *Frankfurter Diaries*, pp. 218–19 (entry for March 17, 1943).

17. Letter, FF to Halifax, May 14, 1943, FF/LC, Box 62.

18. Letter, Henry L. Stimson to FF, June 19, 1944, FF/LC, Box 104; see also letter, FF to Halifax, May 19, 1943, FF/LC, Box 44.

19. Henry L. Stimson Diary, May 7, 1941, May 25, 1941, and May 26, 1941, Henry L. Stimson papers, Sterling Library, Yale University; and letter, FF to Charles C. Burlingham, June 12, 1941, Charles C. Burlingham papers, Harvard Law School, Box 5.

20. Richard Casey, *Personal Experience, 1939–46* (New York: McKay Co., 1962), p. 51. Frankfurter had earlier reviewed these paragraphs. See undated memorandum, FF/LC, Casey file, Box 53.

On the meeting for Menzies, see letters, FF to Charles C. Burlingham, March 20, 1941, and Charles C. Burlingham to FF, March 27, 1941, Charles C. Burlingham papers, Harvard Law School, Box 5.

21. Freedman, *Roosevelt and Frankfurter*, p. 650.

22. Winston S. Churchill, *Second World War, Vol. III: The Grand Alliance* (Boston: Houghton Mifflin Co., 1950), p. 600.

23. For more on the nature of the relationship between, and work by, these two remarkable men, see Joseph Lash, *Roosevelt and Churchill, 1939–1941* (New York: W. W. Norton and Co., 1975), *passim*.

24. Letter, Benjamin V. Cohen to FDR, July 28, 1939, FDRL, President's Personal File, Box 3509.

25. All the quoted passages in this paragraph are from a memorandum, Herbert Evatt to FF, February 22, 1942, FF/LC, Box 53.

26. Letter, FF to Evatt, February 25, 1942, FF/LC, Box 53.

27. Letter, Hopkins to FF, March 5, 1942, in response to letter, FF to Hopkins, March

2, 1942 (enclosing the memorandum from FF to Evatt, March 27, 1942), Harry Hopkins papers, FDRL, Box 334, Book 9.

28. Letters, Evatt to Casey, March 8, 1942, and Casey to Evatt, March 8, 1942, FF/LC, Box 53.

29. Letter, FF to Hopkins, March 9, 1942, FF/LC, Box 53.

30. Letter, FF to Evatt, March 10, 1942, FF/LC, Box 53.

31. Henry L. Stimson Diary, March 15, 1942 and March 17, 1942, Henry L. Stimson papers, Sterling Library, Yale University.

32. Henry L. Stimson Diary, May 13, 1942, Henry L. Stimson papers, Sterling Library, Yale University.

33. Letters, FF to FDR, March 30, 1942 and May 18, 1942, in Freedman, *Roosevelt and Frankfurter*, pp. 654–55, 659; FDR to Cordell Hull, May 19, 1942, and Hull to FDR, May 20, 1942, FDRL, President's Secretary's File, Box 151; and Benjamin Cohen to FF, August 13, 1945, FF/LC, Box 45. See also, Lash, *Frankfurter Diaries*, pp. 196–97, 208 (entries for February 25, 1943 and March 11, 1943); Kylie Tennant, *Evatt: Politics and Justice* (Sydney, Australia: Angus and Robertson, Ltd., 1970), pp. 141–52.

34. See memorandum by FDR for Missy LeHand (regarding FF's views on Finland), December 2, 1940, FDRL, President's Secretary's File, Box 150; Freedman, *Roosevelt and Frankfurter*, pp. 562–63, 597–98, and 611–15; and Lash, *Frankfurter Diaries*, pp. 145, 194–95, 220–21, 242, 252, and 260–61 (entries for January 5, 1943, February 22, 1943, May 17, 1943, May 19, 1943, May 28, 1943, June 7, 1943, and June 18, 1943).

35. Letter, Niles to FF, February 28, 1940, Charles C. Burlingham papers, Harvard Law School, Box 5, Folder 2; untitled reports by David Niles, April 12, 1943 and April 30, 1943, David Niles papers, Brandeis University; and Lash, *Frankfurter Diaries*, pp. 237–38 (entry for May 12, 1943).

One law clerk recalls Niles as a "constant visitor" to the justice's chambers. Confidential interview, July 10, 1979, Washington, D.C.

36. Henry L. Morgenthau Diary, June 3, 1941, Henry L. Morgenthau papers, FDRL, Volume 404; and Lash, *Frankfurter Diaries*, pp. 152–54, 200–201, 203–5, 208, and 243–44 (entries for January 9, 1943, March 2, 1943, March 5, 1943, March 11, 1943, and May 20, 1943).

37. Frankfurter donated all his Zionist papers to the Hebrew University. A review of those documents, and his private papers in other locations, reveals that Frankfurter did nothing in the actual organization during his Court tenure.

38. For a revealing account of Frankfurter's ambivalence toward his Jewish heritage, see H. N. Hirsch, *The Enigma of Felix Frankfurter* (New York: Basic Books, Inc., 1981), pp. 11–64, and *passim*; and Lash, *Frankfurter Diaries*, pp. 3–90.

39. Letter, Roosevelt to Churchill, November 5, 1942, quoted in Winston S. Churchill, *Second World War, Vol. IV; Hinge of Fate* (Boston: Houghton Mifflin, Co., 1951), p. 605.

40. This section benefited from the accounts in Monnet, *Memoirs*, pp. 182–95; and Robert Sherwood, *Roosevelt and Hopkins: An Intimate History* (New York: Harper and Bros., 1948), pp. 667–97.

41. Letter, FF to FDR, December 19, 1940 (containing a memorandum from Monnet on the "New Order" in Europe dated December 18, 1940 and an unsigned memorandum on Vichy France), in Freedman, *Roosevelt and Frankfurter*, pp. 567–73; Henry L. Stimson Diary, June 5, 1941, Henry L. Stimson papers, Sterling Library, Yale University; and letter, Stimson to FF, June 19, 1944, FF/LC, Box 104 (containing FF's views on the situation in Great Britain).

42. Henry L. Morgenthau Diary, November 17, 1942, Henry L. Morgenthau papers, FDRL, Vol. 404.

43. Several of these undated memoranda and speeches are in FF/LC, Monnet file, Box 85. One of these memoranda is reprinted in Sherwood, *Roosevelt and Hopkins*, pp. 680–81, and Monnet identifies this statement as his own in his *Memoirs*, pp. 181–82.

44. Undated letters and memoranda, FF/LC, Monnet file, Box 85; Lash, *Frankfurter Diaries*, pp. 164–65, 69–73, 181–85, 222 (entries for January 21, 1943, January 25, 1943, January 27, 1943, February 3, 1943, February 5, 1943, February 7, 1943, and March 20, 1943).

45. Monnet, *Memoirs*, pp. 182–92.

46. Ibid., p. 190.

47. *The New York Times*, March 19, 1943, p. 5. There is no evidence that Monnet was indirectly responsible for the writing of this article, but based on his character and previous actions, it is not beyond the realm of possibility.

48. Cable, Murphy to "Secretary of State," March 21, 1943, FF/LC, Box 85; also printed in Lash, *Frankfurter Diaries*, p. 223 (entry for March 25, 1943).

49. *The New York Times*, March 28, 1943, p. 15.

50. Cable, Murphy to "Secretary of State," March 22, 1943, FF/LC, Box 85.

51. Any doubts that this is the correct interpretation of Monnet's message are quickly removed by the account in his *Memoirs* of his reasons for advocating the restoration of the Cremieux Decree. See Monnet, *Memoirs*, p. 190.

52. Letter, FF to Acheson, March 27, 1943, FF/LC, Box 85.

53. *The New York Times*, April 4, 1943, p. 7.

54. Cable, "Memorandum from 'Wiley' to Secretary of State," April 17, 1943, FF/LC (also contains the memorandum from Monnet to Frankfurter).

55. Memorandum, Ray Atherton to Dean Acheson, April 23, 1943, FF/LC, Box 85.

56. Letter, FF to Acheson, May 3, 1943, FF/LC, Box 85.

57. *The New York Times*, April 25, 1943, sect. IV, p. 10.

58. Undated memorandum, FF/LC, Monnet file, Box 85.

59. Letter, FF to Acheson, May 3, 1943, FF/LC, Box 85.

60. Henry L. Stimson Diary, Novembe 6, 1943, Henry L. Stimson papers, Sterling Library, Yale University.

61. Letters, FF to FDR, October 20, 1943 and January 7, 1944, in Freedman, *Roosevelt and Frankfurter*, pp. 714–17.

62. Memoranda, April 26, 1945 and May 6, 1945, written by Frankfurter for Secretary of State Henry L. Stimson, J. Robert Oppenheimer papers, LC, Box 34.

    For more on the general background concerning the association of Frankfurter and the atomic bomb, an account which also relies on these documents but with which I will differ in part because of the information gleaned from my interview sources, see Martin Sherwin, *A World Destroyed: The Atomic Bomb and the Grand Alliance* (New York: Alfred A. Knopf, 1975), pp. 91–114.

63. Interview with John J. McCloy, August 10, 1979, New York, N.Y.

64. Memorandum from FF to Stimson, May 6, 1945, J. Robert Oppenheimer papers, LC, Box 34.

65. Freedman, *Roosevelt and Frankfurter*, p. 725; and Sherwin, *A World Destroyed*, p. 99.

66. Interview with Philip Elman, July 10, 1979, Washington, D.C.

67. All the quotes in this paragraph come from memorandum by FF, April 26, 1945, J. Robert Oppenheimer papers, LC, Box 34.

68. Sherwin, *A World Destroyed*, pp. 100–104.

69. Letters, Ambassador de Kauffmann to FDR, June 26, 1944, Bohr to FF, July 5, 1944, July 6, 1944, and July 14, 1944, and Bohr to FDR, September 7, 1944, memorandum by Bohr, July 3, 1944 (with a March 24, 1945 addendum), and memorandum by FF, May 6, 1945, J. Robert Oppenheimer papers, LC, Box 34. See also letters, FF to FDR, July 10, 1944 (including memorandum on the subject) and September 18, 1944, in Freedman, *Roosevelt and Frankfurter,* pp. 728–36.

    Prime Minister Churchill argued against revealing the secret to Stalin because he did not trust the Russians and he also wanted to maintain a preeminent position for Great Britain in this field. See Sherwin, *A World Destroyed,* pp. 110–14, and Freedman, *Roosevelt and Frankfurter,* pp. 724–26.

70. FF sent this packet of material to Stimson on May 3, 1945, J. Robert Oppenheimer papers, LC, Box 34.

71. Letter, Stimson to Truman, September 11, 1945 (including the memorandum), J. Robert Oppenheimer papers, LC, Box 34. See also Henry L. Stimson Diary, June 12, 1945, Henry L. Stimson papers, Sterling Library, Yale University; and Sherwin, *A World Destroyed,* pp. 177–84.

72. For more on the political actions of these justices during wartime and the normative standards governing them, see the appendix and chapter 2.

73. Learned Hand, *The Spirit of Liberty* (Cambridge, Mass.: Harvard University Press, 1952), p. 138.

74. Freedman, *Roosevelt and Frankfurter,* pp. 496–97.

75. Undated draft pages of manuscript, Samuel Rosenman papers, FDRL, Box 1.

76. Letter, FF to Bruce Bliven (editor of *The New Republic*), December 15, 1944, FF/LC, Box 25. Here FF objected to a statement in *The New Republic* that he had helped to select the new secretary of state. Bliven agreed to print a retraction, but he maintained that the statement was accurate. See letter, Bliven to FF, December 18, 1944, FF/LC, Box 25.

    For another example of this behavior see the exchange of correspondence with historian Henry Steele Commager regarding a claim in a published volume that FF had convinced the Republicans to call off their national convention in 1940 if Henry L. Stimson was named as secretary of state. FF's immediate response to this charge was, "Who's looney now?" Letters, Commager to FF, January 3, 1952, and FF to Commager, January 8, 1952, FF/LC, Box 37.

    For more examples of the justice's behavior on these occasions, see the introduction of the following chapter.

77. Letter, FF to Jerome Frank, September 14, 1956, FF/LC, Box 56 (responding to a request for the justice's views regarding a pending habeas corpus bill).

78. Dean Acheson, "Removing the Shadow Cast on the Court," *American Bar Association Journal* 55 (1969), p. 921; Louis Jaffe, a former Brandeis clerk and a friend of FF, agrees with this view in "Professors and Judges as Advisors: Reflections on the Roosevelt-Frankfurter Relationship," 83 *Harvard Law Review* (1969), pp. 366–72.

Chapter 9

1. William O. Douglas, *Go East, Young Man* (New York: Random House, 1974), pp. 285, 445; Arthur Schlesinger, *Robert Kennedy and His Times* (Boston: Houghton Mifflin Co., 1978), pp. 68–69. Walter J. Cibes, Jr., "Extra-Judicial Activities of the United States Supreme Court, 1790–1960" (Unpublished Ph.D. dissertation, Princeton University, 1975), pp. 1191–96.

2. The Chief Justice refused to serve on the Hague Arbitration panel, the National

Traffic Safety Commission, and the Atomic Energy Commission. For more, see Alpheus T. Mason, *Harlan Fiske Stone: Pillar of the Law* (New York: Viking Press, 1946), p. 714; and Alpheus T. Mason, "Extrajudicial Work for Judges: The Views of Justice Stone," 67 *Harvard Law Review* (1953), pp. 208–9, 214–15.

3. Letter, Jackson to FF, January 25, 1946, FF/HLS, Box 170, Folder 2. Alpheus T. Mason also notes from his research that Jackson was generally reluctant to enter into the extrajudicial realm. See Mason, "Extrajudicial Work for Judges," p. 211n.

4. Letter, Jackson to FF, April 28, 1946, FF/HLS, Box 170, Folder 2.

5. Letter, Jackson to FF, January 25, 1946, FF/HLS, Box 170, Folder 2.

6. There is controversy over Stone's position on this issue. Frankfurter later reported that the Chief Justice initially accepted Jackson's work, but then changed his mind. This interpretation seems to be supported by a report from Jackson to Frankfurter in a letter dated January 25, 1946 that the Chief Justice had been saying that Jackson's absence was not causing the Court to "suffer." However, Alpheus T. Mason reports from his research on Stone that the Chief Justice disliked Jackson's involvement from the start. Either way, both men agree that a short while later Stone was unhappy with Jackson's endeavors. Despite these views, Stone, like Frankfurter, also sent a letter to Jackson saying that he should remain in Germany because he would not be able to function as a part-time Supreme Court justice. See letters, FF to Paul Freund, July 1, 1964, FF/HLS, Box 215, Folder 3; FF to Charles C. Burlingham, October 27, 1952, Charles C. Burlingham papers, Harvard Law School, Box 5; Stone to Jackson, March 1, 1946, FF/HLS, Box 170, Folder 2; and Jackson to FF, January 25, 1946, FF/HLS, Box 170, Folder 2. See also Mason, "Extrajudicial Work for Judges," pp. 209–13.

7. Letter, FF to Jackson, January 16, 1946, FF/LC, Box 69.

8. Letter, FF to Jackson, February 6, 1946, FF/HLS, Box 170, Folder 2.

9. Letter, FF to Jackson, May 11, 1946, FF/HLS, Box 170, Folder 2.

10. Letters, FF to Charles C. Burlingham, October 27, 1952, Charles C. Burlingham papers, Harvard Law School, Box 5; Max Lerner to FF, October 13, 1953, Max Lerner papers, Sterling Library, Yale University, Box 3; FF to Paul Freund, July 1, 1964, FF/HLS, Box 215; FF's Memorandum Response to Eugene C. Gerhart's Manuscript on Robert Jackson, April 9, 1957, FF/HLS, Box 170.

11. Eugene C. Gerhart, *America's Advocate: Robert H. Jackson* (New York: Bobbs-Merrill Co., Inc. 1958), p. 258. Frankfurter confirmed the truth of this report in two letters: FF to Paul Freund, September 24, 1963, FF/HLS, Box 215; and FF to Charles C. Burlingham, October 27, 1952, Burlingham papers, Harvard Law School, Box 5.

This action prompted Jackson to protest by cable from Nuremberg that Black himself was guilty of impropriety in the *Jewell Ridge Case*, (325 U.S. 161 (1945), which was argued by Black's ex-law partner. This charge was answered by Black's former law clerk, John P. Frank in "Disqualification of Judges," 56 *Yale Law Journal* (April, 1957), pp. 605–31. Frankfurter, however, vigorously supported Jackson in his letters. See letters, FF to Jackson, June 12, 1946, and Jackson to FF, June 19, 1946, FF/HLS, Box 170.

Frankfurter desperately wanted a man with such "true judicial equipment" as Jackson to be appointed to the center chair because, as he told Burlingham later, it demanded very special skills:

> What is most wanted in a C.J. is what the Germans call *ein Tonangeber*—a tone giver: one who by his example generates in the others complete dedication to the work of the Court, with a deep sense of humility, that is, a realization . . . of the responsibility and entire disinterestedness.

Letter, FF to Charles C. Burlingham, September 12, 1953, Burlingham papers, Harvard Law School, Box 6, Folder 12. If "complete dedication to the work of the Court" was the requirement, then the highly political Secretary of the Treasury Fred Vinson obviously did not fill that qualification. In fact, contrary to his image of himself, neither did Felix Frankfurter.

12. Letter, FF to Black, September 30, 1950, FF/LC, Box 50. The report can be found in Robert Allen and Robert Shannon, *The Truman Merry-Go-Round* (New York: Vanguard Inc., 1950), pp. 366–67.

13. Ibid.

14. Letter, FF to Jackson, June 12, 1946, FF/LC, Box 69.

15. Letter, Jackson to FF, June 19, 1946, FF/HLS, Box 170, Folder 2.

16. Hugo L. Black, "Mr. Justice Frankfurter," 78 *Harvard Law Review* (June, 1965), p. 1522.

17. Letter, Learned Hand to FF, April 14, 1946, FF/LC, Box 64.

18. Letter, Learned Hand to FF, May 6, 1952, Learned Hand papers, Harvard Law School, Box 105.

19. Letters, Learned Hand to FF, July 6, 1953 and June 5, 1954, Learned Hand papers, Harvard Law School, Box 105.

20. Letter, Learned Hand to FF, February 25, 1951, Learned Hand papers, Harvard Law School, Box 105. Five years before, in a letter of his own to Hand, Frankfurter had acknowledged the differences between them on this matter. See letter, FF to Learned Hand, June 27, 1946, Learned Hand papers, Harvard Law School, Box 105.

21. Max Freedman, ed., *Roosevelt and Frankfurter: Their Correspondence, 1928–1945* (Boston: Little Brown and Co., 1967), p. 662.

    A search of the unpublished letters could not verify this statement. Also, Hand's biographer, Gerald Gunther, has not discovered such a letter. Letter to author from Gerald Gunther, March 7, 1978. Still, the comment could have been made in conversation.

22. Freedman, *Roosevelt and Frankfurter*, p. 662.

23. See Walter Millis, ed., *The Forrestal Diaries* (New York: The Viking Press, 1951), pp. 357–59 (January 9, 1948 entry). This incident was confirmed in a letter to this author dated August 9, 1977 from Loy Henderson.

    Forrestal also reported that Frankfurter approached Assistant Secretary Robert Lovett on the U.S. vote on December 13, 1947 (pp. 348–49). In a personal letter, however, Mr. Lovett could not remember this incident. Letter to author, dated September 15, 1977.

24. Unless otherwise noted, the following quotations are from a letter, FF to Walter Millis, January 19, 1953, FF/LC. This letter and related documents have also been reprinted in Joseph Lash, ed., *From the Diaries of Felix Frankfurter* (New York: W. W. Norton and Co., 1975), 345–49.

    This first argument on the duties of being a judge might partially reveal why FF supported Brandeis's political work.

25. The originals of these letters are now in the Frankfurter papers. FF to Marshall, March 10, 1948, and Marshall to FF, March 15, 1948, FF/LC, Box 40.

26. Letters, FF to Niles, October 13, 1947, December 3, 1947, May 17, 1948, and May 15, 1949, David Niles papers, Brandeis University. For more on this relationship, see David B. Sachar, "David K. Niles and United States Policy Toward Palestine: A Case Study in American Foreign Policy" (Unpublished Senior Honors thesis, Harvard University, 1959), *passim*.

27. Report of Joint Anglo-American Commission was signed in Lausanne, Switzerland,

on April 20, 1946. A copy can be found in the David Niles papers at Brandeis University.

28. Letter, FF to Buxton, July 25, 1946, FF/LC, Box 40. See also letters, FF to Buxton, July 17, 1946 and September 5, 1946, Buxton to FF, February 15, 1946, February 24, 1946, March 13, 1946, April 4, 1946, April 19, 1946, April 23, 1946, and July 23, 1946, and Joseph Hutcheson to Buxton, July 19, 1946, FF/LC, Box 40.

29. *The New York Times*, September 9, 1953, p. 26, col. 1. Also see Harry S. Truman, *Memoirs*, vol. I (New York: New American Library, 1965), p. 363; and Truman, *Memoirs*, vol. II, p. 553.

30. Truman, *Memoirs*, vol. II, pp. 248–54. Years later, in a letter to former law clerk Philip Kurland, Frankfurter indicated that the very thought of this trip offended his ethical sensibilities. In comparing this planned journey to Chief Justice Warren's trip to India in 1956, Frankfurter argued that only Warren's trip was ethical because it was: (a) at India's request, (b) not a diplomatic mission, and (c) not in conflict with assigned judicial duties. As was true on other occasions, however, it seems that Frankfurter's ethical judgments were colored by his personal relationships with the two men. The one factor which Frankfurter conveniently overlooked was that Vinson only considered taking the diplomatic mission, while Warren actually went to the foreign country (see letter, FF to Kurland, August 29, 1956, FF/LC, Box 72).

31. Letter, FF to Charles C. Burlingham, April 24, 1945, Burlingham papers, Harvard Law School, Box 5, Folder 6.

32. Henry Wallace Diary, October 16, 1945 entry, COHC, p. 4156.

33. Letter, FF to Learned Hand, April 23, 1946, Learned Hand papers, Harvard Law School, Box 105.

34. Letter, FF to Learned Hand, April 15, 1952, Learned Hand papers, Harvard Law School, Box 105. See also letters, FF to Truman, January 24, 1949, January 29, 1949, February 11, 1949, and Truman to FF, January 26, 1949, February 1, 1949, February 12, 1949, President's Secretary's files, Truman Library.

35. The account of the Acheson-Frankfurter "walking talks" is drawn from confidential interviews with Mr. Justice Frankfurter's law clerks: July 10, 1979, Washington, D.C. and on July 26 and 27, 1979, Cambridge, Mass. Also, interviews with Professor Gerald Gunther, August 15, 1979, Palo Alto, Ca; and with Elliot Richardson, April 29, 1981, State College, Penn.

This account of the Acheson-Frankfurter "walking talks" also relies upon a variety of published sources: Dean Acheson, "Felix Frankfurter," 76 *Harvard Law Review* (November, 1962), pp. 14–16; Monnet, *Memoirs*, pp. 301–2; Reminiscences of Henry Wallace, COHC, p. 270; and FF's record of several of these chats in his diary, see Lash, *Frankfurter Diaries*, (entries for October 15, 1946, October 18, 1946, October 21, 1946, October 24, 1946, November 7, 1946, and November 18, 1946).

Still, the record on these talks is sparse. The recently published volume *Among Friends: Personal Letters of Dean Acheson* by David S. McClellan and David C. Acheson (New York: Dodd Mead and Co., 1980), sheds little light on this subject. Also Dean Acheson's papers at Yale University are only now being opened and were not available for this research effort.

36. For more on the developing normative standard governing this type of activity, see the book's appendix.

37. The remainder of this chapter uses some of the same research as appears in my article "A Supreme Court Justice as Politician: Felix Frankfurter and Federal Court Appointments," XXI *The American Journal of Legal History* (1977), pp. 316–34. After reading a draft of this article, Professor Dean Alfange of the University of

Massachusetts suggested a revision along the lines presently used. My thanks to him, despite the fact that it has taken me years to see the wisdom of his remarks.

38. See letters, FF to FDR, November 17, 1939 (Microfilm of FF-FDR correspondence), FDRL; FF to FDR, May 18, 1938, and FF to Missy Le Hand, February 4, 1941, in Freedman, *Roosevelt and Frankfurter*, pp. 457–60, 580–81. One of FDR's requests was for a Frankfurter memorandum regarding the possible appointment of United States Court of Appeals Judge John J. Parker for the Supreme Court. Parker had been nominated for the Supreme Court in 1930 but failed to receive Senate confirmation for the position.

39. Much has been written about this incident. For details, see Mason, *Harlan Fiske Stone*, pp. 566–67; Gerhart, *America's Advocate*, p. 230; and Merlo Pusey, *Charles Evans Hughes*, (New York: Macmillan Co., 1951), pp. 787–88.

40. Unless otherwise noted, the following quotations are from a memorandum entitled "H.F.S. and the C.J. 'Ship,'" June 9, 1941, FF/HLS, Box 172, Folder 1.

41. This statement was also quoted in Mason, *Harlan Fiske Stone*, pp. 566–67.

42. This account of the conversation seems to weaken Justice Murphy's charge that Frankfurter had actively blocked his reappointment as attorney general. (For more, see chapter 7.)

43. Letter, FF to Philip Kurland, September 21, 1964, FF/HLS, Box 186.

44. Letter, FF to Biddle, September 2, 1941, FF/LC, Box 24. The two men were old friends and had much earlier conferred on possible appointees for assistant attorney general. See letter, FF to Biddle, November 26, 1934, FF/LC, Box 24.

45. Letter, FF to Biddle, October 16, 1941, FF/LC, Box 24. The letter from Burlingham could not be located in the files.

46. Letter, Biddle to FF, October 17, 1941, FF/LC, Box 24. Fahy was later named a judge on the United States Court of Appeals for the District of Columbia.

47. Letter, FF to Learned Hand, February 16, 1939, FF/LC, Box 64. See also a letter which indicates that Hand himself was actively seeking Wyzanski's appointment: Learned Hand to FF, February 11, 1939, FF/LC, Box 64.

48. Andrew Kaufman, "Charles C. Burlingham: Twentieth Century Crusader," in Harvard Law School library exhibits catalog, prepared by Erika S. Chadbourn (Cambridge, Mass.: Harvard Law School library, 1980), p. i.

49. Letter, FF to Charles C. Burlingham, September 26, 1941, Burlingham papers, Harvard Law School, Box 5, Folder 3. There is no record that Burlingham wrote FDR on this matter.

50. Letter, FF to Frank Buxton, undated, FF/LC, Box 39. This letter, since it refers to McClellan's resignation and is cited by another letter from FF to Buxton on September 10, 1941 (FF/LC, Box 39), was probably written in the first week of September, 1941.

51. Letter, Buxton to FF, March 14, 1941, FF/LC, Box 39.

52. This philosophy is developed in great detail in two letters: FF to Charles Wyzanski, November 22, 1954, FF/LC, Box 52; FF to Learned Hand, February 21, 1957, Learned Hand papers, Harvard Law School Box 105. A more systematic expression of Frankfurter's philosophy can be found in his article, "The Supreme Court in the Mirror of Justices, 105 *University of Pennsylvania Law Review* (1957), pp. 781–95.

53. Letter, FF to Frank Buxton, September 10, 1941, FF/LC, Box 39. This story is retold frequently. See FF to Learned Hand, December 4, 1939 and December 2, 1940, FF/LC, Box 64; FF to Learned Hand, April 24, 1951 and October 24, 1953, Learned Hand papers, Harvard Law School, Box 105; and FF to Charles C. Burlingham, April 25, 1941, FF/LC, Box 36.

54. Letter, FF to Max Lerner, May 21, 1952, Max Lerner papers, Sterling Library, Yale University, Box 3. Here Frankfurter was describing Justice Owen Burton, who possessed this quality in his opinion. For more on Frankfurter's views on "merit selection," see letter, FF to Charles C. Burlingham, February 21, 1957, Burlingham papers, Harvard Law School, Box 6. Here Frankfurter said the emphasis must be on "the quality of judges" and not on the appointment "machinery."
55. Letter, FF to Buxton, September 10, 1941, FF/LC, Box 39.
56. Letter, FF to Buxton, September 24, 1941, FF/LC, Box 39.
57. Frances Biddle, In Brief Authority, vol. II (Garden City, N.Y.: Doubleday, 1962), pp. 201–2. The incident is verified in a letter to author from Charles E. Wyzanski, Jr., October 7, 1976.
58. Biddle, In Brief Authority, vol. II, pp. 201–2.
59. This paragraph benefited from the excellent analysis of the relationship between these two men in Gerald Gunther's William Winslow Crosskey Lecture in Legal History at the University of Chicago Law School entitled, "Some Reflections on the Learned Hand-FF Correspondence," delivered November 18, 1976. For more on Hand, see Marvin Schick, Learned Hand's Court (Baltimore, Md.: Johns Hopkins Press, 1970). Hand's philosophy is evident in his volume, The Spirit of Liberty (Cambridge, Mass.: Harvard University Press, 1952). A fascinating study of the psychological warfare on the Supreme Court during Frankfurter's tenure can be found in H. N. Hirsch, The Enigma of Felix Frankfurter (New York: Basic Books, Inc., 1981), pp. 127–201.
60. Letter, FF to FDR, September 30, 1942, in Freedman, Roosevelt and Frankfurter, pp. 670–72.
61. Stone approached FDR through journalist Irving Brant; see Cibes, "Extra-Judicial Activities of Judges," pp. 1222–23; and Biddle, In Brief Authority, vol. II, p. 193.
62. Letter, FF to FDR, November 3, 1942, in Freedman, Roosevelt and Frankfurter, p. 672. For more on the general details of this selection incident, see Michael Kahn, "The Politics of the Appointment Process: An Analysis of Why Learned Hand Was Never Appointed to the Supreme Court," 25 Stanford Law Review (1973), pp. 251–84.
63. Letter, FF to FDR, December 3, 1942, in Freedman, Roosevelt and Frankfurter, p. 673.
64. Letter, FDR to FF, December 4, 1942, in Freedman, Roosevelt and Frankfurter, pp. 673–74.
65. Letter, FF to FDR, December 7, 1942 (includes a memorandum by FF on Judge Hand), in Freedman, Roosevelt and Frankfurter, pp. 674–75.
66. Douglas, Go East, Young Man, p. 332.
67. Letter, Learned Hand to FF, January 11, 1943, Learned Hand papers, Harvard Law School, Box 105.
68. See Memoirs by Frank Buxton entitled "Chum Felix Frankfurter," FF/LC, Box 256; letters, FF to Buxton, April 26, 1939, FF/LC, Box 39; FF to James Byrnes, March 17, 1944 and March 27, 1944, FF/LC, Box 41; FF to Frances Biddle, May 4, 1942, Biddle to FF, May 1, 1942 and May 22, 1942, FF/LC, Box 24.
69. Letter, FF to Charles C. Burlingham, May 25, 1950, FF/LC, Box 36. Burlingham requested help in letter, Burlingham to FF, May 9, 1950, Burlingham papers, Harvard Law School, Box 5. The request was a result of Judge George M. Hulbert's death and Judge Simon H. Rifkind's resignation. Moreover, Burlingham claimed that Judge John C. Knox was sick and Judge William Bondy was deaf. The U.S. attorney general at the time was J. Howard McGrath.
70. Letter, FF to Charles C. Burlingham, June 1, 1950, FF/LC, Box 36.

71. Burlingham's reputation was well known to Brownell, though the two men had not met personally. Letter to author from Herbert F. Brownell, October 21, 1976.

72. 333 U.S. 203 (1948).
    Frankfurter had been corresponding with this venerable lawyer on a weekly basis since 1924.

73. Letter, FF to Burlingham, April 13, 1951, FF/LC, Box 36. The main case on this issue—*Abington School District v. Schempp*, 374 U.S. 203 (1963)—did not come to the Supreme Court until after Frankfurter had retired.

74. Letter, FF to Burlingham, April 18, 1951, FF/LC, Box 36.

75. *Sacco and Vanzetti v. Commonwealth of Massachusetts*, 275 U.S. 574 (1927). For more on Brandeis's actions in this instance, see the discussion in chapter 3.

76. Letter, FF to Burlingham, April 18, 1951, FF/LC, Box 36.

77. 343 U.S. 306 (1952).

78. 343 U.S. 306 (1952), at 308–9. Frankfurter's dissent can be found on pp. 320–23.

79. Until otherwise noted, the following quotations are from a letter, FF to Burlingham, November 24, 1952, FF/LC, Box 36.

80. Ibid. Dewey was governor of New York from 1942–1954.

81. Letter, Burlingham to Thomas Dewey, November 26, 1952, FF/LC, Box 36.

82. Burlingham reported on his statements in a letter, Burlingham to FF, December 30, 1952, FF/LC, Box 36. See also, Burlingham to FF, December 4, 1952, FF/LC, Box 36.

83. Letter to author from Herbert F. Brownell, October 21, 1976.

84. 343 U.S. 579 (1952).

85. All the quotations in this paragraph are from a letter, FF to Burlingham, January 5, 1953, FF/LC, Box 37.

86. Letter, Burlingham to Brownell, January 15, 1953, Burlingham papers, Harvard Law School, Box 5, Folder 12.

87. Brownell's response is quoted in a letter, Burlingham to FF, January 27, 1953, FF/LC, Box 37.

88. Letter, FF to Burlingham, June 12, 1953, FF/LC, Box 37. Augustus Hand had retired from the Court on June 30, 1953, and Thomas Swan retired on July 1, 1953.

89. Letter, FF to Learned Hand, June 9, 1953, FF/LC, Box 65.

90. Letter, FF to Burlingham, July 4, 1953, FF/LC, Box 37.

91. Letter, Burlingham to FF, July 27, 1953, FF/LC, Box 37.

92. Letters, FF to Burlingham, August 12, 1953 and August 20, 1953, FF/LC, Box 37. There is no evidence that Burlingham did pass along these objections.

93. Letter, FF to Burlingham, March 24, 1958, FF/LC, Box 37.

94. Letter, FF to Attorney General Herbert Brownell, January 14, 1957, Learned Hand papers, Harvard Law School, Box 105.

95. Harlan was appointed on November 8, 1954, but consideration of the appointment by the Senate was postponed. So, the nomination was resubmitted to the new Senate on January 10, 1955, and confirmation came on March 16, 1955.

96. Letter, FF to Learned Hand, January 4, 1955, FF/LC, Box 65. Hand's letter in favor of the candidacy was Hand to FF, December 30, 1954, FF/LC, Box 65. Of course, FF's "rule not to initiate any suggestions" was well known by Hand to be a facade; after all, it was FF who had so actively sought to elevate him from the Appeals Court to the Supreme Court.

97. Letter, FF to Ives, January 4, 1955, FF/LC, Box 56.

98. Letter to author from Henry Friendly, November 6, 1977. Friendly, a close friend of Brownell and later a judicial colleague of both Lumbard and Moore, was in a position to assess the accuracy of this story.

99. Letter, FF to Herbert Brownell, January 14, 1957, Learned Hand papers, Harvard

Law School, Box 105. A copy of this letter is also present in the judicial appointments files of the deputy attorney general's office. The author is indebted to Professor Sheldon Goldman of the University of Massachusetts for providing these excerpts from his research materials.

100. Letter, Brownell to FF, January 16, 1957, FF/LC, Box 30.

101. Letter, Learned Hand to FF, January 15, 1957, FF/LC, Box 65. The copy of FF's letter to Brownell with his handwritten note to Hand can be found in Learned Hand's papers at the Harvard Law School, Box 105.

102. Letter, FF to Brownell, January 18, 1957, FF/LC, Box 30.

103. Letter, FF to Learned Hand, January 25, 1958, Learned Hand papers, Harvard Law School, Box 105. See also letters, FF to Hand, February 1, 1957, and Hand to FF, February 3, 1957, Learned Hand papers, Harvard Law School, Box 105.

104. This case, United States v. Dennis was decided by the jury on October 14, 1949, appealed to the United States Court of Appeals (Dennis v. United States, 183 F 2d 201), and then to the United States Supreme Court (341 U.S. 494 (1951)).

105. Smith Act, 54 U.S.C. Section 670, 671, Chapter 439, Section 2 and 3, 1946 edition.

106. Letter, FF to Learned Hand, April 24, 1951, Learned Hand papers, Harvard Law School, Box 105.

107. Letter, FF to Learned Hand, April 22, 1951, Learned Hand papers, Harvard Law School, Box 105.

108. Letters, FF to Charles C. Burlingham, April 25, 1951, FF/LC, Box 36; FF to Learned Hand, April 24, 1951, Learned Hand papers, Harvard Law School, Box 105. FF also sent other letters revealing the depth of his opposition to Medina, both personally and professionally, e.g. FF to Burlingham, April 21, 1951, FF/LC, Box 36.

109. Letter, FF to Charles C. Burlingham, April 25, 1951, FF/LC, Box 36.

110. Letter, FF to Herbert Brownell, February 18, 1957, FF/LC, Box 30. The response was to The New York Times, February 18, 1957, p. 16, col. 3.

111. The New York Times, September 7, 1957, p. 37, col. 2.

112. Letter, FF to Burlingham, January 11, 1957, Burlingham papers, Harvard Law School, Box 5, Folder 16.

113. Letter, FF to William P. Rogers, February 26, 1957, FF/LC, Box 97.

114. Letter, FF to Attorney General Rogers, January 28, 1958, FF/LC, Box 97. The report on Medina appeared in The New York Times, January 29, 1958, p. 17, col. 8. At the time of FF's letter, Rogers had not even been confirmed for the position yet. He was a recess appointment on October 23, 1957 and was not confirmed by the Senate until January 29, 1958.

115. Ibid.

116. Letter, FF to Learned Hand, February 13, 1958, FF/LC, Box 65. Learned Hand was in full agreement with this position. See letter, Hand to FF, January 19, 1958, Learned Hand papers, Harvard Law School, Box 105.

117. The directive was issued on April 4, 1959. See The New York Times, April 5, 1959, p. 1, col. 4 and p. 19, col. 2. FF's response is an undated note to Rogers, FF/LC, Box 97.

118. Letter, FF to Burlingham, March 24, 1958, FF/LC, Box 37. General background on this incident comes from The New York Times, March 24, 1958, p. 1, col. 5, p. 16, col. 3; June 2, 1958, p. 16, col. 1; February 8, 1959, p. 76, col. 1; and March 11, 1959, p. 1, col. 7.

119. Letters, Charles C. Burlingham to FF, May 2, 1958, Burlingham papers, Harvard Law School, Box 6; and Burlingham to Charles E. Wyzanski, Jr., June 17, 1958; Wyzanski papers, Harvard Law School, Box 1.

120. Letter to author from Judge Charles E. Wyzanski, Jr., October 7, 1976. It is inter-

esting to note that despite FF's abhorrence of the political considerations involved in such appointments, it was just such an "irrelevant" factor which was holding up the nomination. See also *The New York Times*, January 16, 1959, p. 25, col. 1 and February 8, 1959, p. 76, col. 1.

121. Hand told Eisenhower that he was "volunteering" his recommendation because he was "interested in getting the very best man we can." See *The New York Times*, February 17, 1959, p. 34, col. 4.

122. Letter, FF to Burlingham, March 11, 1959, FF/LC, Box 38.

Another slightly veiled attack against Kaufman came in an exchange of correspondence in May, 1959, with Attorney General Rogers. Here Frankfurter delivered his standard lecture on the inadvisability of appointing judges for political reasons. Unlike his past sermons, however, this time the justice emphasized in particular his view that prior judicial experience did not necessarily indicate the ability of an individual to function on a higher court. Frankfurter's philosophical argument here had a very practical application. Having secured an appointment to the Court of Appeals for *Attorney* Henry Friendly, he was still opposing by implication one for *Judge* Irving Kaufman. No doubt, then, the justice was greatly pleased by Rogers's closing letter in this discussion, stating that he was in "complete agreement" with Frankfurter's views. Letter, Rogers to FF, May 29, 1959, FF/LC, Box 97. Rogers was responding to two FF letters: FF to Rogers, May 13, 1959 and May 27, 1959, FF/LC, Box 97.

123. Letters, Learned Hand to FF, August 10, 1959, Learned Hand papers, Harvard Law School, Box 105; FF to Bickel, April 1, 1959, FF/HLS, Box 206.

124. Letter, Learned Hand to FF, August 10, 1959, Learned Hand papers, Harvard Law School, Box 105.

125. Letter, FF to Learned Hand, August 19, 1959, Learned Hand papers, Harvard Law School, Box 105.

126. Friendly took the oath of office on September 30, 1959. The judiciary bill was passed on May 19, 1961 (Public Law 87-36), and Kaufman was appointed to the Appeals Court on September 22, 1961. For more see *The New York Times*, August 26, 1959, p. 15, col. 1; September 5, 1959, p. 6, col. 1; September 8, 1959, p. 41, col. 1; September 10, 1959, p. 16, col. 5; and October 1, 1959, p. 12, col. 4.

127. See letters, FF to Herbert Brownell, March 19, 1957, FF/LC, Box 30; acknowledged by letter, Brownell to FF, March 22, 1957, FF/LC, Box 30; FF to Vincent McKusick, March 18, 1958, FF/LC, Box 53; and FF to H. Chapman, March 18, 1958, FF/LC, Box 53.

128. *The New York Times*, February 23, 1965, p. 1, cols., 6, 7; and Lash, *Frankfurter Diaries*, p. 89.

129. Max Isenbergh, "Reminiscences to FF as a Friend," 51 *Virginia Law Review* (1965), p. 573.

130. Garson Kanin, "FF Toward the End," 51 *Virginia Law Review* (1965), p. 561.

131. Earl Warren, *The Memoirs of Earl Warren* (Garden City, N.Y.: Doubleday and Co., Inc., 1977), p. 358.

132. See letters, FF to Philip Kurland, October 16, 1964, FF/HLS, Box 186. FF's comments indicate that this is the second note sent to Kurland on this subject. FF to Alexander Bickel, December 17, 1963, FF/HLS, Box 206. FF suggests three Supreme Court cases which support his position. However, Bickel never wrote the article. The quoted statement is from Freedman, *Roosevelt and Frankfurter*, pp. 662-63.

Appendix

1. The evidence for this survey is drawn from the entire collection of judicial biographies and general historical studies of the Supreme Court. The author found several summary works to be quite helpful in suggesting volumes and articles to study. These works all give various summaries of incidents of extrajudicial behavior by members of the Supreme Court. However, none of them attempt to derive a continuous normative standard of propriety for Supreme Court justices. See William J. Cibes, Jr., "Extrajudicial Activities of the United States Supreme Court, 1790–1960," (Unpublished Ph.D. dissertation, Princeton University, 1975); Walter F. Murphy, *Elements of Judicial Strategy* (Chicago: University of Chicago Press, 1964); Robert McKay, "The Judiciary and Non-Judicial Activities," 35 *Law and Contemporary Problems* (1970), pp. 9–36; "Extrajudicial Activities of Judges," 47 *Iowa Law Review* (1962), pp. 1026–48; Solomon Slonim, "Extrajudicial Activities of Supreme Court Justice," 22 *Stanford Law Review* (1970), pp. 587–617; and Henry J. Abraham and Bruce Allen Murphy, "The Influence of Sitting and Retired Justices on Presidential Supreme Court Nominations," 3 *Hasting Constitutional Law Quarterly* (winter, 1976), pp. 37–65.
2. For more on the meaning of the judiciary to the separation of powers, see Baron de Montesquieu, *The Spirit of the Laws*, transl. Thomas Nugent, vol. I (New York: Colonial Press, 1899), book X, sec. 6, pp. 152ff.
3. Alexander Hamilton, John Jay, and James Madison, *The Federalist Papers*, number 78 (New York: Random House, 1937), p. 505.
4. Russell Wheeler, "Extrajudicial Activities of the Early Supreme Court," 1973 *Supreme Court Review* (1973), p. 128. Wheeler provides a fine analysis of the "intent of the Founders" and the early Supreme Court members on the extrajudicial activities of that body in "Extrajudicial Activities of United States Supreme Court Justices: the Constitutional Period, 1790–1809" (Unpublished Ph.D. dissertation, University of Chicago, 1971), especially chapter III. The section of this chapter on the Court prior to 1803 draws upon these works especially.
5. Max Farrand, ed., *The Records of the Federal Convention* (New Haven: Yale University Press, 1937), at vol. 1, p. 21; vol. II, pp. 341, 342–344, 427.
6. Hamilton et al., *The Federalist Papers*, number 73, p. 481.
7. United States Constitution, Article III, Section I.
8. United States Constitution, Article I, Section 6.
9. The only issues mentioned here concern the judicial appointment process and the tenure of office for the position. See Hamilton et al., *The Federalist Papers*, number 51, p. 33, and number 78, pp. 505–6.
10. Wheeler, *Supreme Court Review*, p. 145.
11. See Charles Warren, *The Supreme Court in United States History*, vol. 1 (Boston: Little, Brown and Co., 1926), passim.
12. Books by several scholars depict these early codes of behavior: Richard Ellis, The Jeffersonian Crisis: Courts and Politics in the Young Republic (New York: Oxford University Press, 1976); and Henry Steele Commager, *The Empire of Reason: How Europe Imagined and America Realized the Enlightenment* (New York: Anchor Press/Doubleday, 1977).
13. Wheeler, *Supreme Court Review*, p. 145.
14. An example of this behavior occurred when Washington was planning his State-of-the-Union address in 1790. He wanted to know "every matter which may occur to the heads of Departments." So he wrote to Jay requesting "anything in the judiciary line, [and] anything of a more general nature," which should be included in

the speech. See John C. Fitzpatrick, ed., *The Writings of Washington*, vol. 31 (Washington, D.C.: Government Printing Office, 1931–44), pp. 155–157. See also vol. 31, pp. 44–46, and pp. 102–3. Also see Fitzpatrick, ed., *The Diaries of George Washington*, vol. 4 (Boston: Houghton Mifflin Co., 1925), pp. 15–16, 90, 122; Cibes, "The Extrajudicial Activities," pp. 82–84; and Henry P. Johnston, ed., *The Correspondence and Public Papers of John Jay*, vol. 3 (New York: G.P. Putnam's Sons, 1890–93), pp. 405–9.

15. Congressional Acts of July 20, 1790, Chapter 29, Section 3, *United States Statutes*, Vol. 1., p. 132; Act of January 23, 1978, Chapter 8, Section 1, *Statutes*, Vol. 1, p. 537; Act of May 26, 1790, Chapter 12, *Statutes*, Vol. 1, pp. 122–23; and Act of January 29, 1795, Chapter 20; *Statutes*, Vol. 1, pp. 414–15.

16. Wheeler, *Supreme Court Review*, pp. 139–141; and Wheeler, "Extrajudicial Activities," chapter IV.

17. 2 Dallas 409 (1792).

18. Wheeler, *Supreme Court Review*, pp. 131–39, was very helpful in this section of the essay.

19. Slonim, "Extrajudicial Activities," p. 404.

20. Johnston, *Public Correspondence to John Jay*, vol. 3, p. 389; see also pp. 387–395. Also partially quoted in Wheeler, "Extrajudicial Activities," p. 79.

21. Johnston, *Public Correspondence of John Jay*, vol. 3, p. 486.

22. Johnston, *Public Correspondence of John Jay*, vol. 3, pp. 486–88.

23. Johnston, *Public Correspondence of John Jay*, vol. 3, pp. 488–89. Also quoted in Cibes, "The Extrajudicial Activities," p. 102.

24. Joseph Story, *Commentaries on the Constitution*, vol. 3 (Boston: Hilliard, Gray and Co., 1833), p. 651.

25. Indicating the ambiguity here, when he became governor of New York, John Jay asked the chancellor and judges of the New York Supreme Court for an advisory opinion. He wanted to know whether he had the exclusive power under the New York Constitution to nominate individuals for the Council of Appointment to accept or reject. His request differed from the earlier one by Jefferson in that it was limited to one specific issue at one time. Further, he requested the advice "unless a mode of having [the question] judicially determined should occur to you, and in that case, that you will be pleased to indicate it." The chancellor refused, for fear of setting a dangerous precedent of advice-giving. See letter, John Jay to Supreme Court Judges, March 18, 1801, quoted in Wheeler, *Supreme Court Review*, p. 156.

26. Johnson, *Public Correspondence of John Jay*, vol. III, p. 488.

27. Charles Warren, *The Supreme Court*, vol. 1, p. 275; Frank Monaghan, *John Jay* (New York: The Bobbs-Merrill Co., 1935), pp. 318, 325–27; and Albert Beveridge, *The Life of John Marshall* (Boston: Houghton Mifflin Co., 1919), vol. III, pp. 30, 49.

28. Monaghan, *John Jay*, pp. 365–68; William G. Brown, *The Life of Oliver Ellsworth* (New York: The Macmillan Co., 1905), p. 215; and Cibes, "The Extrajudicial Activities," pp. 174–76.

29. I Cranch 137 (1803).

30. Cibes, "The Extrajudicial Activities," pp. 174–76.

31. Justice Nelson served as an intermediary in bringing peace proposals to the confederacy. Then he served on a commission arbitrating British claims over ships such as the *Alabama*. See Henry G. Connor, *John A. Campbell, Associate Justice of the United States Supreme Court, 1853–1861* (Boston: Houghton Mifflin Co., 1920), p. 163; Charles Fairman, *Reconstruction and Reunion, 1864–88*, vol. 1, vol. 6 of the Oliver Wendell Holmes Devise History of the Supreme Court of the United States

(New York: The Macmillan Co., 1971), p. 753; and Cibes, "The Extrajudicial Activities," pp. 755–63.

32. Gerald Dunne, *Justice Joseph Story and the Rise of the Supreme Court* (New York: Simon and Schuster, 1970), p. 96.

33. Donald G. Morgan, *Justice William Johnson, The First Dissenter* (Columbus, Ohio: University of South Carolina Press, 1954), pp. 97–98.

34. Irving Brant, *James Madison: Commander in Chief* (Indianapolis, Ind.: The Bobbs-Merrill Company, Inc., 1961), pp. 83–84.

35. Freeman Cleaves, *Old Tippecanoe: William Henry Harrison and his Time* (New York: Charles Scribner's Sons, 1939), pp. 121–22.

36. Charles Warren, *The Supreme Court*, vol. 1, pp. 87–89.

37. 7 Cranch 32 (1812).

38. William Wetmore Story, ed., *Life and Letters of Joseph Story*, vol. 1 (Boston: Charles C. Little and James Brown, 1851), pp. 243–45 (letter, Joseph Story to Nathaniel Williams, May 27, 1813).

39. William Story, *Letters of Joseph Story*, vol. 1, p. 254 (letter, Joseph Story to Nathaniel Williams, February 22, 1815); also Dunne, *Joseph Story*, pp. 106–9.

40. William Story, *Letters of Joseph Story*, vol. 1, p. 300 (letter, Joseph Story to William Pinckney, 1816); also vol. 1, p. 293; and Dunne, *Joseph Story*, pp. 144–48.

41. I Wheat. 304 (1816).

42. I Wheat. 304 at 310 (1816).

43. Story sent Webster ideas for reform in the areas of bankruptcy, criminal laws, and maritime crimes. Moreover, he would feed Webster information to be used on the floor of the Senate in opposition to the president. See William Story, *Letters of Joseph Story*, vol. II, pp. 316, 374, 372–39, 404–6, 155–58.

44. Dunne, *Joseph Story*, pp. 161–69.

45. At this time Story was pushing for two bills, both of which he had personally drafted: "A Bill further to extend the judicial System of the United States," and "A Bill to provide for the Punishment of certain crimes against the United States, and for other purposes." The first bill was enacted quickly, but action on the second measure was delayed. See William Story, *Letters of Joseph Story*, vol. 1, p. 315, 401, 437; and R. Kent Newmyer, "Justice Joseph Story: A Political and Constitutional Study," (Unpublished Ph.D. dissertation, University of Nebraska, 1959), pp. 173–75.

46. Wheat. 122 (1819).

47. 4 Wheat. 518 (1819).

48. 4 Wheat. 316 (1819).

49. Warren, *The Supreme Court*, vol. 1, *passim*.

50. The account of the following incident is drawn from Gerald Gunther, ed., *John Marshall's Defense of McCulloch v. Maryland* (Stanford, Calif.: Stanford University Press, 1969), pp. 1–21.

51. William Story, *Letters of Joseph Story*, vol. 1, pp. 435–39 (letter, Joseph Story to Webster, January 4, 1824).

52. Dunne, *Joseph Story*, pp. 253–55; and William Story, *Letters of Joseph Story*, vol. II, pp. 402–3, 405–6.

53. Morgan, *William Johnson*, pp. 123–24; Cibes, "The Extrajudicial Activities," pp. 248–49, 263–64. Johnson was referring to the Court's decision in *McCulloch v. Maryland*, 4 Wheat. 316 (1819).

54. Johnson was quite active in advising Adams. When the latter was secretary of state, the two men conferred on the question of slavery. Letter, Johnson to Adams, June

12, 1821, quoted in Morgan, *Johnson*, p. 172n, also pp. 135n and 136n; also Charles Francis Adams, ed., *Memoirs of John Quincy Adams*, vol. 7 (Philadelphia: J.B. Lippincott & Co., 1874–77), pp. 223, 236–37.

55. Adams, *Memoirs of John Quincy Adams*, vol. VII, pp. 236, 314; and Cibes, "The Extrajudicial Activities," pp. 256–58.

56. Francis P. Weisenburger, *The Life of John McLean: A Politician on the United States Supreme Court* (Columbus, Ohio: Ohio State University Press, 1937), pp. 103–5, 69–77.

57. Weisenburger, *John McLean*, pp. 177, 68–69, 147, 136, 183, 91; Warren, *The Supreme Court*, vol. II, pp. 210, 222, 271; William Story, *Letters of Joseph Story*, vol. II, pp. 373–74, 407; Alexander A. Lawrence, *James Moore Wayne: Southern Unionist* (Chapel Hill, N.C.: University of North Carolina Press, 1943), pp. 86n, 90; Carl Swisher, *The Taney Period, 1836–64*, vol. V of the Oliver Wendell Holmes Devise History of the Supreme Court of the United States (New York: Macmillan Co., 1974), p. 565n.

58. William Story, *Letters of Joseph Story*, vol. II, pp. 330–32 (letter, Story to Webster, May 10, 1840); Cibes, "The Extrajudicial Activities," pp. 397–401. The treaty concerned the boundary for New England.

59. The realignment of circuits was made necessary by the acquisition of new states in the West. This bill passed a year later. Swisher, *The Taney Period*, pp. 25–28, 62–63, 254–55.

60. Carl Swisher, *Roger B. Taney* (New York: Macmillan Co., 1935), pp. 326–30, 339–40, 335–67, 216–17, and 389–90.

61. Catron began this relationship by sending Polk advice on policy and ways to advance his political career as Speaker of the House. Swisher, *The Taney Period*, pp. 113, 223; Cibes, "The Extrajudicial Activities," pp. 403–413; Eugene I. McCormac, *James K. Polk: A Political Biography* (New York: Russell and Russell, 1965), pp. 660–61, 61, 114–15.

62. 19 How. 393 (1857).

63. Quote from Swisher, *Taney*, p. 502.

64. David M. Silver, *Lincoln's Supreme Court* (Urbana, Ill.: University of Illinois Press, 1956), pp. 60–70.

65. Several administration figures were used as intermediaries by the Court: Secretary of State William Seward, Attorney General William Bates, Secretary of the Treasury Salmon P. Chase (prior to his elevation to the Court), and Postmaster General Montgomery Blair. See Henry Connor, *John A. Campbell*, pp. 114–15, 122–32, 138–40; Philip G. Clifford, *Nathan Clifford, Democrat* (New York: Putnam's, 1922), pp. 277–78.

66. Lawrence, *Wayne*, pp. 200–203; and David F. Hughes, "Salmon P. Chase—Chief Justice" (Unpublished Ph.D. dissertation, Princeton University, 1963), pp. 157, 214, and 278.

67. The Chief Justice helped to draft sections two and four of the Fourteenth Amendment. See Hughes, "Chase," p. 40; Jacob W. Schuckers, *Life and Public Services of Salmon P. Chase* (New York: D. Appleton and Co., 1874), pp. 516–18, 520–23, 533; Fairman, *Reconstruction and Reunion*, vol. I, pp. 118, 121; and David Donald, ed., *Inside Lincoln's Cabinet: The Civil War Diaries of Salmon P. Chase* (New York: Longmans, Green and Co., 1954), pp. 268–70.

68. William Gillette, "Noah Swayne," in Leon Friedman and Fred L. Israel, eds., *The Justices of the United States Supreme Court 1789–1969: Their Lives and Major Opinions* (New York: Chelsea House Publishers and R. R. Bowker Co., 1969), p. 998.

69. Fairman, *Reconstruction and Reunion*, pp. 160–65; Swisher, *The Taney Period*, pp. 836–37; Charles Fairman, *Mr. Justice Miller and the Supreme Court 1862–1890* (Cambridge, Mass.: Harvard University Press, 1960), p. 192.

70. Swisher, *The Taney Period*, pp. 22–23; Swisher, *Roger B. Taney*, pp. 311–12; John P. Frank, "The Appointment of Supreme Court Justices," 1941 *Wisconsin Law Review* (1941), pp. 178–79; and Willard L. King, *Lincoln's Manager: David Davis* (Cambridge, Mass.: Harvard University Press, 1960), p. 192.

71. Daniel McHargue, "Appointments to the Supreme Court, 1789–1932" (Unpublished Ph.D. dissertation, UCLA, 1949), p. 189; Fairman, *Reconstruction and Reunion*, pp. 11–12, 14, 16–17, 18; Silver, *Lincoln's Supreme Court*, p. 191 and 200–201.

72. Fairman, *Reconstruction and Reunion*, pp. 515–538; and Hughes, "Chase," pp. 120–147, 166.

73. *Newsweek*, July 20, 1981, p. 17; and *Time Magazine*, July 30, 1981, pp. 10–11.

74. Fairman, *Reconstruction and Reunion*, pp. 1466–72; King, *David Davis*, pp. 277–82; Fairman, *Mr. Justice Miller*, pp. 297–306; and Carl B. Swisher, *Stephen J. Field, Craftsman of the Law* (Washington, D.C.: The Brookings Institution, 1930), pp. 220–22, 300–310.

75. C. Peter Magrath, *Morrison R. Waite: The Triumph of Character* (New York: The Macmillan Co., 1963), pp. 147–49, 285–89. Alan Westin, "The First Justice Harlan and the Constitutional Rights of Negroes," 66 *Yale Law Journal* (1957), pp. 675–77, 637.

76. King, *Davis*, pp. 291–93; and Swisher, *Field*, p. 281.

77. Bruce Trimble, *Chief Justice Waite, Defender of the Public Interest* (Princeton, N.J.: Princeton University Press, 1938), pp. 147–49; Magrath, *Waite*, pp. 285–92.

78. On eight occasions members of the Court lobbied for appointments of their colleagues. For more, see Abraham and Murphy, "Presidential Supreme Court Nominations," chart, pp. 40–49. On the 1875 act, see Fairman, *Justice Miller*, pp. 403–4; Swisher, *Field*, pp. 318–19.

79. Paul L. Haworth, *The Hayes-Tilden Disputed Presidential Election of 1876* (Cleveland, Ohio: Burrows Bros., Co., 1906), chapter 10. Justice David Davis, who was originally offered the swing seat on the commission, declined to serve because he had just been elected by the Illinois legislature as that state's new senator.

80. In the following instances the assignment was accepted: Justice Harlan on the 1892 Bering Sea Arbitration; Justices Brewer and Fuller on an arbitrating commission in 1895 examining the boundary between Venezuela and British Guiana; Justice Fuller in 1900 on the Permanent Court of Arbitration; and Justice Moody in 1909 on the Moody-Mahan Commission. In the following instances the assignment was refused: Justices Fuller and White in 1898 on the Spanish-American Peace Commission; and Justices Oliver Wendell Holmes and Edward White in 1903 on the Alaskan Boundary Commission. See Willard King, *Melville Weston Fuller: Chief Justice of the United States, 1888–1910* (New York: Macmillan Co., 1950), pp. 182–84, 251–53; Russell R. Wheeler, "Extrajudicial Behavior and the Role of the Supreme Court Justice," *University Programs Modular Studies* (Morristown, N.J.: General Learning Press, 1975), pp. 6–7; Cibes, "The Extrajudicial Activities," p. 938; Philip C. Jessup, *Elihu Root* (New York: Dodd Mead and Co., 1938); and Elting E. Morison, ed., *The Letters of Theodore Roosevelt*, vol. III (Cambridge, Mass.: Harvard University Press, 1951–54), pp. 248–67.

81. 198 U.S. 45 (1905).

82. There were fourteen incidents of justices attempting to influence appointments of their colleagues during this period. For more, see Abraham and Murphy, "Presi-

dential Supreme Court Appointments," chart, pp. 40–49. On the plethora of attempts to appoint individuals to the executive branch, see Cibes, "The Extrajudicial Activities," pp. 1001–38.

83. Murphy, *Elements of Judicial Strategy*, p. 136; and King, *Fuller*, pp. 150–51.

84. Morison, *Letters of Theodore Roosevelt*, vol. V, pp. 801–4; and Henry F. Pringle, *Theodore Roosevelt* (New York: Harcourt, Brace and Co., 1931), p. 403.

85. On the Judicial Reform Acts, see Murphy, *Elements of Judicial Strategy*, p. 136; and Alpheus T. Mason, *William Howard Taft: Chief Justice* (New York: Simon and Schuster, 1964), pp. 38–39, 108–9. The Court under White was not terribly active in efforts to put people on the Supreme Court. There were only eight instances of such behavior, and four of these revolved around efforts to fill Chief Justice Fuller's post. See Abraham and Murphy, "Presidential Supreme Court Nominations," chart, pp. 40–49. On efforts to place people in the executive branch, see Cibes, "The Extrajudicial Activities," pp. 1001–38. In the period from 1910 to 1916 there were three instances of appointing judicial members to official government tribunals, and all were accepted: Justice Hughes in 1911 on the Postal Rate Commission; Justices White, Furton, and Van Devanter in 1911 on the Delegate to the A.B.C. Conference. See Merlo J. Pusey, *Charles Evans Hughes*, vol. I (New York: The Macmillan Co., 1951), p. 296; Mason, *William Howard Taft*, p. 119.

86. Pusey, *Hughes*, vol. I, pp. 302–20.

Selected Bibliography

Source Abbreviations

FF/LC   Felix Frankfurter Papers,
Manuscripts Division,
Library of Congress

FF/HLS   Felix Frankfurter Papers
(Court-related), Manuscripts
Division, Harvard Law School

LDB/LLS   Louis D. Brandeis Papers,
Manuscripts Division,
Louisville Law School

LDB/HLS   Louis D. Brandeis Papers
(Court-related), Manuscripts
Division, Harvard Law School

LC   Manuscripts Division,
Library of Congress

FDRL   Manuscripts Division,
Franklin Delano Roosevelt Library

COHC   Columbia Oral History Collection,
Butler Library, Columbia University

453

Unpublished Sources

Manuscripts and Oral Histories
American Zionist Archives. New York, New York
        Louis D. Brandeis Papers (personal)
Brandeis University. Waltham, Massachusetts
        David Niles Papers
Columbia University. New York, New York
        Frances Perkins Papers
Columbia University, Oral History Collection. New York, New York
        George W. Alger
        Adolf A. Berle, Jr.
        Harvey H. Bundy
        Charles C. Burlingham
        Marquis W. Childs
        James F. Curtis
        Thomas I. Emerson
        Jerome N. Frank
        Felix Frankfurter
        Edward S. Greenbaum
        Learned Hand
        Gardner Jackson
        James M. Landis
        Chester T. Lane
        David A. Morse
        John Lord O'Brian
        Frances Perkins
        Louis H. Pink
        Paul and Elizabeth Raushenbush
        Bernard G. Richards
        Samuel I. Rosenman
        George Rublee
        William J. Schieffelin
        Arthur Schlesinger, Sr.
        Rexford G. Tugwell
        Henry A Wallace
        James P. Warburg
        James T. Williams, Jr.
        Leo Wolman
        Charles E. Wyzanski, Jr.
Harvard Law School. Cambridge, Massachusetts
        Louis D. Brandeis Papers (Court-related)
        Charles C. Burlingham Papers
        Felix Frankfurter Papers (Court-related)
        Felix Frankfurter Papers (Zionist-related; on microfilm)
        Learned Hand Papers
        Calvert Magruder Papers
        Charles E. Wyzanski, Jr., Papers
Harvard University, Houghton Library. Cambridge, Massachusetts
        Jay Pierrepont Moffat Papers and Diary
Hoover Institution on War, Revolution and Peace. Stanford, California

Raymond W. Moley Papers and Diary
James Grafton Rogers Papers
John F. Kennedy Library. Waltham, Massachusetts
John F. Kennedy Presidential Papers
James P. Warburg Papers
Dean Acheson Oral History
Abram Chayes Oral History
Felix Frankfurter Oral History
Library of Congress. Washington, D.C.
Ray Stannard Baker Papers
Wendell Berge Papers
Harold Burton Papers and Diary
Bainbridge Colby Papers
Josephus Daniels Papers
Felix Frankfurter Papers and Diary (personal)
Emanuel Goldenweiser Papers
Harold Ickes Papers
James M. Landis Papers
William McAdoo Papers
Herbert Marks Papers
George W. Norris Papers
J. Robert Oppenheimer Papers
Gifford Pinchot Papers
Donald Richberg Papers
Harlan Fiske Stone Papers
Huston Thompson Papers and Diary
Woodrow Wilson Papers
Franklin D. Roosevelt Library. Hyde Park, New York
Adolf A. Berle, Jr., Papers and Diary
Morris L. Cooke Papers
Oscar Cox Papers and Diary
Wayne Coy Papers
Mary W. Dewson Papers
Mordecai J. B. Ezekiel Papers
Felix Frankfurter-Franklin D. Roosevelt Letters (on microfilm)
Harry Hopkins Papers
Louis M. Howe Papers
Gardner Jackson Papers
Herbert H. Lehman Papers
Lowell Mellett Papers
R. Walton Moore Papers
Henry M. Morgenthau, Jr. Papers and Diary
Franklin D. Roosevelt Papers
Samuel I. Rosenman Papers
Rexford G. Tugwell Papers and Diary
Louis B. Wehle Papers
Harry Truman Library. Independence, Missouri
Dean Acheson Papers
Harry Truman Papers
University of Kentucky, Fred Vinson Oral History Project, Lexington, Kentucky
W. E. Crutcher

John W. McCormack
Newton N. Minow
Willard H. Pedrick
Paul Porter
Howard J. Triennes
University of Louisville Law School. Louisville, Kentucky
  Louis D. Brandeis Papers (personal)
University of Virginia, Alderman Library. Charlottesville, Virginia
  Homer Cummings Papers and Diary
  Carter Glass Papers
  James C. McReynolds Papers
Yale University, Sterling Library. New Haven, Connecticut
  Jerome Frank Papers
  Edward M. House Papers and Diary
  Max Lerner Papers
  Henry L. Stimson Papers and Diary (on microfilm)

Author Interviews

Benjamin V. Cohen
William T. Coleman
Thomas Corcoran
Philip Elman
Paul A. Freund
Henry J. Friendly (telephone)
Gerald Gunther
Milton Katz
Andrew L. Kaufman
John J. McCloy
Carl McFarland (telephone)
Carl McGowan
Robert Nathan
Edward F. Prichard, Jr.
Joseph L. Rauh, Jr.
Elliot Richardson
David Riesman, Jr.
Albert M. Sacks
Frank E. A. Sander
Donald T. Trautman
James Vorenberg
Charles E. Wyzanski, Jr.

Unpublished Studies

Ashby, John G. "Supreme Court Appointments Since 1937." Unpublished Ph.D. dissertation, University of Notre Dame, 1972.

Blackmun, Paul H. "Judicial Biography and Public Law: An Analysis with Emphasis on the New Deal Court." Unpublished Ph.D. dissertation, University of Virginia, 1970.

Burke, Richard. "The Path to the Court: A Study of Federal Judicial Appointments." Unpublished Ph.D. dissertation, Vanderbilt University, 1958.

Cibes, Walter J., Jr. "Extra-Judicial Activities of the United States Supreme Court, 1790–1960." Unpublished Ph.D. dissertation, Princeton University, 1975.

Dawson, Nelson L. "Louis D. Brandeis, Felix Frankfurter and the New Deal." Unpublished Ph.D. dissertation, University of Kentucky, 1975.

Hirsch, Harry Nathan. "The Uses of Psychology in Judicial Biography: Felix Frankfurter and the Ambiguities of Self-Image." Unpublished Ph.D. dissertation, Princeton University, 1978.

Hughes, David F. "Salmon P. Chase—Chief Justice." Unpublished Ph.D. dissertation, Princeton University, 1963.

Levinson, Sanford Victor. "Skepticism, Democracy, and Judicial Restraint: An Essay on the Thought of Oliver Wendell Holmes and Felix Frankfurter." Unpublished Ph.D. dissertation, Harvard University, 1969.

McHargue, Daniel S. "Factors Influencing the Selection and Appointment of Members of the United States Supreme Court, 1789–1932." Unpublished Ph.D. dissertation, University of California at Los Angeles, 1949.

Massaro, John. "Advice and Dissent: Factors in the Senate's Refusal to Confirm Supreme Court Nominees, with Special Emphasis on the Cases of Abe Fortas and Clement Haynsworth." Unpublished Ph.D. dissertation, Southern Illinois University, 1973.

Newmyer, R. Kent. "Justice Joseph Story: A Political and Constitutional Study." Unpublished Ph.D. dissertation, University of Nebraska, 1959.

Rusch, Jonathan J. "William H. Hastie and the Vindication of Civil Rights." Unpublished Master's thesis, University of Virginia, 1978.

Sachar, David B. "David K. Niles and United States Policy Toward Palestine, A Case Study in American Foreign Policy." Unpublished Senior Honors thesis, Harvard University, 1959.

Spencer, Samuel, Jr. "A History of the Selective Training and Service Act of 1940." Unpublished Ph.D. dissertation, Harvard University, 1949.

Wheeler, Russell. "Extrajudicial Activities of United States Supreme Court Justices: The Constitutional Period, 1790–1809." Unpublished Ph.D. dissertation, University of Chicago, 1971.

Other Unpublished Materials

Berns, Walter. "The Least Dangerous Branch, But Only If . . ." Paper delivered at the National Legal Center for the Public Interest, 1977.

Goldman, Jerry. "Jurisdictional Politics: Congressional Attention to Federal Court Power." Unpublished manuscript, 1975.

Gunther, Gerald. "Some Reflections on the Learned Hand—Felix Frankfurter Correspondence." William Winslow Crosskey Lecture in Legal History. University of Chicago Law School, delivered November 18, 1976.

Strum, Philippa. "Brandeis and the Exercise of Judicial Power." Paper delivered at the American Political Science Association convention, September 1977.

Transcripts of wiretap placed by Massachusetts State Police on Felix Frankfurter and Sacco-Vanzetti Defense League. August 9, 1927 to October 3, 1927. Secretary of State's Office, Government Center, Boston, Massachusetts.

Published Sources

Books

Abraham, Henry J. *The Judicial Process: An Introductory Analysis of the Courts of the United States, England, and France.* New York: Oxford University Press, 1975.

————. *Justices and Presidents: A Political History of Appointments to the Supreme Court*. New York: Oxford University Press, 1974.

Acheson, Dean. *Morning and Noon*. Boston: Houghton Mifflin Co., 1975.

————. *Present at the Creation; My Years in the State Department*. New York: Norton, 1969.

Adams, Charles Francis, ed. *Memoirs of John Quincy Adams*. Philadelphia: J. B. Lippincott and Company, 1874–77.

Auerbach, Jerold S. *Unequal Justice: Lawyers and Social Change in Modern America*. New York: Oxford University Press, 1976.

Baker, Liva. *Felix Frankfurter*. New York: Coward-McCann, Inc., 1969.

Baker, Ray Stannard. *Woodrow Wilson: Life and Letters*. 6 vols. New York: Doubleday, Page and Company, 1927–39.

Barnard, Harry. *The Forging of an American Jew: The Life and Times of Judge Julian W. Mack*. New York: Herzl Press, 1974.

Berle, Beatrice B., and Jacobs, Travis B. *Navigating the Rapids, 1918–1971: From the Papers of Adolf A. Berle, Jr*. New York: Harcourt Brace Jovanovich, Inc., 1973.

Beveridge, Albert J. *The Life of John Marshall*. Boston: Houghton Mifflin Co., 1916.

Biddle, Francis. *In Brief Authority*. Garden City, N.Y.: Doubleday, 1962.

Brandeis, Louis D. *Business—A Profession*. Boston: Small, Maynard and Co., 1914.

————. *Other People's Money, and How Bankers Use it*. New York: F. A. Stokes and Co., 1914.

Brown, William G. *The Life of Oliver Ellsworth*. New York: The Macmillan Co., 1905.

Burns, James M. *Roosevelt: The Lion and the Fox*. New York: Harcourt, Brace and World, 1956.

Byrnes, James. *All in One Lifetime*. New York: Harper and Row, 1958.

————. *Speaking Frankly*. New York: Harper & Brothers, Publishers, 1947.

Carter, John F. *The New Dealers*. New York: Simon and Schuster, 1934.

Casey, Richard G. *Friends and Neighbors*. East Lansing, Mich.: Michigan State College Press, 1955.

————. *Personal Experience, 1939–1946*, New York: David McKay Co., Inc. 1962.

Clifford, Phillip G. *Nathan Clifford, Democrat*. New York: Putnam's, 1922.

Collins, Larry and Dominique La Pierre. *O Jerusalem!* New York: Simon and Schuster, 1972.

Conklin, Paul. *The New Deal*. New York: 1968.

Connor, Henry G. *John A. Campbell, Associate Justice of the United States Supreme Court, 1853–1861*. Boston: Houghton Mifflin Co., 1920.

Cronon, E. David, ed. *The Cabinet Diaries of Josephus Daniels 1913–21*. Lincoln, Neb.: University of Nebraska Press, 1963.

Cuff, Robert D. *The War Industries Board*. Baltimore: Johns Hopkins University Press, 1973.

Dalfiume, Richard. *Desegregation of the U.S. Armed Forces*. Columbia, Mo.: University of Missouri Press, 1969.

Dallek, R. *F.D.R. and American Foreign Policy, 1932–1945*. New York: Oxford University Press, 1979.

Danelski, David S. and Tulchin, Joseph S., eds. *The Autobiographical Notes of Charles Evans Hughes*, Cambridge, Mass.: Harvard University Press, 1973.

Danelski, David J. *A Supreme Court Justice is Appointed*. New York: Random House, 1964.

Daniels, Josephus. *The Wilson Era: Years of Peace 1910–1917*. Chapel Hill, N.C.: University of North Carolina Press, 1944.

Dawson, Nelson Lloyd. *Louis D. Brandeis, Felix Frankfurter, and the New Deal.* Hamden, Conn.: Archon Books/The Shoe String Press, Inc., 1980.

DeHaas, Jacob. *Louis D. Brandeis.* New York: Block, 1929.

Dilliard, Irving. *Mr. Justice Brandeis, Great American.* St. Louis: The Modern View Press, 1941.

Donald, David, ed. *Inside Lincoln's Cabinet: The Civil War Diaries of Salmon P. Chase.* New York: Longman's Green and Co., 1954.

Donovan, Robert J. *Conflict and Crisis: The Presidency of Harry S. Truman, 1945–1948.* New York: W. W. Norton and Co. Inc., 1977.

Douglas, William O. *Go East, Young Man.* New York: Random House, 1974.

————. *The Court Years, 1939–1975.* New York: Random House, 1980.

Dunham, Allison and Kurland, Philip B., eds. *Mr. Justice.* Chicago: University of Chicago Press, 1964.

Eidelberg, Paul. *The Philosophy of the American Constitution.* New York: Free Press, 1968.

Fairman, Charles. *Mr. Justice Miller and the Supreme Court, 1862–1890.* Cambridge, Mass.: Harvard University Press, 1939.

————. *Reconstruction and Reunion, 1864–88.* vol. 1. Oliver Wendell Holmes Devise History of the Supreme Court of the United States. (Paul A. Freund, General Editor). New York: The Macmillan Co., 1971.

Farrand, Max, ed. *The Records of the Federal Convention.* New Haven: Yale University Press, 1937.

Feingold, Henry L. *The Politics of Rescue: The Roosevelt Administration and the Holocaust, 1938–1945.* New Brunswick, N.J.: Rutgers University Press, 1970.

Fish, Peter G. *The Politics of Federal Judicial Administration.* Princeton, N.J.: Princeton University Press, 1973.

Fitzpatrick, John C., ed. *The Diaries of George Washington,* 4 vols. Boston: Houghton-Mifflin Co., 1925.

————. *The Writings of Washington.* Washington, D.C.: Government Printing Office, 1931–44.

Fraenkel, Osmond K., ed. *The Curse of Bigness: Miscellaneous Papers of Louis D. Brandeis.* New York: Viking Press, 1934.

Frank, John P. *Mr. Justice Black: The Man and His Opinions.* New York: Alfred A. Knopf, 1949.

————. *Justice Daniel Dissenting.* Cambridge, Mass. Harvard University Press, 1964.

————. *The Warren Court.* New York: Alfred A. Knopf, 1964.

Frankfurter, Felix. *Mr. Justice Brandeis.* New Haven: Yale University Press, 1932.

Freedman, Max, ed. *Roosevelt and Frankfurter: Their Correspondence 1928–1945.* Boston: Little Brown and Col, 1967.

Friedel, Frank. *Franklin D. Roosevelt: Launching the New Deal.* Boston: Little Brown and Co., 1973.

————. *Franklin D. Roosevelt: The Triumph.* Boston: Little Brown and Co., 1956.

Friedman, Leon and Israel, Fred L., eds. *The Justices of the United States Supreme Court: Their Lives and Major Opinions,* 4 vols. New York: Chelsea House Publishers, 1969.

Friendly, Henry J. *Benchmarks.* Chicago: University of Chicago Press, 1967.

Funigiello, Philip. *Toward A National Power Policy: The New Deal and the Electric Utility Industry, 1933–41.* Pittsburgh, Pa.: University of Pittsburgh Press, 1973.

Gal, Allon. *Brandeis of Boston.* Cambridge, Mass.: Harvard University Press, 1980.

Gerhard, Eugene C. *America's Advocate: Robert H. Jackson.* New York: Bobbs-Merrill Co., Inc., 1958.

Gibbs, George. *Memoirs of the Administration of Washington and John Adams.* New York: William Van Norden, 1846.

Graham, Otis. *Encore for Reform: The Old Progressives and the New Deal.* New York: Oxford University Press, 1967.

Grubbs, Donald H. *Cry from the Cotton: The Southern Tenant Farmers' Union and the New Deal.* Chapel Hill, N.C.: University of North Carolina Press, 1971.

Halberstam, David. *The Powers That Be.* New York: Alfred A. Knopf, 1979.

Hamilton, Alexander; Jay, John; and Madison, James. *The Federalist Papers.* New York: Random House, 1937.

Hand, Learned. *The Spirit of Liberty.* Cambridge, Mass.: Harvard University Press, 1952.

Harper, Fowler V. *Justice Rutledge and the Bright Constellation.* Indianapolis, Ind.: Bobbs-Merrill Co., 1965.

Harrod, Roy. *The Life of John Maynard Keynes.* New York: St. Martin's Press, 1963.

Hawley, Ellis Wayne. *The New Deal and the Problem of Monopoly: A Study in Economic Ambivalence.* Princeton, N.J.: Princeton University Press, 1966.

Hirsch, H. N. *The Enigma of Felix Frankfurter.* New York: Basic Books, 1981.

Hofstadter, Richard. *The Age of Reform: From Bryan to F.D.R.* New York: Alfred A. Knopf, 1969.

Howard, J. Woodford, Jr. *Mr. Justice Murphy: A Political Biography.* Princeton, N.J.: Princeton University Press, 1968.

Howe, Mark de Wolfe, ed. *The Holmes-Laski Letters, 1916–35,* 2 vols. Cambridge, Mass.: Harvard University Press, 1941.

———. *The Holmes-Pollock Letters: The Correspondence of Mr. Justice Holmes and Sir Frederick Pollack, 1874–1932,* 2 vols. Cambridge, Mass.: Harvard University Press, 1941.

Huthmacher, J. Joseph. *Senator Robert F. Wagner and the Rise of Urban Liberalism.* New York: Atheneum, 1968.

Ickes, Harold L. *The Secret Diary of Harold L. Ickes,* 3 vols. New York: Simon and Schuster, 1954.

Jacobsohn, Gary J. *Pragmatism, Statesmanship and the Supreme Court.* Ithaca, N.Y.: Cornell University Press, 1977.

Johnston, Henry P., ed. *The Correspondence and Public Papers of John Jay,* 4 vols. New York: G. P. Putnam's Sons, 1890.

Kelly, Alfred H. and Harbison, Winfred A. *The American Constitution; Its Origins and Development.* New York: W. W. Norton & Co. 1963.

King, Willard. *Lincoln's Manager: David Davis.* Cambridge, Mass.: Harvard University Press, 1960.

———. *Melville Weston Fuller: Chief Justice of the United States, 1888–1910.* New York: Macmillan Co., 1950.

Konefsky, Samuel J. *The Legacy of Holmes and Brandeis: A Study in the Influence of Ideas.* New York: Macmillan Co., 1956.

Kurland, Philip B., ed. *Mr. Justice Frankfurter and the Constitution.* Chicago, University of Chicago Press, 1971.

———. *Mr. Justice Frankfurter on the Supreme Court.* Cambridge, Mass.: Harvard University Press, 1970.

———. *Of Law and Life and Other Things That Matter: Occasional Papers of Mr. Justice Frankfurter, 1956–1963.* New York: Harcourt, Brace and World, 1939.

Lamar, Clarinda. *The Life of J. R. Lamar, 1857–1916.* New York: G. P. Putnam's Sons, 1926.

Langer, William L. and Gleason, S. Everett. *Challenge to Isolation.* New York: Harper and Brothers, 1952.

Lash, Joseph, ed. *From the Diaries of Felix Frankfurter.* New York: W. W. Norton and Co., 1975.

———. *Roosevelt and Churchill, 1939–41.* New York: W. W. Norton and Co., 1976.

Lathan, Frank B. *The Great Dissenter: John Marshall Harlan, 1833–1911.* New York: Chester Book Co., 1970.

Lawrence, Alexander A. *James Moore Wayne, Southern Unionist.* Chapel Hill, N.C.: University of North Carolina Press, 1973.

Leuchtenburg, William E. *Franklin D. Roosevelt and the New Deal.* New York: Harper and Row, 1963.

Lief, Alfred. *Brandeis: The Personal History of an American Ideal.* New York: Stackpole Sons, 1936.

———. *The Social and Economic Views of Mr. Justice Brandeis.* New York: Vanguard Press, 1930.

Lilienthal, David. *TVA: Democracy on the March.* New York: Harper and Row, 1964.

———. *The Journals of David Lilienthal.* New York: Harper and Row, 1964.

Link, Arthur A. *Woodrow Wilson and the Progressive Era, 1910–1917.* New York: Harper and Bros., 1954.

———. *Wilson: The New Freedom.* Princeton, N.J.: Princeton University Press, 1956.

———. *Wilson: The Road to the White House.* Princeton, N.J.: Princeton University Press, 1947.

Lodge, Henry Cabot, ed. *The Works of Alexander Hamilton,* 12 vols. New York: G. P. Putnam's Sons, 1904.

Lowitt, Richard. *George W. Norris.* Urbana, Ill.: University of Illinois Press, 1979.

McClellan, David S. and Acheson, David C., eds. *Among Friends: Personal Letters of Dean Acheson.* New York: Dodd, Mead & Co., 1980.

McCormac, Eugene I. *James K. Polk: A Political Biography.* New York: Russell and Russell, 1965.

McGraw, Thomas K. *Morgan vs. Lilienthal.* Chicago: Loyola University Press, 1970.

Magrath, C. Peter. *Morrison R. Waite: The Triumph of Character.* New York: Macmillan Co., 1963.

Mann, Arthur. *LaGuardia: A Fighter Against His Times, 1882–1933.* Philadelphia: publisher 1959.

Martin, George. *Madam Secretary: A Biography of Frances Perkins.* Boston: Houghton Mifflin Co., 1976.

Mason Alpheus T. *Brandeis: A Free Man's Life.* New York: Viking Press, 1946.

———. *Harlan Fiske Stone: Pillar of the Law.* New York: Viking Press, 1956.

———. *William Howard Taft: Chief Justice.* New York: Simon and Schuster, 1964.

Mendelson, Wallace, ed. *Felix Frankfurter: A Tribute.* New York: Reynal, 1964.

———. *Felix Frankfurter: The Judge.* New York: Reynal, 1964.

Menzies, Robert G. *Afternoon Light: Some Memories of Men and Events.* Melbourne, Australia: Cassell Australia, Ltd., 1967.

Millis, Walter, ed. *The Forrestal Diaries.* New York: Viking Press, 1951.

Moffat, Jay Pierrepont. *The Moffat Papers.* Cambridge, Mass.: Harvard University Press, 1952.

Moley, Raymond. *After Seven Years.* New York: Harper and Brosl, 1939.

———. *The First New Deal.* New York: Harcourt, Brace and World, 1966.

————. *27 Masters of Politics*. New York: Funk and Wagnalls, 1949.

Monaghan, Frank. *John Jay: Defender of Liberty*. New York: Bobbs-Merrill Co., 1935.

Monnet, Jean. *Memoirs*, (translated by Richard Mayne). St. James Place, London: William Collins Sons & Co., Ltd., 1978.

de Montesquieu, Charles L. *The Spirit of the Laws* (translated by Thomas Nugent), 2 vols. New York: Colonial Press, 1899.

Morison, Elting E., ed. *The Letters of Theodore Roosevelt*. Cambridge, Mass.: Harvard University Press, 1951–54.

————. *Turmoil and Tradition: A Study of the Life and Times of Henry L. Stimson*. New York: Houghton Mifflin Co., 1960.

Murphy, Walter F. *Elements of Judicial Strategy*. Chicago, University of Chicago Press, 1964.

Nelson, Daniel. *Unemployment Insurance: The American Experience, 1915–35*. Madison Wis.: University of Wisconsin Press, 1969.

Nelson, Donald M. *Arsenal of Democracy: The Story of American War Production*. New York: Harcourt, Brace and Company, 1946.

Pangle, Thomas L. *Montesquieu's Philosophy of Liberalism*. Chicago, University of Chicago Press, 1973.

Parrish, Michael E. *Securities Regulation and the New Deal*. New Haven: Yale University Press, 1970.

Perkins, Frances. *The Roosevelt I Knew*. New York: Viking Press, 1946.

Phillips, Harlan, ed., *Felix Frankfurter Reminisces*. New York: Reynal and Co., 1960.

Pringle, Henry F. *The Life and Times of William Howard Taft*, 2 vols. New York: Farrar and Rinehart, Inc., 1939.

Pritchett, C. Herman. *The Roosevelt Court: A Study in Judicial Politics and Values, 1937–47*. Chicago: Quadrangle Books, 1969.

Pusey, Merlo. *Charles Evans Hughes*, 2 vols. New York: Macmillan Co., 1951.

Rabinowitz, Ezekiel. *Justice Louis D. Brandeis, the Zionist Chapter of His Life*. New York: The Philosophical Library, 1968.

Ratner, Sidney. *American Taxation, Its History as a Social Force in Democracy*. New York: W. W. Norton Co., 1942.

Rauch, Basil. *The History of the New Deal, 1933–38*. New York: Creative Age Press, 1944.

Richberg, Donald. *My Hero, The Indiscreet Memoirs of an Eventful but Unheroic Life*. New York: G. P. Putnam's Sons, 1954.

Rosen, Elliot A. *Hoover, Roosevelt and the Brains Trust: From Depression to New Deal*. New York: Columbia University Press, 1977.

Rosenman, Samuel I. *Public Papers and Addresses of Franklin D. Roosevelt*, 9 vols. New York: Random House, 1938.

————. *Working with Roosevelt*. New York: Harper and Bros., 1952.

Schick, Marvin. *Learned Hand's Court*. Baltimore, Md.: Johns Hopkins University Press, 1970.

Schlesinger, Arthur M. *The Age of Roosevelt*. Vol. I: *The Crisis of the Old Order 1919–1933*. Boston: Houghton Mifflin Co., 1957.

————. ———— II: *The Coming of the New Deal*. Boston: Houghton Mifflin Co., 1958.

————. ————. III: *The Politics of Upheaval*. Boston: Houghton Mifflin Co., 1960.

Schuckers, Jacob W. *Life and Public Services of Salmon P. Chase*. New York: D. Appleton and Co., 1874.

Scigliano, Robert. *The Supreme Court and the Presidency*. New York: Free Press, 1971.

Shapiro, Yonathan. *Leadership of the American Zionist Organization, 1897–1930*, Urbana, Ill.: University of Illinois Press, 1971.

Sherwin, Martin. *A World Destroyed: The Atomic Bomb and the Grand Alliance.* New York: Alfred A. Knopf, 1975.

Sherwood, Robert. *Roosevelt and Hopkins: An Intimate History.* New York: Harper and Bros., 1948.

Silver, David M. *Lincoln's Supreme Court.* Urbana, Ill.: University of Illinois Press, 1956.

Silverberg, Robert. *If I Forget Thee O Jerusalem.* New York: Pyramid Books, 1970.

Simon, James F. *Independent Journey: The Life of William O. Douglas.* New York: Harper and Row 1980.

Sternsher, Bernard. *Rexford Tugwell and the New Deal.* New Brunswick, N.J.: Rutgers University Press, 1964.

Stimson, Henry L. and Bundy, McGeorge. *On Active Service in Peace and War.* New York: Harper and Bros., 1947.

Story, Joseph. *Commentaries on the Constitution,* 3 vols. Boston: Little Brown and Co., 1851.

Swisher, Carl B. *The Taney Period, 1836–64.* The Oliver Wendell Holmes Devise History of the Supreme Court of the United States (General editor, Paul A. Freund). New York: Macmillan Co., 1974.

———. *Roger B. Taney.* New York: Macmillan Co., 1935.

———. *Stephen J. Field, Craftsman of the Law.* Washington, D.C.: The Brookings Institution, 1930.

Syrett, Harold C., ed. *The Papers of Alexander Hamilton.* New York: Columbia University Press, 1961.

Tennant, Kylie. *Evatt: Politics and Justice.* Sydney, Australia: Angus & Robertson Ltd., 1970.

Thomas, Helen S. *Felix Frankfurter: Scholar on the Bench.* Baltimore, Md.: Johns Hopkins University Press, 1960.

Trimble, B. R. *Chief Justice Waite: Defender of the Public Interest.* Princeton, N.J.: Princeton University Press, 1938.

Tugwell, Rexford G. *The Act of Politics.* Garden City, N.Y.: Doubleday, 1958.

———. *The Brains Trust.* New York: Viking Press, 1968.

———. *The Democratic Roosevelt, A Biography of FDR.* Garden City, N.Y.: Doubleday, 1957.

———. *Roosevelt's Revolution: The First Year—A Personal Perspective.* New York: Macmillan, 1977.

Tully, Grace. *F.D.R., My Boss.* New York: Charles Scribner's Sons, 1949.

Urofsky, Melvin I. *A Mind of One Piece: Brandeis and American Reform.* New York: Charles Scribner's Sons, 1971.

———. *American Zionism from Herzl to the Holocaust.* New York: Doubleday and Co., 1975.

———. *Louis D. Brandeis and the Progressive Tradition.* Boston: Little Brown and Co., 1981.

Urofsky, Melvin I. and Levy, David W., eds. *Letters of Louis D. Brandeis,* 5 vols. Albany, N.Y.: State University of New York, 1975.

Vile, M.J.C. *Constitutionalism and the Separation of Powers.* Oxford, U.K.: Clarendon Press, 1967.

Warren, Charles. *The Supreme Court in United States History,* 3 vols. Boston: Little Brown and Co., 1926.

Weaver, John D. *Warren, the Man, the Court, the Era.* London: Victor Gollancz Ltd., 1968.

Wehle, Louis B. *Hidden Threads of History: Wilson Through Roosevelt.* New York: Macmillan Co., 1953.

Weisenburger, Francis P. *The Life of John McLean: A Politician on the United States Supreme Court.* Columbus, Ohio: Ohio State University Press, 1937.

Westin, Alan F. *An Autobiography of the Supreme Court; Off-the-Bench Commentary by the Justices.* New York: Macmillan Co., 1963.

White, G. Edward. *The American Judicial Tradition.* New York: Oxford University Press, 1976.

Witte, Edwin. *The Development of the Social Security Act.* Madison, Wis.: University of Wisconsin Press, 1963.

Woodward, Bob and Armstrong, Scott. *The Brethren: Inside the Supreme Court.* New York: Simon and Schuster, 1979.

Articles

————. "The Association and the Supreme Court." 32 *American Bar Association Journal* (December 1946), 862–63.

————. "Extrajudicial Activities of Judges." 57 *Iowa Law Review* (1962), 1026–48.

————. "Mr. Justice Brandeis, Competition and Smallness: A Dilemma Re-examined." 66 *Yale Law Review* (1956), 69–96.

————. "New Dealers Still Wanted: Reports about Corcoran and Cohen." *The New Republic,* January 13, 1941, p. 40.

————. "Twins: New Deal's Legislative Architects: Corcoran and Cohen." *Newsweek,* July 13, 1935, pp. 24–25.

Acheson, Dean. "Removing the Shadow Cast on the Courts." 55 *American Bar Association Journal* (1969), 919–20.

Beaver, Daniel R. "Newton D. Baker and the Genesis of the War Industries Board, 1917–18." 1965 *The Journal of American History* (1965), 43–58.

Bell, Peter Alan. "Extrajudicial Activity of Supreme Court Justices." 22 *Stanford Law Review* (1969–70), 587–607.

Bolles, Blair. "Cohen and Corcoran: Brain Twins." *American Mercury,* January 1938, pp. 38–45.

Braeman, John. "The New Deal and the 'Broker State': A Review of the Recent Scholarly Literature." 46 *Business History Review* (Winter, 1976), 409–29.

Brandeis, Elizabeth. "Security for Americans." *The New Republic,* Dec. 1934, pp. 295–96.

————. "Employment Reserves vs. Insurance." *The New Republic,* May 27, 1933, pp. 177–79.

Carmen, Ira Ho. "The President, Politics and the Power of Appointments: Hoover's Nomination of Mr. Justice Cardozo." 55 *Virginia Law Review* (1969), pp. 620–51.

Coleman, William T. "Mr. Justice Felix Frankfurter: Civil Libertarian as Lawyer and as Justice." 1978 *Law Forum* (1978), 279–99.

Danzig, Richard. "How Question Begot Answers in Felix Frankfurter's First Flag Salute Opinion." 1977 *The Supreme Court Review* (1977), 257–74.

Eliot, Thomas H. "The Social Security Bill: 25 Years After." *Atlantic Monthly,* Aug. 1960, 72–76.

Epstein, Abraham. "Enemies of Unemployment Insurance." *The New Republic,* September 16, 1933, pp. 94–96.

Ervin, Sam J., Jr. "Separation of Powers: Judicial Independence." 35 *Law and Contemporary Problems* (1970), 108–27.

Frank, John P. "The Appointment of Supreme Court Justices." 1941 *Wisconsin Law Review* (1941), 172–202, 343–73, 461–91.

————. "The Legal Ethics of Louis D. Brandeis." 17 *Stanford Law Review* (1965), 683–709.

Frankfurter, Felix. "Distribution of Judicial Power Between United States and State Courts." 13 *Cornell Law Quarterly* (1928), 449–530.

———. "The Federal Securities Act." *Fortune Magazine*, August 1933, pp. 53–55, 106–11.

———. "Personal Ambitions of Judges: Should A Judge 'Think Beyond the Judicial?' " 34 *American Bar Association Journal* (1948), 656–59, 747–49.

———. "The Supreme Court in the Mirror of Justices." 105 *University of Pennsylvania Law Review* (1957), 781–95.

———. "What We Confront in American Life." *Survey Graphic*, March 1933, pp. 133–6.

Freund, Paul. "Justice Brandeis: A Law Clerk's Remembrance." *American Jewish History*, 1978, 7–18.

Graham, Fred. "The Many Sided Justice Fortas." *The New York Times Magazine*, June 4, 1967, p. 94.

Graham, Otis L. "Historians and the New Deals: 1944–1960." 54 *The Social Studies* (1963), pp. 133–40.

Howard, J. Woodford. "Fluidity of Judicial Choice." 62 *American Political Science Review* (March 1968), 43–57.

Isenberg, Max. "Felix Frankfurter as a Policymaker." 85 *Yale Law Journal* (1975), 280–98.

Jaffe, Louis. "Professors and Judges as Advisors: Reflections on the Roosevelt-Frankfurter Relationship." 83 *Harvard Law Review* (1969), 366–72.

James, Dorothy. "Role Theory and the Supreme Court." 30 *Journal of Politics* (March 1968), 160–86.

Johnson, Alva. "White House Tommy." *Saturday Evening Post*, July 31, 1937, pp. 5, 65–67.

Kahn, Michael. "Politics of the Appointment Process: An Analysis of Why Learned Hand Was Never Appointed to the Supreme Court." 25 *Stanford Law Review* (1973), 251–73.

Keyserling, Leon. "The Wagner Act: Its Origins and Current Significance." 29 *George Washington Law Review* (1960–61), 199–233.

Kommers, Donald. "Professor Kurland, The Supreme Court, and Political Science." 15 *Journal of Public Law* (1966), 230–50.

Kurland, Philip B. "The Lord Chancellor of the United States." *Trial*, Nov./Dec. 1971, pp. 10–17.

Landever, Arthur. "Chief Justice Burger and Extra-Case Activism." 20 *Journal of Public Law* (1971), 523–41.

Landis, James. "The Legislative History of the Securities Act of 1933." 28 *George Washington Law Review* (Oct. 1959), 29–49.

Lerner, Ralph. "The Supreme Court as Republican Schoolmaster." 1967 *The Supreme Court Review* (1967), 127–80.

Leuchtenburg, William. "The Origins of Franklin D. Roosevelt's 'Court-Packing' Plan." 1966 *The Supreme Court Review* (1966), 347–400.

Levinson, Sanford. "The Democratic Faith of Felix Frankfurter." 25 *Stanford Law Review* (1973), 430–57.

Levy, David W. "The Lawyer as Judge: Brandeis' View of the Legal Profession." 22 *University of Oklahoma Law Review* (1969), 391–411.

McClennen, Ned. "Louis D. Brandeis as a Lawyer." *Massachusetts Law Quarterly*, 1947, 4–28.

McCloy, John J. "Owen J. Roberts' Extra-Curiam Activities." 104 *University of Pennsylvania Law Review* (Dec. 1955), 350–54.

McKay, Robert. "The Judiciary and Non-Judicial Activities." 35 *Law and Contemporary Problems* (1970), 9–36.

Mason, Alpheus T. "Extrajudicial Work for Judges: The Views of Chief Justice Stone." 67 *Harvard Law Review* (1953), 202–31.

Murphy, Walter F. "In His Own Image: Mr. Chief Justice Taft and Supreme Court Appointments." 1961 *Supreme Court Review* (1961), 159–93.

––––––. "Chief Justice Taft and the Lower Court Bureaucracy." 24 *Journal of Politics* (1962), 453–59.

––––––. "Marshaling the Court: Leadership, Bargaining, and the Judicial Process." 29 *University of Chicago Law Review* (1962), 640–54.

Parker, John. "The Judicial Office in the United States." 23 *New York University Law Quarterly* (1948), 225–48.

Peek, George N. "In and Out: The Experiences of the First AAA Administrator." *Saturday Evening Post*, May 16, 1936, pp. 7–15.

Rauh, Joseph L. "Felix Frankfurter: Civil Libertarian." II *Harvard Civil Rights–Civil Liberties Law Review* (1976), 496–520.

Raushenbush, Paul. "Starting Unemployment Compensation in Wisconsin." 4 *Unemployment Insurance Review* (April–May 1967), 16–28.

Roberts, Owen. "Now is the Time: Fortifying the Supreme Court's Independence." 35 *American Bar Association Journal* (January 1949), 1–4.

Rosen, Elliot A. "Roosevelt and the Brains Trust: An Historiographical Overview." 87 *Political Science Quarterly* (Dec. 1972), 531–57.

Rosenfarb, Joseph. "Reflections on a Visit to Mr. Justice Brandeis." 27 *Iowa Law Review* (1942), 359–66.

Slonim, Solomon. "Extrajudicial Activities and the Principle of the Separation of Powers." 49 *Connecticut Bar Journal* (1975), 391–410.

Spector, Robert. "Judicial Biography and the United States Supreme Court: A Bibliographical Appraisal." II *Journal of Legal History* (Jan. 1967), 1–24.

Swindler, William F. "The Chief Justice and Law Reform, 1021 71." 1971 *Supreme Court Review* (1971), 241–64.

Westin, Alan. "Out of Court Commentary by United States Supreme Court Justices, 1790–1961: Of Free Speech and Judicial Lockjaw." 62 *Columbia Law Review* (1962) 633–53.

Wheeler, Russell. "Extrajudicial Behavior of the Early Supreme Court," 1973 *Supreme Court Review*, (1973), 123–58.

––––––. "Extrajudicial Behavior and the Role of the Supreme Court Justice." *University Programs Modular Series*, General Learning Press, 1975.

Wyzanski, Charles E., Jr., "Brandeis." *Atlantic Monthly*, November 1956, pp. 69–77.

Government Documents

"Nonjudicial Activities of Supreme Court Justices and Other Federal Judges." Hearing before the Subcommittee on Separation of Powers of the Senate Committee on the Judiciary. 91st Congress, 1st Session, 1969.

"Hearings on Nomination of Abe Fortas to be Chief Justice." Senate Committee on the Judiciary. 90th Congress, 2nd Session, 1968.

"Report Together with Individual Views to Accompany the Nomination of Abe Fortas." Senate Committee on the Judiciary. Executive Report Number 8. 90th Congress, 2nd Session, 1968.

Index